Praise for *JUNOS High Availability*

"*JUNOS High Availability* contains all the technical building blocks necessary to plan and maintain a medical grade network."

> —Jonathan Yantis, Network Engineer, Medical University of South Carolina

"At Townsend Analytics, our trading clients, using our RealTick trading suite, demand that our global network maintain an extremely high level of availability. Downtime translates directly into lost money. *JUNOS High Availability* has great tips and guides to help support this environment. It includes everything from conceptual details on software and hardware, very detailed routing protocol examples, security and auditing, and everything in between. This book is a must for anyone who is in any way involved in maintaining a high level of service on their network!"

> —Chris Rizzo, Senior Network Engineer, Townsend Analytics

"*High availability* is such a buzz phrase these days. It's refreshing to see an approach that breaks down all of the various conversations and shows what is required for an overall continuous system. Getting the building blocks right is crucial to having a network that is truly highly available, and *JUNOS High Availability* will help you get it right and keep it right."

> —Scott Stevens, Vice President, Technology, Juniper Networks

"With *disaster recovery* and *business continuity* the current buzzwords in our state government network as well as in most corporate networks around the world, this book has come along at the perfect time to spur conversations on high availability, not only for networks built on Juniper Networks equipment, but on other vendor equipment as well. The topics covered in *JUNOS High Availability* are broad enough for engineers looking to design an overarching high availability posture in their network, but also detailed enough to allow engineers to implement their designs through protocol tweaks and JUNOS tools. The transition between authors keeps topics interesting and provides amusing quips along the way."

> —Aaron Robel, Systems Engineer, Washington State Department of Information Services

JUNOS High Availability

JUNOS High Availability

James Sonderegger, Orin Blomberg, Kieran Milne, and Senad Palislamovic

O'REILLY®

Beijing · Cambridge · Farnham · Köln · Sebastopol · Tokyo

JUNOS High Availability

by James Sonderegger, Orin Blomberg, Kieran Milne, and Senad Palislamovic

Published by O'Reilly Media, Inc., 1005 Gravenstein Highway North, Sebastopol, CA 95472.

O'Reilly books may be purchased for educational, business, or sales promotional use. Online editions are also available for most titles (*http://my.safaribooksonline.com*). For more information, contact our corporate/institutional sales department: 800-998-9938 or *corporate@oreilly.com*.

Editor: Mike Loukides	**Indexer:** Lucie Haskins
Production Editor: Sarah Schneider	**Cover Designer:** Karen Montgomery
Copyeditor: Audrey Doyle	**Interior Designer:** David Futato
Proofreader: Kiel Van Horn	**Illustrator:** Robert Romano

Printing History:

August 2009:   First Edition.

ISBN: 978-0-596-52304-6

[LSI]   [2011-11-18]

1320750155

Table of Contents

Part II. JUNOS HA Techniques

Part III.   Network Availability

Preface

At a recent meeting of network admins, the talk turned to uptime, and some bragged about the high availability of services in their network; they had 100% uptime. Wow, this normally is unthinkable. After more discussion, the truth came out. This figure is based on the fact that the service provider did not take into account outages in the network that made their service unavailable, because their service was still "up," though totally unreachable. The same admins also admitted that they really didn't keep records of actual outages. In their opinion, they had no reliability issues, but their customers would disagree with that.

This book is not about reliability theory. Theory addresses the full range of possibilities. This book is for those of us who have to keep the network working. It is a guide for students of the art of creating self-sustaining continuous systems.

As such, we fought to keep the book grounded not necessarily in what you *can* do, but more importantly, in what you *should* do as an administrator to protect availability and to keep the customers, internal or external, connected and happy. Most of the chapters include case studies that show you how things work and provide pointers on where you might investigate if your results differ. The topologies included are realistic and in many cases reflective of actual networks that we, the authoring team, have worked with at some point in our careers.

There are four authors on this book, and while we tried to homogenize the writing, you will see different styles and different approaches. Ultimately, we think that's a good thing. It's like working with your peers who are also maintaining the same network and who have different methods of working. The team shares a common goal and the variation in approaches brings strength through diversity.

Ultimately, this book is about Juniper Networks JUNOS Software and Juniper Networks boxes. You need to design a continuous system, and you need the right mix of equipment placed ideally on your topology, but eventually you come back to the network OS. And our chapters all come back to roost with JUNOS.

What Is High Availability?

How often in your life have you picked up a phone and *not* heard a dial tone? Not very often, right? Every time you did it was certainly a cause for concern. This is a classic example of the definition of *availability*. People do not expect the network to be in use constantly, 365 days a year, but they do expect the network to be available for use every time they try to use it. With a high number of users expecting availability as needed, we begin to approach the point of constant availability. But is that realistic? Statistically speaking, no; over a long enough timeline every system eventually fails. So, what is a realistic solution for systems whose purpose means they can't be allowed to fail?

A classic concern with high availability was the difficulty in measurement. The notion was that any measurement tool had to be more available than the system being measured. Otherwise, the tool would potentially fail before the system being measured. These days the most highly available systems are processing constant and ever-increasing volumes of user traffic, such as credit card transactions, calls connected, and web page hits. Any disruption in service would immediately be noticed and felt by end users. The users themselves have become the most effective availability monitoring tool.

Five 9s is easily dismissed as a marketing term, but the math behind the term is sound and wholly nonmarketing. The 9s concept is a measure of availability over a span of a year. It is a percentage of time during the year that the system is guaranteed to be functional. The following table is often drawn to describe the concept:

Availability	Downtime in one year
90%	876 hours
99%	87.6 hours
99.9%	8.76 hours
99.99%	52.6 minutes
99.999%	5.26 minutes
99.9999%	31.5 seconds

 In this book we cite five 9s as a concept rather than as the recommended target. In financial enterprises, five 9s could be unacceptable and the target may instead be seven 9s, or eight 9s. Whenever you see "9s" in this book, whether your target is five, seven, or even nine 9s, please read it as a measurement of a continuous system rather than as a figurative number we recommend for all networks.

The table about 9s gets the message across, but it doesn't really tell the story of *where* availability should be measured. Chapter 1 of this book talks about dependencies within redundancy schemes: redundant components protect chassis, redundant chassis protect systems, redundant systems protect services, and redundant services protect the enterprise. Some vendors would have you believe that availability should be measured at the chassis level. Others tout the availability of specific components in their chassis.

User experience is reality. This reality means that neither component nor system levels are appropriate points to measure availability. Relying on hardware availability as a measure of system, service, and enterprise availability ignores the importance of network architecture planning and site design, effective monitoring, and a highly trained and proactive support staff. In the modern world of constant transactions, it is the services and the enterprise that must be available 99.999999% of the time. This is the approach we've taken in this book.

So, are we saying that the component and chassis availability are irrelevant? Hardly. The strength and resilience of components are critical to the chassis. The availability of chassis is critical to the availability of services. The point is that even with best-in-class components and chassis it is possible to make poor design and configuration decisions. The fact that you have chosen to buy Juniper means that you have already secured best-in-class components and chassis. The purpose of this book is to help you make the most of this investment and build truly continuous systems and services.

How to Use This Book

We are assuming a certain level of knowledge from the reader. This is important. If you are not familiar with any of the assumptions in the following list, this book will occasionally veer over your head. The JUNOS documentation site (*http://www.juniper.net/techpubs*) is a great place to start. It's thorough, well written, and free.

OSI model
> The Open Systems Interconnection (OSI) model defines seven different layers of technology: Physical, Data Link, Network, Transport, Session, Presentation, and Application. This model allows network engineers and network vendors to easily discuss and apply technology to a specific OSI level. This segmentation allows engineers to divide the overall problem of getting one application to talk to another into discrete parts and more manageable sections. Each level has certain attributes that describe it, and each level interacts with its neighboring levels in a very well-defined manner.

Switches
> These devices operate at Layer 2 of the OSI model and use logical local addressing to move frames across a network. Devices in this category include Ethernet, ATM, and Frame Relay switches.

Routers
> These devices operate at Layer 3 of the OSI model and connect IP subnets to each other. Routers move packets across a network in a hop-by-hop fashion.

Ethernet

These broadcast domains connect multiple hosts together on a common infra-structure. Hosts communicate with each other using Layer 2 Media Access Control (MAC) addresses.

Point-to-point links

These network segments are often thought of as wide area network (WAN) links in that they do not contain any end users. Often these links are used to connect routers together in disparate geographical areas. Possible encapsulations used on these links include ATM, Frame Relay, Point to Point Protocol (PPP), and HDLC.

IP addressing and subnetting

Hosts using IP to communicate with each other use 32-bit addresses. Humans often use a dotted decimal format to represent this address. This address notation includes a network portion and a host portion that is normally displayed as 192.168.1.1/24.

TCP and UDP

These Layer 4 protocols define methods for communicating between hosts. TCP provides for connection-oriented communications while UDP uses a connection-less paradigm. Other benefits of using TCP include flow control, windowing/buffering, and explicit acknowledgments.

ICMP

This protocol is used by network engineers to troubleshoot and operate a network, as it is the core protocol used by the ping and traceroute (on some platforms) programs. In addition, ICMP is used to signal error and other messages between hosts in an IP-based network.

JUNOS CLI

This is the command-line interface used by Juniper Networks routers, and is the primary method for configuring, managing, and troubleshooting the router. JUNOS documentation covers the CLI in detail and is freely available on the Juniper Networks website (*http://www.juniper.net*).

What's in This Book?

The ultimate purpose of this book is to be the single, most complete source for working knowledge related to providing high availability with Juniper Networks equipment. Though you may not find detailed configurations for all protocols and interfaces, you will find those tweaks and knobs that will provide high availability.

This book is divided into four parts, with a total of 25 chapters, and some general reference items put into the appendixes. The chapters are written by four different authors, although all of us tended to review each other's work. You'll be able to tell different voices in the writing styles, and we hope that is generally refreshing rather than a hindrance. Here is a detailed account of what's in this book.

Part I, *JUNOS HA Concepts*

Chapter 1, *High Availability Network Design Considerations*
> This chapter provides real-world perspective on the relative cost associated with making a network highly available and is the only nontechnical chapter in the book. It opens by describing a very simple, small enterprise network and then adds layers of redundancy, each designed to protect against a wider range of threats to continuity. The chapter concludes with a chart comparing the relative cost of the cumulative layers.

Chapter 2, *Hardware High Availability*
> This chapter focuses on the foundation of Juniper Networks high availability: the hardware. It starts by discussing the divided architecture available on all systems and expands to the specific hardware redundancy features of the Juniper product lines.

Chapter 3, *Software High Availability*
> This chapter builds on the hardware knowledge gained in Chapter 2 to highlight the features of the Juniper software that ensure high availability. The chapter looks at the stable operating system on which the system is built and the divided software architecture that keeps the network running.

Chapter 4, *Control Plane High Availability*
> This chapter provides in-depth understanding of control plane and forwarding plane interactions. Then it covers details of the different high availability features: Graceful Routing Engine Switchover (GRES), Graceful Restart (GR), Non-Stop Active Routing (NSR), and Non-Stop Bridging (NSB). The chapter concludes with a list of protocol and platform support for different high availability tools.

Chapter 5, *Virtualization for High Availability*
> This chapter provides an overview of advanced applications of the control plane in a data center environment. The chapter also discusses the latest developments in control plane scalability and provides solutions to control plane scaling problems present at large service providers.

Part II, *JUNOS HA Techniques*

Chapter 6, *JUNOS Pre-Upgrade Procedures*
> This chapter provides an overview of the things a user needs to keep in mind when preparing to upgrade JUNOS. Then it dives into configuration and use of unified In-Service Software Upgrade (ISSU). The chapter concludes with a handy collection of protocol mechanisms that can be used to divert traffic around a non-ISSU chassis that is being upgraded.

Chapter 7, *Painless Software Upgrades*
> This chapter is the second of a three-chapter series on software upgrades. It covers the syntax and options available for upgrading software on JUNOS platforms and

describes the importance of a fallback procedure and fallback authority. The chapter concludes with special considerations for Juniper Networks J Series chassis, including rescue configurations.

Chapter 8, *JUNOS Post-Upgrade Verifications*
This chapter provides an overview of JUNOS commands used to verify network device state after an OS upgrade. The chapter then describes how to gracefully undo the traffic diversion techniques described in Chapter 6, and is an important companion to that chapter.

Chapter 9, *Monitoring for High Availability*
This chapter provides an overview of JUNOS features and industry standards that can be used to monitor network equipment to ensure network uptime. Juniper-specific features, such as JUNOScript, are introduced.

Chapter 10, *Management Interfaces*
This chapter details the different interfaces, including the command-line interface (CLI), GUIs, and application programming interfaces (APIs), that are used to manage Juniper Networks equipment to ensure high availability.

Chapter 11, *Management Tools*
This chapter builds on the previous two chapters by discussing tools available for managing network equipment. The chapter discusses both Juniper Network tools as well as open source tools that can interact with the APIs in JUNOS Software.

Chapter 12, *Managing Intradomain Routing Table Growth*
This chapter opens with a discussion of intelligent IP address allocation for networks with a high availability focus. The chapter then looks at the configuration options available for controlling the size of the intradomain routing table while at the same time protecting the availability of the network.

Chapter 13, *Managing an Interdomain Routing Table*
A companion to Chapter 12, this chapter looks at configuration elements that an administrator would use to control the locally received content of the interdomain routing table. Border Gateway Protocol (BGP)-related policy and configuration options are the focal point in this chapter, and it is one of several that discuss how BGP scalability mechanisms can be used to manage the local network.

Part III, *Network Availability*

Chapter 14, *Fast High Availability Protocols*
This chapter provides an overview of several protocols that support high availability by providing fast failure detection and recovery. It discusses protocols for optical and Ethernet networks, and then dives into options for lowering Interior Gateway Protocol (IGP) timers and using Bidirectional Forwarding Detection (BFD). The chapter finishes by covering redundancy protocols, including Virtual Router Redundancy Protocol (VRRP), and several options for Multiprotocol Label Switching (MPLS) path protection.

Chapter 15, *Transitioning Routing and Switching to a Multivendor Environment*
This is the first in a series of chapters that look at how products from Juniper can be added into a single-vendor network to improve the availability of the network. The chapter uses a layered strategy that first compares interface characteristics, then IGPs, and then BGP configuration syntax between JUNOS and IOS devices.

Chapter 16, *Transitioning MPLS to a Multivendor Environment*
This chapter builds on the successes of the previous chapter by adding Resource Reservation Protocol (RSVP) and Label Distribution Protocol (LDP)-signaled MPLS to the multivendor BGP topology. The chapter includes discussion of MPLS interoperability "gotchas" between JUNOS and IOS, and concludes with two case studies that show layered transition and site-based transition to a multivendor state.

Chapter 17, *Monitoring Multivendor Networks*
In this chapter, the authors compare Simple Network Management Protocol (SNMP) and syslog configuration syntax between JUNOS and IOS platforms, and look at best practices for use of the tools to monitor multivendor networks. The chapter concludes with a brief look at the J-Web GUI as a device monitoring tool.

Chapter 18, *Network Scalability*
This chapter opens with a comparison of throughput capabilities of the different product families that run JUNOS. The chapter then looks at additional configuration tweaks that allow the network to grow or shrink as needed to meet changing demands from the user base. A key feature of this chapter is high availability zoning for BGP route reflector schemes. The chapter closes with a look at how traffic engineering can help a network scale while meeting customer availability and bandwidth requirements.

Chapter 19, *Choosing, Migrating, and Merging Interior Gateway Protocols*
This chapter discusses the two most commonly used industry-standard IGPs: Open Shortest Path First (OSPF) and Intermediate System to Intermediate System (IS-IS). The first section examines the advantages and disadvantages of each protocol, and looks at how each one supports high availability. The next section examines what is involved in migrating from one of these IGPs to the other. The chapter finishes with considerations and recommendations for merging separate networks that run the same IGP.

Chapter 20, *Merging BGP Autonomous Systems*
This chapter discusses features of JUNOS and best common practices that can be used to merge Autonomous Systems (ASs) while preserving network uptime. Issues that occur in large-scale BGP deployments are also raised.

Chapter 21, *Making Configuration Audits Painless*
This chapter provides information on using JUNOS Software features to audit network configurations to ensure that human error or misconfiguration does not cause network downtime.

Chapter 22, *Securing Your Network Equipment Against Security Breaches*
> This chapter provides an overview of options to provide strong security for your device. It discusses authentication methods, and then lists a series of features you can implement to harden the device. The chapter then dives into firewall filters, discussing how they are configured and implemented. It ends with several examples using filters to protect the network as well as the device itself.

Chapter 23, *Monitoring and Containing DoS Attacks in Your Network*
> Building on the previous chapter, this chapter discusses strategies for attack detection, as well as steps you can take to lessen the impact of the attack while it is in progress. It then covers strategies for proactively reducing the impact of denial-of-service (DoS) attacks on your network. The chapter concludes by discussing several methods you can use to gather evidence of the attack.

Chapter 24, *Goals of Configuration Automation*
> This chapter discusses how configuration automation can be used to prevent human errors that cause network downtime.

Chapter 25, *Automated Configuration Strategies*
> This chapter provides an overview of how to use the JUNOS tools to conduct configuration automation for various network settings and architectures.

Part IV, *Appendixes*

We include a few items for your perusal: a sample checklist for getting new JUNOS devices operational, a sample audit list, and a JUNOS configuration statement review for high availability operations.

Conventions Used in This Book

The following typographical conventions are used in this book:

Italic
> Indicates new terms, URLs, email addresses, filenames, file extensions, pathnames, directories, and Unix utilities.

`Constant width`
> Indicates commands, options, switches, variables, attributes, keys, functions, types, classes, namespaces, methods, modules, properties, parameters, values, objects, events, event handlers, XML tags, HTML tags, macros, the contents of files, and the output from commands.

`Constant width bold`
> Shows commands or other text that should be typed literally by the user.

`Constant width italic`
> Shows text that should be replaced with user-supplied values.

This icon signifies a tip, suggestion, or general note.

 This icon indicates a warning or caution.

Using Code Examples

This book is here to help you get your job done. In general, you may use the code in this book in your own configurations and documentation. You do not need to contact us for permission unless you're reproducing a significant portion of the material. For example, deploying a network based on actual configurations from this book does not require permission. Selling or distributing a CD-ROM of examples from O'Reilly books does require permission. Answering a question by citing this book and quoting example code does not require permission. Incorporating a significant number of sample configurations or operational output from this book into your product's documentation does require permission.

We appreciate, but do not require, attribution. An attribution usually includes the title, author, publisher, and ISBN. For example: "*JUNOS High Availability*, by James Sonderegger, Orin Blomberg, Kieran Milne, and Senad Palislamovic. Copyright 2009 James Sonderegger, Orin Blomberg, Kieran Milne, and Senad Palislamovic, 978-0-596-52304-6."

If you feel your use of code examples falls outside fair use or the permission given here, feel free to contact us at *permissions@oreilly.com*.

Safari® Books Online

 Safari Books Online is an on-demand digital library that lets you easily search over 7,500 technology and creative reference books and videos to find the answers you need quickly.

With a subscription, you can read any page and watch any video from our library online. Read books on your cell phone and mobile devices. Access new titles before they are available for print, and get exclusive access to manuscripts in development and post feedback for the authors. Copy and paste code samples, organize your favorites, download chapters, bookmark key sections, create notes, print out pages, and benefit from tons of other time-saving features.

O'Reilly Media has uploaded this book to the Safari Books Online service. To have full digital access to this book and others on similar topics from O'Reilly and other publishers, sign up for free at *http://my.safaribooksonline.com*.

Comments and Questions

Please address comments and questions concerning this book to the publisher:

> O'Reilly Media, Inc.
> 1005 Gravenstein Highway North
> Sebastopol, CA 95472
> 800-998-9938 (in the United States or Canada)
> 707-829-0515 (international or local)
> 707-829-0104 (fax)

We have a web page for this book, where we list errata, examples, and any additional information. You can access this page at:

> *http://www.oreilly.com/catalog/9780596523046*

or:

> *http://cubednetworks.com*

To comment or ask technical questions about this book, send email to:

> *bookquestions@oreilly.com*

For more information about our books, conferences, Resource Centers, and the O'Reilly Network, see our website at:

> *http://www.oreilly.com*

Acknowledgments

The authors would like to gratefully and unabashedly acknowledge many of our peers, editors, and advisers over the long course of writing this book. We began naively and finished as book-writing experts mostly because of the leadership of many of our associates.

First, we must thank Patrick Ames, Juniper Networks' editor in chief for its technical book program. Without him you would not be holding this volume in your hand or viewing it on your monitor. Second, Aviva Garrett, author of *JUNOS Cookbook* (O'Reilly), performed a marvelous final edit of our work, putting in countless hours and raining down incredible suggestions. Third, Colleen Toporek, our developmental editor, slogged through our first missives and gently guided us toward the O'Reilly benchmarks of excellence. Finally, our copyeditor, Audrey Doyle, took it all in and masterfully made it sync together. These four, along with Mike Loukides, Marlowe

Shaeffer, Robert Romano, and countless others at O'Reilly, formed a team that helped to create a book that is greater than the sum of its authors. Thank you all.

We would also like to thank Juniper Networks, the employer of three of the four authors, for allowing us the resources and occasional bandwidth to work on this project, and the many people who contributed to this book in a thousand little ways, from hallway conversations to in-depth emails explaining one thing or another; Fred Stringer, who helped us at the very beginning while we were still proposing the book; Chris Hellberg for sparking the book idea—no more busting routers, mate; and Anton Bernal and Gonzalo Gomez Herrero for contributing to the early discussions and providing many fresh ideas. We note that Abhilash Prabhakaran was the original writer and Ben Mann and Joanne McClintock the editors of the material in Appendix C, which we condensed and abbreviated for the reader's benefit. And finally, we want to especially reserve our admiration for the team of additional technical reviewers from Juniper Networks who worked on tight schedules and limited resources: Majid Ansari, Nathan Day, Jasun Rutter, and Jared Gull.

James Sonderegger would personally like to thank his wife, Bonnie, and children, Gabby, Riley, Cat, and William, for their patience and unwavering support through the year it took to finish this project.

Orin Blomberg would personally like to thank his wife, Holly, for all her support during the writing of the book.

Kieran Milne would like to first thank and acknowledge his daughter, Sarah. Then, he would like to extend deep appreciation to Will Pincek, Stacy Smith, and Elna Wells for making Juniper Networks an amazing place to work. He would also like to thank James Sonderegger for inviting him to join this project and Patrick Ames for keeping the project on track and moving forward.

Senad Palislamovic would like to thank his Guide for allowing him to complete this project; and his parents and beautiful wife for their love and support during long sleepless weekends. Special thanks go to James Sonderegger, Orin Blomberg, and Kieran Milne for all the extra cycles devoted to the project; Aviva Garrett for pulling all-nighters rewriting his lines and still meeting the deadline; Fred Stringer for his High Availability mentorship; and his old and new managers for letting him slack, Michael Kozich and Michael Langdon. Final thanks go to all of those who gave him space throughout the past year; Senad is still your friend.

PART I

JUNOS HA Concepts

CHAPTER 1

High Availability Network Design Considerations

Before diving into the details of how JUNOS-enabled networks can be managed to promote high availability, we need to examine networks at the architectural level in order to distinguish a high availability network from other networks.

Redundancy schemes are relative to a layered model and can be described with the following line of simple premises:

Redundant components protect systems
> High availability at the system layer is supported by redundant hardware components such as power supplies, interface cards, and processor engines.

Redundant systems protect services
> High availability at the service layer is supported by redundant systems such as routers, switches, and servers.

Redundant services protect the enterprise
> High availability at the enterprise layer is supported by redundant services such as email, VoIP, the Web, and "shopping carts."

Redundant enterprises protect free-market economies
> Though relevant to the current state of world finances, this premise is beyond the scope of this book.

Each layer in the model can be said to have an associated base cost that represents the price of functionality at that layer. High availability is provided by protecting base functionality with hardware, software, configuration options, staffing, or whatever else is available. In almost every case, adding protection to a layer's functionality increases the cost of that layer.

Why Mention Cost in a Technical Book?

With the exception of some government projects, cost is always a concern when building or upgrading a network, even when high availability is the desired end state. Is it practical to add $500,000 to the cost of creating and supporting services that yield a $50,000 annual revenue stream? Probably not. Would it be more tenable to protect a $50,000 revenue stream with $25,000 in high availability-focused enhancements? An investment like that makes sense.

Most books on the market today that describe "network solutions" do so with little consideration given to the price of equipment and support, and to additional operational expenses (OPEX) tied to space, power, and cooling. Why are these issues so commonly overlooked? Perhaps because prices are subject to change; they can be affected by discount models, and they change over time: some prices could be outdated before this book's shelf life expires. Also, vendors occasionally discourage the release of price information in public forums.

This chapter does not attempt to capture the *actual* cost in real dollars of products from Juniper or any other vendor. Instead, we assign a *baseline* cost to a simple, nonredundant network, and then look at the relative changes that are associated with different forms of redundancy as described in the layered model. Likewise, we do not attempt to place specific makes and models of network products, such as routers, switches, and firewalls, in the design. Doing so could distract you from the true purpose of this chapter, which is to identify the relative cost of different layers of redundancy in a network.

A Simple Enterprise Network

A simple enterprise network design relies on routers, firewalls, and switches, as shown in Figure 1-1. The design provides filtering and separation of traffic to support a pair of employee local area networks (LANs), a pair of sensitive corporate LANs that support connectivity among corporate data stores, and a pair of demilitarized zone (DMZ) LANs that support the company's web presence.

While this design is quite common, you'll notice immediately that it has multiple single points of failure. All Internet connectivity is provided by a single router through a single connection to the Internet. All Internet access to the DMZ LANs is provided by a single firewall. The employee LANs reside behind another router, itself an additional single point of failure. Finally, the sensitive corporate LANs are connected using an additional firewall, which because of the linear design of the network, must push traffic through no fewer than three other single points of failure in order to send data from the corporate LANs to the regular Internet. The complete reliance on multiple single points of failure in this design results in a total lack of fault tolerance on the network.

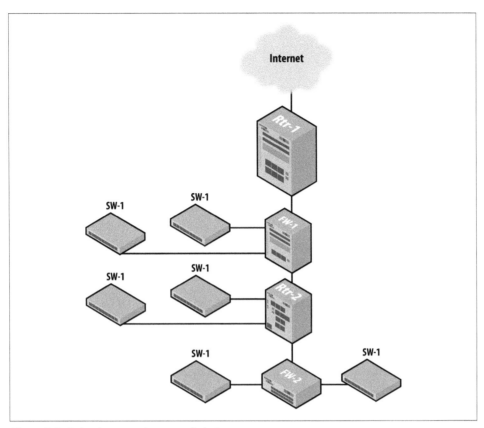

Figure 1-1. A simple enterprise network design

Table 1-1 lists the chassis that provide the base functionality and is used to calculate a representative "cost" for this simple network. The cost calculation includes all switches, routers, and firewall products shown in the data transport path. This calculation also includes a representative cost of labor and materials for fiber optic connections within the office in which the network is located.

Table 1-1. Representative cost of a simple network

Line item	Description	Qty
1	Router 1 with interface cards and one year of vendor support	1
2	Firewall 1 with interface cards and one year of vendor support	1
3	Router 2 with interface cards and one year of vendor support	1
4	Firewall 2 with interface cards and one year of vendor support	1
5	Switch 1 and one year of vendor support	6
6	Multimode fiber trunk (materials and installation)	10

Line item	Description	Qty
7	Facility power and cooling for one year	1

Total representative cost = $100,000

Redundancy and the Layered Model

Because most corporations have come to rely on data communications as a means of generating profit, we can safely assume that the simple design shown in Figure 1-1, with its complete lack of fault tolerance, is inadequate for the majority of corporate needs. Redundancy is necessary, so we must redesign the simple transport network.

Redundant network architectures fall into one of four basic categories:

Redundant site architectures
> Rely on identical systems and services, placed in geographically disparate locations, to support enterprise-level redundancy.

Redundant system architectures
> Rely on paired groupings of systems (routers, switches, servers) to provide service resiliency when chassis or components fail.

Redundant component architectures
> Rely on additional interface cards, processor boards, power supplies, and other major components within individual chassis to provide chassis resiliency when components fail.

Hybrid redundancy schemes
> Use a combination of system, component, and site redundancy elements to provide resilient services. This is by far the most common category.

Redundant Site Architectures

Figure 1-2 shows the simple network design from Figure 1-1 replicated at a site that is geographically distant from the primary site. The advantage of having the same architecture at two different sites is that it provides resilient routing of traffic during system or component failure, as well as during catastrophic disasters at the primary site. Also, this scheme allows the backup site to serve corporate goals because it is an online, staffed, working office while the primary site is also online.

The disadvantages of this redundancy scheme are based on usage and availability. First, note that all backup systems are physically distant from primary systems, resulting in the added difficulty of the primary site staff using the backup systems. Furthermore, this scheme by itself would require a full site failover to recover from something as simple as an interface failure on a router. Site-based redundancy schemes require constant attention, particularly when the backup site is in active use.

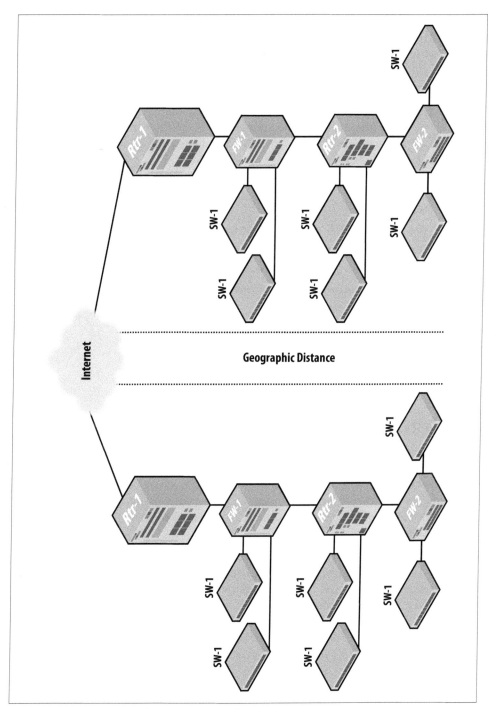

Figure 1-2. Site redundancy for a simple network

Resource availability on the backup system must be kept above the levels required to fully support the processing needs of the primary site. Otherwise, the backup site cannot accurately be called a backup site. For this reason and those previously listed, a site-based redundancy scheme is seldom used *without* some form of component or system redundancy at both the primary and backup sites.

Table 1-2 details the relative cost of a site-based redundancy scheme. Note the added cost of facilities startup as well as the annual cost of staffing, security, Internet connectivity, and utilities. You should keep in mind that any annual costs described in the table recur on a yearly basis.

Table 1-2. Relative cost of site redundancy

Line Item	Description	Qty
1	Router 1 with interface cards and one year of vendor support	2
2	Firewall 1 with interface cards and one year of vendor support	2
3	Router 2 with interface cards and one year of vendor support	2
4	Firewall 2 with interface cards and one year of vendor support	2
5	Switch 1 and one year of vendor support	12
6	Multimode fiber trunk (materials and installation)	20
7	Additional physical facilities startup costs	1
8	Facility power and cooling for one year	2
Total relative cost = $540,000		

Redundant Component Architectures

Use of redundant components within a network requires significant planning by the network architects. Equipment should be chosen that supports the component redundancy scheme required at both the physical and logical levels. To provide link redundancy, chassis should be selected that support at least twice as many physical interfaces as are needed for nonredundant connectivity. Future growth plans should also be taken into consideration.

Physical component redundancy is supported by original equipment manufacturers (OEMs) when they design a chassis to hold multiple power supplies and multiple processor boards. Logical redundancy is supported by the protocols implemented in a network. Virtual Router Redundancy Protocol (VRRP), for example, allows multiple routers or multiple interfaces on a single router to serve as virtual redundant gateways off a LAN. The Internet Engineering Task Force (IETF) standard 802.3ad, which supports bundling of multiple physical Ethernet interfaces to a single logical address, is another way to take advantage of redundant component architectures.

A disadvantage to redundant component architectures is the lack of protection in the event of complete system failure. For example, regardless of the number of redundant components within a router, a single bucket of mop water can still destroy the system. Furthermore, redundant component architectures provide no resilience against regional disasters.

Figure 1-3 shows the addition of redundant components including power supplies, processor boards, and physical connections to the simple transport network described in Figure 1-1.

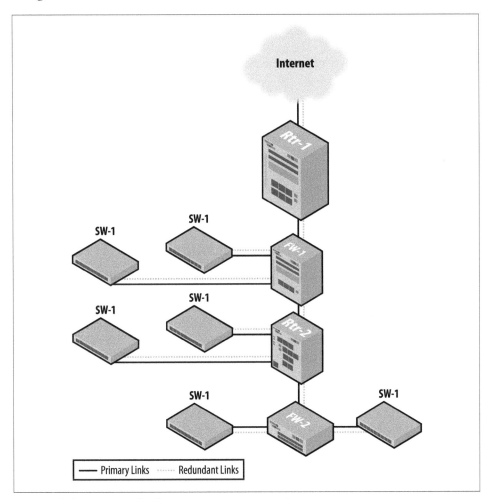

Figure 1-3. Component redundancy in a transport network

Table 1-3 details the cost of the network after complete component redundancy is added. Again, costs listed are an estimate at the time of this book's writing and may not reflect actual vendor pricing.

Note that no additional cost is associated with the implementation of logical redundancy protocols such as VRRP and 802.3ad. These protocols are relatively simple to implement and require little ongoing adjustment by network administrators. Furthermore, neither requires modification to the IP address scheme used for nonredundant connectivity.

Table 1-3. Relative cost of component redundancy

Line item	Description	Qty
1	Router 1 with additional interface cards and redundant power and processor and one year of vendor support	1
2	Firewall 1 with additional interface cards and redundant power and processor and one year of vendor support	1
3	Router 2 with additional interface cards and redundant power and processor and one year of vendor support	1
4	Firewall 2 with additional interface cards and redundant power and processor and one year of vendor support	1
5	Switch 1 and one year of vendor support	6
6	Multimode fiber trunk (materials and installation)	20
Total relative cost = $150,000		

Combined Component and Site-Redundant Architectures

A combination of component and site redundancy provides better network resilience than either component or site schemes do by themselves. Under the tenets of this scheme, failure of multiple components does not automatically trigger a failover to the backup site. This scheme is therefore much friendlier to both staff members and application systems. As with a simple site-based scheme, this hybrid still requires administrative attention to make sure the backup system can support resource use levels if the primary system fails.

Figure 1-4 illustrates the architectural principles of the hybrid component and site redundancy scheme applied to the simple transport network, and Table 1-4 details the relative cost associated with this scheme.

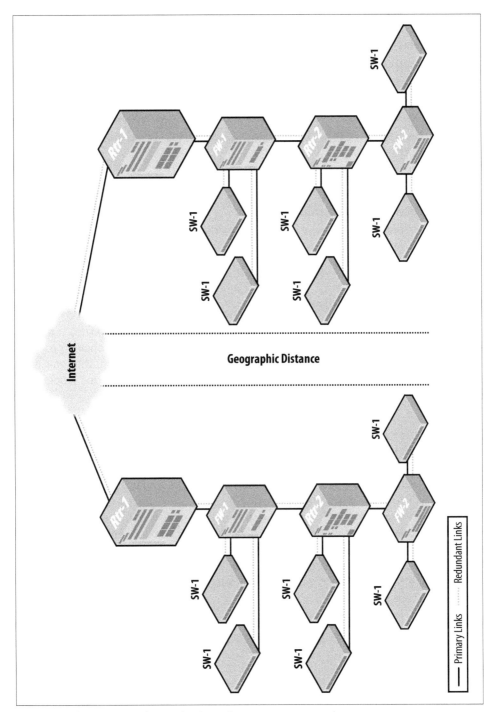

Figure 1-4. Component and site redundancy for a transport network

Table 1-4. Relative cost of component and site redundancy

Line item	Description	Qty
1	Router 1 with additional interface cards and redundant power and processor and one year of vendor support	2
2	Firewall 1 with additional interface cards and redundant power and processor and one year of vendor support	2
3	Router 2 with additional interface cards and redundant power and processor and one year of vendor support	2
4	Firewall 2 with additional interface cards and redundant power and processor and one year of vendor support	2
5	Switch 1 and one year of vendor support	12
6	Multimode fiber trunk (materials and installation)	40
7	Additional physical facilities startup costs	1
8	Additional physical facilities operational costs for one year (electricity, Internet connectivity, staffing, and support)	1

Total relative cost = $660,000

Redundant System Architectures

Use of redundant systems within the network architecture provides protection from both component failure and complete system failure. However, this scheme provides no protection from regional disaster. You should also take into account that on top of the cost of additional systems, the power and cooling requirements of this scheme are twice those of a simple, nonredundant architecture.

The redundant system architecture requires careful planning before deployment and requires ongoing administrative scrutiny for the life of the network because, assuming traffic load is balanced across paired systems, no single physical system or single physical link is permitted to exceed 50% utilization. If any system or link does exceed 50% utilization, failure of the paired device could result in loss of data. Loss of data is not synonymous with high availability. For example, let's say we have a traffic load evenly balanced between a pair of switches. If throughput across each of the individual switches is at 60% of individual switch capacity, then the two cannot accurately be described as a "redundant pair." If one of the switches in the pair were to fail, then a load equivalent to 120% of single-device capacity would be placed on the remaining switch (60% + 60% = 120%). Clearly many packets would spill out on the floor, making a terrible mess!

Figures 1-5 and 1-6 show two system redundancy principles applied to infrastructure links and user LANs. These diagrams also include physical cross connection among components.

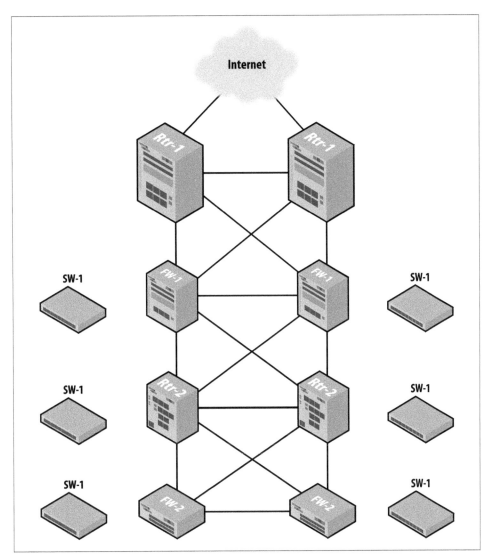

Figure 1-5. System redundancy for transport networks

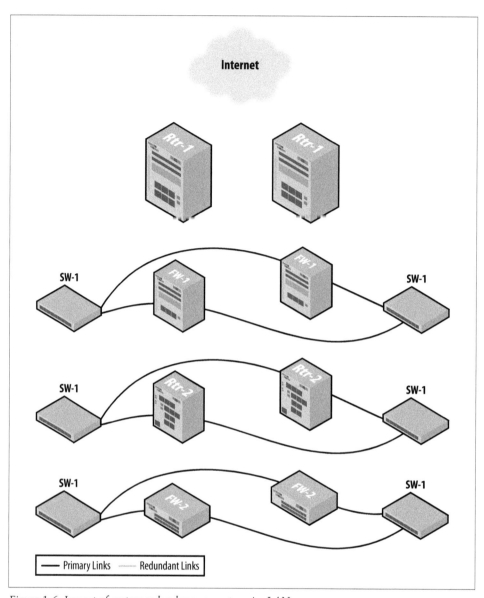

Figure 1-6. *Impact of system redundancy on enterprise LANs*

Table 1-5 shows the relative costs associated with use of redundant systems. Note the added cost of space cooling and electricity shown in the table.

Table 1-5. Relative cost of system redundancy

Line item	Description	Qty
1	Router 1 with interface cards and one year of vendor support	2
2	Firewall 1 with interface cards and one year of vendor support	2
3	Router 2 with interface cards and one year of vendor support	2
4	Firewall 2 with interface cards and one year of vendor support	2
5	Switch 1 and one year of vendor support	6
6	Multimode fiber trunk (materials and installation)	28
7	Additional space, cooling, and electrical use for second system	1

Total relative cost = $200,000

Combined System- and Site-Redundant Architectures

In modern network designs, redundant systems and redundant sites are commonly used to provide effective transport network resilience. This scheme is among the more expensive; however, it does protect users from component and system failure on a local basis, as well as from regional disasters. Furthermore, this scheme allows the enterprise to take advantage of system capabilities at both the primary and backup sites. As with other architectures featuring redundant systems, care must be taken to make sure that failure of a system or a component does not result in an excessive burden on the paired device.

Figure 1-7 illustrates these system and site redundancy principles applied to our simple transport network, with Table 1-6 giving details of the relative cost of the scheme.

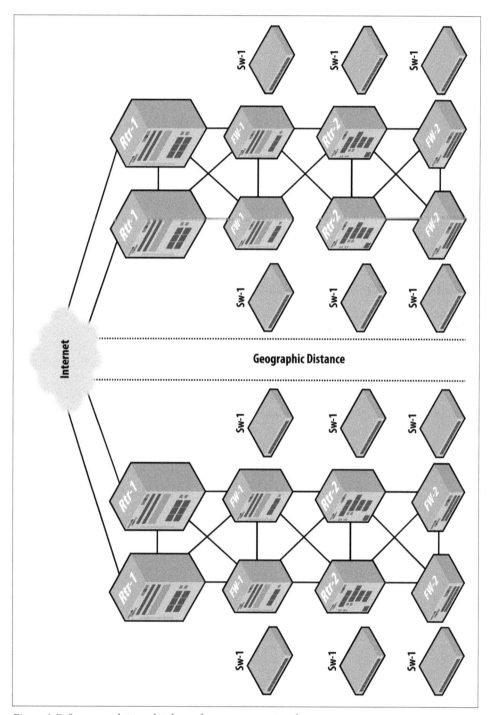

Figure 1-7. System and site redundancy for transport networks

Table 1-6. Relative cost of system and site redundancy

Line item	Description	Qty
1	Router 1 base bundle with interface cards and one year of vendor support	4
2	Firewall 1 with interface cards and one year of vendor support	4
3	Router 2 with interface cards and one year of vendor support	4
4	Firewall 2 with interface cards and one year of vendor support	4
5	Switch 1 and one year of vendor support	12
6	Multimode fiber trunk (materials and installation)	56
7	Additional physical facilities startup costs	1
8	Additional physical facilities operational costs for one year (electricity, Internet connectivity, staffing, and support)	1

Total relative cost = $720,000

Combined System- and Component-Redundant Architectures

Figures 1-8 and 1-9 show the combination of redundant systems and redundant components applied to the simple transport network model from Figure 1-1. This type of architecture is generally used only in situations in which an extremely strong resiliency scheme is required but site redundancy is *not* an option. And as itemized in Table 1-7, this scheme carries the added expense of double the amount of space, power, and cooling that would be required from a network that did not include redundant systems.

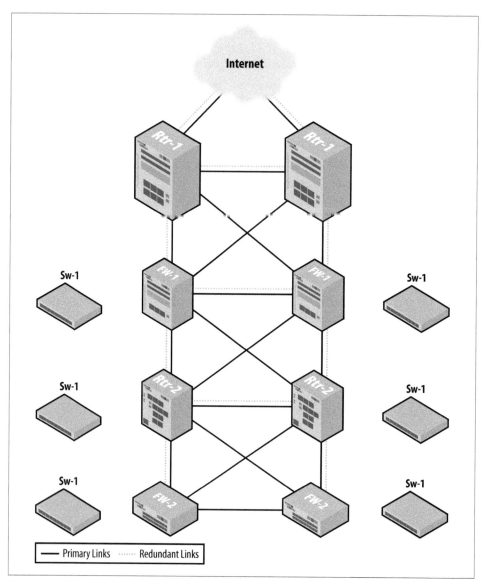

Figure 1-8. System and component redundancy for transport networks

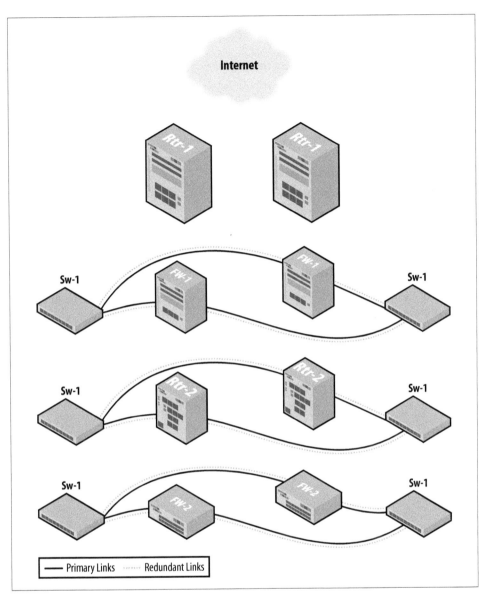

Figure 1-9. Impact of system and component redundancy on enterprise LANs

Table 1-7. Relative cost of system and component redundancy

Line item	Description	Qty
1	Router 1 with additional interface cards and redundant power and processor and one year of vendor support	2
2	Firewall 1 with additional interface cards and redundant power and processor and one year of vendor support	2
3	Router 2 with additional interface cards and redundant power and processor and one year of vendor support	2
4	Firewall 2 with additional interface cards and redundant power and processor and one year of vendor support	2
5	Switch 1 and one year of vendor support	6
6	Multimode fiber trunk (materials and installation)	56
7	Additional space, cooling, and electricity for second system	1
Total relative cost = $320,000		

Combined System-, Component-, and Site-Redundant Architectures

The model shown in Figure 1-10 provides the greatest protection possible from equipment failure and regional disaster, though at significant cost (you'll have to decide the price of failure for your network), as listed in Table 1-8. In comparison with the dollar amounts in Table 1-1, we can see that this scheme is almost 10 times the relative cost of a simple transport network.

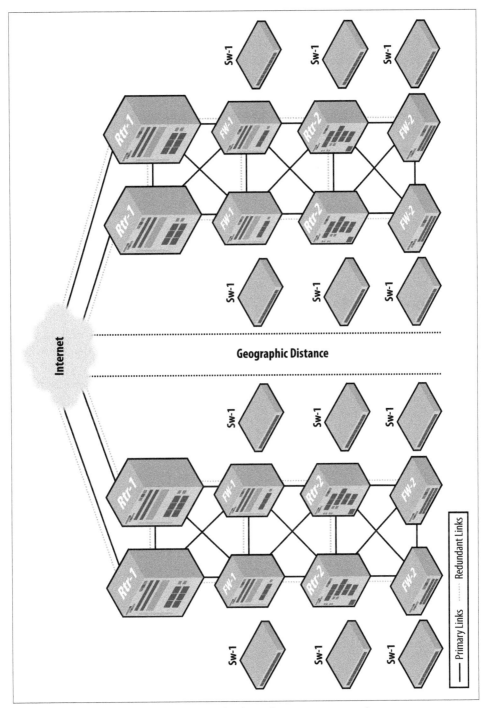

Figure 1-10. System, component, and site redundancy for transport networks

Table 1-8. Relative cost of system, component, and site redundancy

Line item	Description	Qty
1	Router 1 with additional interface cards and redundant power and processor and one year of vendor support	4
2	Firewall 1 with additional interface cards and redundant power and processor and one year of vendor support	4
3	Router 2 with additional interface cards and redundant power and processor and one year of vendor support	4
4	Firewall 2 with additional interface cards and redundant power and processor and one year of vendor support	4
5	Switch 1 and one year of vendor support	12
6	Multimode fiber trunk (materials and installation)	112
7	Additional physical facilities startup costs	1
8	Additional physical facilities operational costs for one year (electricity, Internet connectivity, staffing, and support)	1

Total relative cost = $970,000

What Does It All Mean?

You don't need to be a rocket scientist to figure out that the more protection your network has, the greater its cost. Fortunately, there is no rule requiring that every network be set up with the maximum amount of redundancy technologically available. Typically, networks are somewhere in between on the scale of "no protection" to "complete and redundant protection." Indeed, this book assumes you are in a gradual transition toward a higher availability and thus might find the final analysis useful.

Table 1-9 allows you to compare relative costs among the different redundancy schemes described in this chapter. Note that the relative dollar amounts are not as important (and indeed were manipulated for ease of comparison) as the cost represented as a multiplier of the simple nonredundant scheme. The relative cost number listed in the "Base system multiplier" column allows you to predict the cost of redundancy schemes for other enterprise network projects. You can then compare the cost estimates to the anticipated value of the services the network provides, or for nonprofits and government agencies, the importance of the purpose for which the network is being built.

Table 1-9. Relative cost comparison

Table #	Redundancy scheme	Provides protection from...	Total relative cost	Base system multiplier
1	None	Provides *no* protection	$100,000	1
2	Site redundancy	System failure, component failure, and regional disaster	$540,000	5.4
3	Component redundancy	Component failure	$150,000	1.5
4	Component and site redundancy	Component failure and regional disaster	$660,000	6.6
5	System redundancy	System failure and component failure	$200,000	2.0
6	System and site redundancy	System failure, component failure, and regional disaster, as well as regional disaster and single-system and single-component failure combinations	$720,000	7.2
7	System and component redundancy	System failure and component failure	$320,000	3.2
8	System, site, and component redundancy	System failure, component failure, and regional disaster, as well as regional disaster and single-system and multiple-component failure combinations	$970,000	9.7

CHAPTER 2

Hardware High Availability

Within networks, there are normally three roadblocks to high availability: hardware failures, software failures, and user-based configuration errors. Before we dive into the nitty-gritty details of how a string of acronyms (VRRP, ISSU, etc.) can improve the high availability of your network, we need to look at the hardware on which your network is based.

No matter how well designed a network is, if you're missing a few key features in the hardware design all the protocol hacks, routing tips, and best common practices offered up in the networking books on your shelf may be useless. Let's say that you have a set maintenance window for a bug scrub on your new router operating system, and you have tested the upgrade in the lab environment 10 times, but when you complete the upgrade, you discover that your routing engine (RE) is not booting. You will have to replace it and get your router running again before the maintenance window closes and calls start coming in from customers. To accomplish this task, it is vital that you have a way to smoothly replace hardware.

Any network design that is to provide high availability must be built on a solid foundation that offers stability, resiliency, and redundancy. Without such a foundation, the efforts of your team will be wasted on attempting to solve or mitigate issues through the use of complex redundancy protocol configurations or traffic engineering, when you and your customers would be better served by having the hardware in place to mitigate those issues so that your team can focus their time on adding or improving services on the network.

This chapter provides insight into the feature set of JUNOS devices that ultimately provide the resilient and stable hardware foundation upon which your network will thrive.

Divide and Conquer

Have you ever had someone in management, three tiers above you, send you email because you didn't use the new report cover or you missed some checkbox on a minor network form? This type of micromanagement can hamper efficiency, forcing individuals in an office to be responsible for a wide range of tasks and making them less efficient on the core tasks for which they are responsible.

Just as with the overworked employees in the micromanaged office, data processing chips in network equipment based on generalized designs, performing a multitude of functions such as routing protocols, packet forwarding, encryption, and system management, are less efficient in each of those processes because they are doing them all. By incorporating application-specific integrated circuits (ASICs) that perform very specific tasks, Juniper Networks equipment is able to provide efficient processing of packets and a stable foundation on which to build networks that provide high availability.

Since the beginning, Juniper's hardware design has steered clear of the monolithic processor trying to perform every task in the network device. The design architecture has instead been divided into the RE as the brain and the forwarding engine as the brawn.

Imagine if you will that all packages transiting a post office were required to be examined by the head postmaster to ensure that they were being handled properly. Package delivery would be totally unfeasible, which is why the head postmaster is responsible for high-level management and the mail sorters and carriers are responsible for getting the mail out to the right address. This *separation of tasks* provides the high availability for the post office, and it is the same philosophy that applies to network equipment. Figure 2-1 illustrates the separation of the Packet Forwarding Engine (PFE) and the RE.

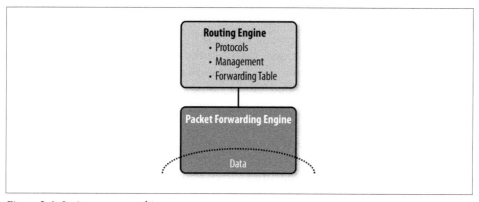

Figure 2-1. Juniper router architecture

While Figure 2-1 is a simplified look at the Juniper Networks router architecture, the RE serves the purpose of the head postmaster in our post office metaphor. Though the RE is responsible for managing the overall processes of the system, such as processing the routing and management protocols, it is not responsible for actually forwarding the packets. Without the packet forwarding responsibilities, the processor cycles of the RE are used to process the routing and management protocols present on the network, performing the calculations to determine the best path to an address, and create a forwarding table tree that the ASICs in the forwarding engine can easily parse.

This type of architecture quickly proves itself in a network, especially when you have a full Internet routing table feed and, possibly, Multiprotocol Label Switching (MPLS) virtual private networks (VPNs). Looking at older-generation routers, the toll on the CPU caused by processing all the management protocols, as well as forwarding the packets, led to lower throughputs and performance even on high-end equipment. It is not uncommon to see a router advertised with 4 Gbps bidirectional throughput pass fewer than 100 Mbps while its CPU spikes to 100% utilization in this type of situation. With processor cycles being split between packet forwarding and management protocols, the CPU is overworked to the point where protocol processes may die or packets may be dropped. The divided architecture ensures that packet processing does not impact CPU performance and the reconvergence of routing protocols does not affect packet throughput.

The PFE serves the purpose of the sorters and carriers in our snail mail example. It is responsible for comparing the addresses on incoming packet headers and determining their next hop based on the forwarding table pushed from the RE. Without the need to understand the routing and management protocols, the PFE is able to process all the transit packets efficiently. The only packets that are ever sent to the RE are those of local significance, such as routing protocol and management packets, or other packets of special interest such as packets with the IP option bits set.

By dividing the processes of routing and packet forwarding, the RE remains stable during times of unusually high network activity, and the PFE remains stable during times of network and routing table churn. When you provide this stability in your networking equipment, you have taken the first step in guaranteeing that the network achieves your high availability goals.

The architecture is further divided with the use of Adaptive Services Physical Interface Cards (PICs) in Juniper Networks M and T Series equipment, and Services Processing Cards (SPCs) in the Juniper Networks SRX Series, to offload highly intensive processing used for services such as stateful firewalls, VPNs, and intrusion detection and prevention. Again, by removing these new calculations from the work of the RE and PFE, the chassis is able to provide high availability and throughput even with a multitude of services running on the equipment.

The Brains: The Routing Engine

If you were to pull one of the REs out of the device—preferably a device that has a redundant RE—it would look strangely familiar. Unlike some routing products that cloak their deep magic in jumbles of unidentifiable chips and wires, the Juniper RE looks just like a PC motherboard, with all the standard features: Intel-based processor, hard drive, RAM, and Ethernet port. Here is a brief description of the role each component plays:

General processor

Ranging from Pentium III to Pentium 4 and Intel Celeron, the processor provides the power for running the kernel and performing the routing and management functionality of the router. In the Juniper Networks EX Series, the PowerPC processor is used.

Random access memory

The random access memory performs the normal RAM functionality of the processor and is sized to scale to allow storage of routing tables with millions of routes, which is hundreds of times the size of the current Internet routing tables.

Hard disk drive

This is a standard hard drive on which a backup of the Juniper operating system (JUNOS) is stored. Including a hard drive in the system allows for flexibility in logging and system configuration management. More importantly, the hard disk drive is used to store the Unix logs from the underlying FreeBSD operating system.

CompactFlash drive

The CompactFlash storage on the Juniper RE stores the JUNOS software and the current configurations.

Ethernet port

The Ethernet port on the RE allows for direct access to the RE's management processes for Out of Band (OoB) management.

RE comparison

Some people new to Juniper equipment are surprised that the processors in the RE can be earlier models than those in their PCs. Because of the efficiency of BSD-based operating systems and the JUNOS software, the earlier Pentium and Celeron processors are more than powerful enough to run the protocols and keep track of the routing tables. Remember, these processors are not responsible for forwarding traffic—the ASICs handle that.

An additional advantage with the older general processors is that they require less electrical supply and cooling than the more modern chips. This allows the equipment to be in a better high availability posture during times of high heat or electrical grid disruption.

Though based on a common architecture, the REs within various Juniper Networks devices have unique throughput and traffic requirements that correspond with their specific usage. Understanding how the RE was designed for specific network equipment is worth a few moments of inspection. By reviewing the design of each of these REs, you can see how they are scaled and scoped to ensure that they remain stable during the most extreme network conditions, thus allowing your network to maintain its high availability status.

M Series. The first of the core networking routers in the Juniper product line, and thus a general-purpose routing device, the M Series provides flexibility in its RE deployment.

Table 2-1 shows the available REs for the various M Series equipment. Though the M7i does not offer RE redundancy, the M10i, M120, and M320 all offer the ability to install redundant REs in an active/standby mode. As you can see in Table 2-1, some of the REs are interchangeable among different equipment within the series. With a lack of redundancy in REs and with its throughput levels, the M7i is very well suited for branch offices where redundancy is not needed or provided through multihomed connections to an ISP. The full redundancy in the rest of the M Series allows the devices to form the core of an enterprise network or the edge of a service provider.

Table 2-1. M Series REs

Specifications	M7i	M10i	M120	M320
400 MHz Intel Celeron processor	X	X		
768 MB SDRAM	(NR)[a]			
1 GB CompactFlash				
20 GB IDE hard disk drive				
850 MHz Intel Pentium III processor	X	X		
1536 MB SDRAM	(NR)			
1 GB CompactFlash				
40 GB IDE hard disk drive				
1 GHz Intel Celeron M processor			X	
2 GB DRAM				
1 GB CompactFlash				
40 GB IDE hard disk drive				
1.6 GHz Intel Pentium 4 M processor				X
2 GB DRAM				
1 GB CompactFlash				
40 GB IDE hard disk drive				
2 GHz Intel Celeron M processor			X	X
4 GB DRAM				
1 GB CompactFlash				
40 GB IDE hard disk drive				

[a] (NR) = No redundancy available

MX Series. The Juniper Networks MX Series routers are positioned for use in the Metro Ethernet realm, and provide high throughput and various services. The REs in this line are based on the Intel Celeron chipset. All models of equipment within the MX Series offer the ability to install redundant REs.

It is important to remember that the resiliency and redundancy of the hardware are only as good as the rest of your network design. No number of redundant parts can ensure high availability in your network when a backhoe cuts your only fiber cable to a distant site.

Imagine that for your network you have just been put in charge of ensuring that service-level agreements (SLAs) are maintained and that they include guarantees not only for high availability, but also for rapid response if any of the equipment fails. With interchangeable REs in the MX Series and optional hardware redundancy, you are able to meet the high availability requirements either by having seamless failover between the redundant equipment or by reducing your Mean Time to Repair (MTTR) by having a general spare RE to install in case of a hardware failure in a nonredundant system. Table 2-2 lists the REs for the MX Series.

Table 2-2. MX Series REs

Specifications	MX240	MX480	MX960
1.3 GHz Intel Celeron M processor	X	X	X
2 GB DRAM			
1 GB CompactFlash			
40 GB IDE hard disk drive			
2 GHz Intel Celeron M processor	X	X	X
4 GB DRAM			
1 GB CompactFlash			
40 GB IDE hard disk drive			

T Series. In the core network "big iron" range of routers, the T Series is designed for high throughput and redundancy. The T Series REs are based on the Pentium 4 chipsets, can be fully redundant in all models of the series, and are interchangeable among all chassis. The TX Matrix, which allows multiple T1600s or T640s to be connected to form a virtual router chassis, requires redundant REs. The T Series REs are covered in Table 2-3. The *virtual router chassis* or *routing node* created by the T Series adds important high availability features to the routing core. With all the routers attached through the matrix appearing as a single router, the systems offer multiple redundant paths across the node. If a single RE fails, the other REs in the node are available to continue managing the routing information. Only in the rare case that a full chassis fails would a large number of links be affected, but of course, this too could be mitigated with redundant links to multiple chassis in the node.

Table 2-3. T Series REs

Specifications	T320	T640	T1600	TX Matrix
1.6 GHz Pentium 4 processor	X	X	X	X
2 GB DRAM				(RR)[a]
1 GB CompactFlash				
40 GB IDE hard disk drive				
2 GHz Pentium 4 processor	X	X	X	X
4 GB DRAM				(RR)
1 GB CompactFlash				
40 GB IDE hard disk drive				

[a] (RR) = Redundancy required

EX Series. Unlike the other devices in the Juniper Networks line, the EX Series does not rely on a removable RE. In the EX Series, the RE is built into the chassis itself. To provide for RE redundancy, the switches can be connected to provide a single virtual switch chassis. This Virtual Chassis (VC) uses one RE as the master of the system and another one as a backup to provide high availability for the switching network.

Though the EX Series has been designed to fit into your network within the data center, or in any area that relies on traditional Ethernet switching systems, it also includes an RE so that it can participate in the routing protocols running on the core or distribution layer routers to which it is attached. The ability of the EX Series to work at Layer 3 as well as Layer 2 moves the platform away from the typical switch's reliance on Spanning Tree Protocol (STP), which was designed merely to prevent loops in a Layer 2 architecture but was not designed to provide the deterministic packet forwarding or resiliency necessary in a high availability architecture. Table 2-4 shows the details of the EX Series.

Table 2-4. EX Series REs

Specifications	EX3200	EX4200	EX8200
600 MHz Power PC processor	X	X	X
512 MB DRAM	(NR)[a]		
1 GB CompactFlash			
20 GB IDE hard disk drive			

[a] (NR) = No redundancy available

SRX Series. The most recent addition to the Juniper Networks product line is the SRX Series of security gateways which not only provide full routing capabilities, but also provide for VPNs, high-throughput stateful firewalls, and industry-leading intrusion detection and prevention. As with the rest of the product lines discussed in this book, the SRX uses the JUNOS operating system running on an RE, which in the case of the

SRX is located in its System Control Board (SCB). Though a detailed explanation of the SRX Series is beyond the scope of this book, its architecture mirrors that of the router and switch product lines.

J Series. The RE within the J Series is different from all others in the other product lines because of this platform's position in the enterprise routing arena. With a focus on accessibility, cost savings, and the provision of services to lower bandwidths in branch offices, the J Series divided architecture is based on software modules instead of discrete hardware. This difference makes the choice of an RE for the J Series far simpler. The RE within the J Series can come with upgraded RAM or an additional hardware encryption accelerator, but no other options. High availability for the J Series can be provided through the use of Virtual Router Redundancy Protocol (VRRP) or other protocols, as well as multihoming to several ISPs.

> For small offices with little or no IT support, sometimes the best way to provide high availability is simplicity in the deployment and configuration of the network device. The J Series, with web configuration and limited configurations, is appropriate for your most distant offices, whereas the more complex systems may require you to spend hours on the phone walking someone through configuration or troubleshooting.

The Brawn: The Packet Forwarding Engine

Having the RE responsible for the management and routing tasks on the device frees the PFE to forward data packets as efficiently as possible.

Unlike the RE, which uses a general processor for calculations and processes, the PFE consists of ASICs designed to perform specific jobs as efficiently and accurately as possible. The jobs within the PFE, such as Layer 2 header decoding, IP longest-prefix match lookup, and buffer memory management, are divided among these ASICs.

At lower levels of throughput, the Juniper device relies on a single PFE per chassis to perform packet processing tasks, but as the device's bandwidth needs grow, device throughput is scaled by using multiple PFEs per chassis—even to the point where multiple PFEs exist on a single interface card.

Hardware components

Throughout the entire line of Juniper products, the PFE performs the function of handling the processing of media signaling, Layer 2 encapsulation, Layer 3 routing and filtering, and packet forwarding. Though the overarching architecture for the PFE and the router is the same, how individual products in the line perform this duty is slightly different. The roles that individual components play in the PFE are as follows:

Layer 2 Processor ASICs

These provide Layer 2 header processing for packets across the network.

Internet Processor ASICs

The heart of the PFE, the Internet Processor ASIC provides efficient and quick packet processing at Layer 3 and higher.

PIC

In the M Series and T Series routers, the PICs provide ports and processing for specific media types. The Controller ASICs on the PIC perform framing and line-speed signaling specific to the media type.

Flexible PIC Concentrator (FPC)

In the M Series and T Series, the FPC provides connectivity between the PICs and the midplane of the device. In the T Series and in the M320, M120, and M40e, the FPC also provides an Internet Processor ASIC for longest-prefix match lookups.

Services Processing Cards (SPCs)

The SPCs of the SRX Series host Services Processing Units (SPUs) that are used to offload the processing of security-related features, such as stateful firewalling and denial-of-service (DoS) mitigation.

Control boards

In the M Series, the control boards provide the Internet Processor to process the Layer 3 (and higher) headers of the packets. In the T Series and MX Series, the control boards provide the Switch Interface ASIC for data and notification cell switching across the backplane.

Midplane

The midplane provides connectivity between the various components that make up a single PFE, or between PFEs in systems with multiple PFEs.

Buffering and memory control

Each product has ASICs specifically designed to buffer data packets and to switch data packets across the midplane of the device.

Model comparison

Though the PFE provides the same functionality in each model in the product line, the architecture in each series is slightly different, depending on the market use Juniper initially intended it to serve. At the lower end of the product line, the packet forwarding components are built into the chassis. Products at the higher end provide options allowing for PFE scaling and hardware redundancy. For more comprehensive coverage of individual hardware components, see the hardware guides at *http://juniper.net/tech pubs*.

M Series. The M Series PFEs consist of an FPC and a control board. At the lower end of the M Series (the M7i and M10i), the FPCs are built into the chassis. At the high end of the M Series, the PFE is divided among removable FPCs and removable Forwarding Engine Boards (FEBs). In order to support the high throughput needed by the M320, the highest in the M Series, the M320 is identically architected to the T640. By having control boards and packet forwarding components that can be replaced without causing a full network outage, it is possible to maintain high availability even during hardware failures.

The M Series has the following combination of FPCs and control boards:

M7i/M10i FPC
> The FPC on the low-end M Series equipment is built into the router chassis.

M120FPC-1, 2, 3
> Three revisions of the standard M120 FPC exist for the various revisions of PICs.

M320FPC-1, 2, 3
> Three revisions of the standard M320 FPC exist for the various revisions of PICs.

cFPC
> This is a *compact FPC* with a single built-in interface. cFPCs are available with OC-192 and 10 Gigabit Ethernet interfaces.

M7i/M10i cFEB
> The *compact FEB* is the control board within the M7i and M10i. A single board is present in the M7i, but the M10i can support two cFEBs in an active/standby mode for RE redundancy.

MX Series. Within the MX Series, the concept of the FPC is replaced with the Dense Port Concentrator (DPC), which provides four PFEs per DPC. The SCBs within the MX Series provide the Switch Interface ASIC for the management of data packets across the midplane of the system. The DPCs are interchangeable among the MX240, MX480, and MX960. The interchangeable nature of the MX Series components makes it easier to maintain high availability in the Metro Ethernet environment, because a limited number of spares can be stored to mitigate any threat from hardware failures.

The DPCs in the MX Series Ethernet Services Routers are designed to supply the most efficient performance based on the services they are to provide. The MX Series has three DPC models:

DPCE-X
> Designed for distributed and centralized office Ethernet and Metro Ethernet aggregation. The cards provide both virtual LAN (VLAN) and MPLS aggregation.

DPCE-R
> Provides for a full suite of routing protocols and upper-layer packet processing capabilities.

DPCE-EQ
> A DPCE-X or DPCE-R card providing more advanced queuing capabilities.

Table 2-5 lists the basic features available on the DPCE-X and DPCE-R (advanced queuing is in addition to these features).

Table 2-5. DPC differentiation

Feature	DPCE-X	DPCE-R
IP multicast	Yes	Yes
Layer 2 switching and STP	Yes	Yes
Virtual Private LAN Service or VPLS (Layer 2 VPNs)	Yes	Yes
RFC 2547 VPNs (Layer 3 VPNs)	No	Yes
Border Gateway Protocol (BGP)	No (limited scaling)	Yes
uRFP	No	Yes
Source class usage/destination class usage (SCU/DCU)	No	Yes
Filter scalability	Limited	Very large

> The midplane communication in the MX Series is controlled by the SCB, which has a Switch Interface ASIC that communicates with a Switch Interface ASIC on the DPC.

T Series. As with the M Series, the T Series relies on the concept of FPCs, but like the MX Series, its control board is in the system (the T Series Switch Interface Board) and provides for connectivity between the FPCs. Within the T Series, as well as the M120 and M320, the Internet Processor is on the FPC itself. This change in architecture facilitates the system's higher packet throughput, as well as allowing the T Series to be connected to other T Series routers through the T Series matrix.

Through the use of the T Series matrix switch, the equipment attached to the switch appears as a single routing node. The routing node provides multiple redundant paths, REs, and systems to ensure that the node remains available.

EX Series. Because the EX Series was designed to be a switch and to work efficiently at Layer 2 and Layer 3, the EX architecture is based on the new EX-PFE ASIC. Depending on the size, chassis, and number of ports on the switch, the EX Series can contain from one to three PFEs. To make the EX Series more efficient at forwarding Layer 2 traffic, the RE in the system not only pushes down the standard forwarding table with Layer 3 information, but also pushes a bridging table.

In existing networks, STP and Layer 2 switching are used at the access layer and sometimes at the core to provide packet forwarding. In accordance with STP rules, loops are prevented in the Layer 2 switching network by forwarding packets across only a single forwarding path. This restriction results in reduced efficiency and increased complexity in troubleshooting and scalability, which in turn affects the high availability of the network. However, by using uplink modules, you can combine the EX Series switches in your network to form a VC, providing for redundancy of the RE as well as eliminating the need for STP between the switches. Creating a VC eliminates extraneous packet processing and allows the chassis to build a shortest-path tree for packets moving between PFEs, which allows for a more deterministic forwarding of packets and a higher high availability profile for the switch.

SRX Series. The SRX Series of security gateways possess separate REs and PFEs to provide the same throughput and high availability as the rest of the product line. To ensure that the stateful firewall and security features also realize the same high availability posture, the SRX Series uses SPCs to offload the processing. You can find more information on the SRX Series on the Juniper website.

J Series. In the J Series RE, the PFE components are not discrete pieces of hardware, but are instead virtualized within software modules. These software modules handle the Layer 2 header processing and longest-prefix match lookups. Interfaces on the J Series are provided by either Physical Interface Modules (PIMs) or Enhanced Physical Interface Modules (E-PIMs), which can be interchanged with other J Series equipment or with the Juniper Secure Services Gateway (SSG). The first-generation J Series equipment, including the J4300 and J6300, accept the PIM cards, whereas the second generation—the J2350, J4350, and J6350—support both the PIM and E-PIM cards. For more information on card compatibility, see the "Physical Interface Module Compatibility Matrix for J Series Routers and Secure Services Gateways" at *http://juniper.net/ us/en/products-services/routing/j-series/*.

The design of the J Series provides high availability for networks without incurring the higher expense or complexity of M Series equipment. The simplicity of the J Series allows it to sit in your network at branch offices or in smaller portions of the network where full redundancy of connectivity is not available, and provides the highest level of availability possible in this position.

Packet Flows

From a high availability perspective, the divided architecture affects how packets flow through the different equipment. As with the hardware, the way packets flow through the network varies slightly across the equipment lines. It is important to understand how packets are passed through the components to fully realize what impact a component failure might have on the high availability of an individual piece of equipment and of the entire network.

Packet flows throughout the Juniper equipment line are similar, with differences that are primarily the result of hardware size and scalability. At the enterprise routing level, J Series packets travel through a virtualized environment mimicking the hardware of the larger pieces of equipment. Beginning with the M Series (the M7i and M10i) and extending into the entire Juniper router and switch product line, packet flow depends on ASICs to perform very specialized tasks, such as Layer 2 processing, data buffering, and most importantly, longest-prefix match lookup and packet header processing.

In all Juniper architecture, packet processing is not performed on the packet itself; instead, the routers use a copy of the key information within the IP header. As each incoming packet is processed, the packet is split into 64-byte J-cells, which are stored in the RAM of the forwarding engine. The key information from the IP header, as well as local information, such as the incoming interface, is copied into a Juniper-specific cell of information. This *notification cell* is processed through the entire array of hardware components and points to the location where the rest of the packet contents are retained in storage. Through this separation of control data from the IP header and actual data, the system is not required to transfer whole packets to and from the Internet Processor ASIC, allowing the bus systems to remain free to switch the notification cells. This limited transfer of full data packets allows for less writing to and reading from buffers, and leads to faster processing of individual packets, which translates into higher availability of bandwidth for users.

M Series

To better understand how the M Series architecture allows for high availability, we will follow a packet through the system. Figure 2-2 is an example of the hardware layout for the M Series routers.

In the smaller boxes of the M Series, the M7i and M10i, the PFE is contained within the cFEB.

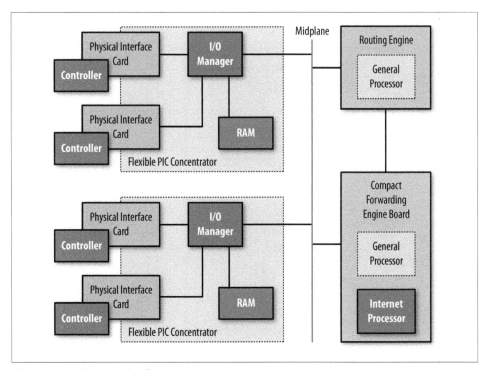

Figure 2-2. M Series packet flow

When a packet first arrives at the PIC, ASICs on the card verify that the link layer information is valid. If it is, the packet is forwarded to the FPC, which validates the data link and network layer information and copies the key information into a notification cell. After the notification cell is pushed to the Internet Processor for route lookup, the rest of the packet is segmented in 64-byte J-cells, which are written into memory. By writing packets across all FPCs in the system, the M Series routers prevent single sessions from being punished during hardware failures. With the correction and control methods in TCP/IP, the end user should never see any indication of a failure in the system—which of course is the goal of high availability.

The Internet Processor conducts a longest-prefix match lookup on the notification header, and performs other functionality such as packet filtering. After the packet is processed, the resulting cell, cleverly called the *result cell*, is sent to the outgoing FPC. It is the result cell that is queued at the FPC until the packet is ready to be transmitted. Then, the first J-cell of the packet is called from memory, any network layer header modifications are made, and the packet is given a data link layer header. Pointers within the first J-cell point to the next memory location, and each subsequent J-cell points to the next in line; thus, the packet is rebuilt before transmission.

Figure 2-3 is an example of the architecture in the M120 family. You can see that the architecture is the same as that of the other M Series equipment. The only difference is in the naming of the control board.

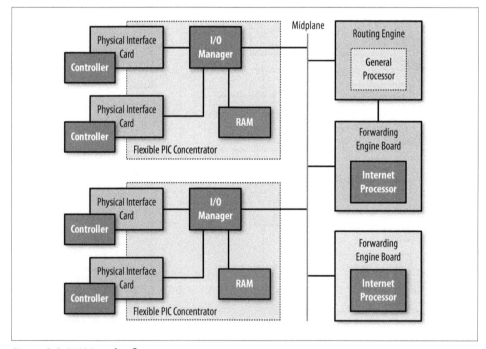

Figure 2-3. M120 packet flow

MX Series

Following the original design of the M Series, the T Series and eventually the MX Series were created with redundancy in the PFEs to ensure that high availability would be maintained. Within the MX Series, the Switch Interface ASIC controls the flow of packets across the midplane. Before packets are sent from the ingress PFE to the egress PFE, the system requests the proper bandwidth for the transmission. This interaction guarantees the efficient flow of packets. By deploying the features of redundant PFEs and switch control boards, the MX Series is scaled to handle the large packet through-puts necessary for the Metro Ethernet realm while maintaining high availability. Figure 2-4 shows the packet flow of the MX Series.

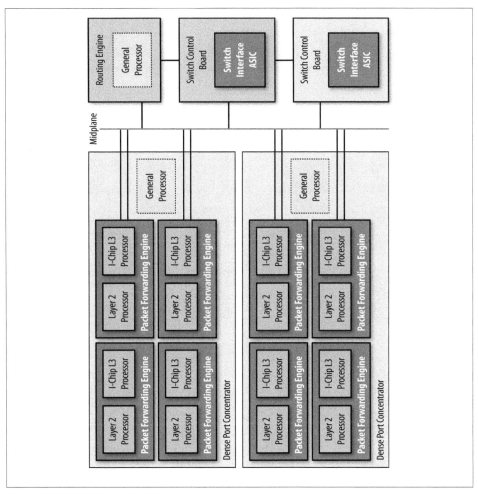

Figure 2-4. MX Series packet flow

T Series

Figure 2-5 shows the components that make up the packet flow for the T Series routers. As you can see, the T Series also uses redundant control boards and PFEs to maintain the high level of throughput necessary in the core. The Queuing and Management Interface ASIC is unique to the T Series; it performs the management necessary to read and write the data packets from the buffer memory. Through the use of the notification cell, the T Series also maintains the integrity of the data across the chassis so that packets are not lost in buffers.

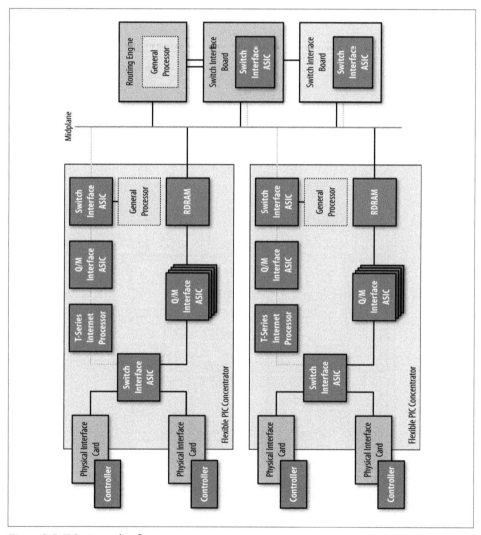

Figure 2-5. T Series packet flow

EX Series

The EX Series is Juniper's first venture into enterprise switching, and thus the packet flow within the EX places more emphasis on Layer 2 addressing than the other routers. The RE of the EX Series calculates both a forwarding table and a bridging table and pushes both to the PFEs that support the individual Ethernet ports. The RE builds the bridging table using the Source Media Access Control (Source MAC or SMAC) addresses it receives from the network. As packets are received, if the EX Series knows the Destination MAC (DMAC) address, the packet is switched to the appropriate PFE and forwarded. If the SMAC address of the packet is not known, a copy of the header information is forwarded to the RE and the address is added to the bridging table, which is then pushed to the PFE. For the packets that arrive with an unknown DMAC address, the PFE automatically floods the packet to all ports on the switch, except for the ingress port. When the reply to the Address Resolution Protocol (ARP) call is received, the SMAC address from the reply is copied and sent to the RE for inclusion in the bridging table. Figure 2-6 shows the EX Series packet flow.

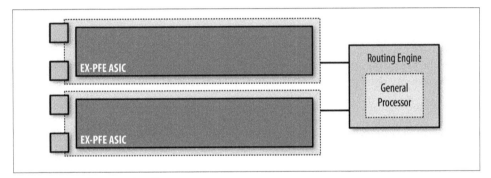

Figure 2-6. EX Series packet flow

SRX Series

With the additional functionality of stateful firewalling, intrusion detection and prevention, and VPNs, packets in the SRX Series have an extra step of being processed by SPCs. The SPCs are designed to efficiently perform all the security functions for the product line.

J Series

The J Series routers, which sit at the enterprise routing level of the Juniper product line, have the same overall packet flow as the rest of the equipment we have discussed. The major difference with the J Series is that the specific hardware functionality, such as the PFE, the RE, and their respective ASICs, has been virtualized into software processes to provide the same stability and efficiency for networks that require less overall throughput.

Redundancy and Resiliency

While Juniper's divided architecture keeps networks stable during times of network churn or high throughput, it is still possible that hardware failures may decrease the high availability of the network. To counter the possible downtime created by the rare occurrence of hardware failure, all the carrier-class platforms include the availability of hardware redundancy for key components, including the power supplies, REs, and SCBs. For other components, such as PICs, FPCs, and fans, the system provides the ability to swap parts while the network is operational, without affecting the performance of the entire system.

Each of these Field Replaceable Units (FRUs) can be categorized into one of two types:

Hot-swappable/hot-insertable
  Can be removed and replaced without powering down the system and without disrupting the routing function

Hot-pluggable
  Can be removed and replaced without powering down the system, but routing functions are disrupted if a redundant FRU is not available or is not active

 Keeping spare FRUs that are compatible among chassis can drastically reduce MTTR.

M Series

The M Series provides the option of power supply redundancy at all levels of the system, and offers full redundancy of the RE and PFE beginning at the M10i router. This redundancy in the system mitigates the threat of hardware failures in your network reducing your high availability. The ability to hot-swap or hot-plug the gear also ensures that a hardware failure does not have to affect the packet processing being performed by the entire system. Table 2-6 illustrates the resilient and redundant nature of the M Series.

Table 2-6. M Series redundancy and resiliency

FRU	M7i	M10i	M120	M320
Fan tray	Hot-swappable	Hot-swappable	Hot-swappable	Hot-swappable
PIC	Hot-swappable	Hot-swappable	Hot-swappable	Hot-swappable
FPC	Hot-swappable	Hot-swappable	Hot-swappable	Hot-swappable

FRU	M7i	M10i	M120	M320
Power supply	Hot-swappable (if redundant)	Hot-swappable (if redundant)	Hot-swappable (if redundant)	Hot-swappable (if redundant)
RE	Hot-pluggable	Hot-swappable (if redundant)	Hot-swappable (if redundant)	Hot-swappable (if redundant)
PFE components	Hot-pluggable	Hot-swappable (if redundant)	Hot-swappable (if redundant)	Hot-swappable (if redundant)

MX Series

The MX Series provides the option of full redundancy in all chassis. Again, full redundancy mitigates hardware failures in the network. However, as with the other series in the Juniper line, redundancy is optional when budget constraints outweigh the need for the highest levels of high availability. Table 2-7 highlights the FRUs for the MX Series.

Table 2-7. MX Series redundancy and resiliency

FRU	MX240	M480	M960
Fan tray	Hot-swappable	Hot-swappable	Hot-swappable
Power supply	Hot-swappable (if redundant)	Hot-swappable (if redundant)	Hot-swappable (if redundant)
Backup SCB	Hot-swappable (if redundant)	Hot-swappable (if redundant)	Hot-swappable (if redundant)
Backup RE	Hot-swappable (if redundant)	Hot-swappable (if redundant)	Hot-swappable (if redundant)
DPC	Hot-swappable	Hot-swappable	Hot-swappable
Master SCB	Hot-pluggable (if redundant)	Hot-pluggable (if redundant)	Hot-pluggable (if redundant)
Master RE	Hot-pluggable (if redundant)	Hot-pluggable (if redundant)	Hot-pluggable (if redundant)

T Series

The T Series also provides the option of full redundancy in all chassis. For the T640 and T1600, additional redundancy is provided by the TX Matrix. As with the rest of the routers that offer full redundancy, the T Series ensures high availability in the network through the use of components that do not affect the packet forwarding of the entire system if a hardware failure occurs. Also, if a component does fail, the entire router does not have to be taken out of service to replace it. Table 2-8 highlights the FRUs for the T Series.

The T Series takes redundancy a step further, though, with the concept of a routing node, or virtual routing chassis. In the core of your network, the T Series can be connected to other T Series routers through the TX Matrix to form a routing node with a single virtual control plane. This additional redundancy ensures that the core networks that it supports are always available.

Table 2-8. T Series redundancy and resiliency

FRU	T320	T640	T1600
Fan tray	Hot-swappable	Hot-swappable	Hot-swappable
PIC	Hot-swappable	Hot-swappable	Hot-swappable
FPC	Hot-swappable	Hot-swappable	Hot-swappable
Power supply	Hot-swappable (if redundant)	Hot-swappable (if redundant)	Hot-swappable (if redundant)
Switch Interface Board	Hot-swappable	Hot-swappable	Hot-swappable
T640 Switch Interface Board	Hot-swappable	Hot-swappable	Hot-swappable
Backup T-Control Board	Hot-swappable (if redundant)	Hot-swappable (if redundant)	Hot-swappable (if redundant)
Backup RE	Hot-swappable (if redundant)	Hot swappable (if redundant)	Hot-swappable (if redundant)
Master T-Control Board	Hot-pluggable (if redundant)	Hot-pluggable (if redundant)	Hot-pluggable (if redundant)
Master RE	Hot-pluggable (if redundant)	Hot-pluggable (if redundant)	Hot-pluggable (if redundant)

J Series

Because the J Series Enterprise Router is positioned for smaller networks, such as branch offices, that normally do not have redundant links or the cooling and cabling facilities for a larger routing platform, it does not provide for full hardware redundancy. If you need high availability in a branch office, the J Series does support VRRP to allow it to work in tandem with a second J Series router, as well as full routing functionality to allow it to be used to also multihome with separate ISPs for redundancy.

SRX Series

With the SRX Series performing functions ranging from security SOHOs to ISP-level data centers, redundancy of the systems varies greatly. At the basic security gateway level, redundancy is available on a network level with multiple gateways being able to work in either an active/active or an active/standby configuration. Beginning with the SRX650 and up through the SRX3400, SRX3600, SRX5600, and SRX5800, component and power redundancy along with network redundancy is available.

EX Series

With the introduction of the EX Series, Juniper moves its high availability design to the switching infrastructure. The chassis of the entry-level EX3200 switch does not provide for internal redundant power supplies, but it can be attached to an external power supply that provides the redundancy needed for high availability. At the current pinnacle of switches, the EX8208, the hardware supports multiple redundancy designs and an optional redundant Switching and Routing Engine (SRE) Module. Table 2-9 indicates the FRUs for the EX Series.

Table 2-9. EX Series redundancy and resiliency

FRU	EX3200	EX4200	EX8208
Fan tray	Hot-swappable	Hot-swappable	Hot-swappable
Power supply	Hot-swappable (when an external redundant power supply is used)	Hot-swappable (if redundant)	110 V 3+3 redundancy
			110 V 5+1 redundancy
			220 V 3+3 redundancy
			220 V 3+1 redundancy
SRE	N/A	N/A	Hot-swappable

CHAPTER 3

Software High Availability

In many networks, there seems to be a very clear divide in administration levels between those who consider themselves server experts and those who consider themselves networking experts. The problem is that the actual pieces of our networking equipment are merely computers designed specifically to pass traffic as quickly as possible. Though a network engineer does not require the knowledge to recompile kernels in order to maintain high availability in his network, he should have at least a basic understanding of how the operating system software that is running on his network equipment is designed.

By understanding how JUNOS software is designed and operates on your equipment, you are able to more accurately plan and prepare for critical situations, such as network-wide software upgrades, when high availability needs to be maintained. These are the times when the software is placed under the greatest strain.

This chapter provides an overview of the software design decisions and the software architecture of JUNOS devices, for it is the JUNOS software that provides the stable software foundation for the control of resilient and redundant hardware.

Software Architecture

Just as with the Juniper hardware, as discussed in Chapter 2, the software operating on Juniper Networks routing equipment has been specifically designed for stability and resiliency. Starting from a known stable base, JUNOS software has been designed and coded to provide maximum stability. It also incorporates features to mitigate errors that might lead to reduced uptime.

Stable Foundations

Just as the routing engine (RE) of the Juniper Networks routers is built upon proven and standard technologies, it was consistent for Juniper Networks to build its JUNOS operating system on a stable and proven software product. Instead of reinventing code and building a proprietary operating system from scratch, Juniper adopted the Berkeley Software Distribution, better known as BSD, as its foundation. The choice of BSD as the operating systems of the Juniper network equipment was logical because of its long history of stability. It is a Unix version from the University of California, Berkeley, and based on the sixth-edition Unix code released by AT&T in 1975. The BSD world has also prided itself on the early adoption and stabilization of networking protocols for IP. Its stability in networking has allowed it to become ubiquitous in hosting and service providers, as well as in academic and research settings. The licensing and documentation of the BSD software also lends itself to companies wishing to build software on a strong, stable base.

Modular Design

Like most modern operating systems, BSD segregates virtual memory into *kernel space* and *user space*. The BSD kernel space is a monolithic structure that is strictly reserved for running the kernel, kernel extensions, and device drivers. The memory of the kernel space is never swapped to disk.

BSD user space is a memory segment in which the daemons running the user software reside. In the case of JUNOS software, processes such as routing protocols, system management, and the command-line interface (CLI) reside in user space. The memory within the user space is not monolithic, but is further divided into virtual segments occupied by individual daemons.

Daemons

In the Unix and BSD world, the background services providing functionality for the operating system are called *daemons*. Daemons are responsible for providing a conduit process in user space to interact with the kernel.

In JUNOS, each daemon has been designed to be as focused and self-sufficient as possible to eliminate interprocess communication (IPC) between the daemons. To provide additional protection for high availability in network equipment, each daemon in JUNOS software runs in its own portion of protected memory. Any interactions between the daemons within JUNOS are routed through system calls to the kernel.

The kernel, in turn, communicates directly to the microkernel on the system's Packet Forwarding Engine (PFE), which is running its own autonomous daemons. By preventing the user space daemons from directly interacting with the daemons in the microkernel, JUNOS software prevents errors and failures in an individual daemon from affecting other daemons or the packet flow through the system. Mitigating the effect of daemon failures on either packet flow or other daemons ensures that high availability is maintained, even in times of high resource usage by the individual daemons. Figure 3-1 illustrates the interaction between the daemons in JUNOS and the kernel.

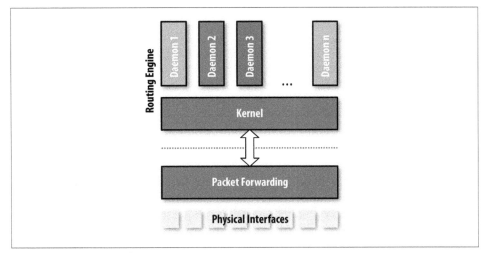

Figure 3-1. JUNOS architecture

As you can see in Figure 3-1, the kernel interacts with the PFE microkernel and keeps communication between the daemons in the RE and the PFE to a minimum. Within the operating system itself, the daemons are also designed to prevent software issues from affecting other daemons, thus lessening the high availability of the system. To provide for the most efficient high availability in a network, it is also important to know how the daemons coordinate transactions and handle resources such that they do not affect the proper operation of the system. In modern programming, daemon interaction can be divided into one of two main states:

Loosely coupled daemons
> The daemons coordinate transactions and system calls but do not share system resources, such as memory. If a single daemon is killed or restarted in this situation, it will not affect the resources of other daemons in the system.

Tightly coupled daemons
> The daemons not only coordinate transactions and system calls, but also share resources in the system. Because of the shared resources, a failure in a single daemon could lead to failures in other daemons. These daemon failures could also result in a cascading error, in which the entire operating system is compromised.

The JUNOS software is built to use loosely coupled daemons for all the processes necessary to keep the networking equipment functioning normally. By having the daemons run independently and in protected memory, the system can maintain its high availability even when one or more daemons are in a period of high resource usage or failure.

Although some network engineers never worry about how their daemons are coupled or how their operating system works, we have all had software installed that seems to steal resources from other software running on the machine—locking up the computer and forcing a reboot. You don't want to see a mistake in a Simple Network Management Protocol (SNMP) process stealing resources from Border Gateway Protocol (BGP) and possibly crashing the router.

One OS to Rule Them

Even with the most stable of software, it is sometimes necessary to upgrade to provide for new features or to fix a minor bug. In your network, this type of upgrade should be simple and should not impact your high availability, but it seems that in most networks, software upgrades are a Sisyphean task that diverts the attention of one or more network engineers from normal operations to the task of developing upgrade implementation and testing plans. When upgrading the operating system of your networking equipment, it is necessary to do the following:

Feature set
Determine which set of networking features is required in the deployed device, such as IPv6, Multiprotocol Label Switching (MPLS), or certain routing protocols.

Software versioning
Determine which version of networking software is required to provide the fixes and features necessary. Versioning information can include:

- Chassis type
- Major release number
- Minor release number
- Maintenance release number
- Software train, including general deployment, early deployment, special release, or deferred release (none of which apply to JUNOS releases)

Hardware requirements
Determine whether the hardware onto which the software is to be loaded has the proper amount of memory and processing power, and the correct firmware and hardware versions.

Interoperability
Determine whether the software release supports all the hardware versions in the device onto which the software is to be loaded, and whether it is interoperable with the devices attached to the device being upgraded.

CLI retraining
Determine whether the new code is based on the same code as previous versions. With the number of mergers and acquisitions we are seeing in the networking

world, it is possible to run across CLIs that work very differently even though they are from the same company.

Bug scrubs

Finally, after you decide on the upgraded software, review the list of known bugs in the software to determine whether any of the bugs directly affect features that you require. If the bugs for the desired features are considered "showstoppers," you must begin the process of choosing software again.

The complex nature of attempting to manually cross-reference known bugs, features, and hardware requirements for each separate code train for a piece of network equipment creates an inherent risk that the upgrade will not efficiently perform every function that is required in the network. With each upgrade, the high availability of the network is on the line as the upgrades may work differently on different pieces of equipment and major changes to the CLI may be introduced. In Juniper Networks equipment, the solution to this complexity is the use of a single operating system across multiple lines of hardware.

Single OS

One of the key features that enable JUNOS software to ensure high availability is the fact that all the major equipment rests on a single source code. This use of a single code across product lines and systems allows Juniper to mitigate many of the risks inherent in software upgrades and allows it to be able to deliver upgrade functionality on a stable release schedule.

Forks and trains

Those in the software development culture are quite familiar with the concept of *forks* and *trains* (or *branches*). In normal software development, a fork is useful for taking a piece of source code and mutating it into something entirely new. The issue in an operating system is that each branch that is forked from the mainline code must have its own set of developers to develop, test, and validate the code. With each branch forming a separate train and moving in its own direction, separate integration and regression testing must be done to ensure that all the branches of code are still backward compatible, communicate properly, and are free of bugs. Each code train makes the development of stable and interoperable software exponentially more difficult.

To avoid any effects caused by the forking of code and multiple code trains, JUNOS software has been consistently developed in a single software train with a single source code. This single train of software is run through batteries of regression and quality testing to ensure that new features do not break previous features and that no new errors are introduced into the code. With all development engineers focusing on the single code base, the testing of the code is much more effective and you are guaranteed a stable network operating system to support your networking equipment.

Because the single code train is used in almost all Juniper hardware—on the J, M, MX, EX, T, and SRX Series—it is possible to upgrade large portions of your network without worrying about some of the equipment being required to remain on older code that may not have the necessary features.

No reeducation through labor

Working in a typical network with a multitude of different switches, routers, and firewalls, engineers must be able to quickly manipulate the nuances of configuration syntax for each piece of equipment, even if they are from the same company. With JUNOS software providing the same operating system across switching, routing, and security equipment, it is possible for an engineer to learn a single, standard syntax for configuring all network components.

> Though Juniper does have product lines with different CLIs because of acquisitions, the company is actively working to bring those systems into the JUNOS fold, as you can see with the SRX Series of security devices, which includes firewall and intrusion detection and prevention, all of which now run JUNOS software.

Within most networks having separate departments for security and overall routing, the use of the same CLI allows closer interaction between the two groups to ensure that network high availability is not optimized at the expense of security, or vice versa.

One Release Architecture

The modular nature of the JUNOS architecture not only provides stability to ensure high availability, but also allows the same OS to be used across all of the products in the M, T, EX, MX, J, and SRX Series equipment, with all core features supported in all series. As we mentioned before, when selecting software for upgrade with other vendors, it is necessary to ensure that all features, such as MPLS and Intermediate System to Intermediate System (IS-IS), are available in the specific release to be downloaded. With JUNOS software, though, the core functionality and CLI exist in the operating systems for all lines of equipment, including the J, EX, and SRX Series, which have their own code downloads. The ability to deploy functionality in a similar manner across all systems in the network allows the system architect to shift focus from interoperability to carefully designed high availability.

Automation of Operations

One of the major causes of network downtime is the introduction of simple mistakes in a configuration through typos or lack of configuration experience. Though there is no way to prevent all human error in your network, JUNOS software has features that attempt to mitigate the effects of these types of errors.

Configuration Management

A key strength of the software is the fact that configuration changes must be explicitly committed to the system and that they do not take effect without some form of basic validation, either through the automated configuration checks built into the commit function of the CLI or through network-specific commit scripts developed using the JUNOS application programming interfaces (APIs). The JUNOS operating system also stores previously used configurations, and either changes can be manually rolled back or the JUNOS software can be set to automatically roll back the changes if connectivity is lost.

Application Programming Interfaces

Although you have probably used SNMP in a network, it may not have provided the flexibility and information that were critical in protecting the high availability of your network. To provide high availability reporting and information, JUNOS supports standards such as SNMP, but it also provides APIs that allow client/server applications to be designed and built to read and write configuration and operating information from the Juniper Networks device using the Juniper Extensible Markup Language (XML) API.

The JUNOScript API is a Juniper-designed application that can be used to connect a client to a device running JUNOS to retrieve or change configuration information using XML. The JUNOScript API server runs natively in JUNOS software and clients can be written in either Perl or the C programming language to connect to it. The API is also used to connect Juniper written software, such as JUNOScope, to the network equipment and read and write information.

NETCONF Configuration Protocol is a client/server application that also runs natively within JUNOS. NETCONF, which was defined in the Internet Engineering Task Force (IETF) RFC 4741, can also be used to develop custom monitoring and management systems for Juniper equipment.

The ability to develop specifically tailored clients using the JUNOScript or NETCONF API allows network engineers to create meaningful data about their network and monitor situations and nodes that could affect the network's high availability.

Scripting

If you have worked in networks for any length of time, you have definitely seen a case where a minor user error crashed an individual node or even created cascading errors that brought down portions of the network. Though it is impossible to totally prevent humans from making mistakes when configuring equipment, it is possible to mitigate the effect of errors on the network through careful scripting and monitoring of network changes. To aid network managers in guaranteeing that their uptime is not affected by simple error, JUNOS contains a single Extensible Stylesheet Language Transformation (XSLT) processor to parse the XML files that contain the configuration and logging files. The use of the processor enables the creation of scripts for double-checking configurations and providing event notification. XSLT is the primary language used to parse the files. However, two languages exist for scripting:

Stylesheet Language Alternative Syntax (SLAX)
> A scripting language developed by Juniper engineers to use with XML for developing scripts for network devices running JUNOS. The SLAX language is similar to Perl in its syntax and constructs; thus, those familiar with Perl can pick up SLAX rather quickly. When processing scripts written in SLAX, the scripts are first automatically converted to native XSLT for the processor.

XSLT
> The standard scripting language used to parse the XML files. Unfortunately, many people find it more difficult to read and write.

Through the use of either SLAX or XSLT in the networking equipment, three types of scripts can be written and applied to the system. In Chapters 10 and 25, we cover in more detail the use of these scripts in high availability architectures.

Commit scripts

The most basic of all scripting in JUNOS software is the *commit script*, which parses configuration changes before they are committed to ensure that potential errors are caught before being applied. When errors are found in a configuration, the script can either alert the user of the error and fail the commit, or correct the configuration automatically. Going beyond configuration checking, commit scripts can be used to develop macros that use simple configuration variables to create a complete and more complex application.

Through the use of commit scripts, senior-level network engineers can develop macros and checks for a network to ensure that junior-level engineers do not introduce errors during maintenance windows and to prevent these possible errors from affecting the network's high availability.

Operation scripts

Operation scripts provide a way for your network engineers to create scripts that monitor the router during operations. The script can be developed to take very specific actions ranging from simple notification to automated diagnosis and correction of issues that have appeared, or it can be developed into a series of step-by-step diagnostic procedures that can aid junior technicians in troubleshooting, diagnosing, and fixing network issues.

 It may appear that we are picking on junior network engineers, but we have all been in situations where our experience and expertise don't really match the task that needs to get done. The use of commit and operation scripts extends the knowledge of upper-tier engineers to everyone struggling to get the job done, and prevents lack of experience from creating network downtime. It also protects senior engineers from tripping on their own typos.

Event policy scripts

Event policy scripts define policies for a specific action to be taken when a particular event notification is received from one of the JUNOS software modules. These scripts can be used in conjunction with operation scripts to act as an early warning system that not only detects emerging problems but also takes immediate steps to avoid network downtime. Using the event policy and operation scripts, remediation and troubleshooting tools can be developed in your network to pare the amount of time it takes to discover, diagnose, and fix a network outage.

CHAPTER 4

Control Plane High Availability

The explosion of technology and the world's dependence on it means that the reliability of a network is incredibly important. As the bits and bytes carried across networks become more valuable, the high availability of these networks is more relevant than ever. The revenue stream of a major financial customer who purchases managed virtual private network (VPN) services from a global ISP depends on the network's availability. When the chairman of the Federal Reserve finally delivers good news after weeks of market turmoil, news that sparks a buying frenzy, older peering routers at the provider's Point of Presence (POP) could get overloaded. This strain on the older devices could, in turn, ramp up the CPU, causing the routing protocols to fail, which in turn would delay market orders, causing the loss of millions of dollars.

At the same time, in another part of town, another customer of the ISP is experiencing issues. A hospital's ER department needs to access a patient's medical records to pre-scribe appropriate medication. Because of the nature of the medication, access to the patient's medical history is imperative. Time is ticking and, all of a sudden, the ER loses access to the central database. The local IT department reports that the core network router has crashed, and meanwhile the patient is suffering.

These two failure scenarios emphasize the importance of high availability features in next-generation networks and services to minimize the effect of such network failures. This chapter addresses *system-based* availability; specifically, high availability and re-dundancy of the routing engine (RE) and the routing protocols that run on the router or switch.

Under the Hood of the Routing Engine

To utilize the robust high availability toolkit provided in JUNOS, one must fully un-derstand the software components of the RE and how they work together to build a highly available operating system. As we discussed in Chapter 3, JUNOS provides a clear separation between the forwarding and control planes. This separation creates an environment in which the router can still forward the traffic when its control plane is down. As long as the traffic is actually flowing through the router, users do not experience any network-related issues.

The RE is the brain that stores the building blocks of system availability, providing all the necessary tools for routing protocols and route calculations. The main function of the RE is to perform route management, using a vastly modified Unix Routing Protocol Daemon (RPD). Because route management is a complex function, the RPD divides its work into many tasks and runs its own scheduler to prioritize them, ensuring that each protocol and route calculation receives the appropriate resources to perform its job.

The primary goal of the RPD is to create and maintain the *Routing Information Base* (RIB), which is a database of routing entries. Each routing entry consists of a destination address and some form of next hop information. RPD maintains the routing table and properly distributes routes from the routing table into the kernel and the hardware complexes used for traffic forwarding.

While almost all network equipment vendors use the concept of a RIB for Border Gateway Protocol (BGP), JUNOS uses a RIB-based structure for all of its routing tables. To understand routing for high availability in your network, it is important to know the table names and to understand the role of each table. Table 4-1 describes the JUNOS routing tables.

Table 4-1. Routing tables implemented in JUNOS

Routing table name	Description
bgp.isovpn.0	BGP reachability information for International Organization for Standardization (ISO) VPNs.
bgp.l2vpn.0	BGP Layer 2 VPN routes.
bgp.l3vpn.0	BGP Layer 3 VPN routes.
bgp.rtarget.0	BGP route target information.
inet.0	IP version 4 (IPv4) unicast routes.
inet.1	IP multicast routes. Contains an entry for each (S,G) pair in the network.
inet.2	IPv4 unicast routes. Used by IP multicast-enabled routing protocols to perform Reverse Path Forwarding (RPF).
inet.3	Accessed by BGP to use Multiprotocol Label Switching (MPLS) paths for forwarding traffic.
inet.4	Routes learned by Multicast Source Discovery Protocol (MSDP).
inet6.0	IP version 6 (IPv6) unicast routes.
inet6.3	Populated when the resolve-vpn statement is enabled to allow a router whose VPN control plane is undergoing a restart to continue to forward traffic while recovering its state from neighboring routers.
inetflow.0	BGP flow destination (firewall match criteria) information.
invpnflow.0	BGP flow destination (firewall match criteria) information within an RFC 2547 Layer 3 VPN.
iso.0	Intermediate System to Intermediate System (IS-IS) and End System to Intermediate System (ES-IS) routes.

Routing table name	Description
l2circuit.0	Layer 2 circuit routes.
mpls.0	MPLS label-switched paths (LSPs). Contains a list of the next label-switched router in each LSP. Used by transit routers to forward packets to the next router along an LSP.
<instance-name>.inet.0	Table that JUNOS software creates each time you configure an IPv4 unicast routing instance.
<instance-name>.inet.3	Table that JUNOS software creates for each BGP instance that is configured to use MPLS paths for forwarding traffic.
<instance-name>.inet6.0	Table that JUNOS software creates each time you configure an IPv6 unicast routing instance.
<instance-name>.inetflow.0	Table that JUNOS software creates each time you configure a routing instance. This table stores dynamic filtering information for BGP.
<instance-name>.iso.0	Table that JUNOS software creates each time you configure an IS-IS or ES-IS instance.
<instance-name>.mpls.0	Table that JUNOS software creates each time you configure MPLS LSPs.

The RPD stores routes in these tables and moves routes among the tables as needed. For example, when the router receives routing information from a routing protocol in the form of newly advertised routes, such as a BGP update message, the routing update is stored in the table called RIB-IN. The RPD runs BGP import policies and the BGP best route selection algorithm on the received routes to create an ordered set of usable routes. The final results of the route selection process are stored in the routing main JUNOS RIB, inet.0. As BGP prepares to advertise BGP routes to its peers, the export policy is run against the routes and the results are moved into the outgoing table, RIB-OUT.

The RPD stores routes for BGP-based Layer 3 VPNs in the table bgp.l3vpn.0, which is populated by Multiprotocol BGP (MP-BGP). As JUNOS software runs the configured policies against the information in the table, all acceptable routes are sent to one or more routing-instance tables while any routing information that is unacceptable to the policies is marked as hidden. After the RPD route selection process is finalized, the RPD daemon copies the selected routes into the kernel's copy of the routing table using IPC messages. JUNOS does not rely on BSD's default routing socket for IPC; instead, it uses a specialized socket that allows any daemon within the box to communicate with the kernel. For example, the RPD uses routing sockets to signal the addition, deletion, or change of routes to the kernel. Similarly, the dcd daemon, responsible for interface management, also communicates with the kernel using the same routing socket type when it signals an interface addition, deletion, or change of its status. And again, the chassisd daemon updates the kernel with any new or changed hardware status using the same routing socket type.

The protocol used for this IPC is Trivial Network Protocol (TNP). TNP is a Layer 3 protocol (like an IP) and uses Ethernet II encapsulation. Like any Layer 3 protocol, it uses source and destination addresses, and it forms and maintains neighbor relationships using Hello messages. The TNP Hello message contains Hello timers and dead intervals, which are used to discover the failure of other hardware components (REs, Packet Forwarding Engines or PFEs, and Flexible PIC Concentrators or FPCs). While you cannot configure most of the TNP Hello timers, you can configure the Hello and dead time intervals between two REs through the command-line interface (CLI) keepalive command.

 Although the netstat commands do work in JUNOS, because JUNOS uses a raw socket type, the IPC is not visible with the plain Unix netstat-a command. Communication is formed using rtsock messages and can be viewed using the rtsockmon command.

Continuing our look at the RE's processes, the next step is that the kernel copies the RPD's forwarding table to the PFE. The table structure is modified so that it can be stored in the PFE's application-specific integrated circuits (ASICs), which make forwarding decisions. These decisions are based on proprietary Radix tree route lookups (called J-Tree route lookups) that are performed on each ASIC. As inet.0 and subsequent forwarding table routes are modified, the RE kernel *incrementally* updates the copy stored in the PFE that is used for forwarding. Because the microkernel of each ASIC contains all routes and their respective next hops, the actual forwarding process continues even when the primary RE is brought down, as shown in Figure 4-1. The fact that forwarding can continue while the control plane is unavailable—such as during an RE switchover—is important for understanding high availability solutions.

Routing Update Process

To understand how you can use the routing features of JUNOS high availability in your network, it is best to actually visualize the routing update process that we discussed in the previous section. The following steps and code snippets explain the control plane and forwarding plane interactions, as they also serve as an excellent troubleshooting tool for diagnosing issues that might occur during network degradation.

Step 1: Verify that the RE and PFEs are up

During normal operation, one of the REs should be online and labeled as master. The master RE should have open, active connections with the rest of the hardware components. The following commands verify the state of the hardware, as seen by the RE.

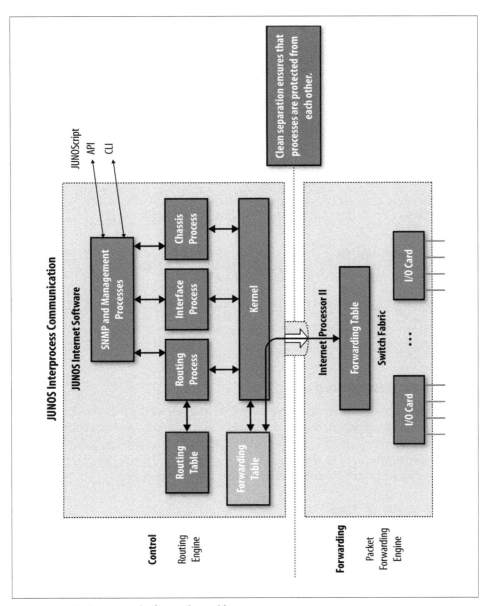

Figure 4-1. ASICs storing the forwarding table routes

```
lab@r1> show chassis routing-engine
Routing Engine status:
  Slot 0:
    Current state           Master
    Election priority       Master (default)
    ......
    Uptime                  2 days, 1 hour, 55 minutes, 53 seconds
    Load averages:          1 minute   5 minute  15 minute
                              0.00       0.00       0.00
Routing Engine status:
  Slot 1:
    Current state           Backup
    Election priority       Backup (default)
    ......
    Start time              2008-09-17 05:59:19 UTC
    Uptime                  17 hours, 53 minutes, 38 seconds


lab@r1> show chassis fpc
            Temp CPU Utilization (%)   Memory    Utilization (%)
Slot State  (C)  Total  Interrupt     DRAM (MB) Heap     Buffer
  0  Online  21    7         0         1024      24         31
  1  Online  21    4         0         1024      24         31
  2  Online  22    5         0         1024      18         31
  3  Online  22    5         0         1024      17         31
  4  Empty
  5  Empty
```

Step 2: Verify that the socket is built

All hardware components should now be online, and one of the REs should be listed in the Master state. If any hardware component is not online, you can start trouble-shooting by examining the IPC performed by TNP between different hardware components. Specifically, look at the connections between the RE and the PFE and make sure you see an RPD OPEN state for each online PFE component:

```
lab@r1>start shell
lab@r1% netstat -a -f tnp
Active TNP connections (including servers)
Proto Recv-Q Send-Q  Local Address      Foreign Address        (state)
<...>
rdp      0      0  master.pfed        feb0.46081             OPEN
rdp      0      0  master.chassisd    feb0.46080             OPEN
rdp      0      0  master.pfed        fpc2.24577             OPEN
rdp      0      0  master.chassisd    fpc2.24576             OPEN
udp      0      0  *.sampled          *.*
udp      0      0  *.sampled          *.*
rdp      0      0  *.1013             *.*                    LISTEN
rdp      0      0  *.chassisd         *.*                    LISTEN
```

Step 3: Verify that there is a valid TNP communication

If you see state issues in step 2, research them further by monitoring the internal management interface:

```
lab@r1> monitor traffic interface em1
verbose output suppressed, use <detail> or <extensive> for full protocol decode
Listening on em1, capture size 96 bytes

02:51:40.239754 Out TNPv2 master.1021 > re1.1021: UDP, length 8
02:51:40.397159  In TNPv2 re1.1021 > re0.1021: UDP, length 8
02:51:41.249676 Out TNPv2 master.1021 > re1.1021: UDP, length 8
02:51:41.407092  In TNPv2 re1.1021 > re0.1021: UDP, length 8
02:51:42.259578 Out TNPv2 master.1021 > re1.1021: UDP, length 8
02:51:42.416900  In TNPv2 re1.1021 > re0.1021: UDP, length 8
02:51:43.269506 Out TNPv2 master.1021 > re1.1021: UDP, length 8
02:51:43.426834  In TNPv2 re1.1021 > re0.1021: UDP, length 8
```

Step 4: Verify that BGP adjacencies are established

Once the RE is online, if you configured a BGP neighbor, you next verify the state of
the BGP adjacency:

```
lab@r1> show bgp summary
Groups: 1 Peers: 1 Down peers: 0
Table      Tot Paths  Act Paths Suppressed  History Damp State Pending
inet.0           28         28          0        0          0       0
bgp.l3vpn.0      13         13          0        0          0       0
bgp.mvpn.0        5          5          0        0          0       0
Peer             AS    InPkt   OutPkt    OutQ   Flaps Last Up/Dwn State|#Activ
e/Received/Damped...
69.191.3.199  33181      68       24       0       0  8:21 Establ
  inet.0: 28/28/0
  bgp.l3vpn.0: 13/13/0
  bgp.mvpn.0: 5/5/0
  vpn.inet.0: 13/13/0
  vpn.mvpn.0: 5/5/0
```

Step 5: Verify that BGP updates are being received

Next, verify that the route updates are being received. The following command peeks
into the BGP RIB-IN table:

```
lab@r1> show route receive-protocol bgp 69.191.3.199

inet.0: 64 destinations, 64 routes (63 active, 0 holddown, 1 hidden)
  Prefix           Nexthop        MED   Lclpref   AS path
* 3.3.3.3/32       69.191.3.201   2000      100   13908 I
* 4.4.4.4/32       69.191.3.201   2000      100   13908 I
* 69.184.0.64/26   69.191.3.201   2025      100   13908 I
* 69.184.25.64/28  69.191.3.201             100   13908 I
* 69.184.25.80/28  69.191.3.201             100   13908 I
* 69.184.25.96/28  69.191.3.201             100   13908 I
* 101.0.0.0/30     69.191.3.201             100   13908 ?
* 128.23.224.4/30  69.191.3.201             100   13908 ?
... output truncated...
```

Step 6: Verify that route updates are processed correctly

The following CLI output proves that a route has gone through the BGP selection process and has been marked as active:

```
lab@r1> show route 3.3.3.3

inet.0: 64 destinations, 64 routes (63 active, 0 holddown, 1 hidden)
@ = Routing Use Only, # = Forwarding Use Only
+ = Active Route, - = Last Active, * = Both

3.3.3.3/32      *[BGP/170] 1w6d 21:55:50, MED 2000, localpref 100, from 69.191.3.199
                  AS path: 13908 I
                > to 172.24.160.1 via fe-1/3/1.0
```

Step 7: Verify that the correct next hop is being selected

The following output gives more details about the actual BGP selection process, including the reasons the route was activated or deactivated, the BGP next hop, the physical next hop, and the state of the route:

```
lab@r1> show route 3.3.3.3 extensive

inet.0: 64 destinations, 64 routes (63 active, 0 holddown, 1 hidden)
3.3.3.3/32 (1 entry, 1 announced)
TSI:
KRT in-kernel 3.3.3.3/32 -> {indirect(262148)}
        *BGP    Preference: 170/-101
                Next hop type: Indirect
                Next-hop reference count: 75
                Source: 69.191.3.199
                Next hop type: Router, Next hop index: 462
                Next hop: 172.24.160.1 via fe-1/3/1.0, selected
                Protocol next hop: 69.191.3.201
                Indirect next hop: 89bb000 262148
                State: <Active Int Ext>
                Local AS: 33181 Peer AS: 33181
                Age: 1w6d 21:54:56  Metric: 2000 Metric2: 1001
                Announcement bits (2): 0-KRT 7-Resolve tree 2
                Task: BGP_33181.69.191.3.199+179
                AS path: 13908 I (Originator) Cluster list: 69.191.3.199
                AS path: Originator ID: 69.191.3.201
                Communities: 13908:5004
                Localpref: 100
                Router ID: 69.191.3.199
                Indirect next hops: 1
                        Protocol next hop: 69.191.3.201 Metric: 1001
                        Indirect next hop: 89bb000 262148
                        Indirect path forwarding next hops: 1
                                Next hop type: Router
                                Next hop: 172.24.160.1 via fe-1/3/1.0
                        69.191.3.201/32 Originating RIB: inet.0
                          Metric: 1001                    Node path count: 1
                          Forwarding nexthops: 1
                                Nexthop: 172.24.160.1 via fe-1/3/1.0
```

Step 8: Verify that the correct copy of the route is being selected for kernel update

This output shows the kernel copy of the forwarding table. This table, which is present on the RE, is sent to the PFE complex by means of routing update messages:

```
lab@r1> show route forwarding-table destination 3.3.3.3 extensive
Routing table: inet [Index 0]
Internet:

Destination:  3.3.3.3/32
  Route type: user
  Route reference: 0                Route interface-index: 0
  Flags: sent to PFE, prefix load balance
  Next-hop type: indirect           Index: 262148   Reference: 26
  Nexthop: 172.24.160.1
  Next-hop type: unicast            Index: 462      Reference: 47
Next-hop interface: fe-1/3/1.0
```

Step 9: Verify that the correct copy of the route is being sent to the forwarding plane

This step looks at the rtsock messages being used to replicate the kernel table into the PFE complex:

```
lab@r1> start shell
% rtsockmon -t
         sender   flag    type      op
[20:07:40] rpd     P     nexthop    add     inet 172.24.160.1 nh=indr
flags=0x1 idx=262142 ifidx=68 filteridx=0
[20:07:40] rpd     P     route      add     inet 69.184.0.64 tid=0
 plen=26 type=user flags=0x10 nh=indr nhflags=0x4 nhidx=262142 filtidx=0
[20:07:40] rpd     P     route      add     inet 199.105.185.224 tid=0
 plen=28 type=user flags=0x10 nh=indr nhflags=0x4 nhidx=262142 filtidx=0
[20:07:40] rpd     P     route      add     inet 160.43.3.144 tid=0
 plen=28 type=user flags=0x10 nh=indr nhflags=0x4 nhidx=262142 filtidx=0
[20:07:40] rpd     P     route      add     inet 172.24.231.252 tid=0
 plen=30 type=user flags=0x10 nh=indr nhflags=0x4 nhidx=262142 filtidx=0
[20:07:40] rpd     P     route      add     inet 4.4.4.4 tid=0
 plen=32 type=user flags=0x10 nh=indr nhflags=0x4 nhidx=262142 filtidx=0
[20:07:40] rpd     P     route      add     inet 172.24.95.208 tid=0
 plen=30 type=user flags=0x10 nh=indr nhflags=0x4 nhidx=262142 filtidx=0
[20:07:40] rpd     P     route      add     inet 172.24.95.204 tid=0
 plen=30 type=user flags=0x10 nh=indr nhflags=0x4 nhidx=262142 filtidx=0
[20:07:40] rpd     P     route      add     inet 172.24.231.248 tid=0
 plen=30 type=user flags=0x10 nh=indr nhflags=0x4 nhidx=262142 filtidx=0
[20:07:40] rpd     P     route      add     inet 172.24.95.196 tid=0
 plen=30 type=user flags=0x10 nh=indr nhflags=0x4 nhidx=262142 filtidx=0
[20:07:40] rpd     P     route      add     inet 3.3.3.3 tid=0
 plen=32 type=user flags=0x10 nh=indr nhflags=0x4 nhidx=262142 filtidx=0
[20:07:40] rpd     P     route      add     inet 160.43.175.0 tid=0
 plen=27 type=user flags=0x10 nh=indr nhflags=0x4 nhidx=262142 filtidx=0
[20:07:40] rpd     P     nexthop    add     inet 172.24.160.1 nh=ucst
flags=0x85 idx=494 ifidx=68 filteridx=0
```

Step 10: Verify that the correct copy of the route is being installed into the forwarding plane on the PFE complex

Using a VTY session to access the PFE complex, you can determine which actual forwarding entries are present in the PFE's ASICs. The following output shows that the routing entry for destination 3.3.3.3 is present and has a valid next hop:

```
lab@r1> start shell
% su
Password:
root@r1% vty feb


CSBR platform (266Mhz PPC 603e processor, 128MB memory, 512KB flash)

CSBR0(r1 vty)# show route ip prefix 3.3.3.3 detail
IPv4 Route Table 0, default.0, 0x0:
Destination                 NH IP Addr       Type      NH ID Interface
------------------------    ---------------  --------  ----- ---------
3.3.3.3                     172.24.160.1     Indirect  262142 fe-1/3/1.0
  RT flags: 0x0010, Ignore: 0x00000000, COS index: 0, DCU id: 0, SCU id: 0
  RPF ifl list id: 0,  RPF tree: 0x00000000
  PDP[0]: 0x00000000

     Second NH[0]: 0x00000000
```

The exercise in this section verified the state of the control plane and followed the routing update process from the initial establishment of a BGP peering session all the way to installing the routing entry into the forwarding ASIC on the PFE. Now that you understand the control and forwarding plane processes and their interactions, we can discuss the different high availability solutions available through JUNOS software.

Graceful Routing Engine Switchover

Graceful Routing Engine Switchover (GRES) takes advantage of the separation between the control and forwarding in JUNOS software to provide system redundancy. GRES allows the control plane, in this case the RE, to switch over to its backup RE without any interruption to the existing traffic flows in the PFE. When GRES is configured on the router, the kernel state on both REs is synchronized to preserve routing and forwarding state on both REs. Any changes to the routing state on the primary RE result in an automatic incremental update of kernel state on the backup RE. As you can see, the GRES concept is very simple.

However, the limitation of GRES is that, by itself, it cannot provide router redundancy. Even though traffic continues to flow through the router during a switchover between REs, the flow occurs for only a limited time. As soon as any of the protocol timers expire, the neighbor relationship between routers is dropped and traffic is stopped at the upstream router. To maintain high availability, networks must quickly discover when a neighbor goes down and must implement the lowest possible timers. Because

GRES provides an intact forwarding plane, it is to our advantage not to drop any of the adjacencies, but rather to continue sending traffic toward the failed router.

The solution to this limitation is to use the Graceful Restart (GR) *protocol extension*. GR signals all supporting protocols that the failing router is capable of forwarding even though it is having control plane problems and needs help maintaining protocol adjacencies. GRES provides zero loss only when supplemented with the GR protocol running between a failed router and all its neighbors. For more about GR, see "Graceful Restart" on page 75.

 As we will see later in this chapter, the key factor for using GR is to have a stable topology. Any topology change results in adjacency loss.

Implementation and Configuration

Enabling GRES on the router changes the information flow from the RE to the PFE. By default, without GRES enabled, the RE signals any state change or routing update directly to the PFE. However, when GRES is enabled, these changes must first be duplicated on the backup RE. This action must be taken first to avoid any potential corner cases where the PFE and the backup RE might be out of sync. For example, if the backup RE is updated last and the primary RE crashes after it updates the PFE, but before updating the backup RE, the backup RE and the PFE would be out of sync. The problems that would result would be immense, so the replication order used makes sure that this condition never happens.

Because *state replication* is a broad term, let's examine further what exactly is being replicated. From the user perspective, all the interfaces and their states are replicated when the interfaces restart. Additionally, all Layer 2 protocol states are preserved, such as ATM, Frame Relay, and Point to Point Protocol (PPP) states. All routes from the kernel table, as well as Address Resolution Protocol (ARP) entries and firewall states, are preserved as well. However, TCP state and actual RPD routes are not preserved because they are rebuilt either locally by means of a kernel copy or through new neighbor discovery.

From the JUNOS perspective, three states are being replicated. Understanding them will help you to configure and troubleshoot the state replication process used in GRES. The three states are:

Configuration database
> The configuration database is the repository of the router's configuration files. Different daemons query this database as needed. The dcd daemon, which manages interfaces, queries it as an interface is brought online. At the same time, the chassisd daemon uses this database when it manages hardware components. The RPD also uses this database, using the configuration information stored in

the database to control all routing protocols. To ensure that this state is preserved and the database is always in sync, you must use the `commit synchronize` command when committing a change in a redundant RE configuration. JUNOS displays an error prompt when GRES is enabled but you fail to commit configuration changes with a `commit synchronize` command.

Kernel with all its entries

Configuring GRES starts the `ksyncd` daemon, which is responsible for all kernel state replications. `ksyncd` is a custom JUNOS daemon used only for replication tasks between different hardware components. Here, it is used to replicate the kernel state. `ksyncd` uses regular IPC `Rtsock` messages to carry information from the kernel on the primary RE to the kernel on the backup RE. When a GRES restart event occurs, the RPD starts up on the backup RE and it reads all saved routes from the kernel and puts them into routing tables as kernel routes (KRT). These routes stay active for a maximum of three minutes. Any routing changes resulting in routing updates, even those as simple as ARP entries, are signaled incrementally to the backup RE by means of `ksyncd`.

PFE state

PFE state replication is done by `chassisd`. When a GRES restart event occurs, `chassisd` does a soft restart of all the hardware, querying it for an inventory. The hardware that responds is reattached to the backup RE and brought online without any disruption. However, if certain hardware fails to respond, it is restarted anyway. To make the replication process as efficient as possible, local user files, accounting information, logs, and `traceoptions` files are not replicated to the backup RE.

Figure 4-2 illustrates the state replication components and the flow of communication between them.

While the replication of all states is important, let's look further at the role of kernel state replication, because all routing entries, including ARP-derived next hop addresses, depend on successful replication of the kernel state. Once the user makes a change and implements it with the `commit sync` command, all the state replication takes place. All routing and next hop entries derived from the RPD and found in routing tables `inet.0`, `inet.6`, `mpls.0`, and `inet.3` are replicated from the primary RE's kernel routing table to the secondary RE's kernel table. All these routes become "active" routes with duplicate forwarding entries in the PFE. The routes and forwarding entries stay active for about three minutes and then are purged. Once the RPD on the backup RE initializes itself, it populates its routing table with the existing kernel routes. We can then say that the GRES event has successfully completed. From a high availability perspective, the RPD acquires the most up-to-date network state information and refreshes its routing tables. Figure 4-3 illustrates the GRES state replication process.

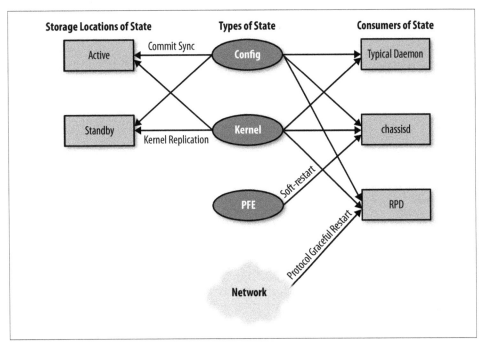

Figure 4-2. State replication process

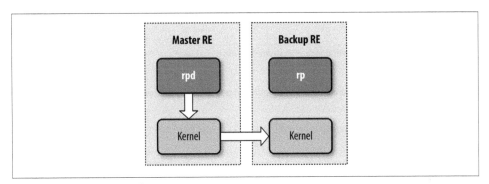

Figure 4-3. GRES state replication process

Configuration examples

GRES is supported only on the routers with two REs running the same JUNOS version. Use the show version command to verify the software version on the RE; by default, when you log in, you are on the master RE:

```
lab@r1> show version
Hostname: r1
Model: mx480
JUNOS Base OS boot [9.2R2.15]
```

```
JUNOS Base OS Software Suite [9.2R2.15]
JUNOS Kernel Software Suite [9.2R2.15]
JUNOS Crypto Software Suite [9.2R2.15]
JUNOS Packet Forwarding Engine Support (M/T Common) [9.2R2.15]
JUNOS Packet Forwarding Engine Support (MX Common) [9.2R2.15]
JUNOS Online Documentation [9.2R2.15]
JUNOS Routing Software Suite [9.2R2.15]
```

From the master RE, you can log in to the backup RE and verify its software version:

```
lab@r1> request routing-engine login other-routing-engine

--- JUNOS 9.2R2.15 built 2008-10-03 19:32:58 UTC

lab@r1> show version
Hostname: r1
Model: mx480
JUNOS Base OS boot [9.2R2.15]
JUNOS Base OS Software Suite [9.2R2.15]
JUNOS Kernel Software Suite [9.2R2.15]
JUNOS Crypto Software Suite [9.2R2.15]
JUNOS Packet Forwarding Engine Support (M/T Common) [9.2R2.15]
JUNOS Packet Forwarding Engine Support (MX Common) [9.2R2.15]
JUNOS Online Documentation [9.2R2.15]
JUNOS Routing Software Suite [9.2R2.15]
```

If the systems are running the same JUNOS version, you can configure GRES using the redundancy statements under the chassis hierarchy:

```
[edit]
lab@r1# set chassis redundancy graceful-switchover

[edit]
lab@r1# set chassis redundancy failover on-disk-failure

[edit]
lab@r1# set chassis redundancy failover on-loss-of-keepalives

[edit]
lab@r1# set chassis redundancy routing-engine 0 master

[edit]
lab@r1# set chassis redundancy routing-engine 1 backup

[edit]
lab@r1# show chassis redundancy
routing-engine 0 master;
routing-engine 1 backup;
failover {
    on-loss-of-keepalives;
    on-disk-failure;
}
graceful-switchover;
```

RE failure is one type of failure that GRES monitors. The primary RE sends keepalive messages every second to the backup kernels. If the backup RE does not receive keepalives for two consecutive seconds, it presumes that the primary RE has failed and attempts to acquire mastership by starting the RE failover process. Another type of failure handled by GRES is *media corruption*. The kernel is intelligent enough to recognize storage media problems, both with the hard drive and with the CompactFlash drive. Because JUNOS software is built on a modified FreeBSD kernel, it requires constant writing to the logfiles. When the kernel senses problems with writing or reading from the hard drive, it registers this as an RE failure and starts up a GRES event.

 In newer JUNOS releases, another configuration step is required to enable GRES: configuring the backup router. Although the backup router is not part of the redundancy mechanism, it is required so that the control plane is always reachable when the primary router is loading or recovering a configuration, or when this router is being configured. The backup router serves as a default route for the control plane, even though this route is never installed into the forwarding plane. Here is an example of configuring the backup router:

```
lab@re1# set system backup-router destination 184.12.1.12
```

Once GRES is enabled, verify its status by executing the show system switchover command from the backup RE:

```
{backup}
lab@r1> show system switchover
Graceful switchover: On
Configuration database: Ready
Kernel database: Version incompatible
Peer state: Out of transition
```

The preceding output shows that the router is running different JUNOS versions on the primary and backup REs. Once you upgrade JUNOS on the backup RE, verify GRES again:

```
{backup}
lab@r1> show system switchover
Graceful switchover: On
Configuration database: Ready
Kernel database: Ready
Peer state: Steady State
```

Troubleshooting GRES

As the previous section shows, the steps to implement GRES are simple. However, there wouldn't be such a high demand for skilled IT employees if everything always worked as configured and expected. Sometimes it will be necessary to troubleshoot how the protocols are working in your network.

As an example, let's consider a scenario in which the entire configuration is in place and the kernel replication states look fine, but during a lab RE switchover test you observe traffic loss. Because GRES is enabled, no packets should be dropped—at least, that's what Juniper promised us. Well, let's analyze the situation and see what is happening.

To troubleshoot the actual problem, first verify the configuration. Enabling traceoptions on all the protocols and GRES knobs helps us get to the root of the problem:

```
lab@r1# show protocols ospf
traceoptions {
    file ospf.trace;
    flag all detail;
}

[edit]
lab@r1# show protocols bgp
traceoptions {
    file bgp.trace;
    flag all detail;
}
```

It is not recommended to have flag all turned on under any protocol traceoptions in the production network. Logging all protocol events takes a toll on RPD processing, which could jeopardize real-time protocol managements such as BGP keepalives or OSPF Hellos. flag all was acceptable in this case since it is a lab environment.

Then check the traceoptions output with the show log command. If you see from the logs that the protocols are working correctly and that it was not a protocol error that caused the issue, the next step is to debug the actual GRES communication:

```
[edit]
lab@r1# show chassis
redundancy {
    routing-engine 0 master;
    routing-engine 1 backup;

    failover {
        on-loss-of-keepalives;
        on-disk-failure;
    }
    graceful-switchover {
        traceoptions {
            flag all;
        }
        enable;
    }
}

[edit]
lab@r1# show routing-options
static {
    route 66.129.243.0/24 next-hop 172.18.66.1;
```

```
    }
    forwarding-table {
        traceoptions {
            flag all detail;
        }
    }
}
```

When you enable `traceoptions` in the GRES portion of the chassis redundancy configuration and on the forwarding table, JUNOS software begins placing debugging information about redundancy and the forwarding engine into logfiles, which you can then review.

Because `ksyncd` is the daemon responsible for kernel route replication, its logs usually reveal a lot of information about state, potential errors, misconfigurations, and software bugs. Check the logs with the following command:

```
lab@r1> show log ksyncd
```

The logs themselves contain much information that can point you in the proper direction when troubleshooting. The following code snippet shows log output from `ksyncd`:

```
lab@r1> show log ksyncd

Sep 10 23:27:09 Terminated: 15 signal received, posting signal
Sep 10 23:27:09 inspecting pending signals
Sep 10 23:27:09 SIGTERM posted, exiting
Sep 12 17:12:27 KSYNCD release 9.0R3.6 built by builder on 2008-08-01 05:05:43
UTC starting, pid 4564
Sep 12 17:12:27 Not runnable attempt 0 reason: not configured (errors: none)
Sep 12 17:12:27 Setting hw.re.is_slave_peer_gres_ready: 0
```

Near the end of the following output, an error message points to a configuration error, specifically that the `commit sync` command is not configured on the master RE:

```
lab@r1> show log ksyncd

Sep 15 21:57:52 KSYNCD release 9.1R2.10 built by builder on 2008-07-01
05:06:40 UTC starting, pid 4566
Sep 15 21:57:52 Not runnable attempt 0 reason: undefined mode (errors: none)
Sep 15 21:58:01 Terminated: 15 signal received, posting signal
Sep 15 21:58:01 inspecting pending signals
Sep 15 21:58:01 SIGTERM posted, exiting
Sep 18 02:17:16 KSYNCD release 9.1R2.10 built by builder on 2008-07-01 05:06:40
UTC starting, pid 8998
Sep 18 02:17:16 Commit sync knob is NOT configured on master RE
Sep 18 02:17:16 Stop attempting to perform initial sync
Sep 18 02:17:16 config state: ready
```

Another problem that occurs quite often is that the REs on the router are running different versions of JUNOS software. In the `kysncd` logfile, you see this as a *version mismatch* error. You could easily search for this message when parsing the logfiles:

```
lab@r1> show log ksyncd

Sep 18 02:17:17 Register timer to wait for version info from master
```

```
Sep 18 02:17:17 recv RE msg subtype RE_MSG_RTSOCK_VERSION_REPLY
Sep 18 02:17:17          RE_MSG_RTSOCK_VERSION_REPLY :
Sep 18 02:17:17                  rtm_n_msg_types : 0x00000059
Sep 18 02:17:17                  rtm_version_checksum : 0x86496873
Sep 18 02:17:17 Received RTSOCK version message from master
Sep 18 02:17:17 Rtsock version checksum mismatch: master 2252957811, slave 1789492047
Sep 18 02:17:17 Version mismatch detected: Slumber time
Sep 18 02:17:17 Suspending due to unrecoverable error: version_mismatch
Sep 18 02:17:17 Not runnable attempt 0 reason: hard error (errors: version_mismatch )
Sep 18 02:17:17 closing connection to master
Sep 18 02:17:17 cleaning up kernel state
Sep 18 02:17:17 delete all commit proposals seqno 1658:
Sep 18 02:17:17 delete route rtb 0 af 2 rttype perm: skip not supported
Sep 18 02:17:17 delete route rtb 0 af 2 0.0.0.0 rttype perm: skip not supported
Sep 18 02:17:17 delete route rtb 0 af 2 66.129.243.0 rttype user: skip private
```

Sometimes issues may not be obvious in the ksyncd logs, or the log may not reveal anything specific. A further step in troubleshooting ksyncd is to log in to the backup RE and run the Unix command rtsockmon from the shell to view the actual route replication process:

```
lab@r1> start shell
% rtsockmon -t
        sender   flag    type        op
[20:07:40] rpd       P    route       add     inet 4.4.4.4 tid=0
plen=32 type=user flags=0x10nh=indr nhflags=0x4 nhidx=262142 filtidx=0
[20:07:40] rpd       P    route       add     inet 172.24.95.208 tid=0
plen=30 type=user flags=0x10 nh=indr nhflags=0x4 nhidx=262142 filtidx=0
[20:07:40] rpd       P    route       add     inet 172.24.95.204 tid=0
plen=30 type=user flags=0x10 nh=indr nhflags=0x4 nhidx=262142 filtidx=0
[20:07:40] rpd       P    route       add     inet 172.24.231.248 tid=0
plen=30 type=user flags=0x10 nh=indr nhflags=0x4 nhidx=262142 filtidx=0
[20:07:40] rpd       P    route       add     inet 172.24.95.196 tid=0
plen=30 type=user flags=0x10 nh=indr nhflags=0x4 nhidx=262142 filtidx=0
[20:07:40] rpd       P    route       add     inet 3.3.3.3 tid=0
plen=32 type=user flags=0x10 nh=indr nhflags=0x4 nhidx=262142 filtidx=0
```

This output shows that the route replication process seems to be fine. If the configuration and logfiles do not reveal anything out of the ordinary, you next look at the bigger picture, such as networkwide issues. For example, investigate the protocol traceoptions logs to see whether an adjacency dropped during a GRES event on a failed router. If this appears to be the case, analyze the neighbor's configuration for Graceful Restart extensions. If you see very similar config without a Graceful Restart knob, the neighbor is missing the GR configuration:

```
lab@r1# show routing-options
static {
    route 66.129.243.0/24 next-hop 172.18.66.1;
```

As you will see in the next section, the GRES concept alone is not sufficient to keep the network running during RE failures. GRES must be complemented with Graceful Restart.

Graceful Restart

No doubt you have experienced some sort of routing meltdown in your networking career. Unfortunately, it is a fact that failures are inevitable, whether software or hardware or a combination of the two. The challenge is to make them as painless as possible.

Let's take a simple routing process failure as an example, in which a routing daemon restarts on one of the core routers. The restart causes a networkwide disruption to many of the network processes and brings down all protocol adjacencies. While the router is recovering, all its neighbors shift their traffic in different directions, using redundant links or paths. It is possible that the shifted traffic, now on oversubscribed links, causes congestion and potential traffic drops. When the failed router recovers, it establishes new adjacencies and advertises new routing information, which in turn causes another traffic shift back to the original paths. This is actually how basic routing handles failures; according to the protocol definitions, each step in this scenario happened as it was designed to. But how does this situation affect the users?

The traffic churn has substantial impact on the user experience. This is especially true with the content being delivered using modern next-generation networks, which consist primarily of video and voice communication, in which any delay and jitter can cause havoc. If you have seen a distorted or frozen picture on your cable TV, it was likely caused by jitter. Moreover, if the next-generation telephone network is riding on top of an IP network, a 911 emergency call (or any other call) could be distorted—just enough for the operator to misunderstand a street location, house number, or other important detail.

Because most modern routers are capable of forwarding, even when the control plane is incapacitated, the traffic churn resulting from a routing process hiccup is absolutely unnecessary. In certain scenarios, it might be better if the neighbors refuse to establish a new adjacency that shifts traffic to a new path after a neighboring router fails.

Graceful Restart (GR) allows you to address this scenario. In a nutshell, GR allows the failure of a neighboring router to go undetected for a period of time so that traffic continues to be forwarded along the already established paths, and no adjacencies are broken. This small detail helps in both software and hardware failures. The period of nondetection was originally designed to support software failures. However, with advances in hardware design and in the separation of the control and forwarding planes, this concept has found its real purpose as a technology complementing nonstop forwarding models. If all the router's neighbors somehow ignore the loss of communication and continue forwarding toward the troubled router, which is still capable of forwarding, all problems induced by routing churn—including convergence time issues, delays, and jitter—simply go away. Figure 4-4 illustrates the basic concepts of GR.

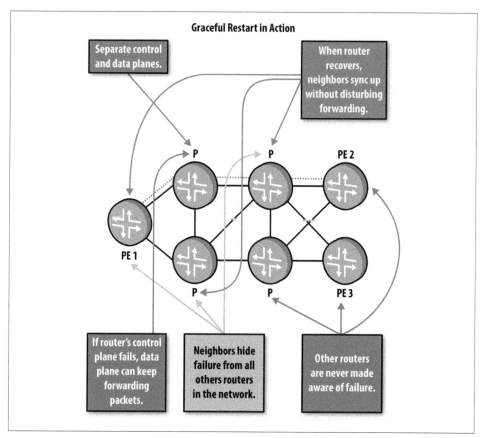

Figure 4-4. GR protocol extension steps

While different protocols implement GR slightly differently, from a high availability point of view the concept is the same for all protocols. The rest of this chapter examines how the various protocols implement GR. Before we begin, however, it is important to point out two crucial conditions that are the prerequisites for successfully deploying GR:

- The router must support Non-Stop Forwarding (NSF). During a failure, this router must be able to forward the traffic based on old forwarding entries found in its forwarding table.

- No topology changes must occur during the failure event.

> Topology changes can occur with certain network designs without any impact on traffic and quality of information. We cover the actual configuration steps for such scenarios later in this chapter.

Graceful Restart in OSPF

To understand how GR is implemented in Open Shortest Path First (OSPF), let's first analyze the basics of OSPF protocol communications. Neighbor adjacency between two OSPF speaking routers is formed by exchanging OSPF Hello messages. After the initial Hello messages, OSPF passes through several states and then establishes full neighbor adjacencies. OSPF advertises routing information using link-state update messages called link-state advertisements (LSAs). For normal routing, OSPF uses standard LSAs. With the integration of MPLS traffic engineering and GR into OSPF, opaque LSAs were created to carry information for these protocol extensions. Depending on the scope of advertisement, these LSA updates can be link-local, area-wide, or across the entire OSPF domain, which is LSA type 9, 10, or 11, respectively. Because GR involves communication between a router and its direct neighbors, it is implemented using link-local scope messages.

Grace (type 9) LSAs negotiate and exchange restart information between OSPF neighbors. The information relevant to the restarting event is carried in the body of the message using the type, length, value (TLV) system:

- Type (two octets):
  - 1 (grace period)
  - 2 (restart reason)
  - 3 (interface IP address)
- Length (two octets):
  - Grace period (four octets)
  - Restart reason (one octet)
  - Interface IP address (four octets)
- Value (open)

Here are more details about the information carried in the TLV message:

Grace period
  This value signals how long a helper should help the router in question. When this period expires, the helper brings down the adjacency with the restarting router, flushes its LSAs from the database, and floods new LSAs to the rest of the network informing the other routers that it has lost its adjacency to the neighbor.

Restart reason
  This is a required field. Four different values are defined:
  - 0 (unknown)
  - 1 (software restart)
  - 2 (software upgrade)
  - 3 (control plane switchover)

Interface IP address
> This is the IP address of the interface sending an update.

RFC 3623 suggests that three modes of operation should be supported, and JUNOS supports all three:

Possible helper
> By default, every router running JUNOS is in this mode, without any configuration. If no network activity exists, all routers stay in this mode forever.

Helper
> Upon receiving a Grace-LSA from the neighboring router, a possible helper is promoted to the helper role. It maintains the adjacency, marks all neighbors' routes as stale, and continues to forward traffic toward the restarting router for a limited period of time. Once the neighbor finishes its restart event, or after the restart timer expires, the helper router flushes the old routes from its routing table. If the neighbor does not recover before the restart timer expires, the adjacencies are also brought down.

Restart candidate
> The router that has undergone a restart event, or is about to undergo one, marks all its routes as stale, in a form of kernel route, and sends a Grace-LSA to its neighbors requesting the help until its control plane is fully recovered.

Let's analyze two different types of failures and the steps OSPF takes to signal the failures. In the case of software restart, OSPF sends a Grace-LSA prior to the restart event. This message ensures that all neighbors keep the adjacency in the "full" state until the router recovers its control plane. In the case of a hardware failure or a GRES event, OSPF sends a Grace-LSA after the control plane has recovered, even before it generated the first Hello message. This order of messages is critical. If the Hello message is received before the Grace-LSA, the original adjacency is destroyed and OSPF attempts to establish a new one.

In either of these two failure cases, after an OSPF adjacency has been established, the restarting router requests help from its neighbors to rebuild its link-state database. All neighbors flood back the original LSAs advertised by the restarting router. After the restarting router receives all LSAs and has updated its LSA database, the GR event is complete and all kernel routes are removed from the routing and forwarding entries.

Configuration

Because JUNOS supports GR for all major routing protocols, there is a single configuration statement that enables it for all of the protocols at once. However, in some network topologies, because of the different GR capabilities of particular routers, you might want to enable GR for some protocols and disable it for others. The following set of commands gives us the ability to do just that.

In the routing-options hierarchy, turning on GR enables it for all running protocols that support it:

```
[edit]
lab@r1# set routing-options graceful-restart
```

In the protocol hierarchy, you can disable GR specifically for OSPF, and you can modify any of the GR parameters for OSPF:

```
[edit]
lab@r1# set protocols ospf graceful-restart ?
Possible completions:
 disable            Disable OSPF graceful restart capability
  helper-disable    Disable graceful restart helper capability
  notify-duration   Time to send all max-aged grace LSAs (1..3600 seconds)
  restart-duration  Time for all neighbors to become full (1..3600 seconds)
```

The `disable` statement disables GR for OSPF. As mentioned earlier, helper mode is enabled by default; use the `helper-disable` statement to disable this mode. The remaining two statements, `notify-duration` and `restart-duration`, allow you to modify the default values of OSPF GR timers.

Immunizing against topology change

There is one additional requirement for GR protocol extensions. Once all the neighbors enter into GR helper mode, any subsequent topology change forces the neighbor to terminate the helper state and bring down OSPF adjacencies. However, certain network designs can safely ignore the fact that the network topology has changed. Depending on how network traffic flows, flaps on out-of-the-way interfaces do not impact network traffic flowing through the failed router. So, in this scenario, you want to prevent GR from terminating and bring down OSPF adjacencies. To work around unnecessary GR termination, configure OSPF to ignore any topology changes and to ignore new LSA updates by configuring the `no-strict-lsa-checking` statement:

```
[edit]
lab@r1# set protocols ospf graceful restart no-strict-lsa-checking
```

All the tools provided in JUNOS allow you to implement a complete model of high availability in OSPF networks by combining a GRES design with GR and BFD in periodic packet management (PPM) mode.

Graceful Restart in IS-IS

To understand how GR is implemented in IS-IS, we'll again start by analyzing the basics of IS-IS protocol communications. Neighbor adjacencies between two IS-IS routers are formed through the exchange of IS-IS Hello messages. After this, IS-IS goes through several states and eventually establishes full neighbor adjacencies. IS-IS advertises its routing information using link-state update messages called link-state Protocol Data Units (PDUs), or LSPs. After routers establish adjacency, they send out Complete Sequence Number PDUs (CSNPs) containing a summary of the link-state information available for advertisement. The neighbors receiving the CSNPs check them against their own database; if there is any discrepancy, the neighbors send a Partial Sequence Number PDU (PSNP) requesting a specific subset of the information that is out of sync with its database. The response to the PSNP is an LSA in the form of either a PSNP on P2P links or a CSPN on broadcast links. Eventually, all routers in the same area synchronize their link-state databases.

IS-IS provides GR support through use of the GR TLV, type code 221, which is carried in the Hello PDU. Two important bits in this message are the request restart (RR) bit and the restart acknowledgment (RA) bit. Under normal conditions, both bits are clear and are set to 0. When a router restarts, it requests support from its neighbors by sending a type 221 TLV with the RR bit "on" (set to 1). Helpers capable of helping acknowledge this PDU with a response that clears the RR bit, setting it back to 0 and setting the RA bit to 1. Additionally, the PDU response also contains the default hold-time value of 90 seconds. This time is how long the neighbor will keep the adjacency up and will keep all entries in the link-state database intact.

RFC 3847 suggests that three modes of operation be supported, and JUNOS supports all three:

Possible helper
> By default, every router running JUNOS is in this mode, without any configuration. If no network activity exists, all routers stay in this mode forever.

Helper
> Upon receiving a Grace-TLV (type 221) from the neighboring router, a possible helper will be promoted into this role. It will maintain the adjacency, mark all neighbors' routes as stale, and continue to forward the traffic toward the restarting router for a limited period of time. Once the neighbor finishes its restart event, or after the restart timer expires, the old routes are flushed from the routing table. If the neighbor does not recover before the restart timer expires, the adjacencies are also brought down.

Restart candidate
> The router that has or is about to undergo the restart event marks all of its routes as stale, in a form of kernel route, and sends the Grace-TLV to its neighbors requesting help until its control plane is fully recovered.

Configuration

As we mentioned in the section about OSPF and GR, you configure GR globally, for all routing protocols, in the routing-options hierarchy or in the IS-IS configuration hierarchy, you can disable it just for IS-IS, and you can set GR timers specific to IS-IS:

```
[edit]
lab@r1# set protocols isis graceful-restart ?
Possible completions:
  disable          Disable graceful restart
```

```
helper-disable     Disable graceful restart helper capability
restart-duration   Maximum time for graceful restart to finish (seconds)
```

 Currently, IS-IS does not support an "ignore topology change" statement similar to that supported by OSPF.

Graceful Restart in BGP

The Internet is where we can see the real advantage of GR protocol extensions. At the time of this writing, the Internet routing table contains approximately 276,000 BGP routes, as shown in Figure 4-5 (and as graphed at *http://bgp.potaroo.net*). Consider a peering router at a major ISP peering point with three or four or five copies of this Internet table. Now imagine a control plane going down on this router and then recovering within a matter of one or two minutes. With incremental route update processing, that's at least 550,000 (276,000 routes × 2 copies of the table) or more routes that need to be recalculated. Events such as this can have a drastic effect on the stability of the global Internet, but implementing GR in BGP can be a large component in helping to solve the instability problem.

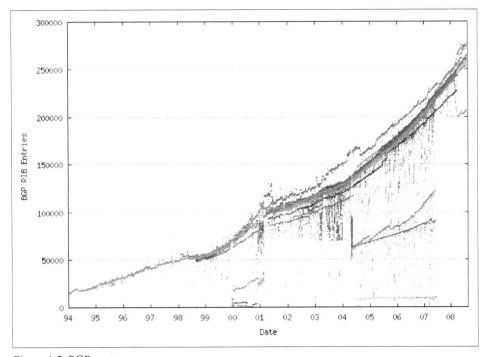

Figure 4-5. BGP routes

As we did with OSPF and IS-IS, let's start by looking at how BGP manages its peering sessions. A BGP neighbor session is established through BGP open messages, and is maintained by BGP keepalive messages. Routing information is advertised with BGP update messages, and a neighbor session is torn down with BGP notification messages. To finalize the routine update process, the peer sends an end-of-RIB marker message (EOR), which is a simple BGP update message with no prefixes. The session itself is maintained through BGP keepalives sent at periodic intervals. Loss of keepalives for the period of the dead interval results in a BGP session being torn down.

A capability announcement for the BGP GR is signaled using special bits. A restart bit (RS) signals that the router is going through the restart event, while a forwarding bit (FS) signals that the router is capable of retaining the forwarding state during a restart event. During initial GR negotiation, both bits are set to 0. In contrast to the OSPF implementation, the restarting router signals the restart event after the restart procedure has begun.

Additionally, GR for BGP is negotiated for each BGP family. Different vendors, and even different JUNOS versions, may support a limited set of families. Therefore, the actual negotiation comes in handy. You can check what is being proposed and what is negotiated by displaying information about the BGP neighbor:

```
lab@r1> show bgp neighbor

Peer: 192.168.36.1+3098 AS 65010 Local: 192.168.24.1+179 AS 65010
Type: Internal State: Established Flags: <>
Last State: OpenConfirm Last Event: RecvKeepAlive
Last Error: None
Options: <Preference LocalAddress HoldTime GracefulRestart Refresh>
Local Address: 192.168.24.1 Holdtime: 90 Preference: 170
Number of flaps: 2
Error: 'Cease' Sent: 2 Recv: 0
Peer ID: 192.168.36.1 Local ID: 192.168.24.1 Active Holdtime: 90
Keepalive Interval: 30
NLRI for restart configured on peer: inet-unicast
NLRI advertised by peer: inet-unicast
NLRI for this session: inet-unicast
Peer supports Refresh capability (2)
Restart time configured on the peer: 120
Stale routes from peer are kept for: 300
Restart time requested by this peer: 120
NLRI that peer supports restart for: inet-unicast
NLRI peer can save forwarding state: inet-unicast
NLRI that peer saved forwarding for: inet-unicast
NLRI that restart is negotiated for: inet-unicast
NLRI of received end-of-rib markers: inet-unicast
NLRI of all end-of-rib markers sent: inet-unicast
Table inet.0 Bit: 10000
```

To understand the BGP GR process, let's examine the signaling involved in a single restart event.

Restarting the node

Let's assume that both GR and GRES are enabled on the restarting router. During the GRES event, all existing routing entries are saved in the router's forwarding table. As soon as the RPD on the newly restarted control plane comes up, it sends an open message to all its neighbors with the RS and FS bits set to 1, requesting continuation of forwarding based on existing routing entries and requesting help in building a new routing table. The RPD marks all previous entries as stale routes and continues processing update messages received from its neighbors. After all the neighbors finish sending their routing update messages, they send end-of-RIB markers to actually mark the successful completion of the update process. The restarting router waits until IGP convergence is complete. Only then does it run the BGP route selection algorithm and activate the received routes. The active routes are pushed to the forwarding table on the PFE complex. Stale routes expire in three minutes, after which they are flushed from the forwarding table. The presence of duplicate routes during this time is not an issue because the stale routes are marked with the preference of 255, and BGP routes have a default preference of 170.

Peers

When a peer receives a new BGP open message with the RS and FS bits set to 1, it closes the TCP session belonging to the old BGP peering session. It then marks all the old BGP routes as stale routes and retains them for three minutes while it continues forwarding based on old routes. When the new BGP session is established and the new update message with the end-of-RIB marker is received, the peer uses the new routes and flushes all the stale routes.

Configuration

For BGP, you configure GR globally for all BGP groups and neighbors, or selectively for individual groups or neighbors. The following code snippet highlights the supported features for BGP GR:

```
[edit]
lab@r1# set protocols bgp graceful-restart ?
Possible completions:
  <[Enter]>           Execute this command
  disable             Disable graceful restart
  restart-time        Restart time used when negotiating with a peer (1..600)
  stale-routes-time   Maximum time for which stale routes are kept (1..600)
  |                   Pipe through a command
```

You verify the configuration with the bgp neighbor command. The truncated output should be similar to the following:

```
NLRI for restart configured on peer: inet-unicast
NLRI advertised by peer: inet-unicast
NLRI for this session: inet-unicast
Peer supports Refresh capability (2)
Restart time configured on the peer: 120
```

```
Stale routes from peer are kept for: 300
Restart time requested by this peer: 120
NLRI that peer supports restart for: inet-unicast
NLRI peer can save forwarding state: inet-unicast
NLRI that peer saved forwarding for: inet-unicast
NLRI that restart is negotiated for: inet-unicast
NLRI of received end-of-rib markers: inet-unicast
NLRI of all end-of-rib markers sent: inet-unicast
```

MPLS Support for Graceful Restart

Many large network deployments use MPLS as an underlying encapsulation technology on top of the Layer 2 frames. While this concept adds some complexity to the design of a GR deployment, it is perfectly doable. Network designers need to look for support for GR protocol extensions among the signaling protocols intended for use with MPLS. For an LDP-based network, support of GR within LDP is necessary. For Resource Reservation Protocol (RSVP)-signaled point to multipoint (P2MP) LSPs, GR must be supported for those LSPs.

Graceful Restart in RSVP

RSVP advertises its ability to support GR protocol extensions during the initial process of establishing adjacencies. The RSVP Hello message contains an additional object, the Restart Capability Object (ResCapObj), which is used to signal both the capability and the desire for GR support.

In addition, ResCapObj contains values for two important timers: the *restart timer* and the *recovery timer*. The restart timer advertises how long a neighbor should wait to receive a Hello from the restarting router before it declares it dead. The JUNOS default value is 60 seconds. The recovery timer defines the maximum time allocated for GR support. During this time, all supporting neighbors (helpers) send Path messages to the failed router containing either the Recover Label Object or the list of labels previously advertised by the restarting router.

If the node sends the RSVP Hello message with both restart and recovery timers set to 0, it means the node is capable of acting only as a helper and of supporting the failed router with the Recovery Label Object. If the two timers have nonzero values, it means that the router is capable of forwarding while its control plane is down, and is basically a request for help when it is needed.

Configuration

You configure individual RSVP parameters for GR under the RSVP protocol stanza:

```
[edit]
lab@r1# set protocols rsvp graceful-restart ?
Possible completions:
disable              Disable RSVP graceful restart capability
```

```
helper-disable          Disable graceful restart helper capability
maximum-helper-recovery-time  Maximum time restarting neighbor states are kept
maximum-helper-restart-time   Maximum wait time from down event to neighbor dead
```

To verify what capabilities RSVP is advertising or has negotiated, use the following command:

```
lab@r1> show rsvp version
Resource ReSerVation Protocol, version 1. rfc2205
  RSVP protocol       = Enabled
  R(refresh timer)    = 30 seconds
  K(keep multiplier)  = 3
  Preemption          = Normal
  Graceful restart    = Enabled
  Restart helper mode = Enabled
  Restart time        = 60000 msec
```

Check on a restarting MPLS-enabled router to see how much recovery time is left:

```
lab@r1> show rsvp version
Resource ReSerVation Protocol, version 1. rfc2205
  RSVP protocol       = Enabled [Restarting]
  R(refresh timer)    = 30 seconds
  K(keep multiplier)  = 3
  Preemption          = Normal
  Graceful restart    = Enabled
  Restart helper mode = Enabled
  Restart time        = 60000 msec
  Recovery time       = 116000 msec
```

Use the show rsvp neighbor detail command to see information about an RSVP neighbor's restart capabilities. If the neighbor is not able to restart, no additional information is displayed; otherwise, the following output shows the restart time and recovery time advertised by a neighbor:

```
lab@r1> show rsvp neighbor detail
RSVP neighbor: 2 learned
Address: 192.168.207.61  via: t3-0/3/3.0    status: Up
  Last changed time: 2:04, Idle: 5 sec, Up cnt: 2, Down cnt: 1
  Message received: 0
  Hello: sent 294, received: 294, interval: 9 sec
  Remote instance: 0x6432682e, Local instance: 0x643ee9dc
  Refresh reduction:  not operational
  Link protection:  disabled
    Bypass LSP: does not exist,  Backup routes: 0,  Backup LSPs: 0
  Restart time: 60000 msec, Recovery time: 0 msec

Address: 192.168.207.65  via: t3-0/3/2.0    status: Up
  Last changed time: 2:05, Idle: 10 sec, Up cnt: 2, Down cnt: 1
  Message received: 139
  Hello: sent 299, received: 299, interval: 9 sec
  Remote instance: 0x3271a074, Local instance: 0x3275e3d8
  Refresh reduction:  not operational
  Link protection:  disabled
    Bypass LSP: does not exist,  Backup routes: 0,  Backup LSPs: 0
  Restart time: 60000 msec, Recovery time: 0 msec
```

Note that the recovery time may be nonzero if the neighbor is in the process of a GR.

Graceful Restart in LDP

The implementation of GR in LDP is very similar to the OSPF implementation, explained earlier in this chapter. GR capabilities are advertised when the LDP session is established, and three different protocol timers directly reflect the GR behavior of LDP:

Reconnect time
> This is how long the restarting router wants its peers to wait for the session to be reestablished, from the time the neighbors realized the session had failed. The reconnect time is 60 seconds, and it cannot be changed.

Recovery time
> This is the time during which both restarting and helper routers should preserve their MPLS LDP-based forwarding entries with old label values.

Maximum recovery time
> A router can send an update with the recovery time set to infinity and force the restarting router to keep its old database forever. This could be a security threat in a form of denial-of-service (DoS) attack on router resources, because the number of label mapping entries is a finite number. Therefore, the restarting router keeps the state intact for the lesser of the two time values—the recovery time sent by its neighbor or the maximum recovery time configured on the router itself.

During the restart, all involved routers—the restarting router and its neighbors—keep the stale routes intact. Once the session is reestablished, new entries are created based on new labels. JUNOS software keeps forwarding entries for both old and new labels. As specified earlier, old labels are removed based on the values of the restart and recovery timers. To keep the forwarding state intact, a helper must receive a nonzero recovery time value in the Hello message. When the router receives the message with a value of 0 in the recovery time field, it means the router was not able to preserve its forwarding state. The result is that the router signals its neighbors to delete their forwarding states for the failed router.

Configuration

As with the other protocols, if you enable the GR under the routing options configuration, you enable it for all supporting protocols, including LDP. The router helper role is enabled by default. You configure LDP-specific parameters for GR in the LDP protocol stanza:

```
[edit]
lab@r1# set protocols ldp graceful-restart ?
Possible completions:
```

```
disable              Disable RSVP graceful restart capability
helper-disable       Disable graceful restart helper capability
maximum-helper-recovery-time  Maximum time restarting neighbor states are kept
maximum-helper-restart-time   Maximum wait time from down event to neighbor dead
recovery-time        Time required for recovery (120..1800 seconds)
```

Look at the output of the show ldp session detail command to verify the GR values that LDP has negotiated:

```
lab@r1> show ldp session detail
Address: 10.168.66.2, State: Operational, Connection: Open, Hold time: 20
  Session ID: 10.168.66.1:0--10.168.66.2:0
  Next keepalive in 0 seconds
  Passive, Maximum PDU: 4096, Hold time: 30, Neighbor count: 1
  Keepalive interval: 10, Connect retry interval: 5
  Local address: 10.168.66.1, Remote address: 10.168.66.2
  Up for 00:00:49
  Local - Restart: enabled, Helper mode: enabled, Reconnect time: 60000
  Remote - Restart: enabled, Helper mode: enabled, Reconnect time: 60000
  Local maximum recovery time: 140000 msec
  Next-hop addresses received:
    10.0.1.2
    10.0.2.2
```

Here is sample output showing a neighbor that does not support GR:

```
lab@r1> show ldp session detail
Address: 10.168.66.2, State: Operational, Connection: Open, Hold time: 28
  Session ID: 10.168.66.1:0--10.168.66.2:0
  Next keepalive in 8 seconds
  Passive, Maximum PDU: 4096, Hold time: 30, Neighbor count: 1
  Keepalive interval: 10, Connect retry interval: 5
  Local address: 10.168.66.1, Remote address: 10.168.66.2
  Up for 00:00:11
  Local - Restart: enabled, Helper mode: enabled, Reconnect time: 60000
  Remote - Restart: disabled, Helper mode: disabled
  Local maximum recovery time: 140000 msec
  Next-hop addresses received:
    10.0.1.2
    10.0.2.2
```

If the restart is in process, this command displays no information:

```
lab@r1> show ldp session detail
Address: 10.168.66.3, State: Operational, Connection: Open, Hold time: 29
  Session ID: 10.168.66.2:0--10.168.66.3:0
  Next keepalive in 9 seconds
  Passive, Maximum PDU: 4096, Hold time: 30, Neighbor count: 1
  Keepalive interval: 10, Connect retry interval: 5
  Local address: 10.168.66.2, Remote address: 10.168.66.3
  Up for 00:00:01
  Restarting, recovery time: 174000 msec
  Local - Restart: enabled, Helper mode: enabled, Reconnect time: 60000
  Remote - Restart: enabled, Helper mode: enabled, Reconnect time: 60000
  Local maximum recovery time: 140000 msec
  Next-hop addresses received:
```

```
    10.0.2.3
    10.0.3.3
```

When displaying the LDP database for the neighbor of a restarting MPLS-enabled router, the bindings learned from the restarting neighbor are displayed as (Stale). If they are not refreshed within the recovery time, these bindings are deleted (as specified in the draft):

```
lab@r1# run show ldp database
Input label database, 10.168.66.1:0--10.168.66.2:0
  Label     Prefix
  100000    10.168.66.3/32 (Stale)
       3    10.168.66.2/32 (Stale)
  100001    10.168.66.4/32 (Stale)
  100002    10.168.66.1/32 (Stale)

Output label database, 10.168.66.1:0--10.168.66.2:0
  Label     Prefix
  100008    10.168.66.4/32
  100006    10.168.66.2/32
  100007    10.168.66.3/32
       3    10.168.66.1/32
```

Graceful Restart in MPLS-Based VPNs

The most frequently used MPLS application is a Layer 3 VPN service provided by the carriers, usually referred to as 2547bis or L3VPNs. While the customer sees only a basic routing update at its customer premises equipment, the actual routing of information through the provider network is quite complex. It not only involves IGP routing to support BGP routes, but also integrates MPLS-based signaling using RSVP, LDP, or both. Every single route sent to the customer depends on correct routing information and stable routing adjacencies for all of the protocols. Therefore, the GR support for a Layer 3 VPN environment is built on many contingencies, and is naturally a little more complex than what we've discussed so far.

The goal is to preserve all uninterrupted services for all sides benefiting from the VPN environment. This means that all involved parties and protocols must support GR protocol extensions, as must all provider BGP sessions. Moreover, the BGP families involved in the VPN services must be configured and supported, such as family L3VPN, family L2VPN/VPLS, and family MVPN. Additionally, all IGPs and the respective MPLS signaling protocols have to be configured and supported. This holds true for both sides—the provider's core network, commonly referred to as the P network, as well as the customer-facing side, or the C network.

When all protocols are supported and GR is configured appropriately, the keys to providing uninterrupted services are the actual dependencies and the order of operations. The PE router first waits until all P-based BGP and IGP states have been stabilized and reconverged, and until all forwarding states related to MPLS tunnels are reconverged and stabilized. This means that all previously advertised labels and label mappings are still found in the forwarding tables, as are the new label values and mappings. Additionally, all BGP and IGP neighbors and the adjacencies in all Virtual Routing and Forwarding (VRF) tables to the C side of the network must be stabilized. Only then can the GR process be marked as completed and the old routing and forwarding entries be flushed.

Configuration

In addition to the configuration requirements on the P side of the network, you must also configure GR support within all routing instances. For Layer 3 VPNs, use the following syntax and help file:

```
[edit]
lab@r1# set routing-instances vpn-junos-ha routing-options
graceful-restart
[edit routing-instance vpn-green routing-options]
        graceful restart {
            ...
        }
```

 In each GR section in the preceding code, you can configure instance-specific GR parameters. You can also move configuration-specific or protocol-specific parameters in the respective protocol hierarchy in that instance.

To verify the GR state on either the provider or the customer side, use the following set of commands. Check the restart completion status for all protocols in each instance; you can see in the following code that some protocols have not completed their restart:

```
lab@r1> show route instance detail
master:
  Router ID: 192.168.1.111
  Type: forwarding       State: Active
  Restart State: Pending  Path selection timeout: 300
  Tables:
    inet.0               : 11 routes (10 active, 0 holddown, 1 hidden)
    Restart Pending: LDP
    inet.3               : 2 routes (2 active, 0 holddown, 0 hidden)
    Restart Pending: LDP
    mpls.0               : 8 routes (8 active, 0 holddown, 0 hidden)
    Restart Pending: LDP VPN
    bgp.l3vpn.0          : 2 routes (2 active, 0 holddown, 0 hidden)
    Restart Pending: BGP VPN
__juniper_private1__:
  Router ID: 0.0.0.0
  Type: forwarding       State: Active
vpn-green:
  Router ID: 11.156.0.5
  Type: vrf              State: Active
  Restart State: Pending  Path selection timeout: 300
  Interfaces:
```

```
    fxp2.0
    Route-distinguisher: 11.156.0.5:506
    Vrf-import: [ vpn-green-import ]
    Vrf-export: [ vpn-green-export ]
    Tables:
      vpn-green.inet.0      : 8 routes (7 active, 0 holddown, 0 hidden)
      Restart Pending: VPN
```

To check BGP restart status in the master instance (for inetvpn/L2VPN peers), use the following command:

```
lab@r1> show bgp summary
Groups: 2 Peers: 2 Down peers: 0
Table            Tot Paths  Act Paths Suppressed    History Damp State    Pending
bgp.l3vpn.0            2          2          0          0        0            0
Peer             AS      InPkt    OutPkt    OutQ   Flaps Last Up/Dwn State|
#Active/Received/Damped...
4.4.4.4          10045      39        43       0       0      18:02 Establ
  bgp.l3vpn.0: 2/2/0
  vpn-green.inet.0: 2/2/0
11.156.0.6       26         42        43       0       0      19:12 Establ
  vpn-green.inet.0: 3/4/0

lab@r1> show bgp neighbor
Peer: 4.4.4.4+179    AS 10045 Local: 5.5.5.5+1214   AS 10045

... output suppressed...

  NLRI for restart configured on peer: inet-vpn-unicast
  NLRI advertised by peer: inet-vpn-unicast
  NLRI for this session: inet-vpn-unicast
  Peer supports Refresh capability (2)
  Restart time configured on the peer: 120
  Stale routes from peer are kept for: 300
  Restart time requested by this peer: 120

  NLRI that peer supports restart for: inet-vpn-unicast
  NLRI peer can save forwarding state: inet-vpn-unicast
  NLRI that peer saved forwarding for: inet-vpn-unicast
  NLRI that restart is negotiated for: inet-vpn-unicast
  NLRI of received end-of-rib markers: inet-vpn-unicast
  NLRI of all end-of-rib markers sent: inet-vpn-unicast
  Table bgp.l3vpn.0 Bit: 10000
    RIB State: BGP restart is complete
    RIB State: VPN restart is complete
    Send state: in sync
    Active prefixes:           2
    Received prefixes:         2
    Suppressed due to damping: 0
  Table vpn-green.inet.0 Bit: 20001
    RIB State: BGP restart is complete
    RIB State: VPN restart is complete
```

```
Peer: 11.156.0.6+179 AS 26    Local: 11.156.0.5+1210 AS 10045
  NLRI for restart configured on peer: inet-unicast
  NLRI advertised by peer: inet-unicast
  NLRI for this session: inet-unicast
  Peer supports Refresh capability (2)
  Restart time configured on the peer: 120
  Stale routes from peer are kept for: 300
  Restart time requested by this peer: 120

  NLRI that peer supports restart for: inet-unicast
  NLRI peer can save forwarding state: inet-unicast
  NLRI that peer saved forwarding for: inet-unicast
  NLRI that restart is negotiated for: inet-unicast
  NLRI of received end-of-rib markers: inet-unicast
  NLRI of all end-of-rib markers sent: inet-unicast
  Table vpn-green.inet.0 Bit: 20000

    RIB State: BGP restart is complete
    RIB State: VPN restart is complete
    Send state: in sync
    Active prefixes:              3
    Received prefixes:            4
    Suppressed due to damping:    0
```

Graceful Restart in Multicast Protocols, PIM, and MSDP

As multicast technology has evolved, the protocols supporting it have evolved as well. From many original multicast protocols, industry has settled to build multicast technology based on Protocol-Independent Multicast (PIM) for single-domain communication and MSDP for any large-scale inter-Autonomous System (AS) multicast delivery. Therefore, we focus on the GR support of these two multicast protocols.

GR in the JUNOS PIM implementation is a proprietary solution that has not yet become a standard. However, the fact that the solution is still not an RFC but a retired draft means only that not all parties in the Internet Engineering Task Force (IETF) can agree that it is the best solution. Of course, not having an alternative means it consequently becomes the de facto solution.

To understand the GR implementation, let's analyze the process of establishing and maintaining the neighbor relationship in PIM. PIM sends Hello messages to all PIM speakers every so often. As long as a message is received before the dead timer expires, the PIM neighbor state is maintained. Only after the neighbor state is established can PIM join and prune messages be received and processed. The value that allows GR implementation in PIM is the 32-bit number called the Generation_ID (GEN_ID). It is a number that stays the same in all PIM messages throughout the neighbor session. It is reset only when either the routing process or the entire router has been restarted.

The receipt of a new Gen_ID value in a PIM Hello message signals to the recipient that the neighbor has restarted. This new Gen_ID value is the signal to all helpers to help rebuild previously known PIM states in the form of PIM join messages. All original entries in multicast cache are marked as stale and are maintained in the forwarding table for three minutes as kernel routes. If the new PIM join messages signal the same (S,G) or (*,G) entries, the forwarding state stays unchanged even after three minutes. However, if there is any discrepancy, all old entries are deleted afterward.

As long as a new Hello message is received before the dead interval, GR saves the multicast forwarding cache, resulting in zero traffic loss.

One fact that guarantees the stability of the forwarding cache is that neither new groups nor sources are supported during a GR event.

To modify any of the GR parameters within PIM, use any of the following statements:

```
[edit]
lab@r1# set protocols pim graceful-restart ?
Possible completions:
  disable              Disable PIM graceful restart capability
    restart-duration   Maximum time for graceful restart to finish (seconds)
```

 As with most of the link-state protocols, topology changes negatively affect the GR process and the outcome within the PIM environment. Specifically, unicast routing instability and topology changes will most likely result in failure of RPF checks. While the GR process is not affected, the actual multicast routing will be.

Table 4-2 describes the JUNOS software support for GR in other PIM mechanisms.

Table 4-2. GR support in PIM

Supported	Not supported
RP functionality (PIM Registers, *,G, pd)	RP advertisements
Source DR functionality (pe)	IGMP (relearned during restart)
RPF based on inet.2	MSDP (relearned during restart)
PIM Hello	STP/RTP overlapping
DR election and priority	Auto-RP
L3VPNs (PE with DR/RP in VRF, pe, pd)	BSR
GRES	Anycast RP

 Any security issue is a high availability issue. For instance, from a security standpoint, spoofed messages with different Gen_IDs could result in a DoS attack. To prevent these issues, JUNOS software limits how quickly join and prune messages can be received.

There are many different ways to deliver multicast traffic. Choosing a particular approach depends on the mix of the network devices being used in a particular network segment, the device control, customer versus provider segmentation, and many other political issues. Since the support for GR is not equally implemented across all equipment models, software versions, and vendors, network designers must evaluate all the choices and feature support before enabling GR PIM protocol extensions.

Non-Stop Active Routing

Having a highly available routing node in the middle of your network running GRES with two REs is a great way to build a core infrastructure supporting seven 9s network uptime. The problem is that ensuring a zero-loss environment requires GRES to be supplemented with GR protocol extensions on all running protocols on all surrounding routers. This is easily done in the core network, where you have the control of platform selection, protocol support, and software version. However, that is not the case at the edge of the network, where you face customer-controlled devices. More often than not, you do not know the hardware type or software versions and protocol support of your customer peering routers. Moreover, even if you do know, you cannot control their hardware and software selection. Thus, you cannot rely on GR protocol extensions to integrate seamlessly into your node redundancy design with GRES.

A provider also cannot always rely on network-based availability by means of redundant network paths toward the customer. Often, the customer is dual-homed to different service providers for better redundancy. It is most likely that catastrophic events, such as a natural disaster, will not affect different service providers in the same manner. While one ISP might lose portions of its data center and upstream peerings, another ISP might be located far away from the disaster site and will be able to preserve all routing state with the rest of the Internet.

Additionally, you do not want your customers to have any idea that your router has gone through a failure event at all. You'd really prefer to provide as little negative information about your network to your customers as you possibly can.

All of these reasons create a strong case for a different implementation of high availability on edge devices. Non-Stop Active Routing (NSR) is the perfect solution, not only for the edge of the network, but also for the core. With its seamless work in the background, NSR should be used wherever applicable. Figure 4-6 shows a network design based on high availability tools.

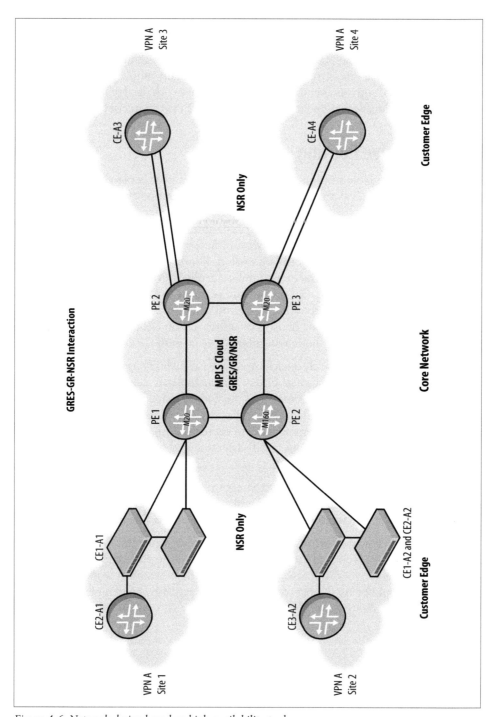

Figure 4-6. Network design based on high availability tools

Implementation Details and Configs

NSR is a relatively new software feature available in JUNOS, included since the JUNOS 8.4 release on platforms with dual REs. The basic concept of NSR is that the backup RE can maintain all peering relationships with its neighbors during an RE switchover event, without the help of protocol extensions such as GR. While NSR takes care of routing protocols, forwarding redundancy is still built on the concept of GRES. Therefore, to provide minimal traffic loss, GRES must be supported and configured in addition to NSR.

The backup RE provides support for NSR by actively running an RPD process. The aim is that the RPD on the backup RE is initially in sync with the primary RPD and in sync with the rest of the network afterward. Figure 4-7 illustrates the NSR state replication process.

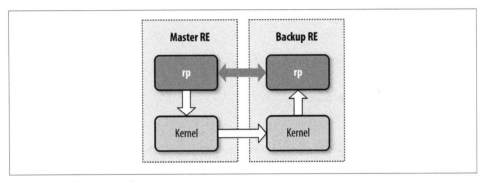

Figure 4-7. NSR state replication process

During the initial startup of the RPD process on the backup RE, all routing state from the primary RE is copied by means of `rtsock` messages using TCP. The private routing instance `_private_instance` is used as a means of RPD replication, ensuring that the RPD on the backup RE does not start routing from the null state. This routing instance also prevents delays in updates, because the backup RPD might have to wait for a long time for all neighbors' states to be refreshed. Certain protocols never readvertise their routing information to neighbors unless specifically requested, with the result that the backup RE remains out of sync with the rest of the world.

Once the RPD is up and running and all of its routing information is populated in the relevant tables, it actively snoops on all incoming and outgoing protocol messages. Moreover, it processes all incoming messages, and adds routes to or removes routes from the backup routing table as needed. During this process, the RPD resolves next hop information as needed, just as the primary RPD does. The RPD also snoops all locally generated messages from the primary RE to its neighbors. Therefore, the backup RE does not keep its state up-to-date with the primary RE. Rather, it keeps its state up-to-date with the rest of the network.

With NSR, the forwarding state and active kernel state are replicated the same way they are replicated in GRES: using the ksyncd daemon, which provides Non-Stop Forwarding (NSF) support.

To configure NSR support, use the following command:

```
[edit]
lab@r1# set routing-options nonstop-routing
```

As stated earlier, NSR is closely tied to GRES and uses GRES for NSF support. Thus, you must configure GRES as well:

```
[edit]
lab@r1# show chassis
chassis {
    redundancy {
        routing-engine 0 master;
        routing-engine 1 backup;
        failover {
            on-loss-of-keepalives;
            on-disk-failure;
        }
        graceful-switchover;
    }
    routing-engine {
        on-disk-failure reboot;
    }
}
```

Because both of the REs have the same configuration, you do not need to enable commit synchronization. In earlier releases, omitting the commit synchronize statement would generate a reminder to use the commit synchronize command for all commits. To avoid potentially forgetting to use this command, you must include the actual command in the router configuration file, and then each time you execute a commit command, JUNOS executes the commit synchronize command:

```
{master}[edit]
lab@r1# set system commit ?
Possible completions:
synchronize          Synchronize commit on both Routing Engines by default
{master}[edit]
lab@r1# set system commit synchronize
```

NSR and GR Helpers

NSR and GR extensions are mutually exclusive, and you cannot configure them together.

The primary goal of NSR is to have the router rebuild its routing and forwarding information without any impact on the actual forwarding and routing. In an ideal scenario, no neighbors would discover that the router has rebooted.

The goal of NSR conflicts with the primary goal of the GR extensions, which is to alert all the neighbors that the router is restarting and needs help from the neighbors. It is a

---

request to neighbors not to drop protocol adjacency and to help rebuild the lost routing table.

If you attempt to configure both NSR and GR, JUNOS displays a warning message:

```
[edit]
lab@r1# show routing-options
##
## Warning: Graceful restart and Nonstop routing may not be enabled simultaneously
##
graceful-restart;
```

Even though you may imagine a scenario in which not all routers can run NSR, but are capable of running GRES with GR, the fact is that all protocols capable of GR are also capable of being GR helpers without any extra configuration steps. As noted earlier in this chapter, they are all helpers by default.

To verify and troubleshoot NSR, use the following command:

```
{master}[edit]
lab@r1# run show task replication
        Stateful Replication: Enabled
        RE mode: Master

    Protocol                Synchronization Status
    IS-IS                   Complete

{master}[edit]
lab@r1#
```

Also execute show route, show bgp neighbor, show ospf database, and similar commands, and compare the output.

The reason network engineers have jobs is that not everything works as expected. Sometimes the problem is a deficiency in the system; however, often the issue is that our expectations are not aligned with the intended design goal of the JUNOS feature.

 "Unlike great literature, routing protocol functionality is not subject to personal interpretation." — Matthew Shaul, 2001

Because JUNOS supports traceoptions in many portions of the configuration, you might expect to find something similar for NSR support. In fact, you can turn on the nsr flag under traceoptions in all major protocols:

```
[edit]
lab@r1# set protocols isis traceoptions flag nsr-synchronization detail
```

Non-Stop Bridging

While most of the Juniper-deployed infrastructure on the Internet provides only routing functionality, more and more networks are deploying Juniper gear for switching purposes as well. Having a highly available switch is as important as the router. The bottom line is that networks provide only a medium for bits and bytes to move across. The failure of the forwarding card or control plane on the switch or the router has the same, unpleasant effect on the network. Therefore, it is necessary to provide some sort of system resilience for switches as well. JUNOS does it with the concept of Non-Stop Bridging (NSB), which, at the time of writing, is available only on the MX platforms. NSB is equivalent to NSR in the bridging world. The goal of NSB is to provide support for control plane failures while maintaining the forwarding state and keeping all neighbors blissfully in the dark about any failure. None of the Layer 2 control protocols should be able to detect the failure of the neighboring switch. The under-the-hood infrastructure of this concept is very similar to the NSR infrastructure.

Implementation Details and Configurations

NSB relies heavily on GRES for its forwarding state maintenance. As described in the previous section, kernel entries must be copied from the primary RE to the secondary RE. However, in this case, kernel entries contain Media Access Control (MAC) addresses and their respective next hops. Nevertheless, the replication process is the same. The ksyncd daemon is responsible for this replication. Once you configure GRES on the router in the chassis redundancy hierarchy, ksyncd is initialized on the backup RE and syncs up all of its state, including next hops with the primary RE. This replication takes care of keeping the forwarding state intact during the switchover.

However, to maintain the control plane replication, a different daemon is used. In the MX Series, all Layer 2 functionality is managed by the l2cpd process. Therefore, all the Layer 2 control protocols as well as the state replication are managed similarly to the way the RPD manages all routing management information and replication between primary and secondary REs. This daemon ensures that all Layer 2 protocol states stay intact during the switchover and afterward. Figure 4-8 shows the NSB state replication process.

As mentioned earlier in this chapter, to configure NSB, you must also configure GRES to ensure that the forwarding redundancy is replicated and routing protocols stay active. Then configure NSB:

```
{master}[edit]
lab@r1# set protocols layer2-control nonstop-bridging
```

As with everything in our network field, things don't always work as expected. To verify the replication state and further troubleshoot the problem, use the following command:

```
lab@r1# run show l2cpd task replication
        Stateful Replication: Disabled
```

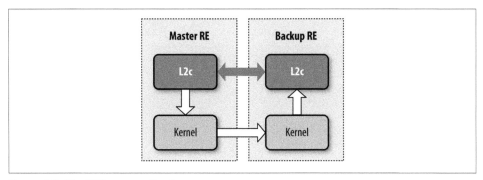

Figure 4-8. The NSB state replication process

Choosing Your High Availability Control Plane Solution

From the high availability perspective, among all the redundancy implementations discussed in this chapter, NSR and NSB are the two best choices: they provide full standalone routing, switching, and forwarding redundancy. In the event of a control plane failure, traffic continues to flow, and no neighbors observe any change in control protocol maintenance.

However, because we all have multivendor network environments, and not all features are supported on all platforms or software versions, we have to assess each design separately to find the optimal redundancy solution. Because of tight protocol interaction, we must analyze each network requirement separately, and based on supported software and platforms, use some or all of the available high availability. Table 4-3 lists the JUNOS release support requirement information needed for you to make these choices.

Table 4-3. High availability redundancy implementations

Platform	GRES	GR	NSR	NSB
T640	5.6	5.6	9.0	N/A
M320	6.0	6.0	9.0	N/A
M120	8.4	8.4	9.0	N/A
M10/7	6.0	6.0	9.6	N/A
J Series	8.4	8.4	10.0	N/A
MX Series	8.4	8.4	9.2	9.0

CHAPTER 5

Virtualization for High Availability

Picture this: you have just left a meeting with the CTO. During the meeting, you were informed that, by order of the CFO, there is no more money, but your customer support manager says the company must improve customer satisfaction statistics by increasing, and most importantly delivering, higher uptime levels in customer service-level agreements (SLAs). Everyone is looking at you to deliver service improvements with empty pockets.

Regardless of your particular business, you have a single goal: to provide reliable access to information. Whether you are in charge of a purpose-built enterprise data center or collocation facilities selling data access, specific uptime levels are defined in your customers' SLAs. While 99.9% uptime was an acceptable measure of reliability a decade ago, the increased importance of mission-critical information demands even higher availability. Many of today's network deployments require an uptime of 99.999%, commonly referred to as "five 9s" of availability. Some networks have even more stringent requirements, approaching an uptime of 99.99999%, or "seven 9s" of availability.

This chapter discusses how the consolidation of resources can improve your network's high availability. Why consolidate? The bottom line is that having fewer devices in your network results in fewer opportunities for potential errors and hence in fewer failures. Here are a few specific reasons for consolidation:

Ease of management
> Reducing the number of devices that IT must manage lowers network complexity, yielding increased availability through more uptime and greater operational efficiency, as well as through increased productivity. The result is a reduction in operational expenses (OPEX) and a decrease in Mean Time Between Failure (MTBF) averages.

Power and cooling efficiency
> Having fewer devices reduces the probability of power failure, resulting in increased availability. The decrease in power consumption is directly proportional to a decrease in cooling costs.

Scalable growth
> Consolidating resources allows for future controlled network growth that is both cost-effective and space-efficient.

While there is ongoing discussion about the best consolidation technologies to use in the data center—iSCSI, Fiber Channel (FC), FC over Ethernet, and InfiniBand are examples of various technological concepts—they all have the same goal: consolidation of operating resources.

A key component to successful consolidation of IT resources is *virtualization*, the combining of multiple network functions and/or components into a single, usually software-based, administrative entity. All the applications being delivered by next-generation data centers have only two needs: access to CPU and I/O. Technology has evolved significantly such that the old concept of a single data center server has been replaced with many virtual entities that access portions of allocated resources. While most virtualization focuses on servers, databases, email, storage, and even end-user client components, we cannot ignore the infrastructure component based around network resource virtualization.

This chapter covers two different, but important, scenarios of network resource virtualization: virtualization of the low-end switching control plane by EX Series switches that are used for host connectivity in data centers, and virtualization of the high-end routing control plane by T Series routers that are used in the core routing domain and in remote mega-Point of Presence (POP) locations. Both types of virtualization are part of the data center infrastructure, but each operates at a different network layer.

Virtual Chassis in the Switching Control Plane

The Juniper EX Series is the newest addition to the Juniper routing and switching portfolio. Lower-end models include the EX3200 and EX4200 series; the EX8200 series are larger switches. The EX3200 and EX4200 are stackable switches targeted as a solution for data centers, campuses, and branch office deployments. As we discussed in Chapter 2, each switch runs JUNOS software and has a routing engine (RE). With these low-end switches, you can create *Virtual Chassis* (VCs) of up to 10 switches to provide high availability of network resources. VC technology allows the RE on one of the switches in the group to manage all the other switches in the stack. The RE uses proven technologies, such as Graceful Routing Engine Switchover (GRES), Non-Stop Active Routing (NSR), and Non-Stop Bridging (NSB), to fully manage and operate the rest of the switches in the stack. These other line card switches have their own Packet Forwarding Engine (PFE) containing proprietary switching application-specific integrated circuits (ASICs).

Figure 5-1 illustrates a VC composed of stackable switches.

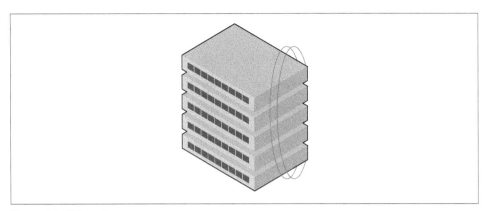

Figure 5-1. VC stack

As you can see in Figure 5-1, five switches are stacked together and joined by a VC backplane connection. This stack provides the equivalent throughput of a 128 Gbps high-speed backplane. The switches are connected using VC cables that can create a stack or ring topology. We discuss different VC connectivity design methods later in this chapter. VC cables can be up to 3 feet long. Member switches can also interconnect through the switch's standard 1GE or 10GE uplink ports, which increases the distance between the switches in a single chassis. Using long-range (LR) optics with these uplinks, there can be up to 1 km between individual switch chassis, so a single VC can span up to 10 km. Note that 1/10GE uplink ports that are dedicated to providing intermember chassis connectivity can no longer be used as regular Ethernet ports because they are running an internal JUNOS protocol, Trivial Network Protocol (TNP). This is the same protocol used on other Juniper equipment for communication between the RE and the PFE. In the VC, TNP carries all the data along the interchassis links.

Each switch in a VC is a member of that chassis. The methodology of master and backup REs that is used on other Juniper equipment is also applied in the VC world. Because each switch has its own built-in RE, any of the 10 switches is eligible to become a master RE through the election process. From the switches that do not become the master, a single switch is elected as the backup RE. The rest of the switches function like line cards. The VC in Figure 5-1 has one master, one backup, and three line cards. Using the JUNOS command-line interface (CLI), you see that all switches appear as Flexible PIC Concentrators (FPCs), starting with FPC 0. As you can see in the following output, one of the FPCs (here, FPC 0) is the master and the other (FPC 1) is the backup. The remaining three switches are also listed in the output as FPCs, starting with FPC 2, and with the role of line card:

```
lab@s1> show virtual-chassis status

Virtual Chassis ID: 0019.e257.3d80
                                      Mastership            Neighbor List
Member ID Status Serial No    Model     priority  Role     ID  Interface
  0 (FPC 0) Prsnt  BQ0208138247 ex4200-48p     255  Master*   1   vcp-0
```

```
                                                          1   vcp-1
  1 (FPC 1)  Prsnt   BR0208211823  ex4200-24f     255   Backup    0   vcp-0
                                                          0   vcp-1
  2 (FPC 2)  Prsnt   BR0208211213  ex4200-24f     128   Linecard  0   vcp-0
                                                          0   vcp-1
  3 (FPC 3)  Prsnt   BR0208218363  ex4200-24f     128   Linecard  0   vcp-0
                                                          0   vcp-1
  4 (FPC 4)  Prsnt   BR0208217183  ex4200-24f     128   Linecard  0   vcp-0
                                                          0   vcp-1


  Member ID for next new member: 5 (FPC 5)
```

You can remotely manage the entire VC in two ways: either through the console of any of the five VC members, or by using a single Ethernet management interface, called a VME, which is manually assigned an IP address. Regardless of the point of entry, console or Ethernet, all roads lead to the master RE. Once you are connected to the VC, all the switch ports are accessible through the CLI.

The master RE manages all control plane protocols for the line cards. The routing and forwarding tables created on the master RE are pushed down to all the VC line cards by means of TNP updates, which is the same method used by other Juniper chassis, as described in Chapter 4.

VCs also support the same high availability control plane features as other Juniper equipment. A VC can use GRES and NSR for control plane failures. Then, if the master RE fails, a backup RE takes over and the rest of the line cards continue to forward the traffic. VCs also support In-Service Software Upgrade (ISSU), which allows each line card to be upgraded during regular operating hours rather than during a maintenance window. These features allow a properly designed and configured EX Series VC to provide a reliability of five 9s.

VC Roles

A VC is created by connecting 2 or more (up to 10) switches and then configuring them as though they were a single chassis. By default, one switch in the VC takes the role of master switch, acting as the brain for all other members of the chassis. This role is identical to the role of master RE on other Juniper routing platforms. The master switch runs all routing and switching daemons and runs chassisd to manage the other VC members. Using its replication daemon, the kernel on the master switch pushes its forwarding entries to the backup switch and to the rest of the line cards as needed.

The backup switch is "the sleeping brain," having the role of backup RE. Depending on the high availability tool set you are using, the backup can be totally asleep, as is the case with GRES and Graceful Restart (GR), or it can be actively listening, as in the case of NSR and NSB. In both scenarios, the backup switch is waiting to take over control of the entire VC if the master switch fails.

The rest of the member switches are in line card mode, in which they act as dumb devices and simply forward traffic based on routing and forwarding table entries created on the master switch. If the master or backup switch fails, one of the line card switches is elected as the next backup switch.

IDs for VCs

Each set of switches connected in a VC has the same VC identifier (ID) value to signal membership in that particular VC. The following CLI output shows how to display the VC ID:

```
lab@s1> show virtual-chassis status
Virtual Chassis ID: 0000.e255.00e0
Mastership Neighbor List
Member ID Status Serial No Model Priority Role ID Interface
0 (FPC 0) Prsnt abc123 ex4200-48p 255 Master* 1 vcp-0
                                          2 vcp-1
1 (FPC 1) Prsnt def456 ex4200-24t 255 Backup 2 vcp-0
                                          0 vcp-1
2 (FPC 2) Prsnt abd231 ex4200-24p 128 Linecard 0 vcp-0
                                          1 vcp-1
```

Each switch also has a member ID, which is a unique identifier within that VC. By default, a switch in standalone mode is assigned a member ID of 0. When the switch joins a chassis group and is used in VC mode, a nonzero member ID is assigned to the switch. The first switch to join the VC has a member ID of 0, the second switch that joins is assigned a member ID of 1, and so forth. The assigned member ID value is sticky and is retained even after the switch leaves the VC group. For example, if the member IDs in a three-switch VC are set in order, 0, 1, and 2, if Switch 1 fails and is replaced with another switch, the new switch is assigned a member ID of 4 and the ID of 1 remains unused. You can clear the member ID manually with the following command:

```
lab@s1> request virtual-chassis renumber member-id 4 new-member-id 1
```

While you can leave the default member IDs unchanged, it is a good practice to pay attention to the ID values and manually modify them as necessary, because they play a significant role in the VC mastership election process.

Priorities and the Election Process

While you can easily slap together and connect switches to create a VC that works in your network, it is better to go the extra mile and plan the VC configuration beforehand and check that the configuration is working properly. As always, planning is better for high availability than not planning.

When you boot the switches in a VC, the following steps determine the master RE:

1. The member with the highest mastership priority value becomes the master VC.
2. If the mastership priority values are equal, the member that was the master the last time the VC booted becomes the master.
3. If there is no record of a previous master, the member that has been part of the VC the longest becomes the master.
4. If several chassis have been part of the VC for the same amount of time, the member with the lowest Media Access Control (MAC) address becomes the master.

How to rig an election

Each switch is assigned a mastership priority value between 1 and 255, and the switch with the highest value is elected master. By default, all switches are assigned a value of 128. While you could configure one switch with 200, configure another with 150, and leave the rest of the switches to the default of 128, this setup is not recommended. The mastership ownership is preemptive, so once the original master comes back online after a failure, it takes back the VC mastership because of its higher priority, which may disrupt VC operations.

 To prevent mastership preemption, it is best to configure both master and backup REs with priorities of 255 and leave the rest of the switches with the default value. Because membership uptime within the VC is also relevant, you should power on the master switch first and configure its priority; then power up and configure the backup switch, and finally bring up the rest of the line card switches.

Basic VC Setup and Configuration

Let's verify the most basic setup of a VC consisting of two member switches. The members are connected using VC ports (VCPs) over proprietary Juniper cable, as shown in Figure 5-2.

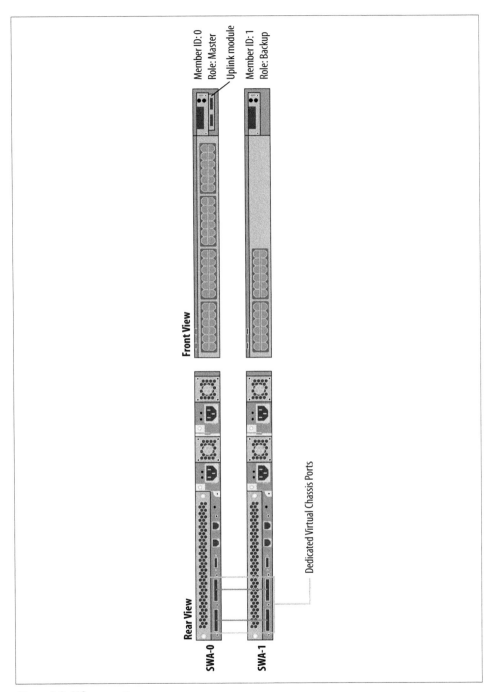

Figure 5-2. VC connection

As recommended earlier, power on the intended master first because this guarantees the default assigned priorities, therefore making the switch a master. After the second switch is online, the VC should be working with the correct mastership assignment, as you can check from the CLI:

```
lab@s1> show virtual-chassis status

Virtual Chassis ID: 0019.e257.3d80
                                              Mastership       Neighbor List
Member ID  Status Serial No    Model          priority  Role   ID  Interface
0 (FPC 0)  Prsnt  BQ0208138247 ex4200-48p         128   Master*  1  vcp-0
                                                                  1  vcp-1
1 (FPC 1)  Prsnt  BR0208211823 ex4200-24f         128   Backup   0  vcp-0
                                                                  0  vcp-1

Member ID for next new member: 2 (FPC 2)

{master}
lab@s1> show virtual-chassis vc-port all-members
fpc0:
--------------------------------------------------------------------
Interface    Type            Status
or
PIC / Port
vcp-0        Dedicated       Up
vcp-1        Dedicated       Up

fpc1:
--------------------------------------------------------------------
Interface    Type            Status
or
PIC / Port
vcp-0        Dedicated       Up
vcp-1        Dedicated       Up

{master}
lab@s1>
```

You see that both switches are present and that Switch 0 has been chosen to be the master of this VC. Because it was the first switch to come online, its member ID is 0 and it is referred to as FPC 0. You also see that both VC cables are in the "up" state and are being used for VC connectivity. In this case, you need only one cable because the connection runs in full duplex (FD) mode. However, using a second cable provides redundancy.

To guarantee that Switch 0 is always the master switch, change its priority to 255:

```
lab@s1# set virtual-chassis member 0 mastership-priority 255
```

To prevent mastership preemption after Switch 0 restarts or its hardware is replaced, change the mastership priority of Switch 1 as well:

```
lab@s1# set virtual-chassis member 1 mastership-priority 255
```

```
lab@s1# commit
fpc0:
configuration check succeeds
fpc1:
commit complete
fpc0:
commit complete
```

To verify the changes, which ensures that the proper mastership election occurs the next time the VC boots up, use the following commands:

```
lab@s1> show virtual-chassis member-config
fpc0:
--------------------------------------------------------------------------

  Member ID:          0
  Mastership priority: 255

fpc1:
--------------------------------------------------------------------------

  Member ID:          1
  Mastership priority: 255

lab@s1> show virtual-chassis status

Virtual Chassis ID: 0019.e257.3d80
                                          Mastership          Neighbor List
Member ID Status Serial No    Model       priority  Role     ID  Interface
0 (FPC 0) Prsnt  BQ0208138247 ex4200-48p       255  Master*  1   vcp-0
                                                             1   vcp-1
1 (FPC 1) Prsnt  BR0208211823 ex4200-24f       255  Backup   0   vcp-0
                                                             0   vcp-1

Member ID for next new member: 2 (FPC 2)
```

When you add more switches to the VC, they all have a line card role and the default mastership priority of 128:

```
lab@s1> show virtual-chassis status

Virtual Chassis ID: 0019.e257.3d80
                                          Mastership          Neighbor List
Member ID Status Serial No    Model     priority  Role       ID  Interface
0 (FPC 0) Prsnt  BQ0208138247 ex4200-48p     255  Master*    1   vcp-0
                                                            1   vcp-1
1 (FPC 1) Prsnt  BR0208211823 ex4200-24f     255  Backup     0   vcp-0
                                                            0   vcp-1
2 (FPC 2) Prsnt  BR0208211213 ex4200-24f     128  Linecard   0   vcp-0
                                                            0   vcp-1
3 (FPC 3) Prsnt  BR0208218363 ex4200-24f     128  Linecard   0   vcp-0
                                                            0   vcp-1

Member ID for next new member: 4 (FPC 4)
```

Eliminating Loops Within the VC

At this point, you may be wondering about potential loops across the VCP intermember links. Since Juniper recommends creation of a VC ring topology, we are in fact creating a loop by default. This is OK. For redundancy purposes, you *should* be connecting VCPs in a ring topology as we described earlier in this chapter. So, how do we solve the issue of looping within the virtual backplane? Simply stated, this is not a problem the user has to solve. EX switches use a proprietary modification of the Intermediate System to Intermediate System (IS-IS) protocol across the VC links to prevent loops. Users can catch a glimpse of it in action by running show virtual-chassis protocol database:

```
{master}
lab@s1> show virtual-chassis protocol database
fpc0:
--------------------------------------------------------------------
LSP ID                    Sequence Checksum Lifetime
0019.e256.5880.00-00      0x6a3ba   0x434d    116
0019.e256.5881.00-00      0x6a359   0x5c9f    114
0019.e257.3d80.00-00      0x6a37e   0xd5bf    118
0019.e257.3d81.00-00      0x6a3bf   0xb434    118
0019.e257.3d82.00-00      0x1f4bb   0x39d1    118
  5 LSPs

fpc1:
--------------------------------------------------------------------
LSP ID                    Sequence Checksum Lifetime
0019.e256.5880.00-00      0x6a3ba   0x434d    118
0019.e256.5881.00-00      0x6a359   0x5c9f    116
0019.e257.3d80.00-00      0x6a37e   0xd5bf    116
0019.e257.3d81.00-00      0x6a3bf   0xb434    116
0019.e257.3d82.00-00      0x1f4bb   0x39d1    116
  5 LSPs
```

This output shows the link-state database that is used to create active backplane routes toward each individual switch that is a member of the VC. Each switch member has a unique IS-IS link-state packet (LSP).

The following output lists each member switch as a separate FPC with individual interfaces that are used for interconnection. Each interface has a metric value that is based on its bandwidth. For example, a standard VCP has a metric of 10, while 10 GB uplink interfaces configured as VCPs have a metric of 30 and a 1 GB interface configured as a VCP has a metric of 300:

```
lab@s1> show virtual-chassis protocol interface
fpc0:
--------------------------------------------------------------------
IS-IS interface database:
Interface           State       Metric
internal-0/24       Up            10
internal-1/25       Up            10
internal-2/24       Up            10
```

```
internal-2/27          Up             10
vcp-0                  Up             10
vcp-1                  Up             10

fpc1:
----------------------------------------------------------------------
IS-IS interface database:
Interface              State          Metric
internal-0/27          Up             10
internal-1/24          Up             10
vcp-0                  Up             10
vcp-1                  Up             10
```

From the perspective of Switch 0 (sw0), sw1 is accessible along a route that has a metric of 10:

```
lab@s1> show virtual-chassis protocol route
fpc0:
----------------------------------------------------------------------

Dev 0019.e257.3d80 ucast routing table          Current version: 1462
----------------
System ID        Version   Metric Interface     Via
0019.e256.5880   1462          10 vcp-0         0019.e256.5880
0019.e256.5881   1462          20 vcp-0         0019.e256.5880
0019.e257.3d81   1462          20 internal-0/24 0019.e257.3d82
0019.e257.3d82   1462          10 internal-0/24 0019.e257.3d82

...
```

On each VC, the VCCPd daemon, which is responsible for backplane link management, contains built-in reconvergence elements that speed up IS-IS backplane routing to a recovery time of just less than one second. Detecting and successfully reconverging the ring-based VC topology takes about 300 milliseconds. This time is the same as the fast-hello Virtual Router Redundancy Protocol (VRRP) interval used in standard IP routing and is significantly faster than many spanning tree implementations.

Local-repair

While 300 milliseconds is acceptable for many data applications, new video and voice solutions require convergence times to be closer to the SONET convergence times of about 50 milliseconds. Starting with Release 9.3, JUNOS software supports enhanced VCCPd "local-repair," which guarantees a backplane reconvergence time of approximately 50 milliseconds. When a VCP interface failure is discovered in the VC, the switch adjacent to the interface creates a local loopback interface and starts sending traffic in the other direction around the VC ring. At the same time, the rest of the VC members recompute the new VC topology.

Depending on the VCPs being used for VC backplane connectivity, you might have to enable the local-repair feature. By default, built-in dedicated VCPs are enabled. However, you must explicitly configure 1GE or 10GE interfaces using the following commands:

```
[edit]
lab@s1# set system virtual-chassis fast-failover xe  enable

[edit]
lab@s1# set system virtual-chassis fast-failover ge  enable
```

Highly Available Designs for VCs

So far in this chapter, we have discussed the hardware and software architecture of the EX Series switches and you have seen that VCs offer many cool features. This section discusses how to use these features to improve your network's availability.

The examples in this section describe tools to optimize link-based redundancy at the network layer. As mentioned earlier, even though different types of redundancy solutions and third-party appliances are currently available, the solutions discussed in this section use product features you already have. They do not require additional purchases, only time for configuration testing and deployment.

Manipulating a split VC

While you can connect all member switches with the single VC backplane cable in a braided VC configuration, for the most optimal high availability design it is highly recommended that you use both VCPs and that you create ring-based virtual backplane connectivity. The ring topology can tolerate a single link failure: when such a failure occurs, control traffic is just rerouted in another direction using interlink IS-IS routing. For example, in Figure 5-3, traffic moving from Switch 0, port ge-0/0/1 to Switch 3, port ge-3/0/5 would normally take Link A because this is the shortest path. If Link A fails, traffic moves in the opposite direction of the ring and follows Link B. As mentioned earlier, the convergence time of a single VCP link failure is about 300 milliseconds, which is fast enough for most data applications.

The likelihood of two VC backplane links failing simultaneously is very slim, however; redundancy built into the VC design minimizes the impact of a dual failure. Simultaneous failure of two VC links is referred to as a *VC split* failure. If this type of failure occurs, each separate section elects its own master and continues running. If the master and backup switches are both on one side of the split, the other side does not have an active master or backup for the time that it takes to elect a new master. To minimize the chance of a split resulting in the master and backup switches being on the same side of the split, we recommend that you configure the master and the backup switches as far as possible from each other, in terms of routing hops. For example, Figure 5-3 shows recommended placement of the master and backup in a ring topology.

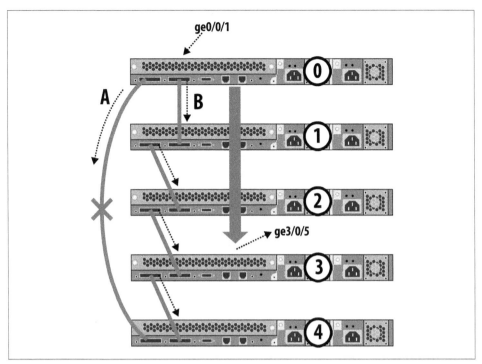

Figure 5-3. Ring-based VC backplane topology

Recovery from dual-link failures in a ring-based VC topology has one potential problem that is observed in only certain scenarios. If the network design architecture uses a globally assigned IP addressing scheme and if switches are participating in Interior Gateway Protocol (IGP) routing protocols, duplicate IP address and router IDs could potentially black-hole traffic and cause networkwide outages. Just imagine the VC split scenario after both halves have recovered. They both would have the same management IP address and the same router ID, resulting in duplicate entries in domainwide routing tables and IGP databases.

To mitigate this problem, the recovery algorithm for VC dual-link failure has been modified in JUNOS Release 9.3 and later. After a VC split, only one-half of the chassis remains active and continues forwarding. The other half of the VC is taken offline until the VCP link is repaired.

The VC routing protocol algorithm uses the following rules to decide which VC side should stay active:

- If both the master and the backup switches are in the same half, that half stays active and the other half is deactivated and its switches stop forwarding.
- If master and backup are in different VC halves, the half with the most members stays active. The other half is deactivated and its switches stop forwarding.

- If master and backup are in different VC halves, and both halves have the same number of active members, the half with the original backup switch stays active. The backup switch is promoted to master and a new backup is elected on that half. The other VC half is brought offline and its switches stop forwarding.

Server resilience with VCs

The need for highly available access to applications has led to further advances in server-based technologies. Even when the entire end-to-end network data path is globally and locally redundant, a single point of failure still exists: the last connection from the switch port to the application server. This problem can be solved by having many different clustering and load-balancing systems, or it can be addressed with application-level redundancy. However, a fairly inexpensive solution is already sitting in many data centers.

Most new chassis or shelf-based blade servers have two or four Ethernet interfaces that can all be used simultaneously. With some extra configuration on both sides, we can utilize all available interfaces on these servers, thus increasing the bandwidth capacity as well as filling in the last gap of network layer redundancy. As a matter of fact, with VCs, we can actually provide both link and switch redundancy.

The EX Series supports a link-bundling concept called Link Aggregated Group (LAG). Up to eight individual interfaces can be bundled into a single LAG. As shown in Figure 5-4, the links between Switch 0 and Switch 1 are simply bundled together. Both links are active at all times, and traffic is load-balanced across both according to the load-balancing hashing algorithm. Active bundling is interoperable with all vendors that support the 802.3ad Ethernet standard. To enable LAG on Ethernet interfaces, you configure the following:

```
[edit]
lab@s1# set chassis aggregated-devices ethernet device-count 2

[edit]
lab@s1# set interfaces ae0 aggregated-ether-options minimum-links 1

[edit]
lab@s1# set interfaces ae0 aggregated-ether-options link-speed 10g
```

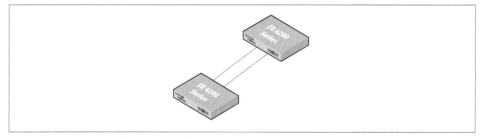

Figure 5-4. Separating the master and backup switches in a VC

While this initial configuration example uses only two interfaces, a single VC domain can support up to 64 LAGs. We have defined the minimum number of links to be 1. If your particular network design has a bandwidth requirement and your topology provides additional redundant paths, you would set the minimum number of links to 2. With that configuration, the aggregated Ethernet interface would be brought down and traffic would shift over to the second redundant path if the first path fails.

The next configuration step is to add interfaces to the LAG bundle. The following configuration joins the xe-0/1/0 and 1/1/0 interfaces to the ae0 interface and assigns a single IP address to this bundle:

```
[edit]
lab@s1# set interfaces xe-0/1/0 ether-options 802.ad ae0

[edit]
lab@s1# set interfaces xe-1/1/0 ether-options 802.ad ae0

[edit]
lab@s1# set interfaces ae0 unit 0 family inet address 192.168.133.1/24
```

To complete the last leg of redundant connectivity, you configure LAGs on the server side of the connection, using the *NIC teaming* feature that is provided with many server platforms (see Figure 5-5). You can configure LAGs between either two or all four of the server's network interface cards (NICs) and VC switch members. However, to provide full switch resiliency, you should connect the NICs to two different switch members. Because both switches are part of a single VC, they are just two different ports on the same virtual switch. This configuration is identical to the previous one, except that the aggregated Ethernet member ports are 1G Ethernet interfaces connected to the servers.

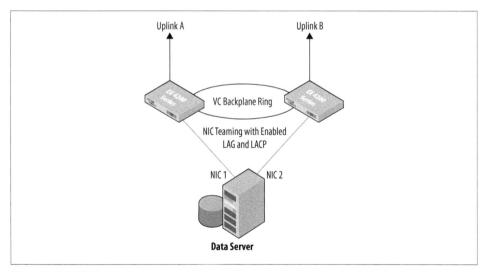

Figure 5-5. NIC Teaming

```
[edit]
lab@s1# set chassis aggregated-devices ethernet device-count 6

[edit]
lab@s1# set interfaces ae2 aggregated-ether-options minimum-links 1

[edit]
lab@s1# set interfaces ae2 aggregated-ether-options link-speed 1g

[edit]
lab@s1# set interfaces ge-3/1/0 ether-options 802.ad ae1

[edit]
lab@s1# set interfaces xe-1/1/0 ether-options 802.ad ae1

[edit]
lab@s1# set interfaces ae2 unit 0 family inet address 192.168.134.1/24
```

To verify the configuration, you can use the following commands. In the show
interfaces ae0 terse command, we care only that both the Admin and Link states are
up. The show interfaces ae0 statistics command gives more detailed information
about the aggregated interface, including the traffic load:

```
lab@s1> show interfaces ae0 terse
Interface              Admin      Link Proto      Local           Remote
ae0                    up         up
ae0.0                  up         up   inet       192.168.133.1/24

lab@s1> show interfaces ae0 statistics
Physical interface: ae0, Enabled, Physical link is Down
Interface index: 153, SNMP ifIndex: 30
Link-level type: Ethernet, MTU: 1514, Speed: Unspecified, Loopback: Disabled,
Source filtering: Disabled, Flow control: Disabled, Minimum links needed: 1,
Minimum bandwidth needed: 0
Device flags : Present Running
Interface flags: Hardware-Down SNMP-Traps Internal: 0x0
Current address: 02:19:e2:50:45:e0, Hardware address: 02:19:e2:50:45:e0
Last flapped : Never
Statistics last cleared: Never
Input packets : 0
Output packets: 0
Input errors: 0, Output errors: 0
Logical interface ae0.0 (Index 71) (SNMP ifIndex 34)
Flags: Hardware-Down Device-Down SNMP-Traps Encapsulation: ENET2
Statistics Packets pps Bytes bps
Bundle:
Input : 0 0 0 0
Output: 0 0 0 0
Protocol inet, MTU: 1500
Flags: None
Addresses, Flags: Dest-route-down Is-Preferred Is-Primary
Destination: 192.168.133/24, Local: 192.168.133.1/24, Broadcast 192.168.133.255
```

The IEEE 802.3ad Ethernet standard does not define LAG liveness detection or LAG
auto-configuration. If a single link fails, it is removed from the bundle and traffic

continues forwarding using another interface. To improve on this, the Internet Engineering Task Force (IETF) has standardized another protocol, called Link Active Connection Protocol (LACP), which supports LAG liveness and auto-configuration. LACP is not just a switch protocol, but is also widely accepted and supported by many different server platform vendors.

With LACP, each side of the connection sends periodic Hello packets. The default Hello time is one second. LACP supports active and passive modes. You should configure one side of the connection as active and the other as passive.

 LACP passive mode stops any Hello advertisements. Make sure you do not configure both ends as passive. Otherwise, neither of the ends will initiate any communication, and LAG will never come up.

LACP is not enabled on LAGs by default. To turn it on, you configure the following:

```
[edit interfaces]
lab@s1#set ae0 aggregated-ether-options lacp active periodic fast

[edit interfaces]
lab@s1#set ae1 aggregated-ether-options lacp active periodic fast
```

To verify that LAG with fast LACP is enabled, use the show lacp interfaces xe-0/1/0 command:

```
lab@s1> show lacp interfaces xe-0/1/0

Aggregated interface: ae0

    LACP state:       Role  Exp Def Dist Col Syn Aggr Timeout Activity

    xe-0/1/0          Actor  No  Yes  No  No  No  Yes   Fast   Active

    xe-0/1/0        Partner  No  Yes  No  No  No  Yes   Fast   Passive

    LACP protocol:   Receive State    Transmit State      Mux State

    xe-0/1/0            Defaulted     Fast periodic        Detached
```

Control System Chassis

In today's tight market space, service and application providers have to maintain their competitiveness through constant innovation. New services, faster time-to-market deployment schedules, and tighter SLA requirements create more pressure on existing network resources. Consolidation of resources and access to CPU and I/O in server-based application space has already been in the works for several years. Just as it makes absolute business sense to consolidate at the application level, it also makes strong business sense to lower the cost and high availability pressure by consolidating the routing and forwarding planes and by creating a new concept of a service-driven network infrastructure.

With this service-driven network you can consolidate all services into a shared IP/Multiprotocol Label Switching (MPLS) backbone while providing strict separation of services in terms of quality and reliability. All voice applications can be entirely separated from video traffic and virtual private network (VPN) transit data services. Additionally, if applicable, the same converged IP/MPLS backbone can provide a secure and reliable transit path for financial market data and stock tickers. The bottom line is that all services can use the same infrastructure without affecting each other's reliability and high availability.

Consolidation need not be limited to revenue-generating services. Supporting network infrastructure should be consolidated, yielding higher capital expenditure (CAPEX) and OPEX savings. A multiple-POP and mega-POP routing infrastructure can be collapsed into a single platform. Likewise, continental and intercontinental uplinks can be collapsed and shared by all services, yielding further cost reduction. Border Gateway Protocol (BGP)-based network services such as route reflection, network peering, and policy management can be collapsed into a single platform as well.

Building network solutions based on the virtualized router concept allows for faster service deployment and higher operational efficiency. Migration and provisioning of geographically dispersed wide area network (WAN) infrastructure built on a single device in each POP is far more efficient. You do not have to build a separate lab or run separate continental links for the pre-staging exercise and deployment testing. As a result of the concise separation of the control domain, you can safely use the existing infrastructure for testing and preprovisioning without affecting data paths in the live network. This particular approach decreases the time needed to bring new products to market.

From the high availability perspective, strict separation of IP/MPLS-based services results in better fault isolation, thus increasing network uptime. Having fewer devices results in easier management and a clear separation between different management groups. Additionally, upgrade cycles and software deployment are far less complex because of the consolidation of network resources.

Most of these issues are addressed by logical routers, which were introduced in JUNOS 6.0. While this control plane separation has been widely accepted, the relatively new Juniper platform called Juniper Control System (JCS) 1200 takes services and management separation to the next level. The JCS1200 works in conjunction with T Series routers to provide scaling of control and forwarding plane resources.

Requirements and Implementation

The JCS1200 is a separate routing node that can host up to 12 REs each running its own version of JUNOS software. The JCS connects to a single or to multiple T Series platforms as an external virtual router. In this configuration, a single T Series router with its own REs becomes a Root System Domain (RSD). Both REs on the T Series router run their own version of JUNOS independently of the JUNOS version on the JCSs. Either one or two REs on the JCS join together to create a hardware-based virtual router, called the Protected System Domain (PSD). All the forwarding resources (i.e., the FPCs and Physical Interface Cards or PICs) of single or multiple RSDs become available to any of the REs on the JCS, resulting in the possibility of up to 12 standalone PSDs (i.e., routers) that each has access to any of the available FPCs. Even though the PSD is a virtual entity because it is composed of separate hardware components, it still feels, looks, and operates like a single JUNOS router. When combined with 16 logical routers—the number supported by a single copy of JUNOS software—and a maximum of 12 PSDs per JCS, a single JCS1200 can support up to 192 logical routers.

Figure 5-6 shows two PSDs consisting of two REs each and two FPCs that are separated from the rest of the forwarding hardware in this RSD, a T Series router. The T Series router is connected to the JCS1200 through an Ethernet connection across which all control traffic is passed to the RE or set of REs in the JCS chassis.

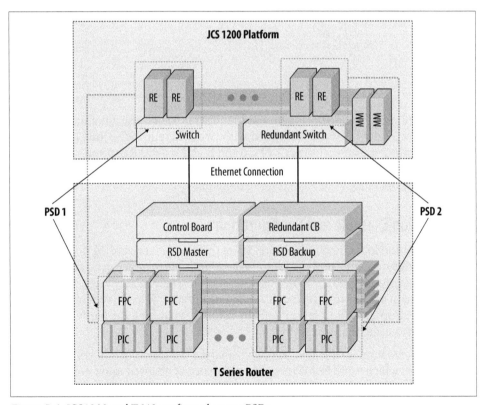

Figure 5-6. JCS1200 and T640 configured as two PSDs

Because each RSD and PSD is a separate entity running its own version of JUNOS, neither PSD nor RSD failures or switchovers affect each other. Control traffic destined to individual REs is isolated between RSDs and PSDs. Both the RSD and PSD support all high availability features such as GRES, NSR, and ISSU. With a fully populated JCS, you would actually end up with 12 different hardware routers, and you would be able to access any of the forwarding components in all three RSDs. Each of the 12 partitions can have its own administrator, yet they all could share uplinks when needed.

To create an RSD on a T Series router you configure the following:

```
[edit]
lab@r1# show
chassis {
    system-domains {
        root-domain-id 1;
        protected-system-domains {
            psd1 {
                fpcs [0 1];
                control-system-id 1;
                control-slot-numbers [0 1];
                }
            psd2 {
                fpcs [6 7];
                control-system-id 2;
                control-slot-numbers [10 11];
                }
            }
        }
    }
}
```

In this configuration, the RSD has a unique identifier of 1, because it is a single T Series chassis. However, its FPCs are associated with two different PSDs, psd1 and psd2, as shown in Figure 5-6. psd1 owns rsd1's FPC 0 and 1, and it owns REs 0 and 1 on the JCS. psd2 owns rsd1's FPC 6 and 7 and JCS REs 10 and 11. This configuration results in two different, fully operational JUNOS routing domains.

Consolidation Example and Configuration

The configuration in the previous section splits the T Series forwarding node into two different routing domains from the administrative and control plane perspective. While you could have configured most of this separation using logical routers, you can accomplish certain aspects of partitioning, including different JUNOS versions, and high availability and strict fault isolation, only by actually separating the hardware control plane resources using the JCS1200.

To take consolidation to the next step, let's analyze the example of a collapsed POP deployment in which P and PE MPLS services have been collapsed into four redundant PSDs using one JCS and two T Series nodes, as shown in Figure 5-7.

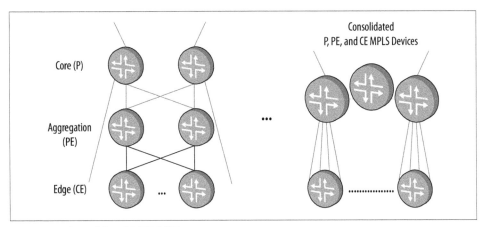

Figure 5-7. Consolidated P/PE POP

As you can see in Figure 5-7, connectivity to the core network is provided by MPLS-enabled uplinks. This POP uses two T640s and two M320s as the P and PE MPLS-enabled routers, respectively. The P and PE routers are interconnected with meshed interfaces for redundancy. With the JCS1200 control system we can eliminate both M320s from the picture. Additionally, we can eliminate the meshed redundant links in favor of internally provisioned tunnel interfaces between the PSDs. The consolidated POP now consists of two T640 RSDs, rsd1 and rsd2, and a single JCS1200 control system. Each RSD services the two PSDs that are used for different MPLS applications. rsd1-psd1 and rsd2-psd1 combinations are used as core facing P routers. rsd1-psd2 and rsd2-psd2 combinations are used as aggregation PE routers. For redundancy purposes, each PSD is managed with two redundant REs; therefore, with eight REs in use, the JCS1200 control system is able to fully serve two more fully redundant PSDs, thus providing scalable growth potential.

Now, let's look at the configuration of the consolidation deployment shown in Figure 5-7:

```
[edit]
lab@r1# show
chassis {
    system-domains {
        root-domain-id 1;
        protected-system-domains {
            psd1 {
                fpcs [0];
                control-system-id 1;
                control-slot-numbers [0];
            }
            psd2 {
                fpcs [1 2 3];
                control-system-id 2;
                control-slot-numbers [1 2 3];
            }
```

```
        }
    root-domain-id 2;
        protected-system-domains {
            psd1 {
                fpcs [0];
                control-system-id 1;
                control-slot-numbers [0];
                }
            psd2 {
                fpcs [1 2 3];
                control-system-id 2;
                control-slot-numbers [1 2 3];
            }
        }
    }
...
```

Two T640s are configured as rsd1 and rsd2, each providing P and PE services. psd1 in both JCSs is used as the P node and consists of FPC 0 connections. psd2 in both JCSs acts in the PE role and consists of FPCs 1, 2, and 3. To verify the configuration, issue the show chassis hardware command on each PSD:

```
lab@psd1> show chassis hardware
rsd-re0:
--------------------------------------------------------------------
Hardware inventory:
Item Version Part number Serial number Description
Chassis S19068 T640
Midplane REV 04 710-002726 AX5666 T640 Backplane
FPM GBUS REV 02 710-002901 HE3251 T640 FPM Board
FPM Display REV 02 710-002897 HE7860 FPM Display
CIP REV 05 710-002895 HC0474 T-series CIP
PEM 1 Rev 03 740-002595 MH15367 Power Entry Module
SCG 0 REV 04 710-003423 HF6042 T640 Sonet Clock Gen.
SCG 1 REV 11 710-003423 HW7765 T640 Sonet Clock Gen.
Routing Engine 0 REV 04 740-014082 1000660098 RE-A-2000
Routing Engine 1 REV 01 740-005022 210865700324 RE-3.0
CB 0 REV 06 710-007655 WE9377 Control Board (CB-T)
CB 1 REV 06 710-007655 WE9379 Control Board (CB-T)
FPC 4 REV 02 710-002385 HC0619 FPC Type 2
CPU REV 06 710-001726 HB1916 FPC CPU
MMB 1 REV 03 710-004047 HE3195 MMB-288mbit
ICBM REV 04 710-003384 HC0377 FPC ICBM
PPB 0 REV 02 710-003758 HC0585 PPB Type 2
PPB 1 REV 02 710-003758 HC0574 PPB Type 2
SPMB 0 REV 10 710-003229 WE9582 T-series Switch CPU
SPMB 1 REV 10 710-003229 WE9587 T-series Switch CPU
SIB 0 REV 05 750-005486 HV8445 SIB-I8-F16
SIB 1 REV 05 750-005486 HW2650 SIB-I8-F16
SIB 2 REV 05 750-005486 HW7041 SIB-I8-F16
SIB 3 REV 05 750-005486 HV4274 SIB-I8-F16
SIB 4 REV 05 750-005486 HV8464 SIB-I8-F16
Fan Tray 0 Front Top Fan Tray
Fan Tray 1 Front Bottom Fan Tray
Fan Tray 2 Rear Fan Tray
```

```
psd1-re0:
------------------------------------------------------------------------
Hardware inventory:
Item Version Part number Serial number Description
Chassis 740-023156 SNJCSJCSAC00 JCS1200 AC Chassis
Routing Engine 0 REV 01 740-023157 SNBLJCSAC004 RE-JCS1200-1x2330
```

As you can see, the hardware inventory is very similar to the output of the show chassis
hardware command on a regular T640. However, the output shows several new items.
All the chassis hardware of a single T640 is listed under rsd-re0. The new section
psd1-re0 lists the JCS1200 hardware and the REs associated with psd1. The following
shows the hardware components belonging to psd2:

```
lab@psd2> show chassis hardware
rsd-re0:
------------------------------------------------------------------------
Hardware inventory:
Item Version Part number Serial number Description
Chassis S19068 T640
Midplane REV 04 710-002726 AX5666 T640 Backplane
FPM GBUS REV 02 710-002901 HE3251 T640 FPM Board
FPM Display REV 02 710-002897 HE7860 FPM Display
CIP REV 05 710-002895 HC0474 T-series CIP
PEM 1 Rev 03 740-002595 MH15367 Power Entry Module
SCG 0 REV 04 710-003423 HF6042 T640 Sonet Clock Gen.
SCG 1 REV 11 710-003423 HW7765 T640 Sonet Clock Gen.
Routing Engine 0 REV 04 740-014082 1000660098 RE-A-2000
Routing Engine 1 REV 01 740-005022 210865700324 RE-3.0
CB 0 REV 06 710-007655 WE9377 Control Board (CB-T)
CB 1 REV 06 710-007655 WE9379 Control Board (CB-T)
FPC 5 REV 01 710-010233 HM4187 E-FPC Type 1
CPU REV 01 710-010169 HS9939 FPC CPU-Enhanced
MMB 1 REV 01 710-010171 HR0833 MMB-288mbit
SPMB 0 REV 10 710-003229 WE9582 T-series Switch CPU
SPMB 1 REV 10 710-003229 WE9587 T-series Switch CPU
SIB 0 REV 05 750-005486 HV8445 SIB-I8-F16
SIB 1 REV 05 750-005486 HW2650 SIB-I8-F16
SIB 2 REV 05 750-005486 HW7041 SIB-I8-F16
SIB 3 REV 05 750-005486 HV4274 SIB-I8-F16
SIB 4 REV 05 750-005486 HV8464 SIB-I8-F16
Fan Tray 0 Front Top Fan Tray
Fan Tray 1 Front Bottom Fan Tray
Fan Tray 2 Rear Fan Tray
psd2-re0:
------------------------------------------------------------------------
Hardware inventory:
Item Version Part number Serial number Description
Chassis 740-023156 SNJCSJCSAC00 JCS1200 AC Chassis
Routing Engine 0 REV 01 740-023157 SNBLJCSAC006 RE-JCS1200-1x2330
Routing Engine 1 REV 01 740-023157 SNBLJCSAC005 RE-JCS1200-1x2330
```

To enable the JCS to fully control all of its routing nodes and to remotely control the RSD hardware using the JCS, you must configure a set of special "blade bay data" commands. The blade bay configuration is then passed from the JCS to the REs used in the RSDs. The blade bay data configuration uses a special 60-byte test string in the following format:

```
Vn-JCSn-SDn-PSDn-REPn-REBn-PRDplatform-type
```

For our example, you execute the following blade bay configuration commands on the JCS management console of both JCSs.

To assign the REs in slots 1 (primary) and 2 (backup) to rsd1 and psd1:

```
system> baydata -b 01 -data "V01-JCS01-SD01-PSD01-REP01-REB02-PRDT640"
system> baydata -b 02 -data "V01-JCS01-SD01-PSD01-REP01-REB02-PRDT640"
```

To assign the REs in slots 3 (primary) and 4 (backup) to rsd1 and psd2:

```
system> baydata -b 03 -data "V01-JCS01-SD01-PSD02-REP03-REB04-PRDT640"
system> baydata -b 04 -data "V01-JCS01-SD01-PSD02-REP03-REB04-PRDT640"
```

Essentially, the blade bay configuration file and the allocation of REs to PSDs must match what is provided in the JUNOS CLI configuration. Because a blade bay is not a typical JUNOS-style configuration, we do not elaborate on its syntax and command availability. To further use and manipulate blade bay configuration options, refer to the JCS1200 documentation guide found at the Juniper Networks Technical Support website at *http://www.juniper.net*.

Taking Consolidation to the Next Level: Scalable Route Reflection

Many of you are probably already familiar with the specifics of BGP and how BGP redistributes learned routes to its peers. For those who have forgotten it, here's a quick review. BGP never readvertises routes learned from IBGP to other IBGP peers. This property mandates that your network have a full-mesh IBGP peering among all IBGP speakers. The scalability of the full mesh can be solved with two different, yet equally well-designed, methods: using route reflectors or confederations. Chapter 13 provides detailed explanations of these solutions.

While both solutions are viable, the market has turned toward route reflection as the more popular IBGP scaling solution. Most networks build IBGP peering based on redundant pairs or quadruples of route reflectors. Some larger-scale networks even use hierarchical route reflection designs with multiple planes of route reflectors.

Service providers, large-scale enterprises, and even smaller enterprises are in the process of or have already deployed MPLS-based solutions for their networks. The most widespread MPLS application is Layer 3 VPNs, also known as 2547 VPNs (named after the original IETF draft, draft-ietf-l3vpn-rfc2547bis), now standardized under RFC 4364. An important property of this application is that all customer VPN routes are stored on route reflectors.

A second widely implemented MPLS application is Virtual Private LAN Service (VPLS). Here, all Layer 2 MAC addresses are stored in the form of BGP routes on route reflectors. A third application, providing scalable solutions, is multicast-enabled Layer 3 VPNs, known as NGEN MVPN and defined in draft-ietf-l3vpn-2547bis-mcast-bgp-07. Most multicast content requests and advertisements known as PIM joins and PIM register messages have found their way into the BGP control plane, thus adding to the scalability requirement of route reflectors. You can see that in addition to regular IBGP peering, the widespread use of MPLS applications places extra strain on the scalability of route reflectors. While this is not a problem for networks with a small number of customer routes, Tier 1 and Tier 2 service providers might reach the limits of control plane scalability if they use regular routers as route reflectors.

The key fact to remember is that route reflection is an application of the control plane. Thus, traffic forwarding is not a requirement. Therefore, you can safely take one RE, or two for redundancy, from the pool of 12 REs in the JCS1200 to serve as a route reflector pair. Designing a route reflector in this way provides the most scalable solution for converged MPLS networks, without incurring additional infrastructure costs for the forwarding plane.

PART II

JUNOS HA Techniques

CHAPTER 6

JUNOS Pre-Upgrade Procedures

Because JUNOS software is provided as a package, software upgrades are relatively straightforward, low-risk events. However, major upgrades still require that you fully reset the updated routing engine (RE), and some planning is necessary to ensure that traffic continues to be transported across the network during the upgrade. In this chapter, we discuss device and network considerations and preparations that you should make before performing a software upgrade.

JUNOS Package Overview

Before looking at how or when to upgrade, we need to talk a bit about the naming conventions used to identify a JUNOS software package.

Software Package Naming Conventions

Most commercially available JUNOS software packages follow a naming convention based on the following model:

> *Package_name-M.NZNumber-Audience-Validation.tgz*

In this model:

Package_name
> Identifies the type of package and platform family to which the JUNOS software applies. The software has two major categories of packages: jbundle and jinstall. jbundle comprises just the JUNOS components, while jinstall contains the JUNOS components as well as a revised FreeBSD. The jinstall and jbundle packages are provided in platform-specific variations, as shown in Table 6-1.

M.N
> Represents the software major release number.

Z

Indicates the type of software release. In most cases, it is an *R*, to indicate that this is *released* software. While not appropriate for a high availability network, alpha and beta software is made available to some customers for testing purposes. Such software is tagged with an *A* (for alpha-level software), *B* (for beta-level software), or *I* (for internal, test, or experimental versions of software) in the *Z* position.

Number

Describes the incremental release of the major revision or the internal build number for non-R releases.

Audience

Identifies the software package as being suitable for a worldwide audience (marked as export) or as being suitable for a domestic audience. This distinction is made because the domestic version contains strong encryption algorithms, which are considered to be munitions by the U.S. government, and as such, their export is controlled.

Validation

Indicates whether the software has been "signed." An MD5 hash of the software image is available for packages that have been signed. This hash is used during the software load process to verify the integrity of the image. If the image has been tampered with, the hash of the image will no longer match the signature.

Table 6-1. JUNOS package_names and platforms

Name	Description and relevant platform
jbundle-	M and T Series
jinstall-	M and T Series
jinstall-ex-	EX Series
junos-jseries-	J Series
junos-jsr-	J Series with enhanced services

As an example, let's take a look at a currently available software package:

jbundle-9.1R3.5-domestic-signed.tgz

jbundle

Indicates that this is a JUNOS release appropriate for M and T Series routers.

9.1

The major release number.

R

Indicates that this is a general release rather than an alpha, beta, or experimental release.

3.5

The revision number (or minor release number).

-domestic
> Indicates that this release includes strong encryption components that are appropriate for use in the United States and Canada, but whose export must be controlled.

-signed
> Indicates that an MD5 hash of the operating system image is available and can be used to confirm the integrity of the image.

When to Upgrade JUNOS in a High Availability Environment

As we mentioned, upgrading JUNOS is an easy task that you can complete with a single simple command. So, "How do I upgrade?" is not the first question an administrator needs to ask. The important question is, "*When* should I upgrade?" Software upgrades should be performed for a reason, preferably for several. Valid reasons for a software upgrade include the following:

- The current release of code being used in production is approaching end of life (EOL) and will no longer be supported by the Juniper Technical Assistance Center (JTAC). JTAC service agreements usually require the devices under contract to run a supported version of JUNOS to qualify for support.

- The current release of code being used in production does not support a necessary feature. Networks tend to grow over time, and as the number of users increases, the demands placed on the network increase. Requirements evolve over time as well. High availability requirements are a perfect example. High concentrations of users or growth of business-critical services may make unified In-Service Software Upgrade (ISSU) a requirement. So, it might become necessary to upgrade devices in the network to a newer release capable of supporting ISSU functionality.

- The current release of code being used in production is found to have a bug or vulnerability. Compared to offerings from other vendors, JUNOS is an incredibly stable and resilient operating system. However, bugs and vulnerabilities are occasionally discovered. In a few cases, the bugs and vulnerabilities may be so severe or threatening to the availability of the network that a JUNOS upgrade is needed.

- All Juniper devices in a network are being moved to a common code release. JUNOS is common across all platforms. As new platforms are released, however, they are not always compatible with older revisions of JUNOS. Therefore, to maintain a single revision of JUNOS across all platforms in the network, it may be necessary to upgrade to a newer software revision.

The Right Target Release for a High Availability Environment

Once you have identified a definite need for an upgrade, the next step is to choose a software revision. In some cases, when a business requirement demands a specific new feature, you may have little choice. In other situations, such as EOL of the currently deployed production release, you have a choice of many options. Given a selection among a number of possible releases, the administrator of a high availability network should consider the following:

Review release documentation
> Each release of JUNOS has an accompanying "feature guide" and "release notes" publication. The feature guide describes the configuration of all new and notable features in the release. The release notes document describes any changes in default behavior as well as all known bugs and issues present in the release.

Talk to the experts
> The account and support staffs have a vested interest in helping customers maintain network availability. Consult a Juniper sales representative or JTAC engineer about release options well in advance of the upgrade date.

Remember that higher R numbers are usually better than lower R numbers
> While Juniper makes every effort to eliminate bugs from the operating system, statistically speaking an R1 version of the operating system probably has more issues than a later release. For high availability networks, we recommend R3 and later revisions of JUNOS because the release has had enough time in the field so that most major issues have been identified and resolved.

Extended end of life (EEOL)
> In 2007, Juniper began an EEOL program that features an extended life span revision of the JUNOS software version released in Q4 of every year. Whereas most revisions of JUNOS are supported for only 13 months, EEOL releases are supported by JTAC for 37 months.

High Availability Upgrade Strategy

It is important to choose an upgrade strategy that minimizes risk. Furthermore, you should document that strategy and thoroughly test it in a lab environment that includes the same devices currently in the production network. These devices should be arranged, as much as possible, to match the neighbor relationships currently in use in production.

Conduct a lab trial

Once you determine that a JUNOS release is a candidate for the production network, you should install the release in a lab that mimics the devices, protocols, and topology that is used in the production network, and then test it thoroughly. The testing should include all protocols and services currently in use in the production network, as well as any functions or protocols planned for future addition. Appendix A includes a sample lab test plan. Your actual plan should be based on protocols and platforms found in the production network.

Choose the device to upgrade

The choice of target device for an upgrade is based on several factors, including network design, device redundancy schemes, traffic patterns, need, and perhaps even politics. For a detailed explanation of redundancy scheme considerations when planning an upgrade, see Chapter 1.

Ensure router steady state

We cannot overemphasize the importance of making a backup copy of the known good working configuration before beginning a JUNOS upgrade. Of even greater importance is keeping that copy easily accessible during the software upgrade. Occasionally, problems arise during an upgrade that mandate a fallback to the pre-upgrade state of the network. You may need to quickly undo any configuration changes that were made to accommodate the upgrade. You can accomplish this easily by reloading the known good working configuration.

Save the working configuration. The save command does not require a lot of explanation, but it bears mentioning that this command is relative to the position from which it is executed. To make a *complete* backup copy of the configuration, you must run the save command from the top-tier hierarchy.

In this example, the existing working configuration is saved on both the local chassis and an administrative workstation using an FTP command. This save command ensures that the device configuration is readily available should anything go wrong during the upgrade process, and also makes returning to a steady state much easier if you need to back out of a software upgrade:

```
[edit]
lab@r5# save r5-backup-20-october-2008
Wrote 869 lines of configuration to 'r5-backup-20-october-2008'
```

System-archive a copy of the working configuration. The system archive command has two options that have the chassis create an archive copy of the working configuration. The archive-on-commit option creates a copy of the configuration each time the commit command is executed. The interval option creates a copy of the configuration at specific user-configurable intervals, typically every 24 hours. Both handle the configuration (send it somewhere) based on additional configuration settings at the system level of the hierarchy. This configuration example shows that a copy of the configuration is sent using FTP to the identified hosts each time a configuration change is made:

```
lab@r5> show configuration system archival
configuration {
    transfer-on-commit;
    archive-sites {
        "ftp://james:password@199.98.97.217:21";
        "ftp://backup:password@202.45.45.12:21";
    }
}
```

While a backup configuration from a regularly scheduled run of a configuration archive may be available, it is always best to create an additional backup immediately before a router upgrade. This backup captures any configuration changes that were made since the last archive run.

Establish a quarantine period

The idea of a quarantine period is common among network administrators, but the implementation details vary. Some administrators view the predeployment lab testing as part of the quarantine period. The majority of network administrators, however, do not, and selectively upgrade chassis to minimize risk to the production network.

Pre-Upgrade Verifications

Before performing a software upgrade, a competent network administrator checks the state of the chassis, including hardware integrity, peering relationships with adjacent devices, and stability of the routing tables. You do this beforehand, because there are often problems confirming stability after a software upgrade. If you have not performed a pre-upgrade check, it is impossible to know whether any problems are related to the software upgrade or whether they existed prior to the software upgrade. Commands to use and results to expect will vary by platform and by network topology.

 Pre-upgrade and post-upgrade verifications should be nearly identical, as it is necessary to know what normal behavior is in order to spot the abnormal behavior. Appendix B provides a checklist that you can use for both pre-upgrade and post-upgrade verification.

Filesystems and Logs

Network problems tend to be intermittent. As a result, you may not be able to directly observe device or network problems when performing a pre-upgrade verification. This situation is where logfiles come in very handy. A few searches through selected files can show recent past problems that could potentially return. Again, failure to identify a preexisting problem could result in the problem being mistakenly attributed to the software upgrade, which wastes valuable troubleshooting time.

Logfile information is commonly stored in the *messages* file. Additional logfiles to look at depend on syslog settings for the chassis. Here is selected content from the *messages* file on **r1**. Notice that there appears to be a link flapping issue. This type of event is one that could be mistakenly attributed to a software upgrade if it is not noted and hopefully resolved beforehand:

```
[edit]
lab@r1# run show log messages | match down
```

```
Nov 15 19:01:23  r1:[2649]: EVENT <Bandwidth UpDown>
index 128 <Broadcast Multicast> address #0 0.2.b3.10.af.1e
Nov 15 19:01:23  r1:[2648]: EVENT <UpDown> ge-0/1/0.0
index 85 <Broadcast Multicast> address #0 0.2.b3.10.af.1e
Nov 15 19:01:23  r1:[2648]: EVENT UpDown ge-0/1/0.0
index 85 7.6.5.1/24 -> 7.6.5.255 <Broadcast Multicast Localup>
Nov 15 19:01:23  r1:[2648]: EVENT UpDown ge-0/1/0.0
index 85 <Broadcast Multicast>
Nov 15 19:01:23  r1:[2648]: EVENT UpDown ge-0/1/0.0
index 85 <Broadcast Multicast>
Nov 15 19:01:23  r1:[2648]: EVENT <Bandwidth UpDown>
index 128 <Broadcast Multicast> address #0 0.2.b3.10.af.1e
Nov 15 19:01:23  r1:[2648]: EVENT <UpDown> ge-0/0/1.0
index 86 <Broadcast Multicast> address #0 0.2.b3.24.25.f4
Nov 15 19:01:23  r1:[2648]: EVENT UpDown ge-0/0/1.0
index 86 172.17.0.5/30 -> 172.17.0.7 <Broadcast Multicast Localup>
```

After reviewing syslog settings, look in the */var/log* directory for content of interest:

```
[edit system syslog]
lab@r5# show
file cli {
    interactive-commands any;
}
file messages {
    any info;
}
 file proc {
    daemon error;
    kernel error;
    pfe error;
}


lab@r5-main# run file list /var/log

/var/log:
access.aprobed
access.dcd
access.sampled
amsterdam/
aprobed
apsd
auditd
bfdd
bfdd.0.gz
bfdd.1.gz
chassisd
cli
cli.0.gz
cli.1.gz
cli.2.gz
cli.3.gz
cli.4.gz

<output truncated>
```

Checklist

Creating a procedural checklist is an important part of preparing to upgrade software in a high availability network. The checklist should include methods of confirming the successful upgrade and stability of the network, along with the commands required to perform the upgrade and those required to back out of the upgrade if necessary.

Moving Services Away from a Router

High availability requirements are so common these days that pretty much all network hardware manufacturers have developed ways to support software upgrades without interrupting service. One method of doing this is to move traffic away from a router prior to a software upgrade. This way, any device downtime associated with the software upgrade is invisible to the end user. In this section, we describe configuration tweaks appropriate for redirecting traffic in a high availability network.

Interface Configuration

In some situations, simply disabling an interface is the most efficient and desirable way to force traffic onto an alternative path through the network. In Figure 6-1 (shown later), both r3 and r4 support connections to r5. Disabling ge-0/0/0 on r4 by using set disable would effectively force all traffic destined for r5 (and r6) to transit r3:

```
[edit interfaces ge-0/0/0]
lab@r4# set disable

[edit interfaces ge-0/0/0]
lab@r4# commit
commit complete

[edit interfaces ge-0/0/0]
lab@r4# show
description "r4 ge-0/0/0 to r5 ge-0/0/0";
disable;
unit 0 {
    family inet {
        address 10.0.1.14/30;
    }
    family mpls;
}

[edit interfaces ge-0/0/0]
lab@r4# run show interfaces terse ge-0/0/0
Interface           Admin Link Proto Local            Remote
ge-0/0/0            down  up
ge-0/0/0.0                up   down inet  10.0.1.14/30
                                    mpls
```

If you choose to use the **set disable** command remember to change the interface description accordingly:

```
[edit interfaces ge-0/0/0]
lab@r4# show
description "r4 ge-0/0/0 to r5 ge-0/0/0 DISABLED for JUNOS 9.4 UPGRADE";
disable;
unit 0 {
    family inet {
        address 10.0.1.14/30;
    }
    family mpls;
}
```

It is equally important to remember to resume traffic flow on the interface by deleting the **disable** tag once the software upgrade is completed:

```
[edit interfaces ge-0/0/0]
lab@r4# delete disable

[edit interfaces ge-0/0/0]
lab@r4# set description "r4 ge-0/0/0 to r5 ge-0/0/0"

[edit interfaces ge-0/0/0]
lab@r4# commit
commit complete

[edit interfaces ge-0/0/0]
lab@r4# run show interfaces terse ge-0/0/0
Interface               Admin Link Proto Local             Remote
ge-0/0/0                up    up
ge-0/0/0.0              up    up   inet  10.0.1.14/30
                                   mpls
```

Switching Ownership of a VRRP Virtual IP

Virtual Router Redundancy Protocol (VRRP), discussed in detail in Chapter 12, allows multiple routers to serve as redundant default gateways off a local area network (LAN) segment. These redundant gateways support high availability by preventing the default gateway router from being a single point of failure in the network. The redundant design also allows software upgrades on the routers without loss of connectivity to the protected LAN. In Figure 6-1, r1 and r2 are serving as redundant gateways for the Bastion Server LAN.

The relevant configuration elements from r1 and r2 show that both routers are participating in a VRRP group that provides redundancy for the Bastion Server LAN.

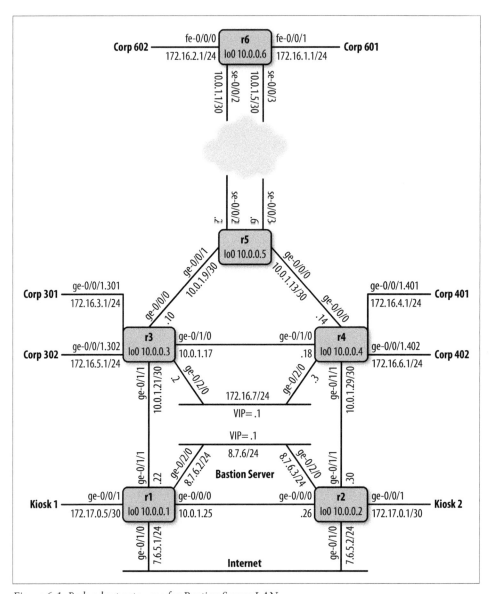

Figure 6-1. Redundant gateways for Bastion Server LAN

On r1 we see:

```
[edit interfaces]
lab@r1# show ge-0/2/0
 unit 0 {
     description "Bastion Server LAN";
     family inet {
         address 8.7.6.2/24 {
```

```
            vrrp-group 1 {
                virtual-address 8.7.6.1;
                priority 101;
                preempt;
                accept-data;
                track {
                    interface ge-0/1/0 priority-cost 5;
                    interface ge-0/1/1 priority-cost 5;
                }
            }
        }
    }
}
```

On r2 we see:

```
[edit interfaces]
lab@r2# show ge-0/2/0
 unit 0 {
     description "Bastion Server LAN";
     family inet {
         address 8.7.6.3/24 {
             vrrp-group 1 {
                 virtual-address 8.7.6.1;
                 preempt;
                 accept-data;
                 track {
                     interface ge-0/1/0 priority-cost 5;
                     interface ge-0/1/1 priority-cost 5;
                 }
             }
         }
     }
}
```

The run show route command confirms that r1 is the current owner of the virtual IP (VIP), 8.7.6.1. Router r1 owns the VIP because its priority is set at 101, which is higher than the default priority of 100:

```
[edit]
lab@r1# run show route 8.7.6/24

inet.0: 32 destinations, 32 routes (32 active, 0 holddown, 0 hidden)
+ = Active Route, - = Last Active, * = Both

8.7.6.0/24          *[Direct/0] 00:27:44
                     > via ge-0/2/0
8.7.6.1/32          *[Local/0] 00:27:37
                        Local via ge-0/2/0
8.7.6.2/32          *[Local/0] 00:27:44
                        Local via ge-0/2/0

[edit]
lab@r2# run show route 8.7.6/24

inet.0: 31 destinations, 31 routes (31 active, 0 holddown, 0 hidden)
```

```
+ = Active Route, - = Last Active, * = Both

8.7.6.0/24          *[Direct/0] 00:27:49
                     > via ge-0/2/0
8.7.6.3/32          *[Local/0] 00:27:49
                        Local via ge-0/2/0
```

Assuming that all host systems on the LAN are configured correctly, having r1 own the VIP allows a software upgrade to occur on r2 with no impact to traffic leaving the protected Bastion Server LAN. However, notice that although the r1 configuration has a priority of 101, it is penalized 5 points for the loss of a link on ge-0/1/0 or ge-0/1/1. With the current priority setting on r2, failure of a link on r1 could trigger a VIP switch to r2. So, for added security, make a slight change to the VRRP configuration on r2:

```
[edit interfaces ge-0/2/0 unit 0]
lab@r5-main# set unit 0 family inet address 8.7.6.3/24 vrrp-group 1 priority 50

[edit interfaces ge-0/2/0 unit 0]
lab@r2# show
description "Bastion Server LAN";
family inet {
    address 8.7.6.3/24 {
        vrrp-group 1 {
            virtual-address 8.7.6.1;
            preempt;
            priority 50;
            accept-data;
            track {
                interface ge-0/1/0 priority-cost 5;
                interface ge-0/1/1 priority-cost 5;
            }
        }
    }
}
```

This change permits r1 to retain the VIP in the event that the ge-0/1/0 or ge-0/1/1 interface fails.

IGP Traffic Control Tweaks

The previous section showed how to configure VRRP to "encourage" traffic leaving the Bastion Server LAN to use r1 as the exit point. In this section, we modify Open Shortest Path First (OSPF) and Intermediate System to Intermediate System (IS-IS) configuration elements to make traffic destined for the LAN, as well as other traffic transiting other interfaces on r2, prefer to use r1 as a transit point.

OSPF and the overload bit

An OSPF tweak known as the *overload bit* allows us to effectively make r2 appear unattractive to transit traffic. A textbook explanation of what is accomplished by setting the overload bit can be found using the help topic option in the command-line interface (CLI):

```
[edit protocols ospf]
lab@r2# help topic ospf overload
Configuring the Router to Appear Overloaded

  If the time elapsed after the OSPF instance is enabled is less than the
  specified timeout, overload mode is set.

  You can configure the local router so that it appears to be overloaded.
  You might do this when you want the router to participate in OSPF routing,
  but do not want it to be used for transit traffic. (Traffic to directly
  attached interfaces continues to transit the router.)

  You configure or disable overload mode in OSPF with or without a timeout.
  Without a timeout, overload mode is set until it is explicitly deleted
  from the configuration. With a timeout, overload mode is set if the time
  elapsed since the OSPF instance started is less than the specified
  timeout.

  A timer is started for the difference between the timeout and the time
  elapsed since the instance started. When the timer expires, overload mode
  is cleared. In overload mode, the router LSA is originated with all the
  transit router links (except stub) set to a metric of 0xFFFF. The stub
  router links are advertised with the actual cost of the interfaces
  corresponding to the stub. This causes the transit traffic to avoid the
  overloaded router and take paths around the router. However, the
  overloaded router's own links are still accessible.

  To mark the router as overloaded, include the overload statement:
    [edit protocols (ospf | ospf3)]
    overload;
```

You can observe the result of this configuration change on r2 directly by comparing the output of a show route command before the overload bit is set to the content of the routing table after the bit is set. Notice the route metrics before the bit is set:

```
[edit protocols ospf]
lab@r2# run show route protocol ospf

inet.0: 31 destinations, 31 routes (31 active, 0 holddown, 0 hidden)
+ = Active Route, - = Last Active, * = Both

10.0.0.1/32        *[OSPF/10] 00:14:36, metric 1
                    > to 10.0.1.25 via ge-0/0/0
10.0.0.3/32        *[OSPF/10] 00:14:25, metric 2
                    > to 10.0.1.29 via ge-0/1/1
                      to 10.0.1.25 via ge-0/0/0
10.0.0.4/32        *[OSPF/10] 00:14:36, metric 1
                    > to 10.0.1.29 via ge-0/1/1
10.0.0.5/32        *[OSPF/10] 00:14:30, metric 2
                    > to 10.0.1.29 via ge-0/1/1
10.0.0.6/32        *[OSPF/10] 00:14:30, metric 3
                    > to 10.0.1.29 via ge-0/1/1
```

```
10.0.1.0/30          *[OSPF/10] 00:14:30, metric 3
                      > to 10.0.1.29 via ge-0/1/1
10.0.1.4/30          *[OSPF/10] 00:14:30, metric 3
                      > to 10.0.1.29 via ge-0/1/1
10.0.1.8/30          *[OSPF/10] 00:14:20, metric 3
                      > to 10.0.1.29 via ge-0/1/1
                        to 10.0.1.25 via ge-0/0/0

(output truncated)
```

Now let's set the overload bit and take a look at the impact to the local routing table. Notice the dramatic change in OSPF metrics in the r2 local database:

```
[edit protocols ospf]
lab@r2# set overload

[edit protocols ospf]
lab@r2# commit
commit complete

[edit protocols ospf]
lab@r2# run show route protocol ospf

inet.0: 31 destinations, 31 routes (31 active, 0 holddown, 0 hidden)
+ = Active Route, - = Last Active, * = Both

10.0.0.1/32          *[OSPF/10] 00:00:06, metric 65535
                      > to 10.0.1.25 via ge-0/0/0
10.0.0.3/32          *[OSPF/10] 00:00:06, metric 65536
                      > to 10.0.1.29 via ge-0/1/1
                        to 10.0.1.25 via ge-0/0/0
10.0.0.4/32          *[OSPF/10] 00:00:06, metric 65535
                      > to 10.0.1.29 via ge-0/1/1
10.0.0.5/32          *[OSPF/10] 00:00:06, metric 65536
                      > to 10.0.1.29 via ge-0/1/1
10.0.0.6/32          *[OSPF/10] 00:00:06, metric 65537
                      > to 10.0.1.29 via ge-0/1/1
10.0.1.0/30          *[OSPF/10] 00:00:06, metric 65537
                      > to 10.0.1.29 via ge-0/1/1
10.0.1.4/30          *[OSPF/10] 00:00:06, metric 65537
                      > to 10.0.1.29 via ge-0/1/1
10.0.1.8/30          *[OSPF/10] 00:00:06, metric 65537
                      > to 10.0.1.29 via ge-0/1/1
                        to 10.0.1.25 via ge-0/0/0

(output truncated)
```

You see the real impact of this change in the routing tables of the other routers in the network—in this case, r1, r3, and r4:

```
[edit]
lab@r1# run show ospf database router detail advertising-router  10.0.0.2

    OSPF link state database, area 0.0.0.0
 Type       ID             Adv Rtr       Seq        Age  Opt  Cksum  Len
 Router   10.0.0.2       10.0.0.2     0x80000009   276  0x2  0x3226  96
   bits 0x0, link count 6
```

```
  id 10.0.1.29, data 10.0.1.30, Type Transit (2)
  TOS count 0, TOS 0 metric 65535
  id 10.0.1.26, data 10.0.1.30, Type Transit (2)
  TOS count 0, TOS 0 metric 65535
  id 8.7.6.0, data 255.255.255.0, Type Stub (3)
  TOS count 0, TOS 0 metric 1
  id 172.17.0.0, data 255.255.255.252, Type Stub (3)
  TOS count 0, TOS 0 metric 1
  id 7.6.5.0, data 255.255.255.0, Type Stub (3)
  TOS count 0, TOS 0 metric 1
  id 10.0.0.2, data 255.255.255.255, Type Stub (3)
  TOS count 0, TOS 0 metric 0

[edit]
lab@r3# run show ospf database router detail advertising-router  10.0.0.2

    OSPF link state database, area 0.0.0.0
 Type       ID            Adv Rtr      Seq      Age Opt Cksum  Len
Router   10.0.0.2      10.0.0.2     0x80000009  288 0x2 0x3226 96
  bits 0x0, link count 6
  id 10.0.1.29, data 10.0.1.30, Type Transit (2)
  TOS count 0, TOS 0 metric 65535
  id 10.0.1.26, data 10.0.1.26, Type Transit (2)
  TOS count 0, TOS 0 metric 65535
  id 8.7.6.0, data 255.255.255.0, Type Stub (3)
  TOS count 0, TOS 0 metric 1
  id 172.17.0.0, data 255.255.255.252, Type Stub (3)
  TOS count 0, TOS 0 metric 1
  id 7.6.5.0, data 255.255.255.0, Type Stub (3)
  TOS count 0, TOS 0 metric 1
  id 10.0.0.2, data 255.255.255.255, Type Stub (3)
  TOS count 0, TOS 0 metric 0

[edit]
lab@r4# run show ospf database router detail advertising-router  10.0.0.2

    OSPF link state database, area 0.0.0.0
 Type       ID            Adv Rtr      Seq      Age Opt Cksum  Len
Router   10.0.0.2      10.0.0.2     0x80000009  292 0x2 0x3226 96
  bits 0x0, link count 6
  id 10.0.1.29, data 10.0.1.30, Type Transit (2)
  TOS count 0, TOS 0 metric 65535
  id 10.0.1.26, data 10.0.1.26, Type Transit (2)
  TOS count 0, TOS 0 metric 65535
  id 8.7.6.0, data 255.255.255.0, Type Stub (3)
  TOS count 0, TOS 0 metric 1
  id 172.17.0.0, data 255.255.255.252, Type Stub (3)
  TOS count 0, TOS 0 metric 1
  id 7.6.5.0, data 255.255.255.0, Type Stub (3)
  TOS count 0, TOS 0 metric 1
  id 10.0.0.2, data 255.255.255.255, Type Stub (3)
  TOS count 0, TOS 0 metric 0
```

Notice that all traffic will avoid r2 because the metrics have been set to the protocol maximum. This configuration effectively urges traffic entering the Bastion Server LAN, as well as all other traffic that would normally transit r2, to pass instead through r1. By encouraging traffic to avoid the local router, r2 minimizes the impact of the software upgrade on the availability of the network.

 For added assurance, always run the `monitor interface traffic` command to confirm that the overload bit setting has had the desired effect and that no traffic is transiting local router interfaces. The `monitor interface traffic` command paints a near-real-time picture of interface input and output statistics that is refreshed at two-second intervals. Don't assume success when you can confirm it!

Moving the designated router

For multiaccess segments with a significant number of gateway routers running OSPF, a designated router (DR) and backup designated router (BDR) are often configured to serve as the "spokesmen" for the segment. To support high availability, the DR and BDR responsibility should be shifted among routers in the group so that all routers can be upgraded without taking the DR offline. Moving the DR among routers may result in less than optimal placement of the DR, but the condition is temporary and is outweighed by the benefits.

DR status is controlled to some extent by the priority setting at the protocol OSPF level of hierarchy. To transfer DR status to the BDR, simply adjust the priority numbers and trigger the transfer. In Figure 6-2, r3 and r4 share ownership for subnet 10.0.1.16/30.

Router r4 is currently the DR for the subnet, and r3 is serving as the BDR, as confirmed by the `show ospf interface` command on r3:

```
[edit protocols ospf area 0.0.0.0]
lab@r3# run show ospf interface
Interface     State    Area       DR ID       BDR ID     Nbrs
ge-0/1/0.0    BDR      0.0.0.0    10.0.0.4    10.0.0.3    1
ge-0/2/0.0    DR       0.0.0.0    10.0.0.3    0.0.0.0     0
ge-0/0/0.0    BDR      0.0.0.0    10.0.0.5    10.0.0.3    1
ge-0/1/1.0    DR       0.0.0.0    10.0.0.3    10.0.0.1    1
ge-0/0/1.301  DR       0.0.0.0    10.0.0.3    0.0.0.0     0
ge-0/0/1.302  DR       0.0.0.0    10.0.0.3    0.0.0.0     0
lo0.0         DRother  0.0.0.0    0.0.0.0     0.0.0.0     0
```

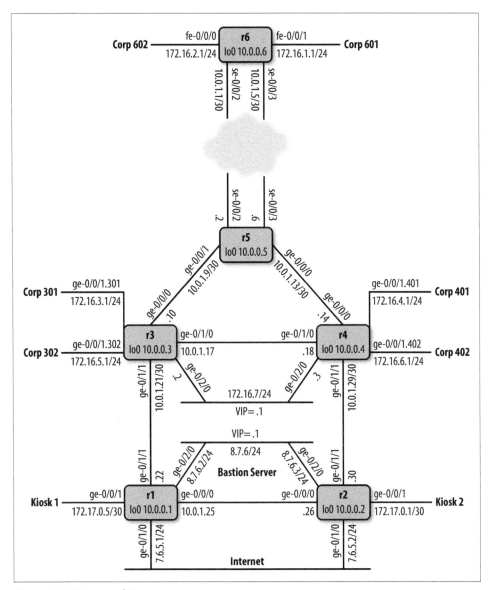

Figure 6-2. DR ownership

Priority settings in the protocol OSPF configuration on both **r3** and **r4** help explain why **r4** is the current DR for the subnet. Router **r4**'s OSPF configuration shows a priority of 255 for the **r4** interface onto the 10.0.1.16/30 subnet. Router **r3**'s priority setting for that interface is only 100. The higher priority number currently holds the DR state:

```
[edit protocols ospf area 0.0.0.0]
lab@r3# show
interface ge-0/1/0.0 {
    priority 255;
}
interface ge-0/2/0.0 {
    passive;
}
interface ge-0/1/1.0;
interface ge-0/0/1.301 {
    passive;
}
interface ge-0/0/1.302 {
    passive;
}
interface lo0.0 {
    passive;
}
interface ge-0/0/0.0;

[edit protocols ospf area 0.0.0.0]
lab@r4# show
interface ge-0/1/0.0 {
    priority 100;
interface ge-0/2/0.0 {
    passive;
}
interface ge-0/1/1.0;
interface ge-0/0/1.401 {
    passive;
}
interface ge-0/0/1.402 {
    passive;
}
interface lo0.0 {s
    passive;
}
interface ge-0/0/0.0;
```

Transfer of ownership can be accomplished by changing the priority setting and forcing a reset of the neighbor state between the two routers involved. First, to make r3 the DR for the selected subnet, give r3 a higher priority value for its interface onto the subnet:

```
[edit protocols ospf area 0.0.0.0]
lab@r3# set interface ge-0/1/0 priority 255

[edit protocols ospf area 0.0.0.0]
lab@r3# show
interface ge-0/1/0.0 {
    priority 255;
}
interface ge-0/2/0.0 {
    passive;
}
interface ge-0/1/1.0;
```

```
interface ge-0/0/1.301 {
    passive;
}
interface ge-0/0/1.302 {
    passive;
}
interface lo0.0 {
    passive;
}
interface ge-0/0/0.0;

[edit protocols ospf area 0.0.0.0]
lab@r3# commit
commit complete
```

An OSPF priority change is nondeterministic; therefore, a neighbor reset is necessary after the priority change to elect a new DR. Confirm this by first looking at the output of the show ospf interface command:

```
[edit protocols ospf area 0.0.0.0]
lab@r3# run show ospf interface
Interface       State   Area      DR ID       BDR ID    Nbrs
ge-0/1/0.0      BDR     0.0.0.0   10.0.0.4    10.0.0.3   1
ge-0/2/0.0      DR      0.0.0.0   10.0.0.3    0.0.0.0    0
ge-0/0/0.0      BDR     0.0.0.0   10.0.0.5    10.0.0.3   1
ge-0/1/1.0      DR      0.0.0.0   10.0.0.3    10.0.0.1   1
ge-0/0/1.301    DR      0.0.0.0   10.0.0.3    0.0.0.0    0
ge-0/0/1.302    DR      0.0.0.0   10.0.0.3    0.0.0.0    0
lo0.0           DRother 0.0.0.0   0.0.0.0     0.0.0.0    0
```

Notice that r4 is still identified by r3 as the DR on interface ge-0/1/0.0. For the shift to take place, manually reset the neighbor relationship on that interface. After doing so, take a look at the command output again:

```
[edit protocols ospf area 0.0.0.0]
lab@r3# run show ospf neighbor
  Address       Interface     State   ID            Pri  Dead
10.0.1.18       ge-0/1/0.0    Full    10.0.0.4      128  31
10.0.1.9        ge-0/0/0.0    Full    10.0.0.5      128  36
10.0.1.22       ge-0/1/1.0    Full    10.0.0.1      128  33

[edit protocols ospf area 0.0.0.0]
lab@r3# run clear ospf neighbor 10.0.1.18

[edit protocols ospf area 0.0.0.0]
lab@r3# run show ospf interface
Interface       State   Area      DR ID       BDR ID    Nbrs
ge-0/1/0.0      DR      0.0.0.0   10.0.0.3    10.0.0.4   1
ge-0/2/0.0      DR      0.0.0.0   10.0.0.3    0.0.0.0    0
ge-0/0/0.0      BDR     0.0.0.0   10.0.0.5    10.0.0.3   1
ge-0/1/1.0      DR      0.0.0.0   10.0.0.3    10.0.0.1   1
ge-0/0/1.301    DR      0.0.0.0   10.0.0.3    0.0.0.0    0
ge-0/0/1.302    DR      0.0.0.0   10.0.0.3    0.0.0.0    0
lo0.0           DRother 0.0.0.0   0.0.0.0     0.0.0.0    0
```

The purpose of this exercise is to show how DR state can be shifted as needed so that all routers in the network can be upgraded without having an impact on the DR's accessibility. These configuration elements are specific to networks running OSPF.

The overload bit and IS-IS

IS-IS supports overload bit and DR (called Designated Intermediate System, or DIS, in IS-IS) functionality that is comparable to OSPF in many ways. In IS-IS, when the overload bit is set, interface metrics are pushed to the highest possible value to discourage transit traffic, just as is done with OSPF. As in the previous example, this use of the overload bit allows traffic to continue to flow through the network as the JUNOS software on r2 is upgraded. First, let's take a look at IS-IS route metrics for r2:

```
[edit protocols isis]
lab@r2# run show route protocol isis

inet.0: 30 destinations, 30 routes (30 active, 0 holddown, 0 hidden)
+ = Active Route, - = Last Active, * = Both

10.0.0.1/32        *[IS-IS/18] 00:00:05, metric 10
                    > to 10.0.1.25 via ge-0/0/0.0
10.0.0.3/32        *[IS-IS/18] 00:00:05, metric 20
                    > to 10.0.1.29 via ge-0/1/1.0
                      to 10.0.1.25 via ge-0/0/0.0
10.0.0.4/32        *[IS-IS/18] 00:00:05, metric 10
                    > to 10.0.1.29 via ge-0/1/1.0
10.0.0.5/32        *[IS-IS/18] 00:00:05, metric 20
                    > to 10.0.1.29 via ge-0/1/1.0
10.0.0.6/32        *[IS-IS/18] 00:00:05, metric 30
                    > to 10.0.1.29 via ge-0/1/1.0
10.0.1.0/30        *[IS-IS/18] 00:00:05, metric 30
                    > to 10.0.1.29 via ge-0/1/1.0
10.0.1.4/30        *[IS-IS/18] 00:00:05, metric 30
                    > to 10.0.1.29 via ge-0/1/1.0
10.0.1.8/30        *[IS-IS/18] 00:00:05, metric 30
                      to 10.0.1.29 via ge-0/1/1.0
                    > to 10.0.1.25 via ge-0/0/0.0
(output truncated)
```

Now set the overload bit, commit, and observe the changes in the routing table:

```
[edit protocols isis]
lab@r2# set overload advertise-high-metrics

[edit protocols isis]
lab@r2# commit
commit complete

[edit protocols isis]
lab@r2# run show route protocol isis

inet.0: 30 destinations, 30 routes (30 active, 0 holddown, 0 hidden)
+ = Active Route, - = Last Active, * = Both
```

```
10.0.0.1/32        *[IS-IS/18] 00:00:03, metric 63
                    > to 10.0.1.25 via ge-0/0/0.0
10.0.0.3/32        *[IS-IS/18] 00:00:03, metric 73
                    > to 10.0.1.29 via ge-0/1/1.0
                      to 10.0.1.25 via ge-0/0/0.0
10.0.0.4/32        *[IS-IS/18] 00:00:03, metric 63
                    > to 10.0.1.29 via ge-0/1/1.0
10.0.0.5/32        *[IS-IS/18] 00:00:03, metric 73
                    > to 10.0.1.29 via ge-0/1/1.0
10.0.0.6/32        *[IS-IS/18] 00:00:03, metric 83
                    > to 10.0.1.29 via ge-0/1/1.0
10.0.1.0/30        *[IS-IS/18] 00:00:03, metric 83
                    > to 10.0.1.29 via ge-0/1/1.0
10.0.1.4/30        *[IS-IS/18] 00:00:03, metric 83
                    > to 10.0.1.29 via ge-0/1/1.0
10.0.1.8/30        *[IS-IS/18] 00:00:03, metric 83
                    > to 10.0.1.29 via ge-0/1/1.0
                      to 10.0.1.25 via ge-0/0/0.0
(output truncated)
```

Notice the dramatic increase in metrics associated with reaching destinations through
r2. Clearly, r1 will now be used for transit traffic.

Moving the DIS

As with OSPF, the IS-IS spokesman for a multiaccess segment can be changed on a per-
interface basis by adjusting the value assigned to the interface. This process allows the
DIS to be moved as needed. In this example, we move it to allow all routers sharing a
multiaccess segment to receive a JUNOS upgrade without becoming the DIS.

> The election of a DIS is a deterministic event. As soon as an IS-IS-enabled
> router with a higher priority comes online on a multiaccess segment, it
> becomes the DIS. No adjacency reset is needed.

In the following command output, we see that r3 is currently serving as the DIS for the
10.0.1.16/30 LAN, accessible on both r3 and r4 through the ge-0/1/0.0 interfaces:

```
[edit protocols isis]
lab@r3# run show isis interface
IS-IS interface database:
Interface        L CirID Level 1 DR   Level 2 DR         L1/L2 Metric
ge-0/1/0.0       2  0x2  Disabled     r3.02                 10/10
ge-0/2/0.0       0  0x1  Disabled     Passive               10/10
ge-0/0/0.0       2  0x3  Disabled     r5.03                 10/10
ge-0/1/1.0       2  0x4  Disabled     0010.0000.0001.02     10/10
ge-0/0/1.301     0  0x1  Disabled     Passive               10/10
ge-0/0/1.302     0  0x1  Disabled     Passive               10/10
lo0.0            0  0x1  Disabled     Passive                0/0

[edit protocols isis]
lab@r4# run show isis interface
```

```
IS-IS interface database:
Interface         L CirID Level 1 DR    Level 2 DR         L1/L2 Metric
ge-0/1/1.0        2  0x2 Disabled       r2.02                10/10
ge-0/1/0.0        2  0x3 Disabled       0010.0000.0003.02    10/10
ge-0/2/0.0        0  0x1 Disabled       Passive              10/10
ge-0/0/0.0        2  0x4 Disabled       0010.0000.0005.02    10/10
ge-0/0/1.401      0  0x1 Disabled       Passive              10/10
ge-0/0/1.402      0  0x1 Disabled       Passive              10/10
lo0.0             0  0x1 Disabled       Passive               0/0
```

The protocol IS-IS configuration on both r3 and r4 explains why r3 holds the DIS responsibility. Notice that the priority for r3 on the ge-0/1/0 interface has been set to 100 but is currently at 50 for r4:

```
[edit protocols isis]
lab@r3# show
interface all {
    level 1 disable;
}
interface ge-0/1/0.0 {
    level 1 disable;
    level 2 priority 100;
}
interface ge-0/2/0.0 {
    level 1 disable;
    level 2 passive;
}
interface ge-0/0/1.301 {
    level 1 disable;
    level 2 passive;
}
interface ge-0/0/1.302 {
    level 1 disable;
    level 2 passive;
}


[edit protocols isis]
lab@r4# show
interface all {
    level 1 disable;
}
interface ge-0/1/0.0 {
    level 1 disable;
    level 2 priority 50;
}
interface ge-0/2/0.0 {
    level 1 disable;
    level 2 passive;
}
interface ge-0/0/1.401 {
    level 1 disable;
    level 2 passive;
}
interface ge-0/0/1.402 {
```

```
        level 2 passive;
        level 1 disable;
```

Prior to upgrading JUNOS on r3, we want to transfer DIS responsibility to r4. Do this
by adjusting priority on either r3 or r4 (either lowering r3's priority or increasing r4's).
In this example, we chose to set r4's priority for the interface to the maximum allowable
value of 127:

```
[edit protocols isis]
lab@r4# set interface ge-0/1/0.0 level 2 priority 127
```

Committing the change and then running a few show commands confirms that the
priority value adjustment on r4 had the desired result:

```
[edit protocols isis]
lab@r4# commit
commit complete

[edit protocols isis]
lab@r3# run show isis interface
IS-IS interface database:
Interface       L CirID Level 1 DR  Level 2 DR          L1/L2 Metric
ge-0/1/0.0      2   0x2 Disabled    0010.0000.0004.03      10/10
ge-0/2/0.0      0   0x1 Disabled    Passive                10/10
ge-0/0/0.0      2   0x3 Disabled    r5.03                  10/10
ge-0/1/1.0      2   0x4 Disabled    0010.0000.0001.02      10/10
ge-0/0/1.301    0   0x1 Disabled    Passive                10/10
ge-0/0/1.302    0   0x1 Disabled    Passive                10/10
lo0.0           0   0x1 Disabled    Passive                 0/0

[edit protocols isis]
lab@r4# run show isis interface
IS-IS interface database:
Interface       L CirID Level 1 DR  Level 2 DR          L1/L2 Metric
ge-0/1/1.0      2   0x2 Disabled    r2.02                  10/10
ge-0/1/0.0      2   0x3 Disabled    r4.03                  10/10
ge-0/2/0.0      0   0x1 Disabled    Passive                10/10
ge-0/0/0.0      2   0x4 Disabled    0010.0000.0005.02      10/10
ge-0/0/1.401    0   0x1 Disabled    Passive                10/10
ge-0/0/1.402    0   0x1 Disabled    Passive                10/10
lo0.0           0   0x1 Disabled    Passive                 0/0
```

Label-Switched Paths

Multiprotocol Label Switching (MPLS) label-switched paths (LSPs) provide a deterministic path through the network—which is fantastic, except when the deterministic
path transits a router that needs a software upgrade. In the event the LSP transits a
router to be upgraded, the network administrator should manually trigger traffic onto
a secondary LSP or trigger the movement of the primary LSP onto a different router.
Your choice of action depends on topology and on the signaling protocol chosen to set
up the LSP.

RSVP-signaled LSPs

In Figure 6-3, **r3** has an LSP running to **r2** with a primary path that passes through **r4** and a secondary path that passes through **r1**. A return LSP from **r2** to **r3** with similar parameters for the primary and secondary paths has also been configured. In this example, the administrators want to upgrade the JUNOS software on **r4**.

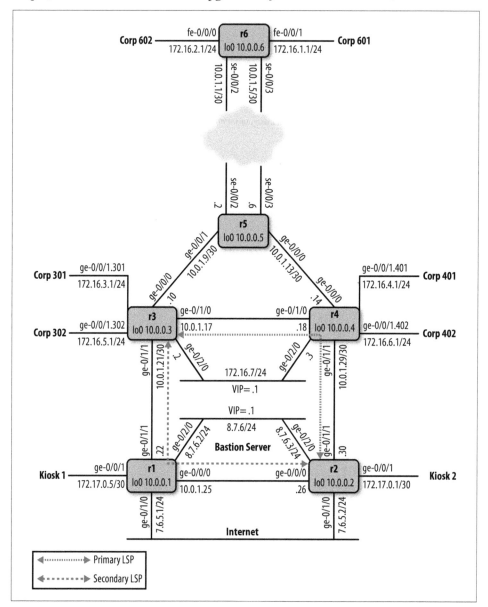

Figure 6-3. Primary and secondary LSPs

Relevant configuration elements on r3 and r2 show how the primary and secondary paths are built and directed through the network. Notice that the standby option is being used with the secondary paths to have the backup LSP signaled as being up and ready for use. Also note that the fast-reroute option is enabled on these LSPs as well:

```
[edit]
lab@r3# show protocols mpls
no-cspf;
label-switched-path to-r2 {
    to 10.0.0.2;
    fast-reroute;
    primary to-r2-primary;
    secondary to-r2-secondary {
        standby;
    }
}
path to-r2-primary {
    10.0.0.4 loose;
}
path to-r2-secondary {
    10.0.0.1 loose;
}
interface all;

[edit]
lab@r2# show protocols mpls
no-cspf;
label-switched-path to-r3 {
    to 10.0.0.3;
    fast-reroute;
    primary to-r3-primary;
    secondary to-r3-secondary {
        standby;
    }
}
path to-r3-primary {
    10.0.0.4 loose;
}
path to-r3-secondary {
    10.0.0.1 loose;
}
interface all;
```

To confirm that both the primary and secondary LSPs are up in both directions, run show mpls lsp from both chassis. First, look at output from the command on r3:

```
edit protocols mpls]
lab@r3# run show mpls lsp
Ingress LSP: 1 sessions
To              From         State Rt ActivePath       P    LSPname
10.0.0.2        10.0.0.3     Up    0 to-r2-primary     *    to-r2
Total 1 displayed, Up 1, Down 0

Egress LSP: 2 sessions, 3 detours
To              From         State    Rt Style Labelin Labelout LSPname
```

```
10.0.0.3      10.0.0.2    Up     0  1 FF       3         - to-r3
10.0.0.3      10.0.0.2    Up     0  1 FF       3         - to-r3
Total 2 displayed, Up 2, Down 0

Transit LSP: 0 sessions, 2 detours
Total 0 displayed, Up 0, Down 0
```

Then look at output from the same command on r2:

```
[edit protocols mpls]
lab@r2# run show mpls lsp
Ingress LSP: 1 sessions
To            From         State Rt ActivePath      P       LSPname
10.0.0.3      10.0.0.2     Up     0 to-r3-primary   *       to-r3
Total 1 displayed, Up 1, Down 0


Egress LSP: 2 sessions, 2 detours
To            From         State  Rt Style Labelin Labelout LSPname
10.0.0.2      10.0.0.3     Up     0  1 FF       3         - to-r2
10.0.0.2      10.0.0.3     Up     0  1 FF       3         - to-r2
Total 2 displayed, Up 2, Down 0

Transit LSP: 0 sessions, 1 detours
Total 0 displayed, Up 0, Down 0
```

The output confirms that both LSPs are up with primary and secondary paths established. Both LSPs have a detour count indicating that fast-reroute is enabled to protect these paths.

 In large, highly complex networks, use the extensive option with the show mpls lsp command to confirm that all LSPs are following the desired paths as defined in the path attributes before you begin the JUNOS upgrade.

As you prepare to upgrade JUNOS on r4, the next step is to check for other transit LSPs on r4. In the following command output, it is apparent that only the bidirectional LSPs between r2 and r3 are transiting r4:

```
[edit protocols mpls]
lab@r4# run show mpls lsp
Ingress LSP: 0 sessions
Total 0 displayed, Up 0, Down 0

Egress LSP: 0 sessions
Total 0 displayed, Up 0, Down 0

Transit LSP: 4 sessions
To            From         State  Rt Style Labelin Labelout LSPname
10.0.0.2      10.0.0.3     Up     1  1 FF   100032        3 to-r2
10.0.0.2      10.0.0.3     Up     1  1 FF   100064        3 to-r2
10.0.0.3      10.0.0.2     Up     1  1 FF   100048        3 to-r3
10.0.0.3      10.0.0.2     Up     1  1 FF   100080        3 to-r3
Total 4 displayed, Up 4, Down 0
```

Because of the LSP protection configuration options and the confirmation that no other LSPs are transiting r4, you can force traffic onto the secondary paths with minimal service interruption by disabling RSVP on r4. LSP traffic between r2 and r3 transfers immediately to the backup paths, which you can confirm using the extensive option on the show mpls lsp command, here shown for r2:

```
[edit protocols mpls]
lab@r2# run show mpls lsp ingress extensive
Ingress LSP: 1 sessions

10.0.0.3
  From: 10.0.0.2, State: Up, ActiveRoute: 0, LSPname: to-r3
  ActivePath: to-r3-secondary (secondary)
  FastReroute desired
  LoadBalance: Random
  Encoding type: Packet, Switching type: Packet, GPID: IPv4
  Primary    to-r3-primary    State: Up
    SmartOptimizeTimer: 180
    Received RRO (ProtectionFlag 1=Available 2=InUse 4=B/W 8=Node
10=SoftPreempt):
          10.0.1.25 10.0.1.21
    17 Nov 15 18:44:34 10.0.1.29: MPLS label allocation failure[8 times]
    16 Nov 15 18:42:40 Deselected as active
    15 Nov 15 18:42:40 Record Route:  10.0.1.25 10.0.1.21
    14 Nov 15 18:42:40 Down
    13 Nov 15 18:42:40 10.0.1.18: MPLS label allocation failure
    12 Nov 15 18:42:40 10.0.1.29: MPLS label allocation failure
    11 Nov 15 18:42:40 10.0.1.18: MPLS label allocation failure
    10 Nov 15 18:42:40 10.0.1.29: MPLS label allocation failure
     9 Nov 15 18:25:49 Fast-reroute Detour Up
     8 Nov 15 18:25:40 Record Route:  10.0.1.29(flag=1) 10.0.1.17
     7 Nov 15 18:25:36 Record Route:  10.0.1.29 10.0.1.17
     6 Nov 15 18:25:36 Up
     5 Nov 15 18:25:36 Originate make-before-break call
     4 Nov 15 17:27:44 Selected as active path
     3 Nov 15 17:27:44 Record Route:  10.0.1.29 10.0.1.17
     2 Nov 15 17:27:44 Up
     1 Nov 15 17:27:44 Originate Call
  *Standby   to-r3-secondary  State: Up
    SmartOptimizeTimer: 180
    Received RRO (ProtectionFlag 1=Available 2=InUse 4=B/W 8=Node
10=SoftPreempt):
          10.0.1.25 10.0.1.21
    12 Nov 15 18:42:40 Record Route:  10.0.1.25 10.0.1.21
    11 Nov 15 18:42:40 Selected as active path
    10 Nov 15 18:42:40 Fast-reroute Detour Down
     9 Nov 15 18:27:15 Fast-reroute Detour Up
     8 Nov 15 18:25:40 Record Route:  10.0.1.25(flag=1) 10.0.1.21
     7 Nov 15 18:25:36 Record Route:  10.0.1.25 10.0.1.21
     6 Nov 15 18:25:36 Up
     5 Nov 15 18:25:36 Originate Call
     4 Nov 15 18:25:36 Clear Call
     3 Nov 15 17:30:10 Record Route:  10.0.1.25 10.0.1.21
     2 Nov 15 17:30:10 Up
```

```
     1 Nov 15 17:30:09 Originate Call
   Created: Sat Nov 15 17:27:44 2008
Total 1 displayed, Up 1, Down 0
```

Running the same command on r3 confirms that the return LSP has also moved to the secondary path:

```
[edit protocols mpls]
lab@r3# run show mpls lsp ingress extensive
Ingress LSP: 1 sessions

10.0.0.2
  From: 10.0.0.3, State: Up, ActiveRoute: 0, LSPname: to-r2
  ActivePath: to-r2-secondary (secondary)
  FastReroute desired
  LoadBalance: Random
  Encoding type: Packet, Switching type: Packet, GPID: IPv4
  Primary   to-r2-primary    State: Up
    SmartOptimizeTimer: 180
    Received RRO (ProtectionFlag 1=Available 2=InUse 4=B/W 8=Node
10=SoftPreempt):
          10.0.1.22 10.0.1.26
   15 Nov 15 18:44:34 10.0.1.18: MPLS label allocation failure[8 times]
   14 Nov 15 18:42:40 Deselected as active
   13 Nov 15 18:42:40 Record Route:  10.0.1.22 10.0.1.26
   12 Nov 15 18:42:40 Down
   11 Nov 15 18:42:40 10.0.1.29: MPLS label allocation failure
   10 Nov 15 18:42:40 10.0.1.18: MPLS label allocation failure[2 times]
    9 Nov 15 18:25:48 Fast-reroute Detour Up
    8 Nov 15 18:25:40 Record Route:  10.0.1.18(flag=1) 10.0.1.30
    7 Nov 15 18:25:36 Record Route:  10.0.1.18 10.0.1.30
    6 Nov 15 18:25:36 Up
    5 Nov 15 18:25:36 Originate make-before-break call
    4 Nov 15 17:27:44 Selected as active path
    3 Nov 15 17:27:44 Record Route:  10.0.1.18 10.0.1.30
    2 Nov 15 17:27:44 Up
    1 Nov 15 17:27:44 Originate Call
 *Standby   to-r2-secondary  State: Up
    SmartOptimizeTimer: 180
    Received RRO (ProtectionFlag 1=Available 2=InUse 4=B/W 8=Node
10=SoftPreempt):
          10.0.1.22 10.0.1.26
   12 Nov 15 18:42:40 Record Route:  10.0.1.22 10.0.1.26
   11 Nov 15 18:42:40 Selected as active path
   10 Nov 15 18:42:40 Fast-reroute Detour Down
    9 Nov 15 18:27:14 Fast-reroute Detour Up
    8 Nov 15 18:25:40 Record Route:  10.0.1.22(flag=1) 10.0.1.26
    7 Nov 15 18:25:36 Record Route:  10.0.1.22 10.0.1.26
    6 Nov 15 18:25:36 Up
    5 Nov 15 18:25:36 Originate Call
    4 Nov 15 18:25:36 Clear Call
    3 Nov 15 17:29:42 Record Route:  10.0.1.22 10.0.1.26
    2 Nov 15 17:29:42 Up
    1 Nov 15 17:29:42 Originate Call
  Created: Sat Nov 15 17:27:44 2008
Total 1 displayed, Up 1, Down 0
```

From an MPLS perspective, r4 is now ready for the JUNOS software upgrade. All LSPs have been moved off the router with minimal downtime.

 It is not uncommon for the admins of a large service provider network to experience problems when trying to move LSPs with high bandwidth constraints (we discuss RSVP bandwidth constraints in Chapter 16). This is because LSP establishment will fail in the absence of adequate reserveable bandwidth. One option would be to temporarily configure the LSP bandwidth requirement to a low value:

```
[edit protocols mpls]
lab@r3# set label-switched-path to-r2 bandwidth 1k
```

Another option could be to use `clear mpls lsp optimize-aggressive`, effectively removing the bandwidth constraint check steps for LSP setup.

CHAPTER 7

Painless Software Upgrades

Juniper Networks recently added features to JUNOS software that dramatically reduce the impact of software upgrades on transit traffic by making it possible to upgrade the router operating system while the router is "in service." In this chapter, we build on the pre-upgrade procedures discussed in the previous chapter and show how unified In-Service Software Upgrade (ISSU) functionality supports high availability goals.

Unified ISSU functionality applies only to platforms with redundant routing engines (REs). And since not all routers have redundant REs, this chapter examines software upgrades for platforms that support unified ISSU and software upgrades for platforms with a single RE or where a release of JUNOS supporting unified ISSU is not in use. Figure 7-1 shows the network topology that we'll upgrade.

In Figure 7-1, routers r5 and r6 have redundant REs and are platforms that support ISSU functionality. Routers r1, r2, r3, and r4 do not have redundant REs but are to some extent paired so as to allow continuity of operations during OS upgrades (i.e., r1 is paired with r2, and r3 with r4).

Snapshots

Immediately before upgrading a chassis using either an ISSU or a non-ISSU image, capture a snapshot of the known stable image and configuration using the `request system snapshot` command. Doing this is important because problems do sometimes arise during the upgrade process, and having a known good fallback point makes it possible to recover quickly.

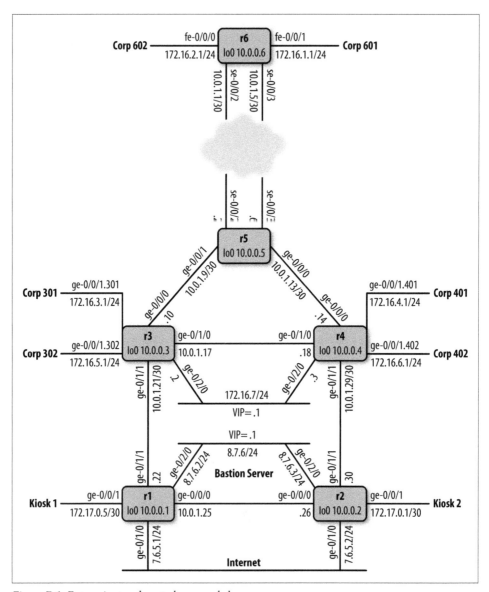

Figure 7-1. Enterprise topology to be upgraded

The `snapshot` command copies the content of */config* and */root* on the boot media to */altconfig* and */altroot* on the alternate boot media. For example, if the router boots from CompactFlash, the `snapshot` command creates the */alt* files on the hard drive. If the router boots from the hard drive, the */alt* files are created on the CompactFlash:

```
[edit]
lab@r5-re0# run request system snapshot
```

The `request system snapshot` command is commonly used with the `partition` option to troubleshoot failed boot media, including CompactFlash or the hard drive. In the following example, the CompactFlash has failed and should be replaced. We know this because of the error message generated:

```
[edit]
lab@r5-re0# run request system snapshot partition
error: s1a media missing or invalid
```

Software Upgrades with Unified ISSU

For routers with redundant REs, unified ISSU allows the administrator to upgrade between two different JUNOS software releases with no disruption on the control plane and with minimal disruption of traffic.

How It Works

Although the goal of this book is to discuss practical application of tools and technologies rather than protocol theory, let's take a quick look at how unified ISSU performs its magic. The process begins when the `in-service-upgrade` command is executed on the master RE:

```
[edit]
lab@r5-re0# run request system software in-service-upgrade /var/tmp/jinstall-9
.3R1.7-domestic-signed.tgz reboot
```

After this command is entered, the router begins an eight-step sequence to complete the upgrade:

1. The router validates the configuration to make sure all elements are compatible with the new revision of code, in this case 9.3R1.7. The router also checks to make sure that all Physical Interface Cards (PICs) are compatible with ISSU. If an incompatible PIC is found, the upgrade continues but the router issues a warning.

2. Kernel state on the backup RE is synchronized with the master RE.

3. The configuration file on the master RE is copied to the backup RE.

4. The backup RE is upgraded with the new operating system, and then kernel state is resynchronized to the master.

5. `chassisd` on the master RE notifies the Packet Forwarding Engine (PFE) on each Flexible PIC Concentrator (FPC) to download the new image from the backup RE.

6. The PFEs download the image, then reboot. Following reboot, they come back online synchronized to the backup RE.

7. Once all PFEs are synchronized to the backup RE, ownership of the chassis transfers to the backup RE and the backup becomes the master.

8. The former master is now upgraded to the new version of code and the process is complete.

Implementation Details

Support for unified ISSU is expanding across the M Series and T Series product lines with most new major releases of JUNOS. Table 7-1 shows unified ISSU platform support by JUNOS release.

Table 7-1. Unified ISSU platform support

Platform	First software release that supports unified ISSU
M120	JUNOS 9.2
M320	JUNOS 9.0
MX240, MX960	JUNOS 9.3
T320	JUNOS 9.0
T640	JUNOS 9.0
T1600	JUNOS 9.1
TX Matrix	JUNOS 9.3

Notice that not every protocol feature of JUNOS is compatible with unified ISSU. Table 7-2 lists protocols that support unified ISSU and the first software release on which unified ISSU for the protocol began being supported.

Table 7-2. Unified ISSU protocol support

Protocol	First software release that supports unified ISSU
Border Gateway Protocol (BGP)	JUNOS 9.0
Open Shortest Path First (OSPF), OSPFv3	JUNOS 9.0
Intermediate System to Intermediate System (IS-IS)	JUNOS 9.0
Label Distribution Protocol (LDP)	JUNOS 9.0
Virtual Private LAN Service (VPLS)	JUNOS 9.3
Layer 2 circuits	JUNOS 9.2
Layer 3 virtual private networks (VPNs)	JUNOS 9.2
Protocol-Independent Multicast (PIM; sparse, dense modes)	JUNOS 9.3

Notice that not all PICs are compatible with unified ISSU. During a unified ISSU operation, legacy PICs that do not support unified ISSU trigger a warning message which indicates that specific PICs in the chassis will be momentarily taken offline during the software upgrade. Once the new firmware is upgraded, the PICs are brought back online.

While a few seconds of interface downtime may sound trivial, it can be significant. During this time, any routing protocol enabled on the interface loses connectivity across that interface to neighbors. This means that while the PIC downtime might last for only a second, the protocols' recovery time could be dramatically longer. It is indeed best to understand potential downtime well in advance of the upgrade. A complete list of legacy PICs that do not support unified ISSU is available in the "High Availability Guide" that accompanies each release of JUNOS software. For JUNOS 9.3, it is available at the following URL:

http://www.juniper.net/techpubs/software/junos/junos93/swconfig-high -availability/unified-issu-pic-support.html#section-issu-supported-pics

Configuration dependencies

To perform unified ISSU, Graceful Routing Engine Switchover (GRES) and Non-Stop Active Routing (NSR) must be enabled on the router. GRES is the component that allows the router to switch between the master and backup REs without interrupting packet forwarding. NSR builds on GRES to preserve routing and switching protocol state information during the transfer between the master and backup REs.

GRES configuration. You add GRES configuration elements at the chassis level of the configuration hierarchy:

```
[edit]
lab@r5-re0# set chassis redundancy graceful-switchover
```

Once committed, this configuration change triggers a marker on the hierarchy label to tell users whether they are on the master or backup RE. You need to know this because you must execute the ISSU command from the master RE:

```
[edit]
lab@r5-re0# commit
commit complete

{master}[edit]
lab@r5-re0#
```

NSR configuration. NSR configuration requires GRES configuration (as shown previously) as well as configuration elements at the system and routing-options hierarchy levels. At the system level of hierarchy, we enable the commit synchronize option to automatically synchronize any configuration changes between REs. The nonstop-routing element under the routing-options level of hierarchy enables NSR:

```
{master}[edit]
lab@r5-re0# set system commit synchronize

{master} [edit]
lab@r5-re0# set routing-options nonstop-routing

{master} [edit]
lab@r5-re0# commit
```

```
re0;
configuration check succeeds
re1;
commit complete
re0;
commit complete
```

Notice that with the commit synchronize feature enabled, all commits result in a configuration update on both the master and backup REs.

Software Upgrades Without Unified ISSU

Chapter 6 looked in detail at configuration elements, such as Virtual Router Redundancy Protocol (VRRP) and the OSPF overload bit, which you can use to "encourage" network traffic to avoid specific routers or links within the network. These configurations deployed chassis in pairs to allow you to perform software upgrades in situations where ISSU is not an option.

If you look at Figure 7-1 again, you might notice that routers r1 and r2 share responsibilities to a great extent. With the exception of the Kiosk LANs, these two chassis effectively serve as a redundant pair. In this scenario, traffic could be shifted from r1 to r2 to permit a JUNOS upgrade on r1 and then from r2 to r1 to permit the r2 upgrade.

Routers r3 and r4 are also redundant in many ways; however, each serves as a nonredundant gateway for a pair of Corp LANs. To upgrade JUNOS on r3 with minimal disruption, transit traffic and ownership of virtual IP (VIP) 172.16.7.1 can be transferred to r4. Once the upgrade to r3 is complete, transit traffic and ownership of the VIP can be transferred back to r3 to permit the r4 upgrade with minimal impact.

Loading a JUNOS Image

Only two steps are needed to load a JUNOS image. First, get the image onto the chassis. Then, make the chassis use it as a boot image.

FTP is commonly used to transfer a JUNOS image. The only real trick to the transfer is to make sure the image is sent to the router using the bin (binary) option available in most FTP client applications. Here's the transfer, using a Microsoft Windows-based host system:

```
Microsoft Windows XP [Version 5.1.2600]
(C) Copyright 1985-2001 Microsoft Corp.

C:\Documents and Settings\jsonderegger>ftp 10.10.13.6
Connected to 10.10.13.6.

220 r5-re0 FTP server (Version 6.00LS) ready.
User (10.10.13.6:(none)): lab
331 Password required for lab.
Password:
```

```
230 User lab logged in.
ftp> bin
200 Type set to I.

ftp> put c:\jinst*
200 PORT command successful.
150 Opening BINARY mode data connection for
'jinstall-9.0R4.5-domestic-signed.tgz'.

226 Transfer complete.
ftp: 163950321 bytes sent in 14.23Seconds 11521.46Kbytes/sec.
ftp>
```

Once the image is on the router, it can be loaded. When upgrading JUNOS without ISSU, it is necessary to reboot the router to load the image. Here we see *jinstall-9.0R4.5-domestic-signed.tgz* loading and the router rebooting and starting the new image:

```
lab@r5-re0> request system software add
/var/home/lab/jinstall-9.0R4.5-domestic-signed.tgz no-validate
Installing package '/var/home/lab/jinstall-9.0R4.5-domestic-signed.tgz' ...
Verified jinstall-9.0R4.5-domestic.tgz signed by PackageProduction_9_0_0
./+INSTALL: /sbin/x509-exts: not found
Adding jinstall...

WARNING:    This package will load JUNOS 9.0R4.5 software.
WARNING:    It will save JUNOS configuration files, and SSH keys
WARNING:    (if configured), but erase all other files and information
WARNING:    stored on this machine.  It will attempt to preserve dumps
WARNING:    and log files, but this can not be guaranteed.  This is the
WARNING:    pre-installation stage and all the software is loaded when
WARNING:    you reboot the system.

Saving the config files ...
Installing the bootstrap installer ...

WARNING:    A REBOOT IS REQUIRED TO LOAD THIS SOFTWARE CORRECTLY. Use the
WARNING:    'request system reboot' command when software installation is
WARNING:    complete. To abort the installation, do not reboot your system,
WARNING:    instead use the 'request system software delete jinstall'
WARNING:    command as soon as this operation completes.

Saving package file in /var/sw/pkg/jinstall-9.0R4.5-domestic-signed.tgz ...
Saving state for rollback ...

lab@r5-re0> request system reboot
Reboot the system ? [yes,no] (no) yes
```

Snapshots Redux

After you complete the software upgrade and confirm that all hardware and protocol behavior is as expected, run the **request system snapshot** command again to copy the new image to the backup boot media. This step is important because the backup media is intended to be redundant to the primary boot media. To be truly redundant, the backup must have the same JUNOS image as the primary media:

```
lab@r5-re0> request system snapshot
```

Image Upgrade Tweaks and Options

The traditional request system software add *<image-name>* command supports options for additional functionality through the upgrade process. The help key (?) lists the options:

```
lab@r5-re0> request system software add jbundle-8.1R1.5-domestic.tgz?
Possible completions:
  <[Enter]>            Execute this command
  delay-restart        Don't restart processes
  force                Force addition of package (ignore warnings)
  no-copy              Don't save copies of package files
  no-validate          Don't check compatibility with current configuration
  reboot               Reboot system after adding package
  validate             Check compatibility with current configuration
  |                    Pipe through a command
```

delay-restart
: Installs the software package but does not restart any software process. This option does not eliminate the need to restart for the upgrade to take effect; it just stops the restart from happening automatically.

force
: Forces the image to be loaded regardless of any system warnings that are generated. This is a dangerous option and can result in a corrupt JUNOS image being loaded as a boot image, effectively making the router inoperable.

no-copy
: Installs the new image but does not save copies of package files.

no-validate
: Installs the new image but suppresses the warning messages that would be generated by the validate function.

validate
: Confirms that all configuration elements and hardware components are compatible with the image being loaded.

reboot
: Automatically reboots the system after finishing the image upgrade.

unlink
: Removes the package after successful installation. This option is very useful on J Series chassis, where storage space is at a premium.

best-effort-load
: Load succeeds if at least one statement is valid.

J Series Considerations

Currently, J Series routers—the chassis most commonly used in the enterprise—are not equipped with a rotating media hard drive. Their on-system memory for storing JUNOS images is limited. As a result, some additional image upgrade commands and options are available as mentioned previously.

Cleanup

J Series chassis support a `cleanup` command that frees up storage space by deleting files in the */cf/var/tmp/* directory that have not been accessed in the past 48 hours, as well as all crash files in the */cf/var/crash* directory. This command also rotates all current logfiles in the */cf/var/log* directory. This command takes a minute or two to complete. You can run it immediately before a software upgrade to free up space for the JUNOS image:

```
lab@r5-re0> request system storage cleanup

List of files to delete:

        Size Date          Name
     2300B Dec  8 09:39 /cf/var/log/interactive-commands.0.gz
     8561B Jun 11 06:00 /cf/var/log/interactive-commands.1.gz
      9.8K Jun 10 09:00 /cf/var/log/interactive-commands.2.gz
     9290B Jun  2  2008 /cf/var/log/interactive-commands.3.gz
     8990B May 20  2008 /cf/var/log/interactive-commands.4.gz
     2408B Dec  8 09:39 /cf/var/log/messages.0.gz
     11.7K Dec  8 08:00 /cf/var/log/messages.1.gz
     14.8K Jul 30 09:00 /cf/var/log/messages.2.gz
     11.1K Jul 25 07:00 /cf/var/log/messages.3.gz
     5550B Jul  9 19:00 /cf/var/log/messages.4.gz
     5527B Jul  9 14:00 /cf/var/log/messages.5.gz
     20.3K Jul  9 09:00 /cf/var/log/messages.6.gz
     17.0K Jun 11 06:00 /cf/var/log/messages.7.gz
     13.0K Jun 10 10:00 /cf/var/log/messages.8.gz
     10.6K Jun 10 06:00 /cf/var/log/messages.9.gz
     8269B May 20  2008 /cf/var/log/sampled.0.gz
     36.3M May 18  2008 /cf/var/tmp/junos-jseries-8.2R4.5-domestic.tgz
Delete these files ? [yes,no] (no) yes
```

Backup Images

J Series chassis support a USB port that allows files, including JUNOS images, to be added and removed from the chassis. Table 7-3 shows the list of officially supported USB thumb drives as of JUNOS 9.3.

Table 7-3. Officially supported USB drives

Manufacturer	Size	Manufacturer part number
SanDisk—Cruzer Mini 2.0	256 MB	SDCZ2-256-A10
SanDisk	512 MB	SDCZ2-512-A10
SanDisk	1,024 MB	SDCZ2-1024-A10
SanDisk—ImageMate USB 2.0 Reader/Writer for CompactFlash Type I and II	N/A	SDDR-91-A15
SanDisk-CompactFlash	512 MB	SDCFB-512-455
SanDisk-CompactFlash	1,024 MB	SDCFB-1000–A10
Kingston	512 MB	DTI/512KR
Kingston	1,024 MB	DTI/1GBKR

Before upgrading an image, you can write the current configuration and image to a USB drive using the `request system snapshot` command. In this example, the USB drive has not previously been used on a JUNOS platform, a FreeBSD environment, so the `partition` option is also necessary. The initial da0 output is generated when the USB drive is inserted into the chassis:

```
da0 at umass-sim0 bus 0 target 0 lun 0
da0: <OPTI3 Flash Disk 2.00> Removable Direct Access SCSI-2 device
da0: 1.000MB/s transfers
da0: 125MB (256000 512 byte sectors: 64H 32S/T 125C)

lab@r5-re0> request system snapshot partition media usb
Clearing current label...
Partitioning usb media (da0) ...
Partitions on snapshot:

  Partition  Mountpoint  Size    Snapshot argument
      a      /           111MB   root-size
      e      /config     13MB    config-size
Running newfs (111MB) on usb media / partition (da0s1a)...
Running newfs (13MB) on usb media /config partition (da0s1e)...
Copying '/dev/ad0s1a' to '/dev/da0s1a' .. (this may take a few minutes)
Copying '/dev/ad0s1e' to '/dev/da0s1e' .. (this may take a few minutes)
The following filesystems were archived: / /config
```

The USB port can also be used as boot media if it is loaded with a jinstall image that meets the install-media guidelines. For the J Series chassis, the install-media packages will have a size indicated in the suffix of the package name to describe system storage requirements for the image, as in this example:

```
Junos-jseries-8.0R2-export-cf256.gz
```

Rescue Configuration

A rescue configuration is a feature specific to J Series routers. Though it is not a true part of the software upgrade procedure, its functionality is directly related. The rescue configuration allows you to create a known stable working configuration and save it in a special memory location in the J Series router. There is no rescue configuration by default. It must be created and saved by the administrator:

```
lab@r4> request system configuration rescue save
```

Once saved, it can be viewed as needed to make sure it is still current and appropriate for the system:

```
lab@r4> show system configuration rescue
version 9.4R2.9;
system {
    host-name r4;
    root-authentication {
        encrypted-password "$1$vky7kvOi$/NeUtRaLSDgDb3we4nPVs/"; ## SECRET-DATA
    }
    login {
        class juniper {
            permissions view;
            allow-commands "show route";
        }
        user lab {
            uid 2003;
            class superuser;
            authentication {
                encrypted-password "$1$pYM5k*hEy_zeUS6rfe32R.4bg.";
                ## SECRET-DATA
            }
        }
    }
}
...
```

Then the rescue configuration can be loaded and committed on the router by momentarily pressing the RESET CONFIG button on the face of the chassis. The rescue configuration can also be loaded through the command-line interface (CLI):

```
[edit]
lab@r4# rollback rescue
load complete
```

 Pressing the RESET CONFIG button momentarily loads and commits the rescue configuration, but be warned: holding the RESET CONFIG button for 15 seconds will delete the active configuration, the rescue configuration, and all rollback configurations, and will reset the system to a factory default.

CHAPTER 8

JUNOS Post-Upgrade Verifications

Congratulations! If you are reading this chapter, you must have followed the pre-upgrade procedures in Chapter 6 and the painless software upgrade recommendations in Chapter 7. You have:

- Identified an appropriate JUNOS release based on current and future network requirements and on the contents of the release notes for that revision.
- Confirmed that the JUNOS release is compatible with your network hardware.
- Formulated a strategy and timeline for rolling the new JUNOS out to the target devices in the network.
- Checked the configuration of the target devices to make sure the proper configuration elements are in place to take advantage of hardware component redundancies and In-Service Software Upgrade (ISSU) features where available.
- Prepared for the upgrade by capturing and storing configuration and state information for each device.
- Downloaded a copy of the new JUNOS release and, using the provided MD5 hash, prepositioned the image on the target chassis.
- Just prior to the upgrade, used Interior Gateway Protocol (IGP)-specific overload bits, metrics adjustments, and virtual IP (VIP) ownership changes to make the target chassis less desirable to transit traffic.
- Confirmed that traffic was indeed following an alternate path through the network.
- Executed the `request system software add` command to load the new operating system and rebooted the routing engines (REs) as needed.
- Did all this with minimal traffic loss during your allocated maintenance window, supporting the service-level agreements (SLAs) guaranteed by your company and protecting the availability of the network.

Well done!

Now that JUNOS has been upgraded to the desired release level, it is time to make sure everything went as smoothly as it appeared. It is time for you to run a *post-upgrade verification*. Performing a post-upgrade verification is the equivalent of double-checking your math. It allows you to spot any mistakes and correct them before they turn into serious problems.

Post-Upgrade Verification

Post-upgrade verification should begin at the Physical layer on the device that has been upgraded, and expand upward through the Open Systems Interconnection (OSI) model and outward through the rest of the network. However, before beginning this process, we recommend confirming that the chassis is currently running on the desired (upgraded) revision of JUNOS.

On more than one occasion, we have been surprised to find a chassis that did not get fully upgraded. Either a hardware or configuration incompatibility occurred that we had overlooked, or we simply failed to reboot the RE to allow it to come up on the new software.

Take a look at the revision of JUNOS the master RE is currently running and make sure it matches the target release:

```
lab@j2300-1-re0> show version
version 9.3R3.8;
```

A commonly overlooked but critical next step is to confirm that the upgrade was also successful on the backup RE. Checking the backup software version is important because a chassis is not really in a fully redundant high availability state unless the backup components (in this case, an RE) are capable of performing the same tasks and supporting the same functionality as the primary components.

Log in to the backup RE and check its release:

```
[edit]
lab@m40-3-re0# run request routing-engine login re1

lab@m40-3-re1> show version
version 9.3R3.8;
```

You can also check the JUNOS revision level from configuration mode, but it is important to keep in mind that what you are viewing in configuration mode is a configuration element that can be changed within the configuration file:

```
[edit]
lab@j2300-1# show version
version 9.3R3.8;

[edit]
lab@j2300-1# set version 867-5309

[edit]
lab@j2300-1# show version
version 867-5309;
```

```
[edit]
lab@j2300-1# run show version
Hostname: j2300-1
Model: j2300
JUNOS Software Release [9.3R3.8] (Export edition)
```

Because of the ability to change the revision tag, the authors strongly recommend that you check the release level from operational mode rather than from configuration mode. Some administrators will, as a standard procedure, simply delete the `version` tag within the configuration file to force all users to rely on the operational mode command to check the true revision level.

Throughout this chapter, we refer to the act of loading JUNOS as an "upgrade." We do this because in most situations the revision of JUNOS being loaded on the chassis is newer than the revision of JUNOS that was already on the chassis. Loading the newer version is considered moving *up* in the code train.

While not explicitly stated in every example, the procedures listed in this chapter also apply to situations in which you are moving *down* in the code train. In other words, you are "downgrading" from a newer release to an older release of JUNOS.

After confirming the successful upgrade of both REs, check the hardware and interface states of the upgraded device.

Device State

You use the `show chassis hardware`, `show chassis alarm`, `show interfaces terse`, and `show chassis fpc pic-status` commands to show the state of the chassis hardware and interfaces. You should run these commands only from the master RE. However, the output from these commands is relevant to the entire chassis.

Verify chassis hardware

In the output from the `show chassis hardware` command, you should check that all components in the chassis are listed. Having them appear indicates they are at least powered on and accessible by the router's management daemon (`mgd`). Output from this command varies in length based on the number of component Field Replaceable Units (FRUs) in the chassis.

Juniper Networks product warranties and service contracts are tied to product serial numbers. All serial numbers have been removed from the output of the `show chassis hardware` commands to protect the service contracts of the owners of the chassis.

For a J2300 chassis, commonly found in small enterprise environments, the output is quite short:

```
lab@j2300-1# run show chassis hardware
Hardware inventory:
Item            Version  Part number Serial#  Description
Chassis                                       J2300
Routing Engine  REV 07   750-009992           RE-J.1
FPC 0           REV 05   750-010738           FPC
  PIC 0                                        2x FE, 2x T1
```

For large enterprise and service-provider-scale chassis, the output is significantly longer. This example is from an M40e:

```
lab@m40-2-re0> show chassis hardware
Hardware inventory:
Item              Version  Part number  Serial#  Description
Chassis                                           M40e
Midplane          REV 04   710-008502
FPM CMB           REV 03   710-001642
FPM Display       REV 04   710-001647
CIP               REV 06   710-002649
PEM 0             Rev 04   740-005165            AC Power Entry Module
PEM 1             Rev 04   740-005165            AC Power Entry Module
PCG 0             REV 06   710-003066
PCG 1             REV 06   710-003066
Routing Engine 0  REV 16   740-005022            RE-3.0
Routing Engine 1  REV 16   740-005022            RE-3.0
MCS 0             REV 15   710-001226
MCS 1             REV 15   710-001226
SFM 0 SPP         REV 09   710-001228
SFM 0 SPR         REV 03   710-007707            Internet Processor IIv2
SFM 1 SPP         REV 10   710-001228
SFM 1 SPR         REV 01   710-011130            Internet Processor IIv2
FPC 1             REV 04   710-005078            M40e-FPC Type 1
  CPU             REV 03   710-004602
  PIC 0           REV 06   750-010240            1x G/E SFP, 1000 BASE
  PIC 1           REV 06   750-010240            1x G/E SFP, 1000 BASE
  PIC 2           REV 06   750-010240            1x G/E SFP, 1000 BASE
  PIC 3           REV 06   750-010240            1x G/E SFP, 1000 BASE
FPC 2             REV 01   710-011165            M40e-FPC Type 1
  CPU             REV 03   710-004602
  PIC 0           REV 06   750-005720            1x OC-12 ATM-II IQ,SMIR
  PIC 1           REV 06   750-005720            1x OC-12 ATM-II IQ,SMIR
  PIC 2           REV 07   750-002911            4x F/E, 100 BASE-TX
  PIC 3           REV 11   750-008431            Adaptive Services
FPC 5             REV 01   710-011165            M40e-FPC Type 1
  CPU             REV 03   710-004602
FPC 6             REV 01   710-011165            M40e-FPC Type 1
  CPU             REV 03   710-004602
  PIC 0           REV 06   750-010240            1x G/E SFP, 1000 BASE
  PIC 1           REV 06   750-010240            1x G/E SFP, 1000 BASE
  PIC 2           REV 05   750-005728            2x OC-3 ATM-II IQ, SMIR
  PIC 3           REV 04   750-005731            4x T3 ATM-II IQ
```

Check for alarms

If the output from the show chassis alarms command matches what is shown in the following output, all the hardware components are operating properly. This output is from J2300-1:

```
[edit]
lab@j2300-1# run show chassis alarms
No alarms currently active
```

However, if alarm conditions are identified by the following command, you need to investigate and remedy them. Output such as this would be disturbing and require investigation:

```
{primary:node0}[edit]
lab@host1-b# run show chassis alarms
node0:
--------------------------------------------------------------------------
7 alarms currently active
Alarm time               Class  Description
2009-04-27 14:17:11 PDT  Minor  ge-3/0/0: Link down
2009-04-27 14:17:10 PDT  Minor  fe-2/0/4: Link down
2009-04-27 14:17:10 PDT  Minor  fe-2/0/3: Link down
2009-04-27 14:17:09 PDT  Minor  fe-2/0/2: Link down
2009-04-27 14:17:09 PDT  Minor  fe-0/0/4: Link down
2009-04-27 14:17:08 PDT  Minor  fe-0/0/3: Link down
2009-04-27 14:17:08 PDT  Minor  fe-0/0/2: Link down

node1:
--------------------------------------------------------------------------
No alarms currently active

{primary:node0}[edit]
lab@host1-b#
```

Verify interfaces

When verifying device state, use the show interfaces terse command to view Link and Admin state for all physical and logical interfaces in the chassis:

```
[edit]
lab@j2300-1# run show interfaces terse
Interface        Admin Link Proto Local              Remote
fe-0/0/0         up    down
fe-0/0/0.0       up    down inet  192.168.50.50/30
gr-0/0/0         up    up
ip-0/0/0         up    up
ls-0/0/0         up    up
mt-0/0/0         up    up
pd-0/0/0         up    up
pe-0/0/0         up    up
sp-0/0/0         up    up
sp-0/0/0.16383   up    up   inet
fe-0/0/1         up    down
fe-0/0/1.0       up    down inet  192.168.50.26/30
```

```
t1-0/0/2            up    down
t1-0/0/3            up    down
dsc                 up    up
gre                 up    up
ipip                up    up
loo                 up    up
loo.0               up    up    inet  152.152.1.1      --> 0/0
loo.16385           up    up    inet  10.0.0.1         --> 0/0
                                      10.0.0.16        --> 0/0

lsi                 up    up
mtun                up    up
pimd                up    up
pime                up    up
ppo                 up    up
tap                 up    up
```

The output shown is likely a genuine cause for concern, because the two physical interfaces fe-0/0/0 and fe-0/0/1 have a logical interface configured with an IP address, but both are showing status of Admin Up and Link Down. A more detailed version of the show interfaces command provides more information, but in this case it is of little help. A physical inspection of the chassis reveals that both Ethernet cables have been disconnected:

```
[edit]
lab@j2300-1# run show interfaces detail fe-0/0/0 | match down
Physical interface: fe-0/0/0, Enabled, Physical link is Down
  Device flags   : Present Running Down
  Interface flags: Hardware-Down SNMP-Traps 16384
  Hold-times     : Up 0 ms, Down 0 ms
    Flags: Device-Down SNMP-Traps Encapsulation: ENET2
      Addresses, Flags: Dest-route-down Is-Preferred Is-Primary
```

As we noted in Chapter 7, if the router detects an incompatibility between a Physical Interface Card (PIC) and the new operating system during a JUNOS upgrade, the PIC may be taken offline. This problem can be difficult to identify because when a PIC is offline, it does not appear in the output of show interfaces commands.

If you suspect a problem with an entire PIC, use the show chassis fpc pic-status command to get more data about interfaces. In the first example, FPC 0 is online:

```
[edit]
lab@j2300-1# run show chassis fpc pic-status
Slot 0   Online       FPC
  PIC 0  Online       2x FE, 2x T1
```

In the second example, FPC 0 is offline:

```
[edit]
lab@j2300-1# run show chassis fpc pic-status
Slot 0   Offline      FPC
```

Notice that when a Flexible PIC Concentrator (FPC) is offline some critical configuration elements vanish from the show interfaces command output:

```
[edit]
lab@j2300-1# run show interfaces terse
Interface              Admin Link Proto Local                Remote
dsc                    up    up
gre                    up    up
ipip                   up    up
lo0                    up    up
lo0.0                  up    up   inet  152.152.1.1          --> 0/0
lo0.16385              up    up   inet  10.0.0.1             --> 0/0
                                        10.0.0.16            --> 0/0

lsi                    up    up
mtun                   up    up
pimd                   up    up
pime                   up    up
ppo                    up    up
tap                    up    up

[edit]
lab@j2300-1# run show interfaces detail fe-0/0/0
error: device fe-0/0/0 not found

[edit]
lab@j2300-1# run show interfaces detail fe-0/0/1
error: device fe-0/0/1 not found
```

To remedy this situation, you can attempt to bring the PIC back online. However, if the problem is a compatibility issue between chassis hardware and the new revision of JUNOS, the operation will fail. In this example there is no compatibility issue and the PIC is easily brought back online:

```
[edit]
lab@j2300-1# run request chassis fpc online slot 0
Online initiated, use "show chassis fpc" to verify

[edit]
lab@j2300-1# run show chassis fpc pic-status
Slot 0   Online       FPC
  PIC 0  Online       2x FE, 2x T1
```

Because the PIC, inseparable from the FPC on a J Series chassis, could be brought back online, it is time to check the logfiles to see what really happened:

```
[edit]
lab@j2300-1# run show log messages | match fpc
Apr 21 14:02:41   chassisd[2361]: CHASSISD_IFDEV_DETACH_FPC: ifdev_detach(0)
May 10 18:34:24   chassisd[2366]: CHASSISD_SNMP_TRAP9:
SNMP trap generated: FRU power on (jnxFruContentsIndex 7,
jnxFruL1Index 1, jnxFruL2Index 0, jnxFruL3Index 0,
jnxFruName FPC @ 0/*/*, jnxFruType 3,
jnxFruSlot 1, jnxFruOfflineReason 2, jnxFruLastPowerOff 0,
jnxFruLastPowerOn 3008)
May 11 18:30:54   fpc0: PFEMAN: Session manager active
May 11 18:30:54   fpc0: PFEMAN: Established connection to Master
May 11 18:30:54   fpc0: PFEMAN: sent Resync request to Master
May 11 18:30:54   fpc0: SNTP: Daemon created
```

```
May 11 18:30:54    fpc0: Version 7.1R1.3 by builder on 2005-02-11 04:39:17 UTC
May 11 18:30:54    fpc0: SNTPD: Initial time of day set.
May 11 18:30:54    fpc0: PFEMAN: received Resync complete.
May 11 18:30:54    fpc0: Installing T1/E1 driver ...
May 19 17:15:15    j2300-1 mgd[3182]: UI_CMDLINE_READ_LINE:
User 'dspitzer', command 'run show chassis fpc pic-status '
May 19 17:15:32    j2300-1 mgd[3182]: UI_CMDLINE_READ_LINE:
User 'dspitzer', command 'run request chassis fpc offline slot 0 '
May 19 17:15:32    j2300-1 chassisd[2371]: CHASSISD_FRU_OFFLINE_NOTICE:
Taking FPC 0 offline: Offlined by cli command
May 19 17:15:32    j2300-1 chassisd[2371]: CHASSISD_IFDEV_DETACH_FPC:
ifdev_detach(0)
May 19 17:15:32    j2300-1 fpc0: CMLC: Master closed connection
May 19 17:15:32    j2300-1 fpc0: Going disconnected;
Routing engine chassis socket closed abruptly
May 19 19:26:20    j2300-1 mgd[3190]: UI CMDLINE READ LINE:
User 'lab', command 'run show log messages | match fpc '
```

In this case, no compatibility issue between the new operating system and the device hardware is reported. The FPC and PIC, taken offline by user dspitzer, can be brought back online and interface information will return to the pertinent show interfaces command output.

On with the verification!

Verify memory

To verify the memory on the REs, execute the show system storage command on both the master and backup REs, assuming the chassis has two REs. You issue the command twice because each RE has separate memory, including CompactFlash, a hard drive, and possibly also removable media. Failure of any memory component on one of the REs negatively impacts the resilience and potentially the availability of the chassis. The following output is from a J2300 router:

```
lab@j2300-1> show system storage
Filesystem     Size     Used     Avail  Capacity  Mounted on
/dev/ad0s1a    213M     59M      152M     28%      /
devfs          1.0K     1.0K     0B      100%      /dev
devfs          1.0K     1.0K     0B      100%      /dev/
/dev/md0       133M     133M     0B      100%      /junos
/cf            213M     59M      152M     28%      /junos/cf
devfs          1.0K     1.0K     0B      100%      /junos/dev/
procfs         4.0K     4.0K     0B      100%      /proc
/dev/bo0s1e    24M      7.0K     24M       0%      /config
/dev/md1       63M      6.2M     52M      11%      /mfs
/dev/md2       58M      10.0K    53M       0%      /jail/tmp
/dev/md3       7.7M     106K     7.0M      1%      /jail/var
devfs          1.0K     1.0K     0B      100%      /jail/dev
/dev/md4       1.9M     6.0K     1.7M      0%      /jail/html/oem
```

When the same command is run on a different chassis, an M40e, the output is in fact different, but still comparable in many ways:

```
[edit]
lab@m40-3-re0# run show system storage

Filesystem       512-blocks     Used   Avail Capacity Mounted on
/dev/ad0s1a          437522    67746  334776      17% /
devfs                    32       32       0     100% /dev/
/dev/vn0              22816    22816       0     100% /packages/mnt/jbase
/dev/vn1              77956    77956       0     100% /packages/mnt/jkernel-
/dev/vn2              20720    20720       0     100% /packages/mnt/jpfe-
/dev/vn3               4492     4492       0     100% /packages/mnt/jdocs-
/dev/vn4              27556    27556       0     100% /packages/mnt/jroute-
/dev/vn5               9620     9620       0     100% /packages/mnt/jcrypto-
mfs:152             4064278        8 3739128       0%
/tmp/dev/ad0s1e       48570       10   44676       0% /config
procfs                    8        8       0     100% /proc
/dev/ad1s1f        52249814   212192 47857638      0% /var
```

In the output from the show system storage command, it is important that you scan the Filesystem column for storage areas. One memory location is visible in the J2300 command output—a CompactFlash drive. Two memory locations, a CompactFlash and a hard drive, are visible in the M40e command output.

The CompactFlash memory is a nonrotating drive. A copy of the JUNOS operating system and recent configuration files are present on the CompactFlash. It is identified as /ad0 in the first column of the command output shown earlier. If the router's CompactFlash has failed or is faulty, no Filesystem listings will be listed for /ad0.

The hard drive is a rotating drive. A copy of the JUNOS operating system and all archived files are present on the hard drive. This drive is also used to store system logfiles and diagnostic dump files. It is identified as /ad1 in the command output shown earlier. Routers with a failed or faulty hard drive will have no Filesystem listings for /ad1.

When redundant components are present in the upgraded chassis, administrators sometimes force the chassis to fail back and forth between the components before making configuration changes to resume actively passing traffic. If you decide to do this, make sure you do it within the established maintenance window:

```
lab@m40-3-re0> request chassis routing-engine master switch
```

Network State (Routes, Peering Relationships, and Databases)

After you confirm that the hardware and all configured interfaces on the device are stable and functional, it is time to check for peering relationships with neighbors and expected routes from other devices in the network. To begin this process, first confirm that no related configuration elements have been disabled or deleted.

For the sake of literary excitement, let's assume we have just completed our hardware and interface and memory verifications for r1. Router r1 is an Internet gateway router in the small enterprise network shown in Figure 8-1.

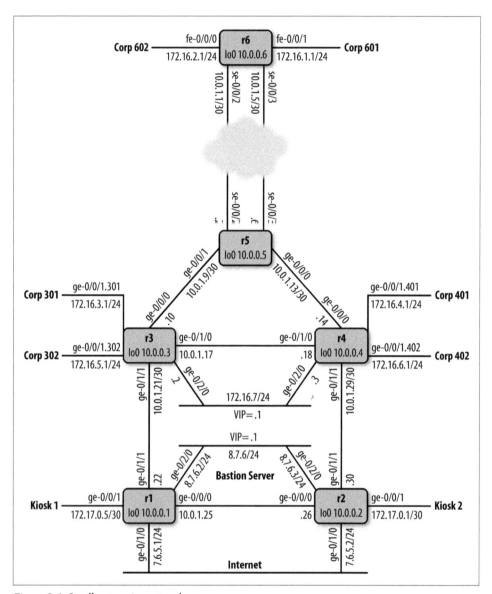

Figure 8-1. Small enterprise network

Now that the device state is verified, we need to check peering relationships, route table content, and protocol databases.

Verify routing

In many cases, a suspected "routing issue" that occurs during a software upgrade or at any other time is nothing more than a configuration error or an overlooked configuration change. Depending on what changes were applied before the upgrade to make the chassis a less desirable choice for transit traffic, it may be necessary to remove some configuration workarounds to bring up peering relationships and populate routing tables:

```
[edit protocols ospf]
lab@r1# show
area 0.0.0.0 {
    interface ge-0/1/1.0;
    interface ge-0/2/0.0 {
        disable;
        passive;
    }
    interface ge-0/0/0.0;
    interface ge-0/0/1.0 {
        passive;
    }
    interface lo0.0 {
        passive;
    }
    interface ge-0/1/0.0 {
        disable;
        passive;
    }
}
```

The output from this command indicates the OSPF protocol has been disabled on several interfaces. This action was most likely taken to stop the router from attracting transit traffic during the software upgrade. Significant time can be wasted attempting to troubleshoot OSPF adjacencies across these disabled links. Let's delete the `disable` tag before moving to the next step:

```
[edit protocols ospf]
lab@r1# show
area 0.0.0.0 {
    interface ge-0/1/1.0;
    interface ge-0/2/0.0 {
        passive;
    }
    interface ge-0/0/0.0;
    interface ge-0/0/1.0 {
        passive;
    }
    interface lo0.0 {
        passive;
    }
    interface ge-0/1/0.0 {
        passive;
    }
}
 [edit protocols ospf]
lab@r1# commit
commit complete
```

Now that the `disable` tag has been removed, use simple `show` commands to check OSPF peering relationships with neighboring routers and awareness of passive interfaces. The output from this command is consistent with the network map in Figure 8-1:

```
[edit protocols]
lab@r1# run show ospf neighbor
Address        Interface       State    ID           Pri  Dead
10.0.1.21      ge-0/1/1.0      Full     10.0.0.3     128  37
10.0.1.26      ge-0/0/0.0      Full     10.0.0.2     128  36

[edit protocols]
lab@r1# run show ospf interface
Interface        State     Area       DR ID      BDR ID      Nbrs
ge-0/1/1.0       BDR       0.0.0.0    10.0.0.3   10.0.0.1     1
ge-0/0/0.0       BDR       0.0.0.0    10.0.0.2   10.0.0.1     1
ge 0/1/0.0       DRother   0.0.0.0    0.0.0.0    0.0.0.0      0
ge-0/1/0.0       DRother   0.0.0.0    0.0.0.0    0.0.0.0      0
ge-0/0/1.0       DRother   0.0.0.0    0.0.0.0    0.0.0.0      0
lo0              DRother   0.0.0.0    0.0.0.0    0.0.0.0      0
```

In small to medium-size enterprise networks, a manual review of the output from these commands is probably enough to let you know whether there is an issue. However, in larger networks with a greater number of interfaces, the chance of missing something important increases.

Because human error is, in fact, the leading cause of network downtime, you should have a copy of the pre-upgrade output of these commands to compare to the post-upgrade list of peering relationships.

Routing table consistency

Assuming that all IGP routing configuration has been returned to its pre-upgrade state, you now check the routing tables for consistency across the network. Although r1 is the focus of this effort, to completely check consistency you must also look at the table on a few other routers in the network.

Many of the changes that were recommended as part of the pre-upgrade and upgrade processes would be "undone" by loading a saved configuration file, checking the differences, and committing. In this section, we'll attempt to address issues on adjacent devices that would impact high availability and might not be remedied by a `rollback` or `load` function on the device being upgraded.

Resuming functionality using a rollback or file load command is still one of the most common methods of configuration recovery and is addressed in the next section of this chapter.

Starting with **r1**, check routes to the loopback addresses of other routers in the network:

```
[edit]
lab@r1# run show route 10.0.0/24

inet.0: 32 destinations, 32 routes (32 active, 0 holddown, 0 hidden)
+ = Active Route, - = Last Active, * = Both

10.0.0.1/32        *[Direct/0] 02:07:42
                    > via lo0.0
10.0.0.2/32        *[OSPF/10] 01:18:14, metric 1
                    > to 10.0.1.26 via ge-0/0/0.0
10.0.0.3/32        *[OSPF/10] 01:18:19, metric 1
                    > to 10.0.1.21 via ge-0/1/1.0
10.0.0.4/32        *[OSPF/10] 01:18:09, metric 2
                      to 10.0.1.21 via ge-0/1/1.0
                    > to 10.0.1.26 via ge-0/0/0
10.0.0.5/32        *[OSPF/10] 01:18:04, metric 2
                    > to 10.0.1.21 via ge-0/1/1.0
10.0.0.6/32        *[OSPF/10] 01:18:04, metric 3
                    > to 10.0.1.21 via ge-0/1/1.0
```

Router **r1** looks fine, but when we run the same command on **r2**, some inconsistencies quickly become apparent:

```
[edit]
lab@r2# run show route 10.0.0/24

inet.0: 31 destinations, 32 routes (31 active, 0 holddown, 0 hidden)
+ = Active Route, - = Last Active, * = Both

10.0.0.1/32        *[OSPF/10] 00:04:58, metric 3
                    > to 10.0.1.29 via ge-0/1/1.0
10.0.0.2/32        *[Direct/0] 02:07:47
                    > via lo0.2
10.0.0.3/32        *[OSPF/10] 00:04:58, metric 2
                    > to 10.0.1.29 via ge-0/1/1.0
10.0.0.4/32        *[OSPF/10] 01:18:24, metric 1
                    > to 10.0.1.29 via ge-0/1/1.0
10.0.0.5/32        *[OSPF/10] 01:18:09, metric 2
                    > to 10.0.1.29 via ge-0/1/1.0
10.0.0.6/32        *[OSPF/10] 01:18:09, metric 3
                    > to 10.0.1.29 via ge-0/1/1.0
```

Router **r2** appears to be transiting **r4** to get to the loopback address of **r1** even though **r2** has a direct connection. A quick configuration check of **r2** shows a high metric setting for the direct link to **r1**:

```
[edit]
lab@r2# edit protocols ospf area 0

[edit protocols ospf area 0.0.0.0]
lab@r2# show
interface ge-0/2/0.0 {
    passive;
}
```

```
interface ge-0/0/0.0 {
    metric 65000;
}
interface ge-0/1/0.0 {
    passive;
}
interface ge-0/0/1.0 {
    passive;
}
interface ge-0/1/1.0;
interface lo0.0;
```

This configuration is most likely a leftover from the efforts to make r1 look less attractive to transit traffic during the software upgrade, and is easy enough to fix:

```
[edit protocols ospf area 0.0.0.0]
lab@r2# delete interface ge-0/0/0.0 metric

[edit protocols ospf area 0.0.0.0]
lab@r2# show
interface ge-0/2/0.0 {
    passive;
}
interface ge-0/0/0.0;
interface ge-0/1/0.0 {
    passive;
}
interface ge-0/0/1.0 {
    passive;
}
interface ge-0/1/1.0;
interface lo0.2;

[edit protocols ospf area 0.0.0.0]
lab@r2# commit
commit complete
```

After the change is committed, the metric and path back to r1 look much better:

```
[edit protocols ospf area 0.0.0.0]
lab@r2# run show route 10.0.0/24

inet.0: 31 destinations, 31 routes (31 active, 0 holddown, 0 hidden)
+ = Active Route, - = Last Active, * = Both

10.0.0.1/32        *[OSPF/10] 00:00:06, metric 1
                    > to 10.0.1.25 via ge-0/0/0.0
10.0.0.2/32        *[Direct/0] 02:13:00
                    > via lo0.2
10.0.0.3/32        *[OSPF/10] 00:00:06, metric 2
                      to 10.0.1.29 via ge-0/1/1.0
                    > to 10.0.1.25 via ge-0/0/0.0
10.0.0.4/32        *[OSPF/10] 01:23:37, metric 1
                    > to 10.0.1.29 via ge-0/1/1.0
10.0.0.5/32        *[OSPF/10] 01:23:22, metric 2
                    > to 10.0.1.29 via ge-0/1/1.0
```

```
10.0.0.6/32          *[OSPF/10] 01:23:22, metric 3
                      > to 10.0.1.29 via ge-0/1/1.0
```

Based on the setting found on r2, we suspect the same setting may be in place on r3, which also has a direct interface connection to r1. A quick look at the r3 configuration confirms the suspicion:

```
[edit protocols ospf]
lab@r3# show
area 0.0.0.0 {
    interface ge-0/1/00 {
    }
    interface ge-0/2/00 {
        passive;
    }
    interface ge-0/1/10 {
        metric 65000;
    }
    interface ge-0/0/1.301 {
        passive;
    }
    interface ge-0/0/1.302 {
        passive;
    }
    interface lo0.0 {
        passive;
    }
    interface ge-0/0/0.0;
}
```

After removing the metric setting on the interface between r3 and r1, routing among the loopbacks in the network looks fine. Issuing a few additional show route commands indicates that intradomain routing is back to where it should be.

The next thing to confirm is routing to destinations external to the local domain. To do this, we start by going as deep into the network as possible. Browsing to *http://www .juniper.net* from host systems on the Corp 601 and 602 subnets is successful and confirms routing to the external destinations. However, because the network has high availability requirements, redundant Internet gateways r1 and r2 have been provisioned. To make sure this redundancy is still in effect, we must confirm that both r1 and r2 are sending the default route out to the Internet. We can check this by looking into the OSPF database. Because the OSPF standard dictates all routers within an area share a common topological view, and all the devices in this network are in the same area, the database can be checked on any of our routers. Here's the output from r5:

```
[edit]
lab@r5# run show ospf database

    OSPF link state database, Area 0.0.0.0
 Type   ID          Adv Rtr       Seq       Age  Opt  Cksum  Len
 Router 10.0.0.1    10.0.0.1    0x8000000c  511  0x22 0x3a09  96
 Router 10.0.0.2    10.0.0.2    0x8000000c  511  0x22 0x80b0  96
 Router 10.0.0.3    10.0.0.3    0x8000000d  510  0x22 0x448b 108
```

```
Router    10.0.0.4       10.0.0.4     0x8000000d  510  0x22 0xa1f5 108
Router   *10.0.0.5       10.0.0.5     0x8000000e  509  0x22 0x52d3  84
Router    10.0.0.6       10.0.0.6     0x8000000c  510  0x22 0x8977  84
Network   10.0.1.1       10.0.0.6     0x80000005 1852  0x22 0xa657  32
Network   10.0.1.5       10.0.0.6     0x80000005  966  0x22 0x7e7b  32
Network  *10.0.1.9       10.0.0.5     0x80000004  965  0x22 0x38c2  32
Network  *10.0.1.13      10.0.0.5     0x80000004 1851  0x22 0x1ed7  32
Network   10.0.1.17      10.0.0.3     0x80000005  966  0x22 0xeb09  32
Network   10.0.1.21      10.0.0.3     0x80000005 1852  0x22 0x995a  32
Network   10.0.1.26      10.0.0.2     0x80000004 1289  0x22 0x658c  32
Network   10.0.1.29      10.0.0.4     0x80000004 1292  0x22 0x5d8c  32
    OSPF AS SCOPE link state database
  Type      ID          Adv Rtr        Seq      Age  Opt  Cksum  Len
  Extern   0.0.0.0      10.0.0.2     0x80000001  716  0x22 0x9a0c  36
```

Because redundant gateways have been configured, the link-state database on r5 should contain two Type External entries for the default route to the Internet. One would come from r1 and the other from r2. Router r5 contains only the link-state advertisement (LSA) from r2. While we do have functionality, at this point we are lacking the type of redundancy necessary for a high availability network. It is time to take a closer look at the r1 OSPF configuration.

In this case, the default route to the Internet is a static route redistributed into OSPF using policy. The policy configuration is still in place on r1:

```
[edit]
lab@r1# show policy-options
policy-statement stat {
    term 1 {
        from {
            protocol static;
            route-filter 0.0.0.0/0 exact;
        }
        then accept;
    }
}
```

However, the export statement for redistribution is not in the OSPF configuration and needs to be added:

```
[edit]
lab@r1# show protocols ospf
area 0.0.0.0 {
    interface ge-0/1/1.0;
    interface ge-0/2/0.0 {
        passive;
    }
    interface ge-0/0/0.0;
    interface ge-0/0/1.0 {
        passive;
    }
    interface lo0.0 {
        passive;
    }
    interface ge-0/1/0.0 {
```

```
            passive;
        }
    }

    [edit]
    lab@r1# set protocols ospf export stat

    [edit]
    lab@r1# edit protocols ospf

    [edit protocols ospf]
    lab@r1# show
    export stat;
    area 0.0.0.0 {
        interface ge-0/1/1.0;
        interface ge-0/2/0.0 {
            passive;
        }
        interface ge-0/0/0.0;
        interface ge-0/0/1.0 {
            passive;
        }
        interface lo0.0 {
            passive;
        }
        interface ge-0/1/0.0 {
            passive;
        }
    }

    [edit protocols ospf]
    lab@r1# commit
    commit complete
```

All routers shown in Figure 8-1 should now show redundant gateway routes, one generated by r1 and the second generated by r2. A quick check of the OSPF database on a few routers confirms this is true. Router r1 looks good at this point:

```
    [edit]
    lab@r1# run show ospf database logical-router r1 | match 0.0.0.0
        OSPF link state database, Area 0.0.0.0
    Extern  *0.0.0.0      10.0.0.1      0x80000001  651  0x22 0xa007  36
    Extern   0.0.0.0      10.0.0.2      0x80000002  226  0x22 0x980d  36
```

Router r5 now has the LSA as well:

```
    [edit]
    lab@r5# run show ospf database | match 0.0.0.0
        OSPF link state database, Area 0.0.0.0
    Extern   0.0.0.0      10.0.0.1      0x80000001  682  0x22 0xa007  36
    Extern   0.0.0.0      10.0.0.2      0x80000002  255  0x22 0x980d  36
```

Router r3 also looks good:

```
    [edit]
    lab@r3# run show ospf database | match 0.0.0.0
        OSPF link state database, Area 0.0.0.0
```

```
Extern   0.0.0.0      10.0.0.1     0x80000001   690  0x22 0xa007  36
Extern   0.0.0.0      10.0.0.2     0x80000002   265  0x22 0x980d  36
```

 Here's an additional step for the big guys: in most enterprise networks, bringing up the IGP and verifying the default gateways leads directly to verifying functionality of services in the network; however, in carrier networks and some large enterprises, it is also necessary to confirm Border Gateway Protocol (BGP) functionality.

As with all verification procedures in this chapter, to accurately verify proper BGP routing, you need to have a good understanding of what is normal for the network. This requires significant preparation and data collection before the JUNOS upgrade begins. Without this data, you could end up spending a lot of time troubleshooting nonproblems while genuine problems are ignored... and Rome burns.

State of Existing Services

While upgrades are often performed to allow the addition of new services to a network, care must be taken not to damage existing services in the process. After all, networks do not exist just to give the mathematically savvy something to do at night. They exist to provide a service to customers. It is in fact services that justify the existence of networks. Keeping the issue of high availability front and center, post-upgrade verifications should extend into the services provided by the network.

Once routing and peering information is confirmed accurate, it is time to check the applications running in the production network. Generally speaking, the applications tend to be fairly immune to changes in the plumbing that carries their packets. However, sometimes there are major problems.

Change in DHCP-Relay Functionality

During a routine JUNOS upgrade a few years ago, a colleague discovered an undocumented change in functionality of the DHCP-relay feature in a Juniper product. In earlier releases of the operating system, DHCP-relay set a very high Time to Live (TTL) on Dynamic Host Configuration Protocol (DHCP) requests forwarded from host systems. Newer versions of the operating system set the TTL for a relayed request to 16, which dramatically reduced the distance DHCP requests could be pushed.

Because JUNOS was upgraded during a late-night maintenance window, very few users were on the network and the issue was not discovered until the next day. After much wringing of hands and gnashing of teeth, the root cause of the problem was discovered and an emergency fallback to the earlier JUNOS version was launched that morning.

The lesson of the story is to *always* confirm functionality all the way through the application layer. Although individual procedures are dictated by services deployed and range far too wide to try to list in this chapter, a good rule of thumb is to include testing

---

of existing services and baseline functionality in the first half of the maintenance window allotted for the upgrade.

Filesystems and Logs

By default, the JUNOS operating system stores event information pertinent to JUNOS upgrade attempts. *Install logs* capture information about JUNOS upgrade successes and failures, and are extremely useful in troubleshooting.

Install logfiles

Our first example is from a successful install on a device with multiple logical routers. The output generated by running this command on R105 is what you would want to see after an install:

```
lab@R105> show log install
2009-01-16 16:51:13 UTC mgd[4537]: /usr/libexec/ui/package
-X update /var/tmp/jbundle-9.0R4.5-domestic.tgz
<output>
Installing package '/var/tmp/jbundle-9.0R4.5-domestic.tgz' ...
...
rpdc: invalid daemon: profilerd
Restarting rmopd ...
Restarting spd ...
Restarting kmd ...
Saving package file in /var/sw/pkg/jbundle-9.0R4.5.tgz ...
Saving state for rollback ...
</output>
<package-result>0</package-result>
```

If a problem is encountered during the upgrade attempt, the install log indicates it with warnings and error messages. The command output from R106 indicates the install was aborted because of an incompatibility between configuration elements on the router and the version of JUNOS the administrator is attempting to load:

```
lab@R106> show log install.0.gz
2008-05-20 16:20:16 UTC mgd[5098]: /usr/libexec/ui/package
-X update -reboot /var/tmp/junos-jseries-8.2R4.5-domestic.tgz
<output>
NOTICE: Validating configuration against junos-jseries-8.2R4.5-domestic.tgz.
NOTICE: Use the 'no-validate' option to skip this if desired.
Checking compatibility with configuration
Initializing...
Verified manifest signed by PackageProduction_8_5_0
Using /var/tmp/junos-jseries-8.2R4.5-domestic.tgz
Checking junos requirements on /
Available space: 118262 require: 43134
mv: rename /cf/sbin/preinit to /cf/sbin/preinit.bak: No such file or directory
Verified manifest signed by PackageProduction_8_2_0
Hardware Database regeneration succeeded
Validating against /config/juniper.conf.gz
mgd: error: Check-out pass for Routing protocols process (
```

```
/usr/sbin/rpd) dumped core (0x86)
&lt;xnm:error xmlns="http://xml.juniper.net/xnm/1.1/xnm"
xmlns:xnm="http://xml.juniper.net/xnm/1.1/xnm"&gt;
&lt;source-daemon&gt;none&lt;/source-daemon&gt;
&lt;message&gt;Opening configuration database:
Could not open configuration database&lt;/message&gt;
&lt;/xnm:error&gt;
mgd: error: configuration check-out failed
Validation failed
WARNING: Current configuration not compatible with
/var/tmp/junos-jseries-8.2R4.5-domestic.tgz
</output>
<package-result>1</package-result>
```

Messages file

The *messages* file captures, among other things, protocol process and daemon restarts as well as changes in interface state and protocol peering state following an upgrade. This information can be useful when troubleshooting interfaces and neighbor relationships after an upgrade. The *messages* file also contains all event information for the boot process that must run after a software upgrade. This information can be used in conjunction with the output from the install log when troubleshooting or simply to confirm there are no upgrade-related issues.

The following is a sample of *messages* file output from a system boot event following a software upgrade. The `copyright` keyword is used for the find operation because it is part of the first message in a boot sequence:

```
lab@r105> show log messages | find copyright
Dec  8 13:27:21  r5-main /kernel: Copyright (c) 1996-2008,
Juniper Networks, Inc.
Dec  8 13:27:21  r5-main /kernel: All rights reserved.
Dec  8 13:27:21  r5-main /kernel: Copyright (c) 1992-2006 The FreeBSD Project.
Dec  8 13:27:21  r5-main /kernel: Copyright (c) 1979, 1980,
1983, 1986, 1988, 1989, 1991, 1992, 1993, 1994
Dec  8 13:27:21  r5-main /kernel:
The Regents of the University  of California. All rights reserved.
Dec  8 13:27:21  r5-main /kernel: JUNOS 9.0R4.5 #0: 2008-11-18 18:59:52 UTC
Dec  8 13:27:21  r5-main /kernel:     builder@nidhogg.juniper.net:
/volume/build/junos/9.0/release/9.0R4.5/obj-i386/sys/compile/JUNIPER
Dec  8 13:27:21  r5-main /kernel:
Timecounter "i8254" frequency 1193182 Hz quality 0
Dec  8 13:27:21  r5-main /kernel:
CPU: AMD Athlon(tm) Processor (908.09-MHz 686-class CPU)
Dec  8 13:27:21  r5-main /kernel:
Origin = "AuthenticAMD"  Id = 0x642  Stepping = 2
Dec  8 13:27:21  r5-main /kernel:
Features=0x183f9ff<FPU,VME,DE,PSE,TSC,MSR,
PAE,MCE,CX8,SEP,MTRR,PGE,MCA,CMOV,PAT,PSE36,MMX,FXSR>
Dec  8 13:27:21  r5-main /kernel:     AMD
Features=0xc0440800<SYSCALL,<b18>,MMX+,3DNow+,3DN
```

The previous command example showed creative use of the | operator in conjunction with an awareness of the content of the logfile. Similar information could be gathered by using the `show system boot-messages` command.

Syslog settings

In networks with high availability requirements, system logs are often stored on the local chassis and sent to a remote syslog server. The collection of syslog information from devices around the network allows you to correlate network events. This speeds up root-cause identification and issue resolution. Chapter 9 describes Network Time Protocol (NTP) functionality and shows how syslog analysis can benefit from having accurate timestamps on log entries.

Removal of Configuration Workarounds

At this point, all devices and services have been confirmed functional.

In many cases, the easiest way to remove configuration workarounds is to copy the saved configuration file, the one created before starting the JUNOS upgrade procedure, back to the router and load it into the candidate configuration file. If the file is stored on the chassis being upgraded, copying the file is unnecessary and you can simply load the configuration into the candidate file. Before launching a `commit`, it is critical to compare the candidate configuration with the active configuration to make sure the changes are desirable:

```
[edit]
lab@r1# load override pre-upgrade-r1
load complete

[edit]
lab@r1# show|compare
[edit]
-   chassis {
-       redundancy {
-           routing-engine 0 backup;
-           routing-engine 1 master;
-       }
-   }

[edit]
lab@r1# commit
commit complete
```

Fallback Procedures

The fallback process is specific to components, topology, and services enabled in the network, but all fallback procedures should include some flavor of the following elements:

- The fallback procedure should be documented and readily available before beginning the upgrade.
- The fallback procedure should include an estimated time duration needed to perform the fallback. General practice is to use only half of a maintenance window for a major change (such as a JUNOS upgrade). The other half of the maintenance window should be reserved for fallback time and to restore devices, connectivity, and services to the premaintenance window state. (As the old saying goes, "How far can a man walk into a forest? Halfway. If he goes further than halfway, he is in fact walking out of the forest.")
- The fallback procedure should identify one person, by name or title, responsible for initiating the fallback procedure. This one person will be responsible for deciding when things have Gone Horribly Wrong. If this occurs, the fallback procedure must be triggered.
- Because there are many degrees of functionality between Horribly Wrong and completely successful, one person should be responsible for determining whether any partial functionality achieved is an acceptable state.
- Because there are occasionally unintended consequences or side effects of reaching full functionality, one person must determine whether any of them are a threat and merit a fallback.

Applicability

The recommendations outlined in this chapter and in Chapter 6 are by no means specific to software upgrades. Any network with high availability requirements should follow a similar planning, execution, and verification pattern for every network change. As we mentioned earlier in the chapter, following a network change, begin at the Physical layer on the device that has been upgraded and expand upward through the OSI model and outward through the rest of the network.

CHAPTER 9

Monitoring for High Availability

High availability is not something that is stumbled upon accidentally. Planning, deploying, and maintaining a network requires a staff of hard-working individuals who actually know what they are doing. The tasks required to maintain high availability in your network do not end with your configuration of Virtual Router Redundancy Protocol (VRRP), Graceful Restart (GR), or routing engine (RE) failover, but encompass the ability of your personnel to monitor the network and head off any errors that could degrade service.

Through the use of logging, Simple Network Management Protocol (SNMP), and traffic flow monitoring, the resourceful network engineer is able to diagnose issues that could lead to network downtime, and plan for a solution to the issue.

I Love Logs

This was actually a bumper sticker that came as swag from a logging software company that sat on a coworker's desk for more than a year—no one really did love logs enough to put it on his car. Logging is one of those necessary evils that exist in a network. Monitoring logs is essential to maintaining high availability in the network, but without proper planning and design of a logging system, it can quickly become a bane of those running the network.

In looking at developing a logging posture that enables increased high availability in your network, it is important to understand the basics of logging and how a little planning can make logging not only more efficient, but also far more effective in achieving your goals of high availability.

Syslog Overview

From its start in the early 1980s to its eventual formalization in 2001 to the current day, syslog has been the standard on which many network monitoring solutions are built. The flexibility and ubiquity of the protocol have allowed networking device makers and operating system manufacturers to create frameworks with which to transmit the minutest events occurring on their systems.

> In its most simplistic terms, the syslog protocol provides a transport to allow a machine to send event notification messages across IP networks to event message collectors, also known as syslog servers. Since each process, application, and operating system was written somewhat independently, there is little uniformity to the content of syslog messages. For this reason, no assumption is made upon the formatting or contents of the messages. The protocol is simply designed to transport these event messages.
>
> —RFC 3164, August 2001

With equipment makers relying on the use of syslog in the network to provide information to network engineers, sometimes syslog collection systems either cannot handle the load of messages, or can handle the load but cannot provide useful information. If your network is anything like most networks, it is possible for the equipment to create thousands upon thousands of messages per second. Those in charge of monitoring these networks with the thousands of messages find it necessary to increase the speed of their syslog servers and the size of the storage devices where the collected messages are saved.

The idea of thousands of syslog messages sitting on a disk supports the goals of high availability within your network, but they are merely messages. To gain any insight into how your network is working, you must collate the data and gauge the health of the network and its equipment.

Some network engineers swear by the magic of grep; they are able to pull out any network information that is needed for maintaining high availability. Others ignore logs altogether and rely on the use of SNMP or ping to monitor the health of the network. Still others purchase multimillion-dollar systems touted to be able to cure all logging woes, only to find that the systems do an excellent job of correlating the security data but do nothing with data for the kernel processes.

Through the use of the syslog framework and JUNOS software, you can deploy well-planned and efficient logging mechanisms in your network. Though no rules are made concerning the format of the content of the individual syslog messages themselves, according to the RFC, the syslog packets must be divided into three parts:

PRI (Priority)
Identifies the priority of the syslog message by combining the facility and severity of the message into either a one-digit, two-digit, or three-digit integer bounded by the open and close brackets; for example, <165>.

Header
Contains the timestamp and either the hostname or the IP address of the device originating the message.

MSG (Message)
> Contains the actual event that is being reported by the syslog message. Though the message can be in any format, containing visible characters, it must not be so long as to make the total syslog packet longer than 1,024 bytes.

Using the information in the various parts of the syslog message, you can filter messages, either when they are transmitted from the device or at your collection agent, to create a system in which engineers, technicians, and managers receive only the information necessary for assigned tasks to ensure high availability.

Facilities

The facilities portion of the PRI indicates from which function, daemon, or process an event was spawned. This facility indicator can be used to sort and collate the messages so that they are delivered to collectors that are monitored by engineers responsible for that functional area. As with the hardware and software of JUNOS, this division of labor (this time among engineers) allows for a more efficient use of resources for the protection of high availability.

Table 9-1 identifies the daemons and processes within JUNOS that can spawn event messages.

Table 9-1. JUNOS system logging facilities

Facility	Type of event or error	Potential high availability issues avoided
any	Messages from all facilities	
authorization	Authentication and authorization attempts	Unauthorized access that could lead to accidental or intentional network downtime
change-log	Changes to the JUNOS configuration	Unexpected configuration changes made intentionally or accidentally
conflict-log	Specified configuration is invalid on the routing platform	
daemon	Actions performed or errors encountered by system processes	Software errors in the RE leading to network downtime
dfc	Dynamic flow capture	
firewall	Packet filtering actions performed by a firewall filter	Network attacks that could lead to downtime
ftp	Actions performed or errors encountered by the FTP process	
interactive-commands	Commands issued at the JUNOS command-line interface (CLI) prompt or invoked by a client application such as a JUNOScript or NETCONF client	Commands that accidentally or intentionally cause network downtime
kernel	Actions performed or errors encountered by the JUNOS kernel	Hardware or software errors in the RE leading to network downtime

Facility	Type of event or error	Potential high availability issues avoided
pfe	Actions performed or errors encountered by the Packet Forwarding Engine (PFE)	Hardware or software errors or failures leading to reduced or no forwarding and network downtime
user	Actions performed or errors encountered in the user space processes	Software errors in the RE leading to network downtime

The JUNOS CLI allows these facilities to be used in determining to which syslog collector the messages are sent.

Severity

To further pare down the amount of information that individual technicians must analyze, it is possible to filter the forwarding of messages by *severity* level in the PRI field. Using the severity level, syslog messages from your network equipment can be sent to either real-time monitoring stations—for the most critical levels—or systems that provide archiving for regulatory compliance or possible forensic tasks. The severity levels of messages within JUNOS are based on the severity conditions defined in RFC 3641 and appear in Table 9-2.

Table 9-2. Syslog messaging severity

Severity level	Description
any	Includes all severity levels
none	Disables logging of the associated facility
emergency	System panic or other condition that causes the network device to stop functioning
alert	Conditions that require immediate correction, such as a corrupted system database
critical	Critical conditions, such as hard drive errors
error	Error conditions that generally have less serious consequences than errors in the emergency, alert, and critical levels
warning	Conditions that warrant monitoring
notice	Conditions that are not errors but might warrant special handling
info	Events or nonerror conditions of interest

When critical messages are sent to real-time monitoring and less important messages are sent to archival or long-term correlation systems, technicians within your network can focus on the current state of the network and events that could possibly degrade high availability.

Header and MSG parts

Though the network devices can filter on the facilities and severity information (the PRI part of the syslog message), the Header and MSG portions are normally used to filter messages within the collectors. The Header is used for quick correlation of the devices from which messages were received and the time period in which the messages were created.

Because the MSG part of the syslog messages is not bound by any rules, except that it must use visible characters and must not make the total syslog message more than 1,024 bytes, it is where the monitoring software vendors attempt to create the most effective algorithms and regular expressions for parsing the messages and correlating the events reported.

Syslog Planning

Without proper planning, the syslog messages produced by equipment in your network can quickly overrun even the most robust logging system. It's not just unnecessary to send all syslog messages to a single device; it's ill-advised. It is almost impossible to do any real analysis, planning, or outage prevention when attempting to parse the millions of messages that may be received within a day. To properly monitor your network to maintain high availability, you must choose the collector to which syslog messages are sent.

Modern network support models normally break technicians into functional areas based on their expertise, such as security, routing, or management. To allow these groups to perform efficiently, many have their own syslog collectors with special properties. Some examples of these organizations and software systems include:

- A Security Information Management (SIM or SIEM) system to collect and collate security and authentication events located in the security group
- A Configuration Management auditing system to collect information on configuration changes or errors in the network located with the network administrators responsible for managing the overall health of the network
- An event correlation system collecting critical chassis or processing syslog events and forwarding them to visual displays or network monitoring equipment in the first-tier technicians' area
- A baselining and trending system set up for the senior engineering team involved with long-term planning and network expansion
- An archive server that receives all syslog messages, and archives, compresses, and stores the messages for possible forensics or public disclosure information

Table 9-3 shows a planning layout that could be used to develop a logging architecture in a network. By carefully examining the facilities supported by JUNOS and the functional areas of network teams, it is possible to eliminate logging bottlenecks that prevent technicians and engineers from discovering events that can lead to degradation in the network and reduce high availability.

Table 9-3. Syslog planning example

Facility	NOC	Security	Network admin	Senior engineers	Archive
any	Emergency		Critical		Any
authorization		Warning	Any		Any
change-log				Any	Any
conflict-log				Any	Any
daemon	Alert		Critical	Warning	Any
firewall		Warning			Any
ftp					Any
interactive-commands				Any	Any
kernel	Alert		Critical	Warning	Any
pfe	Alert		Critical	Warning	Any
user	Alert		Critical	Warning	Any

Using a coherent and logical plan for syslog forwarding, it is possible to turn syslog into a far more useful tool for maintaining high availability.

Pitfalls

Several pitfalls can prevent the syslog in your network from providing the information you need for high availability:

- Collection stations can alter the format of data into proprietary formats; SIM systems are notorious for this. The changed format may not be understood by a division's software solution or may not be used legally during computer forensic investigations. When forwarding messages from a network device, it may be necessary to forward security messages to multiple locations so that an unaltered record is kept.

- Some network management software attempts to write all syslog messages into a relational database, both changing the format and running into issues with transactional rates on the database. In this situation, multiple messages should be forwarded.

- With more and more laws and regulations on network information retention, it is necessary to truly gauge the amount of storage necessary for your system and build a syslog solution that can handle years of syslog messages.

- Syslog forwarding over the network and the practice of not using a secured Out of Band (OoB) management network, such as the RE management interface, allows nefarious people in the network to sniff the unencrypted syslog traffic and conduct reconnaissance.

Implementing Syslog

JUNOS software supports standard syslog, as well as structured format syslog, which is included in Internet Engineering Task Force (IETF) draft documents. Table 9-4 shows the default settings and the overriding statements for the syslog daemon within the JUNOS operating system. By understanding the default operation of the network equipment and how to use the overriding statements, it is possible to develop a logging policy that supports your network's high availability stance.

Table 9-4. JUNOS syslog defaults

Setting	Default	Overrides

Alternative facility for message forwarded to a remote machine	`change-log: local6`
	`conflict-log: local5`
	`dfc: local1`
	`firewall: local3`
	`interactive-commands: local7`
	`pfe: local4`
		Facility overrides can be used to enable more efficient parsing of logs at the collector

Format of messages logged to a file	Standard JUNOS format, based on Unix format	Can be used to select IETF draft structured syslog messages, where appropriate
Maximum number of files in the archived set	10	Can be used to adjust the number of files and file size based on the network situation
Maximum size of logfile	J Series: 128 KB M Series, MX Series, and T Series: 1 MB TX Matrix: 10 MB	Can be used to adjust the number of files and file size based on the network situation
Timestamp format	Month, date, hour, minute, second	Can be used to add milliseconds to the timestamp, which can aid in troubleshooting
Users who can read logfiles	Root user and users with JUNOS maintenance permission	Can allow all users to read select logging files on the network device

In configuring your syslog solution, it will probably be necessary to change some of the default settings to allow for the most efficient use of network resources, but this can easily be done using the JUNOS CLI.

Sample configuration

Using the planning table featured previously, and the JUNOS commands for filtering and forwarding messages, it is possible to deploy a well-planned syslog environment. The following is an example configuration of a filtered syslog environment:

```
system {
    syslog {
        archive size 10240000 files 1000 world-readable;
        user * {
            any emergency;
        }
        host security.example.com {
            authorization warning;
            firewall warning;
        }
        host noc.example.com {
            any emergency;
            daemon alert;
            kernel alert;
            user alert;
            pfe alert;
        }
        host netad.example.com {
            authorization any;
            daemon critical;
            kernel critical;
            user critical;
            pfe critical;
        }
        host engineering.example.com {
            daemon warning;
            kernel warning;
            user warning;
            pfe warning;
            conflict-log any;
            change-log any;
            interactive-commands any;
        }
        host archive.example.com {
            any any;
            log-prefix example.example.com;
        }
        file messages {
            any notice;
            authorization info;
        }
        file interactive-commands {
            interactive-commands any;
        }
        file engineering {
            daemon any;
            kernel any;
            pfe any;
            archive size 10240000 files 1000 no-world-readable;
```

```
            structured-data {
                brief;
            }
        }
        time-format year millisecond;
    }
}
```

As in the previous example, the syslog messages are filtered to their respective collectors within the network management structure. There is also a file to be created called *engineering* that will be used to gather daemon, kernel, and PFE information in the RFC draft structured format to be used by the senior engineers for deep dives into hardware and software process performance. With this kind of syslog design, it is much easier for individual groups to parse and use syslog files to ensure network uptime. The previous syslog configuration allows for the following:

- All warnings either concerning authentication attempts against the device or flagged by the firewall processes will be sent to the syslog server *security.example.com*.
- Any syslog message at the emergency level, or any message at the alert level that relates to system processes and daemons, will be sent to the syslog server *noc.example.com*.
- The syslog server *netad.example.com* will receive any messages regarding authentication attempts against the device and any critical messages concerning the software processes.
- The senior engineering syslog server at *engineering.example.com* will receive warnings concerning the software processes on the device, as well as any messages concerning configuration changes and commands used on the device.
- The syslog server at *archive.example.com* receives all messages from the device for storage.

Monitoring syslog

Even with the carefully developed structure of logging in place, it is nearly impossible to use syslog as the one and only source of network management. To ensure high availability in your network, syslog must be used in conjunction with other management tools.

Simple Network Management Protocol

When logging is a passive endeavor, the collection stations merely sit, waiting for messages to be forwarded by the network devices. Simple Network Management Protocol (SNMP) provides an active exchange of information between network management stations and the network equipment. Building on the foundation of basic well-planned syslog architecture, SNMP can be used to gather and monitor information concerning high availability.

SNMP Overview

If you read RFC 1157, "A Simple Network Management Protocol (SNMP)," you might wonder why it's considered a "simple" network management protocol. However, a closer look at the actual implementation and use of SNMP reveals that it is a fairly simple protocol. The protocol relies on the use of SNMP agents within the networking equipment; these agents understand a common data set and report it to a collection or Network Management Station (NMS). Within SNMP, the agent can both receive and transmit data, thus allowing the NMS to actively pull information from the devices throughout the network. To ensure that equipment from multiple vendors can work with an NMS, the data for managing network equipment is designed into a standardized hierarchy called the Management Information Base (MIB). The MIB uses a tree-based structure: similar data objects are grouped together, and each leaf of the tree is labeled with an Object Identifier (OID).

Using OIDs to identify the information to be processed, SNMP communicates between the agents in one of the following methods:

Get Request
> Used by the management station to request specific information from the networking device. One of three types of "gets" may be used:

> Get
>> Gets a single piece of data related to a single OID; the simplest read function

> Get-Next
>> Gets an iterative series of data based on multiple OIDs

> Get-Bulk
>> A faster version of Get-Next included in Version 2 of SNMP

Set Request
> The basic write command; used to change information on a network device based on a specific OID.

Notification
> Asymmetric message sent from the agent to the Network Management Station. Two forms of notification exist within SNMP:

> *Trap*
>> The best-known notification, and does not require acknowledgment from the NMS

> *Inform*
>> Notifies the NMS of an issue and requires acknowledgment from the NMS

To provide a basic form of security, SNMPv2 uses community strings, or passwords, to identify which NMS can request information from or write information to a network device. The issue is that this community string is passed as plain text, allowing it to be easily sniffed. SNMPv3 is built on a secure architecture with data integrity and authentication built in, to solve some of the issues with SNMPv2.

To prevent network downtime caused by someone sniffing SNMP communities and using them to do network reconnaissance or make changes to network devices, any network concerned with high availability should use SNMPv3, if SNMP is used at all.

 Not only does SNMPv3 provide encryption and authentication, but it also moves away from the community string concept. Hopefully, the additional configuration will allow people to move away from the public/private community strings that are the default on so many pieces of equipment.

SNMPv3 not only supports authentication and encryption, but also uses a user-based security model (USM) for message security and a view-based access control model (VACM) for controlling access to individual MIB strings. Within the SNMPv3 architecture, the USM specifies the authentication and encryption methods used for transporting the data from the agent to the NSM, and vice versa. The VACM is an access-control model that allows you to apply highly granular security policies on which groups can view and change particular MIBs; it can also be used to determine which groups receive notifications.

Notification categories

The simplest form of filtering notifications within the SNMP architecture is through the use of the *category*. Similar to facilities in syslog, categories divide the notifications from a piece of network equipment into functional areas. Using categories can ensure that only NMS devices that require certain information receive that information. Table 9-5 lists the categories that can be used in the SNMP configuration to filter trap messages.

Table 9-5. JUNOS SNMP categories

Category	Description	Potential high availability issues avoided
Authentication	Authentication failures	Attempts at unauthorized access
Chassis	Chassis or environmental notifications	Hardware issues causing network downtime
Configuration	Configuration changes	Intentional or accidental issues causing network downtime
Link	Link-related notifications (such as up/down transitions)	Network device links causing network downtime
Remote operations	Notification concerning remote operations	
Rmon-alarms	Alarms for RMON events	Unexpected or unusual traffic peaks that could indicate other issues in the network

Category	Description	Potential high availability issues avoided
Routing	Routing protocol notifications	Intentional or accidental protocol changes, events, or peerings that could lead to network downtime
SONET-alarms	SONET/SDH notifications	Link outages on SONET networks
Start-up	Cold/warm start notifications	Indications of network reboots
VRRP	Notifications concerning VRRP	Errors with VRRP that could lead to routing issues and network downtime

RMON alarms

In addition to the standard SNMP capabilities, JUNOS uses SNMP in conjunction with Remote Monitoring (RMON) to allow for protocol and traffic analysis. Using MIBs and SNMP as a transport mechanism, you can provide specific traffic data on interfaces, hosts, or specific protocols. Using the RMON alarms, network managers can set thresholds for traffic and be alerted when they are exceeded; alarms can be set for routing, network, or security issues that may affect high availability.

Health monitoring

One of the major factors that contribute to downtime occurs when hardware failure compromises the network devices. Normally, it is possible to diagnose and prevent hardware, and possibly software, errors by monitoring the health of the system. In the past, network health monitoring was performed with the NMS, which polled each network device for system health parameters, such as CPU usage. However, given the size and complexity of current networks, it is now easier for the network devices to alert the NMS of an issue. The JUNOS software monitors the values that are important for maintaining system health and can be configured to alert your network managers when specific thresholds are met. Table 9-6 lists the MIB objects used by the JUNOS health monitoring process.

Table 9-6. Health monitoring objects

Monitored objects	Description
jnxHrStoragePercentUsed.1	Gives the percent of the root filesystem on /dev/ad0s1a in use
jnxHrStoragePercentUsed.2	Gives the percent of the /config filesystem on /dev/ad0s1e in use
jnxOperatingCPU(RE0)	Monitors the CPU usage for RE0
jnxOperatingCPU(RE1)	Monitors the CPU usage for RE1
jnxOperatingBuffer(RE0)	Monitors the amount of memory available on RE0
jnxOperatingBuffer(RE1)	Monitors the amount of memory available on RE1
sysApplElmtRunCPU	Monitors the memory usage for each JUNOS process

SNMP Planning

Just as with syslog, it is best to divide the data received from the network and send it to only the groups that are responsible for a particular area. Because SNMP allows an agent to both send and receive data, it is necessary to do more planning to ensure that notifications are filtered and that get and set requests are secured into functional areas. Table 9-7 provides basic planning necessary to ensure that SNMP functions securely. It also takes into consideration that not all divisions have software that supports SNMPv3.

Table 9-7. SNMP planning

Category	NOC	Security	Network admin	Senior engineers
Authentication		SNMPv3	SNMPv2 traps	SNMPv3
Chassis	SNMPv2 traps	VACM		VACM
Configuration			SNMPv2 traps	
Link	SNMPv2 traps			
Remote operations				
Rmon-alarm				
Routing	SNMPv2 traps			
SONET-alarms	SNMPv2 traps			
Start-up	SNMPv2 traps		SNMPv2 traps	
VRRP	SNMPv2 traps			
RMON	SNMPv2 traps		SNMPv2 traps	
Health monitoring	SNMPv2 traps		SNMPv2 traps	

Implementing SNMP

Though JUNOS software supports all versions of SNMP, it is best to use SNMPv3 because of its security features. In some networks, though, some of the monitoring tools do not operate using SNMPv3. When implementing SNMP in a network, the systems that support SNMPv3 should be configured for that, and SNMPv2c should be used only for traps.

SNMPv3

The following sample configuration uses SNMPv3 to provide security for network management traffic, but also divides the traffic from the network devices to the appropriate work locations. Using both USM and VACM, it is possible to provide granular filtering of SNMP access. Using the view commands, it is also much easier to create a filtered view of the MIB tree for each user or group:

```
[edit snmp]

description "Example.com Router";
location "Example.com Headquarters, WA";
contact "Mr. Example, 555-555-5555";
interface fxp0.0;
filter-duplicates;
v3 {
    usm {
        local-engine {
            user engineering {
                authentication-sha {
                    authentication-key "$9$Nj-VYUj
"; ## SECRET-DATA
                }
                privacy-aes128 {
                    privacy-key "$9$X01xWYaJ
"; ## SECRET-DATA
                }
            }
            user security {
                authentication-sha {
                    authentication-key "$9$61jZAO1
"; ## SECRET-DATA
                }
                privacy-aes128 {
                    privacy-key "$9$GNUqmn/
"; ## SECRET-DATA
                }
            }
        }
    }
    vacm {
        security-to-group {
            security-model usm {
                security-name engineering {
                    group engineering;
                }
                security-name seucurity {
                    group security;
                }
            }
        }
        access {
            group engineering {
                default-context-prefix {
                    security-model usm {
                        security-level privacy {
                            read-view engineering;
                            write-view engineering;
                            notify-view engineering;
                        }
                    }
                }
            }
```

```
            group security {
                default-context-prefix {
                    security-model usm {
                        security-level privacy {
                            read-view security;
                            write-view security;
                            notify-view security;
                        }
                    }
                }
            }
        }
    }
    target-address engineering {
        address 10.0.0.1;
        timeout 10;
        retry-count 3;
        tag-list "noc engineering";
        address-mask 255.255.255.0;
        target-parameters engineering;
    }
    target-address noc {
        address 10.0.0.2;
        tag-list noc;
        address-mask 255.255.255.0;
        target-parameters noc;
    }
    notify engineering {
        type inform;
        tag engineering;
    }
    notify noc {
        type inform;
        tag noc;
    }
}
engine-id {
    use-mac-address;
}
view noc {
    /* INTERFACE MIBS */
    oid 1.3.6.1.2.1.2 include;
    /* OSPF MIBS */
    oid 1.3.6.1.2.1.14 include;
    /* BGP MIBS */
    oid 1.3.6.1.2.1.15 include;
}
view engineering {
    /* IP MIBS */
    oid 1.3.6.1.2.1.4 include;
    /* OSPF MIBS */
    oid 1.3.6.1.2.1.14 include;
    /* BGP MIBS */
    oid 1.3.6.1.2.1.15 include;
}
```

```
view security {
    /* IANA Secuirty MIBS */
    oid 1.3.6.1.5 include;
}
community networkcomm {
    view noc;
    authorization read-only;
}
trap-group noc {
    version v2;
    categories {
        chassis;
        link;
        routing;
        rmon-alarm;
        vrrp-events;
        sonet-alarms;
    }
    targets {
        10.0.0.2;
    }
}
trap-group network-admin {
    version v2;
    categories {
        authentication;
        startup;
        rmon-alarm;
        configuration;
    }
    targets {
        10.0.0.33;
    }
```

Though the configuration of SNMPv3 looks rather daunting in this example, it provides a much more secure and efficient use of SNMP in your network. The use of commands that limit the interfaces on which SNMP is accepted and transmitted allows for the creation of a secured management network. For organizations that have not yet embraced SNMPv3, JUNOS supports all versions of SNMP simultaneously. Other notable features of this configuration that allow for increased visibility into high availability issues include the following:

- Though very basic, the configuration of location and contact in SNMP is invaluable when it comes to troubleshooting and monitoring network uptime.

- Using views, the networking equipment will restrict the use of MIBs to certain groups, thus allowing the division of tasks and resources.

- Using trap groups for SNMPv2, it is possible to restrict the categories of SNMP traps sent to specific workstations.

- As you can see in the example, VACM can be used with the view to further defend the SNMP architecture and provide access to MIBs that are necessary for personnel to monitor network high availability.

RMON

With basic SNMP configured, it is possible to add RMON events to ensure that any large changes in network traffic flows will be alerted to the appropriate network management personnel. Because RMON works with SNMP to alert management stations to changes in network traffic, it is configured under the SNMP hierarchy. In addition to the basic RMON thresholds and monitoring, the event must be configured to alert the network management stations. The following configuration is a basic monitoring of traffic flowing into the fxp0 interface of the RE:

```
[edit snmp]

community networkcomm {
    view noc;
    authorization read-only;
}
rmon {
    alarm 300 {
        description "Input Traffic on fxp0";
        interval 10;
        /* OID for Interface Input Octets for fxp0 */
        variable .1.3.6.1.2.1.2.2.1.10.1;
        sample-type delta-value;
        startup-alarm rising-or-falling-alarm;
        rising-threshold 2000;
        falling-threshold 15000;
        rising-event-index 400;
        falling-event-index 300;
    }
    event 400 {
        type log-and-trap;
        community networkcomm;
    }
    event 300 {
        type log-and-trap;
        community networkcomm;
    }
}
```

In this configuration, we have set up a community name to which the trap will be sent, and the OID that reads input octets on an interface is used. The monitoring for this example is to be run at an interval of 10 seconds and will take a delta of the sample for its calculations. When the octet input increases by more than 2,000 within the interval, the RMON process will write a message to syslog and send a trap.

Health monitoring

The configuration of health monitoring within JUNOS is not nearly as complex as that of RMON, because the OIDs are already configured for the purpose. In the following example, notice that only the interval, the time between samples, and the rising and falling thresholds (in percentages) need to be configured. Events have already been defined for health monitoring, so they are also not necessary in the configuration.

```
[edit snmp]
health-monitor {
    interval 600;
    rising-threshold 75;
    falling-threshold 85;
}
```

In this example, the `health-monitor` MIBs are queried every 10 minutes and an alarm is set to go off if the usage of a device increases by 75% or drops by 85%. By monitoring these swings in usage, network engineers are able to diagnose network device issues early.

Pitfalls

To avoid degradation to your network's high availability, it is necessary to avoid the following pitfalls when configuring SNMP, RMON, and health monitoring:

- Default community strings in SNMPv1 and SNMPv2 exist in many networks, even though we all know better. These default strings can be used to perform reconnaissance on networks with ease, which could result in the worst kind of network downtime.

- In-band management of networking equipment not only allows the less secure SNMP traps to traverse equipment that could be sniffed, but also allows an entrance point for people looking to scout out your network.

- Insane thresholds are one of the most damaging aspects of network monitoring. Deploying thresholds that are activated at small changes in traffic can lead to storms of events being reported, and eventually to network managers ignoring those events, even if one of them is an event leading to network downtime.

Traffic Monitoring

Besides monitoring the hardware and software itself to determine the health of the network, it is also possible to use the traffic flowing through the network and the routing updates received by the network equipment to not only determine the current state of the network, but also create a baseline that can be used to determine issues that in the future could lead to network outages. It is possible to deploy JUNOS or software-based tools to monitor the traffic flows and routing updates and deliver them in a fashion that is usable to network engineers.

Traffic Monitoring Overview

When it comes to the high availability of your network, the purpose of traffic monitoring is twofold:

- To ensure that throughput levels are known and a baseline is created to ensure that anomalies in traffic flow, which could indicate network outages or degradation, are detected as quickly as possible
- To ensure that routing protocols are behaving correctly internally to the network, as well as ensure that neighboring Autonomous Systems (ASs) are not affecting your high availability by sending bogus routing announcements

Though some network engineers never worry about how their daemons are coupled or how their operating system works, it's common to have software installed on machines that seems to steal resources from all the other software—locking up the computer and forcing a reboot. You don't want a mistake in your SNMP process stealing resources from Border Gateway Protocol (BGP) and possibly crashing the router.

 Though political requirements may necessitate proprietary software because it can be supported, the open source community has many traffic and routing monitoring tools that can be used at least for research, if not as the core of your network's traffic monitoring.

When focusing on high availability, you want the tools you introduce into your network to not only be functional, but also provide useful information. Many of the traffic monitoring and routing monitoring tools require secondary software to make the information usable. In developing the traffic monitoring stance for your network, the following protocols are available:

- Traffic sampling and aggregation can be used to provide traffic and protocol analysis across network devices. JUNOS can provide the aggregated sampling information to any system running the cflowd application provided by the Cooperative Association for Internet Data Analysis (CAIDA; *http://www.caida.org*). The data from cflowd can be fed to various open source and proprietary software that can analyze the data and produce graphical representations of it.
- JUNOS supports various counters to monitor and analyze throughput of links and traffic flows. Firewall filters within JUNOS can be configured to count or sample specific flows of traffic.
- Route monitoring can be introduced into the network in many ways. The simplest introduction of monitoring routing protocols includes the use of syslog and SNMP to alert network managers of events, such as adjacency changes.

Traffic Monitoring Planning

The tools used in monitoring traffic in your network are determined by the type of analysis that is to take place. JUNOS supports traffic flow sampling and aggregation, as well as firewall and class usage counters. Syslog, as well as routing monitoring software, can be used to provide a view of the routing health in the network. Table 9-8 shows an example of traffic flow planning.

Table 9-8. Traffic flow planning

Category	Description	Potential high availability issues avoided
cflowd	Analyze protocol and traffic	Anomalies affecting equipment throughput or symptoms of other errors
Class usage	Count traffic based on source or destination addresses	Anomalies in customer networks indicating errors that could lead to network outages
Syslog and SNMP	Monitor routing protocols for changes or errors	Routing outages causing network downtime
Routing software	Monitor advertisements and overall routing	Prefix hijacking by other ASs

Implementing Traffic Monitoring

One important way to ensure high availability in the network is to monitor traffic and traffic types flowing through the network. JUNOS software supports standard traffic monitoring features.

Packet sampling

Packet sampling is a technique for analyzing and characterizing flows of traffic in your network by recording the IP headers of a small percentage of packets that flow through the network device. These sampled packets are then used to create a generalized view of the protocol and traffic types traversing the system. The results of the packet sampling can be viewed using open source software from either *http://www.splintered.net/ sw/flow-tools/* or *http://www.caida.org/*.

In the following code snippet, the device is configured to sample traffic and send it in a format that is readable by the cflowd software. The sampling is configured within JUNOS by creating a firewall filter to sample the traffic, applying it to an interface, and setting up forwarding options to set sampling style and aggregation options:

```
[edit forwarding-options]
sampling {
    input {
        family inet {
            rate 1000;
            run-length 20;
            max-packets-per-second 100;
        }
    }
    output {
        cflowd 10.0.0.1 {
            port 2055;
            source-address 10.0.0.200;
            version 8;
            local-dump;
```

```
        }
        flow-inactive-timeout 50;
        flow-active-timeout 60;
    }
[edit firewall]
family inet {
    filter sampling {
        term sample {
            then {
                sample;
                accept;
            }
        }
    }
}
[edit interfaces]
ge-0/1/0 {
    unit 0 {
        family inet {
            filter {
                input sampling;
            }
        }
    }
}
```

In the configuration sample for packet sampling, the filter is designed to sample and accept all traffic that is being input on the Gigabit Ethernet interface. The sampling is set up to trigger on the first packet out of every 1,000 that match the filter and then collect the 20 packets after that. The information from the aggregated packets is sent to a system running cflowd at the address 10.0.0.1. On the system running cflowd, software such as ntop can be loaded to graph the data to make protocol analysis easier for network managers.

Port mirroring

Unlike packet sampling—which records only key IP header information—port mirroring forwards a copy of the entire packet. With the entire packet being forwarded, very detailed analysis of traffic flows and protocol usage can be performed. Port mirroring is configured in a similar fashion to packet sampling, as you can see here:

```
[edit forwarding-options]
port-mirroring {
    input {
        family inet {
            rate 1000;
            run-length 20;
        }
    }
    output {
        interface ge-1/0/3 {
            next-hop 10.0.0.1;
        }
```

```
}
[edit firewall]
family inet {
    filter mirror {
        term mirror {
            then {
                mirror;
                accept;
            }
        }
    }
}

[edit interfaces]
ge-0/1/0 {
    unit 0 {
        family inet {
            filter {
                input mirror;
            }
        }
    }
}
```

The preceding port mirroring configuration also triggers on the first of every 1,000 packets and forwards the following 20 packets. The major difference is that the entire packet is copied and not just the header information. A packet capture tool, such as Wireshark, can be used to collect the packets.

Counters

One way to ensure high availability is to maintain packet counts based on the entry and exit points for traffic traversing your network. By monitoring network throughputs, anomalies in traffic flows can be revealed and preventive maintenance or reconfiguration can be performed. JUNOS software allows you to introduce both source class usage (SCU) and destination class usage (DCU) to perform accounting on specific source and destination addresses. Configuration of SCUs and DCUs requires configuration of policies, accounting options, and routing options, and they need to be applied to an interface:

```
[edit accounting-options]
file Cust1-usage {
    size 1000k;
    files 50;
    transfer-interval 10;
}
class-usage-profile Customer1 {
    file Cust1-usage;
    interval 30;
    source-classes {
        customer-SCU;
    }
}
```

```
[edit policy-options]
policy-statement Customer-SCU {
    term DMZ {
        from {
            route-filter 192.168.2.0/24 orlonger;
        }
        then source-class customer-SCU;
    }
}

[edit routing-options]
forwarding-table {
    export Customer-SCU;
}

[edit interface ge-1/0/0]
unit 0 {
    family inet {
        accounting {
            source-class-usage {
                input;
            }
        }
    }
}
```

In this example, a Source Class Usage report has been created for packets entering the ge-1/0/0 interface with a source address of 192.168.2.0. The accounting information will be written to a file named *Cust1-usage*, which can be sent to an archive server.

Route Monitoring

High availability is an all-encompassing task, which is affected not only by local hardware or software, but also by the Internet at large and your network peering connections. In February 2008, ISPs in Pakistan began advertising the addresses for YouTube and stopped traffic from reaching the services offered by them. Now, though YouTube had nothing to do with this outage, it is YouTube's high availability stance that was damaged. Many times, network operators do not consider the effects of others' configuration errors, intentional or accidental, on their high availability, but because of the interconnected nature of the Internet, they should.

Route Views

Though JUNOS has many internal tools to ensure that high availability is maintained, there is a great brain pool of network operators in the world who have developed software and scripts for monitoring networks. Many of these tools are open source and are free, as in beer and speech, and can be used as just a single facet of network monitoring. One source for these tools is the Route Views project (*http://www.routeviews.org*), which is provided by the University of Oregon.

Cyclops

The University of California at Los Angeles offers the Cyclops network auditing tool which allows ISPs and enterprises to monitor the behavior of their routes advertised into the Internet routing tables. The tool can be used to monitor against hijacking of an AS number or prefix to ensure that traffic is routed properly to your network. Cyclops can be found at *http://cyclops.cs.ucla.edu/*.

BGPlayer

BGPlayer is a monitoring tool for BGP route advertisements that would have been helpful during the YouTube incident. It provides a graphical representation of how routes are being learned in a network. Based out of Roma Tre University in Rome, the tool is designed to peer with an internal BGP neighbor to receive all the BGP updates from the device. Once a database of routes is built, the routes can be displayed in a matrix showing from where the advertisement was received and how it is advertised to other peers.

After downloading the software, it is possible to configure the network devices to use the computer on which it is running as a BGP route reflector client. To prevent routes from being returned from the server running BGPlayer, a policy can be written to prevent importing routes from the server:

```
[edit policy-options]
policy-statement bgplayer {
    from neighbor 10.0.0.122;
    then reject;
}
[edit protocols bgp]
group bgplayer {
    type internal;
    import bgplayer;
    cluster 1.1.1.1;
    neighbor 10.0.0.122;
}
```

After some time, it is possible to replay advertisements and withdrawals from BGP, allowing for a much better picture of not only how BGP is running, but also how network prefixes are being advertised. With this knowledge it is possible to tweak routing policies to ensure that network outages in neighboring ASs will not degrade high availability in the network.

Pitfalls

As you saw throughout this chapter, the pitfall of all monitoring for high availability is information overload obscuring necessary data. In traffic monitoring, too, the amount of information gathered must be proportionate to the number of people available to monitor the data, as well as the software available for parsing.

CHAPTER 10

Management Interfaces

Although a planned and clearly implemented syslog and Simple Network Management Protocol (SNMP) solution is the first step to ensuring continuous system operation within a network, it removes much of the management intelligence from the networking equipment itself. Using syslog and SNMP configurations does allow you to filter and forward events and messages to specific locations, but the parsing and correlating of information takes place on separate Network Management Stations (NMSs).

With the introduction into JUNOS of intuitive GUI interfaces and powerful onboard scripting, the network management intelligence can be shared by both the NMSs and the networking equipment itself. The variety of interfaces allows all levels of network engineers and technicians—from crusty old-timers who were brought up handcoding assembly language or writing their first BASIC programs for the C64, to kids fresh out of community college who don't comprehend the simple beauty of lines such as "look lantern" and the text-based RPGs to which some of us were addicted—to participate proactively in managing the network to minimize system downtime. Although the debate between GUI and command-line interface (CLI) management tools will no doubt rage on, multiple management interfaces do provide a custom-tailored management tool to network technicians and engineers of all experience levels.

A GUI for Junior Techs

To allow nontechnical people and individuals new to JUNOS to quickly build, deploy, and manage a network of Juniper equipment, a tool called J-Web is bundled with the equipment. J-Web is an HTTP-based GUI-driven tool that has been developed especially for equipment management. The J-Web tool, which comes preinstalled on J Series enterprise routing equipment and is free for download and installation on the EX Series Ethernet switches, the MX Series Ethernet routers, and the M7i, M10i, and M120 router families, provides a graphical interface for many JUNOS commands and tools. Even the big-iron M and T Series routers can use J-Web for an additional licensing fee, but the main purpose of J-Web is to provide simple and quick access for users in remote offices so that they can turn on their systems.

Because J-Web is totally web-driven, you do not need to download a Java client, as with some other vendors' management tools. Although that may seem inconsequential, the fact that you are able to get into the equipment without worrying about Java versions becomes very important when time is of the essence and you see your seven 9s slipping away.

Using J-Web

Because J-Web is preinstalled on the J Series equipment, no configuration tasks are required to use it. On the other JUNOS systems, such as the upper-end M and T Series, you must download, install, and obtain the proper licenses for the J-Web software before you use it. You download the J-Web software from the Juniper Networks Customer Support area and save it to the */var/tmp* directory of the equipment on which it is to be installed.

Once the software is on the network device, install it using the standard `software add` commands, and then add web management to the configuration:

```
user@host> request system software add /var/tmp/j-web-bundle.tgz
user@host> configure
user@host# set system services web-management-http
```

After you issue these commands, you access J-Web through a standard browser using the IP address of the host as the URL. Figure 10-1 shows an example of the J-Web interface.

Although the GUI is designed for lower-level and new users, you can use it to access all JUNOS configuration statements and commands and to monitor the network to ensure high availability.

J-Web for High Availability

The J-Web GUI provides access to the CLI commands and functions that are normally used to ensure continuous system operation. The major advantage of using J-Web is that it provides visual indicators, which can help you to quickly discover issues before you can identify them in the plain-text monitoring formats, such as logfiles. The graphical nature of J-Web lends itself to the following monitoring and management functions:

- Equipment performance, which displays with colored bar graphs
- Syslog events, color-coded to highlight critical errors
- Interface usage, which displays with colored bar graphs

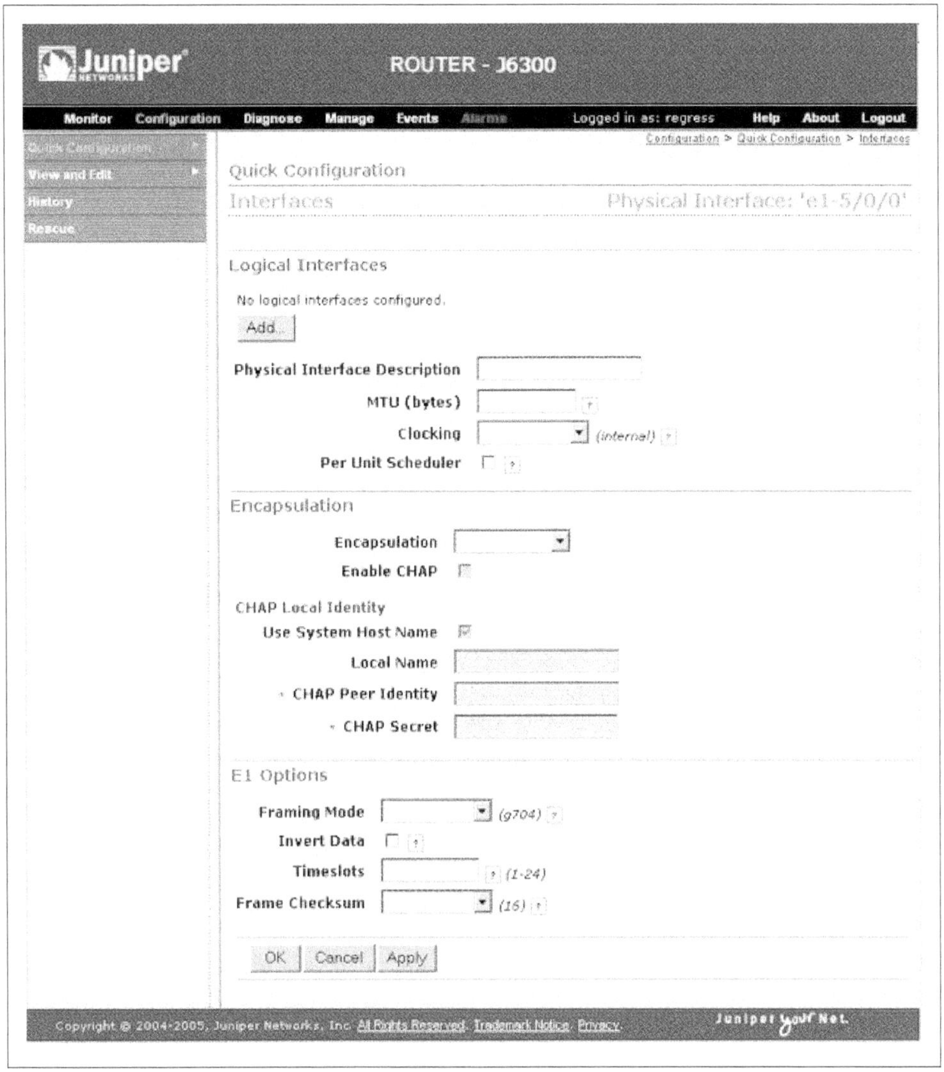

Figure 10-1. J-Web GUI

Mid-Level Techs and the CLI

For those mid-level technicians and engineers in your network who are more comfortable with using the CLI to monitor continuous system operation, JUNOS offers tools in addition to syslog and SNMP for obtaining the information necessary to ensure continuous system operation and high availability. The primary tool for these technicians is event policies, which make it possible to define a list of commands to be run when a trigger event occurs. The output from these commands can be sent to an external source for root-cause failure analysis, for network monitoring, and to develop a network baseline. You configure event policies in the standard configuration file of the network equipment, and they are visible when you display the contents of the configuration.

Event Policy Planning

Just as with syslog and SNMP, you must determine up front exactly what information to retrieve during periodic checks or in the case of an expected or unexpected event. Without proper and thorough planning, the amount of information available from your network equipment can be overwhelming. While you cannot fully customize information gathered from event policies, CLI pipes and other tricks are available to help filter command output. Table 10-1 is an example of an event policy plan.

Table 10-1. Event policy planning

Event	Destination	Commands
Routing failures	Engineers	`show configuration protocols`
		`show system processes	match rpd`
		`show log messages	match rpd`
Daily baseline	Archive	`show interfaces terse`
		`show bgp summary`
		`show ospf overview`
		`show chassis alarms`
Weekly interface baseline	Archive	`show interfaces statistics`
		`clear interface statistics all`
Configuration commit	Archive, engineers	`show configuration`
		`show configuration	compare rollback 1`
		`show configuration	display commit-scripts view`

The event policies shown in this table gather information about the health of routing protocols and interfaces, and track changes in the configuration. The purpose of these policies is to prevent network downtime caused by either software or human errors, and to help guarantee continuous system operation. Notice that pipes are used to limit the amount of information collected by invoking commands such as compare, finding configuration deltas, and matching specific lines from logfiles.

Sample event policy configuration

Once you have a plan for event triggers, you typically build a configuration that both triggers commands when an event appears in the syslog and schedules generated events that force commands to run. The following code creates periodic events—for a daily baseline that runs at midnight and a weekly baseline—and trigger commands that gather information when specific events occur. The code is an example of how to configure the event policy that corresponds to the plan shown in Table 10-1:

```
event-options {
  generate-event {
    Daily_Baseline time-of-day "00:00:00 +0000";
    Weekly_Baseline time-interval 604800;
  }
  policy Routing_Failure {
    events [ rpd_abort rpd_exit rpd_os_memhigh ];
      then {
        execute-commands {
          commands {
            "show configuration protocols";
            "show system processes | match rpd";
            "show log messages | match rpd";
          }
          raise-trip;
          output-filename routing;
          destination Engineering;
          output-format text;
        }
      }
  }
  policy Daily_Baseline {
    events Daily_Baseline;
      then {
        execute-commands {
          commands {
            "show interfaces terse";
            "show bgp summary";
            "show ospf overview";
            "show chassis alarms";
          }
          output-filename Daily_Baseline;
          destination Archive;
          output-format text;
        }
      }
  }
  policy Weekly_Baseline {
    events Weekly_Baseline;
      then {
        execute-commands {
          commands {
            "show interfaces statistics";
            "clear interface statistics all";
          }
          output-filename weekly;
          destination Archive;
          output-format text;
        }
      }
  }
}
```

```
    policy Commit {
      events ui_commit;
      then {
          execute-commands {
              commands {
                  "show configuration";
                  "show configuration | compare rollback 1";
                  "show configuration | display commit-scripts view";
              }
              output-filename commit;
              destination Archive;
              output-format text;
          }
      }
    }
    policy Commit_Engineers {
      events ui_commit;
      then {
          execute-commands {
              commands {
                  "show configuration";
                  "show configuration | compare rollback 1";
                  "show configuration | display commit-scripts view";
              }
              output-filename commit;
              destination Engineering
              output-format text;
          }
      }
    }

    destinations {
      NOC {
          archive-sites {
              "ftp://router@noc.example.com" password "$9$OWOr1RS8X-"; ## SECRET-DATA
          }
      }
      Archive{
          archive-sites {
              "ftp://router@archive.example.com" password "$IEKvxNd"; ## SECRET-DATA
          }
      }
      Engineering {
          archive-sites {
              "ftp://router@engineering.example.com" password "$9$U"; ## SECRET-DATA
          }
      }
    }
}
```

This very basic configuration uses only **show** commands and SNMP traps, and does not invoke any event scripts. The **destination** section of the event policy defines the hosts to which the information collected by the policy is sent. The example configures five policies:

Routing_Failure

Provides routing configuration and possible log messages relating to the routing protocols when a Routing Protocol Daemon (RPD) failure appears in the syslog. The output of the policy is sent to the destination archive.

Daily_Baseline

Provides basic information about Open Shortest Path First (OSPF), Border Gateway Protocol (BGP), interfaces, and any chassis alarms when the specified event is triggered at the set time. The `time-of-day` command generates an event at midnight every night.

Weekly_Int_Baseline

Provides interface statistics weekly and then clears the statistics after gathering them so that each week's information is easy to identify and read.

Commit

Archives the new configuration every time a configuration is committed, along with any changes from the previous configurations and any commit scripts involved in the commit.

Commit_Engineering

Sends the information to a server in the engineering department. It is not sent by the previous scripts because the event policies allow for only a single destination.

After event policies are created, the output files appear on the archive in the format specified. Because no command syntax checking occurs when the `then execute-commands commands` configuration statement is used, testing the policy is mandatory. In the following example, the `show system users` command was misconfigured as `show users`, and the error that occurred was placed into the output file, notated with the string `xnm:error`:

```
<?xml version="1.0" encoding="us-ascii"?>
<junoscript xmlns="http://xml.juniper.net/xnm/1.1/xnm"
xmlns:junos="http://xml.juniper.net/junos/9.1R1/junos"
schemaLocation="http://xml.juniper.net/junos/9.1R1/junos
 junos/9.1R1/junos.xsd" os="JUNOS" release="9.1R1.8"
hostname="router1.example.com" version="1.0">
<!-- session start at 2008-12-09 00:00:00 UTC -->
<!-- No zombies were killed during the creation of this user interface -->
<!-- user root, class super-user -->
<rpc-reply xmlns:junos="http://xml.juniper.net/junos/9.1R1/junos">
<xnm:error xmlns=http://xml.juniper.net/xnm/1.1/xnm
xmlns:xnm="http://xml.juniper.net/xnm/1.1/xnm">
<column>5</column>
<token>users</token>
<message>syntax error, expecting &lt;command&gt;</message>
</xnm:error>
</rpc-reply>
<!-- session end at 2008-12-09 00:00:00 UTC -->
</junoscript>
```

Event Policies for High Availability

Event policies provide a quick and easy way to automate basic troubleshooting on your network equipment. The inability of the event policies to change the command output format itself makes them more suited for times when you require full output from a command. However, the ability of event policies to correlate events, raise traps, and run commands does make them suitable for quickly providing information that might otherwise be lost during an emergency. Some tasks you can perform using the event policies include:

- Forwarding technical support information when major processes restart or when errors with chassis hardware occur
- Collecting configurations and configuration deltas when commits are made
- Creating SNMP traps and collecting data when certain events, such as changes in routing protocol neighbor relationships, occur in quick succession
- Periodically collecting and clearing interfaces, routing, and errors to determine network trending and baselines

Deep Magic for Advanced Techs

For those of you who are intrepid enough to travel beyond the confines of the CLI and GUI, JUNOS software offers a powerful onboard scripting processor that includes application programming interfaces (APIs) for creating scripts and clients capable of providing better coverage and high availability. Using the JUNOScript API and Extensible Markup Language (XML), you can automate monitoring, troubleshooting, and configuration of network equipment, thus possibly preventing human error from leading to network downtime. Full coverage of how to implement JUNOS scripting in your network would require a book of its own. This section provides a good start, explaining how scripting works. The JUNOS documentation itself provides additional explanation, and you can also find example scripts on the Internet that are easy to understand and to modify, especially if you have a basic understanding of Perl scripting.

JUNOS APIs

The key to using the extended JUNOS API capabilities is to understand XML and how it interacts with JUNOS in your network equipment. Network devices natively running the JUNOS software support XML. You can use XML to parse input and output from the device and its software modules. To communicate with the processes on the network device, you use either the JUNOS XML API or the JUNOScript API. Both APIs enable the Juniper networking equipment to accept and respond to request and configuration changes encoded in XML. The APIs take the XML input and perform Remote Procedure Calls (RPCs) to gather or write information.

The APIs allow creation of two types of scripts: *commit* scripts and *automation* scripts. Commit scripts, which are used to parse configurations for human errors or nonstandard items that could lead to network downtime, are called automatically when the `commit` command is issued. These scripts accept only the candidate configuration as input. Automation scripts have no defined input or set execution time, but instead rely on user input during the creation of the script to determine the source of the input data and what will trigger the execution of the script.

Running within the JUNOS software, the JUNOScript and JUNOS XML APIs act as conduits between client software and the information stored in the various software modules of the Juniper Networks equipment. It is this conduit that allows the routers and switches to accept XML-formatted data and return XML-formatted responses. Figure 10-2 illustrates the normal operation of an external client and the JUNOScript server.

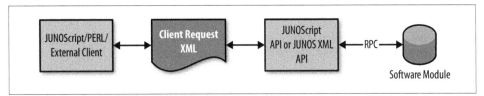

Figure 10-2. JUNOS API processing

As Figure 10-2 shows, when XML-formatted requests are accepted by the API, the requests activate the appropriate RPC, such as the RPC for the `show interfaces` command. After the call is made to the software module in the network device, a series of response tags are crafted that carry the results of the action or the information requested. In both the request and response portions of the call, the API is responsible for translating the RPC information to and from the XML format.

Two languages allow you to call and modify the XML that is at the heart of the interaction between the clients and the RPCs of the network equipment:

XSLT
The Extensible Stylesheet Language Transformation is the World Wide Web Consortium's (W3C) standard language for processing XML language.

SLAX
The Stylesheet Language Alternative Syntax was written specifically for creating JUNOS-based automation scripts and has a simpler syntax, similar to C or Perl.

XSLT

Scripts written in XSLT can be read directly by the native XML capabilities of the JUNOS software. The XSLT transforms the hierarchy in XML files into a new hierarchy, as defined in the XSLT template. Figure 10-3 is an example of XSLT parsing.

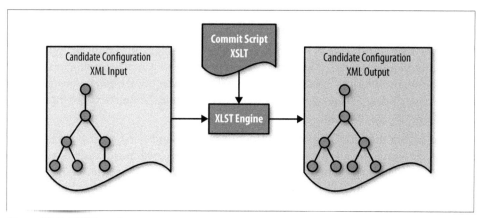

Figure 10-3. XSLT parsing

As Figure 10-3 demonstrates, when the commit command is issued to the network device, the XSLT engine is called and the candidate configuration is compared against the
commit script, which is simply a configuration template written in XSLT. Using the
template, the engine either alerts the user to errors in the configuration that fall outside
the parameters set by the template, or corrects the configuration before it is committed.

The following example from the "JUNOS Internet Software Configuration and Diagnostic Automation Guide" shows that XSLT scripts are written using XML tags. For
JUNOS to understand the tagging within the script, the script must include standard
header lines that call out the location of the JUNOS XML templates:

```
<?xml version="1.0" standalone="yes"?>
<xsl:stylesheet version="1.0"
    xmlns:xsl="http://www.w3.org/1999/XSL/Transform"
    xmlns:junos="http://xml.juniper.net/junos/*/junos"
    xmlns:xnm="http://xml.juniper.net/xnm/1.1/xnm"
    xmlns:jcs="http://xml.juniper.net/junos/commit-scripts/1.0">
    <xsl:import href="../import/junos.xsl"/>
    <xsl:variable name="arguments">
      <argument>
        <name>dns</name>
        <description>Name or IP address of a host</description>
      </argument>
    </xsl:variable>
    <xsl:param name="dns"/>
    <xsl:template match="/">
      <op-script-results>
        <xsl:variable name="query">
          <xsl:choose>
            <xsl:when test="$dns">
              <command>
                <xsl:value-of select="concat('show host ', $dns)"/>
                </command>
            </xsl:when>
            <xsl:when test="$hostname">
```

```
        <command>
          <xsl:value-of select="concat('show host ', $hostname)"/>
          </command>
        </xsl:when>
      </xsl:choose>
    </xsl:variable>
    <xsl:variable name="result" select="jcs:invoke($query)"/>
    <xsl:variable name="host" select="$result"/>
    <output>
      <xsl:value-of select="concat('Name: ', $host)"/>
    </output>
  </op-script-results>
</xsl:template>
</xsl:stylesheet>
```

As this example shows, the XSLT-formatted script can be long and difficult to read for those who are used to more standard scripting languages, such as Perl.

SLAX

To simplify scripting in JUNOS software, Juniper Networks engineers developed SLAX. SLAX uses a more intuitive, Perl-like scripting style that allows network engineers to develop shorter, clearer scripts that leverage the power of the JUNOS APIs. Although it requires additional processing to transform it into XSLT, SLAX provides the same power as scripts written in the standards-based XSLT. Figure 10-4 illustrates how the SLAX parser transforms a SLAX script.

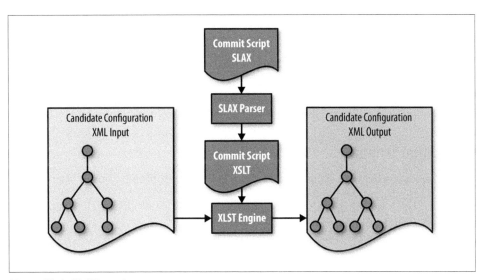

Figure 10-4. SLAX parsing

When scripts written in SLAX are processed, they are first converted to XSLT by the SLAX processor and are then run against the XML files from the network device. This additional processing can either be performed automatically when the script is run or called manually so that the scripts can be tested and converted before they are needed.

The following is an example of the same functionality shown in the previous XSLT script, but written in SLAX:

```
version 1.0;
ns junos = "http://xml.juniper.net/junos/*/junos";
ns xnm = "http://xml.juniper.net/xnm/1.1/xnm";
ns jcs = "http://xml.juniper.net/junos/commit-scripts/1.0";
import "../import/junos.xsl";
var $arguments = {
  <argument> {
    <name> "dns";
    <description> "Name or IP address of a host";
  }
}
param $dns;
match / {
  <op-script-results> {
    var $query = {
      if ($dns) {
        <command> 'show host ' _ $dns;
      } else if ($hostname) {
        <command> 'show host ' _ $hostname;
      }
    }
    var $result = jcs:invoke($query);
    var $host = $result;
    <output> 'Name: ' _ $host;
  }
}
```

The SLAX script provides a much clearer and shorter script, with the same power as the original XSLT, thus making it very useful for building network management systems that run on the Juniper network devices. Those of you who have worked with scripting or programming should find this simplified format easy to understand and to learn.

Automation Scripts

As mentioned earlier, the JUNOS APIs support automation and commit scripts. Automation scripts come in two types:

Operation (ops) scripts
> Execute and inspect router commands and their output using the CLI. Falling under the mgd process, ops scripts can be used to create automated troubleshooting tools.

Event scripts
> Are executed by the eventd process and can be used to automatically execute and inspect router commands when a predefined event occurs.

Using the automation scripts, senior network engineers can build tools to allow more junior engineers and technicians to troubleshoot the network using commands that provide only the necessary information, without displaying extraneous fields in the command output. Unlike event policies, covered in Chapter 9, which supply all information provided by the standard CLI commands, an event script can focus the output on specific areas through the use of the innate XML formatting of the output.

Operation scripts

You write operation scripts to create commands that automate selected monitoring and troubleshooting functions and to customize the output of show commands. In the following example of SLAX code, the standard output from the show bgp summary command is shortened to display only the peer IP address and the number of received and active routes from established users:

```
version 1.0;

ns junos = "http://xml.juniper.net/junos/*/junos";
ns xnm = "http://xml.juniper.net/xnm/1.1/xnm";
ns jcs = "http://xml.juniper.net/junos/commit-scripts/1.0";

import "../import/junos.xsl";

match /
{
    <op-script-results>
    {
        var $peer = { <command> 'show bgp summary'; }
        var $prefix = jcs:invoke($peer);

        <output>"Peer IP\t\tASN\t\tReceived Prefixes\tActive Prefixes\t\tdescription";
        <bgp-information> {
                for-each($prefix/bgp-peer[peer-state='Established']) {
                        <output> peer-address _ "\t\t" _ peer-as _
"\t\t" _ received-prefix-count _"\t" _ active-external-prefix-count _
"\t\t" _ Description;
                }
        }
    }
}
```

Using operation scripts such as this, senior engineers can write commands for junior engineers that supply only the information that falls into their particular purview, making it easier for them to parse the information and find possible indicators of issues that could lead to network downtime. After operation scripts have been added to the network device, they are called by their filename (without the file extension) or by an alias.

Event scripts

Just as with operation scripts, event scripts provide a way to tailor CLI commands and their output to provide information necessary for network management. Unlike operation scripts, event scripts do not require human interaction to run. When the event scripts are loaded into the eventd process, they are called if the network equipment experiences any of the configured triggers. You configure event policies or triggers in the script itself, so the scripts are automatically called when the configured events, timed events, or thresholds, or any combination of events, occur.

Working with Scripts

To work with JUNOS scripts, you need to understand the format of the JUNOS scripting languages, what information needs to be gathered from the network device, and the XML tags for that information. Once the scripts are written, you load them onto the network devices and then call them directly, either from the command line or by event processing. JUNOS also provides commands for refreshing the scripts from a remote location.

Planning scripts

To take advantage of the APIs in the JUNOS software, the scripts you write must call the RPCs providing the information required by the calls. Thankfully, the scripting languages are easily understandable, and you can find the information necessary to build the scripts in the reference material on the Juniper Networks website or in the equipment itself.

The following code example shows the XML version of the show interfaces terse command. The tags displayed in the output are the ones you use in your script to call and process the information necessary for the script:

```
user@host> show interfaces terse | display xml
<rpc-reply xmlns:junos="http://xml.juniper.net/junos/9.1R1/junos">
    <interface-information
xmlns=http://xml.juniper.net/junos/9.1R1/junos-interface
junos:style="terse">
        <physical-interface>
            <name>dsc</name>
            <admin-status>up</admin-status>
            <oper-status>up</oper-status>
        </physical-interface>
        <physical-interface>
            <name>fxp0</name>
            <admin-status>up</admin-status>
            <oper-status>up</oper-status>
            <logical-interface>
                <name>fxp0.0</name>
                <admin-status>up</admin-status>
                <oper-status>up</oper-status>
                <address-family>
```

```
            <address-family-name>inet</address-family-name>
            <interface-address>
                <ifa-local junos:emit="emit">112.2.111.128/27
                </ifa-local>
            </interface-address>
        </address-family>
```

You can use the preceding XML tags as variables to gather information and customize the output of JUNOS commands.

Loading and calling scripts

For scripts to be used by the network device, either you upload them to the hard drive of the network equipment—placing operation scripts in the */var/db/scripts/op* directory and event scripts in the */var/db/scripts/event* directory—or you load them into the flash memory of the equipment. In the configuration file, you call out the filenames of the scripts. When the configuration is committed, the event script is then loaded into the eventd process so that it can be run when triggered. The operation scripts are not loaded into eventd, but are called manually through a user typing the alias or automatically from within an event policy or script.

For network operators to be able to use the scripts, the eventd process must know about them. In the case of an operational script, once it is identified in the configuration, the operator can call it using the CLI. Event scripts, on the other hand, run in the eventd process and are called through event policies, not by an operator using the CLI. If you change an event script, you must reload it into eventd either by modifying the filename in the configuration or by reloading it into the active process. The following code example includes the commands to identify an event script called *routing*, written in the SLAX language, and to load it into the eventd process. The second code example shows an operation script called *trouble* that can be called from the CLI:

```
[edit]
user@host# set system event-options event-script file routing.slax
user@host# commit and-quit
user@host>request system scripts event-scripts reload


[edit system sripts]
user@host# set system scripts op file trouble.slax command trouble
user@host# commit and-quit
user@host>op trouble
```

Because event scripts and operation scripts have the same format, you can store the same script in both the *ops* and *event* directories and the configuration can call both scripts. This deployment style allows operators to retrieve the same data both manually and automatically.

Refreshing scripts

When you update and change scripts, you need to load the new version onto your network equipment. Although it is possible to manually load the new version of the script to each machine in your network, it makes more sense to use the `refresh-from` keyword in the system script ops configuration to refresh the script from an accessible location. The following example shows how to refresh an operation script from a web server:

```
[edit system scripts op]
user@host# set file test.slax refresh-from \
http://engineering.example.com/scripts
refreshing 'test.slax' from 'http://engineering.example.com/ scripts/test.slax'
/var/tmp//...transferring.file.........xsm3bo/100% of  762  B 2194 kBps
```

In your network, you can take the automation even further by using the `refresh-from` keyword along with an event script that triggers at a specific time. The result is that the scripts automatically refresh themselves.

CHAPTER 11

Management Tools

Through the use of ops and event scripts, it is possible to create highly customized management and troubleshooting information to be used to ensure continuous systems, but if this information is not understood or cannot be processed correctly, it is useless. Though most network management systems can be tweaked to handle the information the scripts and the JUNOS software provide, Juniper Networks has worked to provide tools that seamlessly integrate with the power of the JUNOS application programming interfaces (APIs) to provide information in a more easily understood format.

Based on proven open source projects, the Juniper Networks management tools include a GUI for monitoring equipment, software, and networking; tools for interacting with the Juniper Technical Assistance Center (JTAC) for management of tickets and equipment; and partner programs allowing best-in-breed service providers to integrate their protocols and systems into JUNOS.

JUNOScope

Though individual devices in the network can be configured with J-Web for individual management, if you're managing an entire network of routers, use of the web-driven JUNOScope provides a GUI-based tool for collecting and analyzing the information necessary to maintain network high availability. JUNOScope provides access to tools that allow you to monitor information such as system capacity and usage, routing protocols, and interface throughput.

Overview

At the heart of the JUNOScope software are the web-based management functions provided from a Unix/Linux-based server. Using a combination of Perl, Extensible Markup Language (XML), and JUNOScript, the web server interacts with the networking equipment through the use of the APIs built into JUNOS. The JUNOScope server can also interact with remote application servers through standardized communication protocols, such as syslog, Remote Authentication Dial-in User Service (RADIUS), and SQL. Figure 11-1 shows an example of the JUNOScope server in a network and its interactions with network devices.

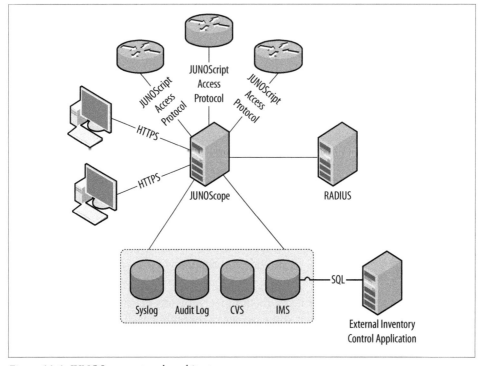

Figure 11-1. JUNOScope network architecture

In Figure 11-1, the JUNOScope server is the hub of the network management architecture, and provides information to the clients through standard web protocols. The JUNOScope server interacts securely with the networking equipment, running JUNOS via the JUNOScript access protocol. Within the JUNOScope server itself, there are syslog and audit log processes, as well as a Concurrent Versions System (CVS) process for maintaining and coordinating configuration information and an Inventory Management System that can interact with external inventory control applications.

The JUNOScope software is divided into six modules, each designed for specific management functions. You interact with each software module through the JUNOScope IP Element Manager via the web GUI. As various processes or modules are called, they interact within the JUNOScope tools and the SQL database on board the JUNOScope server. All requests to and from the network equipment are formed into XML and sent via JUNOScript and the APIs on the machines. The network equipment responds to the requests from JUNOScope by crafting the appropriate Remote Procedure Calls (RPCs) to write or gather the requested information. The function of each module is as follows:

Looking Glass
> A GUI for querying and viewing device status and troubleshooting information

Configuration Manager
> A CVS system for monitoring and managing configurations currently on network devices or within the local repository

Inventory Management System
> Provides tools for scanning and reporting on hardware and licenses throughout the network

Software Manager
> A licensable add-on that provides tools for managing the deployment and upgrade of JUNOS software throughout the network

Monitor
> A module for managing and auditing the functionality of the JUNOScope server

Settings
> Tools for configuring access and monitoring of the JUNOScope server

You can interact with all of the modules through the GUI. Figure 11-2 illustrates the interaction between software processes in JUNOScope.

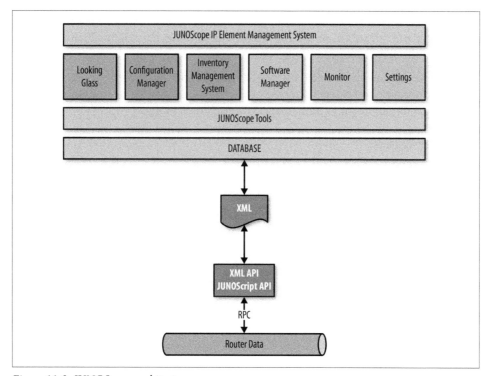

Figure 11-2. JUNOScope architecture

By using the built-in APIs in the network equipment, JUNOScope is able to seamlessly integrate with all network devices running JUNOS software and pull exactly the data necessary for monitoring the network for high availability. Though JUNOScope is not designed to work with the equipment running non-JUNOS software, such as ScreenOS, other management software is available through the NetScreen Security Manager and the Advanced Insight Manager. Also, product lines such as the new SRX security equipment are being built on the JUNOS operating system to allow them to have all the features available from JUNOScript.

JUNOScope and High Availability

JUNOScope works with the previously discussed tools for maintaining continuous systems to provide information to network engineers. Looking through the modules of JUNOScope, four of them stand out as being capable of assisting network engineers in providing the information necessary for ensuring continuous systems.

Looking Glass

The Looking Glass portion of JUNOScope provides access to monitoring and troubleshooting features of the JUNOS equipment and is based on the open source Looking Glass projects accessible through the Internet. Because of the ubiquitous nature of the Looking Glass tools, the module within JUNOScope allows network engineers to more quickly take full advantage of the tool to provide monitoring. Figure 11-3 shows an example of the JUNOScope Looking Glass screen.

The command queries are broken up into device, information category, and command fields. As the device and category options are selected, the available commands appear. The commands can be set to refresh the output incrementally.

Configuration Manager

The Configuration Manager module of JUNOScope provides tools for managing all aspects of configurations on the Juniper Networks equipment that is being managed through the JUNOScope server. Using the open source CVS, the Configuration Manager module offers the ability to scan, audit, compare, and edit configurations. The use of CVS ensures that only a single copy of a configuration is used and that all changes are recorded in the versioning data.

Not only does the Configuration Manager enable management of the configuration files for the network equipment, but it also provides functions to import, upload, edit, and manage scripts on the JUNOS devices. This central repository of JUNOScript files is also included in the CVS so that versioning data is maintained for any changes made to the files.

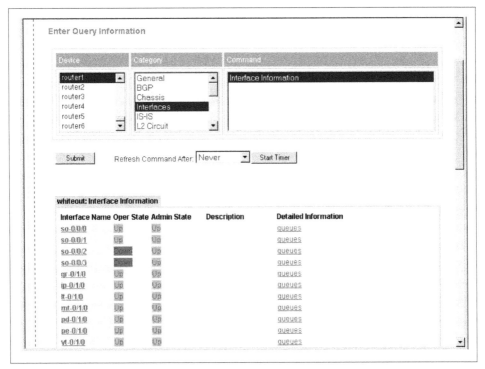

Figure 11-3. Example Looking Glass screen

Inventory Management System

The JUNOScope Inventory Management System allows network engineers to scan, view, and report on equipment and licensing throughout the network. The data retrieved from the networking equipment can be stored within the local database, as well as sent to external inventory control systems through SQL. Reports can also be published to Excel, PDF, and other standard formats.

> In many networks, licensing information is considered one of the less important aspects of inventory control—but it can lead to network outages very quickly. Running into a wall as a result of lack of licensing is an easily avoidable error.

Software Manager

As discussed in previous chapters, the single JUNOS train and the use of JUNOS across the wide spectrum of Juniper Networks gear make software quite easy to upgrade. The Software Manager within JUNOS makes this already easy process even simpler by providing a central repository for the JUNOS software and a way to upload/download the files, as well as upgrade the equipment. Once JUNOS files are downloaded to one of the JUNOScope clients, they can be imported to the JUNOScope server, and from there be deployed to the systems through the network.

Using JUNOScope

As with all of the functionality of JUNOS and Juniper Networks equipment, it is best to determine which high availability issues can be avoided using the various modules within JUNOScope. Table 11-1 compares the JUNOScope modules with the information they provide.

Table 11-1. JUNOScope modules

JUNOScope module	Type of information	Potential high availability issues avoided
Looking Glass		
ASP	Firewall and Network Address Translation (NAT) information	Prevents overconsumption of firewall flows or NAT IP addresses
Chassis	Alarms, routing engine (RE), and hardware information	Checks for hardware or environment issues that cause or could lead to downtime
Interfaces	Interface operations and throughout	Prevents oversubscription of network interfaces
Routing Protocols	Information on routing protocol processes, including Border Gateway Protocol (BGP), Open Shortest Path First (OSPF), and Intermediate System to Intermediate System (IS-IS)	Monitors for configuration errors resulting in routing and network outages
System	Status of storage capacity, users, uptime, and version	Prevents the overuse of system equipment, such as hard drives
Configuration Manager		
Configuration	Provides for viewing and editing of configuration files	Prevents user-caused configuration errors
JUNOScript	Provides for the management of JUNOScript scripts on network devices	Allows network engineers to ensure that the scripts they developed to ensure high availability exist on the system
Inventory Management System		
Hardware	Tracks information on hardware within the chassis of network equipment	Speeds the time for replacement of failed equipment by having a central repository for serial number and other equipment information
Licensing	Tracks information on the licenses for upgraded modules	Provides a central repository for licensing information to prevent service outages caused by lack of licensing or passing license limits
Software Manager		
Import	Allows software to be loaded onto the JUNOScope server	Provides a central repository for JUNOS software so that upgrades can be performed more efficiently

JUNOScope module	Type of information	Potential high availability issues avoided
Upgrade	Pushes software to network equipment from the central repository and upgrade devices	Prevents user error in loading software onto network equipment

JUNOScope installation

Once the hardware requirements of the server are met, the installation of JUNOScope is very straightforward. Installation on a Sun Solaris box requires a simple installation shell script. Installation on a Red Hat Enterprise Linux server requires the standard Red Hat Package Manager (RPM) software. After installation, the software can be configured to scan for network devices.

Juniper AIS

The creation of Juniper Advanced Insight Solutions (AIS) has made Juniper Networks a partner in maintaining continuous systems by providing in-depth support for the Juniper Networks products. AIS, which is built on top of the JUNOScript ability in JUNOS software, allows Juniper to automatically detect events and gather network intelligence information, manage incidents, and provide information to Juniper Support Systems (JSS) to facilitate efficient resolution of incidents, and provide intelligence to prevent future incidents.

Overview

Juniper AIS is made up of three main components that work together to provide proactive and reactive support for your network and allow you to maintain high availability for critical components.

At the heart of AIS are the Advanced Insight Scripts, which are a collection of ops scripts used to detect, collect, and gather incident information and network intelligence. All the information gathered in the scripts is converted into Juniper Message Bundles (JMBs) and sent to archive sites, which can be forwarded to the JTAC so that they can quickly and efficiently correct incidents that cause network downtime and identify situations that could lead to network downtime in the future.

The Advanced Insight Manager (AIM), which installs on Solaris/Linux systems, provides a secure conduit between the locally based archives containing information and the intelligence provided by the Advanced Insight Scripts and JSS. Working as a central hub, the AIM monitors and connects to all local archives of information, and provides controls for managing JTAC cases. The AIM can be configured in one of three modes:

Standard Mode

The users connect directly through the AIM to the JSS to send and receive network information and JTAC case information. This deployment is useful for large network providers with highly technical engineering staffs.

Partner Controller

The users at customer sites connect to a partner-supplied AIM that connects to the JSS. The partner can determine what information is sent to and from the customers. ISPs and other network providers use this as an additional service for ensuring high availability among customers.

End Customer

The customer's AIM server connects to the JSS through a partner's AIM device. The customer has full control of the AIM, but is limited in some functionality. Like the Partner Controller, this option allows ISPs to provide the tools necessary for high availability to customers, but also allows larger customers to have some control over their AIM and have a greater hand in providing continuous systems to their network.

The JSS is a series of tools and databases designed to enable JTAC and network engineers to resolve incidents quickly and to provide proactive monitoring to prevent situations that can lead to future network downtime. The JSS has access to all of the necessary information for maintaining networking equipment and providing continuous systems, including configuration item databases, bug and knowledge base data, and analytic processes. Figure 11-4 illustrates the location of the AIM server in the network in a simple deployment.

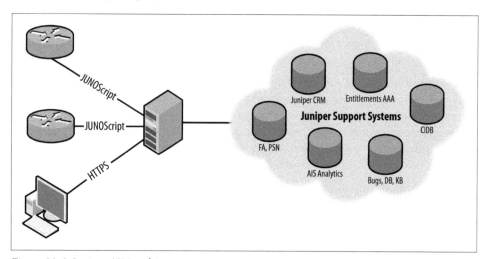

Figure 11-4. Juniper AIM architecture

The AIM is a web-driven tool that provides the convenience of a single access point to data collected through the Advanced Insight Scripts, as well as to the resources of the JSS. Because of mergers and acquisitions, some Juniper Networks equipment does not support JUNOScript (the equipment running operating systems other than JUNOS, such as JUNOSe). The AIM allows for information gathering for these devices, as well as those running older versions of JUNOS, through the use of the Data Collector process. The information from these devices can be used with the JSS and JTAC.

AIS for High Availability

Though the use of the AIS requires licensing, the power it gives network engineers to maintain continuous systems is extraordinary. By increasing the efficiency of interaction between the JTAC and your local network engineers, issues that do arise can be solved quickly and future issues to network downtime can be caught and prevented.

Installation

The first step in the use of AIS is installation of the Advanced Insight Scripts on the network devices. You can load the scripts manually, or automatically using JUNOScope. When you load the Advanced Insight Scripts manually, you must download them from the Juniper website and move the package to the */var/sw/pkg* directory of the networking equipment. Then you can extract them to the appropriate locations using the `request system software add` command. Once you've added them to the system, you can activate the scripts using the JAIS activation script. In the following example code, the activation script is inserting the JAIS scripts into the configuration using the `commit` script function:

```
groups {
  juniper-ais {
    system {
      scripts {
        commit {
          allow-transients;
          file jais-activate-scripts.slax {
            optional;
          }
        }
        load-scripts-from-flash;
      }
    }
  }
  event-options {
    destinations {
      AIS-Archive {
        archive-sites {
          "ftp://anonymous@archive.example.com/AIS";
        }
      }
    }
  }
}
```

The preceding configuration not only calls out where the scripts are located, but also points to the destination for the archived information. This archive can be accessed to provide information to JTAC and JSS directly or through the AIM:

```
user@host# show configuration groups juniper-ais | display commit-scripts
system {
  scripts {
    commit {
      allow-transients;
      file jais-activate-scripts.slax {
        optional;
      }
    }
  }
}
event options {
  event-script {
    file problem-event-pfecrash.slax;
    file problem-event-dcrash.slax;
    file intelligence-event-main.slax;
    file SPD_EVLIB_CREATE_FAILURE.slax;
    file SPD_DAEMONIZE_FAILED.slax;
    [remainder omitted]
  }
  destinations {
    AIS-Archive {
      archive-sites {
        "ftp://anonymous@archive.example.com/AIS";
      }
    }
  }
}
```

Once you have activated the scripts, you can confirm them by using the show configuration commands, and by calling out the specifics of the Advanced Insight Scripts. In the preceding example, the various Stylesheet Language Alternative Syntax (SLAX) scripts have been added to the event-script portion of the hierarchy with the appropriate destination. eventd will now monitor for the described events and send messages to the AIM archive sites. Using AIM, the results from these scripts can also be configured to forward events to third-party network management devices.

You install AIM through a graphical installation binary file available for download from Juniper Networks. The binary file walks you through the entire installation process.

AIS planning

Because AIS is a tool for integration with the JSS and the specialized Insight JTAC, one decision that you must make for AIS is what level of support will be required. Table 11-2 illustrates an example of J-Care levels and features.

Table 11-2. Support levels

	J-Care essential services	J-Care efficiency services	J-Care continuity services	J-Care agility services
Business protection				
Technical support	X	X	X	X
Operational efficiency				
Inventory management assistance		X	X	X
Knowledge transfer		X	X	X
Automated incident management		X	X	X
High availability				
Service desk management			X	X
Access to Insight JTAC			X	X
Evolution and adaptability				
Advanced options				X
Proactive product report				X

Partner Tools

In addition to the tools available to maintain high availability, Juniper also offers APIs to allow Juniper Partners to develop and deploy applications for service creation and management, as well as directly interact with JUNOS and with multiservice Physical Interface Cards (PICs) to provide services built directly on the stable foundation of JUNOS. By allowing service providers that are considered best-in-breed in their respective fields to develop services and software that integrate directly with JUNOS and the other Juniper Networks management software, Juniper Partners can guarantee high availability for their customers.

Open IP Service Development Platform (OSDP)

OSDP allows best-in-breed producers to access APIs in the Service Resource Controller (SRC) software to allow for integration and rollout of new service networks. The OSDP allows direct access to JTAC and software development engineers for the creation and testing of the new software.

Partner Solution Development Platform (PSDP)

PSDP software gives engineers direct access to Juniper to develop software that directly interacts with the JUNOS operating system and the Juniper hardware. Using SDKs and JUNOS APIs, software engineers can build tools to better secure or provide high availability to the network. Some examples of groups taking advantage of the PSDP include:

Customers

Allows for development of applications used on their networks to provide additional security, stability, or unique service offerings

Integration partners and OEMs

Allows channel partners to integrate services, such as VoIP, more intimately in the hardware and software of the networking equipment

Universities and research

Allows for the development and testing of new and cutting-edge services on a stable routing platform

CHAPTER 12

Managing Intradomain Routing Table Growth

This chapter provides a useful collection of methods, tips, and tricks for controlling routing table growth. While controlling the size of routing tables was once imperative because of memory and processor limitations on many vendors' routing platforms, those limitations are no longer the prime reasons to do so. Because modern networks' routing tables are minimized as much as possible to simplify operation and troubleshooting, controlling routing table growth is a much more basic equation—fewer routes equals fewer potential routing issues, and therefore increases uptime.

For example, suppose you came into the operations center to bring up a new local area network (LAN) with a bank of web servers during a routine 2:00 a.m. maintenance window. Shortly after bringing the servers online, you lose remote connectivity to the LAN. The flashing red icon on the network management map confirms the loss and you immediately reverse the changes. You then spend a few hours trying to figure out why the activation of the subnet impacted traffic. After much digging, you determine the issue to be the result of several small factors, the classic "death by a thousand cuts," but it's already 5:00 a.m. The maintenance window closed an hour ago. So, what caused the failure?

- A few static routes that were no longer needed were left configured on a router.
- An IP address conflict existed between the new server LAN and several existing LANs.
- The crisis was exacerbated by lack of a sensible IP addressing scheme, which would have made it possible to distinguish between host LANs and infrastructure links.
- Finally, the massive number of routes in the table helped obscure the problems.

In the end, a new maintenance window has to be scheduled and the launch of some new revenue-generating service, based on the new server LAN, has to be delayed for more than a week.

While not an outage in the classic sense, the end result was the same: loss of service that resulted in loss of revenue.

This chapter focuses on key mechanisms that reduce the number of routes needed to route traffic bound for intradomain destinations, thus promoting high availability. It also addresses the reasons and methods for limiting external advertisement (and therefore reachability) to certain destinations within the Autonomous System (AS). Specific implications of route reduction for both carrier and enterprise networks are also covered in this chapter.

Address Allocation

Intelligent address allocation is arguably the most critical element in controlling the size of the intradomain routing table. While an intelligent addressing scheme is often a byproduct of "good design," and therefore applicable in "greenfield" situations, it is also an element that can be applied to mature networks. Furthermore, the increasing use of multiple logical networks or service overlays, riding on a single collection of physical routers, means that many more architecture and design opportunities for intelligent address allocation exist than did just a few years ago.

Logical Networks As Design Opportunities

Logical networks as a tool for high availability are covered in detail later in this chapter. However, they do merit some immediate discussion to clarify the previous statements on design opportunity being more than a "greenfield" endeavor.

A logical network is a collection of logical components, including IP addresses, routing protocols, routing policies, virtual LAN (VLAN) tags, and ATM PVCs, that are collected together on a group of physical devices and links. Several years ago, businesses were content to have a single logical construct in their physical network, but this is no longer the case. Service providers and medium to large enterprise networks now commonly have multiple logical networks overlaid on the same physical infrastructure.

A network must have a Layer 2 and Layer 3 addressing scheme, as well as a way to share reachability information with other devices in the network, so at least one logical network is necessary. But setting up multiple independent logical networks is a way to separate customer traffic, create independent service domains, and provision Quality of Service (QoS), streaming multicast, or traffic separation for a subset of the existing customer base. These logical networks, sometimes called *logical overlays*, are used to separate and control services for customer billing or to limit the exposure of the network to services that are not needed everywhere in the domain.

The increasing use of logical overlays results in greater network complexity, placing higher demands on the skills of the support staff. Getting the foundational design elements (IP addressing) *right* becomes critical to the integrity and availability of the network.

Seldom does a network retain the shape described by its original architects. Technologies change; applications and services evolve or die out completely. Even in the absence of multiple logical networks or service overlays, engineers have many opportunities throughout the life of a network to properly allocate address space. As a result, it's important to discuss interface addressing in the context of high availability.

Interface Addressing

Interface addressing, or the process of assigning one or more logical identities to a physical port, seems on the surface like a very simple task. If done properly, it is part of the solution to controlling the size of your intradomain routing tables. However, if done improperly, it works against high availability. For example, every network engineer has at one time or another built an entire network using just 192.168.*n*/24 addresses for everything, including all host LANs and infrastructure links. Likewise, nearly every engineer has felt the pain of having to go back and readdress that same network as it expands in scale and complexity—to the point where the addressing scheme hampers growth and makes troubleshooting a slow, cumbersome endeavor. Don't be ashamed. The authors of this book are guilty as well. This mistake is dishonorable only if repeated. So, how do we properly assign network addresses?

JUNOS interface addressing syntax

Interface addressing syntax in JUNOS software is quite intuitive. All logical components related to a single logical connection are grouped under a `unit` number. Logical elements can include a Layer 2 and Layer 3 address, and should always include a description.

> Because this chapter focuses on controlling the size and content of intradomain routing tables, we do not cover the full range of interface configuration options in detail. You can find a thorough list and description of interface-related configuration elements at *http://www.juniper.net/support*.

In this example, interface `fe-0/0/0` has `vlan-tagging` enabled and three VLANs configured. `unit 70` corresponds to VLAN 70, `unit 90` to VLAN 90, and `unit 100` to VLAN 100. Each VLAN carries a `description` as well as an IP address:

```
[edit interfaces fe-0/0/0]
lab@r5# show
vlan-tagging;
unit 70 {
    description "VLAN connection to r3";
    vlan-id 70;
    family inet {
        address 10.0.1.9/30;
    }
```

```
    }
    unit 90 {
        description "VLAN Primary to r6";
        vlan-id 90;
        family inet {
            address 10.0.1.2/30;
        }
    }
    unit 100 {
        description "VLAN Secondary to r6";
        vlan-id 100;
        family inet {
            address 10.0.1.6/30;
        }
    }
```

 The unit numbering scheme in this example is intentional. Successful JUNOS engineers quickly get in the habit of matching the unit number—the logical interface identifier—to the logical interface address. This simplifies protocol configuration (see "Using Protocol Tweaks to Control Routing Table Size" on page 275) and can reduce troubleshooting time and, therefore, downtime.

Intelligent interface addressing requires an understanding of the purpose of the network. Subnet IPs should be allocated based on the purpose of the link to which they are being assigned. For example, in enterprise environments it is almost always necessary to distinguish between IP addresses used for corporate LANs and IP addresses used for connectivity to the Internet and partnering networks. In many networks, the distinction is simple: internal addresses are drawn from the private range and external addresses are drawn from the public range.

Furthermore, the range of addresses used within the corporate network can be divided into subnets used for router-to-router communication and subnets used for host machines. Therefore, one block of IP addresses should be reserved for infrastructure links and device IDs, another block for internal user and server LANs, and a third block for LANs used for connections to kiosks and other areas outside the corporate domain. The network shown in Figure 12-1 demonstrates how addresses can be pulled from different blocks of space based on link purpose. Interface addressing simplifies both traffic engineering and troubleshooting of the network, while conserving address space.

In Figure 12-1, all router and security devices are assigned an IP address that serves as a device ID, commonly referred to as a *loopback address*. All loopback addresses in Figure 12-1 take the form 10.0.0.*<device ID#>*. This numbering scheme permits up to 254 routers and security devices within the network. Considering that there are currently only six, this design leaves adequate room for growth.

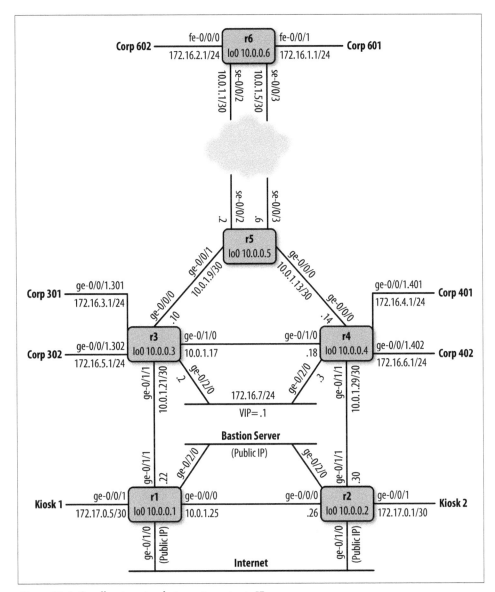

Figure 12-1. Small-enterprise design using private IPs

The infrastructure links in Figure 12-1 begin numbering at 10.0.1.0/30 (recall that the 10.0.0.0/24 space was reserved for device IDs). While address conservation is itself a noble goal, you should also allow adequate space for network growth. With this in mind, only infrastructure links in Figure 12-1 are drawn from the 10/8 addressing space in this design, leaving ample room for network growth, network virtualization, and numerous service overlays.

The addressing scheme used for the Corp LANs in Figure 12-1 draws from the 172.16/12 range of private addresses. In this design, all LANs are in the 172.16/16 space and are subnetted out to 24 bits, resulting in a capacity of 255 subnets with as many as 254 host machines per subnet. While a full /24 was used in this example, user LANs should be appropriately scoped for the number of users that will connect to them. Though commonly used, a 24-bit subnet mask may be overkill in many cases for a segment expected to have few hosts. Table 12-1 is a good quick reference for subnet scoping based on anticipated number of hosts.

Table 12-1. Usable hosts for common subnet masks

Bit mask	Bit mask (dotted decimal notation)	Usable hosts
/24	255.255.255.0	254
/25	255.255.255.128	126
/26	255.255.255.192	62
/27	255.255.255.224	30
/28	255.255.255.240	14
/29	255.255.255.248	6
/30	255.255.255.252	2

Though the number of hosts present on a subnet has an impact on the amount of bandwidth required, keep in mind that this type of planning is in addition to, not a substitute for, capacity planning and trend analysis.

Capacity Planning and Trend Analysis

While diving deep into *bandwidth capacity planning* and *network trend analysis* is beyond the scope of this book, both topics merit some mention as they are related to high availability.

Capacity planning is a greenfield activity that includes elements of both science and art. The scientific piece involves anticipating the number of users, the types of applications they will run, and the times of day they will run them. Once all elements are taken into consideration, network devices, interfaces, and a design (the art piece) can be created. A general rule of thumb is to provision bandwidth (interfaces) for what you expect utilization requirements to be in two years and to select network devices that can support what you expect the network to be in five years. These are merely suggested guidelines. For a more comprehensive method, a great resource is OPNET (*http://www.opnet .com/solutions/network_planning_operations/itguru_net_planner.html*).

Determining the distribution of traffic across devices and links within a network at specific intervals throughout the day and identifying which services or applications are responsible for the traffic is the core of *trend analysis*. In this analysis you go back and see whether the variables factored into the calculations during the capacity planning stage were correct.

Both capacity planning and trend analysis have an impact on high availability. Network architects must accurately predict how much bandwidth will be needed and plan accordingly; otherwise, bottlenecks could cause major service and performance problems. Once the network is operational, it is necessary to examine how it is being used to predict future bandwidth demands and plan accordingly.

Infrastructure Routes

We have described *infrastructure routes* as subnets used for connectivity between routers and security devices within the confines of an AS, but the term also includes any IP addresses that are used to give network-reachable identities to routers and security devices for management purposes.

When allocating infrastructure routes, the first thing a good engineer wants to do is be thrifty—don't waste IP addresses in places where they will never be used. For example, do not waste a few hundred IPs by using a 24-bit subnet mask on a point-to-point link. Instead, use a 30-bit subnet mask. There are several reasons for this thrift:

- It makes efficient use of a finite resource.
- It helps (to a small degree) in securing the network; for example, when a promiscuous routing protocol such as Open Shortest Path First (OSPF) is used. Using Figure 12-1 as a reference, the addressing scheme on the link between r2 and r4 won't prevent a passive monitoring exploit, but it could undermine an unauthorized attempt to bring up an additional OSPF neighbor on the link and sabotaging network routing.
- It can speed up troubleshooting by making infrastructure routes even more clearly distinguishable from customer routes. Rapid troubleshooting is a friend of high availability.

The JUNOS operating system supports a variety of options for the show route command, including the ability to filter output based on prefix length. Here is a way to pull up a report of routes with a /30 subnet mask, which are our infrastructure routes:

```
[edit]
lab@r5# run show route | match /30
10.0.1.0/30        *[Direct/0] 12:58:48
10.0.1.4/30        *[Direct/0] 12:58:48
10.0.1.8/30        *[Direct/0] 12:58:48
10.0.1.12/30       *[Direct/0] 12:58:48
10.0.1.16/30       *[OSPF/10] 12:57:53, metric 2
10.0.1.20/30       *[OSPF/10] 12:57:53, metric 2
10.0.1.24/30       *[OSPF/10] 12:57:53, metric 3
10.0.1.28/30       *[OSPF/10] 12:57:58, metric 2
172.17.0.0/30      *[OSPF/10] 12:57:58, metric 3
172.17.0.4/30      *[OSPF/10] 12:57:53, metric 3
```

Notice that while the command did produce a thorough list of infrastructure routes known by r5, it also listed the kiosk routes configured on r1 and r2. The network administrator chose to configure the mask this way because each LAN currently has only one kiosk system. The mask can be changed to permit more IP addresses as the number of kiosk systems grows.

> Very few networks are built with products from a single vendor. While JUNOS supports the use of a 31-bit subnet mask for point-to-point links, not all vendors support this functionality on all product lines, so we recommend using a 30-bit mask for point-to-point (infrastructure) links. Use of a 31-bit subnet mask is formalized in RFC 3021 (*http://www.faqs.org/rfcs/rfc3021.html*).

Customer Routes

In enterprise environments, almost every subnet within the domain that is not classified as an infrastructure route can be classified as a *customer route*. Customer routes include user LANs, server LANs, and storage LANs (Network Access Servers or NASs), and they are collections of users and tools, represented by IP addresses, for which the network infrastructure exists. In Figure 12-1, these are identified as the Corp LANs.

In a service provider topology, the term *customer LANs* implies the same thing. Again, it is the collection of tools and users for which a service is being provided by the infrastructure. An important distinction between enterprise and service provider topologies is that with a service provider, most commonly the customer routes lay outside the service provider's domain. For this reason, we cover management of these types of routes from a service provider perspective separately, in Chapter 11.

All infrastructure routes mapped in Figure 12-1 were drawn from the 10/8 address space. Likewise, all host LANs, our customer LANs, will be drawn from the 172.16/16 address space. This address allocation scheme allows quick and accurate distinction between host and infrastructure routes. This promotes high availability by effectively reducing the amount of time spent troubleshooting an issue.

> The astute reader should also note that all router interfaces on host LANs were configured with the .1 address of the host LAN subnet. While the address does not always have to be the .1 IP, to promote rapid troubleshooting—and therefore high availability—a competent network administrator should standardize configuration of the router interface on a host LAN. This simplifies configuration of the default gateway on all host systems in the network.

In Figure 12-1, kiosk routes have also been allocated a block of addresses, 172.17/16. This differentiation further simplifies troubleshooting by making kiosk routing easily distinguishable from other types of customer LANs. In Figure 12-1, kiosk LANs are currently using a /30 mask because there is only one kiosk system and one router interface on each subnet. Using what we learned in Table 12-1, this subnet mask could be changed to permit more IP addresses as the number of kiosk systems grows.

Virtual Router Redundancy Protocol

Virtual Router Redundancy Protocol (VRRP) should be used on business-critical LANs to support high availability because it allows multiple routers to share ownership of an interface IP address. This interface IP address is then used by host systems as a default gateway off the LAN. Because two or more routers share ownership of the IP address, failure of a single router would not result in loss of connectivity to the LAN. Additionally, JUNOS allows configuration of interface *tracking*, which can effectively trigger gateway failover when upstream links drop.

In Figure 12-1, VRRP is being used for the 172.16.7/24 LAN. We have chosen to describe this LAN as critical to the operation of the business and have provided it with additional high availability mechanisms. The LAN has connectivity to the rest of the network through both r3 and r4. Routers r3 and r4 share a virtual IP (VIP) address, 172.16.7.1, used by hosts on the LAN as a default gateway. This design is reflected in the ge-0/2/0 interface configuration on r3. The use of the .1 address on the LAN is in keeping with the scheme used in host LANs in the network. Use of the .1 address supports high availability by keeping default gateway configuration consistent. Here's a sample configuration:

```
[edit interfaces]
lab@r3# show ge-0/2/0
 unit 0 {
     family inet {
         address 172.16.7.2/24 {
             vrrp-group 1 {
                 virtual-address 172.16.7.1;
                 priority 101;
                 preempt;
                 accept-data;
                 track {
                     interface ge-0/0/0 priority-cost 5;
                     interface ge-0/1/1 priority-cost 5;
                 }
             }
         }
     }
 }
```

In this configuration sample, the priority for ownership of the VIP address is set to 101. This is one point higher than the default of 100, which is what the r4 configuration has been left at. Also notice that both r3 and r4 are tracking the state of interfaces ge-0/0/0 and ge-0/1/1. Both links have been assigned a priority cost value, which is deducted from the total priority number in the event of a link failure.

If one or both of these interfaces fail, ownership of the VIP transfers from r3 to r4, allowing the host systems on the LAN to continue to communicate with the rest of the network. So, here is the interface configuration on r4:

```
[edit interfaces]
lab@r4# show ge-0/2/0
 unit 0 {
     family inet {
         address 172.16.7.3/24 {
             vrrp-group 1 {
                 virtual-address 172.16.7.1;
                 preempt;
                 accept-data;
                 track {
                     interface ge-0/0/0 priority-cost 5;
                     interface ge-0/1/1 priority-cost 5;
                 }
             }
         }
     }
 }
```

Router r4 now has complementary VRRP configuration elements for Group 1. Notice that no priority has been set for r4. This configuration allows r4 to assume the default VIP ownership priority of 100, which means that, by default, it is serving as a backup gateway for the LAN, with r3 being the primary gateway.

 These configuration samples show two routers serving as primary and backup gateways for the 172.16.7/24 LAN. Additional routers can be configured for added redundancy by configuring them to be in the same VRRP group for the subnet.

Network Virtualization and Service Overlays

One of this book's premises is that in the real world, network design is no longer a greenfield event that occurs only once in the life of a network. These days, all major router and security device OEMs offer products that feature the ability to run multiple logical instances of components of the operating system. These virtual machines are best described as "lots of little routers inside one chassis." In JUNOS software, virtual machines take several forms, including *routing instances* (sometimes referred to as virtual routers or VRs) and *logical routers*.

Logical routers and routing instances are important because they are the mechanisms used to configure the additional logical networks and service overlays discussed at the beginning of this chapter. As we said earlier, these logical abstractions are used to separate and control services for customer billing, or to limit the exposure of the network to services that are not needed everywhere in the domain. If properly configured, they contribute to high availability by partitioning what would be a single large routing table into multiple smaller routing tables that are themselves service-focused.

Routing instances

Routing instances are a means of separating routing information and traffic within the JUNOS operating system. Routing instances come in many flavors, but all share a few common characteristics:

- All routing instances create routing and forwarding tables that feed the same instance of the Routing Protocol Daemon (RPD).
- Routes are not propagated to other routing tables unless explicitly configured to do so.
- Routing instances are used to create nearly all flavors of virtual private networks (VPNs) in common use today.
- Multiple routing instances can be grouped within a single logical router.

 When routing instances are configured on a chassis, the configuration elements that are *not* placed under a routing-instance are said to be in the *primary routing instance*.

You can always use the help topic routing-instances instance-type command to provide an excellent online description of the purpose of the different flavors of routing instances that you can use:

```
[edit routing-options]
lab@main# help topic routing-instances instance-type
Configuring an Instance Type

    You can configure six routing instance types at the [edit
    routing-instances routing-instance-name instance-type] and [edit
    logical-routers logical-router-name routing-instances
    routing-instance-name instance-type] hierarchy levels:
     * Forwarding--Use this routing instance type for filter-based forwarding
       applications. For this instance type, there is no one-to-one mapping
       between an interface and a routing instance. All interfaces belong to
       the default instance inet.0.

     * Layer 2 VPN--Use this routing instance type for Layer 2 VPN
       implementations.

     * Nonforwarding--Use this routing instance type when a separation of
       routing table information is required. There is no corresponding
       forwarding table. All routes are installed into the default forwarding
       table. IS-IS instances are strictly nonforwarding instance types.

     * Virtual router--Similar to a VPN routing and forwarding instance type,
       but used for non-VPN-related applications. There are no VRF import,
       VRF export, VRF target, or route distinguisher requirements for this
       instance type.
```

* VPLS--Use this routing instance type for point-to-multipoint LAN
  implementations between a set of sites in a VPN.

* VRF--Use this routing instance type for Layer 3 VPN implementations.
  For this instance type, there is a one-to-one mapping between an
  interface and a routing instance. Each VRF instance corresponds with a
  forwarding table. Routes on an interface go into the corresponding
  forwarding table.

 Although routing instances do generate separate routing tables, all the
tables generated still rely on a single RPD and a single collection of
routing policies. This means that even though the tables are separate,
they are still somewhat related to each other.

For example, policies can be created that permit routes to be shared
among the tables created by multiple routing instances within a single
logical router. Routing instances do not separate logical elements as
cleanly as logical routers, but routing instances do provide functionality
beyond that available from a logical router.

Logical routers

Unlike a routing instance, a logical router maintains its own independent RPD that
generates an independent set of routing tables. A logical router also maintains its own
routing policies and interfaces, and can support multiple routing instances (as
described in the previous section). A JUNOS router can support up to 15 logical routers.

These features are important because logical routers are a way to control the content
and size of JUNOS routing tables. The features allow the logical separation of configuration elements, control traffic, and user data traffic that would otherwise increase
the size and complexity of the primary logical network. In many ways, logical routers
result in a cleaner separation of logical elements than a routing instance and are therefore easier to troubleshoot.

Figure 12-2 shows some of the same physical devices used in Figure 12-1, but with an
independent IPv4-based service overlay on top of a subset of the existing links. The
router icons in Figure 12-2 represent logical routers, hence the -lr suffix. In this
example, logical routers are configured on r1, r2, r3, and r4 to provide a complete
separation of routing protocol and interface information from the primary IPv4 logical
network. This configuration allows any troubleshooting necessary on the primary logical network to be performed without digging through the additional configuration
elements made necessary by stand-up of the new service overlay.

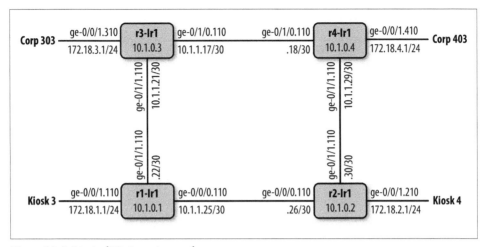

Figure 12-2. Limited IPv4 service overlay

 The logical elements present in Figure 12-1 have not gone away. Figures 12-1 and 12-2 are each simply one of many possible virtual networks that ride on top of the same physical infrastructure.

Enable VLAN tagging in the primary logical router

Before creating the service overlay, we must first enable VLAN tagging and assign our existing logical interfaces to VLANs that will be used in the primary logical router. Figure 12-3 shows that VLAN 100 will be used for interfaces in the primary logical router. Notice that the only real difference between Figures 12-1 and 12-3 is the addition of VLAN tags to the four infrastructure links among r1, r2, r3, and r4—a very small price to pay for the high availability benefits of service-based route table separation.

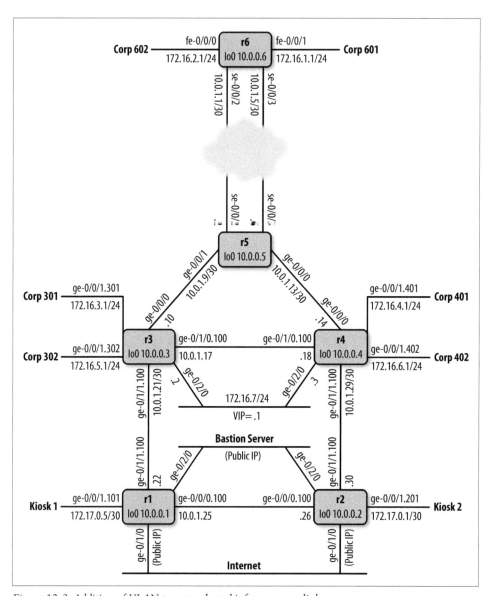

Figure 12-3. Addition of VLAN tags to selected infrastructure links

Begin by changing the configuration on the infrastructure links and on the kiosk LAN on r1 to support vlan-tagging:

```
[edit interfaces]
lab@r1# set ge-0/0/0 vlan-tagging

[edit interfaces]
lab@r1# set ge-0/0/1 vlan-tagging
```

```
[edit interfaces]
lab@r1# set ge-0/1/1 vlan-tagging

[edit interfaces]
lab@r1# show
ge-0/0/0 {
    description "link to r2";
    vlan-tagging;
    unit 0 {
        family inet {
            address 10.0.1.25/30;
        }
    }
}
ge-0/0/1 {
    description "Link to Kiosk 1";
    vlan-tagging;
    unit 0 {
        family inet {
            address 172.17.0.5/30;
        }
    }
}
ge-0/1/1 {
    description "Link to r3";
    vlan-tagging;
    unit 0 {
        family inet {
            address 10.0.1.22/30;
        }
    }
}
```

Use the JUNOS rename function to change unit 0 to unit 100 to match the logical identity to the VLAN tag. After this step is complete, add a VLAN tag to the logical unit on each interface and review the changes:

```
[edit interfaces]
lab@r1# rename ge-0/0/0 unit 0 to unit 100

[edit interfaces]
lab@r1# rename ge-0/0/1 unit 0 to unit 100

[edit interfaces]
lab@r1# rename ge-0/1/1 unit 0 to unit 100

[edit interfaces]
lab@r1# set ge-0/0/0 unit 100 vlan-id 100

[edit interfaces]
lab@r1# set ge-0/0/1 unit 100 vlan-id 100

[edit interfaces]
lab@r1# set ge-0/1/1 unit 100 vlan-id 100
```

Routers running JUNOS can support multiple IPv4 addresses on the same logical interfaces at the same time. The logical separation shown in Figure 12-2 simply demonstrates one possible use of virtual network configuration elements.

We could confirm our work by using the show command. However, in this example we use show | compare to compare the candidate configuration to the active configuration. All of the expected VLAN changes are present; however, notice that another change has been made since the last commit. User james has been deleted from the system login hierarchy. A commit now could have unintended consequences if another administrator is actively adjusting user permission on this chassis. Had we not checked the configuration using the compare option, we could have accidentally locked someone out of the box:

```
[edit]
lab@r1# show | compare
[edit system login]
-    user james {
-        uid 2001;
-        class superuser;
-        authentication {
-            encrypted-password "$1$tAbi_rOseCV5e6irKOFfQmee7mqj.";
-        }
-    }
[edit interfaces ge-0/0/0]
+   vlan-tagging;
[edit interfaces ge-0/0/0]
-    unit 0 {
-        family inet {
-            address 10.0.1.25/30;
-        }
-    }
+    unit 100 {
+        vlan-id 100;
+        family inet {
+            address 10.0.1.25/30;
+        }
+    }
[edit interfaces ge-0/0/1]
+   vlan-tagging;
[edit interfaces ge-0/0/1]
-    unit 0 {
-        family inet {
-            address 172.17.0.5/30;
-        }
-    }
+    unit 100 {
+        vlan-id 100;
+        family inet {
+            address 172.17.0.5/30;
+        }
+    }
```

```
[edit interfaces ge-0/1/1]
+   vlan-tagging;
[edit interfaces ge-0/1/1]
-    unit 0 {
-        family inet {
-            address 10.0.1.22/30;
-        }
-    }
+    unit 100 {
+        vlan-id 100;
+        family inet {
+            address 10.0.1.22/30;
+        }
+    }
```

VLAN tagging is now enabled in the main logical router, and VLAN tags have been assigned to our infrastructure interfaces that continue to be present in the main logical router. Before committing this configuration change, be sure to update the interface names throughout the configuration file. This will include the VRRP and OSPF configuration stanzas. Using r3 as an example, the end result should include the following change to interface ge-0/2/0 to protect the 172.16.7/24 LAN:

```
[edit interfaces]
lab@r3# show ge-0/2/0
 unit 0 {
     family inet {
         address 172.16.7.2/24 {
             vrrp-group 1 {
                 virtual-address 172.16.7.1;
                 priority 101;
                 preempt;
                 accept-data;
                 track {
                     interface ge-0/0/0.100 priority-cost 5;
                     interface ge-0/1/1.100 priority-cost 5;
                 }
             }
         }
     }
 }
```

The OSPF stanza of r3 should also be updated to allow the protocol to continue to function across the new logical interfaces:

```
[edit protocols ospf]
lab@r3# show
area 0.0.0.0 {
    interface ge-0/0/0.0;
    interface ge-0/1/0.100;
    interface ge-0/1/1.100;
    interface ge-0/2/0.0{
        passive;
    }
    interface lo0.0 {
        passive;
```

```
        }
    }
```

Similar configuration changes should be made on r1, r2, and r4 before adding the overlay. One can briefly look at the configuration options available under the logical-router level of the JUNOS hierarchy to see how much functionality is available through logical-routers:

```
[edit logical-routers r1-lr1]
lab@r1# set ?
Possible completions:
+ apply-groups          Groups from which to inherit configuration data
+ apply-groups-except   Don't inherit configuration data from these groups
> interfaces            Interface configuration
> policy-options        Routing policy option configuration
> protocols             Routing protocol configuration
> routing-instances     Routing instance configuration
> routing-options       Protocol-independent routing option configuration
```

Notice that it is possible to configure interfaces, protocols, and policies from within the logical router, just like within the primary logical router. This separation, and the independent tables it creates, controls the size and content of the primary routing table without affecting the ability to support new services—simply by breaking the routing information into smaller, more manageable chunks.

Configuring the service overlay

Referring back to the topology in Figure 12-2, we see a limited deployment of an IPv4-based service to support testing of an application involving two corporate LANs and two kiosk LANs. Notice that the router names have an -lr# suffix to indicate that they are logical routers. Additional VLANs can now be added to r1, r2, r3, and r4, but they are not configured in the main logical router. Instead, they are configured in lr1 on each of the four chassis.

 When logical routers are configured on a chassis, the configuration elements that are *not* placed under a logical router are said to be in the *main logical router* or *primary logical router*.

Using the VLAN tag and interface addressing scheme shown in Figure 12-2, create the necessary interfaces in logical-router r1-lr1 on r1 and assign addresses accordingly. Output from the show command confirms that the configuration changes were accurate:

```
[edit logical-routers r1-lr1 interfaces]
lab@r1# show
ge-0/0/0 {
    unit 110 {
        description "logical router 1 link to r2";
        vlan-id 110;
        family inet {
```

```
                address 10.1.1.25/30;
            }
        }
    }
    ge-0/0/1 {
        unit 110 {
            description "logical router 1 link to kiosk 3";
            vlan-id 110;
            family inet {
                address 172.18.1.1/24;
            }
        }
    }
    ge-0/1/1 {
        unit 110 {
            description "logical router 1 link to r3";
            vlan-id 110;
            family inet {
                address 10.1.1.22/30;
            }
        }
    }
    lo0 {
        unit 1 {
            family inet {
                address 10.1.0.1/32;
            }
        }
    }
}
```

Using the logical topology in Figure 12-2, make similar interface changes on r2, r3, and
r4. Once interfaces are configured, you need to enable only a routing protocol within
the logical-router on each chassis to complete the task:

```
[edit logical-routers r1-lr1]
lab@r1# edit protocols ospf area 0

[edit logical-routers r1-lr1 protocols ospf area 0.0.0.0]
lab@r1# set interface ge-0/1/1.110

[edit logical-routers r1-lr1 protocols ospf area 0.0.0.0]
lab@r1# set interface ge-0/0/0.110

[edit logical-routers r1-lr1 protocols ospf area 0.0.0.0]
lab@r1# set interface ge-0/0/1.110 passive

[edit logical-routers r1-lr1 protocols ospf area 0.0.0.0]
lab@r1# set interface lo0.1 passive

[edit logical-routers r1-lr1 protocols ospf area 0.0.0.0]
lab@r1# show
interface ge-0/1/1.110;
interface ge-0/0/0.110;
interface ge-0/0/1.110 {
    passive;
```

```
}
interface lo0.1 {
    passive;
}
```

By comparing the output from show route with the output from show route logical-router r1-lr1, you can see the clean separation of routing information. This separation allows fast and effective troubleshooting of both logical networks, contributing to high availability in both:

```
lab@r1> show route

inet.0: 33 destinations, 34 routes (33 active, 0 holddown, 0 hidden)
+ = Active Route, - = Last Active, * = Both

0.0.0.0/0          *[Static/5] 00:02:22
                    > to 7.6.5.3 via ge-0/1/0.0
                   [OSPF/150] 00:02:22, metric 0, tag 0
                    > to 10.0.1.26 via ge-0/0/0.100
7.6.5.0/24         *[Direct/0] 00:02:23
                    > via ge-0/1/0.0
7.6.5.1/32         *[Local/0] 00:02:23
                      Local via ge-0/1/0.0
8.7.6.0/24         *[Direct/0] 00:02:23
                    > via ge-0/2/0.0
8.7.6.1/32         *[Local/0] 00:02:14
                      Local via ge-0/2/0.0
8.7.6.2/32         *[Local/0] 00:02:23
                      Local via ge-0/2/0.0
10.0.0.1/32        *[Direct/0] 00:48:25
                    > via lo0.0
10.0.0.2/32        *[OSPF/10] 00:47:35, metric 1
                    > to 10.0.1.26 via ge-0/0/0.100
10.0.0.3/32        *[OSPF/10] 00:47:35, metric 1
                    > to 10.0.1.21 via ge-0/1/1.100
10.0.0.4/32        *[OSPF/10] 00:47:25, metric 2
                    > to 10.0.1.21 via ge-0/1/1.100
                      to 10.0.1.26 via ge-0/0/0.100
10.0.0.5/32        *[OSPF/10] 00:01:18, metric 2
                    > to 10.0.1.21 via ge-0/1/1.100
10.0.0.6/32        *[OSPF/10] 00:01:18, metric 3
                    > to 10.0.1.21 via ge-0/1/1.100
10.0.1.0/30        *[OSPF/10] 00:01:18, metric 3
                    > to 10.0.1.21 via ge-0/1/1.100
10.0.1.4/30        *[OSPF/10] 00:01:18, metric 3
                    > to 10.0.1.21 via ge-0/1/1.100
10.0.1.8/30        *[OSPF/10] 00:01:18, metric 2
                    > to 10.0.1.21 via ge-0/1/1.100
10.0.1.12/30       *[OSPF/10] 00:01:26, metric 3
                      to 10.0.1.21 via ge-0/1/1.100
                    > to 10.0.1.26 via ge-0/0/0.100
---(more)---

lab@r1> show route logical-router r1-lr1
```

```
inet.0: 16 destinations, 16 routes (16 active, 0 holddown, 0 hidden)
+ = Active Route, - = Last Active, * = Both

10.1.0.1/32       *[Direct/0] 01:06:16
                   > via lo0.1
10.1.0.2/32       *[OSPF/10] 00:00:07, metric 1
                   > to 10.1.1.26 via ge-0/0/0.110
10.1.0.3/32       *[OSPF/10] 00:02:01, metric 1
                   > to 10.1.1.21 via ge-0/1/1.110
10.1.0.4/32       *[OSPF/10] 00:00:07, metric 2
                   > to 10.1.1.21 via ge-0/1/1.110
                     to 10.1.1.26 via ge-0/0/0.110
10.1.1.16/30      *[OSPF/10] 00:02:01, metric 2
                   > to 10.1.1.21 via ge-0/1/1.110
10.1.1.20/30      *[Direct/0] 00:02:41
                   > via ge-0/1/1.110
10.1.1.22/32      *[Local/0] 00:02:41
                     Local via ge-0/1/1.110
10.1.1.24/30      *[Direct/0] 00:02:41
                   > via ge-0/0/0.110
10.1.1.25/32      *[Local/0] 00:02:41
                     Local via ge-0/0/0.110
10.1.1.28/30      *[OSPF/10] 00:00:07, metric 2
                   > to 10.1.1.26 via ge-0/0/0.110
172.18.1.0/24     *[Direct/0] 00:02:41
                   > via ge-0/0/1.110
172.18.1.1/32     *[Local/0] 00:02:41
                     Local via ge-0/0/1.110
172.18.2.0/24     *[OSPF/10] 00:00:07, metric 2
                   > to 10.1.1.26 via ge-0/0/0.110
172.18.3.0/24     *[OSPF/10] 00:02:01, metric 2
                   > to 10.1.1.21 via ge-0/1/1.110
172.18.4.0/24     *[OSPF/10] 00:00:07, metric 3
                   > to 10.1.1.21 via ge-0/1/1.110
                     to 10.1.1.26 via ge-0/0/0.110
224.0.0.5/32      *[OSPF/10] 01:06:17, metric 1
                     MultiRecv
```

Address Aggregation

A second task in allocating infrastructure routes for subnets is to make sure your address assignment will support either a protocol-driven aggregation scheme or a manual route aggregation scheme. This allows control of the size of the routing table inside the network and yields efficiency when advertising subnets outside the local domain.

Aggregation may not be necessary at the start of a small network deployment because there just aren't enough subnets to aggregate. However, it does come into play in larger networks and quite commonly in service overlays.

What Is Aggregation?

Aggregation is an address allocation goal for any network requiring high availability. *Aggregation*, or *supernetting* as it is described in Cisco and Microsoft textbooks, is a less specific way to refer to a collection of more specific routes. The ability to aggregate a collection of more specific routes into fewer, less specific routes is based on binary bit patterns in the subnets themselves. Table 12-2 shows a collection of multiaccess subnets that can be aggregated into a single route advertisement, thereby reducing the number of routes that would need to be advertised.

Table 12-2. Route aggregation example

IP address	Binary breakout
192.160.0.0/24	*1100 0000. 1010 0100. 0000 0000.* 0000 0000
192.168.1.0/24	*1100 0000. 1010 0100. 0000 0001.* 0000 0000
192.168.2.0/24	*1100 0000. 1010 0100. 0000 0010.* 0000 0000
192.168.3.0/24	*1100 0000. 1010 0100. 0000 0011.* 0000 0000
192.168.4.0/24	*1100 0000. 1010 0100. 0000 0100.* 0000 0000
192.168.5.0/24	*1100 0000. 1010 0100. 0000 0101.* 0000 0000
192.168.6.0/24	*1100 0000. 1010 0100. 0000 0110.* 0000 0000
192.168.7.0/24	*1100 0000. 1010 0100. 0000 0111.* 0000 0000

Notice that all the italicized bits in the "Binary breakout" column match, and that once you go toward the low-order bits beyond them, the pattern changes among subnets. The italicized portion is used to derive the less specific route to represent reachability to these subnets. In each row, 21 bits are italicized. Therefore, our subnet mask is a /21. The italicized bits also determine the subnet itself. In this case, it is 192.168.0/21, which effectively replaces the need to advertise eight subnets by advertising a single, less specific subnet.

Practical aggregation for a large domain

While it is important to understand the hows and whys of route aggregation (actually calculating aggregate routes for a large service provider or large enterprise network should not be seen as a manual task), the example shown in Table 12-2 is intentionally simple, to illustrate how bit patterns are used as part of the calculation. Running the same calculation for several thousand or even just a few hundred routes could take weeks and would likely be prone to human error.

Numerous tools exist that calculate the minimum number of aggregates required for a list of subnets. Some of the better tools we have worked with are the Subnet/Supernet Calculator, which you can find at *http://www.subnet-calculator.com/cidr.php*, and Advanced IP Address Calculator v1.1, which you can find at *http://advanced-ip-address -calculator.download-99-28194.programsbase.com/*. Both are free downloads.

Is there a risk?

On occasion, we have heard colleagues describe risks associated with route aggregation, the most common being the use of a static default route in conjunction with a calculated aggregate that results in a routing loop when some of the subnets of the aggregate are not reachable. Figure 12-4 illustrates this unfounded phobia.

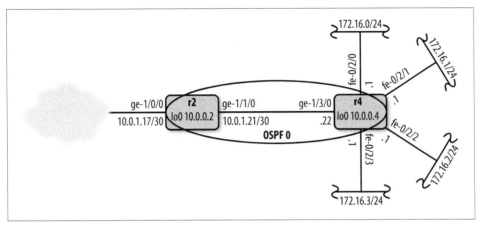

Figure 12-4. Route aggregation example

In this (perhaps oversimplified) example, r2 and r4 are in OSPF Area 0. Router r2 has connectivity to the outside world through interface ge-1/0/0. Router r4 has a connection to r2 through ge-1/3/0, and also four connections to departmental LANs in a small company. The LANs' subnets are allocated in a way that permits them to be rolled up into a single aggregated advertisement. Output from a show interfaces command reveals the IP addressing scheme:

```
[edit]
lab@r4# show interfaces
fe-0/2/0 {
    unit 0 {
        description "Parts Dept LAN";
        family inet {
            address 172.16.0.1/24;
        }
    }
}
fe-0/2/1 {
    unit 0 {
        description "Service Dept. LAN";
        family inet {
            address 172.16.1.1/24;
        }
    }
}
fe-0/2/2 {
    unit 0 {
```

```
                description "Accounting Dept. LAN"
                family inet {
                    address 172.16.2.1/24;
                }
            }
        }
    }
    fe-0/2/3 {
        unit 0 {
            description "Management and HR LAN"
            family inet {
                address 172.16.3.1/24;
            }
        }
    }

    [edit]
    lab@r4# show routing-options
    aggregate {
        route 172.16.0.0/22;
    }
```

 Notice that the administrator of this network followed the recommended practice of assigning a description to each logical connection. This
practice may seem like a trivial step, but in the heat of a troubleshooting
battle it can reduce downtime. Anything that reduces downtime is a
friend of high availability!

Let's assume the administrator responsible for the network in Figure 12-3 has created
a policy called AGG that is used to redistribute the aggregate route into OSPF:

```
    [edit]
    lab@r4# show policy-options policy-statement AGG
    term 1 {
        from protocol aggregate;
        then accept;
    }

    [edit]
    lab@r4# show protocols
    ospf {
        export AGG;
        area 0.0.0.0 {
            interface ge-1/3/0.0;
            interface lo0.0 {
                passive;
            }
        }
    }
```

Seasoned JUNOS engineers often use all-capital letters for user-defined variables. This technique makes the variables easy to spot among the screens full of command-line interface (CLI) syntax and can save time when troubleshooting.

So, r2 and r4 are OSPF Area 0 neighbors, and r2 has a static default route it is redistributing into OSPF to allow both routers to forward traffic into the cloud. If that is the case, the show routing-options command reveals the following:

```
[edit]
lab@r2# show routing-options
static {
    route 0.0.0.0/0 next-hop 10.0.1.18;
}

[edit]
lab@r2# show policy-options policy-statement STAT
term 1 {
    from protocol static;
    then accept;
}

[edit]
lab@r2# show protocols
ospf {
    export STAT;
    area 0.0.0.0 {
        interface ge-1/1/0.0;
        interface lo0.0 {
            passive;
        }
    }
}
```

The unfounded phobia is based on a hypothesis that goes like so: in the event that one of the aggregated subnets on r4 becomes unavailable, traffic bound for the subnet would arrive at r4, find the subnet unavailable, and be forwarded back to r2 because of the existence of the default route. Upon arrival at r2, the traffic would be forwarded back to r4 due to the advertisement of the aggregate. The theory is that r4 would then forward it back to r2 because of the default route causing some sort of evil loop.

This will not happen. Functional attributes of route aggregation make it safe for use in this scenario and prevent the behavior attributed to evil looping, because an aggregate route is active only when one or more active contributing routes exist. More importantly, the default *forwarding* action of an aggregate route is to discard traffic that recognizes the aggregate itself as the longest prefix match. Therefore, if the aggregate is active because of an active contributing route, but other contributing routes are inactive, traffic bound for the inactive contributing routes is discarded.

Truth be told, we have seen one corner case specific to large-scale ISP routing in which an aggregate route does cause problems. In some topologies that include one or more External Border Gateway Protocol (EBGP)-speaking routers in an OSPF not-so-stubby area (NSSA) with redundant area border routers (ABRs), the presence of an aggregated route that encompasses the links in the NSSA causes undesirable consequences for BGP and OSPF. Harry Reynolds does a good job of describing details of this corner case, as well as a few effective workarounds, in his *Juniper Networks Certified Internet Professional (JNCIP) Study Guide*, currently available free of charge from Juniper networks at *http://www.juniper.net/training/certification/books.html*.

Use of the Private Address Space

RFC 1918 defines several ranges of IP addresses that are reserved for private use—they are never to be allocated for addition to the regular Internet routing table. These addresses are commonly used in lab environments, classrooms, and anyplace else that does not require native reachability across the regular Internet. Table 12-3 lists the RFC 1918 addresses.

Table 12-3. The private address space

IP address range	Number of IP addresses
10.0.0.0-10.255.255.255	16,777,216
172.16.0.0-172.31.255.255	1,048,576
192.168.0.0-192.168.255.255	65,536

Private addressing and internal services

Use of the private address space has a few implications for services provisioned internally for users located within the corporate domain. An interesting fact is that these address ranges are commonly blocked by service providers at their domain boundaries when handling regular Internet traffic. This limitation gives use of this space an added benefit of security in some situations.

Private addressing and customer services

Because the addresses are not routable destinations across the regular Internet, use of the private address space has several important implications for companies that use their corporate network to provide a service to customers outside the corporate domain. In most cases, companies stand up a Bastion Server LAN or, for smaller networks, use a mapped IP address (MIP) in conjunction with Network Address Translation (NAT) at the Internet boundary. In some cases both are used.

A *Bastion Server* LAN is a subnet with a publicly routable IP addressing scheme. The Bastion Server LAN is commonly protected from malicious attack by multiple collections of filters and policies facing the regular Internet as well as the intranet. This type of LAN is useful when several servers or discrete services need to be accessed both from within and outside the domain.

Private addressing, NAT, and MIP

NAT and Port Address Translation (PAT) are methods of mapping IP addresses and TCP ports across a defined boundary. Sometimes NAT and PAT are used as a security mechanism to obscure host IPs, though the effectiveness of this method is questionable at best. For a good explanation as to why NAT and PAT are ineffective security mechanisms, take a look at *Security Power Tools (http://oreilly.com/catalog/9780596009632/)*, by Bryan Burns, et al. (O'Reilly).

Today, NAT is commonly used at the boundary between a network using the private IP range and the regular Internet. This design allows the private network to grow and be addressed as needs arise, while still supporting the ability to access resources across the regular Internet. NAT and PAT also allow a number of users to share a smaller number of public IP addresses for Internet connectivity.

Because manual configuration is required, a MIP is appropriate when only one or perhaps just a few servers will be accessed from outside a NAT boundary. A MIP is used to map a single external IP address or port number to a single IP address within the NATed domain. This addressing scheme makes the internal service reachable externally without exposing any infrastructure details.

MIP address allocation and boundary considerations are covered in detail in *ScreenOS Cookbook (http://oreilly.com/catalog/9780596510039/)*, by Stefan Brunner, et al. (O'Reilly).

Use of Public Address Space

All the examples in this chapter so far have used the private address space for infrastructure links. Although this is common practice, there is no written or implied rule that says public IP addresses cannot be used. Allocating public IP addresses for infrastructure links may be appropriate in some circumstances, such as when web services are hosted from a high percentage of the routers in the network. Figure 12-5 shows a service provider network hosting web services from nearly all its routers.

In Figure 12-5, public IP addressing for the four defined infrastructure links may be desirable from a support perspective, although there are some very important implications to consider:

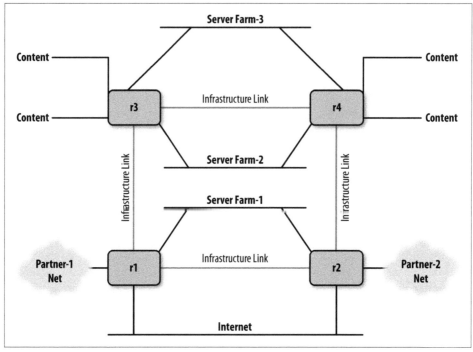

Figure 12-5. Business case for using public IPs

- Public IP addresses cost money and require documentation showing a business justification, while private IP address use is free of charge.
- Public IP addresses are a finite resource. Additional space may be needed as a business grows. Private IP address space, on the other hand, can be consumed and reallocated as needed.
- If purchased and used for infrastructure links, public IP addresses are not available for use in host LANs, where there is a much stronger business case for placement.

Most importantly, however, these links host neither service nor content, so from a security perspective, no valid reason exists for them to be reachable destinations across the Internet. Allowing them to be advertised as such opens them to potential attack. Also, if BGP is used within this domain, the infrastructure routes could be obscured without impacting the ability to reach the public IP destinations.

Static Routes

Static routes are easily configured in JUNOS software, a fact that is rather unfortunate because it often leads to overuse. By their very nature, static routes lack administrative visibility, are subject to human error, and cannot take link or node failures into

---

consideration when forwarding traffic. Generally speaking, these characteristics make them a rather strong enemy of high availability.

When to configure static routes

If used judiciously, static routes can serve a purpose in a production network, such as when a static default route is used in an enterprise network to internally advertise reachability to all external destinations without using a full BGP table. In Figure 12-6, a static default route is being redistributed by r3 into OSPF to advertise to r1 and r2 the default gateway to the Internet.

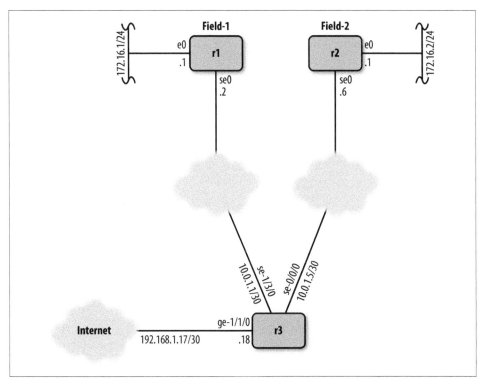

Figure 12-6. Static routing for low-bandwidth applications

Static routing is also used in Figure 12-6 because the chatty nature of a link-state protocol consumes a significant amount of the available link bandwidth between r1 and r3, and also between r2 and r3. In this situation, the dynamic benefits of OSPF or Intermediate System to Intermediate System (IS-IS) are surrendered in favor of increasing the available bandwidth. The configuration file for r3, a Juniper router, would include the static routes needed to advertise the default as mentioned earlier and to reach the Field 1 and Field 2 subnets that are behind r1 and r2, respectively:

```
[edit routing-options]
lab@r3# show
static {
    route 0.0.0.0/0 next-hop 192.167.1.17;
    route 172.16.1.0/24 next-hop 10.0.1.2;
    route 172.16.2.0/24 next-hop 10.0.1.6;
}
```

The static default on r3 provides external connectivity. Routers r1 and r2, both Cisco routers, would likewise have static default routes pointing toward r3. This setup would allow users on the Field 1 and Field 2 subnets to reach destinations off the local LAN, all without running a bandwidth-consuming routing protocol:

```
r1#show run
Building configuration...

Current configuration:
!
...
interface Ethernet0
 ip address 172.16.1.1 255.255.255.0
!
interface Serial0
 ip address 10.0.1.2 255.255.255.252
 clockrate 56000
!
...
ip route 0.0.0.0 0.0.0.0 10.0.1.1
!
...

r2#show run
Building configuration...

Current configuration:
!
...
interface Ethernet0
 ip address 172.16.2.1 255.255.255.0
!
interface Serial0
 ip address 10.0.1.6 255.255.255.252
 clockrate 56000
!
...
ip route 0.0.0.0 0.0.0.0 10.0.1.5
!
...
```

Use of static routes in this case makes sense because the topology is not blessed with diversity. There is only one way in and out of r1 and r2. Furthermore, the low bandwidth available on the links from r3 to r1 and r2 makes routing efficiency a top priority. In this case, static routing is without a doubt the best approach.

Using Protocol Tweaks to Control Routing Table Size

Interior Gateway Protocols (IGPs) come in several flavors—link-state, distance vector, and hybrids—and can serve different functions in a network based on network size and purpose. For example, in an enterprise network, the IGP's primary function is to share route reachability information among the routers. In a service provider network, the IGP's primary function is to enable establishment of BGP neighbors. Because the strengths and weaknesses of the protocol flavors are covered extensively in other chapters, it is sufficient here to say that any network of considerable size runs one of the two dominant link-state protocols, IS-IS or OSPF. Both support features that, when properly used, help to control the size of the intradomain routing table.

IS-IS areas and levels

IS-IS supports use of a two-level hierarchical scheme to control routing table and link-state database size within the IS-IS domain. The two level types are conveniently called Level 1 areas and Level 2 areas. IS-IS is, by default, a friend of routing table control because of the default functionality of its levels. While routers within a Level 2 area each by default maintain a complete collection of routes for the IS-IS domain, routers in a Level 1 area retain routes specific to their area and generate a default route to any immediately attached Level 2 router.

Beyond the described functionality of the Level 1 and Level 2 areas, the IS-IS protocol has no mechanism for summarizing routing information across area boundaries. This fact does not make the protocol any less appropriate for route control or high availability applications; it simply means that an additional tool is required to summarize the routes.

Route aggregation in conjunction with policy statements for redistribution, both described earlier in this chapter, are commonly used to control intra-area advertisements. Chapter 17 provides a detailed look at how routing policy is used to summarize routes across area boundaries.

OSPF areas

OSPF also uses a hierarchical area scheme to control route advertisement within the AS. Unlike IS-IS area types, which rely on manual summarization, aggregation, and policy for control of routing advertisements, OSPF area types have been heavily modified over several decades to enable route control from within the protocol.

OSPF Versus IS-IS

We have chosen not to endorse one link-state IGP over another. Both protocols have characteristic strengths related to controlling routing table size that should be taken into consideration.

With OSPF, the route summarization mechanisms are incorporated in the protocol itself, making external tools such as aggregation and policy-based route filtering less prevalent. However, this design adds to the complexity of the protocol itself.

With IS-IS, the protocol mechanics are kept quite simple. Any desired route summarization is achieved by manually configuring aggregates. This effectively moves complex configuration elements to the JUNOS policy engine.

At the end of the day, the protocol that most effectively supports high availability may be determined by the skill set of the O&M staff. Which protocol are they most comfortable supporting?

Historically, OSPF area types such as stubby, totally stubby, and not so stubby were used in larger networks to reduce the size of routing tables and of the link-state database without impairing reachability. These area types all provide varying degrees of summarization of routing information advertised from other areas within the domain.

For our purpose of controlling the size of the routing table, let's see what the OSPF table looks like for the Figure 12-1 network when all devices are in Area 0. For the sake of brevity, the output of the run show route protocol ospf command is shortened using | match /. This generates just a raw list of routes being advertised by OSPF:

```
[edit]
lab@r5# run show route protocol ospf | match /
7.6.5.0/24          *[OSPF/10] 00:02:05, metric 3
8.7.6.0/24          *[OSPF/10] 00:02:05, metric 3
10.0.0.1/32         *[OSPF/10] 00:02:05, metric 2
10.0.0.2/32         *[OSPF/10] 00:02:05, metric 2
10.0.0.3/32         *[OSPF/10] 00:02:05, metric 1
10.0.0.4/32         *[OSPF/10] 00:02:05, metric 1
10.0.0.6/32         *[OSPF/10] 00:02:05, metric 1
10.0.1.16/30        *[OSPF/10] 00:02:05, metric 2
10.0.1.20/30        *[OSPF/10] 00:02:05, metric 2
10.0.1.24/30        *[OSPF/10] 00:02:05, metric 3
10.0.1.28/30        *[OSPF/10] 00:02:05, metric 2
172.16.1.0/24       *[OSPF/10] 00:02:05, metric 2
172.16.2.0/24       *[OSPF/10] 00:02:05, metric 2
172.16.3.0/24       *[OSPF/10] 00:02:05, metric 2
172.16.4.0/24       *[OSPF/10] 00:02:05, metric 2
172.16.5.0/24       *[OSPF/10] 00:02:05, metric 2
172.16.6.0/24       *[OSPF/10] 00:02:05, metric 2
172.16.7.0/24       *[OSPF/10] 00:02:05, metric 2
172.17.0.0/30       *[OSPF/10] 00:02:05, metric 3
172.17.0.4/30       *[OSPF/10] 00:02:05, metric 3
224.0.0.5/32        *[OSPF/10] 00:03:04, metric 1
```

Now, move r5 and r6 into a separate OSPF area, Area 1, by changing the protocols ospf area configuration statements on r3, r4, r5, and r6. Figure 12-7 shows the protocol area assignment we want to achieve with our configuration changes.

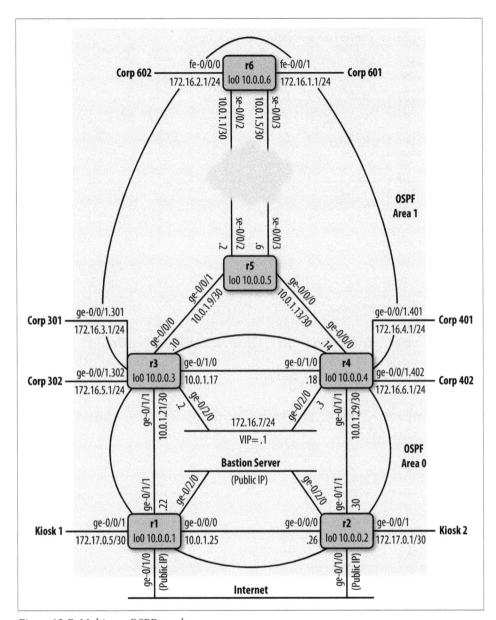

Figure 12-7. Multiarea OSPF topology

Routers r3 and r4 now become ABRs and you'll need to move the ge-0/0/0 interface into Area 1. Change r3 first:

```
[edit protocols ospf]
lab@r3# delete area 0 interface ge-0/0/0
```

```
[edit protocols ospf]
lab@r3# set area 1 interface ge-0/0/0

[edit protocols ospf]
lab@r3# show
area 0.0.0.0 {
    interface ge-0/0/1.301{
        passive;
    }
    interface ge-0/0/1.302 {
        passive;
    }
    interface ge-0/1/0.0;
    interface ge-0/1/1.0 {
    interface ge-0/2/0.0{
        passive;
    }
    interface lo0.0 {
        passive;
    }
}
area 0.0.0.1 {
    interface ge-0/0/0.0;
}
```

Now make comparable changes to the OSPF area configuration on r4:

```
[edit protocols ospf]
lab@r4# delete area 0 interface ge-0/0/0

[edit protocols ospf]
lab@r4# set area 1 interface ge-0/0/0

[edit protocols ospf]
lab@r4# show
area 0.0.0.0 {
    interface ge-0/0/1.401{
        passive;
    }
    interface ge-0/0/1.402 {
        passive;
    }
    interface ge-0/1/0.0;
    interface ge-0/1/1.0;
    interface ge-0/2/0.0 {
        passive;
    }
    interface lo0.0 {
        passive;
    }
}
area 0.0.0.1 {
    interface ge-0/0/0.0;
}
```

Once ABR configuration is complete, change the configuration on r5 and r6 to place them into OSPF Area 1. Since the interface in use does not change, use the JUNOS rename command on both r5 and r6 to expedite the changes, first on r5:

```
[edit protocols ospf]
lab@r5# show
area 0.0.0.0 {
    interface lo0.0 {
        passive;
    }
    interface ge-0/0/0.0;
    interface ge-0/0/1.0;
    interface se-0/0/2.0;
    interface se-0/0/3.0;
}

[edit protocols ospf]
lab@r5# rename area 0 to area 1

[edit protocols ospf]
lab@r5-main# show
area 0.0.0.1 {
    interface lo0.0 {
        passive;
    }
    interface ge-0/0/0.0;
    interface ge-0/0/1.0;
    interface se-0/0/2.0;
    interface se-0/0/3.0;
}
```

Then make a similar change on r6:

```
[edit protocols ospf]
lab@r6# show
area 0.0.0.0 {
    interface fe-0/0/0.0 {
        passive;
    }
    interface fe-0/0/1.0 {
        passive;
    }
    interface se-0/0/2.0;
    interface se-0/0/3.0;
    interface lo0.0 {
        passive;
    }
}

[edit protocols ospf]
lab@r6# rename area 0 to area 1

[edit protocols ospf]
lab@r6# show
area 0.0.0.1 {
    interface fe-0/0/0.0 {
```

```
        passive;
    }
    interface fe-0/0/1.0 {
        passive;
    }
    interface se-0/0/2.0;
    interface se-0/0/3.0;
    interface lo0.0 {
        passive;
    }
}
```

Now take another look at the routing table from the perspective of r5:

```
[edit]
lab@r5# run show route protocol ospf | match /
7.6.5.0/24         *[OSPF/10] 00:00:57, metric 3
8.7.6.0/24         *[OSPF/10] 00:00:57, metric 3
10.0.0.1/32        *[OSPF/10] 00:01:07, metric 2
10.0.0.2/32        *[OSPF/10] 00:00:57, metric 2
10.0.0.3/32        *[OSPF/10] 00:01:07, metric 1
10.0.0.4/32        *[OSPF/10] 00:00:57, metric 1
10.0.0.6/32        *[OSPF/10] 00:00:57, metric 1
10.0.1.16/30       *[OSPF/10] 00:00:57, metric 2
10.0.1.20/30       *[OSPF/10] 00:01:07, metric 2
10.0.1.24/30       *[OSPF/10] 00:00:57, metric 3
10.0.1.28/30       *[OSPF/10] 00:00:57, metric 2
172.16.1.0/24      *[OSPF/10] 00:00:57, metric 2
172.16.2.0/24      *[OSPF/10] 00:00:57, metric 2
172.16.3.0/24      *[OSPF/10] 00:01:07, metric 2
172.16.4.0/24      *[OSPF/10] 00:00:57, metric 2
172.16.5.0/24      *[OSPF/10] 00:01:07, metric 2
172.16.6.0/24      *[OSPF/10] 00:00:57, metric 2
172.16.7.0/24      *[OSPF/10] 00:00:57, metric 2
172.17.0.0/30      *[OSPF/10] 00:00:57, metric 3
172.17.0.4/30      *[OSPF/10] 00:01:07, metric 3
224.0.0.5/32       *[OSPF/10] 00:49:05, metric 1
```

As expected, there is very little change. To reduce the size of the routing table in Area 1, you need to change Area 1's area type and control the advertisement of summarized routes into the area. To accomplish this, change the area type on r3 and r4 to stub and eliminate summaries using the no-summaries command:

```
[edit]
lab@r3# set protocols ospf area 1 stub no-summaries default-metric 5

[edit]
lab@r3# commit
commit complete

[edit]
lab@r4# set protocols ospf area 1 stub no-summaries default-metric 10

[edit]
lab@r4# commit
commit complete
```

The astute reader will notice a `default-metric #` statement on the r3 and r4 OSPF configurations. This command is used with the redundant ABRs, r3 and r4, to assign primary ownership of the default route that is being generated and injected into Area 1. Because of the lower metric of 5, r3 is responsible for injecting the default. If r3 fails, then r4, with a metric of 10, would be responsible for injecting the default route into Area 1.

 The OSPF tweaks in this chapter demonstrate how protocol configuration can support high availability by dramatically reducing the size of the intradomain routing table. A more thorough collection of high availability OSPF configuration elements is available in Chapter 14.

You also need to change the `area-type` on r5 and r6 to match what is configured on the ABRs. The routers within an area must be configured to match the `area-type` defined by the ABRs:

```
[edit]
lab@r5# set protocols ospf area 1 stub

[edit]
lab@r5# commit
commit complete

[edit]
lab@r6# set protocols ospf area 1 stub

[edit]
lab@r6# commit
commit complete
```

Now take a look at the routing table on r5 to see the impact of the changes:

```
[edit]
lab@r5-main# run show route protocol ospf | match /
0.0.0.0/0          *[OSPF/10] 00:01:36, metric 6
10.0.0.6/32        *[OSPF/10] 00:02:21, metric 1
172.16.1.0/24      *[OSPF/10] 00:02:21, metric 2
172.16.2.0/24      *[OSPF/10] 00:02:21, metric 2
224.0.0.5/32       *[OSPF/10] 01:02:17, metric 1
```

Success! The size of the routing table has been effectively reduced within the domain by modifying the OSPF area topology and by eliminating route summarization across the ABRs. The result is a more manageable routing table that is easier to support and more likely to be highly available.

CHAPTER 13

Managing an Interdomain Routing Table

Chapter 12 focused on mechanisms available to control the information that routers and host systems in the local network add to the local routing table. Emphasis was on keeping the table as small as possible through intelligent address allocation, aggregation schemes, and effective use of Interior Gateway Protocol (IGP) scalability tools.

This chapter looks at the current global routing table, which comprises about 230,000 aggregated routes, as a potential addition to the local table. In this chapter, we look at what we can do to control and organize this massive number of potential route additions to the local table. Clearly, the local administrator lacks the authority to control all routes that are added to the global routing table, so measures must be taken on the devices you do control to make sure external factors do not negatively impact internal stability. Controlling how the local Autonomous System (AS) handles the Internet routing table is a fundamental high availability priority for all networks.

When addressing route table content, we must strive for route table stability. Stability has direct implications for high availability, because an unstable routing table results in an unstable network.

With attention to high availability through strong redundancy schemes, this chapter discusses address mechanisms to control *ingestion* and advertisement of interdomain destinations. These methods include configuration of both confederated and route re-flected topologies. This chapter also includes related best practices for several network types, but focuses primarily on large enterprise and carrier networks—those that ingest the most routing table content from external sources.

Enterprise Size and Effective Management

Depending on the size of the network, you must adopt different strategies to obtain the most effective management of content.

Small to Medium-Size Enterprise Perspective

We started out mentioning the need to manage the content of the complete aggregated Internet routing table and hinted at some of the tools that can be used to control that content, but does a network have to run Border Gateway Protocol (BGP) to communicate with the rest of the world? Is it absolutely necessary to retain a copy of that BIG table for a business to function? The answer, actually, is no. The reality is that small networks and most medium-size networks typically do not run BGP at all.

Unnecessary routing protocols just add complexity and are an enemy of high availability. Keep it simple!

Networks that do not run BGP rely on a few fairly simple configuration elements to communicate with external destinations. These elements include a default route on the local AS gateway router and a passive route or possibly some redistribution by the service provider. In Figure 13-1, a small enterprise network composed of r1, r2, and r3 uses a default route on r3, the gateway router, to reach all destinations outside the local network. The ISP in Figure 13-1 has configured a static route on r4 and redistributed it into BGP to advertise a return route to the small enterprise.

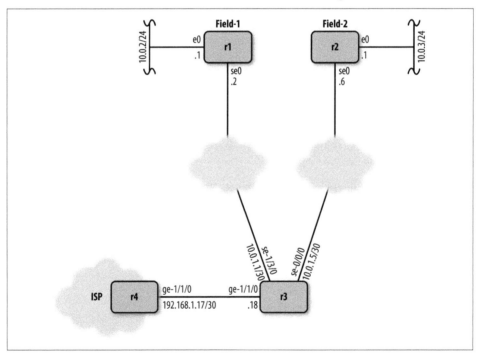

Figure 13-1. Route control for small enterprise networks

The configuration on r3 has r1, r2, and r3 in Open Shortest Path First (OSPF) Area 0 and has a static default pointing to r4 that is redistributed into OSPF:

```
[edit]
lab@r3# show protocols ospf
export STATIC;
area 0.0.0.0 {
    interface se-0/0/0.0;
    interface se-1/3/0.0;
    interface lo0.0 {
        passive;
    }
}

[edit]
lab@r3# show routing-options
static {
    route 0.0.0.0/0 next-hop 192.168.1.17;
}

[edit]
lab@r3# show policy-options policy-statement STATIC
term 1 {
    from {
        protocol static;
        route-filter 0.0.0.0/0 exact;
    }
    then accept;
}
```

The corresponding configuration on r4 advertises the static route so that the rest of the world can reach addresses in the small enterprise. In this case, the static address is redistributed to all Internal BGP (IBGP) peers:

```
[edit]
lab@r4# show routing-options
static {
    route 10.0.0.0/22 next-hop 192.168.18.1;
}

[edit]
lab@r4# show policy-options policy-statement STATIC
term 1 {
    from {
        protocol static;
        route-filter 10.0.0.0/22 exact;
    }
    then accept;
}

[edit]
lab@r4# show protocols bgp group IBGP export
STATIC;
```

This combination of configuration elements shows one simple way a small enterprise can communicate with the rest of the world and allow the world to initiate conversation back by adding a single default route to the local table and a static route on the provider's side. From the perspective of the small enterprise local table, the only interdomain content is the static default route.

Large Enterprises and Service Providers

If you have many internal hosts and connections to external networks, simple static defaults are less practical for large enterprise and service provider networks. Clearly, the local routing tables of these network types need more information to effectively direct traffic to its destination. And as more information is added to the table, more mechanisms are needed to control the table's size, content, and stability.

As everyone learns in Networking 101, large enterprises and service provider networks are separated into administrative domains defined as ASs. An AS is a collection of devices under the control of a common administration. Because BGP is a common way in which ASs communicate with each other, BGP is also the most sensible place to configure mechanisms to control the routes carried among ASs. Mechanisms to control what gets into the local routing table from BGP include AS numbering schemes, policies for route redistribution, and BGP protocol options.

AS Number

As we discussed in Chapter 12, the ability to provision multiple logical networks or service overlays over a single physical infrastructure means that architecture and design decisions are no longer a one-time event in the life of a network. Just as intelligent and scalable IP addressing schemes are needed for each logical overlay, you must also define the BGP specifics of the logical network.

Based on the AS's size and function in the greater Internet, the AS may be numbered. BGP is typically the deciding factor. Each router that participates in BGP routing must belong to an AS. The AS number identifies the logical location of the router, and subsequently the routes that the router advertises in the Internet. Each route that the router advertises using BGP carries with it an AS number.

AS numbers come in two flavors, *public* and *private*. Public AS numbers are just like public IP addresses. They are purchased from one of several allocation bodies, such as the Asia Pacific Network Information Center (APNIC), ARIN, and RIPE, and are recognized throughout the Internet. In use, private AS numbers are comparable to the RFC 1918-defined private IP addresses. According to APNIC, private AS numbers are used for BGP communications when "an AS is only required to communicate via BGP with a single provider. As the routing policy between the AS and the provider will not be visible in the Internet, a Private AS Number can be used for this purpose" (APNIC 2007). All AS numbers from 64,512 to 65,535 are in the private AS range.

In the case of small and medium-size enterprise networks, the decision to go with a private or public AS number may belong to the carrier rather than to the enterprise itself. This is because public AS numbers are expensive and may not be necessary. For example, an ISP may support virtual private network (VPN) connectivity among dozens of medium-size enterprise sites. These sites may use BGP to pass routing information to the ISP. Rather than pay for a public AS number for each site, the service provider could allocate numbers from the private range to support site-to-site communications and could use a single public AS number for communication outside the VPN.

 In response to growing demand for the finite number of possible AS numbers, in January 2007 APNIC began distributing 4-byte AS numbers along with the 2-byte numbers it had been distributing in the Pacific region. This expanded address space can support a little more than 4 billion potential ASs.

In JUNOS, the AS number for the router is configured under the `routing-options` level of hierarchy:

```
[edit]
lab@r2# show routing-options
autonomous-system 22;
```

Border Gateway Protocol (BGP)

While a complete and thorough discussion of BGP theory is well beyond the scope of this chapter, a few functional details critical to high availability merit some discussion. Most importantly, when talking about routing, you have to talk about preventing *routing loops*, the archenemy of high availability. BGP uses two distinct loop prevention mechanisms: one prevents loops in External BGP (EBGP) connections, and the other in IBGP connections.

 For a more in-depth discussion of EBGP and IBGP connection types, take a look at Chapter 13 in *JUNOS Cookbook (http://oreilly.com/cata log/9780596100148/)*, by Aviva Garrett (O'Reilly).

EBGP Loop Prevention

EBGP loop prevention, as a concept, is very easy to understand. Figure 13-2 shows an EBGP-speaking router, r1, receiving a route update from an EBGP neighbor, r2. r1 checks the AS path. If the update contains r1's AS number, in this case 1717, r1 drops the update. The presence of AS 1717 in the advertisement indicates that the route either originated in AS 1717, or has already been advertised through AS 1717 and is a loop.

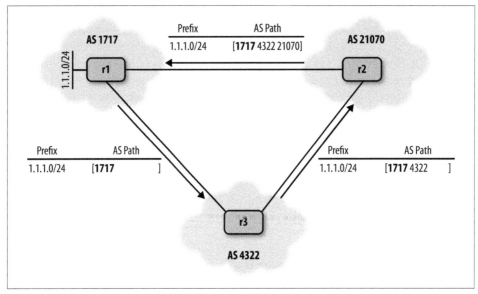

Figure 13-2. EBGP loop prevention

EBGP loop prevention is an inherent function of BGP and does not need to be enabled to prevent loops. It is "on" by default and does not require configuration in JUNOS or IOS.

IBGP Loop Prevention

IBGP loop prevention is a bit more complex and is based on three foundational rules:

- A route received from an EBGP neighbor is forwarded to all IBGP and EBGP neighbors.
- A route received from an IBGP neighbor is forwarded to all EBGP neighbors.
- A route received from an IBGP neighbor is *not* forwarded to other IBGP neighbors.

These three foundational rules are necessary because the AS number does not change from hop to hop in IBGP advertisements. All IBGP hops are, by definition, within the same AS. Therefore, an additional mechanism is required to prevent loops; hence, the foundational rules.

Figure 13-3 shows IBGP route advertisement in all its resplendent glory. In this image, r3 receives a prefix advertisement of 1.1.1.0/24 from r1. Router r3 follows the first foundational rule and forwards the route to all EBGP neighbors, in this case r2, as well as all IBGP neighbors, r4 and r5. Routers r4 and r5 each follow the second foundational rule and propagate the route to their external neighbors in AS 97 and AS 876. In keeping with the third foundational rule, r4 and r5 do not forward the route to each other, effectively preventing an AS-internal routing loop.

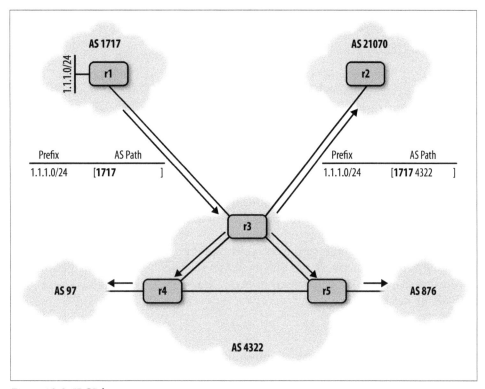

Figure 13-3. IBGP loop prevention

 You might be wondering why this is important for high availability. A solid understanding of EBGP and IBGP route advertisement rules is necessary when attempting to control the size, content, and stability of the local routing table. Without this understanding, you may waste time attempting to configure unnecessary route filters or, worse, troubleshooting a problem that does not exist.

IBGP full-mesh requirements

If you take a closer look at the IBGP route advertisement rules and at Figure 13-3, something may become apparent. IBGP's refusal to advertise IBGP-learned routes to IBGP neighbors mandates a *full mesh* of neighbor relationships among IBGP speakers. Any full mesh is subject to what is commonly known as the *N-squared issue*, a reference to the mathematical equation necessary to calculate the number of links required to connect all points in a given grouping to every other point in the grouping. The formal equation is:

$$N(N-1)/2 = links$$

where N is the number of host systems in the group, and *links* is the number of connections required to establish a full mesh among the hosts. As a practical example, let's take a look at the number of links required for a network with 20 BGP speakers:

$$20(20-1)/2 = 190$$

Clearly, as the BGP implementation grows, the effort required to support the implementation also grows at an alarming rate. If we were to add two BGP speakers to the 20-router topology, we would need to configure 41 additional BGP neighbor relationships to support the full mesh:

$$22(22-1)/2 = 231$$

Implications of full mesh for high availability

As network complexity increases, the difficulty in supporting the network also increases. And while an IBGP neighbor relationship is simple to configure and fairly straightforward to support, configuring and supporting 231 (or even 190) relationships tends to place a burden on the finite resources of the support team. This much configuration spread out across the network not only increases the likelihood of human error, but also ensures that the risk touches many devices. Clearly, if high availability is desirable, an IBGP full mesh is not.

Alternatives to full mesh

Now that we have addressed the administrative complexity of IBGP in a full-mesh configuration, the sensible question to ask is, "Can BGP be implemented without configuring a full mesh of IBGP speakers?" Sure! There are two commonly used ways to get around the full mesh: *route reflection* and *confederation*.

The next two sections in this chapter cover route reflection and confederation. By themselves, neither can reduce the number of routes in the local table. So, why discuss them? To support high availability, deterministic routing is critical. Therefore, controlling the way route advertisements get into the local table is just as important as controlling the contents of the route advertisements themselves. It's all about control.

Route Reflection

Route reflection is a mechanism that allows IBGP speakers to bend the third foundational rule of IBGP loop prevention. In effect, route reflection allows a route received from an IBGP speaker to be advertised to other IBGP speakers. An additional tag, CLUSTER_ID, is added to reflected routes to support loop prevention. Without digging too deeply into protocol theory concepts covered in other books, let's take a look at the components of a route reflector scheme that have an impact on high availability.

Route reflection basics

Route reflection makes use of a *route reflector* entity and a *cluster* entity. A route reflector is an IBGP router configured to act as a route server. A cluster is a collection of IBGP routers acting as clients to the route server. Routes learned by a cluster client are sent to the route reflector for the cluster, where they are then advertised to all other clients in the cluster, as well as to other route reflectors.

High availability design considerations for route reflection

There are some design issues to take into consideration when employing route reflection:

- Because failure of a route reflector would result in the cluster being isolated from the rest of the BGP implementation, you should always configure clusters with redundant route reflectors.
- Routers chosen to be reflectors should have consistently reliable power cooling and network connectivity and should be central to the network design.
- Route reflectors within an AS should themselves be fully meshed. This permits each route reflector to receive all known BGP paths and ensures completeness of the local routing table.
- The logical topology should follow the physical topology. Route reflection simplifies support of the network by reducing the number of required IBGP relationships. However, configuring a logical reflector topology that deviates from the physical topology adds so much complexity that it may be better not to deploy route reflection in the first place.

Turning it on

Figure 13-4 shows a small portion of a carrier network. Routers r1 and r2 serve as route reflectors for this network.

The IBGP configuration on r1 has two BGP groups. Group IBGP maintains a full mesh among the route reflectors in AS 22—in this case, between r1 and r2:

```
[edit protocols bgp]
lab@r1# show
group IBGP {
    type internal;
    description "Full mesh for route reflectors";
    local-address 10.0.0.1;
    neighbor 10.0.0.2;
}
```

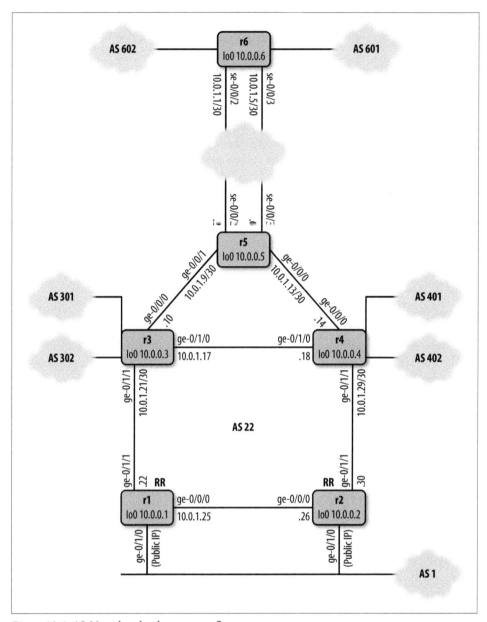

Figure 13-4. AS 22 with redundant route reflectors

A second BGP group, CLUSTER-1, on r1 configures a neighbor relationship with all other routers in the cluster—in this case, routers r3 through r6. These four routers are the neighbors for which r1 serves as a route reflector:

```
[edit protocols bgp]
lab@r1# show
group IBGP {
    type internal;
    description "Full mesh for route reflectors";
    local-address 10.0.0.1;
    neighbor 10.0.0.2;
}
group CLUSTER-1 {
    type internal;
    description "Cluster 1.1.1.1 clients";
    local-address 10.0.0.1;
    cluster 1.1.1.1;
    neighbor 10.0.0.3;
    neighbor 10.0.0.4;
    neighbor 10.0.0.5;
    neighbor 10.0.0.6;
}
```

The BGP group configuration for r2 is comparable in many ways to r1. Again, CLUSTER-1 defines the neighbors for which r2 serves as a route reflector:

```
[edit protocols bgp]
lab@r2# show
group IBGP {
    type internal;
    description "Full mesh of route reflectors";
    local-address 10.0.0.2;
    neighbor 10.0.0.1;
}
group CLUSTER-1 {
    type internal;
    description "Cluster 1.1.1.1 clients";
    local-address 10.0.0.2;
    cluster 1.1.1.1;
    neighbor 10.0.0.3;
    neighbor 10.0.0.4;
    neighbor 10.0.0.5;
    neighbor 10.0.0.6;
}
```

The BGP configuration for r3 through r6 identifies r1 and r2 as neighbors. The presence of the cluster 1.1.1.1 configuration element on r1 and r2 means these two routers include a cluster identifier in routes they advertise to r3 through r6; effectively telling these routers that they, r3 through r6, are clients in a route reflector scheme. Router r3 and r4 configurations are shown as examples in the following code. The configurations on r5 and r6 would be comparable:

```
[edit protocols bgp]
lab@r3# show
group CLUSTER-1 {
    type internal;
    description "Cluster 1.1.1.1 route reflectors";
    local-address 10.0.0.3;
    neighbor 10.0.0.1;
    neighbor 10.0.0.2;
}

[edit protocols bgp]
lab@r4# show
group CLUSTER-1 {
    type internal;
    description "CLUSTER-1 route reflectors";
    local-address 10.0.0.4;
    neighbor 10.0.0.1;
    neighbor 10.0.0.2;
}
```

 In the previous configuration examples, we selected group names that will be helpful when attempting to troubleshoot BGP-related routing issues. We also included description elements to provide additional information about the purpose of both groups. This is a good habit to get into; it can save valuable time when troubleshooting.

Route reflectors and policy configuration

About seven years ago, we heard a class instructor describe policy configuration on a router participating in a redundant hierarchical route reflector scheme. The instructor looked out over the class and told us in a very somber voice, "One day you will configure a policy on a route reflector and it will damage the network. It may even bring it down."

Fortunately, to this day we have not "brought down" any networks, but we have seen our fair share of botched policy configurations. The most destructive mistakes that occur when configuring policy on a route reflector tend to be when you use the next-hop self option.

Route reflection and next-hop self: What not to do. You commonly use a *next hop self policy* to overwrite the protocol next hop on IBGP advertisements with the local address of the advertising router. This policy effectively overcomes what is known as the *BGP next hop reachability issue*. Figure 13-5 adds a few details about the AS external peers to our small carrier topology to illustrate the point.

In Figure 13-5, r3 maintains an EBGP peering relationship to r5. Router r3 also has an IBGP relationship with r1 and r2, the route reflectors in this topology. When r3 receives a route from r5, r3 advertises the route to its IBGP neighbors with the BGP next hop to r5, 172.16.5.2. Because no IGP is running across the EBGP boundary, r3 uses a next hop self policy named NHS to advertise itself as the next hop to reach routes learned from r5. The policy is configured in the export direction to IBGP peers for r3.

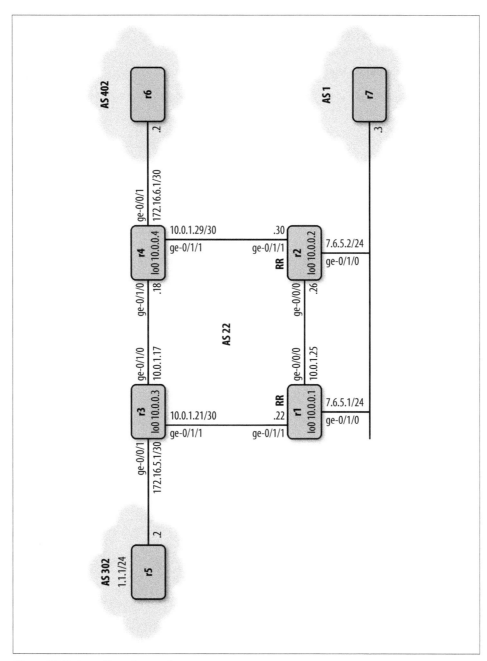

Figure 13-5. A small carrier topology

```
[edit]
lab@r3# show policy-options
policy-statement NHS {
    term 1 {
        from protocol bgp;
        then {
            next-hop self;
        }
    }
}

[edit]
lab@r3# show protocols bgp group CLUSTER-1
type internal;
description "Cluster 1.1.1.1 route reflectors";
local-address 10.0.0.3;
export NHS;
neighbor 10.0.0.1;
neighbor 10.0.0.2;
```

So far, so good; after committing this configuration change, routes from r5 are now reachable from r4.

Notice that r1 and r2 also maintain an EBGP relationship. They are both peers with r6 in AS 1. They too would need to overcome the next hop reachability issue and may configure a next hop self policy to do so. Here is the configuration from r1; r2 would be similar:

```
[edit]
lab@r1# show policy-options
policy-statement NHS {
    term 1 {
        from protocol bgp;
        then {
            next-hop self;
        }
    }
}

[edit]
lab@r1# show protocols bgp group CLUSTER-1
type internal;
description "Cluster 1.1.1.1 neighbors";
local-address 10.0.0.1;
cluster 1.1.1.1;
neighbor 10.0.0.3;
neighbor 10.0.0.4;
neighbor 10.0.0.5;
neighbor 10.0.0.6;

[edit]
lab@r1# show protocols bgp group IBGP
type internal;
description "Full mesh for route reflectors";
```

```
local-address 10.0.0.1;
neighbor 10.0.0.2;
```

After this change is committed, there is still no immediate problem, but the protocol next hop for all routes received from r5 is now being overridden by r3, then again by r1, and r2 (as a backup). In this simple topology, the repeated protocol next hop override does not pose a problem that affects traffic. Only when the network size increases is high availability threatened.

In Figure 13-6, two additional routers, r8 and r9, are added to support connectivity to an internal data center. Routers r8 and r9 are both configured as route reflector clients to r1 and r2.

Soon after the configuration of r8 is complete, traffic coming from r4 is no longer able to reach destinations inside AS 302. Now we have a problem.

What is wrong with this picture?

The problem in Figure 13-6 is that BGP next hops are out of sync with the physical topology of the network. In other words, the contents of the routing table do not correctly describe destination reachability. Here are the details:

1. Routes from AS 302 are advertised by r3 to r1 (the route reflector) using IBGP. Router r3 overrides the protocol next hop and sets it to the r3 loopback address before sending it to r1.

2. Router r1 receives the AS 302 routes and installs them in the local table. Router r1 then exports the routes to all clients, including r8, with the r1 loopback address as the protocol next hop.

3. When r4 has traffic destined for AS 302, it is forwarded to r1.

4. In the r1 local table, the protocol next hop is r3's loopback address, so r1 does a recursive lookup and sees that r8 is the next hop to get to r3, and then forwards the traffic accordingly.

5. Router r8 receives the traffic destined for AS 302, but in r8's local table, r1 is the protocol next hop for AS 302. Router r8 then forwards the traffic back to r1, and a loop is formed.

6. Service-level agreements (SLAs) are violated. Availability suffers. Pain ensues.

Be terrific; be specific. When configuring policy on a route reflector, always designate the neighbor to which the policy should be applied. Simply defining the EBGP neighbor for the next hop self policy permits routes from clients to maintain the protocol next hop.

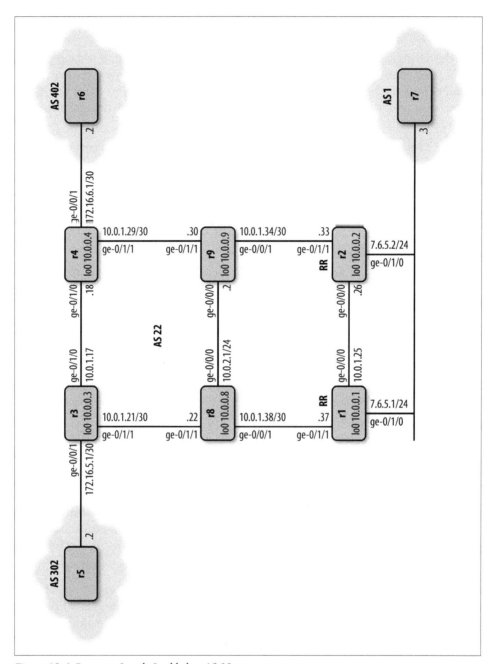

Figure 13-6. Routers r8 and r9 added to AS 22

For the scenario depicted in Figure 13-6, you can resolve the issue by adding neighbor 7.6.5.3 to the NHS policy on r1 and r2:

```
[edit]
lab@r1# show policy-options policy-statement NHS
term 1 {
    from {
        protocol bgp;
        neighbor 7.6.5.3;
    }
    then {
        next-hop self;
    }
}
```

Clearly, making the content of the routing table as accurate as possible is critical to the functioning of the network.

 While designating the BGP neighbor to which the policy should apply is critical to the functioning of a route reflector, it is in fact a great habit to get into for all BGP policy configurations because this specificity can limit the impact of configuration errors to a single BGP connection, the one neighbor explicitly described in the policy.

Confederation

Confederation is a "divide and conquer" approach to the management of interdomain routing. A *confederation* is an AS that has been divided into a collection of smaller ASs. This method dramatically decreases the number of IBGP connections required, but can increase the number of EBGP-like connections. In a confederation scheme, the public AS is retained and used for external peering, but the domain is divided into two or more private AS numbers, as shown in Figure 13-7. In this example, AS 22 is confederated, split into AS 64512 and 64513. Because of configuration elements on all routers in the AS, the confederation is invisible to the outside world.

Confederation syntax

In this confederation example, r5 maintains a classic IBGP relationship with r6, as shown in the group IBGP portion of the configuration. Router r5 also maintains a classic EBGP-type relationship with r3 and r4 in the group CBGP portion. The confederation 22 statement under routing-options creates the confederated BGP scheme. In effect, this configuration element tells the router three things:

- Use AS 64512 when forming an EBGP relationship with a router in 64513.
- Use AS 64513 when forming an EBGP relationship with a router in 64512.
- Use AS 22 for all other EBGP relationships.

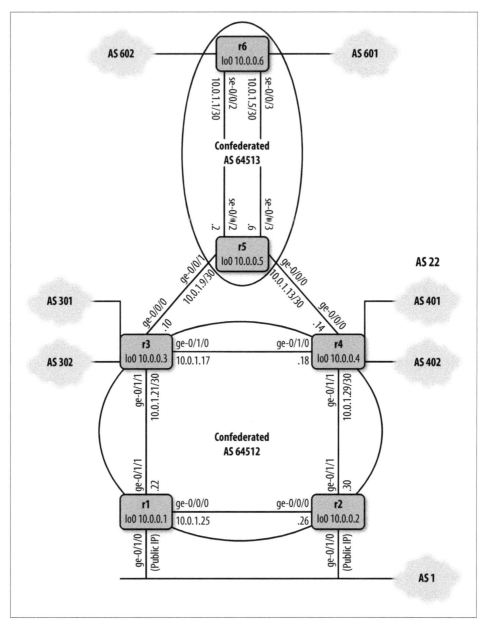

Figure 13-7. AS 22 with confederation

```
lab@r5# show routing-options
autonomous-system 64513;
confederation 22 members [ 64512 64513 ];

lab@r5# show protocols bgp
group IBGP {
    type internal;
    description "IBGP neighbor r6";
    local-address 10.0.0.5;
    neighbor 10.0.0.6;
}
group CBGP {
    type external;
    description "CBGP neighbors r3 and r4";
    peer-as 64512;
    neighbor 10.0.1.10;
    neighbor 10.0.1.14;
}
```

Comparable elements are on r3:

```
[edit]
lab@r3# show routing-options
autonomous-system 64512;
confederation 22 members [ 64512 64513 ];

[edit]
lab@r3# show protocols bgp
group IBGP {
    type internal;
    description "IBGP neighbors r1, r2, r4";
    local-address 10.0.0.3;
    neighbor 10.0.0.1;
    neighbor 10.0.0.2;
    neighbor 10.0.0.4;
}
group CBGP {
    type external;
    description "CBGP neighbor r5";
    peer-as 64513;
    neighbor 10.0.1.9;
}
```

For redundancy, you also configure comparable elements on r4:

```
[edit]
lab@r4# show routing-options
autonomous-system 64512;
confederation 22 members [ 64512 64513 ];

[edit]
lab@r4# show protocols bgp
group IBGP {
    type internal;
    description "IBGP neighbors r1, r2, r3";
    local-address 10.0.0.4;
    neighbor 10.0.0.1;
```

```
        neighbor 10.0.0.2;
        neighbor 10.0.0.3;
    }
    group CBGP {
        type external;
        description "CBGP neighbor r5";
        peer-as 64513;
        neighbor 10.0.1.13;
    }
```

Implications of confederation for high availability

While confederation can be beneficial in reducing the number of IBGP peering relationships necessary for an AS to function, as well as for controlling routing advertisements within the AS, confederation is less common than route reflectors on modern
networks. There are several reasons for this:

- Policies configured at the edge of an AS are typically more complex than those
  configured within the AS, and confederation increases the number of "edge devices" (EBGP speakers), which usually increase the amount of policy configuration
  necessary for the AS to function.

- BGP interaction with the designated IGP (OSPF or Intermediate System to Intermediate System [IS-IS]) is more complicated with confederation because AS
  boundaries no longer follow IGP boundaries.

- Configuration for redundancy requires additional confederated EBGP relationships and modifications to default BGP behavior, which can work against the
  primary reasons for deploying confederations, reducing support demands and
  increasing availability.

Configuration for redundancy

As a warning, based on what the authors have experienced in many years of supporting
production networks, redundant confederation implementations can be extremely
complex to troubleshoot and thus might not be the best choice of scaling mechanisms
for a network with high availability requirements. Confederation is mentioned in this
chapter primarily because it can have an impact on the stability of the local routing
table.

Engineers who deploy confederations often change the default Time to Live (TTL)
expiration on EBGP advertisements (the default is one hop). This change allows the
confederation neighbors to find each other using alternate routes through the network.

You override the default hop limit under the individual neighbor configuration statements; to be effective you should make the change on both neighbors in a peering
relationship. In this configuration example, r5 and r3 agree to use loopback addresses
for their peering relationship and to change the TTL limit to allow up to three router
hops to get to each other:

```
[edit]
lab@r5# show protocols bgp group CBGP
type external;
description "CBGP neighbors r3 and r4 with peering to loopbacks";
local-address 10.0.0.5;
peer-as 64512;
neighbor 10.0.0.3 {
    multihop {
        ttl 3;
    }
}
neighbor 10.0.0.4 {
    multihop {
        ttl 3;
    }
}
```

Router r3 has complementary configuration elements:

```
lab@r3# show protocols bgp group CBGP
type external;
description "CBGP neighbor r5 with peering to loopback";
local-address 10.0.0.3;
peer-as 64513;
neighbor 10.0.0.5 {
    multihop {
        ttl 3;
    }
}
```

There are also similar elements on r4:

```
[edit]
lab@r4# show protocols bgp group CBGP
type external;
description "CBGP neighbor r5 with peering to loopback";
local-address 10.0.0.4;
peer-as 64513;
neighbor 10.0.0.5 {
    multihop {
        ttl 3;
    }
}
```

The astute reader should notice that in the last set of configuration samples, not only did the authors change the TTL, but we also changed the peering points for the confederated BGP relationship from interface addresses to loopback addresses. Changing to loopback-based peering strengthens the availability scheme by allowing the routers to forward/direct traffic around interface failures toward the peer. For example, if the direct link between r3 and r5 were to fail, r3 would maintain its peering relationship to r5 because the relationship would be able to transit r4.

How does multihop affect my routing table?

The stated purpose of the TTL change is redundancy. However, during times of link, interface, or node failure, this configuration tweak often results in routing table content that does not accurately reflect the network's physical topology, which can prolong troubleshooting, delay problem resolution, and, in short, be extremely detrimental to high availability.

Common High Availability Routing Policies

Routing policies are the primary mechanisms available in JUNOS for blocking, modifying, or marking the routes that are advertised into and out of the local AS. Earlier in this chapter, we showed how to configure a next hop self policy, NHS, to overcome the BGP next hop reachability issue. The NHS policy modified routes as they were coming into the local routing table.

NHS is one example of how you can define policies to provide routing table content and stability control to support network high availability. We now look at several other common high availability-focused policies, including local address filtering, prefix length enforcement, default route blocking, and route flap damping.

Local address filters

Every administrator, particularly those interested in supporting high availability of the local network, should implement routing policies that prevent locally used prefixes from being advertised by external peers. While this "spoofing" is typically described as an attack, it is more often the result of a faulty configuration in a neighboring network. Figure 13-8 shows the IP addressing scheme of AS 22.

To protect the integrity of the local network, you can block the prefixes used in the network from being advertised by external sources into the network, as shown in this configuration sample from router r2. The policy is defined under the policy-options level of hierarchy:

```
[edit policy-options]
lab@r2# show
policy-statement LOCAL-ADDRESS {
    term 1 {
        from {
            protocol bgp;
            neighbor 7.6.5.3;
            route-filter 10.0.0.0/23 orlonger;
            route-filter 172.16.0.0/12 orlonger;
            route-filter 8.7.6.0/24 orlonger;
        }
        then reject;
    }
}
```

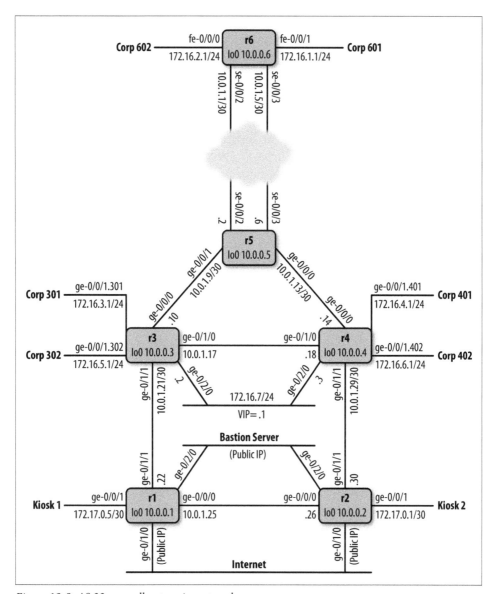

Figure 13-8. AS 22, a small enterprise network

After the policy is configured, apply it on the import direction of the EBGP relationship between r2 and r7:

```
[edit protocols bgp group EBGP]
lab@r2# show
type external;
import LOCAL-ADDRESS;
```

```
    peer-as 1;
    neighbor 7.6.5.3;
```

Prefix-length enforcement

Controlling the prefix length of routes advertised into the local AS allows you to effectively control the size of the local routing table by forcing external routes to be summarized before the routes are advertised to the local router. This not only supports high availability by keeping the local table as small as possible, but it also has an added benefit of displaying "good netizen" behavior, because of the reduction of the overall number of routes propagated by the local AS.

You enforce prefix-length restrictions on inbound advertisements with an import policy on EBGP groups that permits prefixes up to a set size and rejects anything longer. The policy is configured under the policy-options level of hierarchy. In this example, term 1 defines the source protocol bgp and the source neighbor 7.6.5.3 of the route. The route-filter statement in term 1 allows any route with a subnet mask up to 24 bits long to continue to be processed by the policy chain. Any route with a subnet mask longer than 24 bits is explicitly rejected by the reject term in this policy:

```
[edit policy-options policy-statement PREFIX-LENGTH-LIMIT]
lab@r2# show
term 1 {
    from {
        protocol bgp;
        neighbor 7.6.5.3;
        route-filter 0.0.0.0/0 upto /24;
    }
    then next policy;
}
term reject {
    then reject;
}
```

After configuring the policy, you must apply it to have it take effect:

```
[edit protocols bgp group EBGP]
lab@r2# show
type external;
import [ LOCAL-ADDRESS PREFIX-LENGTH-LIMIT ];
peer-as 1;
neighbor 7.6.5.3;
```

Default routes: To block or not to block?

Depending on circumstances, the inbound advertisement of a default route may be desirable. For example, a small enterprise may depend on receipt of a default route from a service provider to reach external destinations. The beauty of this scheme is that when connectivity to the service provider is lost, the default route is automatically removed from the local routing table.

Referring back to Figure 13-1, a default route could have been configured on r4 and advertised by OSPF to r3 to provide reachability to AS external destinations. While this scheme does provide the benefit noted, there is a serious implication. Router r3 must form an OSPF neighbor relationship with r4. Typically, an IGP, particularly one as promiscuous as OSPF, is confined within an AS for security reasons.

However, in some situations when a default route is required, you configure it locally. This method is common in small networks and also in some medium-size enterprise networks that, for redundancy reasons, have EBGP connectivity to multiple providers. In this situation, you may choose to block or at least modify the metrics of a default route received from one of your providers.

Because of the need to maintain full and accurate Internet routing table content and to protect customers, service providers also have a need to prevent default routes from being advertised into the local network.

JUNOS policy options can permit the blocking of inbound advertisement of default routes regardless of prefix length. This blocking is useful because, whether through malice or accidental misconfiguration, default routes often arrive with a subnet mask longer than the zero-length subnet mask commonly associated with default routing.

To block inbound advertisement of default routes regardless of subnet mask length, use the **through** option in conjunction with a **route-filter** statement. In this configuration example, all default routes are rejected by the filter in **term 1**:

```
[edit policy-options policy-statement DEFAULTS]
lab@r2# show
term 1 {
    from {
        protocol bgp;
        neighbor 7.6.5.3;
        route-filter 0.0.0.0/0 through 0.0.0.0/32;
    }
    then reject;
}
```

Then apply the filter as an import policy on the EBGP peering point to block the defaults as they are received, *before* they are added to the local routing table:

```
[edit protocols bgp group EBGP]
lab@r2# show
type external;
import [ LOCAL-ADDRESS PREFIX-LENGTH-LIMIT DEFAULTS ];
peer-as 1;
neighbor 7.6.5.3 {
    family inet {
        unicast {
            prefix-limit {
                maximum 2000;
                teardown 80 idle-timeout forever;
```

```
            }
          }
        }
      }
    }
```

 Notice that in the previous series of configuration samples, we tacked on additional policies rather than replace the previous policy. The last sample includes three policies—LOCAL-ADDRESS, PREFIX-LENGTH-LIMIT, and DEFAULTS—in the processing chain that are evaluated in sequence.

Route damping

Route damping is a way to reward stable EBGP neighbors while penalizing unstable ones. Route damping significantly helps stability in the network, but may have negative implications for high availability, depending on one's perspective.

In Figure 13-9, r3 maintains an EBGP relationship with r5 and is responsible for sharing routes learned from r5 with all other routers in AS 22. The other routers in AS 22 are themselves responsible for sharing the routes learned from r5 with their EBGP peers. Considering that BGP is an event-driven protocol, repeated advertisements and withdrawals of routing information (*flapping*) would result in a flood of advertisements both within AS 22 and to all EBGP neighbors of AS 22.

Fortunately, BGP supports damping, a method of preventing flapping routes from being repeatedly propagated to EBGP peers. BGP assigns a *figure of merit* (FoM) to all received routes, and increments the FoM based on withdrawals, readvertisements, and changes in attributes of the BGP route. The FoM is tracked for each route, and if the FoM exceeds a predefined threshold, the route is no longer advertised to peers. If the route stabilizes, the FoM *decays* (is reduced over time) and the route is eventually readvertised.

All vendor implementations of damping permit modification to the settings that control penalization, FoM at which a route is withdrawn, rate of decay, and FoM at which a route is readvertised. What is important to remember is that in both JUNOS and Cisco IOS, damping is disabled by default and must be explicitly enabled. In JUNOS, you enable it with policy.

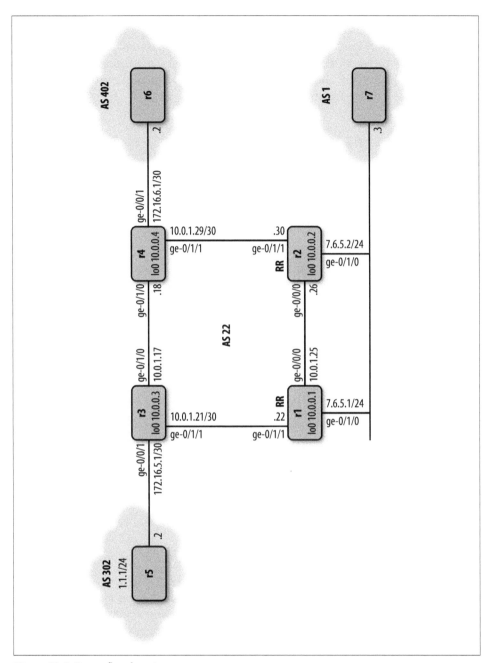

Figure 13-9. Route flap damping

A "damp" policy

This policy effectively implements stability requirements on routes advertised from AS 302 and harshly penalizes any instability. This example configures a route filter that specifies both the protocol and the neighbor and applies damping parameters defined in D1 to all routes received from the neighbor:

```
[edit policy-options]
lab@r3# show
policy-statement DAMP-302 {
    term 1 {
        from {
            protocol bgp;
            neighbor 172.16.5.2;
            route-filter 0.0.0.0/0 upto /32 damping D1;
        }
    }
}
```

The damping parameters associated with D1 suppress the route from advertisement when the FoM for the route exceeds 3,000. D1 readvertises the route when the FoM falls below 1,000. D1 reduces the FoM for the route by 50% every five minutes, but readvertises a route regardless of FoM after 20 minutes of suppression.

```
[edit policy-options]
lab@r3# show damping D1
half-life 5;
reuse 1000;
suppress 3000;
max-suppress 20;
```

To have the desired effect, you apply this policy in the import direction on the EBGP peering relationship to AS 302:

```
[edit protocols bgp]
lab@r3# show group AS302
type external;
import DAMP-302;
peer-as 302;
neighbor 172.16.5.2;
```

Implications of damping

Administrators responsible for high availability on a production network should pay careful attention to route damping implications. When damping is enabled, the local routing table and peer networks are protected from flapping updates, but any route that gets damped becomes unreachable until the FoM drops below the reuse threshold or the maximum suppression timer expires. For commercial routes, this behavior may be desirable, but for critical routes, as defined by purpose or volume of traffic, it may be completely unacceptable.

Because service providers commonly apply damping to customer peering points, administrators responsible for high availability on networks
peering to service providers have a powerful incentive to keep their local
routing tables stable. Be stable or be damped!

BGP Tweak: Prefix Limit

BGP itself provides optional features that, when used correctly, can increase network
availability. BGP supports the prefix limit option, which offers the ability to restrict the
total number of routes being advertised into the local AS. This option supports high
availability by preventing an EBGP neighbor from advertising an undesirably large
number of routes into the local AS. You configure a prefix limit for each EBGP neighbor,
under the protocols BGP level of hierarchy. In this configuration sample, r2 allows no
more than 2,000 prefixes to be advertised by neighbor 7.6.5.3. When the inbound
advertisements reach 80% of this threshold, warning messages are logged. When the
maximum is reached, the EBGP relationship is torn down for one hour (60 minutes):

```
[edit protocols bgp group EBGP]
lab@r2# show
type external;
import [ LOCAL-ADDRESS PREFIX-LENGTH-LIMIT ];
peer-as 1;
neighbor 7.6.5.3 {
    family inet {
        unicast {
            prefix-limit {
                maximum 2000;
                teardown 80 idle-timeout 60;
            }
        }
    }
}
```

Implications of route and prefix limits

Administrators concerned with SLA requirements should pay special attention to optional elements of the prefix limit configuration. Once the limit is reached, the BGP
relationship is torn down for a configurable duration, which stops routing across the
domain boundary. This is "downtime," as defined in any SLA.

PART III

Network Availability

CHAPTER 14

Fast High Availability Protocols

Quick failure recovery within a device is critical to maintaining high availability. In a network, it is equally important for the device to be able to determine what is going on around it. Protocols play a very important role in detecting and recovering from link and neighboring node failures. This chapter discusses several protocols that can help minimize downtime and keep the network running smoothly.

Protocols for Optical Networks

Optical networks provide the highest-speed links in existence today. With that speed comes a requirement for extremely fast failover mechanisms, to ensure that the massive amounts of traffic flowing through these pipes are disrupted for only a minimal amount of time.

Ethernet Operations, Administration, and Maintenance (OAM)

Despite the massive popularity of Ethernet networks, one of Ethernet's greatest shortcomings has been its lack of network management tools. For years, network administrators have wished for a way to monitor and manage Ethernet networks in the same way they can monitor SONET/SDH, ATM, and Multiprotocol Label Switching (MPLS) networks. This need has become more urgent as Ethernet continues to move beyond the local area network (LAN) and into metro area networks.

IEEE 802.1ah and 802.1ag

After years of waiting, a solution is now available to properly monitor Ethernet networks. Ethernet Operation, Administration, and Maintenance (OAM) provides a set of tools that you can use to monitor and manage the state of Ethernet links. The IEEE has defined two standards for Ethernet OAM: 802.1ah and 802.1ag. The 802.1ah standard, also known as link fault management (LFM), provides fault management for a single directly connected link. The 802.1ag standard, also known as connectivity fault management (CFM), provides OAM across multiple nodes.

Ethernet OAM provides three general features: fault monitoring, path discovery, and fault isolation. High availability is provided by the fault monitoring feature. An OAM-enabled node sends periodic OAM Protocol Data Units (PDUs) to the neighboring device to monitor the link. If the receiving device stops receiving PDUs, it declares the link down, which alerts upper-layer protocols that a failure has occurred.

The high availability component of Ethernet OAM is similar in functionality to Bidirectional Forwarding Detection (BFD), covered later in this chapter.

You configure Ethernet OAM as a protocol:

```
[edit]
lab@r1# set protocols oam ethernet ?
Possible completions:
+ apply-groups          Groups from which to inherit configuration data
+ apply-groups-except   Don't inherit configuration data from these groups
> connectivity-fault-management  Configurations related to 802.1ag ethernet oam
> link-fault-management  802.3ah Ethernet OAM configuration
```

At the time of this writing, CFM is supported on MX Series, T Series, and M120 and M320 devices. LFM is supported on 100 Mbps or faster Ethernet interfaces on MX Series, T Series, M Series (except M10 and M7 routers), and EX Series devices.

Configuring link fault management to perform basic link-level fault detection and management requires a simple one-line command on each neighboring device:

```
[edit]
lab@r1# set protocols oam ethernet link-fault-management interface ge-0/0/1
```

As shown in the preceding code, you simply specify `link-fault-management` as the desired OAM method, and then add each interface you wish to monitor and manage. You can optionally modify the default settings used to send PDUs and determine when a neighbor is considered lost:

```
[edit protocols oam ethernet link-fault-management]
lab@r1# set interface ge-0/0/1 pdu-?
Possible completions:
  pdu-interval    Periodic OAM protocol data unit interval (milliseconds)
  pdu-threshold   Number of PDUs missed before declaring peer lost (3..10)
```

The default PDU interval is 1,000 ms, while the default PDU threshold is 3.

Once committed, you can confirm that LFM is working properly by entering the following command:

```
lab@r1> show oam ethernet link-fault-management
Interface: ge-0/0/1.0
Status: Running, Discovery state: Send Any
```

```
Peer address: 00:19:e2:50:3b:e1
Flags:Remote-Stable Remote-State-Valid Local-Stable 0x50
Remote entity information:
Remote MUX action: forwarding, Remote parser action: forwarding
Discovery mode: active, Unidirectional mode: unsupported
Remote loopback mode: supported, Link events: supported
Variable requests: unsupported
```

OAM LFM is configured properly if the output displays the peer Media Access Control (MAC) address and the discover state is Send Any.

CFM provides many of the same general capabilities as LFM, but on a broader level. Because of CFM's end-to-end nature, it is ideal for service providers who need to manage Ethernet wide area network (WAN) and access service offerings, as well as monitor service-level agreements (SLAs). Because the scope of monitoring and management is greater with CFM, so is the configuration:

```
[edit protocols oam ethernet]
lab@r1# show
connectivity-fault-management {
    maintenance-domain Provider {
        level 0;
        maintenance-association Provider-ma {
            continuity-check {
                interval 1s;
                loss-threshold 4;
            }
            mep 100 {
                interface ge-0/0/1;
                direction down;
                auto-discovery;
            }
        }
    }
}
```

As you can see, CFM is not a one-command configuration. Detailed discussion of CFM configuration is beyond the scope of this book. But in short, you can configure administrative and maintenance domains to allow various parties, such as providers, partners, and customers, to perform their own monitoring and management while keeping everyone segregated. Within each maintenance domain, you include the desired interfaces and define timer and threshold values.

Ethernet OAM concepts and configuration are large and detailed topics that could easily take up an entire chapter on their own. Despite being a comparatively new technology, vast amounts of background information on IEEE 802.1ah and 802.1ag are available on the Internet. For detailed information on configuring Ethernet OAM on devices running JUNOS Software, see the "Network Interfaces Configuration Guide" at *http://www.juniper.net/techpubs/software/junos/index.html*.

SONET/SDH Automatic Protection Switching

SONET equipment uses automatic protection switching (APS) to detect and recover from circuit failures. SDH equipment has a similar mechanism, called multiplex section protection (MSP). Both APS and MSP can detect a failed link and recover in 50 milliseconds—perfect for a five 9s environment!

APS and MSP require dual-circuit configurations, with traffic flowing over an active *working* circuit and a second *protect* circuit standing by at all times. If the working circuit fails, traffic is redirected through the protect circuit, effectively making it the active circuit.

JUNOS Software supports 1 + 1 protection switching and can be configured as *revertive* or *nonrevertive*. Protection switching helps with two general scenarios: link failure and device failure. The example in Figure 14-1 shows a single router connected to an optical add-drop multiplexer (ADM). This scenario provides protection against link failure, as well as failure of the physical interface on the router.

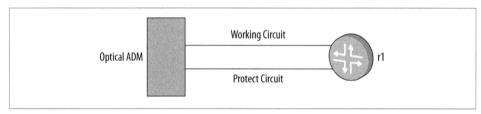

Figure 14-1. APS/MSP protection for link and interface hardware

In Figure 14-2, two separate routers are connected to the ADM, providing protection against failure of the router itself.

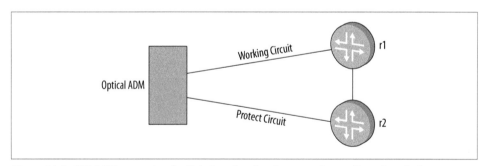

Figure 14-2. APS/MSP protection for link, interface hardware, and overall routing platform

You configure APS and MSP under the sonet-options for an interface:

```
[edit]
lab@r1# set interfaces so-0/1/0 sonet-options aps ?
Possible completions:
  advertise-interval   Advertise interval (1..65534 milliseconds)
```

```
+ apply-groups          Groups from which to inherit configuration data
+ apply-groups-except   Don't inherit configuration data from these groups
> authentication-key    Authentication parameters
  force                 Force circuit state
  hold-time             Hold time (1..65534 milliseconds)
  lockout               Lockout protection
  neighbor              Neighbor address
  paired-group          Name of paired APS group
  preserve-interface    Preserve interface state for fast failover
  protect-circuit       Protect circuit group name
  request               Request circuit state
  revert-time           Circuit revert time (seconds)
  switching-mode        APS switching mode
  working-circuit       Working circuit group name
```

 You configure MSP and APS using the same command-line interface (CLI) commands.

First, configure two interfaces: one as the working circuit and the second as the protect circuit. You must also associate the interfaces to an APS group and specify an authentication key:

```
[edit]
lab@r1# show interfaces so-0/1/0
sonet-options {
    aps {
        working-circuit apsgroup1;
        authentication-key "$9$CivTAOIEhrKvLIR-VY2aJ"; ## SECRET-DATA
    }
}
unit 0 {
    family inet {
        address 10.0.1.1/24;
    }
}

[edit]
lab@r1# show interfaces so-0/1/1
sonet-options {
    aps {
        protect-circuit apsgroup1;
        authentication-key "$9$aTJDk.mTF39kquOREyr"; ## SECRET-DATA
    }
}
unit 0 {
    family inet {
        address 10.0.2.1/24;
    }
}
```

If the circuits are on different routers, you must also add the IP address of the neighboring router:

```
[edit]
lab@r1# show interfaces so-0/1/0
sonet-options {
    aps {
        working-circuit apsgroup1;
        neighbor 192.168.1.2;
        authentication-key "$9$CivTAOIEhrKvLIR-VY2aJ"; ## SECRET-DATA
    }
}
unit 0 {
    family inet {
        address 10.0.1.1/24;
    }
}
```

The "neighbor" is not the device at the other end of the APS-protected link; in this case, the neighbors are the two routers benefiting from APS protection. For example, in Figure 14-2, r1 and r2 are neighbors. The two routers should be directly connected together, and the neighbor parameter should be the IP address of the neighbor's interface connected to this link. Traffic between neighbors should never travel along the APS-protected links.

A key high availability element that makes APS and MSP "fast" is the amount of time it takes for a link to be declared down and to then fail over. By default, Juniper Networks routers send advertisements every second, and failover occurs after three missed advertisements. You can change these values:

```
[edit]
lab@r1# set interfaces so-0/1/0 sonet-options aps advertise-interval ?
Possible completions:
  <advertise-interval>  Advertise interval (1..65534 milliseconds)
[edit]
lab@r1# set interfaces so-0/1/0 sonet-options aps hold-time ?
Possible completions:
  <hold-time>           Hold time (1..65534 milliseconds)
```

The default APS failover settings aren't especially fast for SONET/SDH links. However, you can see from the CLI output that you can modify these parameters to support the SONET standard APS failover time of 50 ms.

By default, APS is *nonrevertive*, meaning that when a working circuit has failed and then recovers, traffic continues to use the protect circuit and does not automatically revert to the working circuit. If you want traffic to move back to the working circuit after it recovers, you can manually force traffic back to the working circuit by using the request or force statement, or you can configure it to happen automatically using the revert-time statement, as shown here:

```
[edit]
lab@r1# set interfaces so-0/1/1 sonet-options aps revert-time ?
Possible completions:
  <revert-time>          Circuit revert time (seconds)
```

 Whether you use this feature depends entirely on your requirements: do you need to have traffic revert back to the working circuit as soon as possible, or is it fine to keep it on the protect circuit as long as traffic is flowing smoothly? Either way, don't set the revert-time too low. You are better off with traffic flowing reliably over the protect circuit than having traffic revert to the working circuit before it is fully stable.

Once you have committed the configuration, you can monitor link status using any of the various show aps commands. Here is an example of the output from the show aps extensive command:

```
lab@r1> show aps extensive
Interface   Group                            Circuit  Intf state
so-0/1/0    apsgroup1                        Working  enabled, up
  Neighbor 0.0.0.0, adj up, neighbor interface disabled, dead 2.788
  Channel state Working
  Protect circuit is on interface so-0/1/1
  Local-mode bidirectional(5), neighbor-mode bidirectional(5)
  Req K1 0x00, rcv K1 0x00, xmit K1 0x00, nbr K1 0x00, nbr paired req 0
  Revert time 0, neighbor revert time 0
  Hello due in 0.663
so-0/1/1    apsgroup1                        Protect  disabled, up
  Neighbor 0.0.0.0, adj up, neighbor interface enabled, dead 2.747
  Channel state Working
  Working circuit is on interface so-0/1/0
  Local-mode bidirectional(5), neighbor-mode bidirectional(5)
  Req K1 0x00, rcv K1 0x00, xmit K1 0x00, nbr K1 0x00, nbr paired req 0
  Revert time 0, neighbor revert time 0
  Hello due in 0.669
```

This example shows two interfaces on the same router that are running APS. Notice that interface so-0/1/0 is enabled as the working circuit, and so-0/1/1 is the protect circuit. Also, notice how each circuit knows about the other, making extremely fast failover possible.

Rapid Spanning Tree Protocol

Spanning tree protocols provide loop prevention for Layer 2 networks with multiple paths. The original Spanning Tree Protocol (STP) does this well; however, it is not up to the requirements of today's high availability networks. Specifically, failure detection takes too long (several seconds) and reconvergence involves several stages, lasting almost a minute, during which time traffic does not flow.

Spanning Tree Fundamentals

This book assumes you have good knowledge of routing and switching protocols. Should you want or need more information on the various spanning tree protocols, you can find a wide range of material on the Internet. You can also learn more about the protocol and its implementation on JUNOS devices by attending Juniper Networks training courses.

For more information on Juniper Networks training, see *http://www.juniper.net/train ing*

As the requirement for minimal downtime has increased, so has the need for an improved protocol. Rapid Spanning Tree Protocol (RSTP) is one of the answers to this requirement. RSTP eliminates the STP phases that require the switch to "listen and learn" after a topology change. Instead, a switch running RSTP knows its alternate path options before the failure occurs. When a failure occurs on a device, this increased "intelligence" allows the switch to provide subsecond failover—talk about a huge improvement for high availability environments!

MX Series and EX Series devices support switching along with Layer 2 protocols such as RSTP. You configure RSTP much like a routing protocol:

```
[edit]
lab@r1# set protocols rstp ?
Possible completions:
  <[Enter]>               Execute this command
+ apply-groups            Groups from which to inherit configuration data
+ apply-groups-except     Don't inherit configuration data from these groups
  bpdu-block-on-edge      Block BPDU on all interfaces configured as edge (BPDU Protect)
  bridge-priority         Priority of the bridge (in increments of 4k - 0,4k,8k,..60k)
  disable                 Disable STP
  forward-delay           Time spent in listening or learning state (4..30 seconds)
  hello-time              Time interval between configuration BPDUs (1..10 seconds)
> interface
  max-age                 Maximum age of received protocol bpdu (6..40 seconds)
> traceoptions            Tracing options for debugging protocol operation
```

Enable the protocol and add the interfaces you wish to include in the spanning tree environment:

```
[edit]
lab@r1# show protocols
rstp {
    interface fe-0/0/0.0;
    interface fe-0/0/1.0;
}
```

To achieve subsecond reconvergence, you must configure the RSTP interfaces as point-to-point:

```
[edit]
root# show protocols
rstp {
    interface fe-0/0/0.0 {
        mode point-to-point;
    }
    interface fe-0/0/1.0 {
        mode point-to-point;
    }
}
```

 Interfaces operating in full-duplex (FD) mode are set as RSTP point-to-point links by default.

You can then set any other RSTP parameters that are relevant for your environment.

Interior Gateway Protocols

IGPs are historically considered to be slow in detecting and recovering from failures in the network. However, this no longer has to be the case. Sure, the default timers for Open Shortest Path First (OSPF) can cause a router to take up to 40 seconds to declare a link down, but did you know that for OSPF and Intermediate System to Intermediate System (IS-IS) you can reduce the dead interval to as low as one second?

```
[edit]
lab@r1# set protocols ospf area 0 interface so-0/1/0 dead-interval ?
Possible completions:
  <dead-interval>      Dead interval (seconds) (1..65535)
```

This capability has the potential to completely change the way networks are designed in relation to protocol failover strategies. Where previously an IGP timer might have been a hindrance, requiring reliance on other mechanisms for fast failure detection and failover, the fast timers for these IGP protocols mean they can now arguably provide high availability capabilities all on their own.

Just because you *can* configure extremely low IGP timers doesn't mean you *should*. While the low timer settings for IGPs on JUNOS devices provide the option to use these protocols to maintain high availability networks, in practice routing protocols are no longer used as a primary means of quick failure detection and recovery. This is true to such an extent that these days it is not recommended to use extremely low timers at all. With the introduction of newer mechanisms that are purpose-built to provide extremely fast failure detection, such as BFD (discussed in the next section), protocol timers can be left at their default settings. In fact, because BFD essentially relieves IGP timers of their high availability duties entirely, some network administrators are even going the other way and *increasing* protocol timers above their default settings, to minimize the load placed on the control plane of network devices due to protocol communication exchanges.

Bidirectional Forwarding Detection

Lowering the timers of OSPF and IS-IS can be a reasonable solution to contain network failures, but it comes at a cost. It is possible to lower the timers to the point that they cause problems for the router. Imagine a scenario in which you have hundreds of in-terfaces all announcing subsecond OSPF Hellos—that's a lot of work for a router! Now, of course, the amount of hardship the router incurs depends on the size and capacity of the router, how many interfaces are in play, and how exactly you configure the timers. But suffice it to say, there comes a point when IGP timers are not the solution to fast link failure detection. And beyond these two IGPs, what about the other protocols that don't have fast failure detection mechanisms? Or what if there is no protocol at all?

BFD is a simple protocol designed to perform one function: link failure detection. BFD provides a mechanism to directly monitor a link and to notify the device if it stops receiving messages from a neighbor on the other end of that link. BFD relieves the IGP of having to provide fast failure detection; in fact, it can alleviate the load that Hello messages can place on a router. With BFD, it is no longer necessary to lower timers, or even to have them run at the default settings. In fact, you can configure higher timer values, virtually eliminating load issues on the router that result from generating Hello messages.

Another benefit of BFD is that it provides a centralized, common, and scalable way to perform fast link failure detection. Instead of modifying and managing timers so each protocol can monitor link status, you use BFD to manage link failure detection, leverage this information within the desired protocols, and leave the protocols themselves to do what they were built to do: determine the best path through the network to a given destination.

BFD also provides a specific solution for static routes. Because a static route uses no routing protocol, it has no natural failure detection mechanism. This means that a link can be down but the router will continue sending traffic along that path indefinitely.

BFD solves this issue by providing a failure detection mechanism where there wasn't one before.

It may seem like BFD is a Layer 3 protocol, or a kind of routing protocol, but it's not. While BFD is closely integrated with protocols (it is configured within each protocol's configuration stanza), it stands alone and is simply used for failure detection. When a failure does happen, BFD immediately notifies the appropriate routing protocol, and that protocol can take action from there, routing traffic around the problem link.

At the time of this writing, BFD works with the following protocols:

- IPv4:
  - Routing Information Protocol (RIP)
  - OSPF
  - IS-IS
  - Border Gateway Protocol (BGP): Internal BGP (IBGP) and External BGP (EBGP)
  - Static routes
  - MPLS (RSVP)
  - PIM
- IPv6:
  - OSPFv3
  - Static routes

The BFD configuration stanza is as follows:

```
[edit]
lab@r1# set protocols bgp group ext-peers bfd-liveness-detection ?
Possible completions:
+ apply-groups            Groups from which to inherit configuration data
+ apply-groups-except     Don't inherit configuration data from these groups
> detection-time          Detection-time options
  holddown-interval       Time to hold the session-UP notification to the client
  minimum-interval        Minimum transmit and receive interval (milliseconds)
  minimum-receive-interval  Minimum receive interval (1..255000 milliseconds)
  multiplier              Detection time multiplier (1..255)
  no-adaptation           Disable adaptation
> transmit-interval       Transmit-interval options
  version                 BFD protocol version number
```

At a minimum, you must define the transmit and receive intervals. You can set each parameter separately or specify both using the `minimum-interval` parameter:

```
[edit]
lab@r1# show protocols bgp
group ext-peers {
    bfd-liveness-detection {
        minimum-interval 300;
    }
    neighbor 10.20.30.40 {
```

```
        peer-as 54321;
    }
}
```

In the preceding example, BFD control packets (Hellos) are sent every 300 ms. The router also expects to receive a control packet from its neighbor every 300 ms.

 Be sure to configure the transmit and receive intervals identically between nodes.

By default, BFD declares a link down when it fails to receive three packets in a row from its neighbor. If this value is too aggressive, you can modify it:

```
[edit]
lab@r1# show protocols bgp
group ext-peers {
    bfd-liveness-detection {
        minimum-interval 300;
        multiplier 5;
    }
    neighbor 10.20.30.40 {
        peer-as 54321;
    }
}
```

In the preceding example, BFD now waits for five missed control packets from the neighboring router before declaring the link down and informing BGP.

Setting the Interval for BFD Control Packets

Since BFD was first implemented, there has been debate over the "correct" settings for BFD. And what quickly became apparent is that there is no single right answer. Set the interval too high, and you don't get especially fast failover. Set the interval too low, and even a slight variance in the quality of the link could cause it to be declared down. Worse yet, continuous flapping could occur as BFD repeatedly declares the link up and then down.

Having had a few years now to work with BFD, network administrators and operators seem to have come to a general consensus that 300 ms is an appropriate interval value, with a multiplier of 3 (that is, 900 ms to link failure detection). These values support a high availability environment nicely, providing subsecond detection as well as an allowance for small variances in link quality, and not causing more harm than good.

In JUNOS releases before 9.4, BFD Hello packets are generated only by the RPD process running on the routing engine (RE), by default. To alleviate the load placed on the RE, you can enable periodic packet management (PPM). PPM directs the Packet Forwarding Engine (PFE) to assist in handling the sending of BFD control packets, allowing your JUNOS device to support a higher number of BFD-enabled interfaces. It can be set using the command `set routing-options ppm delegate-processing`. PPM is supported only on the M120, M320, MX Series, T Series, and TX Matrix routing platforms. Note that as of JUNOS 9.4, this feature is enabled by default.

Virtual Router Redundancy Protocol

The premise of high availability extends end to end in a network, right down to an end user's workstation. A user's PC is configured—statically—with a default gateway, making it a major exposure point in maintaining high availability. Even with multiple routers as exit points from the LAN, if the PC's configured gateway fails, traffic has nowhere to go.

Virtual Router Redundancy Protocol (VRRP) is designed to specifically address this issue, as shown in Figure 14-3. All gateway routers essentially become a single virtual router, sharing a common "virtual" IP (and MAC) address. All hosts on the LAN still have a single static gateway address, but the address is *virtual*, meaning it never goes away. Thus, traffic always has a way out of the network.

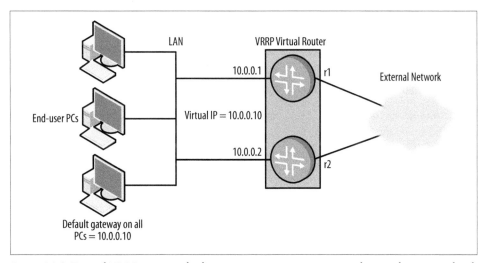

Figure 14-3. Typical VRRP setup: multiple gateway routers acting as a single virtual router, and end-user PCs using the virtual address as their default gateway

VRRP is typically implemented to provide high availability for Ethernet networks.

Of the VRRP-configured routers, one is always the master. This master router is the device that responds to and services traffic from inside the LAN destined for external networks. The other VRRP-configured routers act as backups. If the master fails, one of the backup routers takes over. This new master router takes over responding to and servicing traffic destined for external networks. The key point here is that the hosts on the LAN never know that any failure has occurred. They simply send traffic to their configured gateway (the virtual IP or VIP address) as usual, and the VRRP-enabled routers take care of ensuring that traffic gets to its destination.

VRRP-enabled routers undergo an election process to determine which one becomes the master router. By default, the router containing the VRRP-enabled interface with the highest IP address becomes the master router. Alternatively, the election can be based on a manually configured priority value (1 to 255, default is 100). The router with the highest priority value becomes the master router. If the master router fails, another election takes place and the router with the next highest priority value takes over as the new master router.

You configure VRRP under the interface that acts as a gateway for the LAN:

```
[edit interfaces fe-0/0/0 unit 0]
lab@r1# set family inet address 10.0.0.1/24 vrrp-group 1 ?
Possible completions:
  accept-data           Accept packets destined for virtual IP address
  advertise-interval    Advertisement interval (1..255 seconds)
+ apply-groups          Groups from which to inherit configuration data
+ apply-groups-except   Don't inherit configuration data from these groups
  authentication-key    Authentication key
  authentication-type   Authentication type
  fast-interval         Fast advertisement interval (100..999 milliseconds)
  inet6-advertise-interval  Inet6 advertisement interval (milliseconds)
  no-accept-data        Don't accept packets destined for virtual IP address
  no-preempt            Don't allow preemption
> preempt               Allow preemption
  priority              Virtual router election priority (0..255)
> track                 Interfaces to track for VRRP group
+ virtual-address       One or more virtual IPv4 addresses
+ virtual-inet6-address One or more virtual inet6 addresses
  virtual-link-local-address  Virtual link-local addresses
```

 Juniper Networks routers also support VRRP for IPv6.

The minimum configuration for VRRP includes a group ID to identify the interfaces from the gateway routers that are to work together, a priority number for master router elections, and the VIP address that is shared across the VRRP-enabled interfaces:

```
[edit interfaces fe-0/0/0 unit 0]
lab@r1# show
family inet {
    address 10.0.0.1/24 {
        vrrp-group 1 {
            virtual-address 10.0.0.10;
            priority 150;
        }
    }
}
```

The advertisement interval for the master router is also configurable. By default, a master router sends out advertisement packets each second to indicate that it is up and operating. When the backup routers fail to receive three advertisements, the master router is declared down and an election takes place. You can configure the advertisement interval in seconds using the advertise-interval parameter, or in milliseconds using the fast-interval parameter:

```
[edit interfaces fe-0/0/0 unit 0 family inet address 10.0.0.1/24]
lab@r1# set vrrp-group 1 advertise-interval ?
Possible completions:
  <advertise-interval>  Advertisement interval (1..255 seconds)
[edit interfaces fe-0/0/0 unit 0 family inet address 10.0.0.1/24]
lab@r1# set vrrp-group 1 fast-interval ?
Possible completions:
  <fast-interval> Fast advertisement interval (100..999 milliseconds)
```

 Whether the default failover time (three seconds) is sufficient depends entirely on your network environment and high availability requirements. It may be sufficient if end users are performing tasks that are not time-sensitive, such as using the Internet or sending email. However, if users are running time-sensitive applications, or if the network has devices such as VoIP phones, you likely want to reduce the timers to ensure subsecond failover.

When a master is declared down and a backup router takes over, there is still an item that can hurt high availability. By default, backup routers listen for traffic destined for the VIP address, but they don't retain Address Resolution Protocol (ARP) information and they don't populate their ARP cache. This means that when a backup router takes over as master, it still has some learning to do. In an environment with many hosts, this learning process can become burdensome. To combat this issue, you can alter the backup router's behavior and allow it to learn and retain ARP information. To enable this feature, use the passive-learning parameter under the arp stanza:

```
[edit]
lab@r1# set system arp passive-learning
```

A subtler aspect of high availability involves basic connectivity. For example, as an end user, you might be having trouble reaching a network resource and so you want to confirm basic connectivity to your default gateway. You try to ping the default gateway but receive no response. You have a connectivity issue, right? Wrong. By default, VRRP does not respond to traffic destined to the VIP address. If you wish to receive responses from the VIP address, you must explicitly configure the router to do so:

```
[edit interfaces fe-0/0/0 unit 0]
lab@r1# show
family inet {
    address 10.0.0.1/24 {
        vrrp-group 1 {
            virtual-address 10.0.0.10;
            priority 150;
            accept-data;
        }
    }
}
```

 This feature is not part of the VRRP standard. However, it can be very useful to help verify connectivity and reachability.

VRRP's role is to detect and recover from a LAN-side failure in the gateway devices. But what if the WAN side of the master router experiences a failure? According to VRRP, there is no problem—so traffic flows to the device, only to be dropped because it has nowhere to go. Fortunately, there is a solution to this problem: tracking. Juniper Networks supports two types of tracking: *interface* and *route* tracking. With interface tracking, as shown in Figure 14-4, VRRP can track up to 10 logical interfaces and automatically have VRRP fail over to the backup router if the non-VRRP interface goes down. You can also configure VRRP failover if a non-VRRP interface falls below a given speed threshold. Route tracking works in much the same way, allowing the master router to track reachability, and fail over to the backup router if a given route no longer exists in the routing table.

These features provide a great solution for high availability environments. Traditional VRRP provides only LAN-side protection, but traffic doesn't stop at the router; it flows through to some other destination. Tracking provides a more complete solution by giving VRRP a more complete view of the device's end-to-end monitoring solution.

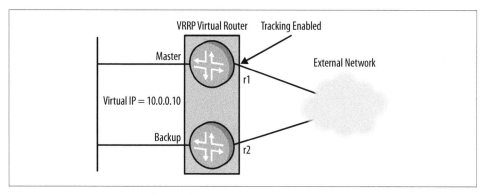

Figure 14-4. VRRP with interface tracking

You configure tracking under the VRRP group, using the track statement:

```
[edit interfaces fe-0/0/0 unit 0 family inet address 10.0.0.1/24]
lab@r1# show vrrp-group 1 track ?
Possible completions:
  <[Enter]>             Execute this command
+ apply-groups          Groups from which to inherit configuration data
+ apply-groups-except   Don't inherit configuration data from these groups
> interface             Interface to track in VRRP group
  priority-hold-time    Priority hold time (0..3600 seconds)
> route                 Route to track in VRRP group
```

To configure interface tracking, identify the interface you wish to track and specify the amount to subtract from the priority value when this interface goes down:

```
[edit interfaces fe-0/0/0 unit 0 family inet address 10.0.0.1/24]
lab@r1# show
vrrp-group 1 {
    virtual-address 10.0.0.10;
    priority 150;
    accept-data;
    track {
        interface so-0/1/0 {
            priority-cost 51;
        }
    }
}
```

Then, if desired, you can also configure a bandwidth threshold for the tracked interface. You can configure up to five thresholds and define how much to reduce the priority value as the bandwidth of the tracked interface falls below each threshold:

```
[edit interfaces fe-0/0/0 unit 0 family inet address 10.0.0.1/24]
lab@r1# show
vrrp-group 1 {
    virtual-address 10.0.0.10;
    priority 150;
    accept-data;
    track {
```

```
      interface so-0/1/0 {
          bandwidth-threshold 10m priority-cost 25;
          bandwidth-threshold 20m priority-cost 25;
          bandwidth-threshold 40m priority-cost 25;
          priority-cost 51;
      }
  }
}
```

Route tracking works much like interface tracking except, of course, you identify a route to track instead of an interface. You must also define an amount to deduct from the priority value when the route goes down:

```
[edit interfaces fe-0/0/0 unit 0 family inet address 10.0.0.1/24]
lab@Bangkok-re1# show
vrrp-group 1 {
    virtual-address 10.0.0.10;
    priority 150;
    accept-data;
    track {
        route 192.168.1.0/24 routing-instance default priority-cost 51;
    }
}
```

In the preceding example, notice the `routing-instance` portion of the configuration. When using interface tracking, you must identify the routing instance that holds the route you wish to track. If you want to track a route in the main routing instance (or if you aren't using routing instances at all), specify the instance as `default`.

After you commit the configuration, you can monitor VRRP using any of the `show VRRP` commands. In the following example, you can see that interface `fe-0/0/0` belongs to VRRP Group 1 with a VIP address of 10.0.0.10. You can also see that this router is the master router for the group:

```
lab@r1> show vrrp
Interface    State    Group   VR state  Timer      Type   Address
fe-0/0/0.0   up           1   master    N  0.278   lcl    10.0.0.1
                                                   vip    10.0.0.10
```

MPLS Path Protection

There are several methods of protecting traffic when using MPLS, including options to protect a single link, an entire node, or the entire path.

The Resource Reservation Protocol (RSVP) provides a way to define MPLS paths across a network. RSVP includes mechanisms to specifically define which nodes the path traverses. You can do this manually, specifying each hop, or you can configure parameters such as bandwidth and link color, and let the router dynamically define certain parts of the path based on resource availability.

Fast Reroute

RSVP is responsible for signaling the MPLS path—that is, establishing and setting it up. It is also responsible for monitoring the path once it has been established. Traditional RSVP failure detection mechanisms are quite slow, on the order of several seconds to detect failures. However, additions to the original protocol provide a detection mechanism that can offer subsecond failover. This feature is called *fast reroute* (FRR).

> Fast reroute provides failure detection and recovery in an incredible 50 ms. That's the same failover time as APS for SONET networks!

FRR is a mechanism that establishes detour label-switched paths (LSPs) at each router along the main MPLS LSP. If a node or link fails, the upstream router immediately sends traffic to its detour LSP. The router also notifies the ingress router for the path that part of the main LSP has failed. The ingress router can then redirect traffic along a new LSP as appropriate. This type of protection is called *one-to-one backup* as the protecting LSPs cannot be shared among active LSPs.

> In practice, administrators configure both primary and secondary MPLS paths. In this case, FRR solves the short-term problem of protecting traffic until the secondary LSP is established. Once established, the ingress router sends traffic down the secondary LSP, and the detour LSP provided by FRR is no longer needed. If there is no secondary LSP, or if constraints don't allow the secondary LSP to be formed, the detour LSP can be used until the failed link is repaired.

You configure FRR only on the ingress node for the MPLS LSP. When RSVP signals the path downstream to the other nodes, it includes information telling each node it should initiate a detour LSP for protection. FRR is very easy to configure:

```
[edit]
lab@r1# show protocols mpls
label-switched-path path-with-FRR {
    to 10.0.5.1;
    fast-reroute;
    primary primary-path;
    secondary secondary-path;
}
path primary-path {
    10.0.1.1 loose;
    10.0.2.1 loose;
}
path secondary-path {
    10.0.3.1 loose;
    10.0.4.1 loose;
}
```

FRR requires that you enable IGP traffic engineering on each node in the MPLS network. IS-IS has traffic engineering enabled by default, and you can enable it for OSPF with a simple command:

```
[edit]
lab@r1# set protocols ospf traffic-engineering
```

You can configure additional parameters for FRR as desired, such as bandwidth reservation and administrative groups (link coloring). You can also define a hop count for the detour LSP, as shown here:

```
[edit protocols mpls label-switched-path path-with-FRR]
lab@r1# show fast-reroute ?
Possible completions:
  <[Enter]>             Execute this command
+ apply-groups          Groups from which to inherit configuration data
+ apply-groups-except   Don't inherit configuration data from these groups
  bandwidth             Bandwidth to reserve (bps)
  bandwidth-percent     Percentage of main path bandwidth to reserve (1..100)
+ exclude               Groups, all of which must be absent
  hop-limit             Maximum allowed router hops (0..255)
+ include-all           Groups, all of which must be present
+ include-any           Groups, one or more of which must be present
  no-exclude            Disable exclude checking
  no-include-all        Disable include-all checking
  no-include-any        Disable include-any checking
```

The FRR feature in JUNOS Software is proprietary; therefore, it is not a widely implemented solution. FRR also has the limitation that it is, by design, an end-to-end solution, which means it doesn't scale all that well. Full protection to each endpoint means a full mesh of LSPs. A more common and efficient mechanism is link protection, which we discuss in the next section.

Node and Link Protection

An alternate method to provide MPLS path protection is to use node and link protection. Each feature functions as you might expect: link protection provides an alternate LSP to reach a neighboring router in case of a failure to a specific link, while node protection provides a bypass LSP around a neighboring router in case the entire node fails. This type of protection is called *facility backup* as the protecting LSPs can be shared by active LSPs.

Node and especially link protection are a more popular solution, as these features are standardized and therefore interoperable with other vendors.

You must first enable IGP traffic engineering on each node in the MPLS network. Since IS-IS has traffic engineering enabled by default, you need to enable it only for OSPF:

```
[edit]
lab@r1# set protocols ospf traffic-engineering
```

Next, enable protection for each LSP you want protected:

```
[edit]
lab@r1# show protocols mpls
label-switched-path path-with-node-protection {
    to 10.0.5.1;
    node-link-protection;
    primary primary-path;
    secondary secondary-path;
}
path primary-path {
    10.0.1.1 loose;
    10.0.2.1 loose;
}
path secondary-path {
    10.0.3.1 loose;
    10.0.4.1 loose;
}
```

The preceding example shows node protection enabled. Note that you could enable just link protection using the link-protection statement.

 Node protection requires that link protection also be enabled.

With protection enabled for the LSP at ingress, the final step is to enable link protection at the RSVP level for every downstream interface across the network that the LSP traverses. There are two ways to configure this on each device: you can use a repetitive series of commands to configure link protection on each interface, or you can simplify things considerably and enter a single command per device, using the all parameter:

```
lab@r2# set protocols rsvp interface all link-protection
```

This statement enables link protection on all interfaces on the device.

You can optionally define additional parameters for bypass LSPs, such as an explicit path for the bypass LSP:

```
lab@r2# set protocols rsvp interface all link-protection ?
Possible completions:
  <[Enter]>            Execute this command
+ apply-groups         Groups from which to inherit configuration data
+ apply-groups-except  Don't inherit configuration data from these groups
> bandwidth            Bandwidth for each bypass (bps)
> bypass               Bypass with specific constraints
  class-of-service     Class of service for the bypass LSP (0..7)
```

```
  disable              Disable link protection on this interface
  hop-limit            Maximum allowed router hops for bypass (2..255)
  max-bypasses         Max number of bypasses permitted for protecting this interface
  no-cspf              Disable automatic path computation
  no-node-protection   Disallow node protection on this interface
  optimize-timer       Interval between bypass reoptimizations (seconds)
> path                 Explicit route of bypass path
  priority             Preemption priorities for the bypass LSP
  subscription         Percent of bandwidth guaranteed when admitting protected
LSPs into bypasses
  |                    Pipe through a command
```

 In practice, link protection is a more effective high availability mechanism than node protection. Node protection relies on protocol timers to determine that a failure has occurred, while link protection is able to declare a failure as soon as the physical link (or interface on the neighboring router) goes down.

It is critically important for network devices to know when failure of another device or a link occurs—the availability of the network depends on it. Protocols play a key role in communicating when these failures occur. The faster devices can learn about, reconverge around, and recover from failures, the higher the uptime for the network as a whole.

CHAPTER 15

Transitioning Routing and Switching to a Multivendor Environment

While most networks begin as single-vendor efforts, very few stay that way. Mature networks, whether owned by an enterprise or by a service provider, are a reflection of the need to reduce costs or expand functionality by taking advantage of products from multiple vendors. Often the transition from a single-vendor network to a multivendor network is painful, involving frustration during the testing, implementation, and support cycles. In this chapter, we give examples, advice, and recommendations for a safe transition to a multivendor network that has no visible impact/effect on the operation of the network.

This chapter starts by explaining, at a high level, how transitioning to (and in some cases through) a multivendor network can be accomplished in the context of two common architectural models. Later sections show some of the configuration elements needed to implement these high-level concepts and describe a few of the more common problems encountered while doing so.

Industry Standards

While writing this book, we frequently shared thoughts with coworkers and fellow network engineers as a sanity check and a way to gather other perspectives. Of all the chapters we discussed, this one drew by far the most queries. The most common question was, "How in the world are you going to write that? Everyone knows that Juniper products don't support EIGRP and HSRP."

True statement. Juniper products do not support Cisco-proprietary protocols. However, both Cisco and Juniper products support implementations of industry-standard protocols such as Open Shortest Path First (OSPF), Border Gateway Protocol (BGP), and Virtual Router Redundancy Protocol (VRRP). Furthermore, while it is not considered a best practice, proprietary protocols are commonly found in some places in multivendor networks.

Actually, the "How?" question is rooted in a major misconception. People, even very experienced engineers, assume that when the terms *system redundancy* and *multivendor* are used to describe a network, the intention is to pair devices from different vendors within the architecture. This is not the case.

Multivendor Architecture for High Availability

In Chapter 1, we described different redundancy models, including component, system, and site redundancy. While the discussion in that chapter implied that redundant pairs of devices should be identical, this condition was not stated outright. For example, when deploying a pair of switches to provide redundancy for a critical corporate local area network (LAN), the switches should at least be from the same vendor, and at best should be identical hardware running identical software. There are several reasons for this recommendation:

- Paired production network devices are expected to perform identically. Identical performance is best facilitated by identical platforms.
- The sparing scheme is simplified. A single collection of redundant components can be stored for the pair of devices.
- Interoperability testing burden is reduced. Identical devices are by default interoperable.
- Network management can focus on a layer in the scheme rather than devices within a layer.

For these reasons, when deploying products from an additional vendor, high availability is best protected by not mixing vendors' products within a high availability pairing of devices.

Two Sensible Approaches

Since pairing devices from different vendors is not desirable, what is the best approach to deploying devices from multiple vendors in a production network? There are two sensible approaches.

Layered approach to multivendor networks

In the *layered* model, the network design team defines layers within the network based on device purpose and function. The two most common models used are Core-Distribution-Access (CDA) and Provider Edge-Customer Edge (PE-CE). Both models are well known and well documented, but they do merit some discussion when applied to high availability networks.

CDA model. This model implies that all devices in the architecture are part of a single Autonomous System (AS) and are under one administration. This model is commonly associated with small to medium-size enterprise networks.

Figure 15-1 shows redundant pairs of devices in a CDA model. With this model in mind, network architects or administrators can choose to designate routers from different vendors in different layers within the architecture. For example, Juniper routers may be selected for the core (`C-router`) and access (`A-switch`) layers, while Cisco products may be used to meet specific needs in the distribution (`D-router`) layer.

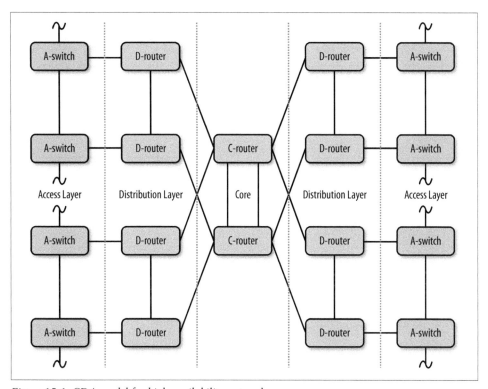

Figure 15-1. CDA model for high availability networks

PE-CE model. This model recognizes the existence of multiple ASs and the presence of multiple administrative domains within the architectural model. The PE-CE model has historically been associated with carrier and service provider networks, but it is becoming more common in large enterprises and campus networks.

Figure 15-2 shows redundant pairs of devices in a PE-CE architectural model. In a layered multivendor approach for this model, the network's architects could select Juniper routers for the provider edge (`PE-router`) role and devices from another vendor for the core (`P-router`) or data center roles.

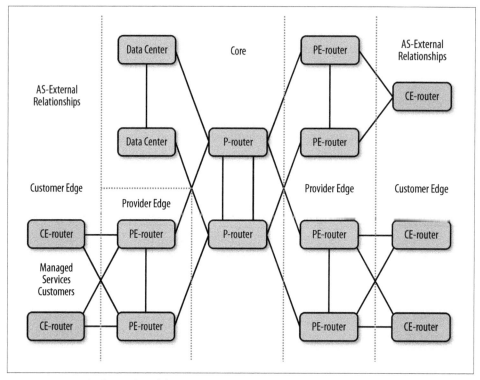

Figure 15-2. PE-CE layered model

 While both models can seldom fit within a single diagram, large-scale network architecture requires both CDA and PE-CE model characteristics. In Figure 15-2, for example, each "CE router" would most likely also be a core device within a CDA modeled topology.

Site-based approach to multivendor networks

Large-scale enterprises and service providers often create and maintain an approved products list. This list identifies products that have been tested or vetted for use in the production network. An "approved products" list approach allows some flexibility in determining which vendor's platforms to use within the network.

This approach is often used in conjunction with a site-based architecture. Site-based architectures allow specific decisions about network devices, protocols, and connection types to be based, to some extent, on factors unique to a deployment site. These factors can include:

- Customer requests for specific vendor hardware in the PE role.

- Presence of specific hardware in the CE role. Customers have been known to deploy hardware in the CE role that does not "play nicely" with equipment from other vendors. It is better for the network's high availability posture to deploy PE devices from the same vendor that provided the customer with the CE devices than to deploy hardware that is known to have interoperability issues.

- Vendor or platform competencies of the local support staff. The notion here is that engineers tend to specialize in just a few or possibly just one vendor's products. There is much less risk in deploying products that the staff is comfortable with supporting.

- Differing collections of functional requirements. Protocol, interface, or other functional requirements, particularly when they are proprietary and specific to a site, can mandate products from a specific vendor. Examples include customer requirements for Cisco CDP or EIGRP on the link between CE and PE devices.

- Price advantage. Product availability, discounts, and shipping costs may make one vendor's products significantly less expensive than another's in some geographic regions.

Figure 15-3 shows application of the PE-CE model to a site-based architecture.

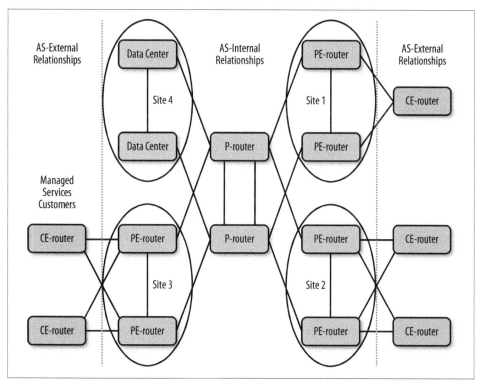

Figure 15-3. Site-based approach to multivendor networks

Figure 15-3 shows several defined sites, 1–4. For the reasons previously discussed, the administrators may choose to deploy different pairs of vendors' products in each site circle even though 1–3 are within the Provider Edge Layer within the architecture. If the administrators had designed a layered approach for multivendor deployment, sites 1–3 would be required to use products from the same vendor.

Multivendor As a Transition State

In some situations, having the network in a multivendor state may simply be a transitional phase that exists because the administrators have chosen to switch hardware vendors. In this case, a multivendor state is more of a temporary necessity, not the desired end result. Interestingly enough, the layered and site-based approaches are also effective and safe ways to transition from one vendor to another.

Layered transitions

User demands for network bandwidth and interface connectivity tend to grow over time. When answering the call for additional bandwidth, CDA networks tend to grow from the core toward the edge. When responding for demands for additional connectivity, CDA networks often grow from the edge back toward the core.

In the layered transition model, you place additional devices at specific layers in parallel to existing devices and they are configured to peer with devices in adjacent layers. In Figure 15-4, the network administrators have chosen to transition from an "all Ericsson" to an "all Juniper" network. Figure 15-4 shows a pair of Juniper routers being added into the core and peering with the existing distribution layer devices.

Once you have confirmed functionality, adjust metrics on the links to the distribution layer routers (D-routers) to make the new core (C-router) devices more desirable than the old ones.

 Chapter 6 provides an extensive tool kit of configuration elements that manipulate metrics and other protocol settings to make specific links more desirable than others.

Then, after confirming that traffic is flowing in a stable manner over the new core, you can decommission the old core.

Although the network that results from a layered transition is not the desired end state, the network is now technically a multivendor network. The core is Juniper and the distribution and edge layers are Ericsson. To achieve the goal of once again having a single-vendor network, you must repeat this process at the distribution layer and, to a lesser extent, at the access layer.

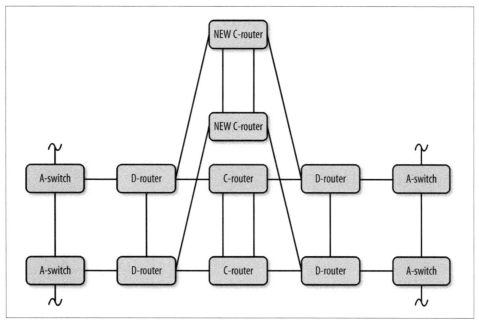

Figure 15-4. Transitioning from an all-Ericsson network to an all-Juniper network, starting with the core

Site-based transitions

By their very nature and purpose, site-based architectures are seldom single-vendor networks. An even rarer event would be the need to change vendors for a single-vendor site-based architecture. However, should the oddsmakers take a beating and the need arise you would begin the process by following a pattern similar to the layered transition:

1. Start up the new provider routers and establish peering sessions to all provider, edge, and data center routers.
2. Manipulate metrics and protocol settings to make traffic "want" to transition the new provider routers instead of the old.
3. Decommission the old provider routers.
4. Enable new provider edge routers that parallel existing sites, and configure peering relationships to the provider chassis.
5. Once you have confirmed that the edge routers are functional, establish peering relationships to customer edge routers and transition the traffic.

The transition is completed when all sites are cut over to the new devices.

Routing Protocol Interoperability

Figure 15-5 illustrates a few issues you may encounter when running common industry-standard routing protocols among Juniper and Cisco routers. In this figure, devices from different vendors have been mixed in a rather haphazard way to trigger certain issues that we want to address. The figure does not necessarily reflect a layered or site-based approach to multivendor networks.

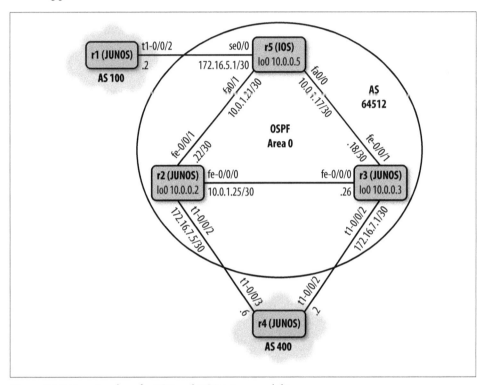

Figure 15-5. Base topology for IGP and BGP interoperability concerns

In Figure 15-5, routers r2, r3, and r5 share OSPF adjacencies, which use MD5 authentication, and Internal BGP (IBGP) relationships within AS 64512. Router r5 is an External BGP (EBGP) peer to r1 in AS 100. Routers r2 and r3 are EBGP peers to r4 in AS 400.

In this example, we assume that AS 64512 contains other Cisco devices that are connected in a partial mesh. Router r5 represents the collection of Cisco routers.

Interface Connectivity

Before bringing up OSPF or BGP relationships among the Cisco and Juniper devices, we must first establish simple Layer 3 connectivity. Assuming that all physical cabling is in place, we add the necessary configuration elements for the Cisco–Juniper connections on **r5**. This snippet shows Fast Ethernet interfaces 0/0 and 0/1 configured with appropriate IP addresses for connectivity to **r3** and **r2**. We also see the appropriate address for serial interface 0/0 and confirm that a loopback address is available for IBGP connectivity:

```
interface Loopback0
 ip address 10.0.0.5 255.255.255.255
 no ip directed-broadcast
!
interface FastEthernet0/0
 ip address 10.0.1.17 255.255.255.252
 no ip directed-broadcast
!
interface Serial0/0
 bandwidth 1544
 ip address 172.16.5.1 255.255.255.252
 no ip directed-broadcast
!
interface FastEthernet0/1
 ip address 10.0.1.21 255.255.255.252
 no ip directed-broadcast
```

Routers **r2** and **r3** host the Juniper side of the Fast Ethernet links. Configuration for **r2** and **r3** is straightforward. Here it is on router **r2**:

```
[edit interfaces]
lab@r1# show
fe-0/0/0 {
    unit 0 {
        family inet {
            address 10.0.1.25/30;
        }
    }
}
fe-0/0/1 {
    unit 0 {
        family inet {
            address 10.0.1.22/30;
        }
    }
}
```

Router **r3** has a similar configuration:

```
[edit interfaces]
lab@r3# show
fe-0/0/0 {
    unit 0 {
        family inet {
            address 10.0.1.26/30;
        }
    }
}
fe-0/0/1 {
```

```
        unit 0 {
            family inet {
                address 10.0.1.18/30;
            }
        }
    }
```

Router r1 hosts the Juniper side of the T1 connection (serial 0/0) to router r5. The interface configuration on r1 includes the necessary elements:

```
[edit interfaces]
lab@r1# show
t1-0/0/2 {
    unit 0 {
        family inet {
            address 172.16.5.2/30;
        }
    }
}
```

Use ping commands on r5 to confirm Layer 3 connectivity on all connected interfaces. Router r5 expects to receive replies from r1, r2, and r3:

```
r5>ping 10.0.1.22

Type escape sequence to abort.
Sending 5, 100-byte ICMP Echos to 10.0.1.22, timeout is 2 seconds:
!!!!!
Success rate is 100 percent (5/5), round-trip min/avg/max = 8/21/68 ms
r5>ping 10.0.1.18

Type escape sequence to abort.
Sending 5, 100-byte ICMP Echos to 10.0.1.18, timeout is 2 seconds:
!!!!!
Success rate is 100 percent (5/5), round-trip min/avg/max = 1/2/4 ms
r5>ping 172.16.5.2

Type escape sequence to abort.
Sending 5, 100-byte ICMP Echos to 172.16.5.2, timeout is 2 seconds:
.....
Success rate is 0 percent (0/5)
```

Routers r2 and r3 responded to the pings, but clearly there is a problem with the connection to r1. Further investigation is required. We use variations of a show interface command on both vendors' platforms to look for compatibility issues. At this point, assume that the physical cabling, a T1 cross-connect that is a standard pin-out recognized by both vendors, has been confirmed to be good. Output from r5 is shown first, followed by output from r1:

```
r5>show int serial 0/0
Serial0/0 is up, line protocol is down
  Hardware is PQUICC with Fractional T1 CSU/DSU
  Internet address is 172.16.5.1/30
  MTU 1500 bytes, BW 1544 Kbit, DLY 20000 usec,
     reliability 255/255, txload 1/255, rxload 1/255
```

```
  Encapsulation HDLC, loopback not set
  Keepalive set (10 sec)
  Last input 00:00:02, output 00:00:00, output hang never
...

[edit interfaces]
lab@r1# run show interfaces t1-0/0/2
Physical interface: t1-0/0/2, Enabled, Physical link is Up
  Interface index: 139, SNMP ifIndex: 36
  Link-level type: PPP, MTU: 1504, Clocking: Internal, Speed: T1,
  Loopback: None, FCS: 16, Framing: ESF
  Device flags   : Present Running
  Interface flags: Point-To-Point SNMP-Traps Internal: 0x4000
  Link flags     : Keepalives
  Keepalive settings: Interval 10 seconds, Up-count 1, Down-count 3
  Keepalive: Input: 0 (never), Output: 0 (never)
  LCP state: Down
  NCP state: inet: Not-configured, inet6: Not-configured,
  iso: Not-configured, mpls:
  Not-configured
  CHAP state: Closed
  PAP state: Closed
  CoS queues     : 8 supported, 8 maximum usable queues
  Last flapped   : 2009-03-21 04:54:48 UTC (00:36:47 ago)
  Input rate     : 0 bps (0 pps)
  Output rate    : 0 bps (0 pps)
  DS1    alarms   : None
  DS1    defects  : None

  Logical interface t1-0/0/2.0 (Index 67) (SNMP ifIndex 40)
    Flags: Hardware-Down Point-To-Point SNMP-Traps Encapsulation: PPP
    Protocol inet, MTU: 1500
      Flags: Protocol-Down, Is-Primary
      Addresses, Flags: Dest-route-down Is-Preferred Is-Primary
        Destination: 172.16.5.0/30, Local: 172.16.5.2, Broadcast: 172.16.5.3
```

Comparing output from the two, the astute reader immediately notices the issue: a Layer 2 encapsulation mismatch. The default encapsulation for a serial interface on a Cisco router is HDLC (Cisco HDLC, to be more specific), whereas the default encapsulation for a serial interface on a Juniper router is PPP (Point to Point Protocol). To resolve the issue, we simply change the encapsulation on one end of the link to match the other. In this case, we change the Juniper side:

```
[edit interfaces t1-0/0/2]
lab@r1# set encapsulation cisco-hdlc

[edit interfaces t1-0/0/2]
lab@r1# show
encapsulation cisco-hdlc;
unit 0 {
    family inet {
        address 172.16.5.2/30;
    }
}
```

```
[edit interfaces t1-0/0/2]
lab@r1# commit
commit complete

[edit interfaces t1-0/0/2]
lab@r1# run show interfaces t1-0/0/2 | match encapsulation
    Flags: Point-To-Point SNMP-Traps Encapsulation: Cisco-HDLC
```

The effectiveness of this change can be confirmed by reissuing the ping command on r5:

```
r5>ping 172.16.5.2

Type escape sequence to abort.
Sending 5, 100-byte ICMP Echos to 172.16.5.2, timeout is 2 seconds:
!!!!!
Success rate is 100 percent (5/5), round-trip min/avg/max = 4/4/4 ms
r5>
```

At this point, r5 has connectivity to all immediately attached subnets shown in Figure 15-5. To go beyond immediately attached subnets, a routing protocol is necessary, and for AS 64512, we have chosen OSPF.

 What's in a name? While we're on the topic of vendor-specific differences in physical media, on Juniper platforms interface media is indicative of throughput. In other words, a 10-Gigabit Ethernet (10GE) interface is capable of connecting to other platforms using the 10-gigabit variant of the Ethernet protocol and is capable of passing traffic at 10 gigabits per second as indicated by the interface's name. For other vendors' platforms, an interface's media naming convention indicates its ability to communicate with other platforms using similar media, but it may not be an accurate reflection of true interface throughput. To put it simply, for non-Juniper platforms a 10GE interface, while capable of connecting to other 10GE interfaces, may not be capable of handling 10 gigabits of transit traffic.

OSPF Adjacencies Between Cisco and Juniper Equipment

Figure 15-6 shows the devices in the OSPF domain of AS 64512. We bring up the simple adjacencies first, and after we confirm the desired state, we add protocol authentication for each neighbor relationship.

On the r5 network, we enable OSPF and bring up adjacencies to r2 and r3. Notice that in IOS, OSPF is enabled on networks:

```
router ospf 10
 network 10.0.0.5 0.0.0.0 area 0
 network 10.0.1.17 0.0.0.0 area 0
 network 10.0.1.21 0.0.0.0 area 0
```

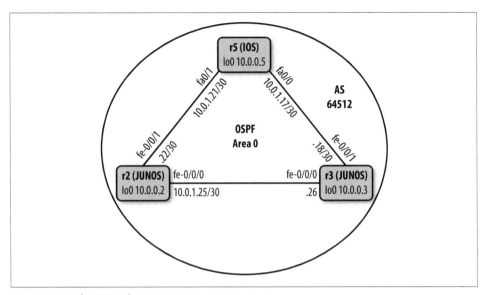

Figure 15-6. The OSPF domain

On r2 and r3, we enable OSPF, but notice that in JUNOS syntax, the protocol is configured on specific physical and logical interfaces:

```
[edit protocols ospf]
lab@r2# show
area 0.0.0.0 {
    interface fe-0/0/0.0;
    interface fe-0/0/1.0;
    interface lo0.0 {
        passive;
    }
}

[edit protocols ospf]
lab@r3# show
area 0.0.0.0 {
    interface fe-0/0/0.0;
    interface fe-0/0/1.0;
    interface lo0.0 {
        passive;
    }
}
```

On the Juniper devices, confirm OSPF adjacencies using the run show ospf neighbor command, first on r2 and then on r3:

```
[edit]
lab@r2# run show ospf neighbor
  Address          Interface        State    ID            Pri  Dead
  10.0.1.26        fe-0/0/0.0       Full     10.0.0.3      128   35
  10.0.1.21        fe-0/0/1.0       Full     172.16.5.1      1   33
```

```
[edit]
lab@r3# run show ospf neighbor
Address          Interface              State   ID            Pri  Dead
10.0.1.25        fe-0/0/0.0             Full    10.0.0.2      128   35
10.0.1.17        fe-0/0/1.0             Full    172.16.5.1      1   39
```

On r5, confirm the adjacencies with the show ip ospf neighbor command:

```
r5# show ip ospf neighbor

Neighbor ID   Pri   State      Dead Time   Address      Interface
10.0.0.3      128   FULL/DR    00:00:33    10.0.1.18    FastEthernet0/0
10.0.0.2      128   FULL/DR    00:00:38    10.0.1.22    FastEthernet0/1
r5#
```

OSPF authentication keys

For added security, the administrators of AS 64512 require MD5 authentication on
OSPF neighbor relationships. Fortunately, the Juniper platforms we are adding to the
network support the MD5 hashing algorithm. Here is the configuration on the Juniper
side for router r2; configuration elements on r3 are similar:

```
[edit protocols ospf area 0.0.0.0]
lab@r2# set authentication-type md5

[edit protocols ospf area 0.0.0.0]
lab@r2# edit interface fe-0/0/0

[edit protocols ospf area 0.0.0.0 interface fe-0/0/0.0]
lab@r2# set authentication md5 0 key Juniper

[edit protocols ospf area 0.0.0.0 interface fe-0/0/0.0]
lab@r2# show
authentication {
    md5 0 key "$9$VxsgajHmFnCZUnCtuEhVwY"; ## SECRET-DATA
}

[edit protocols ospf area 0.0.0.0 interface fe-0/0/0.0]
lab@r2# commit
commit complete
```

When adding protocol authentication to a neighbor relationship, it is a good habit to
confirm the adjacency state for each neighbor pair immediately after adding the authentication syntax. You do this because the JUNOS operating system encrypts the
hash key (in this case, the string Juniper) immediately after you type it into the command-line interface (CLI). While this process is an effective way to protect the hash
key, it does make troubleshooting a typo rather difficult. In this case, the hash key was
successfully added to both r2 and r3, and the adjacency is in the Full state:

```
[edit protocols ospf area 0.0.0.0]
lab@r3# run show ospf neighbor
Address          Interface              State   ID            Pri  Dead
10.0.1.26        fe-0/0/0.0             Full    10.0.0.3      128   37
10.0.1.21        fe-0/0/1.0             Full    172.16.5.1      1   33
```

To complete the operation, add the MD5 hashing function to the links between r5 and r2 and r5 and r3. You can apply the syntax previously shown for interface fe-0/0/0 on r2 to fe-0/0/1:

```
[edit protocols ospf area 0.0.0.0]
lab@r2# set interface fe-0/0/1 authentication md5 1 key Juniper
```

After committing this change, add the corresponding configuration elements on r5:

```
interface FastEthernet0/1
 ip address 10.0.1.21 255.255.255.252
 no ip directed-broadcast
 ip ospf message-digest-key 1 md5 Juniper
!
autonomous-system 64512
!
router ospf 10
 network 10.0.0.5 0.0.0.0 area 0
 network 10.0.1.17 0.0.0.0 area 0
 network 10.0.1.21 0.0.0.0 area 0
 area 0 authentication message-digest
```

Again, it is a best practice to confirm adjacency state immediately after enabling authentication to prevent errant keystrokes from damaging the integrity of the network:

```
r5#show ip ospf ne

Neighbor ID  Pri   State      Dead Time   Address      Interface
10.0.0.2     128   FULL/DR    00:00:39    10.0.1.22    FastEthernet0/1
r5#
```

There appears to be a very serious problem here. Router r5 has a Full adjacency with r2, the neighbor for which authentication was enabled, but the relationship to r3 appears to have dropped. In fact, this is due to the way MD5 was configured on r5: authentication enabled for all Area 0 interfaces in OSPF instance 10. To resolve the issue, we quickly enable MD5 on the r3 interface to r5:

```
[edit protocols ospf area 0.0.0.0]
lab@r3# set interface fe-0/0/1 authentication md5 1 key Juniper

[edit protocols ospf area 0.0.0.0]
lab@r3# commit
commit complete
```

Then enable MD5 on the r5 interface to r3:

```
r5#config t
Enter configuration commands, one per line.  End with CNTL/Z.
r5(config)#interface fastEthernet 0/0
r5(config-if)#ip ospf message-digest-key 1 md5 Juniper
r5(config-if)#^Z
```

And now we confirm the results on both r3 and r5:

```
[edit protocols ospf area 0.0.0.0]
lab@r3# run show ospf neighbor
Address          Interface        State      ID            Pri  Dead
```

```
10.0.1.25      fe-0/0/0.0      Full    10.0.0.2      128    35
10.0.1.17      fe-0/0/1.0      Full    172.16.5.1     1    39
```

r5#show ip ospf neighbor

```
Neighbor ID  Pri   State     Dead Time  Address      Interface
10.0.0.3     128   FULL/DR   00:00:38   10.0.1.18    FastEthernet0/0
10.0.0.2     128   FULL/DR   00:00:34   10.0.1.22    FastEthernet0/1
```

 When you enable authentication between pairs of devices in high availability environments, you should change only one device in each pair at
a time. This practice is necessary because typing errors or unanticipated
protocol behavior has the potential to cause outages. Temporarily moving traffic away from a device within a redundant pair, as discussed in
Chapter 6, is also a sensible move when making major configuration
changes.

IBGP Peering

After enabling OSPF, the next requirement for the Juniper integration into AS 64512
is to enable IBGP peering relationships. Router **r2** is configured to peer using the loopback address with **r3** and **r5**:

```
[edit protocols bgp]
lab@r2# show
group IBGP {
    type internal;
    local-address 10.0.0.2;
    export NHS;
    neighbor 10.0.0.3;
    neighbor 10.0.0.5;
}
```

Router **r3** has similar configuration elements for its relationship with **r2** and **r5**:

```
[edit protocols bgp]
lab@r3# show
group IBGP {
    type internal;
    local-address 10.0.0.3;
    export NHS;
    neighbor 10.0.0.2;
    neighbor 10.0.0.5;
}
```

Cisco-specific configuration elements on **r5** are adequate to bring up the IBGP peering
mesh:

```
router bgp 64512
  neighbor 10.0.0.2 remote-as 64512
  neighbor 10.0.0.2 update-source Loopback0
  neighbor 10.0.0.3 remote-as 64512
  neighbor 10.0.0.3 update-source Loopback0
```

Use show commands on all three chassis to confirm the IBGP peering state. On r5, results are as expected. Juniper neighbors, r2 and r3, are present as IBGP neighbors:

```
r5# show ip bgp summary
BGP router identifier 10.0.0.5, local AS number 64512
BGP table version is 29, main routing table version 29
17 network entries and 24 paths using 2281 bytes of memory
2 BGP path attribute entries using 192 bytes of memory
BGP activity 34/17 prefixes, 48/24 paths
0 prefixes revised.

Neighbor    V   AS MsgRcvd MsgSent TblVer  InQ OutQ Up/Down  State/PfxRcd
10.0.0.2    4 64512    316     324     29    0    0 00:45:38        8
10.0.0.3    4 64512    345     322     29    0    0 00:45:36        8
r5#
```

On r2, the results are similar. Routers r3 and r5 are both listed as IBGP neighbors:

```
lab@r2# run show bgp summary
Groups: 1 Peers: 2 Down peers: 0
Table          Tot Paths  Act Paths Suppressed    History Damp State    Pending
inet.0                25          8          0          0         0           0
Peer        AS    InPkt    OutPkt    OutQ   Flaps  Last Up/Dwn
State|#Active/Received/Damped...
10.0.0.3  64512   426       388        0       0      3:12:22 0/0/0
0/0/0
10.0.0.5  64512   323       325        0       1        48:23 0/0/0
0/0/0
```

A quick check of r3 confirms what we already suspected: the IBGP mesh is fully operational:

```
[edit protocols bgp]
lab@r3# run show bgp summary
Groups: 1 Peers: 2 Down peers: 0
Table          Tot Paths  Act Paths Suppressed    History Damp State    Pending
inet.0                25          8          0          0         0           0
inet.2                 0          0          0          0         0           0
Peer        AS    InPkt    OutPkt    OutQ   Flaps  Last Up/Dwn
State|#Active/Received/Damped...
10.0.0.2  64512   393       434        0       0      3:15:06 0/0/0
0/0/0
10.0.0.5  64512   326       361        0       1        51:05 0/0/0
0/0/0
```

EBGP Peering

The next task is to bring up EBGP peering relationships to ASs 100 and 400. Router r5 supports the relationship to AS 100, as shown in Figure 15-7.

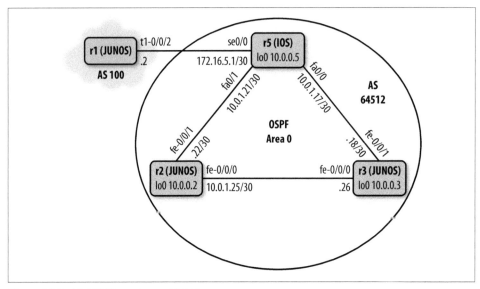

Figure 15-7. AS 64512 peering to AS 100

To bring up the relationship, first add an external neighbor to r5 within the router bgp 64512 configuration stanza:

```
router bgp 64512
 neighbor 10.0.0.2 remote-as 64512
 neighbor 10.0.0.3 remote-as 64512
 neighbor 172.16.5.2 remote-as 100
 no auto-summary
 !
```

Add the complementary configuration elements on r1 to establish the EBGP relationship:

```
[edit protocols bgp]
lab@r1# show
group EBGP {
    type external;
    export STAT;
    peer-as 64512;
    neighbor 172.16.5.1;
}
[edit protocols bgp]
lab@r1# top edit routing-options

[edit routing-options]
lab@r1# show
autonomous-system 100;
```

With the necessary configuration elements in place, we check the state of the relation-ship, first on r1:

```
edit routing-options]
lab@r1# run show bgp summary
Groups: 1 Peers: 1 Down peers: 0
Table          Tot Paths  Act Paths Suppressed    History Damp State    Pending
inet.0                 0          0          0          0        0            0
Peer            AS     InPkt     OutPkt    OutQ    Flaps Last Up/Dwn
State|#Active/Received/Damped...
172.16.5.1   64512       218        249       0        1     1:46:44 0/0/0
0/0/0
```

The relationship looks to be up and usable; however, r1 does not appear to be receiving any BGP routes from r5. This may not be an issue at the moment, but it is something to keep in mind. Router r5 shows the relationship is up and functional as well:

```
r5# show ip bgp summary
BGP router identifier 10.0.0.5, local AS number 64512
BGP table version is 29, main routing table version 29
17 network entries and 24 paths using 2281 bytes of memory
2 BGP path attribute entries using 192 bytes of memory
BGP activity 34/17 prefixes, 48/24 paths
0 prefixes revised.

Neighbor    V    AS MsgRcvd MsgSent TblVer InQ OutQ Up/Down State/PfxRcd
10.0.0.2    4 64512     347     356     29   0    0 01:01:30        8
10.0.0.3    4 64512     380     353     29   0    0 01:01:28        8
172.16.5.2 4    100     249     224     29   0    0 01:47:06        8
r5#
```

For now, we can move on to the next EBGP relationship. In Figure 15-8, both r2 and r3 are peering to r4 in AS 400.

The relevant configuration elements from r2 are shown for reference:

```
[edit protocols bgp]
lab@r2# show group EBGP
type external;
peer-as 400;
neighbor 172.16.7.6;
```

The configuration on r3 is nearly identical:

```
[edit protocols bgp]
lab@r3# show group EBGP
type external;
peer-as 400;
neighbor 172.16.7.2;
```

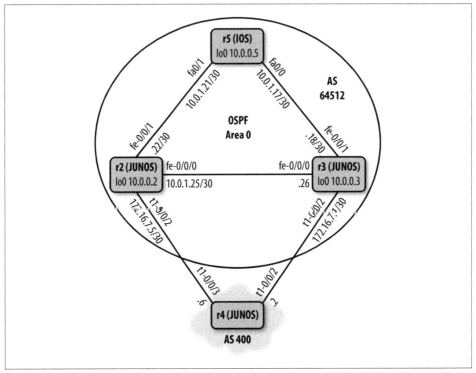

Figure 15-8. AS 64512 peering to AS 400

Router r4 is configured to peer with r2 and r3, and the `multipath` option enables load
sharing across the redundant equal cost paths:

```
[edit protocols bgp]
lab@r4# show
group EBGP {
    type external;
    export STAT;
    peer-as 64512;
    multipath;
    neighbor 172.16.7.5;
    neighbor 172.16.7.1;
}
```

Confirm the functionality of this relationship using `show` commands on r2, r3, and r4.
On r2, the relationship is up and BGP routes are being added to the local routing table.
Output from the same commands on r3 would be nearly identical:

```
[edit protocols bgp]
lab@r2# run show bgp summary
Groups: 2 Peers: 3 Down peers: 0
Table          Tot Paths  Act Paths Suppressed    History Damp State    Pending
inet.0               25          8          0             0          0          0
Peer          AS      InPkt    OutPkt    OutQ  Flaps Last Up/Dwn
```

```
                  State|#Active/Received/Damped...
172.16.7.6     400          498          452        0        0      3:44:51 8/9/0
0/0/0
10.0.0.3        64512        502          456        0        0      3:46:22 0/8/0
0/0/0
10.0.0.5        64512        391          393        0        1      1:22:23 0/8/0
0/0/0

[edit protocols bgp]
lab@r2# run show route protocol bgp terse

inet.0: 27 destinations, 36 routes (19 active, 0 holddown, 8 hidden)
+ = Active Route, - = Last Active, * = Both

A Destination     P Prf  Metric 1  Metric 2  Next hop      AS path
* 10.0.0.4/32     B 170    100                >172.16.7.6   400 I
                  B 170    100                >10.0.1.26    400 I
* 40.40.0.0/24    B 170    100                >172.16.7.6   400 I
                  B 170    100                >10.0.1.26    400 I
* 40.40.1.0/24    B 170    100                >172.16.7.6   400 I
                  B 170    100                >10.0.1.26    400 I
* 40.40.2.0/24    B 170    100                >172.16.7.6   400 I
                  B 170    100                >10.0.1.26    400 I
* 40.40.3.0/24    B 170    100                >172.16.7.6   400 I
                  B 170    100                >10.0.1.26    400 I
* 40.40.4.0/24    B 170    100                >172.16.7.6   400 I
                  B 170    100                >10.0.1.26    400 I
* 40.40.5.0/24    B 170    100                >172.16.7.6   400 I
                  B 170    100                >10.0.1.26    400 I
* 172.16.7.0/30   B 170    100                >172.16.7.6   400 I
  172.16.7.4/30   B 170    100                >172.16.7.6   400 I
                  B 170    100                >10.0.1.26    400 I
```

The show commands on r4 confirm that the expected relationship is up, but no BGP routes have been received from AS 64512:

```
[edit protocols bgp]
lab@r4# run show bgp summary
Groups: 1 Peers: 2 Down peers: 0
Table          Tot Paths  Act Paths Suppressed    History Damp State    Pending
inet.0               0          0          0            0          0           0
Peer            AS     InPkt    OutPkt    OutQ   Flaps Last Up/Dwn
                  State|#Active/Received/Damped...
172.16.7.1     64512    540       544        0        0      4:04:04 0/0/0
0/0/0
172.16.7.5     64512    457       507        0        0      3:47:57 0/0/0
0/0/0

[edit protocols bgp]
lab@r4# run show route protocol bgp

inet.0: 11 destinations, 11 routes (11 active, 0 holddown, 0 hidden)
```

Now that the relationships are completely up, you might expect to see routes received from AS 100 being passed to AS 400, and routes from AS 400 being passed to AS 100.

However, neither AS is receiving routes. There are actually two issues at play in this scenario.

The BGP next hop issue

Some readers may have noticed the presence of an export policy named NHS on the IBGP neighbor group on both r2 and r3. The NHS export statement is a reference to the NHS policy configured on each chassis:

```
[edit policy-options]
lab@r2# show
policy-statement NHS {
    term 1 {
        from {
            protocol bgp;
            neighbor 172.16.7.6;
        }
        then {
            next-hop self;
        }
    }
}
```

The NHS policy syntax is similar on r3:

```
[edit policy-options]
lab@r3# show
policy-statement NHS {
    term 1 {
        from {
            protocol bgp;
            neighbor 172.16.7.2;
        }
        then {
            next-hop self;
        }
    }
}
```

These policies are necessary to overcome the BGP next hop reachability issue. The policies allow r2 and r3 to overwrite the EBGP next hop with their own loopback address. When traffic destined for the EBGP next hop arrives at r2 or r3, r2 or r3 is able to use routes known via protocol Direct to forward the traffic.

Router r5 must also advertise a route to the EBGP protocol next hop. Therefore, either a similar policy must exist on r5, or some other method must be enabled to have the protocol next hop be added to the AS 64512 routing table. In this case, the administrators chose to run OSPF passively across the link between r5 and r1 to get the BGP next hop added as a reachable destination within the AS 64512 routing table:

```
r5#config t
Enter configuration commands, one per line.  End with CNTL/Z.
```

```
r5(config)#router ospf 10

r5(config-router)#network 172.16.5.1 0.0.0.0 area 0
```

 Recognizing that next hop self policy is one of the most common ways
to overcome the BGP next hop reachability issue, Cisco includes an
optional configuration element in IOS that overrides BGP next hop and
replaces it with the loopback address of the local router. The result is
comparable to the result of the JUNOS NHS policy used in the previous
example:

```
router bgp 64512
  neighbor 10.0.0.2 remote-as 64512
  neighbor 10.0.0.2 update-source Loopback0
  neighbor 10.0.0.3 remote-as 64512
  neighbor 10.0.0.3 update-source Loopback0
  neighbor 172.16.5.2 remote-as 100
  no auto-summary
  !
```

Unfortunately, a check of the routing tables shows that r4 is still not receiving routes
from AS 100. There is another issue.

The other issue

The r5 BGP configuration is missing a critical element. By default, an IOS router will
not install any BGP route as active unless the route is known by the underlying IGP, in
this case OSPF. Because the EBGP routes are not known to the router as OSPF routes
they will not by default be advertised to IBGP peers. To overcome this issue we use no
synchronization:

```
router bgp 64512
  no synchronization
  neighbor 10.0.0.2 remote-as 64512
  neighbor 10.0.0.3 remote-as 64512
  neighbor 172.16.5.2 remote-as 100
  no auto-summary
  !
```

Success

A quick check of the r4 routing table confirms that this step resolved the issue, and AS
400 is now receiving BGP routes advertised from AS 100. Router r1 also shows routes
from AS 400 being received in AS 100. Output from the show route command also
confirms load balancing back to r2 and r3 from r4:

```
[edit protocols bgp]
lab@r4# run show bgp summary
Groups: 1 Peers: 2 Down peers: 0
Table     Tot Paths  Act Paths Suppressed History Damp State Pending
inet.0          14         14          0       0        0       0
```

```
Peer          AS   InPkt  OutPkt   OutQ   Flaps Last Up/Dwn
State|#Active/Received/Damped...
172.16.7.1  64512  574      578      0      0     4:18:49 7/7/0
0/0/0
172.16.7.5  64512  487      540      0      0     4:02:42 7/7/0
0/0/0


[edit protocols bgp]
lab@r4# run show route protocol bgp terse

inet.0: 18 destinations, 25 routes (18 active, 0 holddown, 0 hidden)
@ = Routing Use Only, # = Forwarding Use Only
+ = Active Route, - = Last Active, * = Both

A Destination      P Prf Metric 1  Metric 2  Next hop      AS path
* 10.0.0.1/32      B 170    100                172.16.7.1  64512 100 I
                                              >172.16.7.5
                   B 170    100              >172.16.7.1  64512 100 I
* 100.100.0.0/24   B 170    100              >172.16.7.1  64512 100 I
                                              >172.16.7.5
                   B 170    100              >172.16.7.1  64512 100 I
* 100.100.1.0/24   B 170    100              >172.16.7.1  64512 100 I
                                               172.16.7.5
                   B 170    100              >172.16.7.1  64512 100 I
* 100.100.2.0/24   B 170    100               172.16.7.1  64512 100 I
                                              >172.16.7.5
                   B 170    100              >172.16.7.1  64512 100 I
* 100.100.3.0/24   B 170    100              >172.16.7.1  64512 100 I
                                               172.16.7.5
                   B 170    100              >172.16.7.1  64512 100 I
* 100.100.4.0/24   B 170    100              >172.16.7.1  64512 100 I
                                               172.16.7.5
                   B 170    100              >172.16.7.1  64512 100 I
* 100.100.5.0/24   B 170    100               172.16.7.1  64512 100 I
                                              >172.16.7.5
                   B 170    100              >172.16.7.1  64512 100 I
```

CHAPTER 16

Transitioning MPLS to a Multivendor Environment

Though not common in small and medium-size enterprise networks, Multiprotocol Label Switching (MPLS) has a long history (by Internet standards) of use by large enterprises and carriers. Forwarding traffic based on the content of an MPLS label table was originally viewed as faster than forwarding based on a longest-prefix match lookup in a routing table. However, with rapid advances in router hardware and the adoption of the radix tree structure for charting routing table content, the IP-based prefix match quickly caught up. MPLS would have been discarded had its clean separation between control and forwarding not been suitable for other purposes.

Network engineers are, by nature, power-hungry control freaks bent on dominating the traffic that transits their domain. Therefore, the notion of being able to configure paths through the network that allow selected streams of traffic to deviate from the Interior Gateway Protocol (IGP)-dictated "best path" is highly appealing. MPLS—when it is configured statically or deployed with a signaling protocol that supports traffic engineering—provides this functionality.

MPLS and the associated signaling protocols can also provide a means of separating selected traffic streams from other traffic transiting a network to create virtual private networks (VPNs). From a service-provider perspective, VPNs can be used to secure customer traffic streams, create multiservice infrastructures, and promote efficient use of limited resources. From a small-to-medium-enterprise perspective, VPNs enable secure communications across a shared medium and, in some cases, allow legacy and proprietary protocols to communicate across the regular Internet.

Traffic engineering and VPN support are the two primary reasons MPLS has become so pervasive, despite the fact that it is not faster than IP routing. This chapter acknowledges the ubiquity and importance of MPLS, and builds on the considerations described in the previous chapter to show you how to make a safe MPLS transition from a single-vendor to a multivendor network.

Multivendor Reality Check

Before launching into this chapter, we need to pause for a brief reality check. Realistically speaking, network administrators concerned with high availability are not eager to replace a device that is functioning acceptably unless there's a good reason to do so. While achieving a multivendor state may in some cases be viewed as a good reason, it seldom stands as a sole valid justification for a massive undertaking like replacing devices in a network. That being said, here are some valid reasons—reasons that may justify the labor involved in replacing a device in a high availability network:

Improved performance and stability
> Demands for throughput increase over time, and at a certain point the deployed platforms are unable to keep up. Platforms tend to become less stable as they age. Both situations are unacceptable for a high availability network.

Legacy platform replacement
> Platforms that are no longer supported by the manufacturer or are nearing end of life (EoL) are not appropriate for a production network with high availability requirements.

Change in functional requirements
> As time passes, new services emerge and can result in functional requirements that equipment from the incumbent vendor is unable to provide. Though this might not impact high availability for existing customers, the startup of a new service has revenue implications that can't be ignored.

Better network manageability and reduction in support costs
> These two go hand in hand. As a rule, businesses must constantly strive to automate processes and improve efficiency. Management of the network is no exception.

Dissatisfaction with a specific vendor
> All vendors are responsive and eager to interact with customers before and during the sales process. It's what the vendors do after the sale that separates the wheat from the chaff. Over time, the incumbent may become complacent in service or discount provided (or both). Bringing in an additional vendor is a way to get the relationship back on desirable ground.

In most cases, the administrators who choose to move from a single-vendor to a multivendor network do so for a combination of the aforementioned reasons.

Cost Concerns

Chapter 1 introduced the concept of *relative costing*, and offered it as a method of estimating and comparing the cost of different redundancy schemes in relation to the protection each provides. Although this method is still applicable in a multivendor environment, a few additional considerations need to be included in the equation:

- Training for design, implementation, and support staff is necessary if equipment from a different vendor is being introduced to the network for the first time.
- Vendor-specific network management tools may need to be replaced with tools capable of supporting products from multiple vendors.
- Generally speaking, device components are not interchangeable among vendors, so shelf spare schemes may need to be adjusted.

MPLS Signaling for High Availability

As previously mentioned, MPLS is unable to function at scale without the assistance of a signaling protocol. Signaling protocols come in many flavors, including standards-based and vendor-proprietary. Table 16-1 compares Juniper and Cisco support for various MPLS signaling protocols.

Table 16-1. Juniper and Cisco support for MPLS signaling protocols

Signaling protocol	Juniper support	Cisco support	Notes
Tag Distribution Protocol (TDP)	No	Yes	TDP is a Cisco-proprietary protocol.
Label Distribution Protocol (LDP)	Yes	Yes	Both Cisco and Juniper support LDP.
Resource Reservation Protocol (RSVP)	Yes	Yes	Supported by both Juniper and Cisco.
Resource Reservation Protocol with Traffic Engineering (RSVP-TE)	Yes	Yes	Functionality is supported by both Juniper and Cisco. The Juniper protocol naming convention does not draw a distinction between RSVP and RSVP-TE.
Static	Yes	No	Supported on Juniper platforms, though seldom used in high availability environments.
Constraint-Based Routing Label Distribution Protocol (CR-LDP)	No	No	This signaling protocol is supported by neither Juniper nor Cisco. It was deprecated by the Internet Engineering Task Force (IETF) in 2003.

With these considerations in mind, the only realistic choice of MPLS signaling protocols for label-switched paths (LSPs) that can cross between Juniper and Cisco routers is LDP for nontraffic-engineered applications, and RSVP for situations where traffic engineering is desirable. These are the only two signaling methods supported by both vendors.

Static MPLS and High Availability

Although wholly unscalable and nearly unmanageable, it is worth mentioning that in some vendor implementations, MPLS is capable of functioning in the absence of a dynamic path signaling protocol. Some federal agencies prohibit dynamic protocols from being enabled in production networks, yet at the same time need MPLS functionality without compromising high availability to meet specific service requirements.

Some large enterprise networks have the same requirements and follow the same restrictions. Therefore, static MPLS, as troublesome as it may be, does have a place. Static LSP configuration is supported by Juniper products, but not by Cisco.

A Simple Multivendor Topology

Figure 16-1 shows a simple topology that we use to look at the configuration elements relevant to MPLS, RSVP, and LDP between Juniper and Cisco routers. In Figure 16-1, r4 and r5 are Provider Edge (PE) devices that each serve as ingress and egress points for an LSP. Router r4 runs JUNOS and r5 is running IOS. Routers r2 and r6 are provider routers in this topology, and they serve as LSP transit points. Router r6 is a Cisco router, and r2 is a Juniper router.

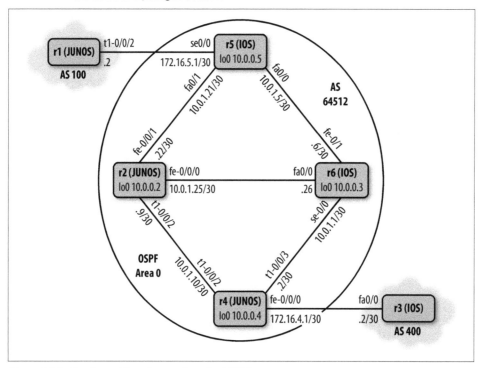

Figure 16-1. Simple multivendor topology for MPLS

To show configuration syntax, we look at two ways to signal setup of LSPs: first with RSVP, then with LDP as the signaling protocol.

RSVP Signaling

RSVP allows a router to act on behalf of an application or another protocol, in this case MPLS, to signal a path through the network. The paths are established and maintained by PATH messages initiated from the ingress router and sent toward the egress, and by RESV messages that are initiated by the egress router and sent toward the ingress. RSVP requires each router in the path to maintain resource reservations for the path. The path adheres to administratively defined characteristics, thereby enabling traffic engineering.

Traffic engineering

Traffic engineering is the ability to cause LSPs to be established contrary to the IGP-dictated best path through the network. Deviation from the IGP could be desirable for any number of reasons, including bandwidth management, service-level agreement (SLA) enforcement, and, most commonly, Quality of Service (QoS).

To deviate from the IGP-dictated best path, the administrator defines attributes, known as *path constraints*, for the path. Administratively defined constraints include:

Explicit Route Objects (EROs)
> EROs permit the definition of IP addresses that must be transited by the LSP. IP addresses used for EROs take two forms: *strict* and *loose*. A strict IP address must be the immediate next hop in LSP construction. A loose IP address must be transited by the LSP prior to egress, but is not required to be the immediate next hop.

Bandwidth
> Administrators have the option of placing a bandwidth requirement on the establishment of the LSP.

Hop count
> Hop count for LSP path selection can be limited to prevent scenic routing of the path. This is most often used for fast reroute (FRR) optimization.

Administrative groups
> RSVP allows administrators to assign "colors" to links within their network. These colors can be referenced in the LSP configuration syntax to describe collections of links that can be transited by the path, and also collections of links that should be avoided by the path.

Priority
> Administrators can assign a priority to LSPs that has meaning in relation to the priority assigned to other LSPs in the network. This is critical in situations where there may be insufficient bandwidth to support all LSPs that may transit the network.

MPLS is IGP-agnostic, but traffic engineering in a multivendor environment requires use of Intermediate System to Intermediate System (IS-IS) or Open Shortest Path First (OSPF) as the IGP. This is necessary to build the traffic engineering database (TED). The TED is initially populated from—and, in truth, is comparable in many ways to—the link-state database maintained by both IGPs. The TED is used exclusively for calculating LSPs through the network. Figure 16-2 maps out a traffic engineering computation and the relationships among the link-state database, the TED, and the Constrained Shortest Path First (CSPF) protocol.

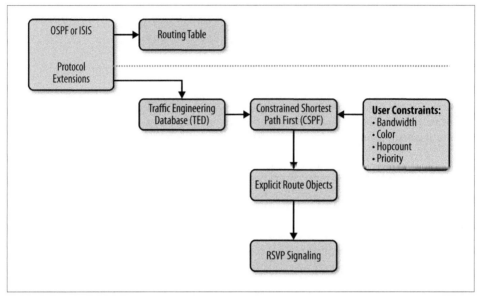

Figure 16-2. Flow of JUNOS traffic engineering computation

Juniper–Cisco RSVP

Figure 16-3 shows that **r4** is the ingress point for an LSP named **r4-to-r5**. Router **r5** is the ingress point for an LSP named **r5-to-r4**. Traffic engineering configuration elements to establish the LSP are added to **r4** and are shown in the JUNOS command-line interface (CLI) examples provided.

 This chapter does not cover MPLS or the associated signaling protocols in depth at the theoretical level. Nor does it describe the full range of configuration statements available in IOS or JUNOS. The purpose of this chapter is to provide enough theory and enough configuration and process recommendations to allow you to safely transition MPLS from a single-vendor to a multivendor environment. Numerous books exist about protocol theory, and both Juniper and Cisco provide technical documentation covering the range of configuration options.

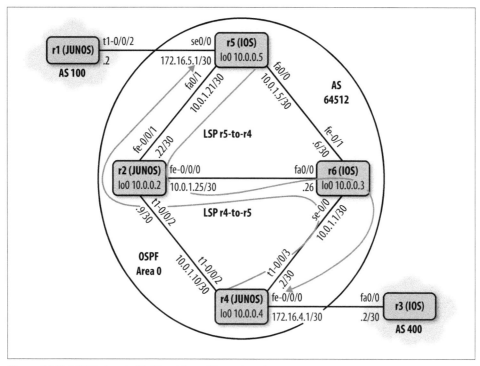

Figure 16-3. RSVP-signaled LSPs with traffic engineering

Router r5 configuration

Router r5 is a Cisco router serving as a PE device in AS 64512. This router is the ingress point for an RSVP-signaled LSP to r4. Router r5 also serves as the egress point for an RSVP-signaled LSP from r4. Interface configuration elements on r5 include `mpls-ip` statements on all interfaces that must support MPLS. Interface `Serial0/0` does not require an `mpls-ip` statement, as the requirements do not call for an LSP to r1:

```
!
interface Tunnel0
 ip unnumbered Loopback0
 tunnel destination 10.0.0.4
 tunnel mode mpls traffic-eng
 tunnel mpls traffic-eng autoroute announce
 no routing dynamic
!
interface Loopback0
 ip address 10.0.0.5 255.255.255.255
 ip ospf 10 area 0
!
interface FastEthernet0/0
 ip address 10.0.1.5 255.255.255.252
 ip ospf 10 area 0
 duplex auto
```

```
  speed auto
  mpls ip
  mpls traffic-eng tunnels
  ip rsvp bandwidth 7500 7500
  ip rsvp resource-provider none
 !
interface Serial0/0
  bandwidth 1544
  ip address 172.16.5.1 255.255.255.252
  no ip directed-broadcast
 !
interface FastEthernet0/1
  ip address 10.0.1.21 255.255.255.252
  ip ospf 10 area 0
  duplex auto
  speed auto
  mpls ip
  mpls traffic-eng tunnels
  ip rsvp bandwidth 7500 7500
  ip rsvp resource-provider none
 !
```

On router r5, the OSPF protocol configuration includes `mpls-traffic-eng` statements to support traffic engineering:

```
router ospf 10
  network 10.0.0.5 0.0.0.0 area 0
  network 10.0.1.5 0.0.0.0 area 0
  network 10.0.1.17 0.0.0.0 area 0
  network 10.0.1.21 0.0.0.0 area 0
  network 172.16.5.1 0.0.0.0 area 0
  mpls traffic-eng router-id Loopback0
  mpls traffic-eng area 0
  log-adjacency-changes
 !
```

Router r4 is a Juniper router serving as a PE device in AS 64512. This router is the ingress point for an RSVP-signaled LSP to r5. Router r4 also serves as the egress point for an RSVP-signaled LSP from r5. Interface configuration elements on r4 include `family mpls` statements on all interfaces that must support MPLS. The `family mpls` statement is not necessary on interface `fe-0/0/0` because there is no requirement to build an LSP to r3:

```
edit interfaces]
lab@r4# show
fe-0/0/0 {
  unit 0 {
    family inet {
    address 172.16.4.1/30;
    }
  }
}
t1-0/0/2 {
  unit 0 {
    family inet {
```

```
    address 10.0.1.10/30;
    }
    family mpls;
  }
}
t1-0/0/3 {
  encapsulation cisco-hdlc;
  unit 0 {
    family inet {
    address 10.0.1.2/30;
    }
    family mpls;
  }
}
lo0 {
  unit 0 {
    family inet {
    address 10.0.0.4/32;
    }
  }
}
```

 Older versions of JUNOS allowed users to configure `family mpls` on the lo0 interface without generating an error message. However, this configuration element never appeared in the configuration file and was in fact completely unnecessary.

The `traffic-engineering` statement in router r4's OSPF configuration allows the creation of the TED and CSPF calculation:

```
[edit protocols]
lab@r4# show ospf
traffic-engineering;
area 0.0.0.0 {
  interface lo0.0 {
    passive;
  }
  interface t1-0/0/3.0;
  interface t1-0/0/2.0;
}
```

Router r4 makes use of a next hop self policy (named NHS in this case) to overcome the Border Gateway Protocol (BGP) reachability issue described in detail in Chapter 15. This is important because using r4's loopback address as the BGP protocol next hop allows the LSP to be used for Autonomous System (AS) transit traffic:

```
[edit protocols]
lab@r4# show bgp
group IBGP {
  type internal;
  local-address 10.0.0.4;
  export NHS;
  neighbor 10.0.0.3;
```

```
  neighbor 10.0.0.2;
  neighbor 10.0.0.5;
}
[edit protocols]
lab@r4# top edit policy-options

[edit policy-options]
lab@r4# show
policy-statement NHS {
  term 1 {
    from {
    protocol bgp;
    neighbor 172.16.4.2;
    }
    then {
    next-hop self;
    }
  }
}
```

Router r4 includes MPLS and RSVP configuration elements to support the LSPs detailed in Figure 16-3. CLI output shows that `label-switched-path` r4-to-r5 uses a path named SCENIC-ROUTE, which has EROs configured to cross IP addresses 10.0.1.1, 10.0.0.2, and 10.0.1.21. This LSP is configured to use r5's loopback address as the egress point:

```
[edit protocols]
lab@r4# show mpls
label-switched-path r4-to-r5 {
  to 10.0.0.5;
  primary SCENIC-ROUTE;
}
path SCENIC-ROUTE {
  10.0.1.1 strict;
  10.0.0.2 loose;
  10.0.1.21 strict;
}
interface t1-0/0/2.0;
interface t1-0/0/3.0;
interface lo0.0;

[edit protocols]
lab@r4# show rsvp
interface lo0.0;
interface t1-0/0/2.0;
interface t1-0/0/3.0;
```

You can use the show command at various points along the path to confirm RSVP neighbor relationships and LSP establishment. From r4, the show mpls lsp detail command confirms that r4 is an ingress and an egress point and shows the path being taken by the LSP:

```
[edit interfaces]
lab@r4# run show mpls lsp detail
Ingress LSP: 1 sessions
```

```
10.0.0.5
  From: 10.0.0.4, State: Up, ActiveRoute: 0, LSPname: r4-to-r5
  ActivePath: SCENIC-ROUTE (primary)
  LoadBalance: Random
  Encoding type: Packet, Switching type: Packet, GPID: IPv4
 *Primary SCENIC-ROUTE    State: Up
  SmartOptimizeTimer: 180
  Computed ERO (S [L] denotes strict [loose] hops): (CSPF metric: 66)
  10.0.1.1 S 10.0.1.25 S 10.0.1.21 S
  Received RRO (ProtectionFlag 1=Available 2=InUse
  4=B/W 8=Node 10=SoftPreempt):
    10.0.1.1 10.0.1.25 10.0.1.21
Total 1 displayed, Up 1, Down 0

Egress LSP: 1 sessions

10.0.0.4
  From: 10.0.0.5, LSPstate: Up, ActiveRoute: 0
  LSPname: r5-to-r4, LSPpath: Primary
  Suggested label received: -, Suggested label sent: -
  Recovery label received: -, Recovery label sent: -
  Resv style: 1 FF, Label in: 3, Label out: -
  Time left:  144, Since: Thu Apr 16 20:18:13 2009
  Tspec: rate 0bps size 0bps peak Infbps m 20 M 1500
  Port number: sender 1 receiver 33755 protocol 0
  PATH rcvfrom: 10.0.1.1 (t1-0/0/3.0) 6 pkts
  Adspec: received MTU 1500
  PATH sentto: localclient
  RESV rcvfrom: localclient
  Record route: 10.0.1.21 10.0.1.25 10.0.1.1 <self>
Total 1 displayed, Up 1, Down 0

Transit LSP: 0 sessions
Total 0 displayed, Up 0, Down 0
```

You can also confirm the establishment and proper path selection from r2 using the
show mpls lsp detail command. As expected, no LSPs are using r2 as an ingress or
egress point, but two LSPs are transiting the router. The output also reflects the EROs
that were used to dictate the path through the network:

```
[edit]
lab@r2# run show mpls lsp detail
Ingress LSP: 0 sessions
Total 0 displayed, Up 0, Down 0

Egress LSP: 0 sessions
Total 0 displayed, Up 0, Down 0

Transit LSP: 2 sessions

10.0.0.4
  From: 10.0.0.5, LSPstate: Up, ActiveRoute: 1
  LSPname: r5-to-r4, LSPpath: Primary
  Suggested label received: -, Suggested label sent: -
  Recovery label received: -, Recovery label sent: 100048
```

```
Resv style: 1 FF, Label in: 100048, Label out: 100048
Time left:  137, Since: Thu Apr 16 08:15:08 2009
Tspec: rate 0bps size 0bps peak Infbps m 20 M 1500
Port number: sender 1 receiver 33755 protocol 0
PATH rcvfrom: 10.0.1.21 (fe-0/0/1.0) 10 pkts
Adspec: received MTU 1500 sent MTU 1500
PATH sentto: 10.0.1.26 (fe-0/0/0.0) 11 pkts
RESV rcvfrom: 10.0.1.26 (fe-0/0/0.0) 10 pkts
Explct route: 10.0.1.26 10.0.1.2
Record route: 10.0.1.21 <self> 10.0.1.26 10.0.1.2

10.0.0.5
  From: 10.0.0.4, LSPstate: Up, ActiveRoute: 1
  LSPname: r4-to-r5, LSPpath: Primary
  Suggested label received: -, Suggested label sent: -
  Recovery label received: -, Recovery label sent: 3
  Resv style: 1 FF, Label in: 100032, Label out: 3
  Time left:  138, Since: Thu Apr 16 08:12:55 2009
  Tspec: rate 0bps size 0bps peak Infbps m 20 M 1500
  Port number: sender 12 receiver 64894 protocol 0
  PATH rcvfrom: 10.0.1.26 (fe-0/0/0.0) 13 pkts
  Adspec: received MTU 1500 sent MTU 1500
  PATH sentto: 10.0.1.21 (fe-0/0/1.0) 14 pkts
  RESV rcvfrom: 10.0.1.21 (fe-0/0/1.0) 13 pkts
  Explct route: 10.0.1.21
  Record route: 10.0.1.2 10.0.1.26 <self> 10.0.1.21
Total 2 displayed, Up 2, Down 0
```

LDP Signaling

Like RSVP, LDP is a method of distributing labels in an MPLS domain. Unlike RSVP, LDP is not capable of deviation from the underlying IGP's dictated best path through the network. When LDP is enabled on a router, it uses the local router's Forwarding Information Base (FIB) to "auto-magically" create LSPs to all reachable host IPs (/32 subnet mask). These characteristics limit LDP's functionality as a QoS mechanism, but they dramatically simplify configuration and make LDP a more scalable protocol than RSVP.

Figure 16-4 shows the resulting LSPs created if LDP is enabled on the devices in the network.

As mentioned, LDP configuration syntax is simpler than RSVP. A sample from r4 is shown. Note that the entire RSVP configuration has been removed. The only LDP elements required are those to identify the interfaces over which the protocol should run:

```
[edit protocols]
lab@r4# show ldp
interface t1-0/0/2.0;
interface t1-0/0/3.0;
interface lo0.0;
```

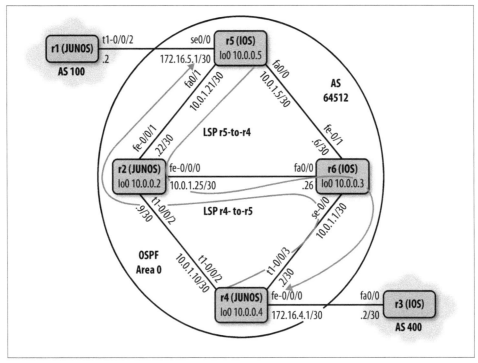

Figure 16-4. LDP-signaled LSPs in the network

The contents of the routing table confirm the presence of usable LSPs to all other routers
in the network:

```
[edit protocols]
lab@r4# run show route protocol ldp

inet.0: 14 destinations, 16 routes (14 active, 0 holddown, 0 hidden)

inet.3: 3 destinations, 3 routes (3 active, 0 holddown, 0 hidden)
+ = Active Route, - = Last Active, * = Both

10.0.0.2/32        *[LDP/9] 00:03:17, metric 1
                    > via t1-0/0/2.0
10.0.0.3/32        *[LDP/9] 00:03:17, metric 1
                    > via t1-0/0/3.0
10.0.0.5/32        *[LDP/9] 00:03:17, metric 1
                      via t1-0/0/2.0, Push 100096
                    > via t1-0/0/3.0, Push 100096
```

A few LDP implementation differences

By default, the IOS LDP session hold time is 180 seconds and the keepalive is 60 seconds. In Juniper, the default hold time is 30 seconds and the keepalive is 10 seconds.
LDP protocol standards dictate that LDP neighbors negotiate to the lowest value.

Therefore, IOS devices, by default, accept the JUNOS hold time and keepalive. If this behavior is undesirable (it can potentially result in LDP neighbor flaps), you can override the defaults to match the IOS defaults:

```
[edit protocols ldp]
lab@r4# show
keepalive-interval 60;
keepalive-timeout 180;
interface t1-0/0/0.0 {
    hello-interval 60;
    hold-time 180;
}
```

By default, JUNOS advertises loopback addresses only into the inet3.0 table. And by default, IOS announces every known route using LDP. If this situation is undesirable, you can filter routes on the IOS platforms to prevent advertisement of nonloopback addresses:

```
!
tag-switching advertise-tags for ldp-filter
!
!
ip access-list standard ldp-filter
remark - IP range for Figure 16-4 loop-back addresses --
permit 10.0.0.0 0.0.0.255
!
```

To further simplify the LDP configuration, newer versions of Cisco IOS support the automatic enabling of LDP on interfaces on which OSPF is enabled, as opposed to having to manually configure LDP on each interface. Although there are notable security concerns with running LDP on customer-facing interfaces on a PE router, when used on provider (P) devices, the automatic configuration feature simplifies LDP configuration without adding security risks. The mpls autoconfig ldp [area number] configuration command enables LDP on all interfaces running OSPF.

MPLS Transition Case Studies

Now that we have looked at vendor-specific configuration characteristics of MPLS and the associated signaling protocols, let's examine how a network can safely transition from a single-vendor to a multivendor MPLS implementation without risking availability. For MPLS transitions, devices that come into play include Provider (P) and Provider Edge (PE). The Provider devices typically serve as transit points for LSPs established between the Provider Edge devices.

This section offers two MPLS transition case studies. Case study 1 demonstrates one alternative for high availability equipment transitions: standing up a redundant pair, bringing up connectivity, transiting traffic, and bringing down the legacy pair. You confirm and monitor stability for a set time at each phase. Case study 2 provides another alternative: replacing devices within a high availability pair one at a time.

Both case studies in this chapter are based on the network shown in Figure 16-5. This topology features redundant P and PE routers that support a primary and secondary pair of LSPs. These LSPs are being used to engineer traffic bidirectionally between PE-router-1 and PE-router-3 to support control of the path used for traffic between Customer Edge (CE) devices at Acme Site 1 and Site 2. The P and PE routers are all in AS 64512 and are fully meshed using BGP. OSPF is used as the IGP, and RSVP is used to signal LSP setup. At this point, we assume that all devices in the network are running Cisco IOS.

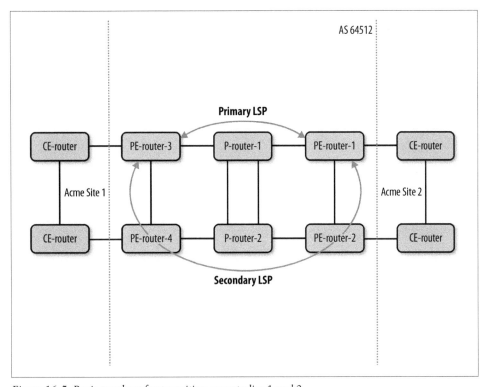

Figure 16-5. Basic topology for transition case studies 1 and 2

To support high availability in this topology, you could configure additional LSPs between PE-router-2 and PE-router-4. However, including them in Figure 16-5 would clutter the diagram and potentially obscure the purpose of the study.

Case Study 1: Transitioning Provider Devices

This case study shows a transition case where you set up a redundant pair, establishing conductivity between them. Then you bring down the legacy pair.

Phase 1: P router transition

In the first case study, the network administrators have decided to replace the IOS-based Provider devices in the network (`P-router-1` and `P-router-2`) with JUNOS platforms. Figure 16-6 shows `NEW P-router-1` and `NEW P-router-2` being added to the network. You first establish connectivity between the `NEW` P routers and the existing PE routers. After confirming the OSPF and BGP peering relationships, configure additional pairs of secondary LSPs between `PE-router-1` and `PE-router-3` and engineer them to transit the new Provider devices, as shown.

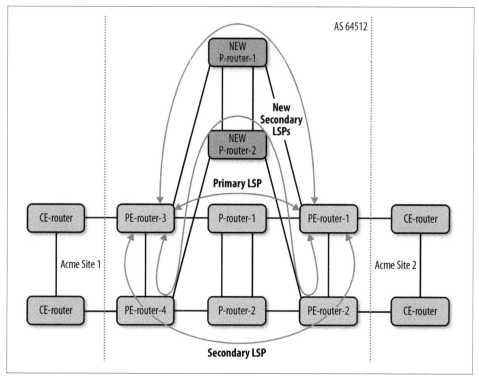

Figure 16-6. Phase 1: addition of NEW P-routers to topology and setup of additional secondary LSPs

Configuration elements on `NEW P-router-1` and `NEW P-router-2` are similar in many ways and include the native IGP, BGP, and RSVP, because this case study requires some traffic engineering. You configure EROs on the `PE-routers` to force LSPs to be established across the `NEW P-routers`.

Phase 2: P router transition

In phase 2 of the transition, you make configuration changes on `PE-router-1` and `PE-router-3` to force the LSPs transiting through `NEW P-router-1` to become the primary LSPs. You retain all other secondary LSPs for redundancy purposes and, as needed, for fallback. RSVP LSP configuration syntax allows configuration of multiple secondary paths. Use this option to support the transition phase shown in Figure 16-7.

 In phase 2 of this transition sequence, multiple redundant secondary LSPs are currently configured. As you can probably predict, some of these will soon be removed. An experienced administrator would save these configurations for later reference or potential fallback should the transition encounter unexpected problems.

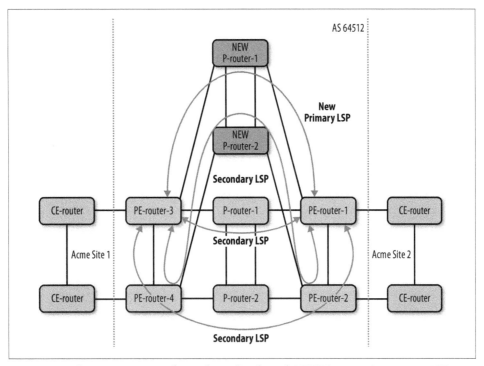

Figure 16-7. Phase 2: promotion of secondary LSPs through NEW P-router-1 to primary LSPs

Devices can remain in phase 2 (Figure 16-7) as long as necessary to confirm expected performance across the new Provider routers. The time period varies from business to business, but for large carrier networks, it is typically 72 hours. Table 16-2 lists what to check for during the time frame.

Table 16-2. JUNOS and IOS commands to confirm stability

Acceptance criteria	JUNOS commands	IOS commands
Device stability	>show chassis alarms	>show (chassis type)
	>show chassis routing engine	

Acceptance criteria	JUNOS commands	IOS commands
Interface stability	>show interface extensive	>show interface
	>show route detail protocol direct	>show ip route connected
	>monitor interface traffic	
Protocol stability	>show ospf neighbor	>show ip ospf neighbor
	>show bgp summary	>show ip route
	>show route detail protocol ospf	
LSP stability	>show rsvp neighbor	>show mpls interfaces
	>show rsvp interface	>show ip rsvp
	>show mpls lsp extensive	

Phase 3: P router transition

Once you have confirmed network and device stability, you can remove P-router-1 and P-router-2 in a graceful manner. After checking to make sure no transit traffic is crossing the old Provider devices, bring down the secondary LSPs that transited P-router-1 and P-router-2 (Figure 16-8). Then bring down RSVP and MPLS, and then the BGP and OSPF neighbor relationships. Finally, shut down the interfaces.

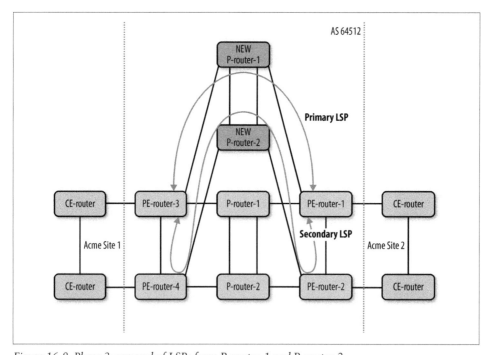

Figure 16-8. Phase 3: removal of LSPs from P-router-1 and P-router-2

Due to the labor involved in decommissioning or repurposing chassis, some network administrators see this phase as another good point to pause and confirm network and device stability. Nothing is more frustrating than removing chassis from the network only to later discover issues that mandate their return.

Final state: P router transition

In the final transition state, P-router-1 and P-router-2 have been completely removed from (or, more likely, repurposed within) the network. Figure 16-9 shows the finished topology, including the newly deployed P-routers.

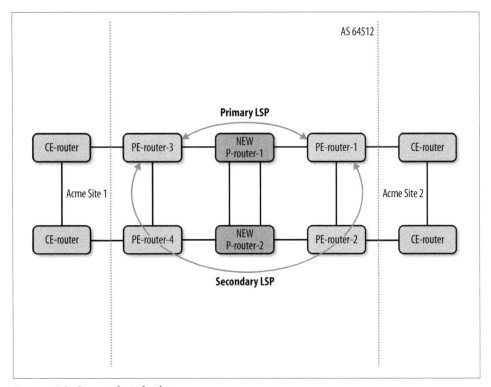

Figure 16-9. Case study 1: final state

Case Study 2: Transitioning Provider Edge Devices

Figure 16-9 serves as the starting point for case study 2. In this case study, we replace the IOS-based PE devices serving Acme Site 2 with JUNOS devices.

Phase 1: PE router transition

In phase 1 of the PE device transition, we added a new pair of chassis (NEW PE-router-1 and NEW PE-router-2). These devices have been physically connected to adjacent P devices and to the PE routers they are replacing. The NEW PE routers are also connected to the existing CE routers at Acme Site 2. Figure 16-10 shows the devices and the new links.

Existing LSPs are not modified in this phase. This allows time to confirm stability and protocol peering relationships.

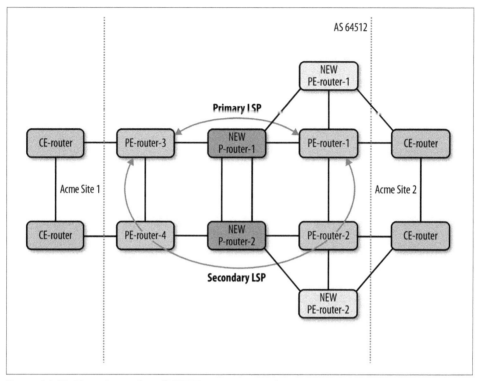

Figure 16-10. Phase 1: standup of NEW PE-routers 1 and 2

Phase 2: PE router transition

In phase 2 of the transition, we add a new secondary LSP from PE-router-1 to PE-router-3. An ERO is used to force the LSP to transit NEW PE-router-1 before continuing on to NEW P-router-1. In Figure 16-11, you see the new secondary LSP between these two NEW routers. The new LSP is providing protection against link and interface failure on the existing primary LSP but is not protecting against more serious failures on the NEW P-router-1. Fortunately, this is only a transitional state as we prepare for phase 3.

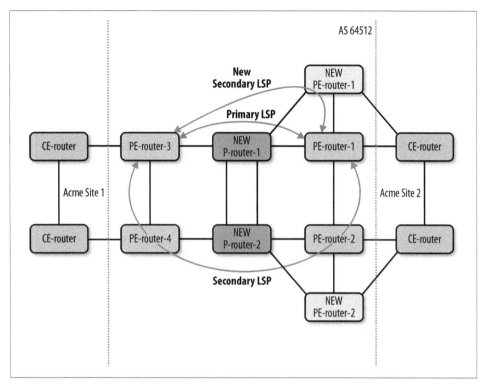

Figure 16-11. Phase 2 of PE router transition

Phase 3: PE router transition

In phase 3, we gracefully decommission PE-router-2 and replace it with NEW PE-router-2. As described in Table 16-2, you use operational mode commands to confirm functionality and stability, including functional establishment of the original secondary LSP through NEW PE-router-2.

Figure 16-12 shows phase 3. In this figure, PE-Router-2 has been completely removed from the network (and the network diagram) and replaced with NEW PE-router-2. The NEW PE router has peering relationships with the existing adjacent P, PE, and CE routers.

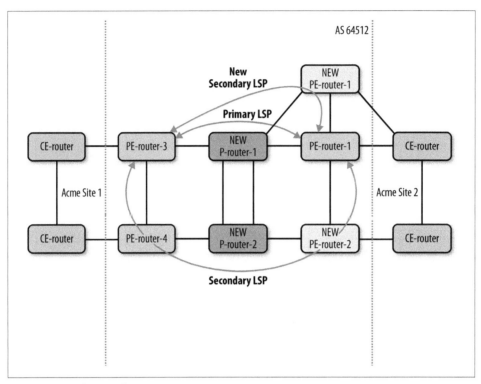

Figure 16-12. Phase 3 of PE router transition

Phase 4: PE router transition

Figure 16-13 shows an additional set of LSPs transiting between r2 and r4. These redundant LSPs emphasize the fact that the other routers in the high availability pairs can be used to support traffic transiting between the Acme sites temporarily while you are replacing PE-router-1. Notice that we have added an additional redundant LSP that transits NEW PE-router-1. As with all steps in this process, this added redundancy is intended to ensure that there are as few single points of failure as possible in the network during the device transition.

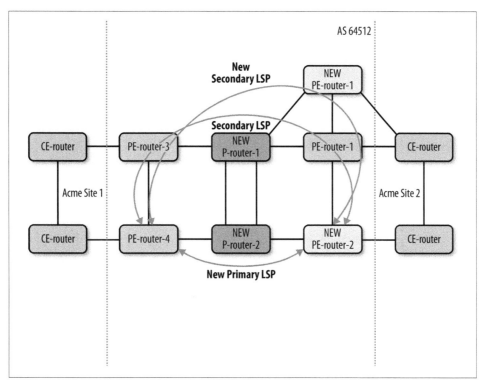

Figure 16-13. Phase 4 of PE router transition

Final state: PE router transition

Once a viable secondary LSP transits the new PE router, it is possible to decommission PE-router-1. Figure 16-14 shows the final state of the devices after PE-router-1 has been decommissioned and removed.

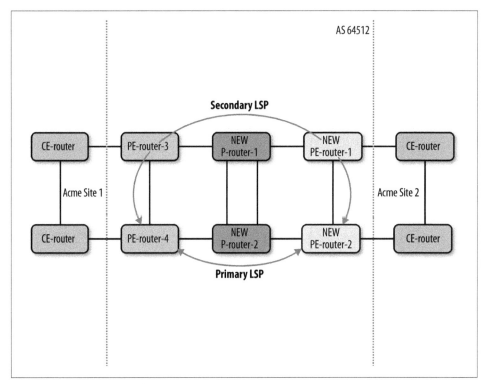

Figure 16-14. Final result of PE router transition

We have now successfully transitioned Provider and Provider Edge chassis in the model topology. The transitions were made in a safe manner with predictable results and adequate pauses along the way to ensure functionality as predicted.

CHAPTER 17

Monitoring Multivendor Networks

Assuming you haven't skipped too many chapters, if you have made it this far into the book you have learned how to transition routing, switching, Multiprotocol Label Switching (MPLS), and the related signaling protocols from a single-vendor to a multivendor environment without risking the availability of the network. A major part of the transition is retaining the ability to monitor the performance and stability of the network. The primary purpose of network monitoring is to protect the availability of the network from hardware failure, configuration error, unauthorized access or activity, and performance degradation—in short, making sure the network is capable of providing performance and services as designed.

This chapter describes configuration elements and gives tips to support classic monitoring and management of fault, configuration, accounting, performance, and security (FCAPS) in a network with high availability requirements. The chapter describes both JUNOS and IOS configuration elements pertaining to Simple Network Management Protocol (SNMP), system logging, remote access, and simple traffic monitoring in relation to their ability to support high availability.

Network monitoring is built on the premise that deviation from a defined *norm* can be detrimental to the network. Therefore, it is critical to establish a baseline of what is normal for the network. It is impossible to identify *abnormal* behavior without an awareness and understanding of what *normal* looks like. How can you accomplish this? Simple: deploy the monitoring mechanisms described in this chapter *before* suspected problems occur on the network.

Are You In or Out?

When you are developing a monitoring and management scheme, it is important to consider the method that the tools use to access the chassis. There are two distinct approaches to network management: *in band* and *Out of Band* (OoB).

In-Band Management

With in-band management, management traffic shares interfaces, links, and other resources with customer traffic. This method is more economical up front because you do not need to purchase additional equipment to support the management network. However, the risks associated with this form of management make it inappropriate for most networks with high availability requirements. The main issue is that when the network is having problems, the router may become inaccessible to management tools.

Out-of-Band Management

With OoB management, you independently provision interfaces and links for the management traffic so that no links are shared with customer traffic. This method requires a greater capital expense, but has a few advantages over in-band management:

- Dedicated interfaces result in clean separation of management traffic from other forms of traffic, and simplify troubleshooting.
- Problems impacting the production network do not automatically degrade the ability to manage the chassis, as is the case with in-band management.

OoB management essentially results in the creation of a second network for the sole purpose of monitoring the production network. Most administrators agree that this is by far the most reliable way to effectively monitor a network; however, there is an associated cost. Additional routers and switches are typically required, and the end result is an additional series of cost calculations, as described in Chapter 1.

 In-band/out-of-band management is a common hybrid in which some resources are dedicated to management traffic, some are dedicated to customer traffic, and some are shared between the two. This method is used in some service provider topologies where the Provider Edge (PE) devices use OoB management and the Provider (P) devices use in-band management.

OoB and fxp0

By definition, OoB management requires a dedicated management interface on the chassis. This interface can be a transit interface or, on M, MX, and T Series chassis, the fxp0 interface. fxp0 is a permanent interface that ties directly into the routing engine (RE) and effectively bypasses the Packet Forwarding Engine (PFE). It exists specifically for OoB management of the system. The fxp0 interface is a Fast Ethernet interface with configuration options similar to fe-*n/n/n* interfaces on the chassis:

```
[edit interface]
lab@r5# show
fxp0 {
    unit 0 {
```

```
            family inet {
                address 172.16.99.56/24;
            }
        }
    }
    ...
```

Configuration groups for high availability

Configuration groups in JUNOS allow you to define a collection of configuration elements in one location that is then referenced, often repeatedly, in other places in the configuration file. This configuration method saves typing time and reduces the risk of configuration mistakes or omissions.

Another use of configuration groups—one that's extremely important for chassis with redundant REs in networks with OoB management—is to place specific configuration elements in a common configuration file, but to have them be applicable to only one of the chassis' two REs. Note that any interface configured under the [edit interfaces] level of hierarchy is applied to both REs when you execute the commit synchronize command. Without configuration groups, both REs would share the same fxp0 IP address. If both REs are connected to the OoB management network, as they should be, the result would be an IP address conflict. To prevent this conflict and for other benefits, JUNOS supports configuration groups specific to RE 0 and RE 1. Through the use of these special groups, you can define specific elements such as chassis names and interface addresses for individual REs. This example defines an fxp0 address for each RE, and also a hostname that includes -RE0 and -RE1. The special group names are re0 and re1:

```
[edit]
lab@r5# show
groups {
    re0 {
        system {
            host-name M40E-1-RE0;
        }
        interfaces {
            fxp0 {
                unit 0 {
                    family inet {
                        address 172.16.99.56/24;
                    }
                }
            }
        }
    }
    re1 {
        system {
            host-name M40E-1-RE1;
        }
        interfaces {
            fxp0 {
                unit 0 {
```

```
                    family inet {
                        address 172.16.99.57/24;
                    }
                }
            }
        }
    }
}
apply-groups [ re0 re1 ];
...
```

With this configuration in place, when you execute the `commit synchronize` command, re0 inherits the hostname M40E-1-RE0 and the IP address 172.16.99.56. re1 inherits the hostname M40E-1-RE1 and the IP address 172.16.99.57. The configuration groups allow both REs to have unique identities in the OoB management network.

SNMP Configuration

SNMP is a topic covered by most books about networking, so we do not discuss it here in detail. However, we can't write a chapter on network monitoring without at least mentioning it. In a nutshell, SNMP helps you monitor the state of devices in the network.

The protocol supports both on-event and on-demand generation of chassis state information. Event-triggered notices are called SNMP *traps*. Traps are triggered when certain conditions, such as link failure, authentication failure, or chassis restarts, occur on a managed chassis. The trap notifications are sent to one or more defined host workstations or servers that have been configured to receive the traps. Chassis state information can be obtained on demand by using variations of `Get` commands issued from host workstations or servers back to the managed chassis.

JUNOS SNMP Configuration

In this configuration sample, SNMP is enabled on router r1. Some SNMP-driven management tools are able to populate a GUI based on content within the `Get` responses and the trap notifications. For this reason, the administrator chooses to define a system name, `r1-J2350`, and the location where the chassis is physically sitting, `Frederick_MD` (arguably the friendliest city in the United States).

The administrator also defines two community strings, `public` and `private`, to control SNMP access to the chassis. A community string acts as a keyword of sorts, in that the host systems must use it to run `Get` commands on the managed device. Community `public` has been given `read-only` access, and community `private` has been given `read-write`.

These community names, public and private, were chosen for illustrative purposes only. In a network with high availability requirements, use more cryptic keywords, because some administrators view the community string as a form of password.

The clients statement, which defines the IP addresses from which Get statements coming to the local chassis must originate, further restricts access for both communities. The configuration sample also shows that SNMP Gets are restricted to the fxp0 interface. SNMP Gets arriving on other interfaces are discarded:

```
[edit snmp]
lab@r1# show
location Frederick_MD;
name r1-J2350;
interface fxp0.0;
community public {
    authorization read-only;
    clients {
        172.16.99.0/24;
    }
}
community private {
    authorization read-write;
    clients {
        172.16.99.213/32;
    }
}
...
```

The next two configuration snippets define SNMP trap parameters for the chassis. These snippets are actually continuations of the previous configuration sample; we've split them out to allow you to focus on specific elements.

In the first sample, the administrator defines lo0 as the source address for all outbound trap notifications. The result is that the primary lo0 address is the source IP for all traps generated by the local chassis. This configuration element is important from a high availability perspective because some SNMP management applications filter traps based on source IP. In the absence of this element, the source address would be the IP address on the interface through which the traps notification leaves the router. Remember that because of groups the address could vary depending on which RE is master. In a high availability environment, redundant REs host different fxp0 interface IP addresses:

```
[edit snmp]
lab@r1# show
...
trap-options {
    source-address lo0
}
```

In the second sample, the administrator defines which categories of events should trigger a trap, as well as the destination IP addresses to which the trap notifications should be sent. Here, trap notifications are sent to host systems residing at 172.16.99.15 and 172.16.99.16:

```
[edit snmp]
lab@r1# show
...
trap-group watcher {
    categories {
        chassis;
        link;
        routing;
        startup;
        configuration;
    }
    targets {
        172.16.99.15;
        172.16.99.16;
```

Trap-related and Get-related configuration elements combine to allow SNMP management in JUNOS.

IOS SNMP Configuration

IOS configuration for SNMP is similar to JUNOS in many ways. In this configuration sample, the communities public and private are both defined. Community public has read-only privileges, as indicated by the ro keyword, and community private has read-write privileges, as indicated by the rw keyword. Access to SNMP data is controlled through the use of access lists. In this example, as in the JUNOS example, read-write access is restricted to a specific IP address, 172.16.99.213, while read-only access is restricted to the entire 172.16.99/24 subnet:

```
r5(config)#access-list 10 permit 172.16.99.0 0.0.0.255
r5(config)#access-list 20 permit 172.16.99.213 0.0.0.0

r5(config)#snmp enable
r5(config)#snmp-server community public ro 10
r5(config)#snmp-server community private rw 20
r5(config)#snmp-server contact Todd_Vaughn
r5(config)#snmp-server location Frederick_MD
```

The next configuration sample enables traps and defines the source address for outbound trap notifications—in this example, lo0. Again, this configuration is imperative for tools that filter inbound trap notices based on the source address of the trap.

```
r5(config)#snmp enable traps
r5(config)#snmp trap-source lo0
```

SNMP and MRTG

The Multi Router Traffic Grapher (MRTG) is a vendor-agnostic tool that is used in conjunction with SNMP to generate pictures of interface utilization. MRTG uses an SNMP Get statement to pull information from the managed devices. It then uses the data returned to populate an HTML-based collection of graphs that show traffic transiting the device. Figure 17-1 is an MRTG-generated view of interface utilization.

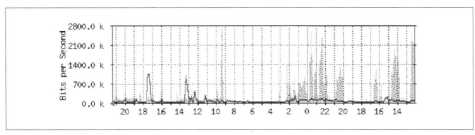

Figure 17-1. Sample MRTG diagram

MRTG operates using SNMP. As a result, no additional router configuration is necessary to support MRTG on either a JUNOS or an IOS system.

> Many visualization tools are available that rely on SNMP to provide the raw data streams needed to monitor conditions in the network. MRTG is mentioned specifically because it is easy to install, widely used, and currently available at no charge. You can download MRTG for free from *http://oss.oetiker.ch/mrtg/*.

Syslog Configuration

System logging, or *syslog*, is a commonly implemented standard for managing and monitoring devices in a network. In many ways, syslog behaves similarly to SNMP traps. When specific events occur, syslog triggers messages that are logged on the local chassis and that are typically also sent to a syslog server. While syslog does have a number of recognized limitations, it is appropriate for multivendor environments because it is standardized by the Internet Engineering Task Force (IETF) and is widely supported among network hardware vendors.

Syslog in JUNOS

In a JUNOS system, logs can be stored on the local chassis, written to the screen of an active user, or written to a remote device. In the following configuration sample, user Pike_Vaughn sees syslog messages of facility (category) any and severity info on his screen when he is logged into the chassis. The host machine at 192.168.17.17 receives system log notices sourced from IP address 10.0.0.5.

As with SNMP, defining the source IP is critical because many syslog servers filter entries based on their source. Definition of source IP is also necessary if you use event correlation tools to parse and analyze entries written to a syslog server. Without a specified source-address, the outbound interface is used as the source of the syslog send back to the server. Depending on what form of management is used (in-band versus OoB), that OoB interface could potentially change in times of network trouble:

```
[edit system syslog]
lab@r5# show
user Pike_Vaughn {
    any info;
}
host 192.168.17.17 {
    daemon info;
}
source-address 10.0.0.5;
...
```

Logfiles can also be written to the local device instead of to a remote server. The files are stored in the */var/log/* directory by filename. By default, JUNOS creates up to 10 files using numbered suffixes of the defined filename, and each file is up to 128 KB in size. In the following code, the file *whodunit* uses the default file settings, and the file *messages* allows the files to be up to 5 MB in size:

```
[edit system syslog]
lab@r5# show
...
file messages {
    any any;
    archive size 5m files 10 no-world-readable;
}
file whodunit {
    authorization info;
    interactive-commands info;
}
```

Syslog messages can be rather cryptic, so use the JUNOS help function for interpreting syslog messages. Here is a sample of a syslog message:

```
May  4 10:47:39  r5 chassisd[2303]: CHASSISD_SNMP_TRAP6: SNMP trap: Power Sup
ply failed: jnxContentsContainerIndex 2, jnxContentsL1Index 1,
jnxContentsL2Index 0, jnxContentsL3Index 0,
jnxContentsDescr Power Supply A, jnxOperatingState/Te
mp 6
---(more 0%)---[abort]
```

The help command reveals further detail:

```
lab@r5> help syslog CHASSISD_SNMP_TRAP6
Name:      CHASSISD_SNMP_TRAP6
Message:   SNMP trap generated: <trap-name> (<argument1> <value1>,
           <argument2> <value2>, <argument3> <value3>, <argument4>
           <value4>, <argument5> <value5>, <argument6> <value6>)
```

```
Help:        chassisd generated SNMP trap
Description: The chassis process (chassisd) generated a Simple Network
             Management Protocol (SNMP) trap with the six indicated
             argument-value pairs.
Type:        Event: This message reports an event, not an error
Severity:    unknown
```

Syslog in IOS

IOS syntax for enabling system logging is similar to JUNOS. In this example, logging is enabled at the debug level. Because the syslog function in both IOS and JUNOS catches everything at the defined severity level, as well as anything more severe, logging at the debug level essentially catches all events. This configuration snippet forwards the logged events to IP address 192.168.17.17:

```
r5(config)#logging trap debugging
r5(config)#logging 192.168.17.17
```

Some IOS versions have a known problem with the syslog implementation that results in redundant timestamp information being prepended to the log entry. Sometimes this problem is merely a nuisance and is easy to avoid using the configuration elements in the following code. However, you want to confirm that not *all* timestamp data is stripped from the syslog entries, particularly when you use event correlation tools:

```
r5(config)#no service timestamps debug uptime
r5(config)#no service timestamps log uptime
```

Syslog and Kiwi

Kiwi is a vendor-agnostic tool that captures and stores syslog notifications from multiple devices. The Kiwi tool also sorts stored syslog entries based on multiple criteria. While it is an effective tool for capturing and sorting, Kiwi has no event correlation capability, which is often required in large multivendor networks. Figure 17-2 shows a Kiwi window.

Because Kiwi operates using received syslog data, no additional router configuration is necessary to support it in either JUNOS or IOS systems. Kiwi is free for download at *http://www.kiwisyslog.com/*.

Many visualization tools are available that rely on syslog to provide the raw data streams needed to monitor network conditions. We mention the Kiwi tool specifically because it is easy to install, widely used, and currently available at no charge. As mentioned earlier, it is appropriate for small to medium-size networks, but it lacks the true event correlation functionality needed for large service provider environments.

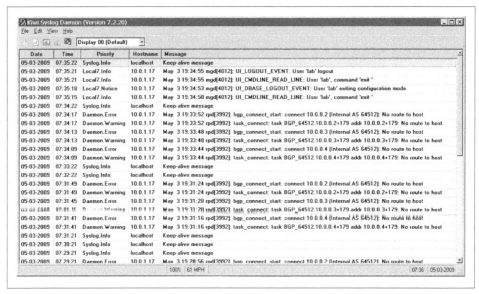

Figure 17-2. Kiwi syslog server

This section made repeated references to the concept of *event correlation*. Event correlation is the process of trying to identify the root cause of a situation or condition when massive amounts of data points, potentially related to the situation, exist. To do this job, the event correlation tool filters through the available data elements, commonly syslog and SNMP data stores, to distinguish issue symptoms from the root cause. The overall purpose of event correlation is to make sure you are resolving the root cause of a problem, not just patching related symptoms. Understanding the difference between symptoms and the root cause is an important concept for high availability, because it can result in reduced downtime.

Configuration Management

JUNOS supports a configuration archiving option that allows a copy of the configuration to be written back to an FTP or SCP server either at periodic intervals or every time a commit is executed. This is critical for high availability networks because it allows all device configurations to be stored in a central location for rapid access. Transferring the configuration at periodic intervals is convenient, but it tends to fill the FTP server with duplicate copies of the configuration. For high availability networks, *transfer-on-commit* is recommended, particularly when managing large numbers of devices.

With the configuration elements shown in this sample, when a commit is typed on
r1, the candidate configuration will be committed and transferred via FTP to
172.16.99.217:

```
lab@r1> show configuration system archival
configuration {
    transfer-on-commit;
    archive-sites {
        "ftp://james:password@172.16.99.217:21";
        "ftp://backup:password@202.45.45.12:21";
    }
}
```

IOS platforms support use of copy run <tftp server>. This sends a manually initiated
write of the current running configuration back to the IP address of a configured TFTP
server, and essentially accomplishes the same thing as the JUNOS configuration
archive function.

Configuration for AAA

The act of configuring and monitoring user authentication, user authorization, and
user activity accounting is collectively referred to as AAA (pronounced "Triple A"). In
a AAA context:

- *Authentication* uses one or more authentication factors to confirm the user is who
  she claims to be. Authentication methods protect the availability of a system by
  preventing unauthorized access.
- *Authorization* uses individual or group profiles to control which features, commands, or system resources the user is permitted to access. Authorization protects
  the availability of a system by restricting user activity to job-specific functions.
- *Accounting* is the act of monitoring what the user is doing while connected to the
  system. Accountability is provided because every configuration change or command executed is recorded and is linked to the user who performed the action.

In small to medium-size networks, AAA functions are often handled on a per-chassis
basis. The elements are simple to configure, few users access the chassis, and the small
number of chassis makes data harvesting a relatively quick process. However, as a
network grows in size, configuring and monitoring AAA on each chassis becomes more
cumbersome and a AAA server based on TACACS or RADIUS standards is needed.

The benefits of a AAA server system are quite clear. A single, managed database of user
IDs and passwords is easier to support than individual user accounts on a large number
of routers. A single repository of profiles allows grouping of users based on duties, and
is easier to support than individual profiles on many routers. In addition, user activity
is easier to track when the data points are in a single location, rather than being scattered
around the network.

There are two common standards for AAA: Terminal Access Control Access-Control System Plus (TACACS+) and Remote Authentication Dial-in User Service (RADIUS). Although they serve similar functions, the two protocols have a few significant differences that have led to different uses in networks.

TACACS+ relies on TCP for its transport, whereas RADIUS relies on UDP. This has led to the notion that TACACS+ is more reliable and secure, which is not entirely true. Also, TACACS+ uses different mechanisms for authentication and authorization, while RADIUS incorporates both functions into a single, simpler mechanism.

For these reasons, TACACS+ is most commonly used by network administrators to monitor and manage network resources for the sake of protecting network availability. RADIUS is generally used by network administrators to monitor and manage customer access to network services and resources for the sake of generating revenue. This chapter focuses on the ability of TACACS+ to provide AAA services for a network with high availability requirements.

TACACS+

To enable TACACS+ in JUNOS, you define `tacplus-server` configuration elements and add `tacplus` to the list of authentication methods for the chassis.

JUNOS authentication

The following configuration sample shows the definition of a `tacplus-server` at IP address 172.16.99.5. An authentication key and `source-address` are defined for authentication attempts to this server. This key is required because most TACACS+ servers maintain an IP address-based list of devices that can request authentication and require that devices submitting requests from a recognized IP submit a valid password with the request:

```
[edit system]
lab@r1# show
authentication-order tacplus;
tacplus-server {
    172.16.99.55 {
        port 2066;
        secret "$9$/wGABby.Ri1EyEyKWxcyoCat.zWiLLevL"; # SECRET-DATA
        timeout 60;
        source-address 172.16.99.50;
    }
}
...
```

A common misconception in JUNOS regarding `authentication-order` is that when `local` is included in the order the local password is tried only when access to the authentication server is not available. In fact, using a local password is the default behavior when the server is not accessible. When adding `local` to the `authentication-order` statement, the administrator is in effect giving users who fail authentication against the

AAA server a chance to authenticate against the router's locally defined user accounts. This may not be desirable in all situations.

IOS authentication

As with JUNOS, IOS authentication is defined on the local chassis and on the TACACS+ server. Here are the elements to accomplish this:

```
r5(config)#enable secret JUNIPER
r5(config)#aaa new-model
r5(config)#aaa authentication login default group tacacs+ enable
r5(config)#tacacs-server host 172.16.99.55
r5(config)#tacacs-server key JUNIPER
```

JUNOS locally defined accounts and authorization

The remote user account is a special account that forces authentication attempts to be forwarded from the chassis to the TACACS+ server. The remote account also defines the maximum permission (level of authorization) that is allowed for users who have been positively authenticated through TACACS+. In this example, two user accounts are configured, lab and remote. User lab is assigned to class superuser and has configured a password. Based strictly on these settings and the previous tacplus-server elements, user lab is the only user able to access this chassis if the TACACS+ server becomes unreachable:

```
login {
    user lab {
        uid 2005;
        class superuser;
        authentication {
            encrypted-password "$1$ZnzWNcTaBi_RoSeJIr6hGL9OfCD/"; # SECRET-DATA
        }
    }
    user remote {
        full-name "for use by TACACS+ tools";
        uid 2020;
        class superuser;
    }

}
```

In this configuration example, user remote is also assigned class superuser; however, users who authenticate through the server have a subset of superuser permissions based on their job duties. In this case, class superuser represents the maximum allowable authorization level that can be granted by the access server. Also of interest, note that user remote has no password configured. In this case, authentication is handled by the TACACS+ server.

IOS authorization

Configuration elements in IOS to have user authorization be controlled by the TACACS+ server include:

```
r5(config)#aaa authorization exec default group tacacs none
r5(config)#aaa authorization commands 0 default group tacacs none
r5(config)#aaa authorization commands 1 default group tacacs none
r5(config)#aaa authorization commands 15 default group tacacs none
```

JUNOS accounting (activity tracking)

You configure TACACS+ accounting, which monitors the activity of users on the sys-tem, under the system accounting level of hierarchy. In this configuration example, as with authorization, you must define the TACACS+ server. A shared secret (a password) is used to authenticate the local system, and a source address for accounting informa-tion is specified. Events for which tracking information is sent to the server include user login attempts, configuration changes (using change-log), and any executable com-mand (using interactive-commands) that generates output:

```
[edit system accounting]
lab@r1# show
events [ login change-log interactive-commands ];
destination {
    tacplus {
        server {
```

```
            172.16.99.55 {
                port 2060;
                secret "$9$lo5MWxY2aji.Lxjq_BONnIE1hLX-Y2a"; # SECRET-DATA
                timeout 60;
                source-address 172.16.99.34;
            }
        }
    }
}
```

IOS accounting (activity tracking)

Configure accounting in IOS with these commands:

```
r5(config)#aaa accounting delay-start
r5(config)#aaa accounting exec default start-stop group tacacs+
r5(config)#aaa accounting commands 15 default start-stop group tacacs+
r5(config)#tacacs-server host 172.16.99.55 key JUNIPER
r5(config)#ip tacacs source-interface lo0
```

JUNOS GUI Support

JUNOS-based platforms support graphics-driven GUI performance monitoring tools. You enable JUNOS GUI support under the system services level of hierarchy. To enable J-Web and other HTML-based management and monitoring tools, add web-management to the configuration. To enable chassis management and monitoring via JUNOScript, add either xnm-clear-text or xnm-ssl:

```
[edit system services]
lab@r1# set ?
Possible completions:
+ apply-groups          Groups from which to inherit configuration data
+ apply-groups-except   Don't inherit configuration data from these groups
> finger                Allow finger requests from remote systems
> ftp                   Allow FTP file transfers
> ssh                   Allow ssh access
> telnet                Allow telnet login
> web-management        Web management configuration
> xnm-clear-text        Allow clear text-based JUNOScript connections
> xnm-ssl               Allow SSL-based JUNOScript connections
```

The J-Web GUI provides a suite of point-and-click tools for management and monitoring of individual devices in the network. Figure 17-3 shows the J-Web home page of an M7i.

Though it may offend some purists, it is important to note that any configuration change that can be made from the JUNOS command-line interface (CLI) can be made from the J-Web GUI. The GUI includes a collection of wizards. A *wizard* is essentially a scripted series of prompts that allows you to get the router up and running quickly without mandating a thorough understanding of the GUI itself.

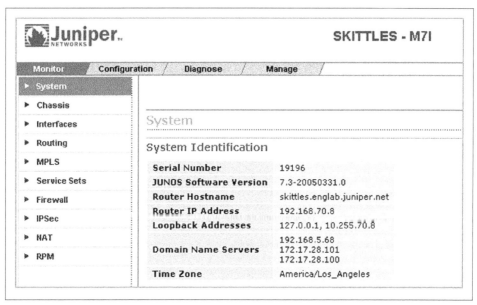

Figure 17-3. J-Web home page

What IS Normal?

As we mentioned at the start of this chapter, network monitoring, whether by CLI commands, remote servers, or device GUIs, is based on the premise that deviation from a defined *norm* can be detrimental to the network. Therefore, it is absolutely critical to establish a baseline of what is normal for the network. Without this awareness, it is impossible to identify *abnormal* behavior.

CHAPTER 18

Network Scalability

Opinions vary widely about the definition of *network scalability*. Some consider it to be the network's ability to handle growing amounts of work and the increasing demands for resources and services. To others, true network scalability must include elements of modularity and mathematical logic. According to this second definition, for a network to be truly scalable, the addition of hardware should yield processing, throughput, and service capacities proportional to the characteristics of the hardware added.

While neither definition is wrong, we'd say they're both missing parts of the picture. The second definition implies that network scalability is a simple byproduct of hardware capacity. Both definitions assume the network will only grow. In the modern economy, it is sometimes necessary for a network to shrink in capacity and cost, while oftentimes retaining all functionality.

A more modern definition of network scalability is the ability of the network to retain all functionality and services while adjusting its capacity and cost to properly fit demand. This definition implies that the network can get bigger *and* smaller. It's with this definition in mind that we approach the discussion in this chapter.

Hardware Capacity

One of the first topics in any discussion of network scalability is hardware. It is imperative that hardware selected for the network can meet the throughput needs and withstand the processing burden of the network. In networks with high availability requirements, chassis are often deployed in pairs. We discuss cost and design implications of pairing devices in Chapter 1, and in this chapter we consider the 50% rule to be gospel. For a high availability network in which chassis are deployed in pairs and in which the load is balanced across the redundant pair of switches, routers, firewalls, and other devices, the 50% rule means that no more than half the resources or capacities of either device in the pair should ever be in use at the same time. If this threshold is exceeded, and especially if it is exceeded consistently, and if one device in the pair fails, the remaining device will be unable to assume the load of both devices and the redundancy scheme will fail.

Device Resources to Monitor

All JUNOS-based products provide functional separation between the control plane, which operates in the routing engine (RE), and the data plane, which operates in the Packet Forwarding Engine (PFE), as discussed in Chapter 3. Trivial Network Protocol (TNP) enables communications between the control and data planes. You must understand the resources and capacities of the RE and the PFE to properly select hardware for a scalable network and to monitor each chassis as the network adjusts to its planned size.

Control plane capacity best practices

Memory and processing power in the control plane are finite resources. The number of variables that tax these resources means it is nearly impossible to make absolute statements about the suitability of placing any particular chassis in a network. Variables that impact processor burden at the control plane include:

Total number of routes in the local routing table
 As the number of routes increases, more memory is required to store them and more processing power is needed to maintain them.

Stability of the local routing table
 If the local routing table is stable, as it should be in a high availability network, less processing power is required for updates.

Total number and stability of Border Gateway Protocol (BGP) peers
 In large service provider networks, the control plane processor burden is directly proportional to the number of BGP peering relationships that must be maintained and the stability of the peers.

Total number of Interior Gateway Protocol (IGP) adjacencies and domain stability
 The control plane processor burden also increases with the number of IGP adjacencies, and the stability of the domain also affects the amount of processing done by the RE.

Total number of routing instances and virtual private networks (VPNs)
 Each routing instance created for a VPN has its own separate routing table within the primary logical router that must be maintained by the control plane processor.

Total number of logical routers enabled
 Configuring a logical router spawns creation of a completely independent routing process and all related routing tables. Therefore, each logical router taxes memory and processor resources relative to the number of BGP and IGP peers, routing instances, and size and stability of the routing table in the logical router.

Amount of system logging enabled

Increasing the amount of information logged about the system requires the RE processor to write that information, which steals time away from other tasks that the processor must perform.

Rate of sampling

If enabled, statistical sampling adds significant burden to the RE.

With all these variables in play, what is the best way to identify a chassis that can adequately scale to network demands? The answer is simple: *testing*. The best practice when selecting a chassis to scale to desired capacity while meeting high availability requirements is to test it in a setting that reflects both the current and anticipated settings for the variables we mentioned in the preceding list. In many cases, equipment vendors actively support this testing because they have a vested interest in it.

 While discussing control plane capacities, we must return to one of the fundamentals of high availability design and consider device pairing from a different perspective. As we discussed in Chapter 1, pairing devices is one way to add redundancy to a design. This method effectively doubles the number of devices that would have to fail before connectivity is impacted. However, deploying redundant devices doubles the number of neighbor relationships that must be maintained by routing protocols and managed by the control plane. As a result, redundant devices tend to add processor burden at the control plane. However, with load sharing enabled across redundant pairs, the "doubling up" effectively decreases the burden on the data plane.

Data plane specifications

When considering classic packet-based routing, forwarding plane capacity has fewer related variables for you to monitor and track. Quite often, the forwarding plane is described simply by its aggregate data transport rate, either in bits per second or in packets per second.

Table 18-1 shows forwarding plane capacity for M Series products. All use classic packet-based forwarding.

Table 18-1. M Series forwarding plane capacity

Chassis	Aggregate half-duplex throughput	Aggregate half-duplex forwarding rate
M7i	10 Gbps	16 Mpps
M10i	16 Gbps	16 Mpps
M40e	51.2 Gbps	40 Mpps
M120	120 Gbps	90 Mpps
M320	320 Gbps	240 Mpps

Table 18-2 shows forwarding plane capacity for MX Series products.

Table 18-2. MX Series forwarding plane capacity

Chassis	Aggregate half-duplex throughput	Aggregate half-duplex forwarding rate
MX240	240 Gbps	180 Mpps
MX480	480 Gbps	360 Mpps
MX960	960 Gbps	720 Mpps

Table 18-3 shows forwarding plane capacity for T Series products.

Table 18-3. T Series forwarding plane capacity

Chassis	Aggregate half-duplex throughput	Aggregate half-duplex forwarding rate
T320	320 Gbps	385 Mpps
T640	640 Gbps	770 Mpps
T1600	1.6 Tbps	1.92 Gpps
TX Matrix (4x T640 multi-chassis system)	2.5 Tbps	3 Gpps
TX Matrix Plus (16x T1600 multichassis system)	25.6 Tbps	30.7 Gpps

J Series products combine routing and security functionality and are capable of classic packet-based forwarding as well as flow-based traffic forwarding. This results in additional capacity variables that must be taken into consideration. These variables are based on the type of forwarding and related features enabled on the chassis. Table 18-4 shows forwarding plane capacity for J Series products.

Table 18-4. J Series forwarding plane capacity

Chassis	Firewall throughput	Routing forwarding rate
J2320	400 Mbps	175,000 pps
J2350	500 Mbps	200,000 pps
J4350	600 Mbps	225,000 pps
J6350	1 Gbps	400,000 pps

A good rule of thumb when selecting devices for a network is to provision for 2.5 times the current anticipated demand. This rule does not mean it is necessary to immediately purchase Physical Interface Cards (PICs) and Flexible PIC Concentrators (FPCs) to support the additional traffic, but it does mean the chassis you select should be able to accommodate the additional PICs and FPCs required to support the increase.

Network Scalability by Design

While choosing the right hardware for a network is critical, more is involved in building a scalable network than simply buying routers with redundant components and a few orders of magnitude more performance than is immediately needed. As important as hardware selection is, it's only about one-third of the task of building a scalable network. The remaining two-thirds of the task comprise the logical design of the network.

Designing a scalable transport network or adding scalability to an existing design can be accomplished by scaling intradomain routing, by scaling interdomain routing, and by engineering transit traffic through the use of Multiprotocol Label Switching (MPLS). Chapter 12 details the IGP mechanisms that allow the network to grow without putting service or connectivity at risk. Chapter 13 addresses methods of controlling domain-external traffic. This chapter ties the two concepts together to provide a big-picture look at scaling networks.

Scaling BGP for High Availability

Any discussion of scaling interdomain routing is, by default, a discussion of BGP scalability mechanisms. This section builds on the Internal BGP (IBGP) configuration basics described in Chapter 13 to show how a simple intelligent route reflection scheme can allow a network to expand or contract to scale as needed.

 As explained in Chapter 13, for networks with high availability requirements the authors strongly recommend scaling using route reflection with clusters instead of using confederations because of the added number and complexity of routing policies that are mandated by IBGP confederations.

Route reflectors and clusters

In Chapter 13, we describe how to configure route reflectors. We also explain how *route reflectors* and *clusters* support high availability by reducing the number of peering relationships that need to be managed by the chassis and that need to be configured and monitored by the network administrators. Chapter 13 includes a collection of high availability-specific design considerations that bear repeating here.

When using route reflection, consider these design issues:

- Because failure of a route reflector would result in the cluster being isolated from the rest of the BGP network, clusters should always be configured with redundant route reflectors.

- Routers chosen to be reflectors should have consistently reliable power, cooling, and network connectivity and should be central to the network design.

- Route reflectors within an Autonomous System (AS) should in most cases be fully meshed. This permits every route reflector to receive all known BGP paths, thus ensuring completeness of the local routing table.

- The logical topology should follow the physical topology. Route reflection simplifies support of the network by reducing the number of required IBGP relationships. However, configuring a logical reflector topology that deviates from the physical topology adds so much complexity that it may be better not to deploy route reflection in the first place.

Route reflection by itself promotes scalability. However, as the network grows in size and geographic coverage, two route reflectors may no longer be adequate to meet high availability requirements. Figure 18-1 shows four routers that are part of a large network. Two are in Dallas, and the other two are in Chicago. Connectivity among these devices forms a physical full mesh.

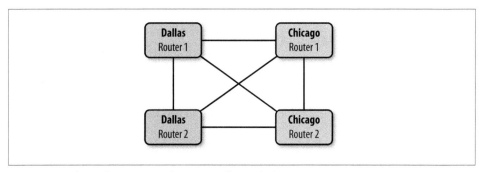

Figure 18-1. Physical connectivity between Dallas and Chicago

Figure 18-2 shows the same four routers, but notice that in this diagram, Dallas Router 2 and Chicago Router 2 have changed places. Because these routers are part of a full mesh, the diagram still accurately reflects their relationships with the other routers. Also notice that Figure 18-2 indicates that the Dallas and Chicago routers are part of an IBGP full mesh.

With the routers arranged in this manner, we can conveniently assign pairs of chassis to serve as route reflector (RR) and backup route reflector (BRR). Furthermore, we can take advantage of the geographic distance between Dallas and Chicago to add another layer of redundancy to our network. Figure 18-3 shows the creation of clusters 1.1.1.1 and 2.2.2.2.

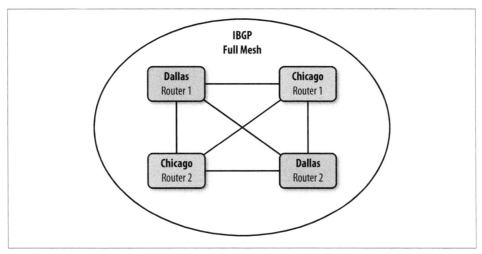

Figure 18-2. Dallas and Chicago IBGP relationships

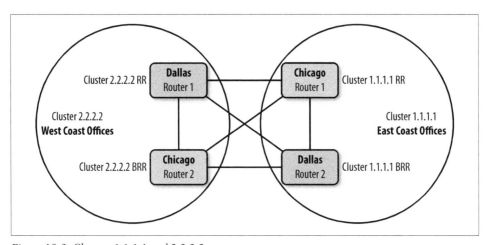

Figure 18-3. Clusters 1.1.1.1 and 2.2.2.2

In Figure 18-3, Chicago Router 1 is serving as the RR and Dallas Router 2 is serving as the BRR for Cluster 1.1.1.1. Dallas Router 1 and Chicago Router 2 are serving as RR and BRR, respectively, for Cluster 2.2.2.2. Not only are both clusters being served by a primary and backup route reflector, but also the route reflector scheme itself features geographic separation for added redundancy and high availability.

The astute reader may notice that two additional geographically separated route reflector pairings are possible with this design. Figure 18-4 shows the placement of clusters 3.3.3.3 and 4.4.4.4.

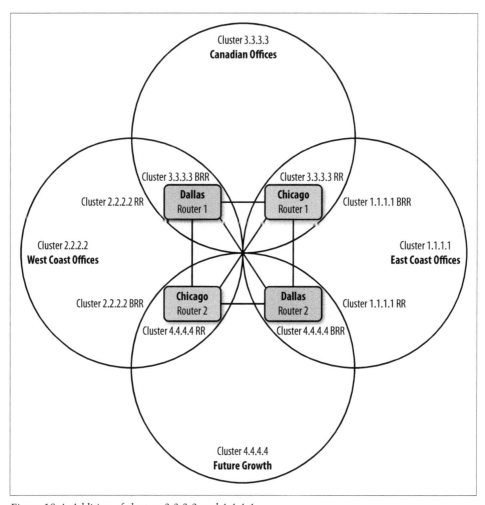

Figure 18-4. Addition of clusters 3.3.3.3 and 4.4.4.4

In Figure 18-4, Cluster 3.3.3.3 has been used for corporate expansion into Canadian markets, and Cluster 4.4.4.4 is reserved for future growth.

What's the point?

Figures 18-1 through 18-4 are cumulative, and demonstrate how route reflection can be used in a scalable manner to promote redundancy and create high availability. This design features a few interesting characteristics that are a direct result of RR and BRR placement:

- No single router is a primary route reflector for more than one cluster.
- Loss of any single router in the top-tier Dallas-Chicago mesh would not isolate any cluster.
- Loss of connectivity to an entire city, Dallas or Chicago, would not isolate any cluster.

Additionally, this design supports the modern definition of scalability because it would be easy to shrink the network as needed. You could decommission individual neighbors or entire clusters with a few simple configuration changes and without impacting peering relationships to other clusters.

 JUNOS route reflector and cluster configuration syntax, along with IBGP configuration options, is covered in Chapter 13.

MPLS for Network Scalability and High Availability

MPLS is a way to establish and maintain engineered paths that are capable of deviating from the IGP-dictated "best path" between any two given points. This concept is critical to network scalability, because in the absence of a traffic engineering tool such as MPLS, there would be no effective way to spread traffic across links to utilize all available bandwidth. Recall that all IGPs identify and use only the lowest-cost path through a network, leaving other links underutilized.

MPLS label-switched paths (LSPs) differ from classic ATM virtual circuits in that LSP configuration is performed only at the point of entry, or ingress, of the traffic-engineered domain. Signaling protocols look at the path characteristics defined on the ingress router and signal the path to the egress point accordingly.

Figure 18-5 shows a small network that we use to demonstrate how MPLS meets network scalability needs and high availability requirements. In this network, routers r1, r2, r3, and r4 are IBGP neighbors within AS 64512. Router r1 has is an External BGP (EBGP) relationship with AS 11, r2 with AS 22, r3 with AS 33, and r4 with AS 44.

In this simplified example, the administrators have decided to enable MPLS to control the path taken by traffic transiting between AS 22 and AS 33. The administrators have decided that this transit traffic should pass through r4 regardless of the IGP-dictated shortest path through the network. Notice that the link between r2 and r1 is a Fast Ethernet segment, whereas the other links in the network are T1. IGP metrics would most likely describe the path through r1 as the best way for packets to travel between r2 and r3.

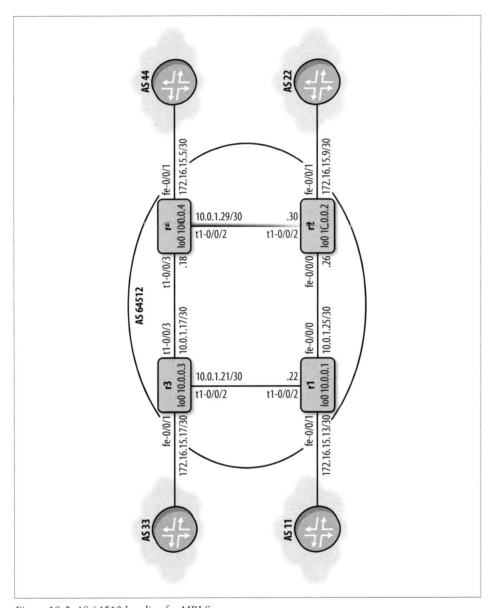

Figure 18-5. AS 64512 baseline for MPLS

Basic LSP configuration syntax

Because MPLS LSPs are unidirectional, you must configure path characteristics on both
r2 and r3 (the ingress routers for each direction), defining r4 as a transit point. Family
MPLS should be enabled on all interfaces participating in MPLS switching. Additional
relevant configuration elements on r2 include:

```
[edit protocols]
lab@r2# show mpls
no-cspf;
label-switched-path to-r3 {
    to 10.0.0.3;
    primary transit-r4;
}
path transit-r4 {
    10.0.0.4 loose;
}
interface all;
```

Relevant configuration elements on r3 include:

```
[edit protocols mpls]
lab@r3# show
no-cspf;
label-switched-path to-r2 {
    to 10.0.0.2;
    primary transit-r4;
}
path transit-r4 {
    10.0.0.4 loose;
}
interface all;
```

The only MPLS-related configuration required for r4 is to enable support for label allocation and path signaling:

```
[edit protocols]
lab@r4# show rsvp
interface all;

[edit r4 protocols]
lab@r4# show mpls
no-cspf;
interface all;
```

With MPLS configured and confirmed, operational transit traffic now follows the LSP. JUNOS show commands demonstrate desired functionality. Let's look first at r2:

```
[edit]
lab@r2# run show mpls lsp
Ingress LSP: 1 sessions
To              From        State Rt ActivePath      P     LSPname
10.0.0.3        10.0.0.2    Up    1 transit-r4       *     to-r3
Total 1 displayed, Up 1, Down 0

Egress LSP: 1 sessions
To              From        State   Rt Style Labelin Labelout LSPname
10.0.0.2        10.0.0.3    Up      0  1 FF    3        - to-r2
Total 1 displayed, Up 1, Down 0

Transit LSP: 0 sessions
Total 0 displayed, Up 0, Down 0
```

Even though the output from r2 appears to be quite positive, it is best to confirm from both ingress points by running the command on r3 as well:

```
[edit]
lab@r3# run show mpls lsp
Ingress LSP: 1 sessions
To              From         State Rt ActivePath      P    LSPname
10.0.0.2        10.0.0.3     Up     1 transit-r4      *    to-r2
Total 1 displayed, Up 1, Down 0


Egress LSP: 1 sessions
To              From         State   Rt Style Labelin Labelout LSPname
10.0.0.3        10.0.0.2     Up       0  1 FF     3        - to-r3
Total 1 displayed, Up 1, Down 0


Transit LSP: 0 sessions
Total 0 displayed, Up 0, Down 0
```

A quick check of the defined transit point confirms that both LSPs have been established and both are using r4 as a transit point as expected:

```
[edit]
lab@r4# run show mpls lsp
Ingress LSP: 0 sessions
Total 0 displayed, Up 0, Down 0

Egress LSP: 0 sessions
Total 0 displayed, Up 0, Down 0

Transit LSP: 2 sessions
To              From         State   Rt Style Labelin Labelout LSPname
10.0.0.2        10.0.0.3     Up       1  1 FF  299792      3 to-r2
10.0.0.3        10.0.0.2     Up       1  1 FF  299776      3 to-r3
Total 2 displayed, Up 2, Down 0
```

Figure 18-6 shows the bidirectional LSPs we have created that transit r4.

Secondary LSPs

Looking at Figure 18-6 and the configuration syntax, a very serious high availability concern becomes quite apparent. Failure of r4 or of any of the links leading to r4 would cause the LSP setup to fail. In a larger network, either because of a routing loop or because the loose hop is simply not reachable (remember, this is a simplified example), loss of the LSP would result in complete loss of deterministic paths for transit traffic, which would more than likely have a negative impact on any service-level agreements (SLAs) tied to the transit traffic. How can we keep this failure from impacting the availability of the network?

By configuring a secondary LSP network, you identify two paths, a primary and a backup, that meet the requirements for the LSP. The primary path is used when available. When this path is not available, transit traffic automatically fails over to the secondary path.

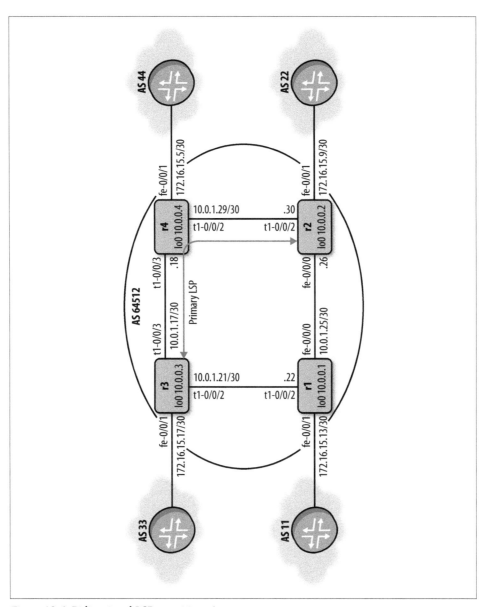

Figure 18-6. Bidirectional LSP transiting r4

To configure a secondary path in this example, we add path signaling and label switching support to r1:

```
[edit protocols]
lab@r1# show rsvp
interface all;
```

```
[edit protocols]
lab@r1# show mpls
no-cspf;
interface all;
```

Then we configure the secondary path. Recall that LSPs are unidirectional, so we need to change the path characteristics on both r2 and r3. Here are the necessary configuration changes on r3:

```
[edit protocols mpls]
lab@r3# show
no-cspf;
label-switched-path to-r2 {
    to 10.0.0.2;
    primary transit-r4;
}
path transit-r4 {
    10.0.0.4 loose;
}
interface all;

[edit protocols mpls]
lab@r3# set label-switched-path to-r2 secondary transit-r1

[edit protocols mpls]
lab@r3# set path transit-r1 10.0.0.1 loose

[edit protocols mpls]
lab@r3# show
no-cspf;
label-switched-path to-r2 {
    to 10.0.0.2;
    primary transit-r4;
    secondary transit-r1;
}
path transit-r4 {
    10.0.0.4 loose;
}
path transit-r1 {
    10.0.0.1 loose;
}
interface all;
```

And here are the necessary configuration changes on r2:

```
[edit protocols mpls]
lab@r2# show
no-cspf;
label-switched-path to-r3 {
    to 10.0.0.3;
    primary transit-r4;
}
path transit-r4 {
    10.0.0.4 loose;
}
interface all;
```

```
[edit protocols mpls]
lab@r2# set label-switched-path to-r3 secondary transit-r1

[edit protocols mpls]
lab@r2# set path transit-r1 10.0.0.1 loose

[edit protocols mpls]
lab@r2# show
no-cspf;
label-switched-path to-r3 {
    to 10.0.0.3;
    primary transit-r4;
    secondary transit-r1;
}
path transit-r4 {
    10.0.0.4 loose;
}
path transit-r1 {
    10.0.0.1 loose;
}
interface all;
```

We now use show commands to verify the existence of the secondary LSP, first on r2, then on r3:

```
[edit protocols mpls]
lab@r2# run show mpls lsp detail
Ingress LSP: 1 sessions

10.0.0.3
  From: 10.0.0.2, State: Up, ActiveRoute: 1, LSPname: to-r3
  ActivePath: transit-r4 (primary)
  LoadBalance: Random
  Encoding type: Packet, Switching type: Packet, GPID: IPv4
 *Primary    transit-r4      State: Up
    SmartOptimizeTimer: 180
    Received RRO (ProtectionFlag 1=Available 2=InUse
    4=B/W 8=Node 10=SoftPreempt):
          10.0.1.29 10.0.1.17
  Secondary transit-r1       State: Dn
    SmartOptimizeTimer: 180
Total 1 displayed, Up 1, Down 0

[edit protocols mpls]
lab@r3# run show mpls lsp detail
Ingress LSP: 1 sessions

10.0.0.2
  From: 10.0.0.3, State: Up, ActiveRoute: 1, LSPname: to-r2
  ActivePath: transit-r4 (primary)
  LoadBalance: Random
  Encoding type: Packet, Switching type: Packet, GPID: IPv4
 *Primary    transit-r4      State: Up
    SmartOptimizeTimer: 180
    Received RRO (ProtectionFlag 1=Available 2=InUse
```

```
        4=B/W 8=Node 10=SoftPreempt):
              10.0.1.18 10.0.1.30
    Secondary transit-r1         State: Dn
       SmartOptimizeTimer: 180
    Total 1 displayed, Up 1, Down 0
```

Notice that in both the show commands, the secondary LSP is tagged as being down. This state is the default behavior of JUNOS. When configured, the secondary LSPs are not signaled until the primary LSP goes down.

Hot standby

From a transit switching perspective, having the secondary LSP remain down until needed may be an acceptable state. After all, *only a few* packets would be lost during LSP switchover from primary to secondary. From a high availability perspective, however, the failover delay is completely unacceptable. Setup and use of the secondary LSP can take several seconds, which equates to an eternity in network time.

JUNOS supports an option that allows the secondary path to be signaled and established before the primary path has failed. This feature, called *hot standby*, reduces traffic loss when the primary LSP fails. You enable hot standby by adding the standby statement to the secondary path attribute of the LSP, as shown here on r3:

```
[edit protocols mpls]
lab@r3# set label-switched-path to-r2 secondary transit-r1 standby

[edit protocols mpls]
lab@r3# show
no-cspf;
label-switched-path to-r2 {
    to 10.0.0.2;
    primary transit-r4;
    secondary transit-r1 {
        standby;
    }
}
path transit-r4 {
    10.0.0.4 loose;
}
path transit-r1 {
    10.0.0.1 loose;
}
interface all;
```

After making the same change on r2, we again look at the paths that have been established between r2 and r3 using the show mpls lsp detail command. Here are both paths established on r3:

```
[edit protocols mpls]
lab@r3# run show mpls lsp detail
Ingress LSP: 1 sessions
```

```
10.0.0.2
  From: 10.0.0.3, State: Up, ActiveRoute: 1, LSPname: to-r2
  ActivePath: transit-r4 (primary)
  LoadBalance: Random
  Encoding type: Packet, Switching type: Packet, GPID: IPv4
 *Primary    transit-r4       State: Up
    SmartOptimizeTimer: 180
    Received RRO (ProtectionFlag 1=Available 2=InUse
    4=B/W 8=Node 10=SoftPreempt):
         10.0.1.18 10.0.1.30
  Standby    transit-r1       State: Up
    SmartOptimizeTimer: 180
    Received RRO (ProtectionFlag 1=Available 2=InUse
    4=B/W 8=Node 10=SoftPreempt):
         10.0.1.22 10.0.1.26
Total 1 displayed, Up 1, Down 0
```

The same state is visible on r2:

```
[edit protocols mpls]
lab@r2# run show mpls lsp detail
Ingress LSP: 1 sessions

10.0.0.3
  From: 10.0.0.2, State: Up, ActiveRoute: 1, LSPname: to-r3
  ActivePath: transit-r4 (primary)
  LoadBalance: Random
  Encoding type: Packet, Switching type: Packet, GPID: IPv4
 *Primary    transit-r4       State: Up
    SmartOptimizeTimer: 180
    Received RRO (ProtectionFlag 1=Available 2=InUse
    4=B/W 8=Node 10=SoftPreempt):
         10.0.1.29 10.0.1.17
  Standby    transit-r1       State: Up
    SmartOptimizeTimer: 180
    Received RRO (ProtectionFlag 1=Available 2=InUse
    4=B/W 8=Node 10=SoftPreempt):
         10.0.1.25 10.0.1.21
Total 1 displayed, Up 1, Down 0
```

To save time, you can also configure hot standby state at the protocol's MPLS level of hierarchy, if you want all secondary LSPs to be actively signaled:

```
[edit protocols mpls]
lab@r2# set standby

[edit protocols mpls]
lab@r2# show
no-cspf;
standby;
...
```

A quick check of the transit routers, r4 and r1, confirms that the primary and secondary LSPs are up. On r4, both of the primary LSPs are visible:

```
[edit]
lab@r4# run show mpls lsp transit detail
Transit LSP: 2 sessions

10.0.0.2
  From: 10.0.0.3, LSPstate: Up, ActiveRoute: 1
  LSPname: to-r2, LSPpath: Primary
  Suggested label received: -, Suggested label sent: -
  Recovery label received: -, Recovery label sent: 3
  Resv style: 1 FF, Label in: 299792, Label out: 3
  Time left:  157, Since: Mon Feb 16 20:20:14 2009
  Tspec: rate 0bps size 0bps peak Infbps m 20 M 1500
  Port number: sender 1 receiver 30045 protocol 0
  PATH rcvfrom: 10.0.1.17 (t1-0/0/3.0) 435 pkts
  Adspec: received MTU 1500 sent MTU 1500
  PATH sentto: 10.0.1.30 (t1-0/0/2.0) 432 pkts
  RESV rcvfrom: 10.0.1.30 (t1-0/0/2.0) 433 pkts
  Record route: 10.0.1.17 <self> 10.0.1.30

10.0.0.3
  From: 10.0.0.2, LSPstate: Up, ActiveRoute: 1
  LSPname: to-r3, LSPpath: Primary
  Suggested label received: -, Suggested label sent: -
  Recovery label received: -, Recovery label sent: 3
  Resv style: 1 FF, Label in: 299776, Label out: 3
  Time left:  159, Since: Mon Feb 16 20:18:03 2009
  Tspec: rate 0bps size 0bps peak Infbps m 20 M 1500
  Port number: sender 1 receiver 55528 protocol 0
  PATH rcvfrom: 10.0.1.30 (t1-0/0/2.0) 439 pkts
  Adspec: received MTU 1500 sent MTU 1500
  PATH sentto: 10.0.1.17 (t1-0/0/3.0) 435 pkts
  RESV rcvfrom: 10.0.1.17 (t1-0/0/3.0) 436 pkts
  Record route: 10.0.1.30 <self> 10.0.1.17
Total 2 displayed, Up 2, Down 0
```

On r1, both of the secondary LSPs are also visible:

```
[edit]
lab@r1# run show mpls lsp transit detail
Transit LSP: 2 sessions

10.0.0.2
  From: 10.0.0.3, LSPstate: Up, ActiveRoute: 1
  LSPname: to-r2, LSPpath: Secondary
  Suggested label received: -, Suggested label sent: -
  Recovery label received: -, Recovery label sent: 3
  Resv style: 1 FF, Label in: 299808, Label out: 3
  Time left:  144, Since: Mon Feb 16 21:06:03 2009
  Tspec: rate 0bps size 0bps peak Infbps m 20 M 1500
  Port number: sender 2 receiver 30048 protocol 0
  PATH rcvfrom: 10.0.1.21 (t1-0/0/2.0) 368 pkts
  Adspec: received MTU 1500 sent MTU 1500
  PATH sentto: 10.0.1.26 (fe-0/0/0.0) 367 pkts
```

```
  RESV rcvfrom: 10.0.1.26 (fe-0/0/0.0) 368 pkts
  Record route: 10.0.1.21 <self> 10.0.1.26

10.0.0.3
  From: 10.0.0.2, LSPstate: Up, ActiveRoute: 1
  LSPname: to-r3, LSPpath: Secondary
  Suggested label received: -, Suggested label sent: -
  Recovery label received: -, Recovery label sent: 3
  Resv style: 1 FF, Label in: 299792, Label out: 3
  Time left:  146, Since: Mon Feb 16 21:05:59 2009
  Tspec: rate 0bps size 0bps peak Infbps m 20 M 1500
  Port number: sender 2 receiver 55533 protocol 0
  PATH rcvfrom: 10.0.1.26 (fe-0/0/0.0) 368 pkts
  Adspec: received MTU 1500 sent MTU 1500
  PATH sentto: 10.0.1.21 (t1-0/0/2.0) 367 pkts
  RESV rcvfrom: 10.0.1.21 (t1-0/0/2.0) 368 pkts
  Record route: 10.0.1.26 <self> 10.0.1.21
Total 2 displayed, Up 2, Down 0
```

Figure 18-7 shows the current state of our bidirectional LSPs. Notice that the primary path transits r4 and that the secondary path transits r1.

Fast reroute. With both the primary and secondary LSPs currently signaled as being up, a thorough lab test reveals a significant improvement in failover time over what was seen without the **standby** option. However, the testing would also show that an unacceptable amount of traffic is still lost during the switchover. Traffic continues to be lost while the network forwards information about the failed primary upstream to the ingress router. With the configuration elements shown so far, only when the ingress router learns that the primary LSP is down does it start using the secondary LSP. The amount of traffic lost is proportional to the hop-count distance between the point of failure and the ingress router. For example, if an LSP transiting nine routers experiences a failure in the seventh router from the ingress, the failover time could be substantial because the signal to fail over would have to be carried across multiple hops back to the ingress router.

Fast reroute works in conjunction with the hot standby LSP to minimize the amount of traffic lost when an LSP fails. Fast reroute allows the router immediately upstream from a failed link or node along an LSP to find an alternate route around the failure and forward traffic, while simultaneously sending notification of the failure back to the ingress node to trigger use of the secondary LSP. To enable fast reroute, add the **fast-reroute** statement to the LSP configuration stanza, as shown here for r2:

```
[edit protocols mpls]
lab@r2# set label-switched-path to-r3 fast-reroute

[edit protocols mpls]
lab@r2# show
no-cspf;
label-switched-path to-r3 {
    to 10.0.0.3;
    fast-reroute;
    primary transit-r4;
```

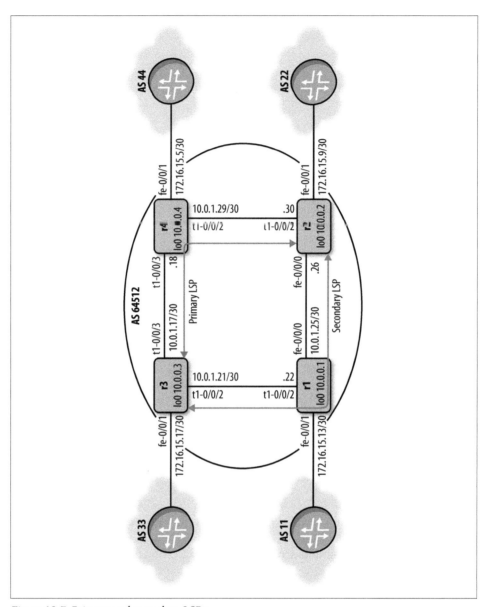

Figure 18-7. Primary and secondary LSPs

```
        secondary transit-r1 {
            standby;
        }
    }
    path transit-r4 {
        10.0.0.4 loose;
    }
    path transit-r1 {
```

```
    10.0.0.1 loose;
}
interface all;
```

After adding the `fast-reroute` statement to both r2 and r3 and committing the con-figuration changes, use the `show mpls lsp ingress detail` command to view the effects of the change. Router r2 shows that fast reroute has been enabled:

```
[edit protocols mpls]
lab@r2# run show mpls lsp ingress detail
Ingress LSP: 1 sessions

10.0.0.3
  From: 10.0.0.2, State: Up, ActiveRoute: 1, LSPname: to-r3
  ActivePath: transit-r4 (primary)
  FastReroute desired
  LoadBalance: Random
  Encoding type: Packet, Switching type: Packet, GPID: IPv4
 *Primary    transit-r4      State: Up
    SmartOptimizeTimer: 180
    Received RRO (ProtectionFlag 1=Available 2=InUse
    4=B/W 8=Node 10=SoftPreempt):
          10.0.1.29 10.0.1.17
  Standby    transit-r1      State: Up
    SmartOptimizeTimer: 180
    Received RRO (ProtectionFlag 1=Available 2=InUse
    4=B/W 8=Node 10=SoftPreempt):
          10.0.1.25 10.0.1.21
Total 1 displayed, Up 1, Down 0
```

Output from this command shows the change was successful on r3 as well:

```
[edit protocols mpls]
lab@r3# run show mpls lsp ingress detail
Ingress LSP: 1 sessions

10.0.0.2
  From: 10.0.0.3, State: Up, ActiveRoute: 1, LSPname: to-r2
  ActivePath: transit-r4 (primary)
  FastReroute desired
  LoadBalance: Random
  Encoding type: Packet, Switching type: Packet, GPID: IPv4
 *Primary    transit-r4      State: Up
    SmartOptimizeTimer: 180
    Received RRO (ProtectionFlag 1=Available 2=InUse
    4=B/W 8=Node 10=SoftPreempt):
          10.0.1.18 10.0.1.30
  Standby    transit-r1      State: Up
    SmartOptimizeTimer: 180
    Received RRO (ProtectionFlag 1=Available 2=InUse
    4=B/W 8=Node 10=SoftPreempt):
          10.0.1.22 10.0.1.26
Total 1 displayed, Up 1, Down 0
```

Testing confirms that life is good. The deployment of hot standby secondary LSPs with fast reroute enabled means the administrators can balance traffic across the topology while maintaining high availability.

Link and node-link protection. Fast reroute is configured on a per-LSP basis and as such each fast reroute LSP protects only one primary LSP, a one-to-one scheme. While fast reroute does work well, in very large-scale networks it is obviously suboptimal.

Link and node-link protection are alternatives to fast reroute that can protect multiple LSPs by using only a single backup LSP. As its name implies, link protection can provide redundancy for links. Node-link protection can provide redundancy for nodes and links. Both types of protection are standards-based and designed to interoperate with other vendors' equipment.

In this example, which is based on Figure 18-7, we will remove the fast reroute statements and enable `node-link-protection` on the `to-r3` LSP:

```
[edit protocols mpls]
lab@r2# show
label-switched-path to-r3 {
    to 10.0.0.3;
    node-link-protection;
    }
interface all;
```

Node-link protection must also be enabled under `protocols rsvp` on all interfaces which the LSP will transit:

```
[edit protocols rsvp]
lab@r2# show
interface all {
    link-protection;
}
```

 Link and node-link protection require Constrained Shortest Path First (CSPF) to be enabled within the MPLS domain to calculate the redundant path. When enabling CSPF in an Open Shortest Path First (OSPF) domain, recall that `traffic-engineering` must also be enabled to allow CSPF to build the traffic engineering database (TED). The highlighted lines in the following output are symptoms of failure to enable traffic engineering, in this case on r2:

```
[edit]
lab@r2# run show mpls lsp extensive
Ingress LSP: 1 sessions

10.0.0.3
  From: 10.0.0.2, State: Dn, ActiveRoute: 0, LSPname: to-r3
  ActivePath: (none)
  Node/Link protection desired
  LoadBalance: Random
  Encoding type: Packet, Switching type: Packet, GPID: IPv4
  Primary                State: Dn
    SmartOptimizeTimer: 180
```

```
             Will be enqueued for recomputation in 26 second(s).
        1 May 21 12:32:22.651 CSPF: could not determine self[7 times]
           Created: Thu May 21 12:29:25 2009
        Total 1 displayed, Up 0, Down 1
```

A quick show mpls lsp on r2 confirms that the LSP to r3 is up. Notice that additional
bypass LSPs have been automatically calculated by CSPF and signaled by RSVP to
protect the path:

```
[edit]
lab@r2# run show mpls lsp
Ingress LSP: 1 sessions
To              From      State Rt ActivePath      P     LSPname
10.0.0.3        10.0.0.2  Up    0                  *     to-r3
Total 1 displayed, Up 1, Down 0


Egress LSP: 2 sessions
To              From      State  Rt Style Labelin Labelout LSPname
10.0.0.2        10.0.0.3  Up     0  1 SE    3        - to-r2
10.0.0.2        10.0.0.4  Up     0  1 SE    3        - Bypass->10.0.1.30
Total 2 displayed, Up 2, Down 0


Transit LSP: 1 sessions
To              From      State  Rt Style Labelin Labelout LSPname
10.0.0.3        10.0.0.4  Up     0  1 SE  299776   299792 Bypass->10.0.1.17
Total 1 displayed, Up 1, Down 0
```

Traffic Engineering Case Study

At the beginning of this section, we explained that MPLS is itself a scalability mechanism, in that it enables *traffic engineering*. Traffic engineering is the act of creating and
assigning traffic flows to deterministic paths through the network that may be contrary
to the IGP-dictated "shortest path." This allows the administrator to control link utilization and traffic patterns regardless of the size of the network.

Figure 18-8 shows a slightly more complex topology than in the previous example to
further demonstrate how to use MPLS to protect availability and scale a network.

In this example, user communities on r4 and r5 have availability-related service agreements within AS 64512. AS 64512 also has bandwidth-related SLAs with peer ASs. By
using MPLS to engineer the user community traffic across the less desirable Fast Ethernet and slower OC-3 ATM links, the network is able to meet both requirements while
optimizing use of available bandwidth.

For both the AS-internal and AS-external customers, availability is protected by allowing traffic to fail over to alternate paths as needed. The higher-bandwidth links are used
for AS-external traffic and the lower-bandwidth links are reserved for traffic with source
and destination addresses internal to the AS.

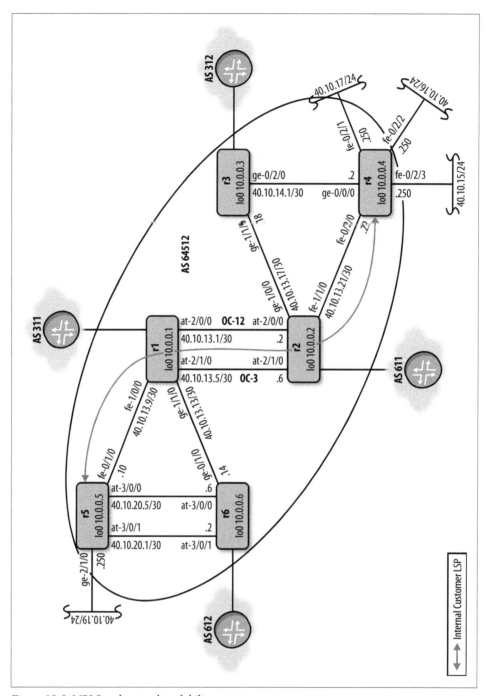

Figure 18-8. MPLS and network scalability

CHAPTER 19

Choosing, Migrating, and Merging Interior Gateway Protocols

Interior Gateway Protocols (IGPs) provide the foundation of traffic flow and control inside an Autonomous System (AS). This chapter discusses the two most commonly used industry-standard IGPs: Open Shortest Path First (OSPF) and Intermediate System to Intermediate System (IS-IS). The first section examines the advantages and disadvantages of each protocol, and also looks at how each one supports high availability. The next section examines what is involved in migrating from one of these IGPs to the other. The chapter finishes with considerations for merging networks running the same IGP.

Choosing Between IS-IS and OSPF

OSPF and IS-IS are two robust and scalable link-state protocols that are used in many networks throughout the Internet. They are based on industry standards, meaning they are available and interoperable with all major vendors' routing equipment. These protocols are also arguably among the earliest forms of high availability. Sure, dynamic routing protocols were designed to ease the administrative burden as networks grow, but the real power is in their ability to dynamically detect an issue in a network and to recover from that issue by rerouting traffic along an alternate path. This is high availability in action!

Since OSPF and IS-IS were first implemented in commercial routers, back in the early 1990s, there has been a great deal of debate over which protocol is superior. Today, many of each protocol's unique features have been implemented by the other, making both protocols very similar in feature set and functionality. That being said, there are still aspects of each that can be considered advantageous or disadvantageous, depending on the situation and environment.

OSPF

OSPF was developed by the Internet Engineering Task Force (IETF) as a reliable routing protocol that runs directly on IP. It was designed specifically with IP networks in mind, and has found a home largely in medium-size to large enterprise networks, although it is used by several service providers as well.

JUNOS Software supports the full range of OSPF features you would expect to find in high-caliber networking devices. JUNOS Software also supports a wide range of OSPF's high availability features. And like any protocol, OSPF has its advantages and disadvantages.

OSPF Fundamentals

This book assumes you have good knowledge of routing and routing protocols. Should you want or need more information on OSPF fundamentals, you can find a wide range of material on the Internet. You can also learn more about the protocol and its implementation on JUNOS devices by attending Juniper Networks training courses.

For more details on Juniper Networks training, see *http://www.juniper.net/training*.

Advantages

First and foremost, OSPF is purpose-built for IP networks. Having been designed by the IETF, OSPF was built for IP networks, by IP networking specialists. It therefore tends to be quite intuitive.

OSPF supports virtual links. Architecturally, OSPF requires that there be a centralized backbone (usually Area 0) and that all nonbackbone areas be directly connected to it. In a case where that's simply not possible, the workaround is virtual links. Virtual links make it possible to join a nonbackbone area across another nonbackbone area to the backbone:

```
[edit]
lab@r1# set protocols ospf area 0 virtual-link ?
Possible completions:
neighbor-id Router ID of a virtual neighbor
transit-area  Transit area in common with virtual neighbor
```

This feature can be particularly handy in situations where two networks are merging and a method is needed to join the networks together when direct physical connectivity is not possible.

> In practice, virtual links are a temporary solution to a larger design issue. Virtual links should not be a long-term solution in an OSPF-designed network.

Another great advantage that simplifies OSPF is its native ability to summarize routes. Unlike IS-IS, OSPF supports the summarization of contiguous routes at area borders using the area-range statement:

```
lab@r1# set protocols ospf area 1 area-range 172.16/16 ?
Possible completions:
<[Enter]>              Execute this command
+ apply-groups         Groups from which to inherit configuration data
+ apply-groups-except  Don't inherit configuration data from these groups
  exact                Enforce exact match for advertisement of this area range
  override-metric      Override the dynamic metric for this area-range
  restrict             Restrict advertisement of this area range
```

With built-in summarization capabilities, no other IGP routing policy configuration is required.

And finally, perhaps OSPF's greatest advantage is that it is simply a more familiar protocol. Networking folks tend to like to work with what they know or can easily learn, and OSPF is more widely deployed and documented than IS-IS.

Disadvantages

OSPF is an excellent routing protocol, but isn't without its flaws and disadvantages.

One disadvantage, at least compared to IS-IS, is that OSPF runs directly on IP (using protocol number 89). As an IP-based protocol, OSPF is subject to malicious attacks, such as IP spoofing or denial-of-service (DoS) attacks.

Another characteristic of OSPF that can be cumbersome is its fairly strict adjacency-forming requirements. While IS-IS has quite relaxed requirements for neighbors to form adjacencies (most parameters *don't* have to match), OSPF requires several parameters to match before neighbors can acknowledge each other's existence. This situation can be a positive in the sense that it ensures that configuration parameters match properly; IS-IS could form an adjacency despite the mismatch of a parameter that, practically speaking, should match. However, the OSPF matching requirement can be a negative in the sense that several parameters must match exactly to allow the routers to share information with one another. For example, in troubleshooting OSPF connectivity between two routers, the correct interfaces could be configured, the subnet mask could be accurate, the Hello timers could match, and the OSPF options could be identical, and yet if the routers' Dead timers are mismatched by one second, the routers can never form an adjacency.

 In practice, OSPF works quite smoothly, and enabling the protocol using its default settings should allow neighboring routers to communicate just fine.

OSPF also has some shortcomings regarding authentication. OSPF supports both simple and MD5-based authentication, with MD5 being a good choice for security purposes. However, where IS-IS supports authentication for all packet types, OSPF authenticates only Hello packets. This means that all other OSPF packet types, such as link-state updates, are not authenticated, thus creating a security exposure.

And finally, OSPF as a protocol is not IPv6-ready. While IS-IS supports IPv6 as readily as IPv4, OSPF (technically, OSPFv2) was built specifically for networks running IPv4, and it is this purpose-built design that makes it incompatible with IPv6.

> To support IPv6 networks, the IETF has developed a new version of the OSPF protocol, OSPFv3.

High availability features for OSPF in JUNOS Software

OSPF provides a number of features that support high availability, among them link and node failure detection, and packet authentication.

Link and node failure detection. A basic feature of OSPF is, of course, its ability to detect link and node failures and reroute around the problem. However, the default timer settings may not be sufficient to support a high availability environment. By default, an OSPF neighbor is declared *down* after 40 seconds (for broadcast networks), but this can be an eternity if the link is a major revenue-generating connection. You can reduce the timers to very low values if desired.

> Use caution when lowering OSPF timers; just because you can configure extremely low values doesn't mean you should. While the low timer settings for IGPs on JUNOS devices provide the option to use these protocols for high availability purposes, in practice routing protocols are no longer used as a primary means of quick failure detection and recovery. This is true to such an extent that it is now not generally recommended to use extremely low timers at all. These days, purpose-built protocols such as Bidirectional Forwarding Detection (BFD) virtually eliminate the need for IGPs to participate in quick failure detection.

Authenticating packets. Authentication plays an important role in high availability: security in a network can only be a good thing. Authentication of OSPF Hello packets ensures that only legitimate routers are on the network and eliminates the possibility of a "rogue" router forming an adjacency with a neighboring router and causing trouble.

Designated routers. OSPF provides high availability support for designated routers (DRs). Each broadcast network running OSPF has a DR, a central point of contact on the subnet to reduce communication traffic between neighboring routers. As part of the DR election process, a backup designated router (BDR) is also elected. Both the DR and the BDR form adjacencies with all routers on the broadcast network, with the BDR sitting quietly in the background. The DR and BDR are shown in the detailed output for OSPF neighbors:

```
[edit]
lab@r1> show ospf neighbor detail
Address         Interface    State    ID              Pri  Dead
10.0.1.2        fe-0/0/2.0   Full     192.168.2.2     128  35
Area 0.0.0.0, opt 0x42, DR 10.0.1.2, BDR 10.0.1.1
  Up 4d 10:45:53, adjacent 4d 10:45:13
```

If the DR goes down, the BDR is in the perfect position to take over the duties and function of the DR.

Graceful Restart. Graceful Restart (GR) is a newer feature in JUNOS Software, allowing a router to restart without affecting the routing topology. The separation of the routing and forwarding planes in Juniper Networks routers allows a routing engine (RE) restart while the forwarding plane continues to forward traffic. (See Chapters 4 and 5 for a complete overview of Graceful Restart.) In practice, a restarting router sends a Grace-LSA (a type 9 link-state advertisement or LSA) to its neighbors, who then ignore that the router is *down* for a given period of time (the grace period). When the RE restarts, the router again forms an adjacency with its neighbors, and the rest of the network is none the wiser. You can configure Graceful Restart globally or just for OSPF:

```
[edit]
lab@r1# show protocols ospf graceful-restart ?
Possible completions:
<[Enter]>             Execute this command
+ apply-groups        Groups from which to inherit configuration data
+ apply-groups-except Don't inherit configuration data from these groups
  disable             Disable OSPF graceful restart capability
  helper-disable      Disable graceful restart helper capability
  notify-duration     Time to send all max-aged grace LSAs (1..3600 seconds)
  restart-duration    Time for all neighbors to become full (1..3600 seconds)
```

Non-Stop Active Routing. Non-Stop Active Routing (NSR) is another newer feature in JUNOS Software that takes the concept of GR to the next level, providing support for an RE restart without affecting the topology *and* without requiring neighboring "helper routers" to assist in preserving the stability of the network.

With a backup RE installed, the router can run routing protocols as normal, and the system maintains neighbor and state information on both REs. This provides excellent high availability support. If the master RE goes down, the backup RE immediately takes over, with routing adjacencies intact, and neighboring routers have no awareness that anything has happened.

You configure NSR globally, and it is extremely easy to set up:

```
[edit]
lab@r1# show routing-options
nonstop-routing;
```

NSR requires that you also enable Graceful Routing Engine Switchover (GRES) and that you configure the router to synchronize all configuration changes between REs:

```
[edit]
lab@r1# show chassis redundancy
graceful-switchover;

[edit]
lab@r1# show system
commit synchronize;
```

If your JUNOS devices have dual REs and your network cannot tolerate even a few seconds of downtime, NSR provides a *huge* benefit.

Overload. Overload, an IS-IS feature that has been added to OSPF, deflects transit traffic away from a router, forcing it to use a different path (unless no other path is available). Consider the network shown in Figure 19-1. Traffic is following normal, shortest-path routing through the r2 router.

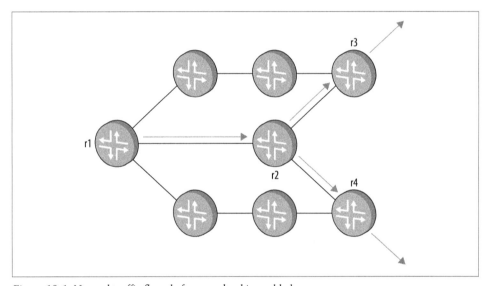

Figure 19-1. Normal traffic flow, before overload is enabled

Now imagine that you want to perform a task on r2 that impacts traffic, such as restarting the routing daemon. You have two choices: either perform the task and let the routing protocols discover the failure in their own time, or preemptively force traffic to use another path, as shown in Figure 19-2.

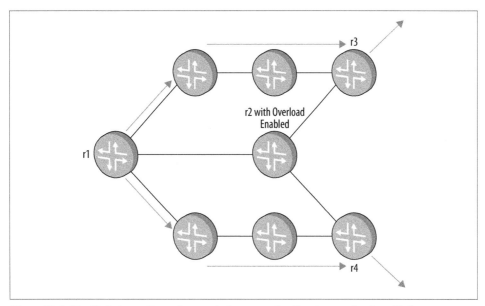

Figure 19-2. Traffic being redirected around r2 as a result of having overload enabled

Using the overload setting does not completely avoid impacting the network, because the process involves Shortest Path First (SPF) recalculations and sending routing updates. However, it's still a more reliable and desirable method than simply putting the router offline and relying on Hello messages to discover the outage and recover from it.

Prefix limits. When you use routing policy, configuration errors are always a possibility. If, for example, a router that is connected to the Internet and receiving a full Border Gateway Protocol (BGP) feed were to redistribute all 230,000 or so routes into OSPF, the router would not be happy! Such redistribution would place a very heavy load on the router, to the point that smaller devices might not function properly. Configuring prefix limits provides a safety mechanism for this situation:

```
[edit]
lab@r1# show protocols ospf
prefix-export-limit 750;
```

Once the prefix limit is configured, the router purges the external prefixes and goes into overload state when that limit is reached. This state ensures that the router is not overwhelmed as it attempts to process more routing information than it can handle.

 It is generally *not* a good practice to redistribute a full BGP table into a network's IGP!

Bidirectional Forwarding Detection. BFD is another relatively new feature that takes significant steps toward achieving high availability. BFD is not directly part of OSPF; rather, it supports routing protocols by providing *liveness detection*. For example, two routers using BFD can detect a failure between them in less than 0.5 seconds, as shown here:

```
[edit]
lab@r1# show protocols ospf
area 0.0.0.0 {
    interface fe-0/0/2.0 {
        bfd-liveness-detection {
            minimum-interval 150;
            multiplier 3;
```

 Use caution when setting BFD timers. BFD is designed for reliable network links and *flapping* can result from even slight delay or loss. See Chapter 14 for more information on BFD.

IS-IS

IS-IS was developed by the International Organization for Standardization (ISO) as the routing protocol for the Connectionless Network Protocol (CLNP) suite, which originally was a competitor to the TCP/IP protocol suite and IP routing protocols. IS-IS was adapted to support IP networks when it became clear that IP would become the standard protocol of the Internet. This new *integrated* IS-IS protocol has now found a home in service provider networks (although there are instances of IS-IS being used in enterprise networks as well).

JUNOS Software supports the full range of IS-IS standards and features. It also supports many high availability features, which we cover later in this chapter. And just like OSPF, IS-IS has its advantages and disadvantages.

IS-IS Fundamentals

This book assumes you have good knowledge of routing and routing protocols. Should you want or need more information on IS-IS fundamentals, you can find a wide range of material on the Internet. You can also learn more about the protocol and its implementation on JUNOS devices by attending Juniper Networks training courses.

For more details on Juniper Networks training, see *http://www.juniper.net/training*.

Advantages

As mentioned earlier, both OSPF and IS-IS have grown to be very similar. However, each still has a set of unique features. If your network uses IS-IS you are probably aware that it has excellent scaling capabilities. But there's more. IS-IS has a deep set of capabilities that are worth exploring.

First off, IS-IS is *not* an IP-based protocol, so it is not affected by issues that affect other routing protocols. For example, you can misconfigure the IP addressing of two neighboring interfaces in a way that puts them on different subnets, but IS-IS doesn't care. As long as you include the interfaces in the IS-IS configuration, the routers can form an adjacency.

A side benefit of IS-IS's non-IP roots is that it is not subject to most malicious attacks, because hackers generally attack networks at the IP level and above.

Another advantage of IS-IS is its looser adjacency-forming requirements. While OSPF requires certain parameters, such as the Hello timer, to match for neighboring routers to form an adjacency, IS-IS has much more flexibility in this regard, specifically that parameters generally don't need to match. For example, imagine a broadcast network such as an Ethernet local area network (LAN). Among the parameters that must match between routers is the subnet mask, right? Wrong! Because IS-IS is not IP-based, matching subnet masks (a requirement for *OSPF* broadcast networks) are irrelevant. IS-IS doesn't care about the IP configuration at all.

Having the freedom to mismatch Hello timers provides nice flexibility in cases where certain routers should detect a failure more quickly. This can also be helpful when changing Hello timers in general, because they can be changed independently of a neighbor, a luxury not offered by OSPF.

IS-IS does not require a "backbone." OSPF architecturally requires that the routes of all areas feed into a centralized backbone (usually Area 0) before being distributed to the rest of the network. Not so for IS-IS. While IS-IS does require all areas to be linked together, it doesn't require a centralized backbone at all. In certain network environments, this can be a huge advantage. For example, imagine a network in which the physical layout doesn't lend itself naturally to a centralized backbone. Instead, there are "islands" of concentrated connectivity, perhaps with lower-speed links joining the islands. In this case, a more distributed architecture that links the areas together would be ideal.

As shown in Figure 19-3, all Level 1 (L1) routers with the same area ID belong to an area. L1 routers feed their routing information to the nearest Level 2 (L2) router, in this case an L1/L2 router. L2 routers share routing information with other L2 routers, providing complete reachability across the entire routing domain—without the use of a centralized backbone.

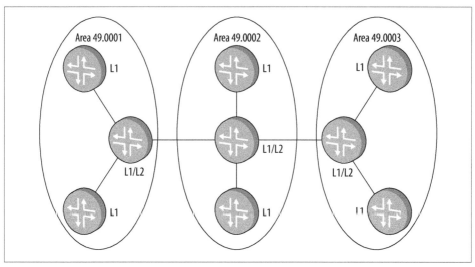

Figure 19-3. An IS-IS network with no centralized backbone

An IS-IS feature that is great for high availability, particularly during area migration or redesign, is the ability to configure a router with multiple area IDs. L1 routers form adjacencies if they are in the same area, as shown in Figure 19-4.

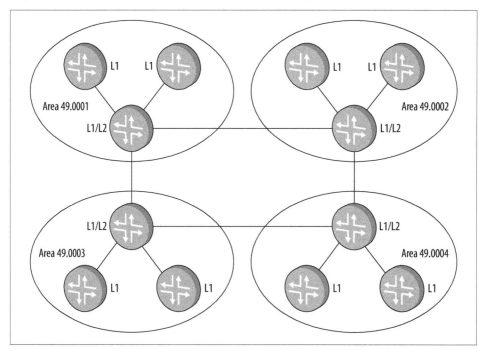

Figure 19-4. IS-IS network with L1 areas and an L2 backbone

In cases where a router is in transition or is being migrated from one area to another, changing the area ID could disrupt the stability of the network. As shown in Figure 19-5, IS-IS supports the configuration of multiple area IDs on a router, which makes transitions and migrations very easy.

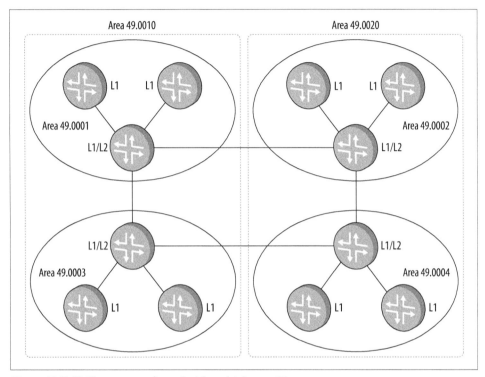

Figure 19-5. IS-IS routers configured with multiple area IDs

A router with an existing area ID can be configured with a second ID, with no requirement or time restriction on synchronizing with neighboring routers. Once the neighboring routers have been configured with the new area ID, and all routers effectively belong in multiple areas simultaneously, the original ID can be removed. Figure 19-6 shows the result of the transition.

Another IS-IS advantage for your high availability network is its large Hello timer range. In situations where Hello traffic is a drain on network resources, such as across a low-speed remote access link or when a router is working at maximum capacity, one solution is to reduce the frequency of the Hellos. IS-IS supports this to the extreme, allowing Hellos to be sent as little as once every 5.5 hours. Now that's granular control!

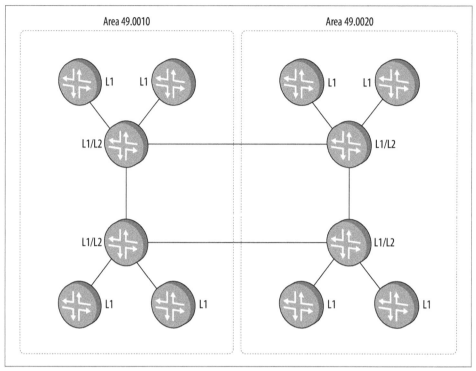

Figure 19-6. IS-IS network after transition

IS-IS has several flexible authentication options that are ideal for environments requiring more than basic authentication between network devices. All IS-IS packets can be sent securely to neighboring routers (OSPF supports only Hello packet authentication), with the additional capability to disable authentication of certain packet types as desired:

```
[edit]
lab@r1# set protocols isis level 1 ?
Possible completions:
+ apply-groups          Groups from which to inherit configuration data
+ apply-groups-except   Don't inherit configuration data from these groups
  authentication-key    Authentication key (password)
  authentication-type   Authentication type
  disable               Disable IS-IS on this level
  external-preference   Preference of external routes
  no-csnp-authentication  Disable authentication for CSN packets
  no-hello-authentication Disable authentication for hello packets
  no-psnp-authentication  Disable authentication for PSN packets
  preference            Preference of internal routes
  prefix-export-limit   Maximum number of external prefixes that
    can be exported
  wide-metrics-only     Generate wide metrics only
```

Furthermore, the router can disregard authentication altogether:

```
[edit]
lab@r1# set protocols isis no-?
Possible completions:
  no-adjacency-holddown     Disable adjacency hold down
  no-authentication-check   Disable authentication checking
  no-ipv4-routing           Disable IPv4 routing
  no-ipv6-routing           Disable IPv6 routing
```

Disabling authentication checking can be helpful when migrating to new authentication parameters, or when bringing a new router online that is configured to run IS-IS but does not have authentication enabled.

And finally, in support of the general evolution of IP networks, IS-IS is IPv6-ready. The protocol requires no special modifications to support IPv6 because it carries IPv6 addressing and routing information alongside IPv4 information. So, as you begin to implement IPv6, IS-IS is already in place and ready to support your rollout.

Disadvantages

Like OSPF, IS-IS is an excellent routing protocol, but it isn't without flaws. For starters, IS-IS isn't "made for IP." Instead, IS-IS has been *adapted* to support IP networks. This fact makes the protocol a bit nonintuitive to use sometimes. For example, you could have the router's interfaces and IS-IS configured correctly, but routing won't work properly until you assign an ISO address to the router.

Another disadvantage for some administrators is the fact that IS-IS has no native summarization ability. OSPF supports the summarization of contiguous routes at area borders, but IS-IS has no such built-in ability. You must completely set up IS-IS summarization using routing policy.

> Interestingly, some administrators actually *prefer* routing policy for route summarization. Route control and redistribution is done for most routing protocols using policy, so having the IGP use policy as well can make things neat and tidy, as well as easy to find, in the policy section of the configuration.

Finally, despite all of IS-IS's advantages, network administrators simply like to work with what they know or can easily learn, and OSPF is more widely deployed and documented than IS-IS.

High availability features for IS-IS in JUNOS Software

Much like OSPF, IS-IS provides a number of features that support high availability.

Link and node failure detection. One of IS-IS's basic features is its ability to detect link and node failures and reroute around the problem. And as with OSPF, the IS-IS default timer settings may not be sufficient to support a high availability environment: by default, a neighboring router is declared *down* after 27 seconds (9 seconds for Designated Intermediate Systems or DISs), but this can be far too long when the link is a high-capacity connection with a service-level agreement (SLA). You can reduce the timers to very low values if desired. In fact, you can technically set the Hello interval to an extremely low 1 second, which means Hello packets are sent every 333 milliseconds!

 Use caution when lowering IS-IS timers; just because you can configure extremely low values doesn't mean you should. While the low timer settings for IGPs on JUNOS devices provide the option to use these protocols for high availability purposes, in practice routing protocols are no longer used as a primary means of quick failure detection and recovery. This is true to such an extent that it is now not generally recommended to use extremely low timers at all. These days, purpose built protocols such as BFD virtually eliminate the need for IGPs to participate in quick failure detection.

Authenticating packets. Authentication plays a part in high availability from the standpoint that security in a network can have only a positive effect on availability. Authentication of IS-IS packets virtually eliminates any chance of downtime in the network due to a malicious attack at the routing protocol level.

Graceful Restart. JUNOS Software supports GR for IS-IS, allowing a router to restart without affecting the routing topology. The separation of the routing and forwarding planes in Juniper Networks routers allows an RE restart while the forwarding plane continues to forward traffic. (See Chapters 4 and 5 for detailed information about GR.) In practice, a restarting router sends a Restart TLV (type, length, value) to its neighbors, who then consider the router to still be *up* for a given period of time. When the RE restarts, the router again forms an adjacency with its neighbors, and the rest of the network is never aware that anything unusual happened. You can configure GR globally or just for IS-IS:

```
[edit]
lab@r1# show protocols isis graceful-restart ?
Possible completions:
<[Enter]>          Execute this command
  disable          Disable graceful restart
  helper-disable   Disable graceful restart helper capability
  restart-duration Maximum time for graceful restart to finish (seconds)
```

Non-Stop Active Routing. NSR uses redundant REs within a router chassis to provide support for an RE restart without affecting the topology. With a backup RE installed, the router maintains neighbor and state information on both REs. If the master RE goes down, the backup RE can immediately take over, making it appear to neighboring routers that nothing has happened.

NSR is not related to a specific protocol, and you configure it globally on the router:

```
[edit]
lab@r1# show routing-options
nonstop-routing;
```

You must also enable GRES and configure the router to synchronize all configuration changes between REs:

```
[edit]
lab@r1# show chassis redundancy
graceful-switchover;

[edit]
lab@r1# show system
commit synchronize;
```

If your JUNOS devices have dual REs, NSR is an absolute *must-have* to ensure minimal downtime.

Overload. The overload bit can be used to deflect transit traffic away from a router before performing a task that affects traffic. Consider the network shown in Figure 19-7. Traffic is following normal, shortest-path routing through r2.

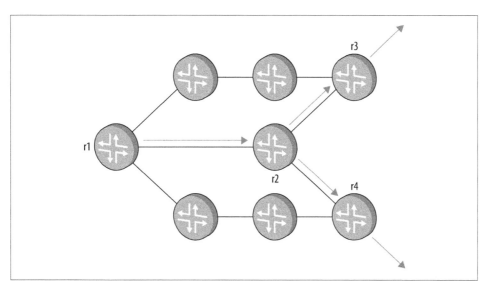

Figure 19-7. Normal traffic flow, before overload is enabled

Now imagine that you want to perform a task on r2 that impacts traffic, such as restarting the routing daemon. You have two choices: you can perform the task and let the routing protocols discover the failure in their own time, or you can preemptively force traffic to use another path, as shown in Figure 19-8.

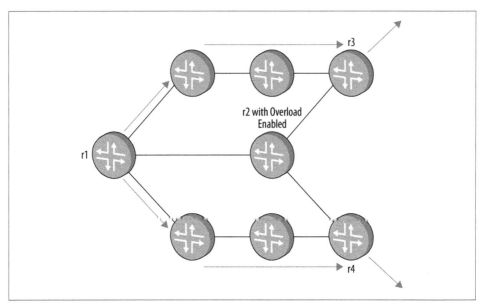

Figure 19-8. Traffic being redirected around r2 as a result of having overload enabled

To be clear, using the overload setting isn't completely impact-free—the process does involve SPF recalculations and sending routing updates. But it is an improvement over simply *downing* the router and letting the network discover that the topology has changed.

Prefix limits. Prefix limits provide a safety mechanism in case a large number of routes (such as a full BGP feed) are imported into IS-IS:

```
[edit]
lab@r1# show protocols isis
level 1 prefix-export-limit 500;
level 2 prefix-export-limit 750;
```

The increased load placed on some devices can slow them down, and even bring them to a halt. When the prefix limit is reached, the router stops transmitting the prefixes in IS-IS and goes into overload state (which is equivalent to setting the overload bit). This state relieves the router of the stress that has been placed on it and ensures that the router will not be brought down by a single action.

 It is generally *not* a good practice to redistribute a full BGP table into a network's IGP!

Bidirectional Forwarding Detection. BFD supports high availability by providing *liveness detection*. BFD is not part of the IS-IS protocol, but it can detect subsecond link failure between routers and inform IS-IS that the link should be considered *down*:

```
[edit]
lab@r1# show protocols isis interface fe-0/0/2.0
bfd-liveness-detection {
    minimum-interval 100;
    multiplier 4
```

In this example, if the router does not hear from its neighbor within 400 milliseconds, it notifies IS-IS that the link should be considered down.

 Use caution when setting BFD timers. BFD is designed for reliable network links and *flapping* can occur from even slight delay or loss. See Chapter 14 for more information on BFD.

Which Protocol Is "Better"?

It is very difficult to crown either the OSPF or IS-IS protocol as the *superior* protocol. They are both solid, robust, scalable protocols that have a deep set of features, and they have become so similar over time that it is truly hard to call one "better" than the other. That being said, here are some general guidelines and recommendations.

OSPF is well suited to situations where:

- An IP-based routing protocol is desired.
- A centralized backbone is desired or required.
- The operational staff is less experienced or not familiar with IS-IS.

IS-IS is well suited to situations where:

- Maximum granularity and control is required.
- A centralized backbone is not required.
- The operational staff is already familiar with IS-IS's terminology, concepts, and functionality.

A final thought

After all the features are compared and the advantages analyzed, the best answer may be the simplest one: OSPF is just more "available." It isn't superior to IS-IS, but it is more available as a standard feature on networking equipment. OSPF is also more widely deployed, making it implicitly more interoperable with other vendors' equipment. In situations where companies are merging, it's a good bet that OSPF is in use in one or both of the networks. And finally, there is more information, support, and knowledge available around OSPF, making it more user-friendly.

Migrating from One IGP to Another

Networks develop and grow over time. Subnets are split up, more equipment and new routes are added, and router configurations become more complex. Changing the IGP of an active network is nothing short of a monumental task—and has the potential to be a nightmare when it comes to preserving high availability.

Five general steps are involved in migrating to another IGP:

1. *Plan for the migration.* Arguably the most important step, proper planning can make or break the entire migration.

2. *Add the new protocol to the network.* The new protocol is added (as the less preferred protocol), mirroring the existing one.

3. *Make the new protocol "preferred."* Once the new protocol is in place it can be made the preferred protocol, effectively taking over from the original protocol.

4. *Verify the success of the migration.* When the new protocol is active it is essential to check the results and look for any problems or issues.

5. *Remove the original protocol.* After the new protocol is in a stable state in the network, the original protocol can be removed.

Migrating from OSPF to IS-IS

Before any migration takes place, it is important to have a good sense of what your current network looks like. In fact, documenting the details of the entire network might be the most important step in the migration!

This section uses the following example to help illustrate the steps of a successful migration:

```
[edit]
lab@r1> show route

inet.0: 9 destinations, 9 routes (9 active, 0 holddown, 0 hidden)
+ = Active Route, - = Last Active, * = Both

10.0.1.0/24        *[Direct/0] 23:46:09
                    > via fe-0/0/2.0
10.0.1.1/32        *[Local/0] 23:46:09
                      Local via fe-0/0/2.0
10.210.0.0/27      *[Direct/0] 2d 10:27:10
                    > via fxp0.0
10.210.0.1/32      *[Local/0] 2d 10:27:11
                      Local via fxp0.0
172.16.1.0/24      *[OSPF/150] 23:43:04, metric 0, tag 0
                    > to 10.0.1.2 via fe-0/0/2.0
172.16.2.0/24      *[OSPF/150] 23:43:04, metric 0, tag 0
                    > to 10.0.1.2 via fe-0/0/2.0
192.168.1.1/32     *[Direct/0] 23:48:55
                    > via lo0.0
```

```
192.168.2.2/32      *[OSPF/10] 23:43:04, metric 1
                    > to 10.0.1.2 via fe-0/0/2.0
224.0.0.5/32        *[OSPF/10] 2d 10:27:11, metric 1
                    MultiRecv
```

This "before" view of the network is from the perspective of r1. In this example, r1 is receiving three routes from its neighbor. Two of them (172.16.1.0/24 and 172.16.2.0/24) are static routes that are being redistributed into OSPF as external routes. The third route (192.168.2.2/32) is an OSPF internal route and happens to be the neighbor's loopback address. With this view of the network in mind, it's time to move on to the first migration step.

Step 1: Plan for the migration

When migrating from one IGP to another, the primary planning step is to consider the design of the existing network and determine the best way to implement that design within the capabilities of the new protocol.

There are several items to consider when moving from OSPF to IS-IS:

Area and backbone design
> IS-IS can simply match the centralized OSPF backbone design, or you can take advantage of the fact that IS-IS doesn't require that its backbone be centralized.

> IS-IS as a protocol scales somewhat better than OSPF. In practice, IS-IS networks often don't use areas at all and simply run as flat L2 networks.

Authentication
> If authentication is in place within OSPF, you can easily mirror it in IS-IS. If authentication is not in place, this would be a good time to add it!

Metrics
> There are two options when migrating metrics to IS-IS:
>
> 1. Set the metrics manually, per interface, using the existing OSPF metrics as reference.
> 2. Set the metrics dynamically. IS-IS (borrowing a feature from OSPF) can use a reference bandwidth and dynamically set the cost of each interface based on link speed.

> In practice, use the method that parallels the current OSPF network. Note that when using manually configured metrics, it is common to scale up the values (e.g., 50 becomes 500) because of IS-IS's larger metric range.

Routing policy

You should mirror any redistribution of routes into OSPF in IS-IS. Some policies may be reusable, while others, such as interarea routes summarized by OSPF itself, require new policies that can be used by IS-IS.

Step 2: Add IS-IS to the network

When the planning step is complete, you can begin adding IS-IS to the network. Configure the protocol, router by router, based on the design considerations determined in the preceding section. If the design is sound, configuration should be fairly straightforward; with a few commands, IS-IS will be in place on the routers.

Start by adding the ISO family under the desired transit interfaces, as well as the NET under the loopback interface:

```
[edit]
lab@r1# show interfaces
fe-0/0/2 {
    unit 0 {
        family inet {
            address 10.0.1.1/24;
        }
        family iso;
    }
}
lo0 {
    unit 0 {
        family inet {
            address 192.168.1.1/32;
        }
        family iso {
            address 49.0001.1921.6800.1001.00;
        }
    }
}
```

Then enable IS-IS and add the appropriate interfaces under the protocol:

```
[edit]
lab@r1# show protocols
isis {
    interface fe-0/0/2.0;
    interface lo0.0;
}
```

Add authentication as desired:

```
[edit]
lab@r1# show protocols isis
level 1 {
    authentication-key "$9$XJlxds2gJUDksYfT3nCA"; ## SECRET-DATA
    authentication-type md5; ## SECRET-DATA
}
level 2 {
    authentication-key "$9$AXPhtORhclvMXREdb2gJZ"; ## SECRET-DATA
```

```
    authentication-type md5; ## SECRET-DATA
}
interface fe-0/0/2.0;
interface lo0.0;
```

In this example, OSPF is using metrics based on link bandwidth. To match this in IS-IS, use the `reference-bandwidth` statement:

```
[edit]
lab@HongKong# show protocols isis
reference-bandwidth 100m;
level 1 {
    authentication-key "$9$XJlxds2gJUDksYfT3nCA"; ## SECRET-DATA
    authentication-type md5; ## SECRET-DATA
}
level 2 {
    authentication-key "$9$AXPhtORhclvMXREdb2gJZ"; ## SECRET-DATA
    authentication-type md5; ## SECRET-DATA
}
interface fe-0/0/2.0;
interface lo0.0;
```

In addition, use `wide-metrics-only` to allow the broadest possible metric-setting capabilities:

```
[edit]
lab@r1# set protocols isis level 1 wide-metrics-only
```

```
[edit]
lab@r1# set protocols isis level 2 wide-metrics-only
```

The neighboring router, r2, is currently using a routing policy to redistribute two static routes into OSPF. You can easily replicate this in IS-IS by reusing the same policy statement:

```
[edit]
lab@r2# show policy-options
policy-statement static-to-IGP {
    term 1 {
        from protocol static;
        then accept;
    }
}
```

It now simply needs to be applied to IS-IS:

```
[edit]
lab@r2# set protocols isis export static-to-IGP
```

One key detail that makes adding IS-IS a nonimpacting step in terms of high availability is its protocol preference. The preference values for IS-IS are higher (i.e., less preferred) than OSPF; therefore, even though IS-IS is configured and running on the routers, it is not the preferred protocol in the network, as shown here:

```
[edit]
lab@r1> show route
```

```
inet.0: 9 destinations, 12 routes (9 active, 0 holddown, 0 hidden)
+ = Active Route, - = Last Active, * = Both

10.0.1.0/24        *[Direct/0] 1d 00:47:49
                    > via fe-0/0/2.0
10.0.1.1/32        *[Local/0] 1d 00:47:49
                      Local via fe-0/0/2.0
10.210.0.0/27      *[Direct/0] 2d 11:28:50
                    > via fxp0.0
10.210.0.1/32      *[Local/0] 2d 11:28:51
                      Local via fxp0.0
172.16.1.0/24      *[OSPF/150] 1d 00:44:44, metric 0, tag 0
                    > to 10.0.1.2 via fe-0/0/2.0
                     [IS-IS/165] 00:00:12, metric 1
                    > to 10.0.1.2 via fe-0/0/2.0
172.16.2.0/24      *[OSPF/150] 1d 00:44:44, metric 0, tag 0
                    > to 10.0.1.2 via fe-0/0/2.0
                     [IS-IS/165] 00:00:12, metric 1
                    > to 10.0.1.2 via fe-0/0/2.0
192.168.1.1/32     *[Direct/0] 1d 00:50:35
                    > via lo0.0
192.168.2.2/32     *[OSPF/10] 1d 00:44:44, metric 1
                    > to 10.0.1.2 via fe-0/0/2.0
                     [IS-IS/18] 00:00:12, metric 1
                    > to 10.0.1.2 via fe-0/0/2.0
224.0.0.5/32       *[OSPF/10] 2d 11:28:51, metric 1
                      MultiRecv
```

Notice how IS-IS is now activated and running in parallel with OSPF. However, IS-IS's protocol preference ensures that it doesn't take over as the primary protocol. The active routes are still provided by OSPF at this point.

Before moving to the next stage, take some time to ensure that IS-IS is working properly *and* advertising the same routes as OSPF. Ensure that both internal and external routes are being advertised properly through the network by comparing the OSPF-specific and IS-IS-specific entries in the routing table:

```
[edit]
lab@r1> show route table inet.0 protocol ospf

inet.0: 9 destinations, 12 routes (9 active, 0 holddown, 0 hidden)
+ = Active Route, - = Last Active, * = Both

172.16.1.0/24      *[OSPF/150] 1d 00:52:44, metric 0, tag 0
                    > to 10.0.1.2 via fe-0/0/2.0
172.16.2.0/24      *[OSPF/150] 1d 00:52:44, metric 0, tag 0
                    > to 10.0.1.2 via fe-0/0/2.0
192.168.2.2/32     *[OSPF/10] 1d 00:52:44, metric 1
                    > to 10.0.1.2 via fe-0/0/2.0
224.0.0.5/32       *[OSPF/10] 2d 11:36:51, metric 1
                      MultiRecv
[edit]
lab@r1> show route table inet.0 protocol isis
```

```
inet.0: 9 destinations, 12 routes (9 active, 0 holddown, 0 hidden)
+ = Active Route, - = Last Active, * = Both

172.16.1.0/24        [IS-IS/165] 00:08:16, metric 1
                     > to 10.0.1.2 via fe-0/0/2.0
172.16.2.0/24        [IS-IS/165] 00:08:16, metric 1
                     > to 10.0.1.2 via fe-0/0/2.0
192.168.2.2/32       [IS-IS/18] 00:08:16, metric 1
                     > to 10.0.1.2 via fe-0/0/2.0
```

 The 224.0.0.5/32 entry is simply the OSPF protocol itself.

If you see any discrepancy between the OSPF and IS-IS advertisements, something isn't properly configured in IS-IS.

Step 3: Make IS-IS the "preferred" IGP

When IS-IS is properly mirroring OSPF, it is time to make IS-IS the preferred routing protocol in the network. You can achieve this in one of two ways: lower the preference of IS-IS or increase the preference of OSPF. In general, it is preferable to leave the new protocol at its default settings (to minimize complexity, should you need to manage protocol preferences again in the future). So, in this case it makes more sense to increase the preference value of OSPF routes to make them less preferred than IS-IS routes:

```
[edit]
lab@HongKong# show protocols ospf
preference 168;
external-preference 169;
```

Once this change is committed, check the routing table to confirm that IS-IS is now the preferred protocol:

```
[edit]
lab@r1> show route

inet.0: 9 destinations, 12 routes (9 active, 0 holddown, 0 hidden)
+ = Active Route, - = Last Active, * = Both

10.0.1.0/24          *[Direct/0] 1d 01:05:54
                     > via fe-0/0/2.0
10.0.1.1/32          *[Local/0] 1d 01:05:54
                       Local via fe-0/0/2.0
10.210.0.0/27        *[Direct/0] 2d 11:46:55
                     > via fxp0.0
10.210.0.1/32        *[Local/0] 2d 11:46:56
                       Local via fxp0.0
172.16.1.0/24        *[IS-IS/165] 00:18:17, metric 1
                     > to 10.0.1.2 via fe-0/0/2.0
                      [OSPF/169] 00:00:05, metric 0, tag 0
```

```
                        > to 10.0.1.2 via fe-0/0/2.0
172.16.2.0/24           *[IS-IS/165] 00:18:17, metric 1
                        > to 10.0.1.2 via fe-0/0/2.0
                        [OSPF/169] 00:00:05, metric 0, tag 0
                        > to 10.0.1.2 via fe-0/0/2.0
192.168.1.1/32          *[Direct/0] 1d 01:08:40
                        > via lo0.0
192.168.2.2/32          *[IS-IS/18] 00:18:17, metric 1
                        > to 10.0.1.2 via fe-0/0/2.0
                        [OSPF/168] 00:00:05, metric 1
                        > to 10.0.1.2 via fe-0/0/2.0
224.0.0.5/32            *[OSPF/10] 2d 11:46:56, metric 1
                        MultiRecv
```

Notice how the preferred protocol has changed, and the IS-IS routes are now active.

Step 4: Verify the success of the migration

Once IS-IS becomes the preferred protocol, your job is simply to watch and wait. If you have executed all of the previous steps properly, there *shouldn't* be many—if any—issues. Nevertheless, some hidden problem is always waiting to be discovered. Monitor the network for issues. Verify that adjacencies are in place and that all routes are being advertised properly:

```
[edit]
lab@r1> show isis interface
IS-IS interface database:
Interface       L CirID Level 1 DR  Level 2 DR   L1/L2 Metric
fe-0/0/2.0      3   0x1 r1.00       r2.02            1/1
lo0.0           0   0x1 Passive     Passive          0/0

[edit]
lab@r1> show isis adjacency
Interface       System   L State  Hold (secs) SNPA
fe-0/0/2.0      r2       2  Up              7  0:14:f6:8c:18:2

lab@r1> show route protocol isis

inet.0: 9 destinations, 12 routes (9 active, 0 holddown, 0 hidden)
+ = Active Route, - = Last Active, * = Both

172.16.1.0/24           *[IS-IS/165] 00:25:50, metric 1
                        > to 10.0.1.2 via fe-0/0/2.0
172.16.2.0/24           *[IS-IS/165] 00:25:50, metric 1
                        > to 10.0.1.2 via fe-0/0/2.0
192.168.2.2/32          *[IS-IS/18] 00:25:50, metric 1
                        > to 10.0.1.2 via fe-0/0/2.0
```

At this stage, a very important detail that can cause later problems is to verify that the active routes in the routers' routing tables are indeed being received from IS-IS and installed as "IS-IS routes." An issue with IS-IS could easily be hidden due to the fact that OSPF is still active and sending routing updates. If you do not check this carefully, the next stage could expose the issue in a very unpleasant way!

A high availability best practice is to now perform connectivity tests to various points in the network to ensure reachability, as well as to confirm proper routing.

Step 5: Remove OSPF from the network

After IS-IS has been made the preferred protocol and has been working smoothly for some time, you can remove OSPF from the network. The process of removing OSPF from the router is simple enough:

```
[edit]
lab@r1# delete protocols ospf
```

Another option is to deactivate OSPF instead of deleting it, using the command `deactivate protocols ospf`. This disables the protocol but leaves the configuration intact in case you need it later.

The process of removing OSPF from all routers may depend on the design of the network as well as your overall migration strategy. For example, perhaps the strategy calls for removing OSPF from nonbackbone areas one by one, to allow for maximum control and containment in case of a problem. This decision is part of the design strategy you created back in step one.

If the worst happens and removing OSPF *does* create a serious problem, it is very easy to recover by using the `rollback` command (don't forget to enter `commit` as well):

```
[edit]
lab@r1# rollback 1
load complete
```

However, with thoughtful planning, careful execution, and close monitoring, the migration should go smoothly.

Migrating from IS-IS to OSPF

As we already mentioned, before any migration takes place, it is important to have a good sense of what your current network looks like. And documenting the details of the entire network might be the most important step of the entire migration.

This section uses the following example to help illustrate the migration steps:

```
[edit]
lab@r1> show route

inet.0: 8 destinations, 8 routes (8 active, 0 holddown, 0 hidden)
+ = Active Route, - = Last Active, * = Both

10.0.1.0/24        *[Direct/0] 1d 01:32:49
                    > via fe-0/0/2.0
10.0.1.1/32        *[Local/0] 1d 01:32:49
                     Local via fe-0/0/2.0
10.210.0.0/27      *[Direct/0] 2d 12:13:50
                    > via fxp0.0
10.210.0.1/32      *[Local/0] 2d 12:13:51
                     Local via fxp0.0
172.16.1.0/24      *[IS-IS/165] 00:00:48, metric 10
                    > to 10.0.1.2 via fe-0/0/2.0
172.16.2.0/24      *[IS-IS/165] 00:00:48, metric 10
                    > to 10.0.1.2 via fe-0/0/2.0
192.168.1.1/32     *[Direct/0] 1d 01:35:35
                    > via lo0.0
192.168.2.2/32     *[IS-IS/18] 00:00:48, metric 10
                    > to 10.0.1.2 via fe-0/0/2.0
```

The preceding example is the "before" view of the network, from the perspective of r1. In this example, r1 is receiving three routes from its neighbor. Two of them (172.16.1.0/24 and 172.16.2.0/24) are static routes that are being redistributed into IS-IS as L2 external routes. The third route (192.168.2.2/32) is an IS-IS L2 internal route; it is the neighbor's loopback address. With this baseline view in mind, it's time to move on to the first migration step.

Step 1: Plan for the migration

When migrating from one protocol to another, the primary planning step is to consider the design of the existing network and determine the best way to implement that design within the capabilities of the new protocol.

There are several items to consider when moving from IS-IS to OSPF:

Area and backbone design
> If the existing IS-IS network has been designed using a centralized L2 backbone, migrating to OSPF is straightforward; you can simply design it to match the existing network. However, if the existing IS-IS network doesn't use a centralized backbone some significant planning may be required. It is not possible to get into all the possible variations in this book, but a good general approach is to make the central area—or areas—Area 0 (the backbone), and make the other areas nonzero areas, feeding into the backbone. Also, don't forget to use OSPF area types as appropriate to match the existing network design. For example, a typical IS-IS L1 (nonbackbone) area is equivalent to an OSPF totally stubby area.

In practice, let natural boundaries determine area boundaries. For example, a remote office that is connected by a low-speed link may make a good stub area.

Authentication

You can take the authentication scheme from the existing network and implement it in OSPF. If it happens that your current network doesn't use authentication, this would be a very good time to start!

 Remember that only OSPF Hello packets are authenticated.

Metrics

You have two options when migrating metrics to OSPF:

1. Set the metrics manually, per interface, using the existing IS-IS metrics as reference.

2. Set the metrics dynamically. By default, OSPF uses a reference bandwidth and dynamically sets the cost of each interface based on link speed.

 In practice, unless you have a specific reason to change the strategy used to determine metrics, use the method that parallels the current IS-IS network.

Routing policy

Any redistribution of routes into IS-IS should be mirrored in OSPF. Some policies may be reusable, while others, such as interarea routes, can be summarized natively by OSPF.

Step 2: Add OSPF to the network

When the planning step is complete, you can add OSPF to the network. The protocol is easy to configure, using settings based on the design considerations in the preceding list. If the design decisions have been made wisely, this should be a straightforward process; with a few commands, OSPF will be in place on the router.

Start by enabling OSPF and adding the appropriate interfaces under the protocol:

```
[edit]
lab@r1# show protocols ospf
area 0.0.0.0 {
    interface fe-0/0/2.0;
    interface lo0.0;
}
```

Then add authentication:

```
[edit]
lab@r1# show protocols ospf
area 0.0.0.0 {
    interface fe-0/0/2.0 {
        authentication {
            md5 1 key "$9$OkzSBEyleWXxdyrYgJZji"; ## SECRET-DATA
        }
    }
    interface lo0.0;
}
```

In this example, IS-IS is using its default method of setting metrics—simply setting a metric of 10 per link. To match this in OSPF, use the `metric` statement:

```
[edit]
lab@r1# show protocols ospf
area 0.0.0.0 {
    interface fe-0/0/2.0 {
        metric 10;
        authentication {
            md5 1 key "$9$OkzSBEyleWXxdyrYgJZji"; ## SECRET-DATA
        }
    }
    interface lo0.0;
}
```

The neighboring router, r2, is using a routing policy to redistribute two routes into IS-IS. Route redistribution can often be replicated easily in OSPF by reusing the same policy statement. However, in this scenario, metrics are being manually configured and OSPF requires additional configuration to alter the metric of an external route:

```
[edit]
lab@r2# show policy-options
policy-statement static-to-IGP {
    term 1 {
        from protocol static;
        then accept;
    }
}
policy-statement static-to-OSPF {
    term 1 {
        from protocol static;
        then {
            metric 10;
            accept;
        }
    }
}
```

Apply this new policy to OSPF:

```
[edit]
lab@r2# set protocols ospf export static-to-OSPF
```

One *critical* item to configure to ensure that there is no impact to the network at this point is to modify OSPF's default protocol preference:

```
[edit]
lab@r1# set protocols ospf preference 168

[edit]
lab@r1# set protocols ospf external-preference 169
```

The default preference values for OSPF are lower (i.e., more preferred) than IS-IS. Implementing OSPF using default settings would immediately make it the preferred protocol, before you have the chance to validate that it is functioning as desired.

When you commit the OSPF configuration, OSPF should *not* appear as the preferred protocol in the routing table:

```
[edit]
lab@r1> show route

inet.0: 9 destinations, 12 routes (9 active, 0 holddown, 0 hidden)
+ = Active Route, - = Last Active, * = Both

10.0.1.0/24        *[Direct/0] 1d 02:07:46
                    > via fe-0/0/2.0
10.0.1.1/32        *[Local/0] 1d 02:07:46
                     Local via fe-0/0/2.0
10.210.0.0/27      *[Direct/0] 2d 12:48:47
                    > via fxp0.0
10.210.0.1/32      *[Local/0] 2d 12:48:48
                     Local via fxp0.0
172.16.1.0/24      *[IS-IS/165] 00:00:04, metric 10
                    > to 10.0.1.2 via fe-0/0/2.0
                     [OSPF/169] 00:02:40, metric 10, tag 0
                    > to 10.0.1.2 via fe-0/0/2.0
172.16.2.0/24      *[IS-IS/165] 00:00:04, metric 10
                    > to 10.0.1.2 via fe-0/0/2.0
                     [OSPF/169] 00:02:40, metric 10, tag 0
                    > to 10.0.1.2 via fe-0/0/2.0
192.168.1.1/32     *[Direct/0] 1d 02:10:32
                    > via lo0.0
192.168.2.2/32     *[IS-IS/18] 00:35:45, metric 10
                    > to 10.0.1.2 via fe-0/0/2.0
                     [OSPF/168] 00:05:57, metric 10
                    > to 10.0.1.2 via fe-0/0/2.0
224.0.0.5/32       *[OSPF/10] 00:07:08, metric 1
                     MultiRecv
```

Notice in the output how OSPF is now activated and running in parallel with IS-IS. However, its modified protocol preference ensures that OSPF doesn't take over as the primary protocol. The active routes are still provided by IS-IS at this point.

Before moving to the next stage, take the time to ensure that OSPF is working properly *and* advertising the same routes as IS-IS. Ensure that both internal and external routes are being advertised properly through the network by comparing the IS-IS-specific and OSPF-specific entries in the routing table:

```
lab@r1> show route table inet.0 protocol isis

inet.0: 9 destinations, 12 routes (9 active, 0 holddown, 0 hidden)
+ = Active Route, - = Last Active, * = Both

172.16.1.0/24      *[IS-IS/165] 00:09:26, metric 10
                    > to 10.0.1.2 via fe-0/0/2.0
172.16.2.0/24      *[IS-IS/165] 00:09:26, metric 10
                    > to 10.0.1.2 via fe-0/0/2.0
192.168.2.2/32     *[IS-IS/18] 00:45:07, metric 10
                    > to 10.0.1.2 via fe-0/0/2.0
```

```
lab@r1> show route table inet.0 protocol ospf

inet.0: 9 destinations, 12 routes (9 active, 0 holddown, 0 hidden)
+ = Active Route, - = Last Active, * = Both

172.16.1.0/24      [OSPF/169] 00:12:05, metric 10, tag 0
                    > to 10.0.1.2 via fe-0/0/2.0
172.16.2.0/24      [OSPF/169] 00:12:05, metric 10, tag 0
                    > to 10.0.1.2 via fe-0/0/2.0
192.168.2.2/32     [OSPF/168] 00:15:22, metric 10
                    > to 10.0.1.2 via fe-0/0/2.0
224.0.0.5/32       *[OSPF/10] 00:16:33, metric 1
                    MultiRecv
```

 The 224.0.0.5/32 entry is simply the OSPF protocol itself.

If you see any discrepancy between the IS-IS and OSPF advertisements, something isn't properly configured in OSPF.

Step 3: Make OSPF the "preferred" IGP

With OSPF properly mirroring IS-IS, make OSPF the preferred routing protocol in the network. You can do this easily by deleting the customized preference settings:

```
[edit]
lab@r1# delete protocols ospf preference
```

```
[edit]
lab@r1# delete protocols ospf external-preference
```

Once you commit this change, OSPF's lower default preference values make it automatically more preferred, and thus it becomes the preferred protocol, as shown here:

```
[edit]
lab@r1> show route
```

```
inet.0: 9 destinations, 12 routes (9 active, 0 holddown, 0 hidden)
+ = Active Route, - = Last Active, * = Both

10.0.1.0/24        *[Direct/0] 1d 02:22:39
                    > via fe-0/0/2.0
10.0.1.1/32        *[Local/0] 1d 02:22:39
                    Local via fe-0/0/2.0
10.210.0.0/27      *[Direct/0] 2d 13:03:40
                    > via fxp0.0
10.210.0.1/32      *[Local/0] 2d 13:03:41
                    Local via fxp0.0
172.16.1.0/24      *[OSPF/150] 00:00:03, metric 10, tag 0
                    > to 10.0.1.2 via fe-0/0/2.0
                    [IS-IS/165] 00:14:57, metric 10
                    > to 10.0.1.2 via fe-0/0/2.0
172.16.2.0/24      *[OSPF/150] 00:00:03, metric 10, tag 0
                    > to 10.0.1.2 via fe-0/0/2.0
                    [IS-IS/165] 00:14:57, metric 10
                    > to 10.0.1.2 via fe-0/0/2.0
192.168.1.1/32     *[Direct/0] 1d 02:25:25
                    > via lo0.0
192.168.2.2/32     *[OSPF/10] 00:00:03, metric 10
                    > to 10.0.1.2 via fe-0/0/2.0
                    [IS-IS/18] 00:50:38, metric 10
                    > to 10.0.1.2 via fe-0/0/2.0
224.0.0.5/32       *[OSPF/10] 00:22:01, metric 1
                    MultiRecv
```

Notice that the preferred protocol has changed and that OSPF routes are now active.

Step 4: Verify the success of the migration

Once OSPF becomes the preferred protocol, the next step simply involves watching and waiting. If the previous steps were carried out properly you *shouldn't* have many—if any—issues. That being said, even the best-planned migration usually involves some unanticipated issue. Monitor the network while OSPF takes over as the preferred protocol. Verify that the router maintains adjacencies with its neighbors and that all routes are advertised correctly:

```
[edit]
lab@r1> show ospf interface
Interface        State   Area      DR ID          BDR ID         Nbrs
fe-0/0/2.0       BDR     0.0.0.0   192.168.2.2    192.168.1.1    1
lo0.0            DR      0.0.0.0   192.168.1.1    0.0.0.0         0

[edit]
lab@r1> show ospf neighbor
Address     Interface    State    ID            Pri  Dead
10.0.1.2    fe-0/0/2.0   Full     192.168.2.2   128   37

[edit]
lab@r1> show route protocol ospf
```

```
inet.0: 9 destinations, 12 routes (9 active, 0 holddown, 0 hidden)
+ = Active Route, - = Last Active, * = Both

172.16.1.0/24        *[OSPF/150] 00:03:58, metric 10, tag 0
                      > to 10.0.1.2 via fe-0/0/2.0
172.16.2.0/24        *[OSPF/150] 00:03:58, metric 10, tag 0
                      > to 10.0.1.2 via fe-0/0/2.0
192.168.2.2/32       *[OSPF/10] 00:03:58, metric 10
                      > to 10.0.1.2 via fe-0/0/2.0
224.0.0.5/32         *[OSPF/10] 00:25:56, metric 1
                       MultiRecv
```

 Verify that the active routes in the routers' routing tables are indeed being received from OSPF and installed as "OSPF routes." If OSPF isn't functioning properly on a router, the issue could easily be hidden because IS-IS is still active and sending routing updates. Missing this situation can lead to a major issue in the next step!

Be sure to conduct connectivity testing to ensure reachability through the network, as well as proper routing.

Step 5: Remove IS-IS from the network

After you have made OSPF the preferred protocol and have verified that it is working properly, you can remove IS-IS from the network. To remove IS-IS, simply delete it from the configuration:

```
[edit]
lab@r1# delete protocols isis
```

 Another option is to deactivate IS-IS instead of deleting it, using the command deactivate protocols isis. This disables the protocol but leaves the configuration intact in case it is needed later.

How you remove IS-IS from all routers in the network likely depends on the design of the network as well as your overall migration strategy. For example, perhaps the strategy calls for removing IS-IS one L1 area at a time, and finally the L2 backbone, to allow for maximum control over the migration and provide containment in case of a problem. At this stage, control is critical.

If the worst happens and removing IS-IS *does* create a problem, the easiest way to recover is to use the rollback command (don't forget to enter commit as well):

```
[edit]
lab@r1# rollback 1
load complete
```

However, if you are thorough in creating the new design, careful in configuring the routers, and watchful during monitoring, the migration should be successful, with minimal problems.

Merging Networks Using a Common IGP

Transitioning from one IGP to another can be quite a challenge. The task of merging two networks that use the same IGP also has its own challenges to overcome. The classic example is the merging of two companies: Company A has bought Company B and the two organizations must now join together. Part of this effort involves merging the companies' IT infrastructure. From a networking perspective, two separate administrative domains must be merged into one, a problem that can be quite a challenge to solve.

Considerations

There are a variety of factors to consider when merging two (or more) networks—primarily area design, but also matching configuration parameters and tunneling.

Area design

The biggest factor in merging the two networks is *area design*, and the most important design consideration is how to deal with the networks' backbones. If the networks are running centralized backbones, as required by OSPF and as shown in Figure 19-9, significant work needs to be done to determine how and where to join the two networks' backbone areas.

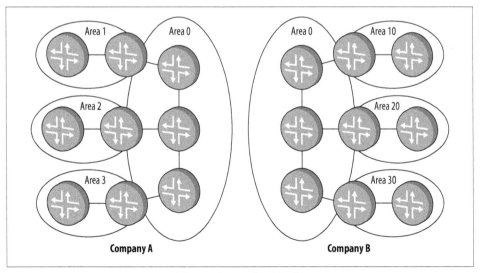

Figure 19-9. Two companies using OSPF and centralized backbones

The simplest solution may involve creating physical links between the backbone areas, effectively creating a single larger backbone, as shown in Figure 19-10.

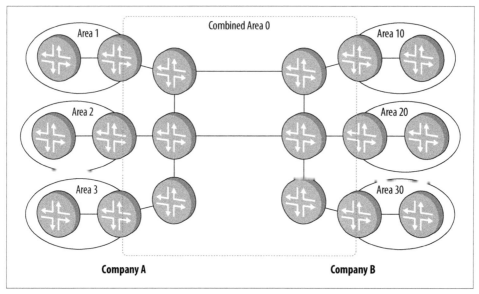

Figure 19-10. Two companies' networks merged by combining backbones

However, the solution depends heavily on access to reliable links with sufficient bandwidth, as well as sufficiently powered routers, to support the increased traffic load. In cases where these conditions don't exist, it may be better to use only a portion of the original backbone areas to create a new combined backbone and repartition the network to absorb the remaining routers. This strategy, shown in Figure 19-11, optimizes the network given the resources available.

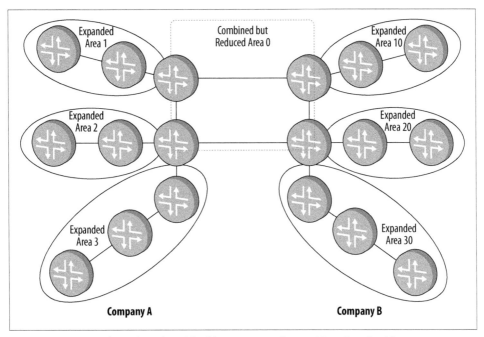

Figure 19-11. Reconfigured combined backbone area, and repartitioned nonbackbone areas

If the networks are running IS-IS, another option is available: because IS-IS doesn't require a contiguous backbone, it may be possible to keep the area structure largely intact and simply join L2 routers from each network, creating a continuous chainlike backbone through both networks. If the architecture supports (or requires) it, joining the routers can be a very efficient solution, as shown in Figures 19-12 and 19-13.

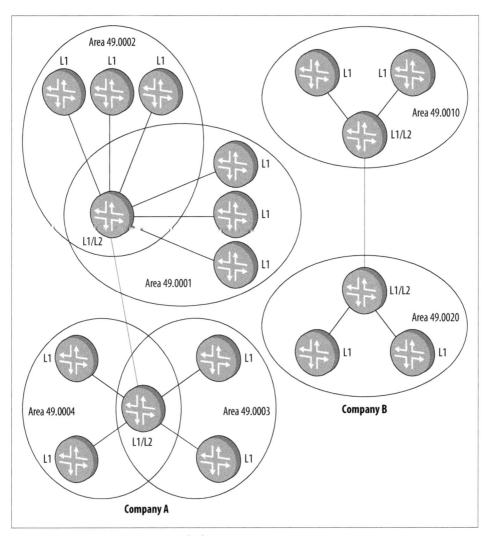

Figure 19-12. Two companies using IS-IS

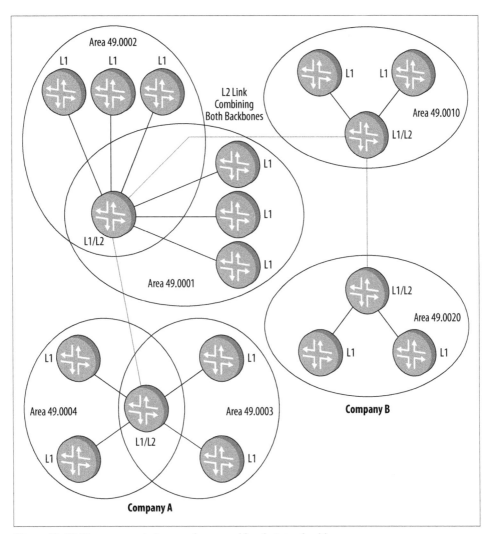

Figure 19-13. Two companies' networks merged by chaining backbones

The treatment of nonbackbone areas depends on how the backbone is impacted when the networks merge. In cases where a backbone is significantly repartitioned, it is reasonable to assume that some of the repartitioning affects nonbackbone areas (as occurred in Figure 19-13) because routers are architecturally repositioned in the network. In cases where the backbones are left largely intact, nonbackbone areas may well require little or no alteration at all (aside from ensuring that they have unique area IDs).

Matching configuration parameters

Of course, a significant factor in "getting it right" is to ensure that all appropriate configuration parameters match—generally this is more applicable to OSPF than IS-IS, but the principle holds for either protocol. The best-laid plans can come crashing down because of simple configuration issues.

A smart approach is to come up with a single strategy for the new combined network. Using the best practices and usage guidelines from each network, define a unified approach and set of requirements for the new domain, including guidelines and rules for Hello timers, authentication types and passwords, metrics, and any other parameters that are relevant for the network. Ensuring that links are using compatible parameters is, of course, critical to ensuring that the network is unaffected during the merge. But the long-term solution to ensure high availability is to standardize the parameters and features across the network *before* the merge takes place. Otherwise, the process of merging the networks will be the start of a long and probably painful exercise.

 Much like earlier topics in this chapter, the key to maintaining high availability is thorough planning and design, attention to detail during reconfiguration, and vigilance in monitoring.

Tunneling

When merging companies together, it is not always possible, at least in the short term, to have the desired physical connectivity between networks. When this happens in OSPF networks, virtual links provide the connectivity required to allow the network to function, as shown in Figure 19-14.

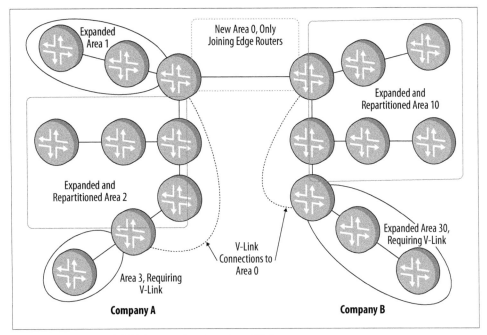

Figure 19-14. Merged OSPF networks using virtual links

Virtual links are generally not recommended as a permanent solution for OSPF networks.

Another option to extend the network is through general *tunneling technologies*. Generic Route Encapsulation (GRE) is a solution that can be helpful in extending and joining networks by allowing discontiguous areas to appear directly connected, despite not being physically connected. For example, the two networks' OSPF backbones could be connected using GRE, creating a single joined backbone despite the lack of direct physical connectivity.

Other Options for Merging IGPs

Sometimes it is simply not feasible to join the networks together, either in the short term or ever. In these cases, other options might be appropriate.

BGP

In certain cases, it might make sense to continue to treat the networks as separate entities. Perhaps there will never be a good solution to physically join them together, or perhaps each company's IT department will continue to manage its own network. In such a situation, an appropriate solution may be to keep the networks separate and join them using BGP. Regardless of whether direct physical connectivity is available, BGP can provide excellent routing and policy control between the networks, while providing the desired connectivity. BGP also provides a variety of high availability features for this scenario, such as redundant routing and failover options, as we discuss in Chapter 20.

Routing instances

In rare cases, connectivity may be available but for some reason it is still desirable to keep the networks separate. In this situation, the solution may be to use the multiple routing instance feature of JUNOS Software. This solution allows a router to join the networks together without requiring that they actually *merge*. A router positioned at the edge of both networks can run two separate routing instances and can send each network's routes to the other network. This effectively provides route redistribution between identical IGPs, allowing sharing of routing information without altering either network's architecture.

 While not an ideal method of joining networks together, using routing instances is functional and you can use it as a short-term solution in certain cases.

CHAPTER 20

Merging BGP Autonomous Systems

It would be nice to be able to plan your network from scratch, taking into account scalability, of course, and to never have to worry about dealing with mergers, or kludges, or one-offs, but that never happens. Sometimes you will be required to bring another network into the fold no matter how messed up you perceive the other network to be.

Although the migration of the Interior Gateway Protocol (IGP) is vital to internal connectivity, errors in Border Gateway Protocol (BGP) can lead not only to internal routing issues, but also to external routing issues that could thrust your network into the listserv annals of groups such as the North American Network Operators Group, which researches, comments on, and, if necessary, sanctions networks affecting Internet routing, or the high availability posture of networks managed by NANOG members.

With careful planning and use of the tools built into JUNOS, it is possible to safely merge Autonomous Systems (ASs) and not only protect your network's uptime, but also mitigate any risk to the high availability of your upstream and downstream neighbors.

Planning the Merge

Unlike the realm of IGPs, where religious wars rage between the noble followers of Open Shortest Path First (OSPF) and heretics of Intermediate System to Intermediate System (IS-IS), or vice versa, interdomain routing sits in a realm where only a single protocol rules. Tomes in all forms of media have been devoted to BGP, and there is no shortage of information available to use to develop a plan for merging networks, including *BGP (http://oreilly.com/catalog/9780596002541/)*, by Iljitsch van Beijnum (O'Reilly), and *Internet Routing Architectures*, by Sam Halabi (Cisco Press).

Architecture

Like most of the other topics covered in this book, planning the architecture for BGP in ASs is normally not a greenfield effort. There are few, if any, large networks that do not already have a BGP architecture. In terms of operating, merging, or maintaining a BGP network, planning is key. It is necessary not only to look to the future to see what design is best for scalability, but also to determine which design will merge most easily and scale most efficiently.

According to RFC 1771, all Internal BGP (IBGP) peers must be fully meshed within the AS to prevent routing loops. Using the full mesh has the advantage of ensuring that all routers in the AS have the same topology information. The disadvantage comes with the configuration and scalability of the IBGP peering. To avoid these issues, the following additional BGP architectures have been created:

Confederations
> The division on an AS into multiple sub-ASs with a full mesh required only in the sub-AS. When confederations are used, the communication across the sub-AS boundaries is called Confederation Border Gateway Protocol (CBGP). CBGP is a slightly modified form of External BGP (EBGP) peering.

Route reflection
> The use of multiple routers as a focal point for routing updates so that most IBGP peers peer only to the route reflectors.

Making the choice

When merging ASs, you must fully understand the advantages and possible trade-offs of each type of architecture. Though both route reflection and confederations solve the full-mesh issues, each has its own peculiarities. Table 20-1 compares the options for IBGP peering.

Table 20-1. Comparing IBGP peering options

Feature	Full mesh	Route reflection	Confederations
Hierarchical roles	None	Uses route reflector and route reflector clients	None formally, but through architectural design, some sub-ASs may work as backbones
Topology	All BGP peers are fully meshed; issues of n * (n − 1)/2 occur	AS is divided into clusters made up of route reflectors and their clients; an AS can contain routers but not within the clusters	AS becomes a confederation of sub-ASs made up of fully peered BGP neighbors; within the sub-AS, all peers *must* be peered
Configuration and peering	All BGP routers are configured to peer with all other BGP peers; JUNOS allows for "dynamic"	Clients are peered to route reflectors and route reflectors are fully meshed; cluster IDs are used to differentiate between route reflector groupings	Sub-ASs are configured with their own ID; within the sub-AS, all peers are fully meshed

Feature	Full mesh	Route reflection	Confederations
	peering to reduce the configuration of peers		
Communications between peers	IBGP is used between all peers	IBGP is used between route reflectors and clients; route reflectors use IBGP with added attributes for peering	IBGP is used between all peers within a sub-AS; CBGP is used between all sub-ASs and uses slightly modified EBGP attributes for the AS-path attribute, local preference, next hop, and MED handling
Changes or additions to the BGP attributes	Standard BGP	Additional mandatory attributes passed within AS: Originator ID (Type 9) Cluster ID (Type 10)	AS-path attribute enhancements passed within AS and between sub-ASs: Type 3: AS Confederation Set Type 4: AS Confederation Sequence
Handling of next hop attribute, local preference, and MED	By design, next hop, local preference, and MED are not changed between IBGP peers	By design, next hop, local preference, and MED are not changed between IBGP peers; thus, there is no change between route reflectors or route reflectors and clients	Though CBGP is "EBGP-like," the next hop is not changed between CBGP peers, and the local preference and MED are preserved; IBGP within the sub-AS follows the full-mesh IBGP rules
Default propagation of learned prefix	IBGP speakers readvertise only those prefixes learned from EBGP	Route reflectors readvertise only routes learned from EBGP or clients—and only to other nonclient peers; route reflectors readvertise EBGP or nonclient peer-learned routes to client peers	IBGP speakers readvertise only prefixes learned from EBGP
Use of multihop parameter	Not needed	Not needed	Because CBGP is based on EBGP, if an IP address other than interface addresses are used, multihop may be necessary

Pitfalls

There are many possible pitfalls when attempting to determine how to architect a newly formed AS made up of merged ASs. In most networks, the full mesh is instantly discounted because of the complexity of its maintenance, but most people overlook the problem of *persistent route oscillation* when dealing with route reflectors and confederations. RFC 3345, "BGP Persistent Route Oscillation Condition," focuses on the two types of churn resulting from route reflection and confederation and how to prevent them. Figure 20-1 illustrates an AS that uses route reflection and accepts multi-exit discriminators from its peers.

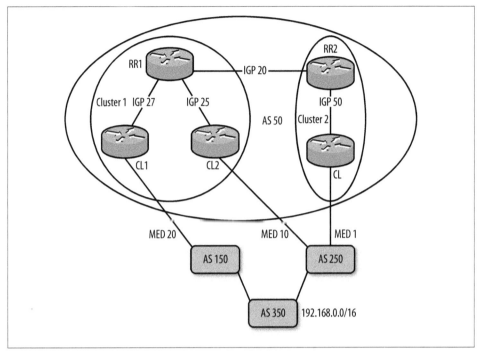

Figure 20-1. Churn in route reflection

Using RFC 3345 as a guide, the following sections illustrate how a situation such as this would result in persistent route oscillation.

> The route oscillation caused by issues such as these can result in networks being advertised, withdrawn, and readvertised within 10 seconds. Although some ignore this issue, calling it a "minor inconvenience," any persistent issues in routing or routing table functions can lead to network downtime. Simple best practices and due diligence can eliminate this issue when you are dealing with providing high availability.

External peering

Looking at Figure 20-1, as the routes for 192.168.0.0/16 are advertised from AS 350 through AS 150 and AS 250 and are then received by AS 50, a `MED` attribute is attached and advertised. The routers that are peered externally—`CL`, `CL1`, and `CL2`—receive the routes from external neighbors and view the routing topology for 192.168.0.0/16 as shown in Table 20-2.

Table 20-2. CL, CL1, and CL2 topology table

Router	MED	AS_PATH
CL	1	250 350
CL1	10	150 350
CL2	20	250 350

Because these routers are the external facing routers, the IGP metric is of no concern in the route decision-making process.

Route reflector 1

The routes that CL1 and CL2 learn are readvertised to the route reflector, which in this case is RR1. Using the MED, RR1 creates the information shown in Table 20-3 for 192.168.0.0/16.

Table 20-3. Route reflector 1 routing table

Best path	AS_PATH	MED	NEXT_HOP	NEXT_HOP IGP cost
*	150 350	20	CL1	27
	250 350	10	CL2	25

The issue with this routing decision is that the IGP cost to CL1 is greater than to CL2; therefore, internal to the AS, CL2 is the best next hop for packets. BGP corrects the routing table within RR1 and sends an update message to RR2 highlighting CL2 as the best next hop for 192.168.0.0/16.

Route reflector 2

When RR2 receives the updates, the information that is received is used to recalculate the next hop against its own table. Using the MED, RR1 creates the information in Table 20-4 for 192.168.0.0/16.

Table 20-4. Route reflector 2 routing table

Best path	AS_PATH	MED	NEXT_HOP	NEXT_HOP IGP cost
*	150 350	1	CL1	50
	150 350	10	CL2	45

Once again, you can see the issue is that the IGP cost for the next hop is less than that of the route currently considered to be the best path. Of course, this has to be changed;

it is, and RR2 sends a withdraw message to RR1 informing it that the path chosen is not the best next hop.

Oscillation commences

This withdraw message is received by RR1 and the next hop is again calculated using the MED as the determining factor for the best path. Because the MED has not changed, RR1 recalculates the best path and creates the routing information shown in Table 20-5.

Table 20-5. Route reflector 1 routing table

Best path	AS_PATH	MED	NEXT_HOP	NEXT_HOP IGP cost
*	150 350	20	CL1	27
	250 350	10	CL2	25

With the recalculation, the routing information is back to where it was in the first step. At this point, BGP must correct its routes again and the route thrashing begins. This thrashing of routes continues until either the MED or the IGP cost is changed in such a way as to make a single route preferable.

Outcomes

Of course, the main goal of merging ASs is to have all the equipment fall under the same administrative control. However, you must consider many underlying issues. Here are a few questions you should ask:

- Will traffic bound for company1 pass through the same ingress point into the new company1/company2 AS, or will routing be diverted such that all traffic passes through combined ingress points?

- During the merger, will a new AS be used for the merged network and, if so, how will the AS numbers of the two ASs be used?

- Will peering change in such a way that it affects routing or creates routing churn in the Internet in general?

- How is the new network to be viewed externally? Will it maintain a look of autonomy for each network being merged, or will the new merged network appear as a single AS externally?

BGP Migration Features in JUNOS

As part of the planning process, we must examine JUNOS features that can smooth the process of merging ASs. This section discusses features related to the operation of BGP, the routing engine (RE), and JUNOS software that ease AS mergers and reduce downtime.

Graceful Restart

Graceful Restart (GR) in routing protocols allows hiccups in network routing to occur without resulting in network downtime. The forgiving nature of GR allows network mergers to proceed without the route flapping, peering issues, and forwarding delays that can accompany peering disruption. If a peering session flags during the merger, with GR other peers can assist the flapping router to relearn the network topology without affecting packet forwarding.

GR is disabled by default. You can configure it for BGP to negotiate GR information with BGP peers. The equipment to which the network device peers must also support GR, as those devices will be the ones helping the peer to relearn its routes.

Here is the basic configuration for GR:

```
routing-options {
    graceful-restart;
}
protocols {
    bgp {
        graceful-restart {
            restart-time 300;
            stale-routes-time 600;
        }
    }
}
```

You must configure GR globally in the routing-options hierarchy, and the `restart-time` and `stale-routes-time` must be configured in either the main BGP instance or the BGP instances of logical routers.

Non-Stop Active Routing

Using the same foundations as GR, *Non-Stop Active Routing* (NSR) allows redundant REs to communicate routing information so that if the master fails, the redundant RE picks up the slack without BGP peers even noticing that the original RE has failed. In JUNOS, you can use NSR with IPv4 and IPv6 to ensure that high availability is maintained even if the network merger causes a routing protocol burp.

Here is the basic configuration for NSR:

```
chassis {
    redundancy {
        graceful-switchover;
    }
}
routing-options {
    nonstop-routing;
}
```

Because NSR provides a graceful failover between REs, you must have redundant REs installed and configured for failover. The `graceful-switching` statement is required in the chassis hierarchy to ensure that failover works correctly.

Full mesh made easy (well, easier)

Because of IBGP's full-mesh architecture, when you add a new IBGP peer to the network, you must add the peer information on every other BGP speaker on the network. This is where the simplicity of a full-mesh architecture to prevent routing loops is overridden by the complexity of the configuration. Also, because you need to make these changes throughout the network, even on the EBGP routers, there is a risk of network-wide downtime caused by human error.

To help mitigate this massive reconfiguration for new peers, JUNOS introduced the concept of "dynamic" BGP peers. The `allow` command within BGP groups allows new peering relationships to be implicitly formed based on IP address ranges. This allows older systems to learn of new peers without requiring their reconfiguration. Figure 20-2 illustrates the addition of routers into an IBGP full mesh. This expansion can be the result of either a merger or simple expansion.

In phase 1 of the illustration, you configure the full mesh very simply, using the loopback addresses. You explicitly call out the IP address of the peer in the configuration. Including the `allow` statement means you can add new peers to the network without having to reconfigure the existing infrastructure.

On router EBGP-Peer:

```
protocols {
    bgp {
        group EBGP {
            type external;
            neighbor 10.0.0.2;
            peer-as 100;
        }
        group IBGP{
            type internal;
            allow 192.168.1.0/24;
            neighbor 192.168.1.2;
        }
    }
}
```

On router IBGP-Peer-1:

```
protocols {
    bgp {
    }
        group IBGP{
            type internal;
            allow 192.168.1.0/24;
            neighbor 192.168.1.1;
        }
    }
}
```

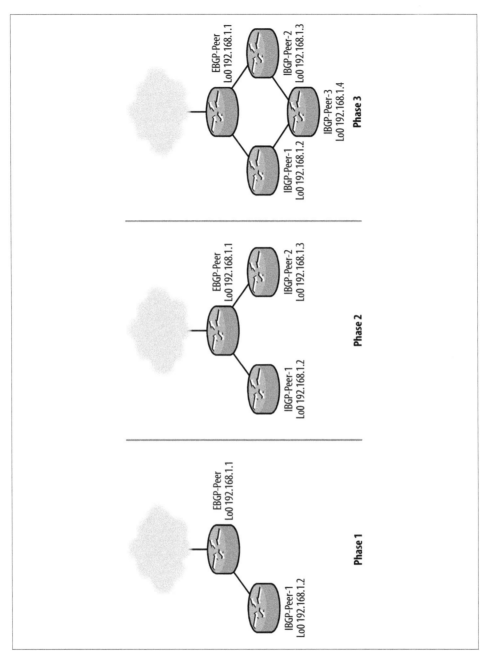

Figure 20-2. Expanding the full mesh

The following code snippet shows the configuration on a newly added router, IBGP-Peer-2:

```
protocols {
    bgp {
    }
        group IBGP{
            type internal;
            allow 192.168.1.0/24;
            neighbor 192.168.1.1;
            neighbor 192.168.1.2;
        }
    }
}
```

As you can see, the loopback interfaces of the existing BGP routers are added to the configuration so that the new router can initiate a peering with each system. Because the infrastructure contains the allow statement for the IP address range that includes the loopback for the new equipment, no changes need to be made to the existing equipment to allow the new equipment to peer.

Again, in phase 3, when you add the new router, IBGP-Peer-3, to the network, no configuration changes are required on the previously installed equipment. The following code snippet for IBGP-Peer-3 explicitly calls out the existing infrastructure so that the router can initiate BGP peering:

```
protocols {
    bgp {
    group IBGP{
            type internal;
            allow 192.168.1.0/24;
            neighbor 192.168.1.1;
            neighbor 192.168.1.2;
            neighbor 192.168.1.2;
        }
    }
}
```

Because the allow statement keeps configurations stable for BGP peering, you can add the new equipment without causing downtime. Using this statement also makes the merging of ASs much easier. The one caveat to the use of the allow statement is that you cannot use it with BGP authentication.

Zen and the art of AS numbers

From Slashdot IDs to JNCIE or CCIE numbers, geeks love to be identified by numbers, and the lower the better. This love of numbered branding seems to extend even to ISPs, which are identified throughout the industry by their AS number. Losing your AS number to a merger, especially if you have something seemingly meaningful, is considered quite a blow by some. Beyond the psychological effect, there are good technical reasons for preserving AS numbers during mergers to protect the network's overall high availability posture:

Limiting configuration changes

Anytime superfluous network configuration changes can be avoided, they should be. Even with commit scripts, JUNOScope, and all the other tools used to limit human error, it still happens.

Mitigating peering issues

Depending on the size of the network you own and the sizes of the neighbors to which your routers peer, it is sometimes nearly impossible to get everything together to conduct a logically staged transition to a new AS number. Preserving the peering relationships based on the AS allows the merger to occur with no interaction by the upstream ISP.

Preserving traffic patterns

Even when one company acquires another, network resources are not going to instantly be combined and controlled by an individual organization. Through the preservation of the AS path information, it is possible to retain traffic patterns that mirror the previously gathered baseline, thus mitigating the possibility that new traffic patterns might overload previously underutilized equipment.

Maintaining consistency of service

For a service provider or a large enterprise, high availability is not only a technical requirement; it is also a service requirement. By preventing Internet routing changes by providing BGP peers with a consistent AS and not renumbering peers with every corporate change, it is possible to create good karma in the network community and allow your peers to be more responsive in how issues affect your network availability.

In JUNOS, you can use the `local-as` statement to preserve an existing peering relationship for a network that is being swallowed by another. In these networks, the BGP peer routers advertise one set of AS numbers to internal peers and a different set to external peers. In Figure 20-3, one company has an AS number it does not want to lose, for obvious reasons. To prevent the loss of such an elite AS number, as well as to mitigate any of the network or bureaucratic churn that may result from changing the peering sessions, the `local-as` statement is included in the configuration.

In this example, the owner of AS 21522 is to merge with AS 1337, but does not want to change the peering relationship with the ISP. The following code illustrates the basic BGP configurations for three routers: router A, the EBGP peer in AS 21522 that communicates with the EBGP peer in 1234; router B, the EBGP peer in 1337 that communicates with the peer in AS 1234; and router C, the EBGP peer in AS 1234 that communicates with the other two peers.

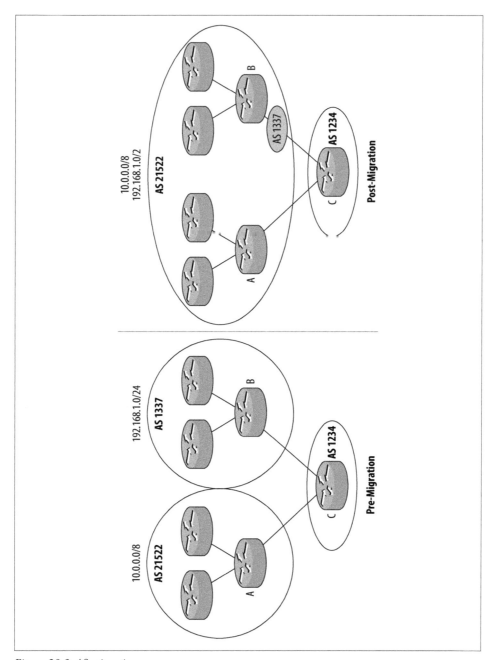

Figure 20-3. AS migration

For router A:

```
routing-options {
    autonomous-system 21522;
}
protocols {
    bgp {
        group internal {
            type internal;
            allow 192.168.1.0/24;
            neighbor 192.168.1.2;
            neighbor 192.168.1.3;
        }
        group external {
            type external;
            neighbor 198.238.112.166;
            remote-as 1234;
        }

    }
}
```

For router B:

```
routing-options {
    autonomous-system 1337;
}
protocols {
    bgp {
        group internal {
            type internal;
            allow 192.168.1.0/24;
            neighbor 10.0.0.2;
            neighbor 10.0.0.3;
        }
        group external {
            type external;
            neighbor 147.56.221.2;
            remote-as 1234;
        }

    }
}
```

For router C:

```
routing-options {
    autonomous-system 1234;
}
protocols {
    bgp {
        group AS21522 {
            type external;
            neighbor 198.238.112.167;
            remote-as 21522;
        }
        group AS1337 {
```

```
                type external;
                neighbor 147.56.221.1;
                remote-as 1337;
            }

        }
    }
```

In this code example, standard EBGP advertisement rules are in play. AS 1234 sees routes from AS 21522 with an AS path of 21522, and sees routes from AS 1337 with an AS path of 1337. To merge these ASs, the following code is configured on the AS 1337 peer (the configuration of IBGP on the AS 21522 routers has been omitted because they are standard).

For router B:

```
routing-options {
    autonomous-system 21522;
}
protocols {
    bgp {
        group internal {
            type internal;
            allow 10.0.0.1/24;
            neighbor 10.0.0.2;
            neighbor 10.0.0.3;
            allow 192.168.1.0/24;
            neighbor 192.168.1.2;
            neighbor 192.168.1.3;
        }
        group external {
            type external;
            neighbor 147.56.221.2;
            remote-as 1234;
            local-as 1337;
        }

    }
}
```

In this example, the internal group is expanded to include the routers in the new parent AS. The AS number for the device has also been changed to the new AS number. The local-as statement is added to the external group to ensure that the peering relationship remains constant and that AS 1234 continues to see AS number 1337.

When you use the local-as statement, it is important to determine how the traffic will flow before and after the migration. This statement adds the AS number to the AS path by default, which can cause traffic to flow differently than planned. Adding the private keyword in the local-as statement overrides the default action of prepending the local-as number to the AS path.

It is necessary to understand how the extra AS in the path affects the flow of incoming packets and whether you can do anything to mitigate the effects of the migration.

Table 20-6 illustrates the possible routing changes caused by the migration we just discussed.

Table 20-6. Migration routing

Route	AS_PATH	Comment
Pre-migration		
10.0.0.0/8	21522	
192.168.1.0/24	1337	
Post-migration		
10.0.0.0/8	21522	
192.168.1.0/24	1337 21522	The AS_PATH for this network has increased because of `local-as`. If both EBGP peers are advertising this route, the chosen route goes through router A because of the AS path. To ensure that router B continues to be the ingress point, routing policies would have to force no advertisement from A or a lengthened AS path.
Post-migration with `private` keyword		
10.0.0.0/8	21522	
192.168.1.0/24	21522	AS number 1337 no longer appears in the AS path for this network. If both EBGP peers are advertising this route, the best route is chosen based on another attribute. To ensure that router B continues to be the ingress point, routing policies would have to force advertisements from A by setting less preferable attributes.

Sometimes loopy is OK

In BGP, it is necessary not only to prevent loops in the full mesh within the AS, but also to prevent loops for external routing. BGP prevents external routing loops for external routes by dropping routes that it has learned from external neighbors when the routes contain its own AS number somewhere in the AS path. Although this does prevent loops, sometimes mergers and BGP/MPLS virtual private network (VPN) deployments require that an AS be seen more than once. You can override this default BGP behavior with the **loops** statement in the AS configuration in the routing-options hierarchy:

```
routing-options {
    autonmous-system 1337 loops 2;
}
```

In this example, AS 1337 has added the **loops** statement to allow its AS to appear up to two times in the AS path.

Merging Our ASs Off

The complexity of merging ASs without causing network downtime requires careful preparation, with an eye on using as many automated tools as possible.

Figure 20-4 shows an example of our merger.

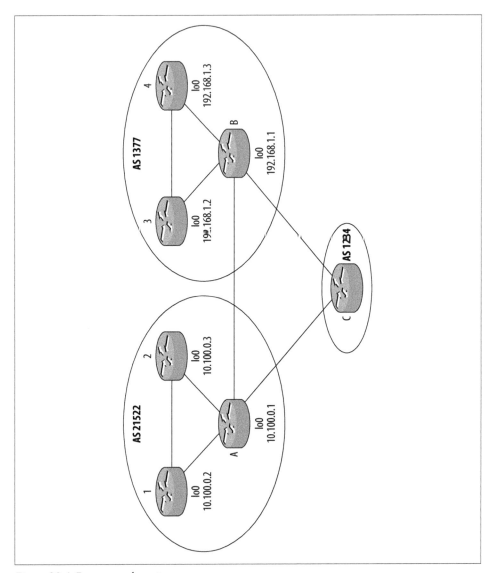

Figure 20-4. Pre-merger layout

Merge with Full Mesh

In the first scenario, the ASs are going to be merged and the result will be a single AS with a full-mesh architecture. To transition to the networks without suffering network downtime, you need to ensure that during the transition, the internal network has access to the external networks, and vice versa, through at least one of the EBGP peers.

IBGP

The first goal of merging our networks while maintaining high availability is to ensure that all hosts internal to the network continue to be able to reach external networks. Chapter 19 discussed merging the IGPs in your network, but with "ships in the night" routing, it is now necessary to ensure that the BGP routing environments are merged.

In the first step of the merge process, the IBGP peers within AS 1337 are fully peered with the routers of AS 21522. Using the `allow` statement enables routers A, 1, and 2 to accept the connections of routers 3 and 4 without being explicitly configured. However, during the configuration changes, you must change the AS number and peering IP addresses on routers 3 and 4.

Once the peering sessions are up and converged, packets on routers 3 and 4 that are about to egress from the network will do so from router A. Packets arriving at router B will also still be able to egress the network. Figure 20-5 illustrates the mid-merger layout.

During this interim step, transit packets begin to use router A as the egress of the network. Packets arriving at router B are also still able to egress the network, and packets bound for AS 1337 are still forwarded to router B.

The following code snippets show the changes in the configuration.

On router 1:

```
protocols {
    bgp {
            group internal {
            type internal;
            allow 192.168.1.0/24;
            allow 10.100.0.0/24;
            neighbor 10.100.0.1;
            neighbor 10.100.0.3;

        }
    }
}
```

On router 3:

```
routing-options {
    autonomous-system 21522;
}
protocols {
    bgp {
            group internal {
            type internal;
            neighbor 10.100.0.1;
            neighbor 10.100.0.2;
            neighbor 10.100.0.3;
        }
    }
}
```

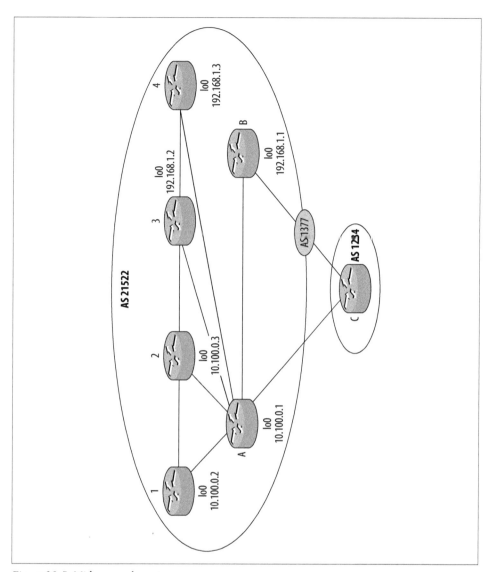

Figure 20-5. Mid-merger layout

The allow statement mitigates the complexity and error-prone nature of configuring every router in the network, bringing us closer to our goal of executing the planned merger and bringing the network to a full mesh with as little disruption as possible.

Bring in the EBGP peer

When all the IBGP neighbors have formed peer relationships, the final EBGP peer can be brought into the network. The first step here is to change the AS number of router B without thrashing the connection to router C. This is where the `local-as` command comes in handy. Figure 20-6 shows the final merger.

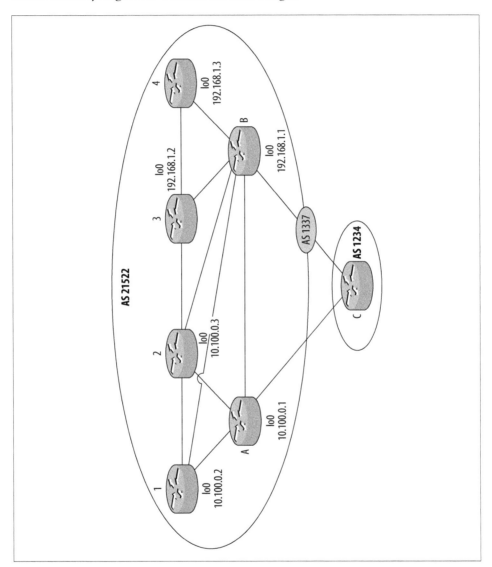

Figure 20-6. Final merger

Not only does the `local-as` statement prevent interruptions with neighbors, but the `allow` command also makes it easier to create the full mesh. The following code shows the changes in router B's configuration:

```
routing-options {
    autonomous-system 21522;
}
protocols {
    bgp {
        group internal {
            type internal;
            allow 10.100.0.0/24;
            allow 192.168.1.0/24;
            neighbor 10.100.0.1;
            neighbor 10.100.0.2;
            neighbor 10.100.0.3;
            neighbor 192.168.1.1;
            neighbor 192.168.1.2
        neighbor 192.168.1.3;
        }
        group AS1234 {
            type external;
            neighbor 147.56.221.2;
            remote-as 1234;
            local-as 1337
        }
    }
}
```

Although merging into a full mesh is possible, sometimes architectures dictate the use of route reflection or confederation.

Merge with Route Reflectors

A second method for merging ASs is to add route reflectors to the network. Although route reflectors do prevent the need for full-mesh networks, as discussed before, they also have issues that affect the merging of networks. In Figure 20-7, the networks have been merged by setting up router A and router B to work as route reflectors, and by having routers 1, 2, 3, and 4 peer to routers A and B in separate clusters to ensure redundancy.

As with the full-mesh merger process, it is best to merge the networks progressively to ensure that no downtime occurs. By using two clusters with redundancy, it is possible to peer routers 3 and 4 to router A to accomplish the same routing patterns as discussed in the full-mesh merger.

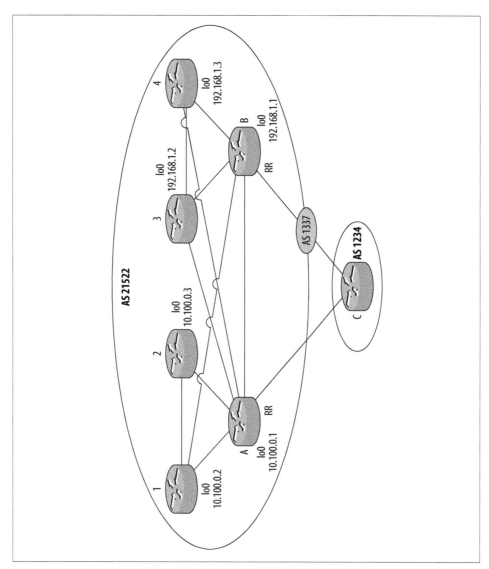

Figure 20-7. Route reflectors

Cluster 1

The following code samples show the statements added to routers 1, 3, and A to set up route reflection.

To router 1:

```
protocols {
    bgp {
            group Cluster1 {
```

```
                    type internal;
                    neighbor 10.100.0.1;
                }
            }
        }
```

To router 3:

```
routing-options {
    autonomous-system 21522;
}
protocols {
    bgp {
        group Cluster1 {
            type internal;
            neighbor 10.100.0.1;
        }
    }
}
```

To router A:

```
protocols {
    bgp {
        group internal {
            type internal;
            allow 192.168.1.0/24;
        }
        group Cluster1 {
            type internal;
            allow 10.100.0.0/24;
            allow 192.168.1.0/24;
            neighbor 10.100.0.1;
            cluster 1.1.1.1;
        }
    }
}
```

As the code demonstrates, router 1 actually needs to peer with only router A at this point and does not require the `allow` statement. The AS number on router 2 has changed and a `neighbor` statement for router A is added. In router A, the `allow` statements are added to allow peering from all the IBGP peers in the network, and the `cluster` statement identifies the `cluster-id`.

The internal group has been added to allow the eventual inclusion of router B as an IBGP peer. Once routers 3 and 4 are configured to use router A as the reflector, they should begin to forward egress packets to it.

Cluster 2

When the first cluster is stable, configure router B with the new AS number so that it becomes an IBGP peer with router A. Once this step is complete, add the `cluster` statement to router B, and configure the `allow` statements to support peering requests from the route reflector clients, routers 1, 2, 3, and 4.

For router 3:

```
routing-options {
    autonomous-system 21522;
}
protocols {
    bgp {
        group Cluster1 {
            type internal;
            neighbor 10.100.0.1;
        }
        group Cluster2 {
            type internal;
            neighbor 192.168.1.1;
        }
    }
}
```

For router B:

```
protocols {
    bgp {
        group internal {
            type internal;
            neighbor 10.100.0.1;
        }
        group Cluster2 {
            type internal;
            allow 10.100.0.0/24;
            allow 192.168.1.0/24;
            neighbor 10.100.0.1;
            cluster 2.2.2.2;
        }
    }
}
```

As you can see in this example, router B now has an IBGP peering with router A and allows IBGP peer requests from all other IBGP routers in the network.

Merge with Confederations

A third way to merge ASs is to use BGP confederations. This type of merge can be very simple to implement, but as we mentioned earlier in this chapter confederations are susceptible to persistent route oscillation. Using RFC 3345 as a guide, you can put in place measures to prevent the type of routing churn that creates oscillation issues. Figure 20-8 illustrates a merger implemented with confederations.

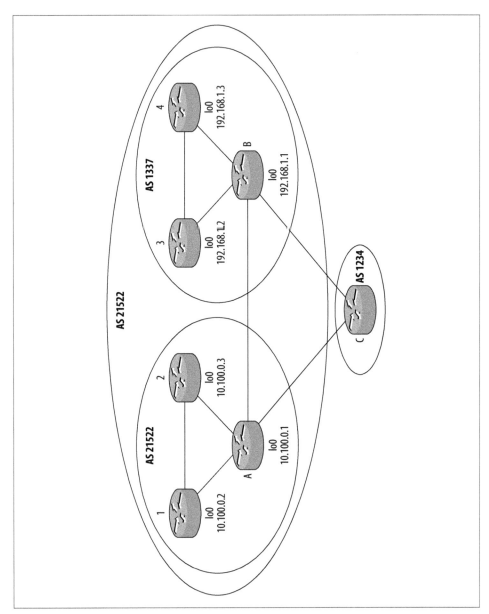

Figure 20-8. Merger with confederations

In Figure 20-8, you see that only a few changes have to be made to the routers. In the following code samples, the `confederation` statement is added to all the systems to identify the AS number that is to be used in the AS_PATH attribute when it is advertised to the peers, as well as to identify the sub-ASs that make up the confederation.

For all routers in AS 21522:

```
routing-options {
    autonomous-system 21522;
    confederation 21522 members [21522 1337];
}
```

For all routers in AS 1337:

```
routing-options {
    autonomous-system 1337;
    confederation 21522 members [21522 1337];
}
```

Once you configure the confederations in the network, configure routers A and B to be EBGP peers. Although the type statement identifies the peering relationship as external, the confederation command overrides the default behavior and allows the relationship to work in the pseudo-EBGP deployment identified as CBGP.

On router B:

```
protocols {
    bgp {
        group CBGP {
        type external;
            neighbor 10.100.0.1 {
            peer-as 21522;
            multihop {
                ttl 3;
                }
            }
        }
        group EBGP {
            type external;
            neighbor 10.0.0.1 {
            peer-as 1234;
            local-as 1337;
            }
        }
    }
}
```

Using the multihop statement in the peering with the CBGP neighbor allows you to still peer using loopback addresses, which is considered a best common practice for internal peering addresses. You can also use the local-as statement again on router B to ensure that the peering information with AS 1234 does not change.

Monitoring the Merge

Of course, the most critical time for high availability is immediately after the merge. Thus, you should use a combination of syslog, Simple Network Management Protocol (SNMP), the command-line interface (CLI), and JUNOScript, as covered in Chapters 9 and 21 of this book and in the technical documentation. To monitor the long-term results of the migration on your network and on your upstream and downstream neighbors, use JUNOScope and JUNOScript and develop simple event policies.

Neighbor Peering

Preventing Internet churn caused by flapping of BGP peers is an easy way to maintain high availability in the whole network, as well as to preserve good karma in the Internet world in general. The following code sample event policy monitors the status of BGP peers:

```
event-options {
    policy BGP-PEER {
        events rpd_bgp_neighbor_state_changed;
        then {
            execute commands {
                commands {
                    "show bgp replication";
                    "show bgp neighbors";
                    "show bgp groups";
                }
                output-filename BGP-PEER;
                destination Engineering;
            }
            raise-trap;
        }
    }
    destinations {
        Engineering {
            archive-sites {
                "ftp://user@engineering.example.com/"
                    password "$9$qP3n1RhclM";
            }
        }
    }
}
```

In the preceding policy, each time a BGP peer flaps, the router sends an SNMP trap and runs a series of commands. These commands provide information about the neighbor relationships, as well as the status of the NSR replication. The command output is written to a file that is then transferred to a management station, where the output can be analyzed.

Persistent route oscillation

A second issue that may arise after an AS merger is persistent route oscillation, which normally goes unnoticed, although it can lead to network downtime. To proactively discover which routes are oscillating so that you can develop a plan to stop the oscillation and prevent it in the future, write the following policy:

```
event-options {
    generate-event {
        Route-Check time-interval 300;
    }
    policy PRO {
        events Route-Check;
        then {
            execute-commands {
                commands {
                    "show route protocol bgp | find '00:0[0-5]:'";
                }
                output-filename PRO-CHECK;
                destination Engineering;
            }
        }
    }
    destinations {
        Engineering {
            archive-sites {
                "ftp://orin@engineering.example.com/" password "$fds";
            }
        }
    }
}
```

This policy generates an event every five minutes. Also, every five minutes, the router
runs a command to look for BGP routes that have been learned within those five minutes and writes the command output to a file on an FTP server. These files can be
parsed to determine whether there is a pattern of constant routing updates for certain
network segments.

CHAPTER 21

Making Configuration Audits Painless

Just as the OS and networking equipment hardware need updates and maintenance, you must also maintain and audit the configuration files on the Juniper devices to ensure that changes in either the configurations or the network architecture have not led to issues that can cause network downtime. Well-planned and proactive auditing systems not only are necessary for maintaining continuous systems, but also are a matter of great importance today when it comes to compliance with data security standards laid out by such groups as the Payment Card Industry and the federal government.

Why Audit Configurations?

In many networks around the globe, the Information Technology Infrastructure Library (ITIL) is being implemented to provide detailed processes for change management and change requests. With these intricate processes, many administrators now swear off configuration auditing as superfluous—but this is not the case. Even if everyone follows the processes to the letter, there is always a need to audit configurations, not just for errors and changes but also for their applicability in the current network architecture.

Knowledge Is Power

Networks do not remain continuous, let alone survive, if no one is able to answer simple questions about how the network is designed or configured. Though some networks struggle along with very little documentation concerning design and configuration, these networks have little high availability. Configuration auditing provides insight into network configuration state to ensure that everything is configured correctly and to provide a foundation for future configuration changes. Configuration auditing has the following advantages:

Configuration standardization
> Having standardized configurations and configuration procedures across the network allows new services to be deployed much more quickly, improves the efficiency of troubleshooting, and can help to prevent network downtime. Through

the use of network auditing, you can ensure that the configurations throughout your network equipment are standardized and that one-off or kludged solutions are highlighted so that they can be eliminated.

Continuous systems

The less time it takes technicians and engineers to find, diagnose, and repair an incident of network downtime, the fewer strikes you have against your goal of high availability. With configuration audits, you can compare baseline configurations and recent changes to quickly determine whether a configuration error is leading to downtime.

Continuous improvement

Using configuration auditing tools, it is much easier to determine what possible changes must be made to the network to ensure high availability. By having a set schedule of configuration audits, you are able to ensure that the configurations are keeping up with the current best common practices and that they reflect any changes in network status, such as formerly bogon addresses being allocated to new customers.

Continuous services

Sometimes it is not physical hardware or software that brings a network service to a halt, but new regulations or policies released by federal agencies or private groups. Through the use of configuration audits, it is possible to demonstrate compliance with the various rules and regulations that are on the services on which you and your customers depend.

JUNOS: Configuration Auditing Made Easy

As we discussed before, the JUNOS operating system was developed with the ISP network in mind. As a result, the OS has features and functionality that allow configuration audits to be performed efficiently. The following features provide an advantage to operators using Juniper Networks equipment:

Single OS

The fact that the code and configuration of JUNOS are standardized across a wide range of products makes planning configurations simpler and allows for efficient configuration auditing. Because of the identical command line, it is not necessary to write auditing rules for individual pieces of equipment or code bases, such as IOS on a router and CATOS on a switch. Instead, audit templates can be written as logical rules for functional areas and shared among the equipment rather than individual rules being written for each piece of equipment to take into account command-line differences.

Configuration groups

JUNOS configuration groups allow you to more easily manage the portions of the configuration that appear on many network systems. Reducing the configuration of items, such as interfaces, to a single group prevents typos by network technicians and provides a single place to audit and correct the configurations.

JUNOScript

Commit scripts allow you to institute specialized configuration audits each time a configuration is committed. Event scripts can provide views of the configurations based on times or events, thus providing a running archive of configurations and configuration changes.

JUNOScope

JUNOScope provides a built-in Concurrent Versions System (CVS) to ensure that configuration files are maintained and versioned so that any changes are readily identifiable.

Configuration Auditing 101

If it were possible, we would have our special Level-40 Night Elf Druid use his inscription skills to create the "Dark Tome of Configuration Auditing" for you, but this being the real world, we will attempt to provide a brief but good foundation for configuration auditing in support of high availability. As with everything about the network, configuration audits require planning before you can implement them successfully. The key to any good configuration audit is to understand that consistency across network device configurations is one of the best and easiest-to-use techniques you can employ to guarantee high availability.

Organizing the Audit

The key to good configuration auditing is to develop rules and a template that create the most useful information, while still being efficient. JUNOScope provides the ability to monitor changes made to each and every configuration on networking equipment in detail, but the information can be unwieldy for an overall view of the network and its high availability stance. Through careful planning of what configuration pieces are most important for continuous systems and the use of audit templates designed for functional areas of the network, not for individual devices, you can more accurately get a snapshot of the overall network condition.

Configuration modules

Dividing the initial templates for audit configurations into the functional areas within the configuration allows you to mix and match modules to build very granular templates for the equipment's functional areas. Here is a list of some of the configuration modules that are important to high availability and those that can be audited to ensure high availability:

Chassis

Through the use of a general template for alarms, hardware information, and routing engine (RE) policy, it is possible to ensure that hardware events are processed for failover properly and that the appropriate alarms are sent for nonredundant systems.

Class of service (CoS)

Ensuring that your network's CoS policies are enforced, not only at your borders but also throughout your entire network, helps to guarantee that high availability for your important customers and packets is maintained, even during times of network saturation.

Firewall filters

A common set of firewall filters can prevent access to REs or deny malicious traffic at borders, ensuring the flow of essential data.

Interfaces

Through the auditing of physical hardware settings, such as speed and duplex, you can ensure that *auto-negotiation failures* and *timing mismatches* do not cause network outages.

Policy options

Because routing is the basis of all packets flowing across the network, you must ensure that routes are learned and distributed properly to all routers in a functional area.

Protocols

Auditing the routing protocols on the network equipment to ensure that high availability features such as Graceful Restart (GR), and security features such as authentication, are in place is a good defense to prevent routing loops or black-holing of traffic because of equipment outages or malicious route advertisements.

Security

Not auditing and updating the encryption protocols and the security stance of equipment is one of the quickest ways to create downtime for services that depend on compliance to federal or standards-based policies.

System

Establishing a consistent configuration for logging and monitoring, as well as authentication, guarantees that only authorized personnel are making configuration changes, and provides information to tools that ensure high availability.

 The most effective technique for ensuring high availability with configuration audits is the consistency of configuration across network devices, which enables technicians to maintain the network more efficiently and troubleshoot issues more quickly.

You can use the preceding configuration modules to develop a common architecture and a style for configuration. These configuration modules can be independent of each other and can change when necessary to meet current best common practices and to deploy new services.

Functional network areas

Using the configuration modules, it is possible to build configuration audit templates that match configuration items necessary to ensure high availability. The problem with this strategy is that you end up trying to create a single, catchall template to audit every piece of equipment within your network. Because the JUNOS command-line interface (CLI) is the same across the EX, J, M, MX, T, and SRX Series hardware, configuration audit templates do not rely on the chassis or software code, but can be divided into the functional areas in which the equipment falls. The requirements of a core Internet router are much different from those of a router acting as a gateway in a SOHO. Table 21-1 shows possible planning for breaking the network into specific functional areas.

Table 21-1. Functional area planning

Functional area	High availability configuration audits
Peering (connectivity to customer networks and external peering points)	Interior Gateway Protocol (IGP) high availability features to prevent internal routing convergence issues and downtime
	Chassis high availability features to maintain continuous systems
	CoS configurations to ensure that customer/peer traffic does not starve internal control or high-priority traffic
	Border Gateway Protocol (BGP) high availability features and routing policy to prevent route flapping or hijacking, or introduction of bogon networks
	Interface high availability and physical hardware features to maintain links to disparate connection types
	Firewall filters to provide very basic packet checking to prevent address spoofing and common attacks
	Standard high availability and monitoring and logging features
Core (internal connectivity within the network cloud providing the efficient transport of packets)	IGP high availability features to prevent internal routing convergence issues and downtime
	Chassis high availability features to maintain continuous systems
	CoS configurations to ensure that customer/peer traffic does not starve internal control or high-priority traffic
	Multiprotocol Label Switching (MPLS) configurations (if needed) to ensure that interfaces are properly configured to handle label switching and protocols to handle traffic engineering
	Standard high availability and monitoring and logging features

Functional area	High availability configuration audits
Data center	Chassis high availability features to maintain continuous systems
	CoS configurations to ensure that high-priority services are treated properly
	High availability configurations for switching, such as Virtual Chassis (VCs) on the EX Series
	Standard high availability and monitoring and logging features
SOHO	High availability features specific to the J Series, such as dial backup through a USB modem
	CoS configurations to ensure that high-priority services are treated properly
	Standard high availability and monitoring and logging features

When you omit unnecessary configuration items from configuration audits for functional areas, the templates are easier to read, and provide only the information necessary to maintain high availability for those types of network devices.

Organization involvement

Once you decide on the configuration items to be audited, you then determine the best course to take to develop the templates. It makes sense for those responsible for configuration of a module to develop the template for it, with the senior network engineers responsible for coalescing each one into a usage template. Table 21-2 illustrates an example of a planning table for organization responsibilities for the audit templates.

Table 21-2. Organization responsibility

Functional organization	High availability configuration audit responsibilities
Security	Packet filtering for external connections
	Security-specific logging
Operations	Chassis high availability features
	Standard high availability and monitoring and logging features
	Interface high availability configurations
Network engineers	IGP and BGP high availability features
	Routing policies
	CoS configuration templates for the core network and for the writing and rewriting of packets entering and leaving the network
	MPLS configurations

After all the functional organizations have completed their portion of the configuration template, it is possible to create the overall templates and begin auditing.

Auditing Configurations

Although having a single JUNOS code train makes it easy to apply common auditing techniques across all levels and functional areas of the network, in planning for configuration audits you must determine what degree of detail and complexity is necessary at each level. For instance, the SOHO staff may not understand the full configuration audit output of a J Series router and how changes to the configuration affect the network, but they must have the ability to determine whether configuration changes have been made. Looking at the various levels of configuration complexity and staffing in different portions of the network makes it possible to discover the best solutions for creating configuration baselines and auditing systems.

Baseline Configurations

For configuration audits to be truly successful, they must be conducted against an accurate baseline configuration. Although you can take the baseline from the production equipment, all network configurations should use templates to guarantee that every device shares a configuration that is consistent in scope and functionality.

Saving a baseline

For offices with few IT staff members and few changes to the configurations of their networking equipment, the simplest way to ensure that a baseline configuration is in place for audits is by simply saving the final deployment configuration to the user directory on the network equipment itself. The following code shows the CLI method for saving a configuration. The J-Web GUI also allows offices with untrained technicians to save the baseline configuration:

```
user@host> show configuration | save /var/home/user/baseline
user@host> file list detail

/var/home/user/:
total 20
drwxr-xr-x  2 user  staff       512 Jan 22 08:08 .ssh/
-rw-r--r--  1 user  staff      2768 Jan 22 08:10 baseline

user@host>
```

As you can see in the code example, the commands are a very simple way to save a baseline configuration so that it can be used for comparison in the future. The issue with such a simple solution for creating the baseline configuration is that while individual copies of the baseline exist on each piece of equipment, there is no guarantee that the configurations are consistent with the other devices in your network. As new services and policies are introduced and the network baseline changes, each piece of equipment must be changed individually at each level of functionality, thus creating a new baseline on each device.

Baseline configuration with JUNOS groups

In the JUNOS CLI, you can create groups that ensure that all functional areas are configured consistently across a single piece of equipment. In the following code, a group named `Standard_Gig_Interface` is created to guarantee that all Gigabit Ethernet interfaces on a single device use consistent settings for speed, duplex, and auto-negotiation:

```
user@host> show configuration
## Last commit: 2009-01-13  12:31:40 PST by root
version 9.1R1.8;
groups {
    interfaces;
    Standard_Gig_Interface {
        interfaces {
            <ge *> {
                speed 1g;
                link-mode full-duplex;
                gigether-options {
                    no-auto-negotiation;
                }
            }
        }
    }
}
apply-groups Standard_Gig_Interface;
```

Though the group in the example must be configured on each piece of equipment, changing the group affects all interfaces to which the group is applied. Through the use of groups, you can prevent human errors, such as misconfiguration of a single interface that could lead to network downtime. As configured in the preceding code, the group provides the first layer of configuration auditing to ensure high availability.

 Tools such as `apply-groups` are invaluable not only to keep your network up, but also when you initially configure the network. The example in the code would be very helpful in networks where million-dollar systems have refused to start communicating because the auto-negotiate settings on two manufacturers' equipment didn't play well.

Baseline configuration with commit scripts

With commit scripts, it is possible to create an automated, preemptive configuration audit that checks for and includes the information required in accordance with your network policies. The following code example is a commit script that ensures that some standard configurations are applied to the configuration each time it is activated. This configuration example applies a standard syslog configuration to all devices in the network. Using a single instance of the syslog template, you can ensure that logging is applied in a uniform manner across your network:

```
version 1.0;
ns junos = "http://xml.juniper.net/junos/*/junos";
ns xnm = "http://xml.juniper.net/xnm/1.1/xnm";
ns jcs = "http://xml.juniper.net/junos/commit-scripts/1.0";
import "../import/junos.xsl";
import "../import/junos.xsl";
var $macro-name = 'config-system.xsl';
match configuration {
s   <transient-change> {
      <system> {
        /* Standard SYSLOG Configuration */
        <syslog> {
          <user> {
            <name> "*";
            <contents> {
              <name> "any";
              <emergency>;
            }
          }
          <host> {
            <name> "security.example.com";
            <contents> {
              <name> "authorization";
              <warning>;
            }
            <contents> {
              <name> "firewall";
              <warning>;
            }
          }
          <host> {
            <name> "noc.example.com";
            <contents> {
              <name> "any";
              <emergency>;
            }
            <contents> {
              <name> "daemon";
              <alert>;
            }
            <contents> {
              <name> "kernel";
              <alert>;
            }
            <contents> {
              <name> "user";
              <alert>;
            }
            <contents> {
              <name> "pfe";
              <alert>;
            }

          }
        }
```

```
                }
            }
    }
```

Once the commit script is installed and loaded on the network devices, it parses the configuration each time the commit command is executed and checks for the appropriate configuration pieces. If the pieces do not exist, they are added to the configuration; if other errors exist, the script can stop the commit and signal the error, depending on how you have written it. Using the commit scripts, it is possible to create a single configuration template that is examined after any change, thus providing for preemptive auditing. The following example is the output showing the inclusion of our configuration template:

```
user@host> show configuration | display commit-scripts
## Last changed: 2009-01-13 11:01:45 PST
version 9.1R1.8;
system {
    host-name host;
    domain-name example.com;
    domain-search example.com;
    time-zone America/Los_Angeles;
    authentication-order [ radius password ];
    root-authentication {
        encrypted-password "$1dfds$.0"; ## SECRET-DATA
    }
    name-server {
        192.168.9.3;
        10.0.0.1;
    }
    radius-server {
        10.0.0.230 secret "$9$0mC4xN"; ## SECRET-DATA
    }
    scripts {
        commit {
            allow-transients;
            file baseline.slax;
        }
        op {
            traceoptions {
                file orin;
                flag all;
            }
            file test.slax {
                source test.slax;
            }
            file test1.xsl;
        }
    }
    services;
    syslog {
        archive size 1000k files 1000 world-readable;
        user * {
            any emergency;
        }
```

```
            host security.example.com {
                authorization warning;
                firewall warning;
            }
            host noc.example.com {
                any emergency;
                daemon alert;
                kernel alert;
                user alert;
                pfe alert;
            }
            file messages {
                any notice;
                authorization info;
            }
            file interactive-commands {
                interactive-commands any;
            }
        }
    }
}
```

Even though you configure the commit scripts, much like configuration groups, on
individual pieces of equipment, updating them is much easier than updating the configuration groups. The commit script itself can point to a source file in which the original
script exists, and can then instruct the network device to update the commit script with
information in the source document. In the following code example, the source code
for the commit scripts exists on a web server in the engineering department:

```
system {
    scripts {
        commit {
            allow-transients;
            file Baseline_audit.slax {
                source http://engineering.example.com/
                    scripts/base_audit_core.slax;
            }
        }
    }
}
```

Once you have added a source of the commit scripts to the configuration, you can
refresh them manually using the following code example—or you can work the commands into automated scripts to provide a scheduled or event-driven refresh:

```
[edit]
user@host#set system scripts commit file Baseline_audit.slax refresh
```

Manually Auditing Configurations

With all network devices running a consistent configuration across the network, using
either groups or commit scripts, we now look at the various methods for performing
the configuration audits themselves. Again, auditing methods can be as simple or as
complex as desired.

Manual auditing through the GUI

J Series and EX Series devices, with their built-in J-Web interfaces, make simple configuration audits quick and easy. By viewing the database commit history on the devices, you can easily determine when the configuration was last changed and how often changes are being made to the device. Data in the configuration database history includes the time the commit was made, the method through which the configuration was edited, and options to either download the configuration or roll back to a previously known good configuration. Figure 21-1 represents the web page for the configuration history. Note that the page also indicates whether anyone is actively editing the configuration.

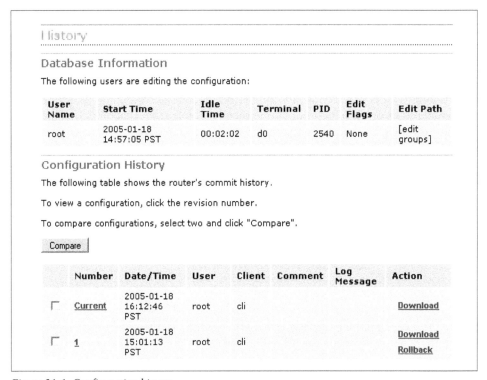

Figure 21-1. Configuration history

Configuration audits consist of more than examining the history of the configuration changes on the devices; they also include a comparison of the configurations that you can use to determine what changes have been made. Figure 21-2 illustrates the configuration comparison screen on the J-Web GUI.

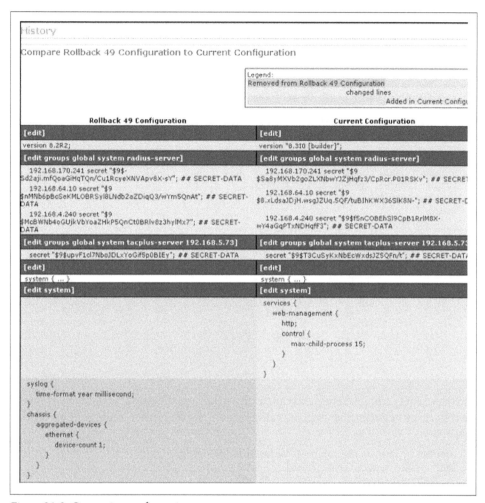

Figure 21-2. Comparing configurations

The J-Web GUI uses color coding, though not readily apparent in Figure 21-2, to highlight any deltas between the current and compared configurations. Using J-Web, it is simple to determine which configuration aspects have been added, deleted, or viewed but not changed.

Manual auditing through the CLI

The simple configuration auditing capabilities in J-Web are also available to junior technicians using the CLI. Automatically saved backups of previously committed configurations or comparisons with saved baseline configurations make it simple to determine when a change was last made and what the change was.

The show system commit command highlights the last configuration commit time, the user, and the management interface through which the change was made:

```
user@host> show system commit
0   2009-01-13 10:40:28 PST by user via cli
1   2009-01-02 09:26:30 PST by user via cli
2   2009-01-10 09:26:22 PST by user via cli
```

The show system rollback command displays the previous configuration. Each time a configuration is committed, the backup is put into a rollback file so that it can be reused, or reloaded, in case a configuration error causes system downtime:

```
user@host> show system rollback 3
## Last changed: 2009-01-22 13:33:15 PST
version 9.1R1.8;
groups {
    Interfaces;
    Standard_Interface {
        interfaces {
            <ge-*> {
                speed 1g;
                link-mode full-duplex;
                gigether-options {
                    no-auto-negotiation;
                }
            }
        }
    }
}
```

The show configuration command can be piped through the compare command to show the difference between the current configuration and any other configuration on the system:

```
user@host> show configuration | compare baseline
[edit system root-authentication]
-    encrypted-password "$1$.XfRw1"; ## SECRET-DATA
+    encrypted-password "$1$ /"; ## SECRET-DATA
[edit system scripts commit file baseline.slax]
+       source http://engineering.wa.gov/baseline.slax;
[edit event-options]
-  generate-event {
-       AUDIT time-of-day "00:00:00 -0800";
-  }
[edit event-options]
+   policy test {
+       events ui_commit;
+       then {
+           execute-commands {
+               commands {
+                   "set system scripts commit refresh";
+               }
+           }
+       }
+   }
```

The preceding example compares the previously saved baseline configuration to the current configuration on the network device. In the output, additions to the current configuration are marked with a plus sign and any deletions are marked with a minus sign.

Automating Configuration Audits

Although it is useful to manually audit configurations on the system, automated configuration auditing is recommended to provide the best posture for high availability. While many software companies have grown up around the process of configuration auditing, JUNOS itself provides many ways to audit configurations, and other Juniper Networks software, such as JUNOScope, makes automated auditing simple.

Event policies

One of the simplest ways to automate configuration auditing is to use event policies to create a file of all the configuration changes every time the configuration is committed. You can do this either with an event script or with a simple event policy. The following code archives the changes between the current configuration and the original baseline configuration, then uses FTP to send the changes to the engineers for more auditing or for archiving:

```
event-options {
    generate-event {
        DAILY time-of-day "01:00:00 -0800";
    }
    policy DAILY {
        events DAILY;
        then {
            execute-commands {
                commands {
                    "show configuration | compare baseline";
                }
                output-filename DAILY;
                destination engineering;
                output-format text;
            }
        }
    }
    destinations {
        engineering {
            archive-sites {
                "ftp://user@engineering.example.com/"
                    password "$9$w3saUq.5F6AfT"; ## SECRET-DATA
            }
        }
    }
}
```

You could write another event policy to fire off the same types of commands every time the configuration is committed. If your network engineers are familiar with Perl or other scripting languages, they could easily develop a set of scripts, templates, and configurations that examine the output of event policy and event scripts and then conduct almost all of the basic auditing of the configurations on the network equipment itself.

JUNOScope

For larger enterprises or ISPs, JUNOScope provides a single location for network engineers to collect, archive, and audit configurations. The JUNOScope software not only audits configurations against rollback or baseline configurations, but also allows you to compare configurations on multiple devices, ensuring that the configurations in place for network high availability are consistent across the network. Figure 21-3 illustrates the Audit Configurations web page of JUNOScope. Use this page to select the devices on which to compare configurations.

Figure 21-3. JUNOScope audit configuration

Like J-Web and the CLI, JUNOScope offers a feature to visually compare changes within the current configuration and other saved configurations. JUNOScope displays both the highlighting colors of J-Web and the plus and minus symbols of the CLI.

Unlike other methods of audit configuration that deal with single network devices, JUNOScope provides scalability to the configuration audit process. Its CVS provides an even greater ability to ensure that network device configurations are consistent. The CVS's check-out, modify, check-in, and deploy processes greatly reduce the introduction of errors into the configuration, thus allowing for a more continuous system.

The JUNOScope software goes even further in simplifying the auditing of configurations by allowing you to audit individual portions of the configuration and audit equipment licensing with its Inventory Management System.

Advanced Insight Solution

The Advanced Insight Solutions (AIS) and Advanced Insight Manager (AIM) add another level of defense against misconfiguration. AIM connects to the Juniper support infrastructure, allowing network engineers to use audits of network device configurations to diagnose possible issues that have occurred in the network, as well as gain intelligence into network operations to determine where the configurations and their baselines can be changed.

Performing and Updating Audits

A single configuration audit run when a service is deployed is good, but does not necessarily add to your network high availability. As changes are made to the network, you must go back and ensure that those changes have not had unexpected consequences. Also, as technology advances, you need to update configurations and, in turn, update the configuration templates and audits that are used to build the network. Just as with the initial planning for configuration templates and audits, it is better to divide the tasks into functional areas. You must also determine how often each functional area needs to be updated and the processes by which ad hoc changes are to be made.

Auditing Intervals

Setting up auditing intervals makes the difference between being overloaded by an avalanche of information and not having the information necessary to make all the proper decisions. In planning the interval for configuration audits, take into account internal organization requirements as well as laws and regulations under which the company may fall, such as Sarbanes-Oxley. For functional areas with glacial or static changes, such as interface physical attributes, an audit every six months may suffice, but for areas where technology and threats change rapidly, it may be necessary to conduct an audit every week, or even more often. Table 21-3 is an example of an audit schedule for configurations.

Table 21-3. Auditing intervals

Configuration module	Audit interval	Comments
Chassis	Quarterly	
Firewall filter	Biweekly	Pay special attention to newly allocated IP address ranges
Interfaces	Quarterly	
Routing policies	Biweekly	Pay special attention to newly allocated IP address ranges
Protocols	Biweekly	Pay special attention to external BGP peering
Security	Biweekly	
Systems	Quarterly	

Analyzing Updates

The first step in determining how to implement configuration templates and their corresponding configuration auditing changes in the system is to analyze how the changes will affect the network. Some changes to the configuration template, such as the rollout of a new service, must be vetted by all groups to ensure that the new service functions properly and does not degrade existing services or network security. Other changes, such as a modification to routing policy for newly allocated IP addresses, generally require only a quick review from those in charge of the peering routers. Table 21-4 is an example planning form for configuration template and audit changes.

Table 21-4. Ad hoc change analysis

Update	Impacted areas	Update reason
Routing policy update for new IP address	Peering connections	Change in networking environment
	Routing	
	Bogon filtering	
Introduction of VoIP into customer node	CoS mapping	Rollout of new service
	Peering connection at customer	
Worm attacking servers	Firewall filters	Issue in network environment

Once you have determined which areas of the configuration template need to be changed, you can develop the changes and decide on the time frame in which to implement them.

Auditing Changes

After the changes to configurations or configuration templates are approved, the resulting changes in the network should immediately be audited to ensure that both the configurations and the new auditing templates are working correctly.

CHAPTER 22

Securing Your Network Equipment Against Security Breaches

Much of this book revolves around concepts of high availability from a networking perspective. But it's equally important to remember that maintaining uptime includes considerations for the device itself. As this chapter discusses, securing the device to prevent it from being attacked or hacked is as important as any other effort put toward constant uptime. Without a strong security implementation on the device itself, all of your other efforts may go to waste.

Authentication Methods

One of the most fundamental ways to secure your device is to require users to log in with a username and password. Each user who accesses the device should have his own user account, and there are three ways you can authenticate that user on a device running JUNOS Software: local password on the device, Remote Authentication Dial-in User Service (RADIUS), and Terminal Access Control Access-Control System Plus (TACACS+).

Local Password Authentication

Local password authentication is very straightforward, involving the creation of a username and password on the device itself. You can create multiple user accounts for different users, and employ user classes to define a variety of access permissions for users accessing the device.

A typical local user account looks something like this:

```
[edit]
lab@r1# show system login user testuser
class super-user;
authentication {
```

```
    encrypted-password "$1$/Nbl7qhu$2dNqBVVauFN..ynv4xa3L0"; ## SECRET-DATA
}
```

 It is always a good practice to use a strong password. We cover password strength in the next section of this chapter.

RADIUS and TACACS+ Authentication

Devices running JUNOS Software can be RADIUS and/or TACACS+ clients. RADIUS and TACACS+ servers support a full range of authentication and authorization capabilities, and these capabilities can be fully leveraged by JUNOS devices. When using a RADIUS or TACACS+ server for authentication, a JUNOS device immediately sends the user's credentials (username/password) to the authentication server to authenticate the user. If successful, the user receives an authorization (permissions) from the server as well.

The following are examples of a device configured to use RADIUS or TACACS+ servers:

```
[edit]
lab@r1# show system
<removed for brevity>
radius-server {
    10.10.10.10 secret "$9$RZ1EyKMWx-dsKvoJDjq."; ## SECRET-DATA
    10.10.10.11 secret "$9$7zNb24oGji.2gTz6/tp"; ## SECRET-DATA
}

[edit]
lab@r1# show system
<removed for brevity>
tacplus-server {
    20.20.20.20 secret "$9$KauvLNdVY4oGN-Hqf5F3"; ## SECRET-DATA
    20.20.20.21 secret "$9$aIJDk.mTF39kquOREyr"; ## SECRET-DATA
}
```

Authentication Order

You can define which methods will be used for login attempts to the device, as well as the order of the authentication methods that will be performed:

```
[edit]
lab@r1# set system authentication-order ?
Possible completions:
  [                   Open a set of values
  password            Traditional password authentication
  radius              Remote Authentication Dial-In User Service
  tacplus             TACACS+ authentication services
```

Simply enter the parameters in the order you wish to have the login attempts performed.

When a user attempts to log in, the device directs the login request to the first server specified in the authentication order list. If the login attempt fails due to an incorrect password or because the server is inaccessible, the device sends the login request to the next server in the authentication order (if there is one listed). If no remote servers are available, the device itself will check the password against its own local user account database.

Devices running JUNOS Software always check the local user account database when external authentication servers fail to respond—even when password is not explicitly specified in the authentication order.

Hardening the Device

A critical element of ensuring high availability for your JUNOS device involves protecting and hardening it from outside attacks. The following are issues to consider.

Use a Strong Password, and Encrypt It

It is amazing how many networking devices in production networks have weak passwords or, worse yet, still have default passwords in place! Ensuring that your devices use strong passwords is one of the simplest steps you can take to harden the device. Every company has its own standard for what constitutes a "strong" password, but a good guideline is to use at least eight characters, and a mix of upper- and lowercase letters, numbers, and symbols.

JUNOS devices require that passwords be at least six characters long and contain at least one change of case or character class (i.e., numbers or symbols).

There are a variety of ways to enter passwords for user accounts on JUNOS devices. The following example shows the password options for an account called testuser:

```
[edit system login]
lab@r1# set user testuser authentication ?
Possible completions:
+ apply-groups          Groups from which to inherit configuration data
+ apply-groups-except   Don't inherit configuration data from these groups
  encrypted-password    Encrypted password string
  load-key-file         File (URL) containing one or more ssh keys
  plain-text-password   Prompt for plain text password (autoencrypted)
> ssh-dsa               Secure shell (ssh) DSA public key string
> ssh-rsa               Secure shell (ssh) RSA public key string
```

As you can see, there are several methods to input a password for a user account, including importing encrypted passwords and SSH strings. But the typical method of entering the password is to simply type it in at the command-line interface (CLI). This is done using the `plain-text-password` option:

```
[edit system login]
lab@r1# set user testuser authentication plain-text-password
New password:
Retype new password:

[edit system login]
lab@r1#
```

When using this option, the password you enter never actually appears on the screen. You simply enter it twice and the system stores the password. But that's not all it does. As an added layer of security, devices running JUNOS Software never show the password as clear text—ever. Notice in the following example that the "plain-text" password is now encrypted.

```
[edit system login]
lab@r1# show user testuser
class super-user;
authentication {
    encrypted-password "$1$O2qv4WXN$lvlz1Ei.rcxEabTwEcVjd."; ## SECRET-DATA
}
```

The device encrypts the password and displays it in the configuration as a hashed value.

> Because the configuration always shows the password as encrypted, it is easy to confuse the plain-text and encrypted password options when configuring a device running JUNOS Software. Use the `plain-text-password` option when you want to manually enter the password into the CLI; use the `encrypted-password` option when you want to use an existing hashed password and paste it into the CLI.

Disable Unused Access Methods

You can access a JUNOS device using a variety of methods, including SSH, Telnet, and HTTP. Each access method has its place, but it is a good practice to disable unused access methods. Consider the following configuration:

```
[edit system services]
lab@r1# show
ftp;
ssh;
telnet;
web-management {
    http;
}
```

This device can be accessed in several ways, not all of which are secure. If, for example, your company mandates using SSH rather than Telnet, you should remove Telnet as a service on the device.

It is a best practice to use only SSH and HTTPS to manage your devices wherever possible. These protocols encrypt their packets and ensure that your username and password are not sent as clear text across the network.

In practice, you can deactivate a service (similar to disabling it) or simply delete it from the device's configuration. Both achieve the same results.

Control Physical Access to the Device

Much effort is spent on securing networking devices from network attacks, but it is equally important to physically secure the device. All of your efforts to control access from the network can be wasted if someone can walk up to the device and connect her laptop directly to the console port! Ensure that the device is in a secure location, such as in a locked closet or a secure server room.

In cases where you are unable to secure a device running JUNOS Software, and the device has a craft interface in the form of a front panel with buttons, you can disable these controls, as shown here:

```
[edit]
lab@r1# set chassis ?
Possible completions:
> alarm                    Global alarm settings
+ apply-groups             Groups from which to inherit configuration data
+ apply-groups-except      Don't inherit configuration data from these groups
> config-button            Config button behavior settings
  craft-lockout            Disable craft interface input
  disable-power-management Disable Power Management in this chassis
> fpc                      Flexible PIC Concentrator parameters
  no-source-route          Don't enable IP source-route processing
> routing-engine           Routing Engine settings
  source-route             Enable IP source-route processing
```

Control Network Access to the Device

You can harden JUNOS devices by controlling how they are accessed over the network. For example, you can control SSH access to the device on a per-host basis:

```
[edit]
lab@r1# set security ssh-known-hosts ?
Possible completions:
+ apply-groups             Groups from which to inherit configuration data
+ apply-groups-except      Don't inherit configuration data from these groups
  fetch-from-server        Fetch the SSH public key interactively from this server
> host                     SSH known host entry
  load-key-file            File containing known hosts in OpenSSH native format
```

You can also limit the number of SSH connections to the device, and allow or deny SSH access using the root account:

```
[edit system services]
lab@r1# set ssh ?
Possible completions:
  <[Enter]>               Execute this command
+ apply-groups            Groups from which to inherit configuration data
+ apply-groups-except     Don't inherit configuration data from these groups
  connection-limit        Maximum number of allowed connections (1..250)
+ protocol-version        Specify ssh protocol versions supported
  rate-limit              Maximum number of connections per minute (1..250)
  root-login              Configure root access via ssh
```

If you are managing a JUNOS device using a web browser, you can define whether the connection can use HTTP or whether it must use HTTPS:

```
[edit]
lab@r1# set web-management http?
Possible completions:
> http                    Unencrypted HTTP connection settings
> https                   Encrypted HTTPS connections
```

You can also control which interfaces will accept management connection requests, as well as which TCP port is to be used for web-based management of the device:

```
[edit]
lab@r1# set web-management http ?
Possible completions:
  <[Enter]>               Execute this command
+ apply-groups            Groups from which to inherit configuration data
+ apply-groups-except     Don't inherit configuration data from these groups
+ interface               Interfaces that accept HTTP access
  port                    TCP port for incoming HTTP connections (1..65535)
```

These last items are less critical elements of hardening your device, but every little bit helps.

Control and Authenticate Protocol Traffic

In any environment where your networking devices are in contact with devices belonging to other parties, or where you share a segment with other companies (such as at an IXP), be very careful that you run only relevant protocols, and that you run them only on appropriate interfaces. If you accidentally enable an internal routing protocol on an external-facing interface, the router may start to learn information from a neighboring device—not a desirable situation! Be sure to control your routing protocols by using them only in desired places in your network.

Another common example where routing protocols can cause problems is when a "rogue" device is added to the network. Consider the following scenario: you configure Open Shortest Path First (OSPF) on your router, but instead of enabling the protocol on specific interfaces, you enable it globally, across all interfaces. One of the router interfaces connects to a local area network (LAN) segment that is used for testing and experimentation with new devices. If a user happens to configure a device and accidentally enables OSPF on that device, information will be passed between that device

---

and the router connecting the LAN segment to the rest of the network. Furthermore, this new routing information will likely be passed from router to router through the entire network—not good. Fortunately, there is an easy solution to this situation: authentication. By simply adding authentication to your device's routing protocols, you eliminate the possibility of this scenario occurring. Should a new device accidentally send out protocol messages, the messages will be dropped because they do not pass the authentication check.

It is quite easy to implement protocol authentication, as shown in this example using OSPF:

```
[edit]
lab@r1# show protocols ospf
area 0.0.0.0 {
    interface ge-0/0/2.0 {
        authentication {
            simple-password "$9$/aZp9pBIRSleWB17-ws4o"; ## SECRET-DATA
        }
    }
}
```

Define Access Policies

A key element of hardening your networking devices and your network in general is determining what traffic to allow and deny. This can be a very involved process, as you must be certain to allow relevant traffic while protecting the network against attacks. A good example of how this can get very tricky is ICMP traffic. It would be easy to deny ping traffic in the name of security; however, the ability to ping a remote host is a key troubleshooting tool. Blocking ICMP traffic can, in some cases, cause more harm than good.

ICMP traffic illustrates the point that defining access policies isn't necessarily a one-size-fits-all solution. Security policies aren't just about what you allow and deny. An equally important factor is *where* you apply them. You may determine that the ability to ping remote hosts is valuable within your own network; however, you may not want to allow inbound ICMP traffic from outside your network. The former is an element of network management, while the latter may well be an attack.

Other situations where access policies can be "location-specific" include RFC 1918 IP addressing, as well as your own public IP address space. Traffic within your network can be allowed to use this addressing. However, inbound traffic should *not* have a source address of your public address space—this is clearly spoofed traffic. In this situation, the access policy must be implemented at the edge of your network, to stop spoofed traffic before it ever gets in.

There are countless examples to illustrate the importance of defining access policies. Ultimately, this is an exercise you must perform within your company, determining guidelines, policies, and best practices based on your own environment.

We cover implementing access policies in the following sections of this chapter.

Firewall Filters

A firewall is a fundamental component in securing any network. Devices running JUNOS Software can filter packets at line rate based on their contents, and perform an action on packets that match the filter.

Firewall Filter Syntax

JUNOS devices filter traffic based on straightforward if-then logic. That is, if an incoming packet matches a given filter parameter, then the device takes some action on that packet.

Here is a basic example of the syntax and structure of firewall filter configuration:

```
[edit]
lab@r1# show firewall
family inet {
    filter samplefilter {
        term A {
            from {
                source-address {
                    192.168.1.0/24;
                }
            }
            then accept;
        }
    }
}
```

 A firewall filter doesn't actually filter traffic until it is applied to an interface. We cover this later in this chapter.

Firewall filters are defined at the firewall family hierarchy level. You can define filters for IPv4, IPv6, or Multiprotocol Label Switching (MPLS), or they can be protocol-independent. Each filter must have its own name, and each filter has one or more terms. A filter can also refer to another filter. In the previous example, a filter called samplefilter has one term, called A.

The following sections explain the remaining components of firewall filters.

Match conditions

The from statement in a firewall filter specifies the conditions the packet must match for the related action to be taken. Match conditions can include any combination of source and destination addresses, protocol numbers, and ports, as well as specific bits in certain packet fields (such as TCP flags). In the previous example, the match condition is a source address of 192.168.1.0/24.

Actions

When a packet matches one of the conditions in a filter, a corresponding action is taken—typically, accepting or denying the packet. Denying the packet can be done in two ways: *discard* and *reject*. When the router discards a packet, it simply drops the packet and takes no other action. When the router rejects a packet, it drops the packet and sends a message back to the source indicating that the traffic has been prohibited.

In addition to the standard accept and deny actions, you can use action modifiers to gather additional information about the traffic that matches a given filter. Action modifiers include logging, counting, and sampling. As an example of where this can be useful, imagine that you have a firewall filter in place to block incoming traffic from a given source address. It would likely be useful to not only drop the traffic, but also know how many packets are coming in from that host. In this case, an action of discard with an action modifier of count would be appropriate.

Firewall filters can also function as a way to "catch" traffic that is interesting to you and do something specific with it. For example, you can add actions that port mirror traffic, assign Quality of Service (QoS) parameters to packets, or redirect traffic to a given logical or virtual router.

Evaluating filters

A filter can contain one or more terms. To match a term, the packet must match all conditions of that term. For instance, using the earlier example, traffic from a host with a source address of 192.168.1.1 matches the condition. The following example is more complex:

```
[edit]
lab@r1# show firewall
family inet {
    filter samplefilter {
        term A {
            from {
                source-address {
                    192.168.1.0/24;
                }
                protocol tcp;
                destination-port 80;
            }
            then accept;
        }
    }
}
```

In this case, traffic from a host with a source address of 192.168.1.1 that is destined for a web server (using the standard HTTP port 80) matches the conditions. Traffic from the same host destined for an FTP server does not match the conditions, and would be dropped.

 Multiple conditions within a term create an "and" scenario. All conditions must match for the packet to be considered a match against the term.

There is one exception to the rule that a packet must match all conditions within a term to be considered a match. Consider the following example:

```
[edit]
lab@r1# show firewall family inet filter anotherfilter
term A {
    from {
        address {
            20.20.20.0/24;
            30.30.30.0/24;
            40.40.40.0/24;
        }
    }
    then accept;
}
```

In this example, it is clearly impossible for a packet to match all the address conditions. When address filters are used, the term is considered a match when any of the addresses matches the packet.

When there are multiple terms, each term is evaluated sequentially. If the packet matches the first term, it takes the corresponding action. If the packet does not match the first term, the router evaluates it against the second term.

Consider the following variation on the previous example:

```
[edit]
lab@r1# show firewall family inet filter samplefilter2
term A {
    from {
        source-address {
            192.168.1.0/24;
        }
    }
    then accept;
}
term B {
    from {
        protocol tcp;
        destination-port 80;
    }
```

```
            then accept;
    }
```

In this example, an incoming packet is evaluated against term A. If the packet does not match the condition, it moves on to term B. So, where the previous example required the traffic to come from a specific subnet *and* be destined for a specific port, this example separates the two parameters. A host with a source address of 192.168.1.1 is a match, regardless of which port the traffic is destined to. And likewise, any traffic toward port 80 is a match, regardless of where it came from.

Multiple terms create an "or" scenario. Conditions within a term are evaluated separately from conditions within another term.

Implicit discard

By default, there is an implicit discard all at the end of a filter. Traffic that does not match any term is dropped.

In general, you want to explicitly configure the traffic you want to accept. This causes all other traffic to be automatically discarded.

There may be rare situations where you want an implicit accept as the final rule. This can be achieved as follows:

```
[edit]
lab@r1# show firewall family inet filter samplefilter3
term A {
    from {
        source-address {
            192.168.1.0/24;
        }
    }
    then {
        discard;
    }
}
term B {
    from {
        protocol tcp;
        destination-port 80;
    }
    then {
        discard;
    }
}
term C {
```

```
        then accept;
    }
```

In this case, the match conditions in terms A and B cause packets to be discarded. The last term, term C, has no from statement, which means it matches all other traffic. This creates an implicit accept as the final match condition.

Applying Firewall Filters

A firewall filter can be well planned and designed, but it doesn't actually do anything until you apply it to an interface on the device. You can apply two filters (or filter lists) to each interface, one inbound and one outbound:

```
[edit]
lab@r1# show interfaces ge-0/0/2 unit 0
family inet {
    filter {
        input samplefilter;
        output anotherfilter;
    }
    address 192.168.1.100/24;
}
```

As the preceding example shows, firewall filters have been applied to the ge-0/0/2 interface, one in each direction.

 The benefit of creating a filter and then applying it as a separate step is that you can apply a filter to more than one interface. In fact, you can reuse filters on as many interfaces as you wish.

Using Firewall Filters to Protect the Network

There are countless ways you can use and apply firewall filters to control traffic flowing into and out of your network. This section shows some examples of how to apply filters to protect the network. The network diagram in Figure 22-1 serves as a reference for the examples that follow.

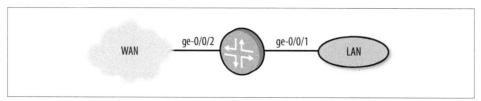

Figure 22-1. Reference diagram for following scenarios

Spoof prevention

In this scenario, you want to deny inbound traffic that is using your own address space as its source address. For example, if your public address space is 100.100.100.0/24, your filter would look like this:

```
[edit]
lab@r1# show firewall family inet filter no-spoof
term A {
    from {
        source-address {
            0.0.0.0/0;
            100.100.100.0/24 except;
        }
    }
    then accept;
}
term B {
    then {
        count no-spoof-counter;
        log;
        discard;
    }
}
```

This example makes use of a very convenient feature, the **except** command. Term A matches all traffic *except* your public address space. Traffic with a source address of your address space moves on to term B. Normally you wouldn't need term B, since all filters end with an implicit discard condition. However, when you let the implicit discard rule drop the traffic, you get no additional information about how much of this type of traffic you are receiving. This example shows how you can implement the implicit discard while also logging and counting traffic that matches your addressing space.

Remember that this filter doesn't actually do anything until you apply it to an interface. Since this filter is designed to block traffic inbound to your network, it should be applied to the wide area network (WAN)-side interface, in the inbound direction:

```
[edit]
lab@r1# show interfaces ge-0/0/2
unit 0 {
    family inet {
        filter {
            input no-spoof;
        }
        address 200.200.200.200/24;
    }
}
```

Your network is now protected from traffic that is illegally using your public addressing.

You can extend this scenario by applying another inbound filter to the ge-0/0/1 interface that allows only traffic with a source address of your public address space. This would ensure that no outbound traffic is being spoofed.

Securing a web/FTP server

In this scenario, you want to control traffic destined to a specific server on your network. External traffic should access the server using only FTP and HTTP. If the server has an IP address of 100.100.100.100, your filter would look like this:

```
[edit]
lab@r1# show firewall family inet filter control-server-access
term allow-FTP_HTTP-access {
    from {
        destination-address {
            100.100.100.100/32;
        }
        protocol tcp;
        destination-port [ ftp ftp-data http ];
    }
    then accept;
}
term deny-server-access {
    from {
        destination-address {
            100.100.100.100/32;
        }
    }
    then {
        count no-server-access;
        log;
        discard;
    }
}
term all-else {
    then accept;
}
```

Several things are going on in this filter. The first term, allow-FTP_HTTP-access, accepts FTP and HTTP traffic destined for the server. Note that JUNOS does not require that you enter port numbers for commonly known services; instead, you can enter the protocol names. Something else to note is a slight quirk in the terminology used to construct filters. As you read the first term, it appears to say "traffic from destination address 100.100.100.100," which sounds rather contradictory. Traffic comes from a source; it doesn't come from a destination. When analyzing firewall filters, it can be helpful to replace the word *from* with *matches*, as that is the actual intent of that section. It makes more logical sense to say, "Traffic that matches destination address 100.100.100.100," and it certainly reduces confusion!

The second term, `deny-server-access`, denies all other traffic to the server. It also counts and logs packets that match this term. This is the term that actually protects the server from unwanted traffic.

The third term is simple but critical. So far this filter allows traffic only to specific ports on a specific host. With only two terms, the implicit discard at the end of the filter will block all other traffic! So, you need to add the third term to allow other traffic through to your network.

As always, firewall filters don't do anything until you apply them. This filter can be applied inbound on the WAN-facing interface of the device:

```
[edit]
lab@r1# show interfaces ge-0/0/2
unit 0 {
    family inet {
        filter {
            input control-server-access;
        }
        address 192.168.1.100/24;
    }
}
```

 It is important to carefully consider where you apply your filter on the device. In the previous examples, there is only one inbound interface, so applying filters to the WAN-side interface inbound works just fine. However, if you have multiple inbound interfaces, it is simpler to apply these filters as output filters on the LAN-side interface of the device to ensure that all inbound traffic gets examined.

The options are endless

As you can imagine, there are countless possibilities when using firewall filters, and full coverage of all aspects and options of filters is beyond the scope of this book. You can find detailed information on firewall filters in JUNOS Software technical publications, which are freely available at *http://www.juniper.net/techpubs/software/junos/index.html*.

Using Firewall Filters to Protect the Routing Engine

When you use firewall filters, you generally think of accepting and denying traffic that passes through the device. However, you can also use filters to protect the device itself—specifically, the routing engine (RE). Protecting and securing the RE from attacks and unwanted traffic is a key component of maintaining five 9s availability.

You implement RE filters in much the same way you would when filtering transit traffic. You can create filters using all the same capabilities you saw earlier. The only difference to the process is where you apply the filter. To protect the RE, you apply filters to the lo0 interface. Filters applied to this interface (in the inbound direction) analyze only traffic destined for the device itself.

A firewall filter for the RE might look something like this:

```
[edit]
lab@r1# show firewall family inet filter protect-RE
term A {
    from {
        destination-port ssh;
    }
    then accept;
}

[edit]
lab@r1# show interfaces lo0
unit 0 {
    family inet {
        filter {
            input protect-RE;
        }
        address 10.0.0.1/32;
    }
}
```

The upper part of the example displays a filter called protect-RE, with a single term that accepts SSH connections. The lower part of the example shows that the filter is applied inbound on the lo0 interface. As with all firewall filters, there is an implicit discard condition at the end of the filter.

However, there is a major problem with this example—a problem that, if not corrected, will cause even bigger problems and will work directly against your efforts to maintain high availability for the network. While it is easy to get caught up in adding all the necessary rules to protect your device, is it critically important to remember a key detail: an input filter on the lo0 interface affects *all* traffic destined to the device. This includes management access, but also includes protocol communications such as routing updates, as well as other management communication protocols, such as Simple Network Management Protocol (SNMP). If you commit the previous configuration, you will actually "break" your network—not a good thing when the goal is constant uptime! Routing protocols will be blocked, causing other devices to think that this device has failed. This will cause reconvergence in the network, and traffic to be rerouted. Management systems will also think the device has stopped responding because communications have been blocked. Another side effect of this situation is that ICMP traffic will be discarded. This means that as you begin to realize there is a problem, any tests you perform using ping to the lo0 interface will only reinforce the impression that the device, or at least the RE, has failed!

Proper implementation of a filter on the lo0 interface requires that you include terms and match conditions for *all* traffic that needs to be able to reach the device. It's perfectly fine to add security to harden the device; however, be very certain you are still allowing required traffic through to the RE.

Here is a more complete version of the protect-RE filter:

```
[edit firewall family inet]
lab@r1# show filter protect-RE
term mgmt-access-in {
    from {
        protocol tcp;
        destination-port [ ssh https ];
    }
    then accept;
}
term mgmt-access-out {
    from {
        address {
            10.0.0.1/32;
        }
        protocol tcp;
        port ssh;
        tcp-established;
    }
    then accept;
}
term ospf {
    from {
        protocol ospf;
    }
    then accept;
}
term bgp {
    from {
        protocol tcp;
        port bgp;
    }
    then accept;
}
term ping {
    from {
        protocol icmp;
        icmp-type [ echo-request echo-reply ];
    }
    then accept;
}
term discard-all-else {
    then {
        count dropped-RE-traffic-inbound;
        log;
        discard;
    }
}
```

This improved filter now contains terms that allow inbound and outbound management traffic, as well as OSPF and Border Gateway Protocol (BGP) traffic. Ping testing will also work properly now. Of course, this filter is still just an example. There are countless options you may need to include, depending on the requirements of your network.

 When committing a configuration that includes a filter on the lo0 interface, it is *strongly* recommended that you use the commit confirmed command. This command temporarily activates the configuration on the device, but requires you to enter commit again within 10 minutes (by default) to permanently implement the new configuration. This feature provides a safety mechanism in case you accidentally lock yourself out of the device you are configuring. If you don't confirm the commit within the allotted time, the device rolls back to the previous committed configuration. If you had blocked your own access to the device, you will now be able to access the device again.

With careful planning, applying a firewall filter to the lo0 interface can be an excellent way to secure and harden the device, and support your goal of five 9s availability.

Stateful Firewalls

The filtering we described in the preceding section uses a *stateless firewall*. Stateless firewalls have their place, and JUNOS devices provide a wealth of excellent options for controlling traffic and protecting the device itself. That being said, stateless firewalls have limitations, the most significant of which is the inability to track a given flow bidirectionally. The packet filter processes each packet as it enters (or leaves) the interface, but it does not keep a record of that transaction beyond the single assessment of the packet. A stateful firewall's primary advantage is that it can keep track of traffic flows. If a JUNOS device assesses a packet and determines that the traffic should be accepted, the device adds an entry to its flow table. Now any traffic belonging to this same flow is automatically accepted, without having to be assessed again by the firewall's filters. This reduces the load on the device's resources and increases throughput.

Stateful firewalls are featured on SRX Series devices and J Series devices using flow-based JUNOS Software. You can also use a stateful firewall on M Series and MX Series devices by installing a services card.

Stateful firewalls are beyond the scope of this book. Although the concepts and general capabilities between stateless and stateful firewalls are the same, the implementation of stateful firewalls is more complex.

You can get complete information on using stateful firewalls on JUNOS devices at *http://www.juniper.net/techpubs/software/junos/index.html*.

CHAPTER 23

Monitoring and Containing DoS Attacks in Your Network

Denial-of-service (DoS) attacks can have a devastating effect on end hosts as well as the networks that service them. Devices can become slow to respond or even crash completely, creating network downtime. DoS attacks are almost impossible to stop at their source, so the focus must be on detecting the attacks and taking steps to limit their impact on the devices in your network. This chapter discusses strategies for attack detection, as well as steps you can take to lessen the impact of an attack while it is in progress. It also covers strategies for proactively reducing the impact of DoS attacks on your network, and concludes by showing you some ways you can gather evidence of the attack.

Attack Detection

You must have mechanisms in place to detect DoS attacks. You can use packet filters to help monitor and detect when an attack is occurring.

Using Filtering to Detect Ping Attacks

A variety of attacks use ICMP traffic. These attacks are designed to either overwhelm the resources of the target device, or fill the bandwidth of the link leading to the target device. In either case, the goal is to make the target device unreachable.

To detect these attacks, you can create firewall filters—not to block traffic, but to count and log it. The filter can be quite simple to create:

```
[edit]
lab@r1# show firewall family inet filter check-for-icmp
term A {
    from {
        destination-address {
            192.168.28.1/32;
```

```
        }
        protocol icmp;
    }
    then {
        count icmp-counter;
        log;
        accept;
    }
}
term B {
    then accept;
}
```

In this example, there is a server, 192.168.28.1, which could be a target for attack. Notice that at this point there is no protection in place; traffic is accepted. However, ICMP traffic destined for the server is counted and logged. This filter, once applied outbound to the JUNOS device's server-facing interface, allows you to view statistics on how much ICMP traffic is being sent toward the server.

Once you have committed the configuration, use the show firewall command to monitor ICMP traffic toward the server:

```
[edit]
lab@r1> show firewall
Filter: __default_bpdu_filter__
Filter: check-for-icmp
Counters:
Name                            Bytes           Packets
icmp-counter                        0                 0
```

In the preceding example, you can see the filter, check-for-icmp, and its related counters, specifically the one named icmp-counter. When monitoring for ICMP attacks, you can reissue the show firewall command a few times and check how quickly the icmp-counter counter is increasing. If the counter values are increasing rapidly, you may be experiencing a DoS attack.

Using Filtering to Detect TCP SYN Attacks

Another type of DoS attack involves a host initiating many TCP sessions to a device. The device responds to the initiating device, but the initiating device doesn't complete the session setup, leaving the session in a partially connected but useless state. This isn't a problem in itself, as the receiving device will eventually tear down the TCP session. However, a TCP SYN attack involves initiating thousands of sessions, none of which are actually used. Eventually, the receiving device becomes overwhelmed and can no longer function properly.

A good way to monitor TCP SYN packets is to create a firewall filter that compares TCP SYN packets to overall TCP traffic:

```
[edit]
lab@r1# show firewall family inet filter check-for-TCP-SYN
```

```
term A {
    from {
        destination-address {
            192.168.28.1/32;
        }
        protocol tcp;
        tcp-flags syn;
    }
    then {
        count syn-counter;
        log;
        accept;
    }
}
term B {
    from {
        destination-address {
            192.168.28.1/32;
        }
        protocol tcp;
    }
    then {
        count tcp-counter;
        accept;
    }
}
term C {
    then accept;
}
```

Notice how this filter accepts all traffic, but counts both TCP SYN packets and general TCP packets destined for the server. Like the ICMP filter, once you apply this filter outbound to the device's server-facing interface and commit the configuration, you can again use the show firewall command to view statistics on how much TCP traffic is being sent toward the server:

```
[edit]
lab@r1> show firewall
Filter: __default_bpdu_filter__
Filter: check-for-icmp
Counters:
Name                              Bytes          Packets
icmp-counter                       1596               19
Filter: check-for-TCP-SYN
Counters:
Name                              Bytes          Packets
syn-counter                           0                0
tcp-counter                           0                0
```

When the network is in a normal state, the tcp-counter value should be much higher than the syn-counter value; that is, there should generally be more TCP packets than TCP SYN packets. If you see the statistics change such that the counters show there are more TCP SYN packets than general TCP packets, you are likely experiencing a DoS attack.

Taking Action When a DoS Attack Occurs

When you determine that a DoS attack is occurring, there is very little chance that you can do much to stop the attack itself. But there are a few ways you can block the traffic from getting to the target device.

Using Filtering to Block DoS Attacks

The most obvious step you can take to block the attack is to use firewall filters. The exact solution will depend on the type and scope of the attack, but a good general approach is to use filters similar to the ones you used to detect the attack in the first place.

Here is a filter similar to the ICMP filter shown earlier, but with a slight variation:

```
[edit]
lab@r1# show firewall family inet filter discard-icmp
term A {
    from {
        destination-address {
            192.168.28.1/32;
        }
        protocol icmp;
    }
    then {
        count icmp-counter;
        log;
        discard;
    }
}
term B {
    then accept;
}
```

In the preceding example, a filter called `discard-icmp` has many of the same parameters as the `check-for-icmp` filter, but with a key difference: ICMP traffic destined for the server is now dropped. Once you apply this filter outbound on the server-facing interface, the attack will be blocked.

Do not deny traffic with the `reject` command. Rejecting traffic causes the JUNOS device to respond with an ICMP message of its own for each packet that matches the filter. This means the device generates as much traffic as it receives during the attack, which doesn't help the situation!

You can implement the same solution for TCP SYN attacks, using a variation of the filter shown earlier:

```
[edit]
lab@r1# show firewall family inet filter discard-TCP-SYN
term A {
```

```
        from {
            destination-address {
                192.168.28.1/32;
            }
            protocol tcp;
            tcp-flags syn;
        }
        then {
            count syn-counter;
            log;
            discard;
        }
    }
    term B {
        from {
            destination-address {
                192.168.28.1/32;
            }
            protocol tcp;
        }
        then {
            count tcp-counter;
            accept;
        }
    }
    term C {
        then accept;
    }
```

In this example, the `discard-TCP-SYN` filter is very similar to the `check-for-TCP-SYN` filter, with a key difference: `term A` discards matching traffic. Once you apply this filter outbound on the server-facing interface, the attack will be blocked.

 It's a best practice to keep in mind that when an attack occurs, time is critical. A good way to minimize downtime resulting from a DoS attack is to create as many of the filters as you can *before* the attack occurs. For example, in the preceding scenarios, you could create the filters in advance. Then, when the attack occurs, you can simply apply the desired filters to the appropriate interfaces and commit the configuration.

Filter some, filter all

Filtering can be an excellent way to block traffic when an attack occurs. However, it comes with a certain cost. When you block traffic to prevent an attack, you block *all* traffic that matches the conditions, including legitimate traffic. For example, if you implement the `discard-TCP-SYN` filter, you block the attack traffic, but you also block any legitimate connections that happen to be trying to establish a session while the attack is going on.

While the issue of blocking legitimate traffic can appear to be significant, in practice it isn't a big issue at all. Why? First, the benefit of blocking the attacking traffic usually far outweighs the issue of blocked legitimate sessions. Second, the reality of the situation is that if you didn't implement the filter, the attack would bring down the device, or at least degrade performance significantly, so the legitimate TCP connection wouldn't be able to connect regardless.

Request Help from Your Upstream Provider

When it becomes clear that your network is under attack, a logical step to take is to contact your service provider for help in blocking the attack (if you have multiple upstream providers, you must determine which direction the attack is coming from). Contact your upstream provider and provide information about the attack, including what you have learned based on the steps discussed previously. Your service provider should be able to help block the attack traffic by using the same filtering mechanisms you have implemented, or they may use routing techniques to black-hole the traffic.

 Some service providers are now charging for this additional "protection."

An Alternative Way to Discard DoS Traffic

Firewall filters are an excellent tool for controlling and blocking DoS attacks. However, in larger-scale environments this may not be a manageable solution. Service providers should consider implementing black hole routing to stop DoS attacks as close to their source as possible. You can preconfigure black hole routing using static routing with a discard next hop or using the *discard* interface. With the main components configured, you can implement black holing easily and at a moment's notice using Border Gateway Protocol (BGP) route advertisements or community strings.

For more information on using black hole routing as a method for controlling DoS attacks, see the presentation by Joe Soricelli and Wayne Gustavus at *http://www.nanog .org/meetings/nanog32/presentations/soricelli.pdf*.

Attack Prevention

It is extremely difficult to actually prevent a DoS attack, since you usually don't own the network from which the attack is originating. That being said, there are some steps you can take to help prevent attacks from bringing down your network and devices.

Eliminate Unused Services

Disabling or removing services that the device is not using gives you a good start toward defeating attacks. Every active service is listening on an open port. Certain attacks, such as TCP SYN floods, rely on this fact. For example, a TCP SYN flood to TCP port 21 will not succeed if the FTP service on the target device is disabled. Of course, you can't disable all services—devices legitimately need some in order to function properly and interact with other devices on the network. But there is no good reason to leave unused services running, and leave the device any more open to attack than it needs to be.

Enable Reverse Path Forwarding

Unicast *Reverse Path Forwarding* (RPF) is a kind of security tool that confirms that traffic is coming from where it's supposed to be coming from. When a packet arrives at a JUNOS device that is configured to use unicast RPF, the device does a route lookup to determine which path it should use to send return traffic to the originating device. If the packet's incoming interface matches the interface the router would use to send return traffic, the packet is considered valid; otherwise, the packet is dropped.

Some attacks use IP spoofing as part of their attack, meaning part of the IP address isn't genuine. You can find an example of this within the mechanics of a *smurf* attack, an attack in which the originating device sends out a large number of pings. To avoid having the ICMP replies come back and bombard the originating device, it sends the pings using a source IP address other than its own. This causes another device to suffer as it receives all the ICMP reply messages.

Unicast RPF can be a great help in stopping this attack without having to perform any action at all. As the packet arrives at the JUNOS device, it is analyzed to see whether it is coming in on the correct interface relative to its source address. Since the source address has been spoofed, there is a reasonable chance the packet will be deemed to be entering on the wrong interface. The packets will be dropped and the attack will end then and there. A simple feature such as unicast RPF can play a significant role in attack prevention.

Unicast RPF is easy to configure; simply add it to each desired interface, as shown here:

```
[edit]
lab@r1# set interfaces so-0/1/1 unit 0 family inet rpf-check
```

Use Firewall Filters

We have covered this topic in some detail at this point, but with good reason. You certainly don't want to put filters in place that will block legitimate traffic from getting through to its destination. But you also shouldn't leave the network any more open to attack than necessary. If you know of a common attack that uses, for example, UDP port 12345, and you don't use that port for any service within your network, of course you want to block that port!

In practice, you should use the "less is more" approach. Start with all traffic blocked and allow only what you need to in order to let legitimate traffic through. By following this approach, you are automatically protecting your network from many attacks.

Use Rate Limiting

Firewall filters provide good protection from DoS attacks, but they have a shortcoming: the filter either accepts or denies traffic; there is no middle ground. You can protect against an attack, but at the expense of blocking other legitimate traffic that also happens to match the filter.

Rate limiting is an excellent solution to this problem. Rate limiting works in conjunction with filtering to provide an additional layer of control over traffic that matches the filter conditions. For example, instead of a strict accept or deny action, a rate limiter allows you to configure a threshold. As long as a given type of traffic is below the threshold, it passes through the device; however, as soon as the volume of that traffic exceeds the threshold, the device can drop it.

This is an excellent solution for attack scenarios. As you saw earlier, you could monitor TCP SYN packets using one firewall filter, but when the attack occurs, you need to change to a different filter. Using rate limiting, you can incorporate these features into one filter.

Rate limiting is performed in JUNOS using a *policer*. Policers are configured under the firewall section of the command-line interface (CLI):

```
[edit]
lab@r1# show firewall policer SYN-policer
if-exceeding {
    bandwidth-limit 100k;
    burst-size-limit 10k;
}
then discard;
```

This policer, called `SYN-policer`, has two parameters of note. The `bandwidth-limit` setting determines the rate (in bits per second) at which traffic can pass through this policer. The `burst-size-limit` setting determines the maximum amount of data (in bytes) that can burst above the bandwidth limit before rate limiting begins. Any data that exceeds these parameters is discarded.

Once you create a policer, you can reference it from within a filter, as shown here:

```
[edit]
lab@r1# show firewall family inet filter police-TCP-SYN
term A {
    from {
        destination-address {
            192.168.28.1/32;
        }
        protocol tcp;
        tcp-flags syn;
    }
    then {
        policer SYN-policer;
        count syn-counter;
        log;
```

```
        }
    }
    term B {
        from {
            destination-address {
                192.168.28.1/32;
            }
            protocol tcp;
        }
        then {
            count tcp-counter;
            accept;
        }
    }
    term C {
        then accept;
    }
```

This example is identical to the check-for-TCP-SYN filter used earlier in this chapter, with one exception. For term A, instead of a match action of accept, the filter now sends matching traffic to a policer called SYN-policer. Once this filter is applied outbound to the server-facing interface on the JUNOS device, an excellent mechanism is in place to detect and dynamically control TCP SYN attacks on the server. And of course, this approach applies to any situation; you can create a filter to match traffic of interest, and use a policer to control the resulting matching action.

Firewall Filters: More Than Meets the Eye

You have seen by now that stateless firewall filters have excellent capabilities when it comes to accepting, denying, and policing traffic. But did you know that traditional firewalling is just one aspect of these filters' capabilities? Filtering is a way to isolate specific types of traffic for any number of specific purposes: applying Quality of Service (QoS) markings, performing filter-based forwarding (also known as source-based routing), traffic mirroring, and sampling, just to name a few.

For more information on the capabilities of firewall filters, see the "Policy Framework Configuration Guide" at *http://www.juniper.net/techpubs/software/junos/index.html*.

Deploy Products Specifically to Address DoS Attacks

This chapter covers DoS monitoring and prevention techniques that are available across all JUNOS devices. However, some devices include additional specialized capabilities for detecting and preventing a wide range of attacks. SRX Series and ISG Series devices provide deep packet inspection using flow-based stateful firewalls, which can manage traffic on a broader level than packet-based filters. They also have intrusion detection and prevention capabilities.

Juniper Networks IDP Series devices provide inline protection that stops network and application-level attacks before they inflict any damage to the network.

These devices are purpose-built to secure the network against attacks. While they involve additional cost, they are often worth it when measured against the cost of a loss in productivity due to a network outage as a result of a DoS attack.

 These features are also available on MX Series devices when installed with a multiservice edge card.

Gathering Evidence

Sometimes you may want to collect information about an attack that has occurred. You might want to analyze the attack further, or perhaps you want to provide data to a law enforcement agency. In either case, there are several tools you can use to gather the appropriate data.

Firewall Logs and Counters

We discussed firewall logs and counters throughout this chapter. They provide direct information about which traffic is being accepted and denied, and how much traffic matches each filter. Using these tools, you can get a good indication of whether attacks are occurring, and capture data to use as evidence of the existence of the attack.

Port Mirroring

You can use port mirroring to capture entire packets and send a copy of them to another device. This can be very useful to gather evidence of an attack.

To configure port mirroring, you must first define parameters for how much data to capture and where to send it:

```
[edit]
lab@r1# show forwarding-options
port-mirroring {
    family inet {
        input {
            rate 100;
            run-length 3;
        }
        output {
            interface fe-0/0/1.0 {
                next-hop 10.10.1.1;
```

```
            }
        }
      }
   }
```

In this example, you can see that port mirroring parameters are configured under the forwarding-options section of the CLI. You must define two input parameters: the rate, which is the capture sampling rate, and the run-length, which is how many packets are captured each time a capture is performed; for example, a rate of 100 means a capture will be triggered for each 100 eligible packets. A run-length of 3 means that each time a capture is triggered, three packets will be captured. You must also define output parameters, including an interface out of which to send the captured packets, and a next hop.

Once the parameters are configured, you can create a filter that matches traffic of interest, and apply that filter to an interface:

```
[edit]
lab@r1# show firewall family inet filter mirror
term A {
    from {
        destination-address {
            192.168.28.1/32;
        }
        protocol icmp;
    }
    then port-mirror;
}

[edit]
lab@r1# set interfaces so-0/1/1 unit 0 family inet filter input mirror
```

In this example, notice that the filter's matching action is set to port-mirror. When you commit the configuration, the device will capture three packets for every 100 ICMP packets destined for the server at 192.168.28.1, and send a copy of these captured packets out interface fe-0/0/1 to a device at 10.10.1.1.

 If you use port mirroring to capture evidence of an attack, be very conservative with the capture rate setting. A device under attack is likely already under heavy stress—the last thing you want to do is to stress it further. Use port mirroring only if the device can handle the additional resource requirements, and keep the capture ratio high (i.e., capture only a few packets per large number of offending packets).

Sampling

If you have a Monitoring Services or Adaptive Services card installed in your JUNOS device, you can sample traffic passing through the routing platform.

Traffic sampling doesn't capture entire packets. It captures only enough information from the headers of matching packets to identify packets belonging to the same flow.

You configure sampling in much the same way as port mirroring. First, configure global sampling parameters, this time under the sampling stanza of the `forwarding-options` section of the CLI:

```
[edit]
lab@r1# show forwarding-options
sampling {
    input {
        family inet {
            rate 100;
            run-length 3;
        }
    }
    output {
        file filename icmp-sample;
    }
}
```

Notice that the output location is a file on the device. Once the parameters are configured, you can create a filter that matches traffic of interest, and apply that filter to an interface:

```
[edit]
lab@r1# show firewall family inet filter sample
term A {
    from {
        destination-address {
            192.168.28.1/32;
        }
        protocol icmp;
    }
    then sample;
}

[edit]
lab@r1# set interfaces so-0/1/1 unit 0 family inet filter input sample
```

 As with port mirroring, if you want to use sampling, be sure the device can handle the resource requirements despite the ongoing attack, and be very conservative with the capture rate setting.

cflowd

Sampled traffic can also be exported to a server running cflowd. This can be an excellent way to capture header information about attack traffic and export it to an external device for storage.

cflowd uses the same configuration as sampling, with the addition of `cflowd` export parameters:

```
[edit]
lab@r1# show forwarding-options
sampling {
    input {
        family inet {
            rate 100;
            run-length 3;
        }
    }
    output {
        file filename icmp-sample;
        cflowd 10.0.1.1 {
            port 12345;
            version 8;
        }
    }
}
```

As you can see in this example, the sampling configuration has additional parameters for cflowd. Note that Version 5 flow records are also supported.

DoS attacks can bring entire networks to a halt. Detecting, controlling, and minimizing the effects of these attacks is a very important component in maintaining high availability. You can find more resources and information about protecting your network at *http://www.juniper.net*.

CHAPTER 24

Goals of Configuration Automation

In the past few years, the size of networks has exploded and the complexity of the protocols on which they are based has had to keep pace. The problem for modern networks is that the number of highly technical engineers has not grown adequately to match this expansion. Engineers have less time to plan, review, and monitor the configuration of devices, and many of these tasks are falling to junior-level engineers who may not have the breadth of experience, but rather have a deep technical understanding of only one or two components of network topology.

With senior engineers spread so thinly and junior technicians possibly dealing with network components outside their area of expertise, it is necessary to prevent human error from causing network downtime. JUNOS Software has specific features that provide automated configuration and validation for network devices that can help a great deal in this area, and tools to better protect against human error for necessary manual configuration.

CLI Configuration Automation

In the realm of network engineers and technicians, it is a badge of honor to be a "CLI guy," someone who is never seen to use a GUI. With some of the legacy operating systems on network devices, this virtue can quickly become a pitfall. Because the operating systems of many network devices apply changes to their active, or running, configuration, simple typos or poorly planned configuration sequences can lead to network downtime. Because these operating systems use instant activation, they lack a way to validate the full command sequence to ensure that all requirements for the configuration are met; instead, they validate only the syntax of individual lines as entered.

Senior network engineers have developed all forms of voodoo rituals, ranging from copying and pasting complete configurations at once to having possibly insecure back doors into equipment, to mitigate the ramifications of errors introduced into the configuration. Although these tricks are often effective, sometimes they themselves cause network downtime or force the engineer to take a trip across the city to reboot a device that is not responding.

 In some networks, the engineers believe the only way to ensure that a major configuration change is implemented properly is to erase the startup configuration, reboot the device, and then cut and paste the whole configuration in one fell swoop. Although this process may ensure that the whole new configuration is applied in order, it results in network downtime during the reload, as well as errors caused by changes introduced after the configuration is pulled from the device and before it is edited and reapplied.

JUNOS Software has many features that have been specifically developed to prevent human error from causing network downtime. These tools not only better protect the device configuration, but also allow for *automated configuration checking* to ensure that the configuration changes that are made do not disrupt the network.

Hierarchical Configuration

Automated configuration makes no difference in a network if the configuration files and structure are too convoluted to make sense to the operator or to the tools used to automate the configuration. To simplify both manual and automated configuration of network devices running JUNOS, use a well-organized hierarchy to ensure consistency within the configuration:

Syntax
A common syntax structure for commands and configuration makes automated validation and creation of scripts for configuration checking simpler and more efficient.

Strings
The parsing of strings at the hierarchy level allows you to use the Tab key to complete strings, thus preventing mistyped strings when referencing user-created objects. It also allows for strings to be called in the various commit scripts developed for the hierarchy level.

Modularity
You can edit, save, and load configuration components in small, manageable sections, thus allowing subject-matter experts to focus on their own portions of the configuration. The modularity is useful not only for the initial configuration by the experts, but also for having a modular structure that commit scripts can be written against.

This hierarchical configuration, in concert with XML storage and parsing, lends itself directly to scripted configuration automation and checking. This scripted checking can be used to enforce network policies or designs to ensure that simple errors are not the root cause of major outages.

Protections for Manual Configuration

Though the goal of any network operator should be to automate as many configuration processes as possible, it is necessary to also have protections in place to prevent human errors from appearing during manual configurations. JUNOS Software includes features to restrict access to certain portions of the configuration hierarchy, allow exclusive configuration of the device, and allow multiple users to configure and commit portions of the configuration.

User access

One way in which JUNOS ensures that human errors are kept to a minimum is by restricting the hierarchy levels or commands a user may access. Through the use of a login class, each user can be assigned a list of commands or functional areas that are explicitly allowed or denied. In the following example, a user has been created that is allowed to only configure and view interface settings:

```
[edit system]
  login {
      class interface {
          permissions [ configure interface ];
          allow-commands "show interfaces";
          allow-configuration interfaces;
      }
          user inteng {
          uid 2002;
          class interface;
          authentication {
              encrypted-password "$1$v5CQbbw.$18MYWw "; ## SECRET-DATA
          }
      }
    }
  }
```

With this example, network engineers can be cordoned off into their functional area to guarantee that any errors they make do not affect the entire system. The login class's permissions can either be configured directly on the JUNOS command-line interface (CLI) or be configured within a Remote Authentication Dial-in User Service (RADIUS) server and passed to the device.

Exclusive configuration

Sometimes it is necessary for a single user to make changes to a JUNOS device without other users simultaneously making changes to the candidate configuration. The configure exclusive command is used to lock the global candidate configuration to one user until the configuration is committed. The command ensures that only a single user makes configuration changes to the device and that the user's changes are discarded if they are not committed:

```
user@host> configure exclusive
warning: uncommitted changes will be discarded on exit
Entering configuration mode
[edit]
user@host# set system host-name R1
[edit]
user@host# quit
The configuration has been changed but not committed
warning: Auto rollback on exiting 'configure exclusive'
Discard uncommitted changes? [yes,no] (yes)
warning: discarding uncommitted changes
load complete
Exiting configuration
```

When other users attempt to move into configuration mode, the user is notified that the configuration is currently locked and is told which user has it locked:

```
user@host> configure
Entering configuration mode
Users currently editing the configuration:
  root terminal p3 (pid 1078) on since 2000-02-30 19:47:58 EDT, idle 00:00:44
      exclusive [edit interfaces ge-3/1/1 unit 0 family inet]
```

The only way to take over the configuration mode is to make the user who has the configuration locked log off.

Private configuration

The configure private command enables multiple users to edit different parts of the configuration at the same time and to commit only their own changes, or to roll back without interfering with changes being made by others. When the command is issued, a private candidate configuration is created from the most recently created configuration and is used for editing:

```
root@host> configure private
warning: uncommitted changes will be discarded on exit
Entering configuration mode

[edit]
root@host# set system host-name R1

[edit]
root@host# exit
The configuration has been changed but not committed
Discard uncommitted changes? [yes,no] (yes)
```

If a second user attempts to configure the device normally, she will be able to view the configuration, but will be unable to make any changes:

```
user@host> configure
Entering configuration mode
Users currently editing the configuration:
```

```
    root terminal d0 (pid 5259) on since 2009-05-15 20:26:03 UTC, idle 00:01:59
        private [edit]
user@host# set system host-name test
error: private edits in use. Try 'configure private' or 'configure exclusive'.

[edit]
user@host#
```

At any time when a user is working with her private candidate configurations, other users may commit their private configurations. For the user to ensure that she has the latest candidate configuration, she uses the update command to merge the committed changes into her private candidate configuration.

Transaction-Based Provisioning

Not all errors in the network occur because of a mistake; some occur as a result of the way changes are applied to a device. For example, when applying access rules to a device, the rules are written in such a way that they block certain access, but grant access lower in the configuration. If this configuration is entered into the device and applied immediately, you may lose access, and it will not be possible to enter the lines that would have allowed you access to the device.

To minimize the immediate effect of human errors on the network, JUNOS uses transaction-based provisioning, in which configuration changes are not made until you manually commit the whole configuration piece at once. In addition, the provisioning tool provides a simplified method of fallback to previous configurations, either manually or automatically.

Standard commits

The basic method of preventing human error during the process of configuring a device is to automate the validation of the configuration before it is applied to the device. This validation process of the entire set of configuration changes prevents single typos and badly designed command sequences from locking the administrator out of a network device or causing protocol or interface errors that could lead to routing loops or black holes.

In JUNOS, even the most basic form of configuration creation and deployment provides automated processes to prevent network downtime caused by configuration issues. Figure 24-1 demonstrates automated features of manual configuration.

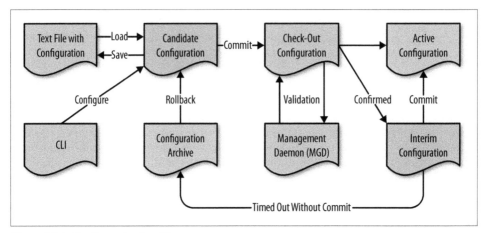

Figure 24-1. Configuration handling

As shown in Figure 24-1, each configuration change passes through at least one automated check before it is allowed to become the active configuration. During a standard commit process, the candidate configuration, which can be created from a text file or CLI configuration or can be pulled from the configuration archive, is copied to the checkout configuration, where it is validated by the management daemon (mgd). The commit confirmed command adds an additional automated step that copies the checkout configuration to an interim configuration. This interim configuration is not copied to the active configuration until a second commit command is entered. If the mgd does not receive the additional commit command, the interim configuration is placed in the configuration archive and the previous active configuration is automatically copied to the candidate configuration, committed, validated, and copied to the active configuration, thus restoring the device to the state of operation before the commit confirmed command was entered:

```
root@host# commit | display detail
2009-03-11 20:03:26 UTC: exporting juniper.conf
2009-03-11 20:03:26 UTC: expanding groups
2009-03-11 20:03:26 UTC: finished expanding groups
2009-03-11 20:03:26 UTC: setup foreign files
2009-03-11 20:03:26 UTC: propagating foreign files
2009-03-11 20:03:26 UTC: complete foreign files
2009-03-11 20:03:26 UTC: dropping unchanged foreign files
2009-03-11 20:03:26 UTC: executing 'ffp propagate'
2009-03-11 20:03:26 UTC: daemons checking new configuration
2009-03-11 20:03:26 UTC: commit wrapup...
2009-03-11 20:03:26 UTC: updating '/var/etc/filters/filter-define.conf'
2009-03-11 20:03:26 UTC: activating '/var/etc/certs'
2009-03-11 20:03:26 UTC: executing foreign_commands
2009-03-11 20:03:26 UTC: /bin/sh /etc/rc.ui ui_setup_users (sh)
2009-03-11 20:03:26 UTC: executing ui_commit in rc.ui
2009-03-11 20:03:26 UTC: executing 'ffp activate'
2009-03-11 20:03:26 UTC: copying configuration to juniper.save
```

```
2009-03-11 20:03:27 UTC: activating '/var/run/db/juniper.data'
2009-03-11 20:03:27 UTC: notifying daemons of new configuration
commit complete
```

This output shows the process of a standard commit with the creation of files for the configuration validation and the inspection of the configuration changes to determine their effect on system daemons. The checkout configuration is made active, and the daemons are notified of any changes.

Commit with scripts

The use of commit scripts adds a layer of complexity to the processing of configuration files, but also adds layers of automation to prevent errors. Within the commit script processing, the mgd will make changes to the configuration. These changes are of one of two change types: *persistent* or *transient*.

Persistent changes. Changes that are not defined as transient in the commit script are considered *persistent* and are placed directly into the candidate configuration. As a result, these changes appear as standard configuration lines in the active configuration when you issue a show configuration command and you can edit these lines in the configuration after the commit:

```
[edit]
root@host# commit | display detail
2009-03-11 20:23:21 UTC: reading commit script configuration
2009-03-11 20:23:21 UTC: testing commit script configuration
2009-03-11 20:23:21 UTC: opening commit script '/var/db/scripts/commit/base.xsl'
2009-03-11 20:23:21 UTC: reading commit script 'base.xsl'
2009-03-11 20:23:21 UTC: running commit script 'base.xsl'
2009-03-11 20:23:21 UTC: processing commit script 'base.xsl'
[edit interfaces interface ge-0/0/0 unit 0]
  warning: Adding 'family mpls' to GE interface.
2009-03-11 20:23:21 UTC: no errors from base.xsl
2009-03-11 20:23:21 UTC: saving commit script changes for script base.xsl
2009-03-11 20:23:21 UTC: summary of script base.xsl: changes 1, transients 0, syslog 0
2009-03-11 20:23:21 UTC: loading commit script changes
2009-03-11 20:23:21 UTC: finished loading commit script changes
2009-03-11 20:23:21 UTC: exporting juniper.conf
2009-03-11 20:23:21 UTC: expanding groups
2009-03-11 20:23:21 UTC: finished expanding groups
2009-03-11 20:23:21 UTC: setup foreign files
2009-03-11 20:23:21 UTC: propagating foreign files
2009-03-11 20:23:21 UTC: complete foreign files
2009-03-11 20:23:21 UTC: dropping unchanged foreign files
2009-03-11 20:23:21 UTC: executing 'ffp propagate'
2009-03-11 20:23:21 UTC: daemons checking new configuration
2009-03-11 20:23:21 UTC: Routing protocols process checking new configuration
2009-03-11 20:23:21 UTC: Firewall process checking new configuration
2009-03-11 20:23:21 UTC: Interface control process checking new configuration
2009-03-11 20:23:21 UTC: Management Information Base II process checking new
status 0 with notification errors enabled
(domain notifications omitted)..
commit complete
```

As this code output demonstrates, the persistent changes are loaded into the configuration before the checkout configuration is created. Through this process, the persistent changes are written into the candidate configuration, and they remain in the configuration after the commit process. Because persistent changes are applied directly to the candidate configuration, you can edit or delete them.

Transient changes. The changes marked as *transient* are added to the checkout configuration before the final validation, but they are not added to the candidate configuration. Here is code output of a commit that uses transient changes:

```
root@host# commit | display detail
2009-03-11 21:20:35 UTC: reading commit script configuration
2009-03-11 21:20:35 UTC: testing commit script configuration
2009-03-11 21:20:35 UTC: opening commit script '/var/db/scripts/commit/mtu.xsl'
2009-03-11 21:20:35 UTC: reading commit script 'mtu.xsl'
2009-03-11 21:20:35 UTC: running commit script 'mtu.xsl'
2009-03-11 21:20:35 UTC: processing commit script 'mtu.xsl'
2009-03-11 21:20:35 UTC: no errors from mtu.xsl
2009-03-11 21:20:35 UTC: saving commit script changes for script mtu.xsl
2009-03-11 21:20:35 UTC: summary of script mtu.xsl: changes 0,
transients 1 (allowed), syslog 0
2009-03-11 21:20:35 UTC: no commit script changes
2009-03-11 21:20:35 UTC: finished loading commit script changes
2009-03-11 21:20:35 UTC: exporting juniper.conf
2009-03-11 21:20:35 UTC: loading transient changes
2009-03-11 21:20:35 UTC: loading commit script changes (transient)
2009-03-11 21:20:35 UTC: updating transient change flags
2009-03-11 21:20:35 UTC: no commit script changes from previous commit
2009-03-11 21:20:35 UTC: finished loading commit script changes
2009-03-11 21:20:35 UTC: expanding groups
2009-03-11 21:20:35 UTC: finished expanding groups
2009-03-11 21:20:35 UTC: setup foreign files
2009-03-11 21:20:35 UTC: propagating foreign files
2009-03-11 21:20:35 UTC: complete foreign files
2009-03-11 21:20:35 UTC: dropping unchanged foreign files
2009-03-11 21:20:35 UTC: executing 'ffp propagate'
2009-03-11 21:20:35 UTC: daemons checking new configuration
2009-03-11 21:20:35 UTC: Routing protocols process checking new configuration
2009-03-11 21:20:36 UTC: Init daemon checking new configuration
2009-03-11 21:20:36 UTC: Chassis control process checking new configuration
2009-03-11 21:20:36 UTC: Booting daemon checking new configuration
2009-03-11 21:20:36 UTC: Firewall process checking new configuration
2009-03-11 21:20:36 UTC: Interface control process checking new configuration
```

Because the changes are applied to the checkout configuration, you cannot edit or delete them. In fact, you must use the show configuration | display commit-scripts command to even see the transient changes in the configuration.

Script processing

Because of the additional steps involved with commit scripts, the process of committing a configuration is slightly more complex. Figure 24-2 illustrates the process of adding script checking to the configuration process.

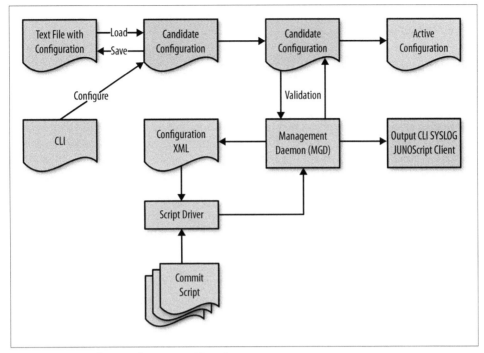

Figure 24-2. Handling configuration with scripts

As with a standard commit, mgd validates all changes before they become part of the active configuration. The additional processing of the commit scripts is performed before the final validation takes place. In the process, once the commit command is used on the candidate configuration, mgd creates an XML formatted copy of the configuration file. The script driver, using the onboard processor, parses the configuration changes against the scripts that are configured on the system. Depending on the commit scripts, various actions can be sent to mgd to perform, including the following:

Error message
> mgd sends an error message to the syslog, CLI, or JUNOScript client, and the commit is rejected.

Persistent changes
> mgd adds to the configuration any change that the commit script makes.

Transient changes
> After all changes have been made to the candidate and the candidate configuration is copied to the checkout configuration, mgd adds to the checkout configuration any changes defined as transient.

When you know the timing and process differences between transient and persistent changes, you can ensure that the commit script's automation process inserts data into the configuration in such a way that errors cannot be introduced later. For example, using transient changes, it is possible to enforce mandatory configuration items that technicians cannot view or change.

Archives and Rollback

Even with automation in place to validate candidate configurations and scrub them against scripts, and even if the JUNOS syntax in the configuration is perfect, it is possible that an error might occur as a result of flawed configuration logic. JUNOS provides archived configuration files and the `rollback` command to ensure that these errors do not lead to extended network downtime.

Configuration stores

As each configuration is committed, the active configuration is copied to the archive before the new checkout configuration is activated. The active configuration and the last three active configurations are stored in the flash of the JUNOS device. The following output displays a list of the current active configuration and the last three configurations on the flash drive in the *config* directory:

```
user@host> file list /config/

/config/:
.snap/
juniper.conf.1.gz
juniper.conf.2.gz
juniper.conf.3.gz
juniper.conf.gz
```

As more commits are made to the systems, the configurations are shifted until they are placed onto the hard drive, where up to 47 more configurations can be saved. This example output shows an abbreviated list of files:

```
user@host> file list /var/db/config/

/var/db/config/:
juniper.conf.10.gz
juniper.conf.11.gz
juniper.conf.12.gz
juniper.conf.13.gz
juniper.conf.14.gz
juniper.conf.15.gz
juniper.conf.16.gz
juniper.conf.17.gz
juniper.conf.18.gz
```

Using the CLI, you can not only roll back to the previous configurations, but also examine the deltas in the configuration files:

```
user@host> show configuration | compare rollback 4
[edit system scripts commit]
+      file mtu.xsl;
-      file encap.xsl;
[edit interfaces]
-    so-0/1/0 {
-        unit 0;
-    }
```

When the configuration is restored from the archive either manually using the `rollback` command or automatically using a remote tool or the `commit confirmed` command, the specified configuration file is loaded and only the objects that differ from the active configuration are marked as changed. The configuration is then validated and activated. This automated rollback process ensures that human error is not introduced in the return to the previous configuration.

Automating Remote Configuration

Although JUNOS contains many features to automate configuration on a device-by-device basis, human error can be introduced when configurations on devices differ in ways that cause unexpected effects in the network. Using the aforementioned strategies in conjunction with the tools for remote administration of the configuration, such as the JUNOScript APIs, it is possible to build systems to make configuration consistent not only across a single device, but also across the entire network. You can find a detailed explanation on using these tools in Chapters 10 and 11.

CHAPTER 25

Automated Configuration Strategies

Automated configuration of networking equipment is becoming a niche market, with companies springing up to develop tools and applications to ensure that human error is mitigated in the quest to achieve high availability. Whether you use external vendor software or the built-in JUNOScript tools to automate configuration of your equipment, it is necessary to develop strategies for the automation. At each level of the design and within each functional area, the key components of high availability may be different and your network automated configuration strategies must reflect this. Although automated configurations normally focus on carefully planned changes that are applied with the deployment of new equipment or services, you must also have strategies to handle automated configuration changes for issues that arise unexpectedly.

Configuration Change Types

When creating strategies for automating the configuration of your systems, it is not possible to take a one-size-fits-all approach. By examining the impact of configuration changes on various parts of the network architecture, as well as on various functional areas, it is possible to develop strategies that give the configuration automation the most impact in terms of improving and maintaining high availability. Separate strategies must be used when the automated configuration changes are designed, not to prevent human error in the configuration of the equipment, but rather to address outside forces that can reduce your network's high availability.

Deployment

When deploying new equipment or services into your network, you must determine what changes the initial deployment of the configurations or the introduction of the service may have on your network high availability. Although it is sometimes impossible to deploy a new piece of equipment without network disruption, introduction of the equipment should not lead to network downtime for a wide range of customers or future network downtime because of incompatibility or misconfiguration. By planning how services and equipment are to be deployed and how the configurations to support the new services and equipment are to be automated, you can create a plan that results in the least impact for your customers, peering points, and infrastructure equipment.

Network equipment

One of the most common uses for automated configuration is for deploying new equipment, either in the core of the network or at its edges. The use of automated configuration and configuration templates ensures that the addition of new equipment does not result in human errors in the configuration that cause network downtime. Once the network equipment is deployed, the infrastructure configuration strategies take over, but during the deployment, the following configuration sections should be automated:

Management interface

Hopefully, your network is using a robust Out of Band (OoB) management system, which is especially easy with the separate interface on the routing engines (REs) of Juniper Networks routers. Quite often, the initial configuration of the management interface is done manually, only to ensure that the tools being used during config- uration automation can access the devices. Once the management interface is reachable, the automated tools can be used to configure the actual information on the interface.

Access

Automated configuration of how, when, and who can access configuration tools on the network equipment is imperative. The goal of automation is to reduce hu- man error during configuration. Therefore, it is necessary to quickly lock down access to the network equipment to only the devices and users allowed to make configuration changes. It is a best common practice to ensure that a network device is brought into the network's Authentication, Authorization, and Accounting (AAA) architecture immediately after it is attached to the network to ensure strong authentication and accounting.

 In all the networks in which I have worked, a common set of default usernames and passwords have existed that are used during the initial configuration of a device. By getting the device into the AAA environment as quickly as possible, it is easy to mitigate the threat caused by users in the network attempting to access new equip- ment using those normally widely known credentials.

Logging

As we discussed in Chapter 9, logging is a great way to maintain network uptime, but it is quite easy to make a typo that leads to logs being sent into the bit bucket. By ensuring that logging is enabled from the start, you can monitor configuration changes and user access during initial deployment of the equipment.

Security

Before automated infrastructure configuration changes are made, it is necessary to ensure that each device is configured with the security policies that are appropriate for its position in the network. By using the management interface and an OoB management network, it is possible to lock down the security of a device to only allow access through the management interface until the entire device is configured and is ready for operation.

Once the basic automated configurations have been made for access to the device and for logging of all future changes to the device, you can view the equipment as a piece of the infrastructure and can start using the automated configuration strategies required of that equipment's place in the network.

Services

Not all new items deployed to networks are hardware; in fact, a majority of new deployments consist of services that may or may not rely on new equipment. When deploying new services, it is often necessary to change the configuration of the underlying networking equipment to allow the service to perform as advertised. Often, your network technicians are on the hook for some aspects of ensuring high availability as a result of the creation and deployment of new services.

 A majority of the time it appears that the individuals deploying a new service do not consider the underlying network and the impact to high availability that it may cause. Consider a streaming video on an oversubscribed line. Although the large amount of streaming traffic may be causing network downtime, the network is normally blamed for any slowdown in other services. Thus, it is up to the network technicians to ensure that enough bandwidth is saved so that everyone has high availability, not just the service owners.

When deploying a new service, you can use the automated configuration to ensure that network traffic, or *control traffic*, is not visibly affected by the new service. For a new service, you should configure the following configuration sections using automated features:

Class of service (CoS) configurations

Depending on the service being introduced, you may need to modify the CoS settings across the network, including code point writing and rewriting, policer and buffer policies, and allowed bandwidth settings. Because CoS configurations are applied on a per-hop basis, they are extremely sensitive to differences in configuration across the network. Thus, it is necessary to ensure that they are consistent. Absolute consistency can be provided only through automated configuration techniques.

Protocol tweaks

Sometimes the new service will necessitate that currently unused knobs for the routing or management protocols are configured across the entire network. As with CoS configurations, the performance of these changes will be greatly affected if the changes are not made consistently across the entire network. The automated configuration functions ensure more consistent deployment.

Multiprotocol Label Switching (MPLS) traffic engineering

If the core over which the new service is to operate includes MPLS, you may need to adjust traffic engineering information across the entire core, or at least confirm that label-switched path (LSP) settings are consistently configured to signal the necessary settings for the path.

Control plane policies

To ensure that the new service does not affect the operation of the routing and other management systems, it is necessary to consistently apply policing of packets to the control plane (e.g., to the RE).

Once the new service is deployed and the configurations have been confirmed to be appropriate, the configuration changes can be transitioned to the infrastructure portion of the automated configurations and can become a baseline configuration of the network.

Infrastructure

At the core of any network attempting to provide high availability are big iron boxes designed to do the heavy lifting of keeping traffic flowing in the network. In looking at automating the configuration for infrastructure equipment for high availability, the focus should rest on the stability and proper functioning of the systems' data and control planes. Because of the nature of the core, the configurations on the devices evolve very slowly and do not require constant updates. However, when configuration changes are made, errors can lead to cascading issues and catastrophic downtime. To prevent human error from causing network downtime for the infrastructure, focus on the following areas when automating configurations:

Interface physical settings

Auto-negotiation and mismatched media can lead to all sorts of errors that not only are difficult to diagnose, but also are sometimes difficult to find. These types of errors can lead to unidirectional traffic on bidirectional links and other very strange behavior that may not really manifest itself until the interfaces start to reach saturation. Though auto-negotiation is a valid option on Juniper devices, it is a best common practice, especially in multivendor environments, to hardcode the link speed and media settings on core gear. The use of automated configuration of physical interface characteristics guarantees more consistent configuration.

Interface logical configurations

For certain protocols to operate properly, it is necessary to ensure that the address family is included on the interface logical configuration. Again, settings such as these, which are required across all interfaces across the core, are perfect candidates for automated configuration.

Interior Gateway Protocol (IGP) settings

Simple human typos in the IGPs, such as incorrect or mismatched subnet masks, authentication, and protocol interface settings, can lead to adjacency issues or routing errors. Other issues, including mismatched reference bandwidth settings, can lead to suboptimal routing and even links being overloaded.

Border Gateway Protocol (BGP) mesh

In networks where BGP is used for peering and transit traffic, or in networks running MPLS, the required full mesh of Internal BGP (IBGP) routers remains constant. Because of the requirement, as the size of the network increases, it becomes much easier to make an error that leads to less than a full mesh of IBGP peers. Using automated configuration to ensure the full mesh, it is possible to mitigate the threat of black-holing traffic.

BGP peering

Automated configuration ensures that BGP policies, attributes, and communities are used consistently across all IBGP and External BGP (EBGP) peering configurations, thus mitigating the threat that local network routing policies cause routing churn across the Internet in general.

The North American Network Operators Group (NANOG) normally discusses the churn created in Internet routing tables introduced by BGP peers that are either established or torn down rapidly, or route information that is mistakenly or purposely injected or withdrawn in a short time period. Though it may not appear to be a high availability issue, after multiple complaints from the Internet routing community in general, it is possible to be sanctioned or to lose peering rights.

RE high availability

Simple errors, such as forgetting to have REs synchronize their configurations, can have a devastating effect on network uptime and can render RE redundancy useless.

CoS

One overlooked portion of high availability is the use of CoS across the network. Although using CoS may not prevent the downtime of particular pieces of network equipment, it does provide the appearance of continuous systems to customers, because their network responses or services do not suffer during a time of actual downtime in your network.

Using the commit scripts, it is possible to provide for an automated audit of these configurations each time the configuration is committed on the system. Event policies can also be written to alert the user anytime the configuration is committed, as well as copy all the results of the commit scripts to a remote workstation for auditing.

Ad Hoc Changes

It is truly unbelievable, but sometimes changes in network configuration are not the result of a carefully planned and reasoned meeting of the minds among technicians in the network, security, and services group. Instead, they are ad hoc changes that are necessary because of an incident, an event, or the revelation of a security hole somewhere in the network. These changes can also be made using configuration automation. Making them just requires a slightly different strategy.

Workarounds

Sometimes hardware or software issues arise that require network engineers to develop a workaround to achieve desired results. The issues can occur in the network gear or in the systems they support, but wherever they exist, the workaround must be applied so that high availability is maintained. Workaround configuration changes normally must be applied to multiple pieces of the network—the main equipment affected by the issue or support equipment affected by the issue. Thus, configuration automation provides the consistency and efficiency necessary.

One-off configurations

Although it may be officially discouraged, most networks have whole areas that are merely "one-offs"; that is, configurations developed solely to serve a corner case. With the uniqueness of these configurations, it is necessary to handle them very specially within a configuration automation scheme and to annotate them quite well, because they fall outside the normal scope of configurations.

Automation Strategies

The main purpose of automating configurations across the network is to ensure that neither human error nor lack of configuration consistency affects network uptime. Using the information we've provided in this chapter, it is possible to model configurations and templates to be used by JUNOScript, or other tools, to deploy the configurations. This section contains examples of using JUNOScript and other tools to confirm the automation of network device configuration.

Global Strategies

The best way to ensure consistent configurations across a network is to have a single source for your configuration scripts. The repository for the scripts should serve as a Concurrent Versions System (CVS) to ensure that all changes are noted, and as a clearinghouse from which the scripts are pulled by the machines. If you remember from previous chapters, the JUNOScope software provides a built-in CVS for configurations.

Luckily, with JUNOScript, you can point network devices to the location of the source script and then reload with the `refresh` command:

```
system {
    scripts {
        commit {
            allow-transients;
            file infrastructure.slax {
                source http://engineering.example.com/infrastructure.slax;
            }
        }
    }
}
```

Deployment

One of the times high availability is most threatened is when you deploy new equipment or services in the network. The engineers are responsible for ensuring that the new systems do not impact the existing network. To do this, automated configuration can be used to guarantee that the proper settings are applied during deployment and to ensure that a human error during deployment does not lead to downtime.

Hardware deployment

Having the ability to apply a single, baseline configuration to all equipment in the network to ensure that settings such as authentication, logging, and access are consistent is a great first step toward ensuring high availability. The best way to ensure that the equipment is configured consistently is to have a commit script to add all the necessary configurations to the device.

A commit script such as the one that follows consists of the basic JUNOScript boilerplate code, a macro and match statement to ensure that all the necessary information has been provided, and the commands to parse through the configuration and configure the baseline settings:

```
version 1.0;
ns junos = "http://xml.juniper.net/junos/*/junos";
ns xnm = "http://xml.juniper.net/xnm/1.1/xnm";
ns jcs = "http://xml.juniper.net/junos/commit-scripts/1.0";
import "../import/junos.xsl";
import "../import/junos.xsl";
var $macro-name = 'deploy.xsl';
```

```
match configuration {
  var $rid = routing-options/router-id;
  for-each (apply-macro[name = 'deploy']) {
    var $hostname = data[name = 'host-name']/value;
    var $fxp0-addr = data[name = 'mgmt-address']/value;
    var $backup-router = data[name = 'backup-router']/value;
    var $bkup-rtr = {
      if ($backup-router) {
      expr $backup-router;
      }
      else {
        var $fxp01 = substring-before($fxp0-addr, '.');
        var $fxp02 = substring-before(substring-after($fxp0-addr, '.'), '.');
        var $fxp03 = substring-before(substring-after(substring-after(
            $fxp0- addr, '.'), '.'), '.');
        var $plen = substring-after($fxp0-addr, '/');
        if ($plen = ??) {
          expr $fxp01 _ '.' _ $fxp02 _ '.' _ $fxp03 div 4 * 4 + 3 _ '.254';
        }
        else if ($plen = 24) {
          expr $fxp01 _ '.' _ $fxp02 _ '.' _ $fxp03 _ '.254';
        }
      }
    }
    if (not($rid) or not($hostname) or not($fxp0-addr)) {
      <xnm:error> {
        <message> "This script requires an ID, host-name, and mgmt-address.";
      }
    }
  }
  else {
    <transient-change> {
      <system> {
        <domain-name> "example.com";
        <domain-search> "example.com";
        <backup-router> {
          <address> $bkup-rtr;
        }
        <time-zone> "America/Los_Angeles";
        <authentication-order> "radius";
        <authentication-order> "password";
        <root-authentication> {
          <encrypted-password>
              "$dfdfsder4&fdsk*$.$fdj9)34556";
        }
        <name-server> {
        <name> "4.2.2.2";
        }
        <radius-server> {
          <name> "10.0.0.1";
          <secret> "$9$4xoDk5T3n/AHkmTQFCAOBIclKWL7sgaRh-bs4GU";
        }
        <login> {
          <class> {
            <permissions> "all";
          }
```

```
<user> {
  <name> "engadmin";
  <uid> "969";
  <class> "superuser";
    <authentication> {
      <encrypted-password>"$1$dfdfsd.k4oivn-hjet9.";
    }
  }
}
<services> {
  <ssh>;
  <xnm-ssl>;
}
<syslog> {
  <user> {
    <name> "*";
      <contents> {
        <name> "any";
        <emergency>;
      }
    }
    <host> {
      <name> "10.0.0.3";
      <contents> {
        <name> "any";
        <notice>;
      }
      <contents> {
        <name> "interactive-commands";
        <any>;
        }
      }
    <archive> {
      <world-readable>;
    }
  }
}
}
<ntp> {
  <boot-server> "example.com";
    <server> {
      <name> "example.com";
    }
  }
}
<snmp> {
  <location> "Engineering";
  <contact> "Orin Blomberg";
  <interface> "fxp0.0";
  <community> {
    <name> "anyone-read";
    <authorization> "read-only";
    <clients> {
      <name> "0.0.0.0/0";
      <restrict>;
    }
```

```
          }
        }
        <community> {
          <name> "shhh-quiet";
        <authorization> "read-write";
          <clients> {
            <name> "0.0.0.0/0";
            <restrict>;
          }
        }
      }
      <routing-options> {
        <static> {
          <junos:comment> "/* Engineering */";
          <route> {
            <name> "10.0.0.0/23";
            <next-hop> $bkup-rtr;
            <retain>;
            <no-readvertise>;
          }
        }
      }
    }
    <apply-groups> "re0";
    <apply-groups> "re1";
    <groups> {
      <name> "re0";
      <system> {
        <host-name> $hostname;
    }
    <interfaces> {
      <interface> {
        <name> "fxp0";
          <unit> {
            <name> "0";
              <family> {
                <inet> {
                  <address> {
                      <name> $fxp0-addr;
                  }
                }
              }
            }
          }
        }
      }
      <groups> {
        <name> "re1";
      }
      <interfaces> {
        <interface> {
          <name> "lo0";
            <unit> {
              <name> "0";
                <family> {
```

```
            <inet> {
              <address> {
                <name> $rid;
            }
          }
        }
      }
    }
  }
}
```

Using scripts such as this one, it is possible to guarantee that all network devices, or at least Juniper Networks devices, are configured consistently, thus making both deployment and troubleshooting progress more smoothly.

Interfaces. Although a baseline interface configuration works with JUNOS devices, not all networks are composed exclusively of Juniper Networks gear. When integrating devices into heterogeneous networks, it is necessary to ensure that default settings, such as encapsulation of interfaces, match, or that one of the systems is configured to use the other device's default. Using the following example script, it is possible to insert a Juniper Networks device into a network with Cisco devices and have the SONET/SDH interfaces default to the Cisco-HDLC, which is the default in Cisco devices:

```
<?xml version="1.0" standalone="yes"?>
<xsl:stylesheet version="1.0"
  xmlns:xsl="http://www.w3.org/1999/XSL/Transform"
  xmlns:junos="http://xml.juniper.net/junos/*/junos"
  xmlns:xnm="http://xml.juniper.net/xnm/1.1/xnm"
  xmlns:jcs="http://xml.juniper.net/junos/commit-scripts/1.0">
<xsl:import href="../import/junos.xsl"/>
<xsl:template match="configuration">
<xsl:for-each select="interfaces/interface[starts-with(name, 'so-')
        and not(sonet-options/aggregate)]">
  <xsl:call-template name="jcs:emit-change">
    <xsl:with-param name="tag" select="'transient-change'"/>
      <xsl:with-param name="content">
        <encapsulation>cisco-hdlc</encapsulation>
      </xsl:with-param>
    </xsl:call-template>
  </xsl:for-each>
</xsl:template>
</xsl:stylesheet>
```

Of course, to use the preceding script, it is necessary to understand the environment into which you are deploying the device and the environment's default settings—or the configuration changes made to devices to which the new device is connecting.

Routing engines. Having redundant REs in your network equipment provides a stable foundation for building high availability. However, the efficacy of the redundancy is lessened if the REs are not configured correctly or if any changes that are made are not applied to both REs. Here are two scripts for automating the process of ensuring that the REs are configured correctly.

This first script ensures that the IP addresses for the management interfaces are not configured directly on the interface itself, but instead are configured in the specialized re0 and re1 apply groups. If this is not the case, the commit script produces an error indicating the issue. By configuring the IP addresses in the apply groups, the REs can properly use the IP addresses.

```
<?xml version="1.0" standalone="yes"?>
<xsl:stylesheet version="1.0"
  xmlns:xsl="http://www.w3.org/1999/XSL/Transform"
  xmlns:junos="http://xml.juniper.net/junos/*/junos"
  xmlns:xnm="http://xml.juniper.net/xnm/1.1/xnm"
  xmlns:jcs="http://xml.juniper.net/junos/commit-scripts/1.0">
  <xsl:import href="../import/junos.xsl"/>
  <xsl:template match="configuration">
    <xsl:for-each select="system/host-name
          | interfaces/interface/unit/family/inet/address
          | interfaces/interface[name = 'fxp0']">
      <xsl:if test="not(@junos:group) or not(starts-with(@junos:group, 're'))">
        <xnm:warning>
          <xsl:call-template name="jcs:edit-path">
            <xsl:with-param name="dot" select=".."/>
          </xsl:call-template>
          <xsl:call-template name="jcs:statement"/>
          <message>
            <xsl:text>statement should not be in target</xsl:text>
            <xsl:text> configuration on dual RE system</xsl:text>
          </message>
        </xnm:warning>
      </xsl:if>
    </xsl:for-each>
  </xsl:template>
</xsl:stylesheet>
```

In the next example, the script checks to see whether a hostname has been configured, and if so, where. If no hostname is configured, an error is produced. If a hostname has been configured in the target group but not in the apply groups for the dual REs, the script moves the hostname to the proper location:

```
version 1.0;
ns junos = "http://xml.juniper.net/junos/*/junos";
ns xnm = "http://xml.juniper.net/xnm/1.1/xnm";
ns jcs = "http://xml.juniper.net/junos/commit-scripts/1.0";
import "../import/junos.xsl";
match configuration {
    for-each (system/host-name | interfaces/interface/unit/family/inet/address
                | interfaces/interface[name = 'fxp0']) {
        if (not(@junos:group) or not(starts-with(@junos:group, 're'))) {
            <xnm:warning> {
                call jcs:edit-path($dot = ..);
                call jcs:statement();
                <message> {
```

```
              expr "statement should not be in target";
              expr " configuration on dual RE system";
            }
          }
        }
      }
    }
  }
```

Using variations of the preceding scripts, you can deploy new devices in the network without disrupting other equipment and services. The key to all the scripts is the same: consistency across the configurations in the network. When deploying new services, the same focus on consistency applies.

Service deployment

One of the biggest threats to high availability when deploying a new service is a disruption to other services in the network. New services that require high bandwidth, low latency, and jitter may not perform well and may affect other services if you do not apply a comprehensive CoS architecture.

Lack of consistency in configuration affects CoS and its use in the network far more than any of the other protocols or technologies because CoS works on a per-hop basis, and failure to configure CoS in any device network negates the effects of the overall CoS configuration. Thus, CoS configuration is another prime candidate for automated configuration.

The following example code illustrates use of automated configuration to ensure that a new forwarding class for CoS is added to all the interfaces of the device. In the code, the script adds the newly created "ef-q1" forwarding class:

```
version 1.0;
ns junos = "http://xml.juniper.net/junos/*/junos";
ns xnm = "http://xml.juniper.net/xnm/1.1/xnm";
ns jcs = "http://xml.juniper.net/junos/commit-scripts/1.0";
import "../import/junos.xsl";
match configuration {
  var $cos-all = class-of-service;
  for-each (interfaces/interface[contains(name, '/')]/unit[family/inet]) {
    var $ifname = ../name;
    var $unit = name;
    var $cos = $cos-all/interfaces[name = $ifname];
    if (not($cos/unit[name = $unit])) {
      call jcs:emit-change($dot = $cos-all) {
        with $message = {
          expr "Adding CoS forwarding class for ";
          expr $ifname _ '.' _ $unit;
        }
        with $content = {
          <interfaces> {
            <name> $ifname;
              <unit> {
                <name> $unit;
                <forwarding-class> "ef-q1";
```

```
                        }
                      }
                    }
                  }
                }
              }
            }
          }
```

By adding the forwarding class to the interfaces as well as updating the entire configuration, it is possible to ensure that the new deployments do not affect existing services.

Infrastructure

Once equipment is deployed, it should fall into an infrastructure configuration automation strategy. The main goal of developing infrastructure scripts for configuration
automation focuses on the foundation of the network. The infrastructure scripts ensure
that the baseline interface and routing configurations are consistent and stable, preventing tiny errors from turning into big problems.

Interfaces

One area where issues can arise in your network is in the legacy Time-Division Multi-
plexing (TDM) circuits, which are normally used to connect remote offices. Though
many network cores are moving to Ethernet or SONET/SDH, there are still many T1-
and E1-type lines that require proper clocking configuration to ensure that they work
effectively. In the following code example, the script notifies the user if the interface
clocking settings on T1s are not set to internal clocking:

```
<?xml version="1.0" standalone="yes"?>
<xsl:stylesheet version="1.0"
 xmlns:xsl="http://www.w3.org/1999/XSL/Transform"
 xmlns:junos="http://xml.juniper.net/junos/*/junos"
 xmlns:xnm="http://xml.juniper.net/xnm/1.1/xnm"
 xmlns:jcs="http://xml.juniper.net/junos/commit-scripts/1.0">
  <xsl:import href="./import/junos.xsl"/>
   <xsl:template match="configuration">
    <xsl:for-each select="interfaces/interface[starts-with(name, 't1-')]">
      <xsl:variable name="clock-source">
       <xsl:value-of select="clocking"/>
     </xsl:variable>
    <xsl:if test="not($clock-source = 'internal')">
    <!-- or xsl:if test="$clock-source != 'internal'" -->
    <xnm:error>
      <xsl:call-template name="jcs:edit-path"/>
      <xsl:call-template name="jcs:statement">
        <xsl:with-param name="dot" select="clocking"/>
      </xsl:call-template>
      <message>This T1 interface should have internal
        clocking.</message>
    </xnm:error>
    </xsl:if>
   </xsl:for-each>
```

```
    </xsl:template>
  </xsl:stylesheet>
```

Though this script does not fully automate the configuration of the clocking on the T1, it does alert the user to a misconfigured clocking setting, thus allowing us to correct the error before the circuit is officially turned up.

Routing

Another major pitfall in infrastructure device configuration is human error in configuring routing protocols. With all devices relying on routing protocols to properly deliver packets, it is again necessary to ensure that the configurations are both consistent and accurate.

In the following example, the router is part of an MPLS cloud and some of its interfaces connect to customer premises equipment. Using a combination of macros and JUNOScript, it is possible to ensure that the IGP settings are correct.

The first code example provides the macros that have been applied to various interfaces to identify the IGP, the interface's class in the hierarchy, and the area, if the interface uses Open Shortest Path First (OSPF):

```
system {
  scripts {
    commit {
      file protocol.xsl;
    }
  }
}
interfaces {
  ge-1/0/3 {
    unit 0 {
      apply-macro igpconf {
        area 0.0.0.0;
        protocol ospf;
        class core;
      }
    }
  }
  ge-2/0/1 {
    unit 0 {
      apply-macro igpconf {
        area 10.0.0.1;
        protocol ospf;
        class area1;
      }
    }
  }
  fe-0/0/0 {
    unit 0 {
      apply-macro igpconf {
        igp isis;
        role customer;
```

```
          }
        }
      }
```

The following commit script is parsed by the management daemon (mgd). If the interface is labeled as a customer interface, its information is placed into the protocol configuration for the Intermediate System to Intermediate System (IS-IS) routing protocol. If the interface uses OSPF, the mgd places the configuration information into the proper configuration hierarchy and identifies the area:

```
version 1.0;
ns junos = "http://xml.juniper.net/junos/*/junos";
ns xnm = "http://xml.juniper.net/xnm/1.1/xnm";
ns jcs = "http://xml.juniper.net/junos/commit-scripts/1.0";
import "../import/junos.xsl";
match configuration {
  for-each (interfaces/interface/unit/apply-macro[name = 'igpconf']) {
    var $class = data[name='class']/value;
    var $protocol = data[name='protocol']/value;
     var $ifname = {
        expr ../../name;
        expr ".";
        expr ../name;
     }
     if ($class = 'customer') {
       <change> {
        if ($protocol = 'isis') {
          <protocols> {
            <isis> {
              <interface> {
                <name> $ifname;
              }
            }
          }
        }
        else if ($protocol = 'ospf') {
          <protocols> {
          <ospf> {
            <area> {
              <name> data[name='area']/value;
              <interface> {
                <name> $ifname;
              }
            }
          }
          }
        }
       }
     }
  }
}
```

Using this combination of macros and commit scripts, it is possible to ensure that configuration consistency, and thus high availability, is maintained across the entire network.

Ad Hoc Changes

Strategies for automating ad hoc changes are far different from strategies for automating infrastructure and deployment changes, because ad hoc changes normally do not offer the same amount of time for planning. In the case of workaround configurations, it is usually necessary to deploy changes to configurations within a few days after the need for the workaround is determined. Other types of configuration changes, such as emergency changes to stop a denial-of-service (DoS) attack, must be deployed even more quickly.

Workarounds

The first goal for designing a strategy for deploying automated configuration changes for a workaround is to determine the systems or devices affected by the issue you are attempting to solve. Workarounds can normally be divided into two groups: those affecting the systems that are internal to the network device, such as the JUNOS software, and those caused by external device issues.

JUNOS issues. If an issue arises in the JUNOS software that requires a workaround, the workaround should be applied to all devices running the same code version. Although the workaround may not be necessary on all devices, the foundation of consistency in configuration demands that you implement the workaround on all of them.

External device issues. Sometimes an issue on an external device requires that you implement a workaround on the devices connected to it. Again, all equipment that can be changed without affecting operation should be changed. Although the argument may be that other devices are currently not connected to the offending device, in the future they may be, and having the configuration in place early saves downtime later:

```
ns junos = "http://xml.juniper.net/junos/*/junos";
ns xnm = "http://xml.juniper.net/xnm/1.1/xnm";
ns jcs = "http://xml.juniper.net/junos/commit-scripts/1.0";

import "../import/junos.xsl";

param $min-mtu = 1024;

match configuration {
    for-each (interfaces/interface[starts-with(name, 'so-') and mtu and
                        mtu < $min-mtu]) {
        <xnm:error> {
            call jcs:edit-path();
            call jcs:statement($dot = mtu);
            <message> {
                expr "SONET interfaces must have a minimum MTU of ";
                expr $min-mtu;
                expr ".";
            }
        }
    }
}
```

One-off workarounds

Sometimes it is either not necessary or not feasible to make a configuration change to all devices in the network—for example, in the event of a DoS attack. In early 2009, many networks were either attacked or participated in Domain Name System (DNS) amplification attacks that were based on misconfigured or out-of-date DNS servers.

Because of the speed at which the attacks occurred and were discovered, it was necessary to immediately deploy policers and policies to lessen the effect of the attacks.

A one-off configuration is sometimes necessary, and should be automated so that it can be quickly deployed, as well as quickly removed if other issues with the configuration are discovered. The key to deploying a one-off configuration is to include detailed commenting in the configuration that explains how, when, and why the configuration changes were made.

PART IV

Appendixes

System Test Plan

This test plan describes Juniper Networks recommendations for testing JUNOS platforms before full implementation in a production network. The purpose of this procedure is to detect hardware problems (e.g., parts damaged in transit) so that you can solve them before they have an impact on transit traffic.

 Because a considerable percentage of hardware failures occur within the first 48 hours of operation, leave the router powered on for at least two days, either on the customer's premises or in a staging location, and then check again.

For most tests, it is necessary to connect to the routing engines (REs) or system boards via a console cable; so, remember to capture all output and keep it for future reference or to help the Juniper Technical Assistance Center (JTAC) in troubleshooting.

Note that the staging procedures might vary for other applications and products.

Physical Inspection and Power On

The purpose of this step is to detect any obvious mechanical damage done to the chassis or to the system boards:

- Check the chassis and the system boards for any sign of mechanical damage.
- Check that all field-replaceable units—Switching and Forwarding Modules (SFMs), Flexible PIC Concentrators (FPCs), REs, MCSs, Compact Forwarding Engine Boards (CFEBs), power supplies, etc.—are correctly seated.
- Connect the power supplies and turn them on one at a time.

Check General System Status

The purpose of this section is to collect data about the router hardware configuration and environment (temperatures and voltages).

 You can run these commands only on the master RE; if you are connected to the backup RE, the commands will fail. In this case, either move your console connection to the master RE or use this command:

```
lab@r1-re0> request routing-engine login other-routing-engine
```

Check for Any Active Alarms

Run the show chassis alarm command on the master RE to display any active alarms. If any alarm is reported, contact JTAC (remember to include all output you collected).

 If the Ethernet management interface (fxp0) is not connected, a red alarm will be triggered. This is the correct behavior; to avoid the alarm, make sure the management interface is connected.

Save the System Hardware Configuration for Future Reference

Connect to the master RE and run the show chassis hardware command. This command allows you to get a snapshot of the actual hardware configuration together with the serial numbers of each component.

Here is sample output from an M40e router; the actual output might vary according to the platform and installed hardware:

```
lab@r1-re0> show chassis hardware
Hardware inventory:
Item              Version  Part number  Serial number  Description
Chassis                                 25979          M40e
Midplane          REV 01   710-005071   AW9739
FPM CMB           REV 03   710-001642   AN5627
FPM Display       REV 03   710-001647   BD0951
CIP               REV 05   710-002649   BA5041
PEM 0             Rev 01   740-003787   MC25400        Power Entry Module
PEM 1             Rev 01   740-003787   MC13653        Power Entry Module
PCG 0             REV 03   710-003066   BD0671
PCG 1             REV 03   710-003066   BD0711
Routing Engine 0  REV 08   740-003239   1000323102     RE-2.0
Routing Engine 1  REV 08   740-003239   1000323004     RE-2.0
MCS 0             REV 12   710-001226   BD0550
MCS 1             REV 12   710-001226   BD0546
SFM 0 SPP         REV 08   710-001228   BB5747
SFM 0 SPR         REV 06   710-002189   BB5595         Internet Processor IIv1
SFM 1 SPP         REV 07   710-001228   HB6333
SFM 1 SPR         REV 05   710-002189   HD4454         Internet Processor IIv1
```

```
FPC 4           REV 07   710-001611   AF1657   FPC Type 2
  CPU           REV 05   710-001217   AE6608
  PIC 0         REV 02   750-001850   HB2063   1x Tunnel
FPC 5           REV 03   710-005078   BE5129   M40e-FPC Type 1
  CPU           REV 01   710-004602   BB8532
  PIC 0         REV 01   750-001897   AF4144   1x OC-12 ATM, MM
FPC 6           REV 02   710-005078   AY7872   M40e-FPC Type 1
  CPU           REV 01   710-004600   BB8809
  PIC 0         REV 01   750-002575   AG7176   4x OC-3 SONET, SMIR
FPC 7           REV 02   710-005078   BD0865   M40e-FPC Type 1
  CPU           REV 01   710-004600   BD0635
  PIC 0         REV 03   750-001894   AF6789   1x G/E, 1000 BASE-SX
```

Here is sample output from an M10i router:

```
lab@r2-re0> show chassis hardware
Hardware inventory:
Item                Version  Part number  Serial number Description
Chassis                                   31977         M10i
Midplane            REV 04   710-008920   CC8226
Power Supply 0      Rev 05   740-008537   QF11226       AC
Power Supply 1      Rev 05   740-008537   QD19413       AC
Power Supply 2      Rev 05   740-008537   QF11383       AC
HCM slot 0          REV 01   710-010580   CE0986
HCM slot 1          REV 01   710-010580   CE0876
Routing Engine 0    REV 09   740-009459   1000500683    RE-5.0
CFEB slot 0         REV 03   750-010465   CC7456        Internet Processor II
FPC 0                                                   E-FPC
  PIC 0             REV 11   750-005653   CA8548        2x EIA-530
  PIC 1             REV 10   750-005653   CC1653        2x EIA-530
  PIC 2             REV 09   750-002992   CC9774        4x F/E, 100 BASE-TX
  PIC 3             REV 09   750-002992   CC9880        4x F/E, 100 BASE-TX
FPC 1                                                   E-FPC
  PIC 0             REV 11   750-005653   CA8538        2x EIA-530
  PIC 1             REV 11   750-005653   BF7328        2x EIA-530
  PIC 2             REV 11   750-005653   CA8525        2x EIA-530
```

 Remember to save the output for future reference; you will need the serial numbers of each component if a Return Materials Authorization (RMA) is opened.

Check Voltages and Temperatures

To check the temperatures and voltages on all boards, use the show chassis environment command. Here is sample output from an M40e router:

```
lab@r1-re0> show chassis environment
Class Item               Status  Measurement
Power PEM 0              OK
      PEM 1              OK
Temp  PCG 0             OK      41 degrees C / 105 degrees F
      PCG 1             OK      45 degrees C / 113 degrees F
      Routing Engine 0  OK      28 degrees C / 82 degrees F
```

```
        Routing Engine 1       OK        26 degrees C / 78 degrees F
        MCS 0                  OK        38 degrees C / 100 degrees F
        MCS 1                  OK        40 degrees C / 104 degrees F
        SFM 0 SPP              OK        36 degrees C / 96 degrees F
        SFM 0 SPR              OK        40 degrees C / 104 degrees F
        SFM 1 SPP              OK        40 degrees C / 104 degrees F
        SFM 1 SPR              OK        42 degrees C / 107 degrees F
        FPC 4                  OK        36 degrees C / 96 degrees F
        FPC 5                  OK        41 degrees C / 105 degrees F
        FPC 6                  OK        38 degrees C / 100 degrees F
        FPC 7                  OK        39 degrees C / 102 degrees F
        FPM CMB                OK        25 degrees C / 77 degrees F
        FPM Display            OK        29 degrees C / 84 degrees F
Fans    Rear Bottom Blower     OK        Spinning at normal speed
        Rear Top Blower        OK        Spinning at normal speed
        Front Top Blower       OK        Spinning at normal speed
        Fan Tray Rear Left     OK        Spinning at normal speed
        Fan Tray Rear Right    OK        Spinning at normal speed
        Fan Tray Front Left    OK        Spinning at normal speed
        Fan Tray Front Right   OK        Spinning at normal speed
Misc    CIP                    OK
```

Commands used to check voltage input vary by chassis. On the M40e platform you
can check voltage input on the various system boards with these commands:

```
show chassis environment fpc
show chassis environment sfm
show chassis environment mcs
show chassis environment pcg
show chassis environment pem
```

Any anomaly (e.g., components that are not online) is flagged in the command output.
Here is an example of show chassis environment sfm output:

```
lab@r1-re0> show chassis environment sfm
SFM 0 status:
  State                       Online
  SPP temperature             36 degrees C / 96 degrees F
  SPR temperature             40 degrees C / 104 degrees F
  SPP Power:
    1.5 V                     1500 mV
    2.5 V                     2471 mV
    3.3 V                     3286 mV
    5.0 V                     5010 mV
    5.0 V bias                4986 mV
  SPR Power:
    1.5 V                     1500 mV
    2.5 V                     2477 mV
    3.3 V                     3299 mV
    5.0 V                     5015 mV
    5.0 V bias                5001 mV
    8.0 V bias                8251 mV
  CMB Revision                12
SFM 1 status:
  State                       Online - Standby
```

```
SPP temperature                 40 degrees C / 104 degrees F
SPR temperature                 42 degrees C / 107 degrees F
SPP Power:
   1.5 V                  1500 mV
   2.5 V                  2471 mV
   3.3 V                  3304 mV
   5.0 V                  5059 mV
   5.0 V bias             4996 mV
SPR Power:
   1.5 V                  1503 mV
   2.5 V                  2477 mV
   3.3 V                  3316 mV
   5.0 V                  5062 mV
   5.0 V bias             5008 mV
   8.0 V bias             8263 mV
CMB Revision               12
```

Check the Status of the Individual Components

Connect to the router and check that the various boards from which the router is composed are in a correct state. On the M40e platform, you can use these commands:

```
show chassis fpc detail
show chassis sfm detail
```

For all active boards, the state field must be online; you can also check how long the board has been online by checking its uptime. Here is a sample of show chassis fpc detail output:

```
lab@r1-re0> show chassis fpc detail
Slot 4 information:
  State                         Online
  Temperature                   36 degrees C / 96 degrees F
  Total CPU DRAM                32 MB
  Total SRAM                     2 MB
  Total SDRAM                  128 MB
  I/O Manager ASIC information     Version 2.0, Foundry IBM, Part number 0
  I/O Manager ASIC information     Version 2.0, Foundry IBM, Part number 0
  Start time:                   2003-12-16 17:36:40 CET
  Uptime:                       2 days, 16 hours, 58 minutes, 57 seconds
Slot 5 information:
  State                         Online
  Temperature                   42 degrees C / 107 degrees F
  Total CPU DRAM                32 MB
  Total SRAM                     4 MB
  Total SDRAM                  128 MB
  I/O Manager ASIC information     Version 3.0, Foundry IBM, Part number 0
  I/O Manager ASIC information     Version 3.0, Foundry IBM, Part number 0
  Start time:                   2003-12-16 17:36:41 CET
  Uptime:                       2 days, 16 hours, 58 minutes, 56 seconds
```

On J Series platforms, use these commands:

```
show chassis fpc detail
show chassis pic fpc-slot <#> pic-slot <#>
```

Here is sample output of both commands on a J2300:

```
lab@j2300-1> show chassis fpc detail
Slot 0 information:
  State                      Online
  Total CPU DRAM             32 MB
  Start time                 2009-05-28 22:24:31 UTC
  Uptime                     29 minutes, 26 seconds

lab@j2300-1> show chassis pic fpc-slot 0 pic-slot 0
PIC fpc slot 0 pic slot 0 information:
  Type                       2x FE, 2x T1
  State                      Online
  PIC version                3.5
  Uptime                     30 minutes, 1 second.
```

Check Routing Engine and Storage Media

The purpose of this section is to check whether the RE and its storage media are working correctly.

Check Routing Engine Status

To check the general condition of the REs, use the show chassis routing-engine command. This command shows the status of both the primary and the backup REs. Here is sample output from an M40e router:

```
lab@r1-re0> show chassis routing-engine
Routing Engine status:
  Slot 0:
    Current state              Master
    Election priority          Master
    Temperature                27 degrees C / 80 degrees F
    DRAM                     768 MB
    Memory utilization        15 percent
    CPU utilization:
      User                     0 percent
      Background               0 percent
      Kernel                   3 percent
      Interrupt                1 percent
      Idle                    97 percent
    Model                      RE-2.0
    Serial ID                  6f000000b3a7e001
    Start time                 2009-03-16 17:34:30 CET
    Uptime                     2 days, 18 hours, 51 minutes, 37 seconds
    Load averages:             1 minute   5 minute  15 minute
                                 0.00        0.01       0.00
Routing Engine status:
  Slot 1:
    Current state              Backup
```

```
Election priority        Backup
Temperature              26 degrees C / 78 degrees F
DRAM                     768 MB
Memory utilization       14 percent
CPU utilization:
  User                   0 percent
  Background             0 percent
  Kernel                 0 percent
  Interrupt              0 percent
  Idle                   100 percent
Model                    RE-2.0
Serial ID                77000000b3a62d01
Start time               2009-03-16 16:02:43 CET
Uptime                   2 days, 20 hours, 23 minutes, 23 seconds
```

Check Storage Media on Each Routing Engine

Use the show system storage command to display storage media and mounted filesystems. Check that the /var, /config, and / (root) directories are correctly mounted. Here is sample output from an M40e platform:

```
lab@r1-re0> show system storage
Filesystem 512-blocks     Used     Avail Capacity Mounted on
/dev/ad0s1a    158174    56516     89006     39% /
devfs              32       32         0    100% /dev/
/dev/vn0        18316    18316         0    100% /packages/mnt/jbase
devfs              32       32         0    100% /dev/
/dev/vn1        45448    45448         0    100% /packages/mnt/jkernel-6.0R1.5
/dev/vn2        20532    20532         0    100% /packages/mnt/jpfe-M160-6.0R1.5
/dev/vn3         3580     3580         0    100% /packages/mnt/jdocs-6.0R1.5
/dev/vn4        20728    20728         0    100% /packages/mnt/jroute-6.0R1.5
/dev/vn5         9252     9252         0    100% /packages/mnt/jcrypto-6.0R1.5
mfs:139       3048670        8   2804770      0% /tmp
/dev/ad0s1e     23742       42     21802      0% /config
procfs              8        8         0    100% /proc
/dev/ad1s1f  34635886  6947870  24917146     22% /var
```

If the directories are correctly mounted, you can run the request system snapshot command to copy JUNOS Software from the CompactFlash memory onto the hard disk. This helps to detect hard disk problems and allows the RE to recover quickly in case of CompactFlash failures.

Repeat the preceding steps on the backup RE. If any error is detected during execution of the request system snapshot command, contact JTAC.

Test Optical Interfaces

The purpose of this section is to do a quick test on all optical interfaces on the router. The configuration might change according to the type of interface being tested; configuration examples are provided for some of the most commonly used interfaces.

You will need a fiber loop and an optical attenuator for Intermediate Reach and Long Haul interfaces. No attenuation is required for multimode Gigabit Ethernet interfaces.

Configure a Private IP Address and Run Ping Tests

You must configure a private IP address to ping through the fiber loop. In this example, we use 10.0.0.1/30 as the private IP address; you can change it if you are already using addresses in the same range (e.g., for the management interface).

To quickly see how many interfaces are present on the router, use the show interfaces terse command. Consider only interfaces whose name is in the form *type-fpc/pic/ port*—for example, so-0/1/0, at-1/2/0, and so on. Ignore the internal interfaces (e.g., pimd, pime, tun, tap, lo0, and dsc).

Run a loopback test on SONET/SDH interfaces

To configure the 10.0.0.1 address on SONET interfaces, use these commands in configuration mode, replacing so-0/0/0 with the actual interface you are configuring:

```
[edit interfaces]
lab@r1-re0# set so-0/0/0 encapsulation cisco-hdlc no-keepalives

[edit interfaces]
lab@r1-re0# set so-0/0/0 unit 0 family inet address 10.0.0.1/30
```

Check that the configuration is correct, and then commit:

```
[edit]
lab@r1-re0# show interfaces so-0/0/0
no-keepalives;
encapsulation cisco-hdlc;
unit 0 {
    family inet {
        address 10.0.0.1/30;
    }
}

[edit]
lab@r1-re0# commit
commit complete
```

The cisco-hdlc and no-keepalive settings are needed to prevent the router from automatically detecting the loop, which would prevent test traffic from being transmitted.

To run the ping test, use this command (replacing so-0/0/0.0 with the actual interface name):

```
[edit]
lab@r1-re0# run ping 10.0.0.1 interface so-0/0/0.0 bypass-routing rapid count 1000
```

Run a loopback test on Fast Ethernet and Gigabit Ethernet interfaces

To configure the 10.0.0.1 address on Gigabit Ethernet or Fast Ethernet interfaces for loopback testing, use these commands in configuration mode, replacing ge-0/0/0 with the actual interface you are configuring. You must configure a dummy Media Access Control (MAC) address to run this test:

```
[edit interfaces]
lab@r1-re0# set ge-0/0/0 mac 00.00.00.00.00.01

[edit interfaces]
lab@r1-re0# set ge-0/0/0 unit 0 family inet address 10.0.0.1/30 arp 10.0.0.2 mac
00.00.00.00.00.01
```

When running a loopback test on Fast Ethernet or Gigabit Ethernet interfaces, you cannot ping your own address, so you must use the remote address (10.0.0.2). The ping will always fail, but you can use the interface counters to check that all packets have been successfully transmitted and received. To clear the interface counters, use this command:

```
lab@r1-re0> clear interface statistic ge-0/0/0
```

Then start a ping test with 10 packets, each of which will loop 255 times through the fiber:

```
lab@r1-re0> ping interface ge-0/0/0 10.0.0.2 bypass-routing count 10 ttl 255
```

While the test is running, you will receive 10 Time to Live (TTL) expired messages; this is normal:

```
lab@r1-re0> ping interface ge-0/0/0 10.0.0.2 bypass-routing count 10 ttl 255
PING 10.0.0.2 (10.0.0.2): 56 data bytes
36 bytes from 10.0.0.1: Time to live exceeded
Vr HL TOS  Len   ID Flg  off TTL Pro  cks      Src      Dst
 4  5  00 0054 a327   0 0000  01  01 0280 10.0.0.1  10.0.0.2

36 bytes from 10.0.0.1: Time to live exceeded
Vr HL TOS  Len   ID Flg  off TTL Pro  cks      Src      Dst
 4  5  00 0054 a32a   0 0000  01  01 027d 10.0.0.1  10.0.0.2
```

Finally, use the show interfaces ge-0/0/0 extensive command to check that no packet was lost:

```
lab@r1-re0> show interface ge-0/0/0 extensive | no-more
Physical interface: ge-7/0/0, Enabled, Physical link is Up
  Interface index: 134, SNMP ifIndex: 26, Generation: 18
  Link-level type: Ethernet, MTU: 1514, Speed: 1000mbps, Loopback: Disabled,
Source filtering: Disabled, Flow control: Enabled
  Device flags   : Present Running
  Interface flags: SNMP-Traps
  Link flags     : None
  Hold-times     : Up 0 ms, Down 0 ms
  Current address: 00:00:00:00:00:01, Hardware address: 00:90:69:fe:67:72
  Last flapped   : 2009-03-16 17:37:05 CET (5d 20:24 ago)
  Statistics last cleared: 2009-03-22 14:00:39 CET (00:00:57 ago)
```

```
Traffic statistics:
  Input  bytes  :              214200                0 bps
  Output bytes  :              214340                0 bps
  Input  packets:                2550                0 pps
  Output packets:                2550                0 pps
```

In this sample output, all 10 packets were looped through the fiber 255 times, resulting in 2,550 input packets and 2,550 output packets. No packets were lost.

Failover and Redundancy Tests

The purpose of the tests described in this section is to verify that the router redundancy and failover functionalities work as expected. Before conducting the tests, make sure that both REs have the correct configuration. If in doubt, log in to the master RE, check its configuration, and run the commit synchronize command.

Routing Engine Redundancy

Use the show chassis routing-engine command to verify the current mastership status:

```
lab@r1-re0> show chassis routing-engine
Routing Engine status:
  Slot 0:
    Current state                 Master
    Election priority             Master (default)
    Temperature                   26 degrees C / 78 degrees F
    DRAM                      768 MB
    Memory utilization         16 percent
    CPU utilization:
      User                        0 percent
      Background                  0 percent
      Kernel                      2 percent
      Interrupt                   0 percent
      Idle                       98 percent
    Model                         RE-2.0
    Serial ID                     6f000000b3a7e001
    Start time                    2009-03-06 14:39:54 CEST
    Uptime                        1 day, 16 minutes, 17 seconds
    Load averages:                1 minute   5 minute  15 minute
                                    0.00       0.00       0.00
  Routing Engine status:
  Slot 1:
    Current state                 Backup
    Election priority             Backup (default)
    Temperature                   26 degrees C / 78 degrees F
    DRAM                      768 MB
    Memory utilization         15 percent
    CPU utilization:
      User                        0 percent
      Background                  0 percent
      Kernel                      0 percent
      Interrupt                   0 percent
```

```
      Idle                         100 percent
   Model                           RE-2.0
   Serial ID                       77000000b3a62d01
   Start time                      2009-03-06 11:11:08 CEST
   Uptime                          1 day, 3 hours, 45 minutes, 2 seconds
```

Connect to the master RE, and trigger a mastership change with this command:

```
lab@r1-re0> request chassis routing-engine master switch
```

Wait a few seconds and verify that the mastership switch is complete:

```
lab@r1-re0> show chassis routing-engine
Routing Engine status:
  Slot 0:
    Current state                  Backup
    Election priority              Master
    Temperature                    26 degrees C / 78 degrees F
    DRAM                           768 MB
    Memory utilization             16 percent
    CPU utilization:
      User                         0 percent
      Background                   0 percent
      Kernel                       0 percent
      Interrupt                    0 percent
      Idle                         100 percent
    Model                          RE-2.0
    Serial ID                      6f000000b3a7e001
    Start time                     2003-12-16 17:34:35 CET
    Uptime                         5 days, 21 hours, 23 minutes, 34 seconds
    Load averages:                 1 minute   5 minute   15 minute
                                      0.00       0.04       0.01

Routing Engine status:
  Slot 1:
    Current state                  Master
    Election priority              Backup
    Temperature                    25 degrees C / 77 degrees F
    DRAM                           768 MB
    Memory utilization             15 percent
    CPU utilization:
      User                         0 percent
      Background                   0 percent
      Kernel                       2 percent
      Interrupt                    0 percent
      Idle                         98 percent
    Model                          RE-2.0
    Serial ID                      77000000b3a62d01
    Start time                     2003-12-16 16:02:43 CET
    Uptime                         5 days, 22 hours, 55 minutes, 24 seconds
```

Connect to the backup RE:

```
lab@r1-re0> request routing-engine login other-routing-engine
```

After the Packet Forwarding Engine (PFE) has completed its initialization, you can check the PFE status from the RE; this might take a few seconds:

```
lab@r1-re1> show chassis hardware
Hardware inventory:
Item            Version  Part number  Serial number  Description
Chassis                               25979          M40e
Midplane        REV 01   710-005071   AW9739
FPM CMB         REV 03   710-001642   AN5627
FPM Display     REV 03   710-001647   BD0951
CIP             REV 05   710-002649   BA5041
PEM 0           Rev 01   740-003787   MC25400        Power Entry Module
PEM 1           Rev 01   740-003787   MC13653        Power Entry Module
...
```

Remember to revert to the previous situation with another request chassis routing-engine master switch.

SFM Redundancy (M40e Platform Only)

Verify the current SFM status by using the show chassis sfm command:

```
lab@r1-re0> show chassis sfm
                  Temp  CPU Utilization (%)  Memory   Utilization (%)
Slot State         (C)  Total  Interrupt    DRAM (MB) Heap    Buffer
   0 Online         36    3        0           64       16      46
   1 Online - Standby 40  3        0           64       16      46
```

You can trigger an SFM switch by using this command:

```
lab@r1-re0> request chassis sfm master switch no-confirm
```

Wait a few seconds, and then verify that the SFM switch was successful:

```
lab@r1-re1> show chassis sfm
                  Temp  CPU Utilization (%)  Memory   Utilization (%)
Slot State         (C)  Total  Interrupt    DRAM (MB) Heap    Buffer
   0 Online - Standby 35  4        0           64       16      46
   1 Online         39    4        0           64       16      46
```

Once the switch is complete, check the system log for any errors with the show log messages command.

Final Burn-In Check

As a final test, if possible, you should power down and then power up the router again, and leave it running for at least 48 hours. After this period, check the system logs and boards status.

Power Down the Router

To power down the router, first stop the backup RE:

```
lab@r1-re0> request routing-engine login other-routing-engine
lab@r1-re1> request system halt
```

After a few seconds, the backup RE will stop, and your Telnet session will fall back to the master RE. After this, stop the master RE:

```
lab@r1-re0> request system halt
```

Both REs are now halted. Turn the power off.

Power On the Router/Burn-In Test

Connect a console cable to RE 0 (capturing any messages on file), and turn the power on. Check for any active alarms and the status of the router boards. Check the content of the *messages* log for any error with the show log messages command.

The router must be left powered on for one or two days.

Final Checks and Power Down

Be sure to check that the uptime for all the FPCs and SFMs is about the same. If it is not, this means one of the boards has restarted during the burn-in period—check in the logs for details. Here is sample output from an M10i router:

```
lab@r1-re0> show chassis fpc detail
Slot 0 information:
  State                         Online
  Logical slot              0
  Temperature               34 degrees C / 93 degrees F
  Total CPU DRAM             8 MB
  Total SRAM                 1 MB
  Total SDRAM              128 MB
  Total notification SDRAM  24 MB
  I/O Manager ASIC information   Version 2.0, Foundry IBM, Part number 0
  Start time:                    2009-03-19 10:15:24 CET
  Uptime:                         2 days, 8 hours, 4 minutes, 2 seconds
Slot 1 information:
  State                         Online
  Logical slot              1
  Temperature               34 degrees C / 93 degrees F
  Total CPU DRAM             8 MB
  Total SRAM                 1 MB
  Total SDRAM              128 MB
  Total notification SDRAM  24 MB
  I/O Manager ASIC information   Version 2.0, Foundry IBM, Part number 0
  Start time:                    2009-03-22 18:19:08 CET
  Uptime:                        1 days, 18 hours, 22 minutes, 54 seconds
```

In this example, FPC2 restarted one day and 18 hours ago; this indicates a possible problem. Check the *system* and *chassisd* logs around the time of the FPC reset; this should provide enough information to understand why the board restarted.

Configuration Audit

The next few pages provide an example of an audit configuration checklist. In any configuration audit, it is important to have the group responsible for the configuration functional area to do quality control against their portion of the template or the configuration scripts used to automate configuration. Once the baseline templates and scripts exist, each portion of the configuration can be compared against the template (in the case of predeployment auditing) or the baseline configuration (in the case of production equipment auditing). The audit itself can be conducted using manual checks of the equipment, configuration audits using JUNOScope, or a combination of both. As each portion of the configuration is audited, the auditor marks how the configuration has been made and audited.

Audit Responsibilities

Configuration module	Audit group	Quality control
Chassis	NOC	
Firewall filter	Security	
Interfaces	Network Engineering	
Routing policies	Network Engineering	
Protocols	Network Engineering	
Security	Security	
Services	Security	
Systems	NOC	

Audit Response Key

Status	Definition	Comments
M	Manually configured and confirmed	Initial comment box
G	Configuration applied through group	Reference group in comment box
S	Configuration added via commit script	Reference script in comment box
N/A	Configuration not applicable	
X	Configuration missing	Identify group responsible for configuration portion in comment box

Audit Checklist

Hierarchy	Configuration	Status	Comments
Chassis	Aggregated devices		
	Cluster		
	Redundancy		
Class of Service	Classifiers		
	Code point aliases		
	Drop profiles		
	Forwarding classes		
	Forwarding policy		
	Interfaces		
	rewrite-rules		
Event Options	Destinations		Access confirmed: YES/NO
	Event script		Refresh access confirmed: YES/NO
	Generate event		
	Policy		
Firewall	Filter		
	Prefix action		
	Service filter		
	Simple filter		
	Interface set		
	Load balance group		
	Policer		
Forwarding Options	Accounting		
	DHCP-Relay		
	Helpers		

Hierarchy	Configuration	Status	Comments
	Load balance		
	Monitoring		
	Next hop		
	Packet capture		
	Port mirroring		
	Sampling		
Groups			
Interfaces	Physical options		
	Clocking		
	Encapsulation		
	Framing		
	Redundancy		
	Schedulers		
	Service options		
	Logical options		
Logical Routers			
Policy Options	AS-Path		
	AS-Path group		
	Community		
	Damping		
	Policy		
	Prefix-list		
protocols-BGP	Authentication		
	Group		
	Neighbor		
	Families		
	Policies		
protocols-IGP	Authentication		
	Interfaces		
	Reference bandwidth		
protocols-switching	MPLS		
	LDP		
	RSVP		
	VSTP		
protocols-multicast	PIM		

Hierarchy	Configuration	Status	Comments
protocols-multicast	MSDP		
routing-instances			
routing-options	Aggregate		
	Auto-export		
	Autonomous		
	Confederation		
	Dynamics		
	Fate-sharing		
	Forwarding table		
	Generate		
	Graceful Restart		
	Multicast		
	Non-Stop Routing		
	RIB		
	RIB groups		
	Route distinguisher		
	Router ID		
	Source routing		
	Static		
	Source routing		
security	Application layer gate-ways		
	Flow		
	Forwarding options		
	IKE		
	IPSEC		
	NAT		
	PKI		
	Policies		
	Screen		
	Zones		
services	CoS		
	Dynamic flow capture		
	Flow collector		
	Flow monitoring		

Hierarchy	Configuration	Status	Comments
	IPSEC-VPN		
	L2TP		
	NAT		
	Stateful firewall		
snmp	Client list		
	Health monitor		
	RMON		
	Trap groups		
	Trap options		
	V3		
system	Accounting		
	Archival		
	Hostname		
	Login		
	NTP		
	RADIUS options		
	Scripts – commit		Refresh access confirmed: YES/NO
	Scripts – op		Refresh access confirmed: YES/NO
	Service		
	Syslog		

Audit Interval

Configuration module	Audit interval	Comments
Chassis	Quarterly	
Firewall filter	Biweekly	Pay special attention to newly allocated IP address ranges
Interfaces	Quarterly	
Routing policies	Biweekly	Pay special attention to newly allocated IP address ranges
Protocols	Biweekly	Pay special attention to external BGP peering
Security	Biweekly	
Systems	Quarterly	

High Availability Configuration Statements

This appendix supplies a summary of JUNOS configuration statements arranged by various high availability features.

Routing Engine and Switching Control Board

cfeb

```
cfeb slot-number (always | preferred);
```

Hierarchy level

[edit chassis redundancy]

Description

On M10i routers only, configure which Compact Forwarding Engine Board (CFEB) is the master and which is the backup.

Default

By default, the CFEB in slot 0 is the master and the CFEB in slot 1 is the backup.

Options

slot-number

Specify which slot is the master and which is the backup.

always

Define this CFEB as the sole device.

preferred

Define this CFEB as the preferred device of at least two.

description

```
description description;
```

Hierarchy level

[edit chassis redundancy feb redundancy redundancy-group name]

Description

Provide a description of the FEB redundancy group.

Option

```
description
```
Provide a description for the FEB redundancy group.

failover on-disk-failure

```
failover on-disk-failure;
```

Hierarchy level

[edit chassis redundancy]

Description

Instruct the backup router to take mastership if it detects hard disk errors on the master routing engine (RE).

failover on-loss-of-keepalives

```
failover on-loss-of-keepalives;
```

Hierarchy level

[edit chassis redundancy]

Description

Instruct the backup router to take mastership if it detects a loss of keepalive signals from the master RE.

Default

If the `failover on-loss-of-keepalives` statement at the [edit chassis redundancy] hierarchy level is not included and Graceful Routing Engine Switchover (GRES) is not enabled, failover cannot occur. When the `failover on-loss-of-keepalives` statement is included and GRES is not configured, failover occurs after 300 seconds (five minutes). When the `failover on-loss-of-keepalives` statement is included and GRES is configured, the keepalive signal is automatically enabled and the failover time is set to two seconds. You cannot manually reset the keepalive time.

failover other-routing-engine

```
failover other-routing-engine;
```

Hierarchy level

[edit system processes process-name]

Description

Instruct the backup RE to take mastership if a software process fails. If this statement is configured for a process and that process fails four times within 30 seconds, the router reboots from the backup RE.

Option

process-name

One of the valid software process names. A few examples are disk-monitoring, ethernet-link-fault-management, kernel-replication, redundancy-interface-process, and vrrp.

feb (Creating a Redundancy Group)

```
feb {
    redundancy-groupgroup-name {
        description description;
        febslot-number (backup | primary);
        no-auto-failoverr;
    }
}
```

Hierarchy level

[edit chassis redundancy]

Description

On M120 routers only, configure an FEB redundancy group.

Options

The remaining statements are described separately.

feb (Assigning a FEB to a Redundancy Group)

```
feb slot-number (backup | primary);
```

Hierarchy level

[edit chassis redundancy feb redundancy-groupgroup-name]

Description

On M120 routers only, configure an FEB as part of an FEB redundancy group.

Options

slot-number

Slot number of the FEB. Range: 0–5.

backup

For each redundancy group, you must configure exactly one backup FEB.

primary

(Optional) For each redundancy group, you can optionally configure one primary FEB.

keepalive-time

```
keepalive-time seconds;
```

Hierarchy level

[edit chassis redundancy]

Description

Configure the time period that must elapse before the backup router takes mastership when it detects loss of the keepalive signal.

Default

If the `failover on-loss-of-keepalives` statement at the [edit chassis redundancy] hierarchy level is not included and GRES is not enabled, failover cannot occur. When the `failover on-loss-of-keepalives` statement is included and GRES is not configured, failover occurs after 300 seconds (five minutes). When the `failover on-loss-of-keepalives` statement is included and GRES is configured, the keepalive signal is automatically enabled and the failover time is set to two seconds. You cannot manually reset the keepalive time.

Option

seconds

Time before the backup router takes mastership when it detects loss of the keepalive signal. Range: 2–10,000.

no-auto-failover

```
no-auto-failover;
```

Hierarchy level

[edit chassis redundancy feb redundancy-groupgroup-name]

Description

Disable automatic failover to a backup FEB when an active FEB in a redundancy group fails.

Default

Automatic failover is enabled by default.

redundancy

```
redundancy {
  cfeb slot-number (always | preferred);
  feb {
    redundancy-group group-name {
      description description;
      feb slot-number (backup | primary);
      no-auto-failover;
    }
  }
  failover on-disk-failure;
  failover on-loss-of-keepalives;
  keepalive-timeseconds;
  routing-engineslot-number (backup | disabled | master);
```

```
    sfmslot-number (always | preferred);
    ssbslot-number (always | preferred);
}
```

Hierarchy level

[edit chassis]

Description

Configure redundancy options.

Options

The statements are explained separately.

---

redundancy-group

```
redundancy-group group-name {
  description description;
  feb slot-number (backup | primary);
  no-auto-failover;
}
```

Hierarchy level

[edit chassis redundancy feb (Creating a Redundancy Group)]

Description

On M120 routers only, configure an FEB redundancy group.

Option

group-name

The unique name for the redundancy group. The maximum length is 39 alphanumeric characters.

Other statements are explained separately.

---

routing-engine

```
routing-engine slot-number (backup | disabled | master);
```

Hierarchy level

[edit chassis redundancy]

Description

Configure RE redundancy.

Default

By default, the RE in slot 0 is the master RE and the RE in slot 1 is the backup RE.

Option

slot-number

Specify the slot number (0 or 1).

Set the function of the RE for the specified slot:

master
> RE in the specified slot is the master.

backup
> RE in the specified slot is the backup.

disabled
> RE in the specified slot is disabled.

sfm

```
sfm slot-number (always | preferred);
```

Hierarchy level
[edit chassis redundancy]

Description
On M40e and M160 routers, configure which Switching and Forwarding Module (SFM) is the master and which is the backup.

Default
By default, the SFM in slot 0 is the master and the SFM in slot 1 is the backup.

Options

slot-number
> Specify which slot is the master and which is the backup. On the M40e router, slot-number can be 0 or 1. On the M160 router, slot-number can be 0 through 3.

always
> Define this SFM as the sole device.

preferred
> Define this SFM as the preferred device of at least two.

ssb

```
ssb slot-number (always | preferred);
```

Hierarchy level
[edit chassis redundancy]

Description
On M20 routers, configure which System and Switch Board (SSB) is the master and which is the backup.

Default
By default, the SSB in slot 0 is the master and the SSB in slot 1 is the backup.

Options

`slot-number`

Specify which slot is the master and which is the backup.

`always`

Define this SSB as the sole device.

`preferred`

Define this SSB as the preferred device of at least two.

Graceful Routing Engine Switchover

graceful-switchover

```
graceful-switchover;
```

Hierarchy level

[edit chassis redundancy]

Description

For routing platforms with two REs, configure a master RE to switch over gracefully to a backup RE without interruption to packet forwarding.

Nonstop Bridging Statements

nonstop-bridging

```
nonstop-bridging;
```

Hierarchy level

[edit protocols layer2-control]

Description

For routing platforms with two REs, configure a master RE to switch over gracefully to a backup RE and preserve Layer 2 Control Protocol (L2CP) information.

Nonstop Active Routing

commit synchronize

```
commit synchronize;
```

Hierarchy level

[edit system]

Description
Configure the `commit` command to automatically result in a commit synchronize action be-tween dual REs within the same chassis. The RE on which you execute the `commit` command (the requesting RE) copies and loads its candidate configuration to the other (responding) RE. Each RE then performs a syntax check on the candidate configuration file being com-mitted. If no errors are found, the configuration is activated and becomes the current opera-tional configuration on both REs. Synchronization occurs only between the REs within the same chassis.

On the TX Matrix platform, when synchronization is complete the new configuration is then distributed to the REs on the T640 routing nodes. That is, the master RE on the TX Matrix platform distributes the configuration to the master RE on each T640 routing node. Likewise, the backup RE on the TX Matrix platform distributes the configuration to the backup RE on each T640 routing node.

 When you configure Non-Stop Active Routing (NSR), you must include the `commit synchronize` statement. Otherwise, the commit fails.

Options

and-quit
> (Optional) Quit configuration mode if the commit synchronization succeeds.

comment
> (Optional) Write a message to the commit log.

and-force
> (Optional) Force a commit synchronization on the other RE (ignore warnings).

nonstop-routing

```
nonstop-routing;
```

Hierarchy level
[edit routing-options]

Description
For routing platforms with two REs, configure a master RE to switch over gracefully to a backup RE and preserve routing protocol information.

traceoptions

```
traceoptions {
  file name <size size> <files number> > <(world-readable | no-world-
  readable)>;
  flag flag <flag-modifier> <disable>;
}
```

Hierarchy level

[edit protocols bfd]
[edit protocols bgp]
[edit protocols isis]
[edit protocols ldp]
[edit protocols ospf]
[edit protocols ospf3]
[edit protocols pim]
[edit protocols rip]
[edit protocols ripng]
[edit routing-options]

Description

Define tracing operations that track NSR functionality in the router. To specify more than one tracing operation, include multiple flag statements.

Default

If you do not include this statement, no global tracing operations are performed.

Options

disable

(Optional) Disable the tracing operation. You can use this option to disable a single operation when you have defined a broad group of tracing operations, such as **all**.

file name

Name of the file to receive the output of the tracing operation. Enclose the name within quotation marks. All files are placed in the directory */var/log*. We recommend that you place global routing protocol tracing output in the file *routing-log*.

files number

(Optional) Maximum number of trace files. When a trace file named *trace-file* reaches its maximum size, it is renamed *trace-file.0*, then *trace-file.1*, and so on, until the maximum number of trace files is reached. Then the oldest trace file is overwritten. Range: 2–1,000 files. Default: two files.

 If you specify a maximum number of files, you also must specify a maximum file size with the **size** option.

flag flag

Tracing operation to perform. To specify more than one tracing operation, include multiple flag statements. The NSR tracing options are:

nsr-packet

Detailed trace information for Bidirectional Forwarding Detection (BFD) NSR only.

`nsr-synchronization`
Tracing operations for NSR.

`flag-modifier`
(Optional) Modifier for the tracing flag. Except for BFD sessions, you can specify one or more of these modifiers:

`detail`
Detailed trace information.

`receive`
Packets being received.

`send`
Packets being transmitted.

`size size`
(Optional) Maximum size of each trace file, in kilobytes (KB), megabytes (MB), or gigabytes (GB). When a trace file named *trace-file* reaches this size, it is renamed *trace-file.0*. When the *trace-file* again reaches its maximum size, *trace-file.0* is renamed *trace-file.1* and *trace-file* is renamed *trace-file.0*. This renaming scheme continues until the maximum number of trace files is reached. Then the oldest trace file is overwritten. Syntax: **xk** to specify KB, **xm** to specify MB, or **xg** to specify GB. Range: 10 KB through the maximum file size supported on your system. Default: 128 KB.

 If you specify a maximum file size, you also must specify a maximum number of trace files with the **files** option.

Graceful Restart

disable

`disable;`

Hierarchy level
[edit logical-systems logical-system-name protocols (bgp | isis | ldp | ospf | ospf3 | pim | rip | ripng | rsvp) graceful-restart]
[edit logical-systems logical-system-name routing-instances routing-instance-name protocols (bgp | ldp | ospf | ospf3 | pim) graceful-restart]
[edit protocols (bgp | esis | isis | ospf | ospf3 | ldp | pim | rip | ripng | rsvp) graceful-restart]
[edit protocols bgp group group-name graceful-restart]
[edit protocols bgp group group-name neighbor ip-address graceful-restart]
[edit routing-instances routing-instance-name protocols (bgp | ldp | ospf | ospf3 | pim) graceful-restart]

[edit routing-instances routing-instance-name routing-Options: graceful-restart]
```
[edit routing-Options: graceful-restart]
```

Description
Disable Graceful Restart.

graceful-restart

```
graceful-restart {
    disable;
    helper-disable;
    maximum-helper-recovery-time seconds;
    maximum-helper-restart-time seconds;
    notify-duration seconds;
    recovery-time seconds;
    restart-duration seconds;
    stale-routes-time seconds;
}
```

Hierarchy level
[edit logical-systems logical-system-name protocols (bgp | isis | ldp | ospf | ospf3 | pim | rip | ripng | rsvp)]
[edit logical-systems logical-system-name routing-instances routing-instance-name protocols (bgp | ldp | ospf | ospf3 | pim)]
[edit logical-systems logical-system-name routing-instances routing-instance-name routing-options]
[edit protocols (bgp | esis | isis | ldp | ospf | ospf3 | pim | rip | ripng | rsvp)]
[edit protocols bgp group group-name]
[edit protocols bgp group group-name neighbor ip-address]
[edit routing-instances routing-instance-name protocols (bgp | ldp | ospf | ospf3 | pim)]
[edit routing-options]

Description
Enable Graceful Restart.

helper-disable

```
helper-disable;
```

Hierarchy level
[edit logical-systems logical-system-name protocols (isis | ldp | ospf | ospf3 | rsvp) graceful-restart]
[edit logical-systems logical-system-name routing-instances routing-instance-name protocols (ldp | ospf | ospf3)] graceful-restart]
[edit protocols (isis | ldp | ospf | ospf3 | rsvp) graceful-restart]
[edit routing-instances routing-instance-name protocols (ldp | ospf | ospf3) graceful-restart]

Description

Disable helper mode for Graceful Restart. When helper mode is disabled, a router cannot help a neighboring router that is attempting to restart.

Default

Helper mode is enabled by default for these supported protocols: IS-IS, LDP, OSPF/OSPFv3, and RSVP.

---

maximum-helper-recovery-time

```
maximum-helper-recovery-time seconds;
```

Hierarchy level

[edit protocols rsvp graceful-restart]
[edit logical-systems logical-system-name protocols rsvp graceful-restart]

Description

Specify the amount of time the router retains the state of its Resource Reservation Protocol (RSVP) neighbors while they undergo a Graceful Restart.

Option

seconds

Amount of time the router retains the state of its RSVP neighbors while they undergo a Graceful Restart. Range: 1–3,600. Default: 180.

---

maximum-helper-restart-time

```
maximum-helper-restart-time seconds;
```

Hierarchy level

[edit protocols rsvp graceful-restart],
[edit logical-systems logical-system-name protocols rsvp graceful-restart]

Description

Specify the amount of time the router waits after it discovers that a neighboring router has gone down before it declares the neighbor down. This value is applied to all RSVP neighbor routers and should be based on the time that the slowest RSVP neighbor requires for restart.

Option

seconds

The time the router waits after it discovers that a neighboring router has gone down before it declares the neighbor down. Range: 1–1,800. Default: 60.

---

maximum-neighbor-reconnect-time

```
maximum-neighbor-reconnect-time seconds;
```

Hierarchy level

[edit protocols ldp graceful-restart]

[edit logical-systems logical-system-name protocols ldp graceful-restart]

[edit routing-instances routing-instance-name protocols ldp graceful-restart]

Description

Specify the maximum amount of time allowed to reestablish connection from a restarting neighbor.

Option

seconds

Maximum time allowed for reconnection. Range: 30–300.

maximum-neighbor-recovery-time

```
maximum-neighbor-recovery-time seconds;
```

Hierarchy level

[edit protocols ldp graceful-restart]

[edit logical-systems logical-system-name protocols ldp graceful-restart]

[edit routing-instances instance-name protocols ldp graceful-restart]

Description

Specify the amount of time the router retains the state of its Label Distribution Protocol (LDP) neighbors while they undergo a Graceful Restart.

Option

seconds

Time, in seconds, that the router retains the state of its LDP neighbors while they undergo a Graceful Restart. Range: 140–1,900. Default: 240.

no-strict-lsa-checking

```
no-strict-lsa-checking;
```

Hierarchy level

[edit protocols (ospf | ospf3) graceful-restart]

Description

Disable strict OSPF link-state advertisement (LSA) checking to prevent the termination of Graceful Restart by a helping router.

Default

By default, LSA checking is enabled.

notify-duration

```
notify-duration seconds;
```

Hierarchy level
>[edit protocols (ospf | ospf3) graceful-restart]
>[edit logical-systems logical-system-name protocols (ospf | ospf3) graceful-restart]
>[edit logical-systems logical-system-name routing-instances instance-name protocols (ospf | ospf3) graceful-restart]
>[edit routing-instances instance-name protocols (ospf | ospf3) graceful-restart]

Description
Specify the length of time the router notifies helper OSPF routers that it has completed Graceful Restart.

Option

seconds
>Amount of time the router notifies helper OSPF routers that it has completed Graceful Restart. Range: 1–3,600. Default: 30.

reconnect-time

```
reconnect-time seconds;
```

Hierarchy level
>[edit protocols ldp graceful-restart]
>[edit logical-systems logical-system-name protocols ldp graceful-restart]
>[edit routing-instances routing-instance-name protocols ldp graceful-restart]

Description
Specify the amount of time required to reestablish an LDP session after Graceful Restart.

Option

seconds
>Time required for reconnection. Range: 30–120.

recovery-time

```
recovery-time seconds;
```

Hierarchy level
>[edit logical-systems logical-system-name protocols ldp graceful-restart]
>[edit logical-systems logical-system-name routing-instances routing-instance-name protocols ldp graceful-restart]
>[edit protocols ldp graceful-restart]
>[edit routing-instances routing-instance-name protocols ldp graceful-restart]

Description
Specify the amount of time a router waits for LDP neighbors to assist it with a Graceful Restart.

Option
seconds
> Time the router waits for LDP to restart gracefully. Range: 120–1,800. Default: 160.

---

restart-duration

```
restart-duration seconds;
```

Hierarchy level
> [edit logical-systems logical-system-name protocols (isis | ospf | ospf3 | pim) graceful-restart]
> [edit logical-systems logical-system-name routing-instances routing-instance-name protocols (ospf | ospf3 | pim) graceful-restart]
> [edit protocols (esis | isis | ospf | ospf3 | pim) graceful-restart]
> [edit routing-instances routing-instance-name protocols (ospf | ospf3 | pim) graceful-restart]
> [edit routing-Options: graceful-restart]

Description
Configure the duration of the Graceful Restart period globally. Additionally, you can individually configure the duration of the Graceful Restart period for the End System-to-Intermediate System (ES-IS), Intermediate System-to-Intermediate System (IS-IS), Open Shortest Path First (OSPF), and OSPFv3 protocols and for Protocol-Independent Multicast (PIM) sparse mode.

Option
seconds
> Time for the Graceful Restart period.

Range
The range of values varies according to whether the Graceful Restart period is being set globally or for a particular protocol:

- [edit routing-options: graceful-restart] (global setting): 120–900
- ES-IS: 30–300
- IS-IS: 30–300
- OSPF/OSPFv3: 1–3,600
- PIM: 30–300

Default
The default value varies according to whether the Graceful Restart period is being set globally or for a particular protocol:

- [edit routing-options: graceful-restart] (global setting): 300

- ES-IS: 180
- IS-IS: 210
- OSPF/OSPFv3: 180
- PIM: 60

restart-time

```
restart-time seconds;
```

Hierarchy level

[edit protocols (bgp | rip | ripng) graceful-restart]
[edit logical-systems logical-system-name protocols (bgp | rip | ripng) graceful-restart]
[edit logical-systems logical-system-name routing-instances routing-instance-name protocols bgp graceful-restart]
[edit routing-instances routing-instance-name protocols bgp graceful-restart]

Description

Configure the duration of the Border Gateway Protocol (BGP), Routing Information Protocol (RIP), or next-generation RIP (RIPng) Graceful Restart period.

Option

seconds

Amount of time for the Graceful Restart period. Range: 1–600.

Default

The range of values varies according to the protocol:

- BGP: 120
- RIP/RIPng: 60

stale-routes-time

```
stale-routes-time seconds;
```

Hierarchy level

[edit logical-systems logical-routing-name protocols bgp graceful-restart]
[edit logical-systems logical-routing-name routing-instances routing-instance-name protocols bgp graceful-restart]
[edit protocols bgp graceful-restart]
[edit routing-instances routing-instance-name protocols bgp graceful-restart]

Description

Configure the amount of time the router waits to receive restart messages from restarting BGP neighbors before declaring them down.

Option

seconds

Time the router waits to receive messages from restarting neighbors before declaring them down. Range: 1–600. Default: 300.

---

traceoptions

```
traceOptions {
file name <size size> <files number> <(world-readable | no-world-
readable)>;
   flag flag <flag-modifier> <disable>;
}
```

Hierarchy level

[edit protocols isis]
[edit protocols (ospf | ospf3)]

Description

Define tracing operations that gracefully restart functionality in the router. To specify more than one tracing operation, include multiple flag statements.

Default

If you do not include this statement, no global tracing operations are performed.

Options

disable

(Optional) Disable the tracing operation. You can use this option to disable a single operation when you have defined a broad group of tracing operations, such as **all**.

file name

Name of the file to receive the output of the tracing operation. Enclose the name within quotation marks. All files are placed in the directory */var/log*. (It's recommended that you place global routing protocol tracing output in the file *routing-log*.)

files number

(Optional) Maximum number of trace files. When a trace file named *trace-file* reaches its maximum size, it is renamed *trace-file.0*, then *trace-file.1*, and so on, until the maximum number of trace files is reached. Then the oldest trace file is overwritten. Range: 2–1,000 files. Default: two files.

 If you specify a maximum number of files, you also must specify a maximum file size with the **size** option.

flag flag

Tracing operation to perform. To specify more than one tracing operation, include multiple flag statements. The NSR tracing option is:

```
graceful-restart
```
Tracing operations for NSR.

```
size size
```
(Optional) Maximum size of each trace file, in KB, MB, or GB. When a trace file named *trace-file* reaches this size, it is renamed *trace-file.0*. When the *trace-file* again reaches its maximum size, *trace-file.0* is renamed *trace-file.1* and *trace-file* is renamed *trace-file.0*. This renaming scheme continues until the maximum number of trace files is reached. Then the oldest trace file is overwritten. Syntax: **xk** to specify KB, **xm** to specify MB, or **xg** to specify GB. Range: 10 KB through the maximum file size supported on your system. Default: 128 KB.

 If you specify a maximum file size, you also must specify a maximum number of trace files with the **files** option.

VRRP

accept-data

```
(accept-data | no-accept-data);
```

Hierarchy level
[edit interfaces interface-name unit logical-unit-number family (inet | inet6) address address (vrrp-group | vrrp-inet6-group) group-id]
[edit logical-systems logical-system-name interfaces interface-name unit logical-unit-number family (inet | inet6) address address (vrrp-group | vrrp-inet6-group) group-id]

Description
In a Virtual Router Redundancy Protocol (VRRP) configuration, determine whether an interface accepts packets destined for the virtual IP (VIP) address.

Options
```
accept-data
```
Enable the interface to accept packets destined for the VIP address.

```
no-accept-data
```
Prevent the interface from accepting packets destined for the VIP address.

Default
If the **accept-data** statement is not configured, the master router responds to ICMP message requests only.

advertise-interval

```
advertise-interval seconds;
```

Hierarchy level

[edit interfaces interface-name unit logical-unit-number family inet address address vrrp-group group-id]

[edit logical-systems logical-system-name interfaces interface-name unit logical-unit-number family inet address address vrrp-group group-id]

Description

Configure the interval between VRRP IPv4 advertisement packets. All routers in the VRRP group must use the same advertisement interval.

Option

seconds

Interval between advertisement packets. Range: 1–255 seconds. Default: one second.

authentication-key

```
authentication-key key;
```

Hierarchy level

[edit interfaces interface-name unit logical-unit-number family inet address address vrrp-group group-id]

[edit logical-systems logical-system-name interfaces interface-name unit logical-unit-number family inet address address vrrp-group group-id]

Description

Configure a VRRP IPv4 authentication key. You also must specify a VRRP authentication scheme by including the authentication-type statement. All routers in the VRRP group must use the same authentication scheme and password.

Option

key

Authentication password. For simple authentication, it can be one through eight characters long. For MD5 authentication, it can be 1 through 16 characters long. If you include spaces, enclose all characters in quotation marks (" ").

authentication-type

```
authentication-type authentication;
```

Hierarchy level

[edit interfaces interface-name unit logical-unit-number family inet address address vrrp-group group-id]

[edit logical-systems logical-system-name interfaces interface-name unit logical-unit-number family inet address address vrrp-group group-id]

Description
Enable VRRP IPv4 authentication and specify the authentication scheme for the VRRP group. If you enable authentication, you must specify a password by including the **authentication-key** statement. All routers in the VRRP group must use the same authentication scheme and password.

Option

authentication
> Authentication scheme:
>
> simple
>> Use a simple password. The password is included in the transmitted packet, making this method of authentication relatively insecure.
>
> md5
>> Use the MD5 algorithm to create an encoded checksum of the packet. The encoded checksum is included in the transmitted packet. The receiving routing platform uses the authentication key to verify the packet, discarding it if the digest does not match. This algorithm provides a more secure authentication scheme.

Default
None (no authentication is performed).

bandwidth-threshold

```
bandwidth-threshold bits-per-second {
  priority-cost priority;
}
```

Hierarchy level
> [edit interfaces interface-name unit logical-unit-number family (inet | inet6) address address (vrrp-group | vrrp-inet6-group) group-id track interface interface-name]
> [edit logical-systems logical-system-name interfaces interface-name unit logical-unit-number family (inet | inet6) address address (vrrp-group | vrrp-inet6-group) group-id track interface interface-name]

Description
Specify the bandwidth threshold for VRRP logical interface tracking.

Option

bits-per-second
> Bandwidth threshold for the tracked interface. When the bandwidth of the tracked interface drops below the specified value, the VRRP group uses the bandwidth threshold priority cost value. You can include up to five bandwidth threshold statements for each interface you track. Range: 1–10,000,000,000,000 bits per second.

The remaining statement is described separately.

fast-interval

```
fast-interval milliseconds;
```

Hierarchy level

[edit interfaces interface-name unit logical-unit-number family (inet | inet6) address address (vrrp-group | vrrp-inet6-group) group-id]

[edit logical-systems logical-system-name interfaces interface-name unit logical-unit-number family (inet | inet6) address address (vrrp-group | vrrp-inet6-group) group-id]

Description

Configure the interval, in milliseconds, between VRRP advertisement packets. All routers in the VRRP group must use the same advertisement interval.

Option

milliseconds

Interval between advertisement packets. Range: 100–999 milliseconds. Default: one second.

hold-time

```
hold-time seconds;
```

Hierarchy level

[edit interfaces interface-name unit logical-unit-number family (inet | inet6) address address (vrrp | vrrp-inet6-group) group-id preempt]

[edit logical-systems logical-system-name interfaces interface-name unit logical-unit-number family (inet | inet6) address address (vrrp | vrrp-inet6-group) group-id preempt]

Description

In a VRRP configuration, set the hold time before a higher-priority backup router preempts the master router.

Default

VRRP preemption is not timed.

Option

seconds

Hold-time period. Range: 0–3,600 seconds. Default: 0 seconds (VRRP preemption is not timed).

inet6-advertise-interval

```
inet6-advertise-interval ms;
```

Hierarchy level

[edit interfaces interface-name unit logical-unit-number family inet6 address address vrrp-inet6-group group-id]

[edit logical-systems logical-system-name interfaces interface-name unit logical-unit-number family inet6 address address vrrp-inet6-group group-id]

Description

Configure the interval between VRRP IPv6 advertisement packets. All routers in the VRRP group must use the same advertisement interval.

Option

ms

Interval, in milliseconds, between advertisement packets. Range: 100–40,950 milliseconds (ms). Default: one second.

interface

```
interface interface-name {
  priority priority;
  bandwidth-threshold bits-per-second {
    priority-cost priority;
  }
}
```

Hierarchy level

[edit interfaces interface-name unit logical-unit-number family (inet | inet6) address address (vrrp-group | vrrp-inet6-group) group-id track]

[edit logical-systems logical-system-name interfaces interface-name unit logical-unit-number family (inet | inet6) address address (vrrp-group | vrrp-inet6-group) group-id track]

Description

Enable logical interface tracking for a VRRP group.

Option

```
interface interface-name
```

Interface to be tracked for this VRRP group. Range: 1–10 interfaces.

The remaining statements are described separately.

preempt

```
(preempt | no-preempt) {
  hold-time seconds;
}
```

Hierarchy level

[edit interfaces interface-name unit logical-unit-number family (inet | inet6) address address (vrrp-group | vrrp-inet6-group) group-id]
[edit logical-systems logical-system-name interfaces interface-name unit logical-unit-number family (inet | inet6) address address (vrrp-group | vrrp-inet6-group) group-id]

Description

In a VRRP configuration, determine whether a backup router can preempt a master router.

Options

preempt

Allow the master router to be preempted.

no-preempt

Prohibit the preemption of the master router.

The remaining statement is explained separately.

Default

If you omit this statement, the backup router cannot preempt a master router.

---

priority

```
priority priority;
```

Hierarchy level

[edit interfaces interface-name unit logical-unit-number family (inet | inet6) address address (vrrp-group | vrrp-inet6-group) group-id]
[edit logical-systems logical-system-name interfaces interface-name unit logical-unit-number family (inet | inet6) address address (vrrp-group | vrrp-inet6-group) group-id]

Description

Configure a VRRP router's priority for becoming the master default router. The router with the highest priority within the group becomes the master.

Option

priority

Router's priority for being elected to be the master router in the VRRP group. A larger value indicates a higher priority for being elected. Range: 1–255. Default: 100 (for backup routers).

---

priority-cost

```
priority-cost priority;
```

Hierarchy level

[edit interfaces interface-name unit logical-unit-number family (inet | inet6) address address (vrrp | vrrp-inet-group) group-id track interface interface-name]

[edit logical-systems logical-system-name interfaces interface-name unit logical-unit-number family (inet | inet6) address address (vrrp | vrrp-inet6-group) group-id track interface interface-name]

[edit interfaces interface-name unit logical-unit-number family (inet | inet6) address address (vrrp | vrrp-inet6-group) group-id track interface interface-name bandwidth-threshold bits-per-second]

[edit logical-systems logical-system-name interfaces interface-name unit logical-unit-number family (inet | inet6) address address (vrrp | vrrp-inet6-group) group-id track interface interface-name bandwidth-threshold bits-per-second]

[edit interfaces interface-name unit logical unit number family (inet | inet6) address address (vrrp-group | vrrp-inet6-group) group-id track route prefix routing-instance instance-name]

[edit logical-systems logical-system-name interfaces interface-name unit logical-unit-number family (inet | inet6) address address (vrrp-group | vrrp-inet6-group) group-id track route prefix routing-instance instance-name]

Description

Configure a VRRP router's priority cost for becoming the master default router. The router with the highest priority within the group becomes the master.

Option

priority

The value subtracted from the configured VRRP priority when the tracked interface or route is down, forcing a new master router election. The sum of all the costs for all interfaces or routes that are tracked must be less than or equal to the configured priority of the VRRP group. Range: 1–254.

priority-hold-time

```
priority-hold-time seconds;
```

Hierarchy level

[edit interfaces interface-name unit logical-unit-number family (inet | inet6) address address (vrrp | vrrp-inet6-group) group-id track]

[edit logical-systems logical-system-name interfaces interface-name unit logical-unit-number family (inet | inet6) address address (vrrp | vrrp-inet6-group) group-id track]

Description

Configure a VRRP router's priority hold time to define the minimum length of time that must elapse between dynamic priority changes. If the dynamic priority changes because of a tracking event, the priority hold timer begins. If another tracking event or manual configuration change occurs while the timer is running, the new dynamic priority update is postponed until the timer expires.

Option

`seconds`
> The minimum length of time that must elapse between dynamic priority changes.

Range: 1–3,600 seconds.

---

route

```
route {
    prefix routing-instance instance-name priority-cost priority;
}
```

Hierarchy level

[edit interfaces interface-name unit logical-unit-number family (inet | inet6) address address (vrrp-group | vrrp-inet6-group) group-id track]

[edit logical-systems logical-system-name interfaces interface-name unit logical-unit-number family (inet | inet6) address address (vrrp-group | vrrp-inet6-group) group-id track]

Description

Enable route tracking for a VRRP group.

Options

`prefix`
> Route to be tracked for this VRRP group.

`routing-instance instance-name`
> Routing instance in which the route is to be tracked. If the route is in the default, or global, routing instance, the value for `instance-name` must be the default.

The remaining statement is described separately.

---

startup-silent-period

```
startup-silent-period seconds;
```

Hierarchy level

[edit protocols vrrp]

Description

Instruct the system to ignore the Master Down Event when an interface transitions from the disabled state to the enabled state. This statement is used to avoid an incorrect error alarm caused by delay or interruption of incoming VRRP advertisement packets during the interface startup phase.

Option

seconds

> Number of seconds. Range: 1–2,000 seconds. Default: four seconds.

traceoptions

```
traceoptions {
  file {
    filename filename;
    files number;
    match regex;
    microsecond-stamp
    size size;
    (world-readable | no-world-readable);
  }
  flag flag;
}
```

Hierarchy level

> [edit protocols vrrp]

Description

Define tracing operations for the VRRP process. To specify more than one tracing operation, include multiple flag statements. By default, VRRP logs the error, DCD configuration, and routing socket events in a file in the directory */var/log*.

Default

If you do not include this statement, no VRRP-specific tracing operations are performed.

Options

filename filename

> Name of the file to receive the output of the tracing operation. Enclose the name within quotation marks. All files are placed in the directory */var/log*. By default, VRRP tracing output is placed in the file *vrrpd*.

files number

> (Optional) Maximum number of trace files. When a trace file named *trace-file* reaches its maximum size, it is renamed *trace-file.0*, then *trace-file.1*, and so on, until the maximum number of trace files is reached. When the maximum number is reached, the oldest trace file is overwritten. Range: 0–4,294,967,296 files. Default: three files.

 If you specify a maximum number of files, you also must specify a maximum file size with the **size** option.

flag flag

> Tracing operation to perform. To specify more than one tracing operation, include multiple flag statements. These are the VRRP-specific tracing options:

---

all
  All VRRP tracing operations.

database
  Database changes.

general
  General events.

interfaces
  Interface changes.

normal
  Normal events.

packets
  Packets sent and received.

state
  State transitions.

timer
  Timer events.

match regex
  (Optional) Refine the output to include only those lines that match the given regular expression.

microsecond-stamp
  (Optional) Provide a timestamp with microsecond granularity.

size size
  (Optional) Maximum size of each trace file, in KB, MB, or GB. When a trace file named *trace-file* reaches this size, it is renamed *trace-file.0*. When the *trace-file* again reaches its maximum size, *trace-file.0* is renamed *trace-file.1* and *trace-file* is renamed *trace-file.0*. This renaming scheme continues until the maximum number of trace files is reached. Then the oldest trace file is overwritten. Syntax: **xk** to specify KB, **xm** to specify MB, or **xg** to specify GB. Range: 10 KB through the maximum file size supported on your routing platform. Default: 1 MB.

 If you specify a maximum file size, you also must specify a maximum number of trace files with the **files** option.

world-readable | no-world-readable
  Specifies whether any reader can read the logfile.

track

```
track {
  interface interface-name {
    priority-cost priority;
    bandwidth-threshold bits-per-second {
      priority-cost priority;
    }
  }
  priority-hold-time seconds;
  route prefix routing-instance instance-name {
    priority-cost priority;
  }
}
```

Hierarchy level

[edit interfaces interface-name unit logical-unit-number family (inet | inet6) address address (vrrp-group | vrrp-inet6-group) group-id],
[edit logical-systems logical-system-name interfaces interface-name unit logical-unit-number family (inet | inet6) address address (vrrp-group | vrrp-inet6-group) group-id]

Description

Enable logical interface tracking, route tracking, or both for a VRRP group.

virtual-address

```
virtual-address [ addresses ];
```

Hierarchy level

[edit interfaces interface-name unit logical-unit-number family inet address address vrrp-group group-id]
[edit logical-systems logical-system-name interfaces interface-name unit logical-unit-number family inet address address vrrp-group group-id]

Description

Configure the addresses of the virtual routers in a VRRP IPv4 group. You can configure up to eight addresses.

Option

addresses

Addresses of one or more virtual routers. Do not include a prefix length. If the address is the same as the interface's physical address, the interface becomes the master virtual router for the group.

virtual-inet6-address

```
virtual-inet6-address [ addresses ];
```

Hierarchy level

[edit interfaces interface-name unit logical-unit-number family inet6 address address vrrp-inet6-group group-id]
[edit logical-systems logical-system-name interfaces interface-name unit logical-unit-number family inet6 address address vrrp-inet6-group group-id]

Description

Configure the addresses of the virtual routers in a VRRP IPv6 group. You can configure up to eight addresses.

Option

addresses

Addresses of one or more virtual routers. Do not include a prefix length. If the address is the same as the interface's physical address, the interface becomes the master virtual router for the group.

---

virtual-link-local-address

```
virtual-link-local-address ipv6-address;
```

Hierarchy level

[edit interfaces interface-name unit logical-unit-number family inet6 address address vrrp-inet6-group group-id]
[edit logical-systems logical-system-name interfaces interface-name unit logical-unit-number family inet6 address address vrrp-inet6-group group-id]

Description

Configure a virtual link local address for a VRRP IPv6 group. You must explicitly define a virtual link local address for each VRRP IPv6 group. The virtual link local address must be in the same subnet as the physical interface address.

Option

ipv6-address

Virtual link local IPv6 address for VRRP for an IPv6 group. Range: 0–255.

The remaining statements are explained separately.

---

vrrp-group

```
vrrp-group group-id {
  accept-data | no-accept-data);
  advertise-interval seconds;
  authentication-key key;
  authentication-type authentication;
  fast-interval milliseconds;
  (preempt | no-preempt) {
    hold-time seconds;
  }
  priority number;
```

```
track {
  interface interface-name {
    priority-cost priority;
    bandwidth-threshold bits-per-second {
      priority-cost priority;
    }
  }
}
priority-hold-time seconds;
route prefix routing-instance instance-name {
  priority-cost priority;
}
}
virtual-address [ addresses ];
}
```

Hierarchy level

[edit interfaces interface-name unit logical-unit-number family inet address address]

[edit logical-systems logical-system-name interfaces interface-name unit logical-unit-number family inet address address]

Description

Configure a VRRP IPv4 group.

Option

group-id

VRRP group identifier. If you enable Media Access Control (MAC) source address filtering on the interface, you must include the virtual MAC address in the list of source MAC addresses that you specify in the **source-address-filter** statement. MAC addresses ranging from 00:00:5e:00:01:00–00:00:5e:00:01:ff are reserved for VRRP, as defined in RFC 2338. The VRRP group number must be the decimal equivalent of the last hexadecimal byte of the virtual MAC address. Range: 0–255.

The remaining statements are explained separately.

vrrp-inet6-group

```
vrrp-inet6-group group-id {
  (accept-data | no-accept-data);
  fast-interval milliseconds;
  inet6-advertise-interval seconds;
  (preempt | no-preempt) {
    hold-time seconds;
  }
  priority number;
  track {
    interface interface-name {
      priority-cost priority;
      bandwidth-threshold bits-per-second {
        priority-cost priority;
      }
    }
  }
  priority-hold-time seconds;
  route prefix routing-instance instance-name {
    priority-cost priority;
```

```
      }
    }
    virtual-inet6-address [ addresses ];
    virtual-link-local-address ipv6-address;
  }
```

Hierarchy level

[edit interfaces interface-name unit logical-unit-number family inet6 address address]

[edit logical-systems logical-system-name interfaces interface-name unit logical-unit-number family inet6 address address]

Description

Configure a VRRP IPv6 group.

Option

`group-id`

VRRP group identifier. If you enable MAC source address filtering on the interface, you must include the virtual MAC address in the list of source MAC addresses that you specify in the **source-address-filter** statement. MAC addresses ranging from 00:00:5e:00:01:00–00:00:5e:00:01:ff are reserved for VRRP, as defined in RFC 2338. The VRRP group number must be the decimal equivalent of the last hexadecimal byte of the virtual MAC address. Range: 0–255.

The remaining statements are explained separately.

Unified In-Service Software Upgrade (ISSU)

To perform a unified ISSU, you must first configure GRES and NSR.

no-issu-timer-negotiation

```
    no-issu-timer-negotiation;
```

Hierarchy level

[edit protocols bfd]
[edit logical-systems logical-system-name protocols bfd]
[edit routing-instances routing-instance-name protocols bfd]

Description

Disable unified ISSU timer negotiation for BFD sessions.

The sessions might flap during unified ISSU or RE switchover, depending on the detection intervals.

traceoptions

```
traceoptions {
  file name <size size> <files number> <(world-readable | no-world-
  readable)>;
  flag flag <flag-modifier> <disable>;
}
```

Hierarchy level

[edit protocols bfd]

Description

Define tracing operations that track unified ISSU functionality in the router. To specify more than one tracing operation, include multiple flag statements.

Default

If you do not include this statement, no global tracing operations are performed.

Options

disable

(Optional) Disable the tracing operation. You can use this option to disable a single operation when you have defined a broad group of tracing operations, such as all.

file name

Name of the file to receive the output of the tracing operation. Enclose the name within quotation marks. All files are placed in the directory /var/log. We recommend that you place global routing protocol tracing output in the file *routing-log*.

files number

(Optional) Maximum number of trace files. When a trace file named *trace-file* reaches its maximum size, it is renamed *trace-file.0*, then *trace-file.1*, and so on, until the maximum number of trace files is reached. Then the oldest trace file is overwritten. Range: 2–1,000 files. Default: two files.

 If you specify a maximum number of files, you also must specify a maximum file size with the size option.

flag flag

Tracing operation to perform. There is only one unified ISSU tracing option:

issu

Trace BFD unified ISSU operations.

size size

(Optional) Maximum size of each trace file, in KB, MB, or GB. When a trace file named *trace-file* reaches this size, it is renamed *trace-file.0*. When the *trace-file* again reaches its maximum size, *trace-file.0* is renamed *trace-file.1* and *trace-file* is renamed *trace-file.0*. This renaming scheme continues until the maximum number of trace files is reached. Then the oldest trace file is overwritten. Syntax: xk to specify KB, xm to specify MB, or

xg to specify GB. Range: 10 KB through the maximum file size supported on your system. Default: 128 KB.

 If you specify a maximum file size, you also must specify a maximum number of trace files with the `files` option.

Index

We'd like to hear your suggestions for improving our indexes. Send email to *index@oreilly.com*.

About the Authors

James Sonderegger (JNCIE-M #130, JNCIS-FWV, JNCIS-ER, and Juniper Certified Instructor) holds an M.S. in IT management and manages the Americas Division of Juniper Networks' Training Delivery organization. James spent five years as an Engineer in Residence for federal customers and has been in the networking industry for the past 13 years. His former employers include The Analysis Corporation (TAC), Ericsson IP Infrastructure, and Automated Data Processing. James is a coauthor of *Juniper Networks Reference Guide: Routing, Configuration, and Architecture* (Addison-Wesley). When not serving the greater glory of the routed packet, James works as a percussionist in several bands in the Washington, D.C., area.

Orin Blomberg (CCNP, CCSP, CCIP, CCVP, CCDP, JNCIS-M, JNCIS-FWV, JNCIS-ER, JNCIS-SSL, JNCI) is the technical lead for the Security Perimeter Planning and Implementation Team at the Washington State Department of Information Services. His primary responsibilities include providing remote access and secure connectivity for state agencies and county, city, and tribal nation governments, as well as connectivity to federal agencies. Orin's former employers include General Dynamics C4 Systems, Ericsson IP Infrastructure, and the U.S. Army. He lives with his wife, two dogs, two cats, and sourdough pot in Olympia, Washington.

Kieran Milne (JNCIE-M #380, JNCIS-ER, JNCIA-WX, JNCIA-EX, JNCIA-E, JNCI, CCNA, Nortel NCTS) is a training developer and technical trainer within the Education Services department at Juniper Networks. With more than 10 years of experience in the networking industry, Kieran has taught all over the world in both corporate and college settings. Before joining Juniper Networks, Kieran spent time at Nortel Networks and Alcatel. He is the author of the forthcoming book *JUNOS Networking Essentials* (O'Reilly), and contributes to exam development for the Juniper Networks Technical Certification Program. Kieran lives and works out of Canada.

Senad Palislamovic (JNCIE-M #145 and JNCIS-E) is a systems engineer at Juniper Networks, where he spends time designing and implementing MPLS-enabled networks for global service providers. Prior to this, he worked as a consultant for Professional Services, where he designed and implemented MPLS-enabled NGEN services for ASPs and financial institutions, specializing in highly available solutions, and at Juniper JTAC, where he troubleshot M/T Series routers. Before Juniper, Senad held various network positions at Weber State University in Utah, designing and implementing scalable network solutions. He holds a double B.S. in telecommunications and IS&T from Weber State University, and has over 13 years of networking experience. Senad contributed to the tech editing of *MPLS-Enabled Applications*, Second Edition (Wiley & Sons). He lives in New York City with his wife, Samera.

Colophon

The animals on the cover of *JUNOS High Availability* are Bohemian waxwings (*Bombycilla garrulus*). The generic name *Bombycilla*, Latin for "silk tail," describes the bird's sleek, soft plumage. *Waxwing* refers to the red tips of the wing feathers that resemble drops of wax. Three species of waxwings exist: Japanese, Cedar, and Bohemian. These species are fairly similar in appearance and are primarily distinguished by geography: the Japanese waxwing lives exclusively in Asia; the Cedar inhabits North America; and the Bohemian—true to its name—travels throughout the sub-Arctic continents in nomadic flocks, particularly in winter as it searches for berries. The two latter waxwings have the most in common, although Cedars are more prevalent in the northeastern United States, whereas Bohemians are numerous in western Canada and the Rocky Mountain region. All three waxwings subsist on a diet of fruit and insects.

Another difference between the species is seen in the edges of the wing feathers: Bohemian and Japanese waxwings have white edges, while Cedars do not. At six to nine inches long, the Bohemian is also larger and grayer than the Cedar, although both have yellow tail feather tips and a pointed crest. The Bohemian waxwing's call is extremely similar to the Cedar's, most likely because the Bohemian has no territory to defend and thus has never needed to develop a true song.

The cover image is from the Dover Pictorial Archive. The cover font is Adobe ITC Garamond. The text font is Linotype Birka; the heading font is Adobe Myriad Condensed; and the code font is LucasFont's TheSansMonoCondensed.

Get even more for your money.

Join the O'Reilly Community, and register the O'Reilly books you own. It's free, and you'll get:

- $4.99 ebook upgrade offer
- 40% upgrade offer on O'Reilly print books
- Membership discounts on books and events
- Free lifetime updates to ebooks and videos
- Multiple ebook formats, DRM FREE
- Participation in the O'Reilly community
- Newsletters
- Account management
- 100% Satisfaction Guarantee

Signing up is easy:

1. **Go to: oreilly.com/go/register**
2. **Create an O'Reilly login.**
3. **Provide your address.**
4. **Register your books.**

Note: English-language books only

To order books online:
oreilly.com/store

For questions about products or an order:
orders@oreilly.com

To sign up to get topic-specific email announcements and/or news about upcoming books, conferences, special offers, and new technologies:
elists@oreilly.com

For technical questions about book content:
booktech@oreilly.com

To submit new book proposals to our editors:
proposals@oreilly.com

O'Reilly books are available in multiple DRM-free ebook formats. For more information:
oreilly.com/ebooks

O'REILLY®

Spreading the knowledge of innovators   oreilly.com

Have it your way.

O'Reilly eBooks

- Lifetime access to the book when you buy through oreilly.com
- Provided in up to four DRM-free file formats, for use on the devices of your choice: PDF, .epub, Kindle-compatible .mobi, and Android .apk
- Fully searchable, with copy-and-paste and print functionality
- Alerts when files are updated with corrections and additions

oreilly.com/ebooks/

Safari Books Online

- Access the contents and quickly search over 7000 books on technology, business, and certification guides
- Learn from expert video tutorials, and explore thousands of hours of video on technology and design topics
- Download whole books or chapters in PDF format, at no extra cost, to print or read on the go
- Get early access to books as they're being written
- Interact directly with authors of upcoming books
- Save up to 35% on O'Reilly print books

See the complete Safari Library at safari.oreilly.com

O'REILLY®